MY SECOND CAMPUS

The Independent Almanac of Study Abroad Programs

The Most Complete Directory of Programs Affiliated with New England Colleges

2012 EDITION

my Second Campus

Washington, DC

About My Second Campus

My Second Campus provides information on study abroad programs. The company was formed on the premise that good study abroad programs exist on many different campuses, not just the ones closest to students at their home campus. The first of its kind, My Second Campus is the only resource that unveils the most complete listing of study abroad programs sponsored by colleges in the United States.

My Second Campus LLC
P. O. Box 15095
Washington, DC 20003

My Second Campus makes every reasonable effort to ensure accuracy and timeliness of the data in this almanac. However, My Second Campus and its affiliates cannot guarantee or make representation or warranty, either expressed or implied, as to the accuracy, timeliness, or completeness of the data or the results to be obtained from using the data. The reader of this book holds My Second Campus harmless by reading this book.

© 2011. All rights reserved. My Second Campus is a registered mark of My Second Campus LLC. No part of this book may be reproduced or used in any form or by any means—graphic, electronic, or mechanical, including photocopying, recording, taping, Web distribution, or information storage and retrieval systems—without the prior written permission of the publisher.

ISBN: 978-0-9834415-0-2

2012 edition

Design by Sensical Design & Communication. Printed in the United States of America.
Cover photo by Aleksandra Yakovleva/istockphoto

Table of Contents

Acknowledgments v

How This Book is Different 1

Once in a Lifetime 3

How to Use this Book 13

The Almanac

Connecticut 17

Maine 69

Massachusetts 99

New Hampshire 259

Rhode Island 269

Vermont 293

Acknowledgments

This work would not have been possible without the contributions of several individuals. The editors would like to thank Arman Rousta, president of Blueliner Marketing LLC, and his associates for their technical expertise. They did an amazing job of creating the data infrastructure for this book. We extend a special thanks to Arbab Hassan and Noman Ismail, project managers of the data infrastructure, for their work efficiency and smooth execution. We also tip our hats to the following individuals for their contributions in the development of the content: Mark Pedretti, faculty member at Case Western University; Jessica Haglund, international development expert; and Nancy Pierce, former director of international programs at St. Lawrence University. Last but not least, we thank Daniel Kohan, principal of Sensical Design and Communication, for bringing all the pieces together in an artistic way.

How This Book is Different

Most college students choose to go on a study abroad program based on limited information available around them. In many cases, choosing a program is a matter of convenience. The campus study abroad office provides a select number of its institution's programs; and from this home program offering, students choose where to go. Surprisingly, there isn't much thoughtful comparison like students would in other academic matters. Take for instance how students meticulously analyze the best college fit among many college choices while still enrolled in high school. In study abroad there really isn't a well-understood market where prospective students can—and should—shop around. A lot of students and parents don't realize that there are other options available.

The lack of careful process in many respects is due to the scant amount of information available on the variety of study abroad programs that exists. No publisher has ever constructed a comprehensive directory of study abroad programs, an authoritative resource that is reliable and exhaustive—that is, until now. *My Second Campus* is the first complete almanac of study abroad programs, unveiling study abroad programs never released by any organization before. It identifies all the major study abroad programs; but more importantly, *My Second Campus* comprises study abroad program information on small, hard to find programs that have eluded the pages of conventional study abroad guidebooks. These programs are often left out of average literature because the institutions that offer them are small and often unfairly overlooked. We believe we can do better.

Another feature that differentiates *My Second Campus* is how it displays the program information. Not all study abroad programs are alike in how they are organized. But no one until now has ever categorized the varying types of programs as completely as *My Second Campus*. For instance, some programs are managed by the home college or university and closely tied to the curriculum of that institution. These programs are often led by a professor employed by the college to lead a

***My Second Campus* is the first complete almanac of study abroad programs, unveiling study abroad programs never released by any organization before.**

group of the institution's students. These home grown programs tend to have more personalized services with additional features in the program, such as internship options and school-sponsored excursions. We call this type of program "self-organized."

At the other end of the spectrum, there are study abroad programs that have substantially less bells and whistles. These programs simply place students in a host institution for a period of study. Students on this type of program have limited support and generally are left to navigate their new environment on their own. Any

How This Book is Different

excursions are planned by the student without any guidance from any study abroad office. We call this type of program "direct enrollment." *My Second Campus* classifies these program differences among others for each of the programs revealed in the book. In the pages that follow, we discuss the full category list of study abroad program types.

Wherever possible, we also show the costs associated with the programs. We hope by including this information, you—the reader—appreciate the amount of choices that you have and the cost differences of various programs.

We hope our work can lead to a better understanding of the diverse study abroad opportunities. Not all programs are identical in design or costs. We begin with an almanac of study abroad programs sponsored by colleges and universities in the New England states. In the future, we will release almanacs of study abroad programs sponsored by institutions in other regions of the United States. So stay tuned. We welcome your comments and suggestions by email or postal mail.

Email: info@mysecondcampus.com

Postal address:
My Second Campus LLC
c/o Customer Relations
P. O. Box 15095
Washington, DC 20003

If you are an administrator, please go to our website—www.mysecondcampus.com—to update your school's study abroad program information. We want to ensure that your programs get included in the next edition of My Second Campus.

With sincere thanks,
Editors of My Second Campus

Once in a Lifetime

You've decided to see the world—to leave your college or university behind for a while and take your studies abroad. The reasons couldn't be more obvious: to experience a different culture, to make new friends, to see all of the places you've only read about up until now, to put all of those foreign language classes to use, or maybe—and maybe best of all—to go on an adventure that you will remember for the rest of your life.

Congratulations! You are joining a rapidly growing community of American students who are making study abroad an integral part of their college experience. Increasingly, spending a summer, semester, or year in another country is becoming *the* premier way for major colleges and universities to offer students the opportunity to expand their cultural horizons while contributing to their education at the same time. And study abroad is no longer just for humanities majors; more and more students in the sciences are finding ways to integrate it into their curriculum without being set back when they return home. Your school will certainly prepare you for your future, but study abroad will prepare you for *the world*; as the global village grows ever smaller, as we interact more and more with people from other cultures on a daily basis, and as career opportunities in other nations appear all the more within reach, it only makes sense to devote part of your education to getting to know the world of which you will be an integral part.

But now that you've taken that first step, you suddenly realize: "the world out there" is enormous, and the opportunities to study in it are extensive. So how do you go from an abstract desire to study abroad to choosing the right program for you? You need a program that will place you where you want to be, contribute to your overall course of study, offer you the right amount of transfer credit, fit your timeframe, and work within your budget. Once you think about all of this, you see that choosing a study abroad program isn't as simple as going to your school's International Education office and seeing what's available. More and more, you don't need to be limited only by the choices offered by your home institution; many colleges and universities are now offering the opportunity to cross-enroll in their study abroad programs, or to participate in consortium programs shared among many institutions. And that's just the tip of the iceberg: there are bilateral exchange programs between particular domestic and foreign institutions, ways to directly enroll at a foreign university, and private companies that offer study abroad programs to college students from all over. So how do you get started?

That's where this book comes in. *My Second Campus* is the first of its kind to offer a comprehensive, one-stop guide to choosing the study abroad program that is right for you. We aim to help students who are eager to look beyond their own institutions and shop around for the right program, based on detailed descriptions of the different program options available to you. We've collected data from literally hundreds of colleges and universities, which details all of their destinations, costs, schedules, and requirements. This is the one and only book that has all of that information in one place. While it's pretty easy to find out about the biggest companies and institutions, this book will also give you a chance to discover hidden gems that offer opportunities you won't get from the big guys. In the pages that follow, you will come to understand the full range of choices open to you and, with some careful reading, to find the program that best suits your needs. We hope that you will come away from reading this book with not only the ability to recognize the programs most appropriate for you, but to differentiate between those that are merely okay from those that are downright excellent. The remaining sections of this introduction are designed to give you a general sense of the types of programs open to you, what you should consider before settling on any one option, the kinds of things you should be prepared for before you go, how to get along in your host country, and how to use our extensive program listings.

The world is waiting for you. Let's get going.

What to Expect

We don't need to tell you that a large part of studying abroad is the challenges it will present to your regular ways of doing things; you're going because you want to shake things up a bit. That's all well and good, but when you actually get to your new temporary home, you still may find yourself feeling a bit of culture shock. This could be something as simple as misunderstanding what your new English friend means when she says she lives "on the first floor" (that's the second floor for Americans), to knowing not to give a "thumbs up" in the Mediterranean (it's an insult), to figuring out how to navigate that toilet contraption you've never seen before (we'll leave that one up to you). The point is that you should *expect to encounter the unexpected*. But don't let this be an obstacle to getting the most of your time abroad—treat it as part of the reason you are there in the first place. Here are some general suggestions to make that possible:

Keep an open mind. Perhaps the greatest virtue of studying abroad is the way it makes you see the particularity of your own customs and habits—that your way, the "American way," is not the *only* way to do things. You are going abroad precisely to see how other people live—but that means that you need to make an effort to understand why they live as they do. No matter what, you should be prepared for some disruptions to your everyday schedule. If you are going to Spain or Mexico, for instance, you might find yourself eating dinner much later than you are used to, or learning to enjoy the quiet bliss of the siesta. Or in Japan you might be asked to eat foods (whale, octopus, raw fish) that you wouldn't otherwise. The best thing you can do when confronted with these situations is to leave yourself open to their possibilities; *this* is the adventure, *this* is the experience. You don't have to "go native," but it's like your mother used to say: you don't have to eat everything on your plate, but you've got to try everything at least once.

Patience is a virtue. Americans are used to living *fast*; from instant messaging to overnight delivery, we want it now, now, now. Abroad, you will rapidly find that this is not the case; shops may be open fewer hours out of the day, restaurants may take extra time to prepare your food, and school offices might take a bit longer to process your paperwork. Take a deep breath and relax— you'll get your food and your forms will be filed. In the U.S., we assume that slow service is bad service, but it can equally mean that people are taking their time to carefully fulfill your requests. Take that extra time to go for a walk around your new city, or to enjoy a conversation with your new friends over drinks.

But there is another sense in which patience can be a virtue too. A decent portion of the time, you will find your encounters with your adopted culture to be frustrating: maybe you can't communicate your wishes effectively or clearly, maybe your interlocutor can't figure out what you are asking of them, maybe you can't find that one simple thing you are looking for in the store. It's enough to blow your lid. So again: take a deep breath and relax. These moments of intercultural friction are actually some of the ones where you will learn the most about cultural differences, about distinct ways of doing things, and about your own beliefs and practices. If you find yourself in a frustrating encounter, take a moment to think about what is at stake, how you are handling it, and what you can learn from the situation. Eventually, you'll work it out, but in the meantime you can at least turn it into a positive learning experience.

Learn to make do. Depending on where you are, you may find facilities—classrooms, houses, toilets—that, shall we say, aren't up to the standards you are used to. Let's face it: when you are abroad, you've got to work with what you have. Especially in poorer or more rural areas, you should not expect to find the modern conveniences that you are accustomed to. Here you have the option to recoil in horror, or to figure out how to embrace your new circumstances and to live happily with them. You may discover a new brand of shampoo that works better than your own, or you may be able to finally understand all of those obscure clothing sizes that have always baffled you at Benetton. Make no mistake, this won't be the life you are accustomed to, but in all of those "inconveniences" lurk opportunities to explore the nooks and crannies of another way of life.

> **Depending on where you are, you may find facilities that, shall we say, aren't up to the standards you are used to. Let's face it: when you are abroad, you've got to work with what you have.**

Get out of your ruts. Be prepared to leave your usual campus life behind. Hanging out exclusively with your American friends, continuing your regular social activities, and thinking that cultural norms and rules will be the same will not serve you well. If you wanted to hang out with Americans and do the same things you did back home, you would have stayed at home. But even once you have settled in to your new home, don't get too comfortable. Avoid becoming a homebody by keeping your TV watching, emails, online communications, and phone calls to a minimum—get outside and greet your new world face to face. Leave campus on campus, and leave home at home.

Do your homework. Before you go, it is probably a good idea to do some reading about the culture and place you are heading to. If you haven't already, acquaint yourself with the customs, practices, and history of your new country; learn about the major newspapers, politics, and governmental structure. Get a map. Prepare a list of the government and academic offices you will likely need to call upon, with addresses, phone numbers, and hours, if you can. And familiarize yourself with your host institution so that you can hit the ground running. A lot of this can be done with a few simple web searches, but it never hurts to hit the library or bookstore either. None of this can fill in for the actual experiences of the adventure you are about to have, but some basic preparation like this can help you avoid those awkward moments of intercultural misunderstanding, and allow you to make the most of the all-too-short time you have there.

Effort counts. Especially if you are traveling to a non-English-speaking country, don't be afraid to draw on all of your foreign language skills, however limited they might be. Even if you still feel a little shaky with your adopted tongue, you will find that most of the locals will appreciate your attempts to speak to them in the language of the land. Moments of potential embarrassment —where you can only muster a phrase or two in order to communicate your basic needs—can quickly turn into opportunities to make new friends or learn more about the language. No one expects you to be perfectly fluent or have a native command of the language, but everyone will recognize how hard you are trying to work it into your daily routine. You're there for the immersion experience, and when in Rome, right?

It never hurts to ask. Of course, you are trying to purvey confidence and knowledge so that you can blend in with your new environs—who knows, eventually you might even be mistaken for a local. But there will be lots of situations where you simply don't or can't understand something, like a particular idiom, a cultural practice, or a joke. At moments like this, don't be afraid to turn to your hosts or program director for help or an explanation of things you don't understand. You'll get a better understanding of what you just saw, heard, or experienced from someone there in the host culture than you will by calling a friend back home and telling him how "weird" something is.

Study hard, play hard. It's easy to think about your time abroad as an excuse for a year-long bender, but remember that you are doing this to contribute to your education and to have some fun. You should plan to take advantage of every moment of your time abroad—going to museums, meeting new people, enjoying the nightlife, or getting out into the countryside. But you should plan to devote equal time to your studies, all the while adjusting to a new institution, a different academic calendar, and a different instructional format. If you don't keep your grades up, your course credit might not transfer back to your home institution and could even affect financial aid (check with your registrar or International Education office about this before you go). Important caveat: it's also probably not worth your time or mental energy to go grade-grubbing, which might even be considered offensive in some academic environments. You don't need to get straight-A's, but don't lose track of the "study" in "study abroad" either.

At the same time, you are likely to get a good part, if not most, of your education outside of the classroom. And you can get credit for it: try to take classes that help you understand your host culture. That's part of the reason you decided to come abroad in the first place, and it will allow you to turn your host city or country into a gigantic, exciting, real-life laboratory.

The Ugly American

Perhaps the other side of the coin here is a word of caution regarding negative stereotypes about Americans. It's no secret that the international reputation of the U.S. has been taking it on the chin a lot lately, but you don't have to contribute to that. It's best to remember that, whether you like it or not, you are an ambassador for your home country as much as your hosts are introducing you to a different culture.

We don't mean to suggest that you always need to be on your perfect behavior, but you can be conscious of some of the most common American stereotypes and how to avoid playing into them. Those include thinking that Americans are: loud and obnoxious (especially when drinking); sexually promiscuous; overly informal or disrespectful of authority; immature and arrogant; and convinced that the United States is the center of the universe. Some of those can negatively affect your interactions with the locals in serious ways, but by and large, you will find that most people will give you the benefit of the doubt; they won't buy into these stereotypes unless you give them reason to do so. You can show them that, by virtue of your very desire to live in their country, you are more than a tourist, and represent an image of an American as a conscientious global citizen.

By the same token, don't believe the stereotypes you've heard about other cultures: not all French people are rude, and not all social exchanges in Japan are full of elaborate ceremonial bowing. As we have suggested, it's a good idea to acquaint yourself with the general customs of your adopted land, but that doesn't mean that everyone you meet will follow them to the letter. Just remember that people are people everywhere, and the best way to avoid stereotypes—in both directions—is to treat each person as an individual.

Packing Light, Packing Long

Remember all of the stuff you packed when you moved to college? Now look around your apartment or dorm room and take note of all that you've accumulated since then. Let's face it: our lives gather belongings like a snowball rolling downhill. Do you need to bring *everything* with you when you go abroad?

The answer, of course, is no. You may be moving to another country, but you don't need to have all of your things *from* home in order to *feel* at home. And, maybe more to the point, you *aren't* at home: if you are staying with a host family, you won't be able to blast your stereo late into the night, and if you are moving into a dorm at your host institution, you may not have as much space as you are used to. You want to be able to settle in to your new environs, but you also want to be able to pack a quick bag for a weekend jaunt. When it comes to packing for your time abroad, our philosophy is simple: *pack light, and pack for the long haul.* That means taking only things that won't weigh you down too much, and that you can use in any number of situations.

Some things to definitely bring along are:

→ **Your passport!** This is the single most important document that you have with you; be sure that it is up to date and won't be expiring during your stay. You should carry your passport on your person on the plane ride over and whenever you make any major changes of location;

→ **Your visa!** Just as your passport lets you leave and return to your home country, your visa lets you enter and leave your host country. Because the process can be long and time-consuming, you should start applying for your entry visa as soon as you are accepted into a study abroad program. And like your passport, don't leave it in your luggage when traveling—keep it with you;

→ **International Student Identity Card,** available from the International Student Travel Confederation (http://www.istc.org) or STA Travel (http://www.statravel.com);

→ **Photocopies of your passport,** and information for the nearest U.S. consulate office;

→ **Travel journal or notebook,** such as Moleskine® journals—we like them for the elastic strap, which can hold all of the memorabilia you accumulate in place;

→ **One or two good guidebooks,** with maps of your host city;

→ **Books for leisure reading**—it's entirely possible that you won't have access to a television or the internet as often as you would like;

→ **Strong backpack** for weekend excursions;

→ **Large, fast drying towel**—also known as *The Hitchhiker's Guide to the Galaxy* rule, since a sturdy towel can, in a pinch, function as a pillow, a blanket, an umbrella, a knapsack, or even a towel;

→ **Electrical adapters/voltage converters**—consider also a power strip if you are bringing multiple electrical devices (iPod, camera, laptop, etc.) so you only need one adapter;

→ **Swiss Army knife** with corkscrew, bottle opener, can opener, and a good blade. Needless to say, you should put this in your checked baggage when traveling;

→ **Money belt;**

→ **Prescriptions** and/or prescription drugs fully-supplied for the duration of your stay;

→ **One "nice" outfit,** for fancy nights out or job/internship interviews (those might not be the same, so you might need two "nice" outfits).

Some things you won't be needing are:

→ **Extensive supplies of toiletries or batteries**—you'll be able to find them (or equivalents) in your host country;

→ **Umbrella**—easily purchased almost anywhere;

→ **Valuable or sentimental items**—this is not a good time to bring along Grandma's heirloom jewelry;

→ **Your cell phone**—we know, we may as well ask you to cut off your right arm, but, unless you already have international calling as part of your cellular package, international calling plans can get very expensive (up to $5 per minute in some places), and there is no guarantee that your phone will be compatible with local cellular services. You'll be better off buying a phone locally with a short-term contract that meets your needs.

→ **Baseball caps**—resist the urge to bring one, even if you have a favorite. Unless you're a kid, most adults don't wear one outside of the U.S., and, besides, they will make you look like the stereotypical American, an easy mark for prejudices and predators when you are out in the streets.

A note about clothing: Consider packing clothing that will be as flexible as you are. That means items that are all-weather, durable, can easily be drip- or line-dried, and that work together in various outfit combinations. Also remember that dark clothing shows fewer stains than light, so you may be able to get away with wearing certain items, even when they are overdue for a wash.

You should also be prepared to wear clothes that might be slightly more adult-like than you are used to. By "more adult-like," we don't mean that you should start pulling your suits and ties out of the closet. Think "chic casual" as your general approach; trade in the T-shirt for the collared shirt, and recognize that in many parts of the world clothing carries more gender-specific connotations. For instance, in many places outside of the United States, adult men are less likely to wear shorts, even when the weather outside begs for them. Women will find that, culturally, it is more acceptable to wear skirts than pants, shorts, or culottes. Even if you find such cultural expectations to be offensive or oppressive, sometimes it is more expedient and effective to follow the customs of your local environment rather than to stake a claim for gender-based—or, for that matter, comfort-based—freedom. (If you want to get involved in organizations that are working to change the gender expectations of your host country, we applaud you. But in the meantime, you might want to find a way to express your individuality within the cultural norms of your new environment.)

A note about computers: You will probably need to bring a laptop computer with you for your studies, but remember that over 1 million laptops are stolen worldwide every year, and particularly on college campuses. We've even had a report from one student whose laptop was taken before she ever left the airport! While you can never entirely eliminate this threat, there are several easy steps that you can take to minimize the risk.

- → **Don't carry your laptop in a traditional laptop case.** Nothing is more inviting to thieves than the typical black square nylon laptop case; you might as well paint a bulls-eye on the side. Consider purchasing a backpack that doesn't look like a laptop case, but has a padded slot to fit your computer inside a more traditional-looking schoolbag. At the very least, this will prevent you from appearing as an obvious mark in public places like cafés and libraries.

- → **Invest in a physical security system.** Many laptops come equipped with a slot to accommodate a chain and lock that can tie the computer to a desk or other immovable object. Devices like the Kensington® Security Slot (http://www.kensington.com) or the Targus DEFCON® Video Port Lock Key (http://www.targus.com) won't prevent 100% of laptop thefts, but they will make it much harder for anyone to grab your computer and go.

- → **Invest in a software security system.** Even if your laptop is stolen, you can protect your sensitive data through various software measures, often available for a reasonable price. The built-in, standard password protection that comes with your computer will no longer do the job; consider a more comprehensive software solution like Bak2U's Phoenix Anti-Theft (available for both Windows and Mac OS X, at http://www.bak2u.com), which runs invisibly in the background to photograph your thief, send out alerts via email, and even physically locate your computer!

- → **Backup and purge sensitive data.** For a more low-tech solution, consider simply stripping your laptop of any vitally sensitive data that you won't be needing while you are abroad (bank records, personal information, etc.) and storing it all on a CD or backup drive to be left at home while you are away. That way, even if your laptop is stolen, you won't have to worry about identity theft and all of the hassles it entails.

Other Considerations Before You Go

Planning a trip like this isn't as simple as packing a bag and heading out; whether we admit it or not, our lives are intimately bound up with a host of bureaucracies and paperwork, and we have to attend to those things before we leave so that we can use them when we need them. Some of this is "worst case scenario" stuff that hopefully will never come into play; some of it is just common sense so that you are prepared in the event of an unexpected situation. Here are some of the additional things you should consider before you go:

Power of attorney. Isn't that for the elderly? No, not really—delegating power of attorney is the process of assigning a trusted representative to take care of your financial and legal obligations, regardless of age. This may come in handy, even necessary, in order to handle your dealings with banks, financial aid, or insurance back home while you are away. But granting power of attorney should not be taken lightly; you are literally assigning someone power over your legal and financial existence, so be sure that it is someone in whom you have the utmost of confidence (in most cases, your parents will do just fine). Delegating power of attorney can be as simple as purchasing a standard form from an office supply store or, if you want to be sure, consulting with an attorney to draft a personalized document. Either way, this can be an essential document to making sure that your legal and financial matters can be taken care of while you are away.

Health insurance. As we all know, health insurance is a precious commodity, and all the more so if you are traveling abroad. Before going, be sure to check with your health insurance provider to see how you are covered while you are abroad. If necessary, consider purchasing supplemental insurance to give you better access to local health care facilities. And you should check with your particular study abroad program to see what additional health insurance is offered to you.

> Chances are, it won't happen to you; but it never hurts to be prepared in case you run into trouble. We don't want to stop you from exploring your new home, but, unfortunately, crime is a fact of life just about anywhere you go.

Other forms of insurance. We hate to say it, but some parts of the world aren't that safe, and being an American can increase your risk. Depending on your destination, consider kidnapping, terrorism, and emergency evacuation coverage. Often, you can get really cheap traveler's insurance to cover these risks through your school insurance.

If you plan on driving in your adopted country, check with your domestic auto insurance provider about your international coverage, and make sure you have the requisite certification for your host country (you might have to take another driver's test).

Health care. As we've already mentioned, be sure that all of your prescriptions medicines are up to date, and that you have substantial supplies of all of them to take with you. Depending on your destination, you might also need to get additional vaccinations, which often require significant (up to six weeks) lead time.

Bank/credit cards. These days, it no longer makes sense to travel with large amounts of local currency or even piles of traveler's cheques—your bank card can do the work for you. But it's not a bad idea to bring about $200 worth of local currency with you; before you go, be sure to check with your bank about the availability of ATMs in your host city, and requirements for your PIN: some countries require PINs of specific lengths, which might be more than your four-digit birth year number.

Exchange rate. Be sure you know the current and common rate of currency exchange before you get off the plane. When you arrive, you'll likely be fatigued, jet-lagged, and disoriented; in such circumstances, it's easy to confuse all of those new coins in your pocket and end up paying $100 for a $10 taxi from the airport. If you can do the mental math, you won't get, well, taken for a ride.

In Case of Emergency

Chances are, it won't happen to you; but it never hurts to be prepared in case you run into trouble—whether you are commuting to class, going home after a late night with friends, coming home from the market, or any of the other myriad reasons why you might be out in the world. We don't want to stop you from exploring your new home, but, unfortunately, crime is a fact of life just about anywhere you go. For the most part, you should be alert for pickpocket thieves and other small-time con artists who may be on the prowl to take your wallet, or worse, especially in large cities where tourists flock. The best policy is to be smart about where you go and who you are with. You should always be with at least another person you know—the more the better—when you are hopping from one place to another on a weekend night out. By being in a group, you won't be singled out and potentially put in a situation where you might get hurt. But if you do get ensnared by dubious characters, don't try to be a superhero; give them whatever belongings they want. There is no reason to take any chances. You probably won't get your wallet back, but at least you'll make it home in one piece.

Be sure to familiarize yourself with the emergency protocols of your particular study abroad program. Your program or university coordinator should explain their established emergency protocol to you—and if they don't have one, you should get out of the program immediately.

Your coordinator will be able to offer more specific "streetwise" advice, but that will surely include:

→ Avoid the lone "sketchy" person weaving in and out of a crowd of tourists, simultaneously spitting on their neck and feeling their back pockets (hint: spitting is only a diversion). While you try to understand what landed on your neck, there goes your wallet!

→ Watch out for groups of cons with one lead who pretends to drop his wallet in front of you. He expects you to pick it up (being the good person that you are) and bring it to him; but then, everything goes topsy-turvy—the lead con artist grabs you to make sure you returned all his money (of all people, right?), and in an instant you are surrounded by two of his accomplices. Now it's your wallet that's gone.

→ *Never, ever, ever, under any circumstances* leave a female friend alone. Study abroad coordinators report that almost every case of sexual assault they see—sadly, all too frequently—the young woman was alone, either because her friends left her behind or because they thought she knew a particular group of men. Never abandon your fellow travelers—you're all in this together, and need to take care of each other.

Rest assured; in most places, the streets are perfectly safe. Just don't take it for granted that they are *always* safe—or, for that matter, that you are never vulnerable. Use common sense and street sense, and approach the streets there the same way you would back home. Listen to your study abroad coordinators' advice and take plenty of precaution. And always know the local emergency telephone number. It is unlikely to be 911, as in the U.S.—England is 999, France is 112.

For Mom and Dad

This section is intended primarily for the parents out there—or, for the potential traveler to talk to their parents in order to put their fears to rest. We want to dispel some of the common anxieties about study abroad so that both you and your parents can enter this adventure with the utmost of confidence.

As parents, you will want to know that there is proper supervision and that your child will stay far from trouble. Rest assured, all colleges conduct extensive studies about the countries in which they plan to send students.

As parents, you will naturally want to know that there is proper supervision and that your child will stay far from trouble. Rest assured, all colleges and universities conduct extensive studies about the countries in which they plan to send students. Prior to actually creating a semester-long study abroad program, for instance, it is not uncommon for college representatives to visit the areas in which their programs operate. If students have the option to live with host families, there are substantial vetting processes to ensure not only good compatibility, but also student safety and welfare. For sure, no one can protect against everything, but a lot goes into creating a study abroad program, and a substantial part of that is in ensuring a safe learning environment.

There are some questions that you should feel free to ask of any study abroad program you are seriously considering:

→ **How much will the program cost?** If your son or daughter is going through their home university, do they pay the same fees, more, or less? If you are going with another institution or third party, be sure to find out what expenses are covered and where you might need to spend some extra money.

→ **Will the credits transfer?** In general, the courses that your son or daughter will take abroad must be assessed by their home institution and approved, so be sure that all of the necessary steps have been taken. Your student should also know the procedures for getting courses approved after they return, if necessary. There are also potentially additional issues related to the length of stay (some institutions require a certain amount of time at the home campus), so knowing these rules is also a good idea.

→ **Who is responsible for making travel arrangements?** Some programs require you to book your own flights to and from the host country, while others will include it in the program fees. Your student will likely have options to travel during their stay as well, so find out if you must commit to them prior to departure or if your student can decide on them on the fly.

→ **What are the living arrangements like?** Will your student live in a dormitory, with a host family, or will they need to find an apartment on their own? Again, the answer to these questions might affect cost calculations, or your own feelings of safety for your child.

→ **What is the program's emergency protocol and who is responsible for implementing it?** As we said, anyone who can't answer this one isn't worth your time. But you should also feel as though *you* have a stable contact person in case you need to reach your son or daughter in a hurry.

But as parents, you've also got to modify your expectations once you send your baby out into the world:

→ **Don't expect a phone call home in the first two days.** Between getting a phone, figuring out international calling, the time difference, and everything your son or daughter will be doing in the first few days, it can be hard for them to find the time. They should be able to let you know they've arrived at their final destination safe and sound, but probably not much more than that at the outset.

→ **Set up a regular time, maybe once a week, to talk on the phone.** Once your son or daughter has settled in, they will be able to check in more frequently, and no doubt they will want to share their new experiences with you.

→ **Don't hover.** Once your child is abroad, they will undoubtedly encounter situations in which they would normally turn to you for help. Wiring some extra money for an apartment deposit is one thing, but try to resist the temptation to solve their problems for them, or even to try to long-distance coach them in the form of "shoulds." It is likely that you will be able to do very little for them at such a remove, and your advice could add layers of frustration to the situation. Be available and encouraging, but let your child enjoy their new circumstances for themselves. Sometimes solving problems can be the most rewarding experiences of all.

→ **Offer support where necessary.** If your child calls in tears or upset, be calm and supportive. Talk through the problem with them, and be there to listen. Encourage him or her to contact the program coordinator or appropriate contact person at their host institution as soon as possible. Someone "on the ground" will be in a much better position to help your child than you will.

Further Resources

We hope that this brief introduction gets you started in planning your study abroad experience, but we also know that there are plenty of other valuable resources out there to further assist in the process. Here are some of the sources we think can offer additional illumination about different aspects of your study abroad adventure.

Resources in Print:

Williamson, Wendy. *Study Abroad 101.* Kalamazoo: Agapy Publishing, 2004. An easy-to-use guide that covers all aspects of the study abroad process (except for the kind of detailed program information you'll find here), broken down into questions and answers.

Dowell, Michele-Marie and Kelly P. Mirsky. *Study Abroad: How to Get the Most out of Your Experience.* New York: Prentice Hall, 2002. This workbook offers exercises for the traveler "to fully capitalize on their study abroad experience," covering all aspects of their time abroad, from personal growth to cultural education and professional development.

Hansel, Bettina. *The Exchange Student Survival Kit.* Boston: Intercultural Press, 2007. An interesting book that emphasizes the personal, social, and cultural aspects of studying abroad. You won't find information here about specific programs, but you will find out how to deal with your host family and how to cope with the loss of Thanksgiving.

Balaban, Mariah and Jennifer Shields. *Study Away: The Unauthorized Guide to College Abroad.* New York: Anchor Books, 2003. A detailed, country-by-country guide to some of the major universities that accept international students. It won't tell you how to get there (providing only basic contact information), but it will give you the lowdown on particular campuses and what to expect.

Loflin, Stephen E. Adventures Abroad: *The Student's Guide to Studying Overseas.* New York: Kaplan Publishing, 2007. Another comprehensive guide, but this one is based on actual testimonials from students affiliated with the National Society of Collegiate Scholars. For anecdotes and practical wisdom, this book has it all.

How to Use this Book

| DESTINATION | HOST INSTITUTION | PRGM SEASON | PRGM TYPE | INTERMEDIARY | HOUSING |

Sample University

Johanna Smith jsmith@sample.edu
Director of International Programs 555.555.5555
1 Main St. http://sample.edu
Springfield, MA 12345

Destination	Host Institution	Prgm Season	Prgm Type	Intermediary	Housing
Austria | Vienna	Theresianum Academy	Fall Spr	Self	n/a	PrivApt
Cost: Fall Costs: T&F: n/a, R&B: n/a, Ttl: $39,000 plus program fees. Spr Costs: T&F: n/a, R&B: n/a, Ttl: $39,000 plus program fees					
Italy | Florence	Firenze Arti Visive	Sum Fall Spr	Intermed	Firenze Arti Visive	n/a
South Korea | Seoul	Yonsei University	Fall	Bilat	n/a	CollRes

My Second Campus contains eight key pieces of information about study abroad programs to help identify the best program for you.

1. Study Abroad Office Contact Information

For colleges and universities that have a central office that manages study abroad programs, we include the contact information of the program director. But for those institutions that do not have a central office yet still have study abroad opportunities for students, we provide the contact information of the chief academic officer (sometimes called provost) who has knowledge of all academic and co-curricular activities. These contacts can help you with any inquiries about applying for the programs mentioned in this guidebook. If it isn't covered in here, don't be afraid to give them a ring.

2. Destination

Destination is the country and city information where the majority of the study abroad program is held. For travel courses where more than two cities and countries are visited, we indicate these as "multiple."

3. Host Institution

Host institution is the receiving school abroad where students enroll for most of their coursework. Some colleges and universities in the U.S. may send their students to a branch campus or classrooms that the schools rent or own in a foreign country. In this instance, we list the U.S. institution's name as the host institution. We also list the U.S. institution as the host institution for travel courses because these courses are normally brief in duration and the programs are not affiliated with any institution during the travel through the foreign country.

4. Program Season

Program season refers to when the study abroad program operates. We convert southern hemisphere academic calendar to northern hemisphere academic calendar. For instance, winter semester in Australia would be considered fall semester in the United States. Abbreviations used are *Spr*, *Sum*, *Fall*, *Win*, and *YrRound*.

5. Program Type

As you browse the following pages, you will notice that our listings refer to several different broad types of study abroad programs. As we have already mentioned, not all study abroad programs are created equal, but each kind has its own advantages. Finding the program that is right for you first involves understanding these basic features, so that you can begin to narrow down your range of opportunities. Study abroad programs generally fall into one of five categories:

Self-Organized (*Self*): As the name implies, these are programs that are organized, managed, and operated directly by a U.S. college or university. Essentially, the home school runs the whole show: its own faculty members go abroad with their students, it builds its own courses in keeping with its curriculum requirements, and it hires its own academics to teach them. Our listings for these programs tend to offer more detailed information (program costs and housing options).

We treat these "self-organized" programs in more detail because we believe homegrown programs offer a stronger student-centered model of study than some of the other options. From providing courses that will easily count towards graduation, to offering excursions woven in between classes and weekends, to recognizing the cultural dimensions of living abroad (i.e. group meals, theatrical outings), we think these programs offer some of the most comprehensive experiences you are likely to find.

Intermediary Company (*Intermed*): These are programs that are organized by third parties or private companies, both non- and for-profit. Certain schools contract with these companies to manage their study abroad offerings, take care of the logistics, and even provide coursework. These programs have the advantage of being managed by folks with a lot of experience from all over—they know what they are doing.

Recognized U.S. College (*USColl*): These are study abroad programs offered at other colleges and universities. In general, most institutions not only allow but encourage students from other institutions to participate in their study abroad programs. Up until now, these programs were largely unknown by prospective students, or only by word of mouth between people in the study abroad business. Now you can access them as well.

Direct Enrollment (*Dir*): Again, pretty self-explanatory; listings with this designation mean that you can enroll directly at the host institution. For all intents and purposes, you will be a student at that school, largely bypassing the structure of an intermediary program. This might give you a more "authentic" immersion experience, but you also may have to figure out more things on your own.

Consortium (*Consrtm*): Oftentimes, smaller schools will pool their resources to create a program that serves all of their needs. This gives you the advantage of working with faculty from other domestic institutions, and of meeting other students from your area. You can get the best that the group has to offer, while still retaining the feel of a personalized experience.

Bilateral/Exchange (*Bilat*): These refer to specific arrangements between domestic institutions and foreign universities, where students from one institution go to the other, and vice versa. This gives you the advantage of two institutions that know how to work with one another and have established lines of communication, but it also means that you will likely encounter a lot of students from your home institution (which can be a good or a bad thing, depending).

6. Name of Intermediary

Intermediaries are study abroad companies that manage abroad programs. These organizations not only coordinate study abroad opportunities on behalf of U.S. colleges and universities, but can also function as freestanding academic institutions stationed abroad. We also provide the name of the U.S. college or university if it sponsors a study abroad program for students from other institutions; many institutions allow their students to enroll in other college or university's study abroad programs.

7. Housing Options

Where you live is an important part of a study abroad experience. You may have a full immersion program by living with a host family. If you prefer a more independent living arrangement, some programs have private apartment or college residence arrangements. For travel courses, there are alternative housing options, such as hotels and hostels.

8. Costs

Program costs are shown separately for tuition and living expenses (room and board) for each term of program availability. When tuition and living expenses are not available separately, comprehensive costs are shown instead, if available.

Connecticut

DESTINATION	HOST INSTITUTION	PRGM SEASON	PRGM TYPE	INTERMEDIARY	HOUSING

Albertus Magnus College

Julia M. McNamaram
Professor of French
700 Prospect Street
Mohun Hall, 1st floor
New Haven, CT 06511

cnamara@albertus.edu
203.773.8529
http://www.albertus.edu/bachelors-degrees/bachelors-degree-programs/foreign-language/faculty.html

[Country Unspecified]	[City Unspecified]	n/a	n/a	n/a	n/a	n/a

Central Connecticut State University

Nancy Weissman
International Education Coordinator
Center for International Education
1615 Stanley Street
Post Office Box 4010
New Britain, CT 06050-4010

weissmannn@ccsu.edu
860.832.2217
http://www.ccsu.edu/page.cfm?p=546

Brazil	Bahia	Central Connecticut State University	Sum	Self	The George R. Muirhead Center for International Education	n/a
Costs: Sum Costs: T&F: $5,150, R&B: n/a, Ttl: n/a					
Chile	(Multiple)	Central Connecticut State University	Win	Self	The George R. Muirhead Center for International Education	n/a
Costs: Win Costs: T&F: $3,700, R&B: n/a, Ttl: n/a					
Chile	Santiago	Central Connecticut State University	Spr	Self	The George R. Muirhead Center for International Education	n/a
Costs: Spr Costs: T&F: $1,995, R&B: n/a, Ttl: n/a					
China	Jinan & Beijing	Central Connecticut State University	Sum	Self	The George R. Muirhead Center for International Education	n/a
Costs: Sum Costs: T&F: $1,295, R&B: n/a, Ttl: n/a					

© 2011 — Updates? Want to be in the next edition? Visit **www.mysecondcampus.com**

Connecticut

DESTINATION	HOST INSTITUTION	PRGM SEASON	PRGM TYPE	INTERMEDIARY	HOUSING
England | (Multiple)	Central Connecticut State University	Sum	Self	The George R. Muirhead Center for International Education	n/a
Costs: Sum Costs: T&F: $4,350, R&B: n/a, Ttl: n/a					
England | London	Central Connecticut State University	Spr	Self	The George R. Muirhead Center for International Education	n/a
Costs: Spr Costs: T&F: $1,995, R&B: n/a, Ttl: n/a					
England | London	Central Connecticut State University	Spr	Self	The George R. Muirhead Center for International Education	n/a
Costs: Spr Costs: T&F: $1,995, R&B: n/a, Ttl: n/a					
England | London	Central Connecticut State University	Sum	Self	The George R. Muirhead Center for International Education	n/a
Costs: Sum Costs: T&F: $3,300, R&B: n/a, Ttl: n/a					
France | Paris	Central Connecticut State University	Sum	Self	The George R. Muirhead Center for International Education	n/a
Costs: Sum Costs: T&F: $4,650, R&B: n/a, Ttl: n/a					
Germany | Berlin	Central Connecticut State University	Spr	Self	The George R. Muirhead Center for International Education	n/a
Costs: Spr Costs: T&F: $1,995, R&B: n/a, Ttl: n/a					
Germany | Berlin	International Center for Journalism at Freie Universitat Berlin	Sum	Intermed	DAAD - German Academic Exchange Service	n/a
Ghana | (Multiple)	Central Connecticut State University	Sum	Self	The George R. Muirhead Center for International Education	n/a
Costs: Sum Costs: T&F: $4,600, R&B: n/a, Ttl: n/a					
Ireland | Dublin	Central Connecticut State University	Spr	Self	The George R. Muirhead Center for International Education	n/a
Costs: Spr Costs: T&F: $1,995, R&B: n/a, Ttl: n/a					
Ireland | Sligo & Dublin	Central Connecticut State University	Sum	Self	The George R. Muirhead Center for International Education	n/a
Costs: Sum Costs: T&F: $5,150, R&B: n/a, Ttl: n/a					
Ireland, Scotland & England | [City Unspecified]	Central Connecticut State University	Sum	Self	The George R. Muirhead Center for International Education	n/a
Costs: Sum Costs: T&F: $7,010, R&B: n/a, Ttl: n/a					
Italy | (Multiple)	Central Connecticut State University	Sum	Self	The George R. Muirhead Center for International Education	n/a
Costs: Sum Costs: T&F: $5,930, R&B: n/a, Ttl: n/a					
Italy | Messina	Central Connecticut State University	Sum	Self	The George R. Muirhead Center for International Education	n/a
Costs: Sum Costs: T&F: $3,870, R&B: n/a, Ttl: n/a					
Italy | Rome	Central Connecticut State University	Spr	Self	The George R. Muirhead Center for International Education	n/a
Costs: Spr Costs: T&F: $1,995, R&B: n/a, Ttl: n/a					
Italy | Rome	Central Connecticut State University	Spr	Self	The George R. Muirhead Center for International Education	n/a
Costs: Spr Costs: T&F: $1,995, R&B: n/a, Ttl: n/a					

© 2011 — Updates? Want to be in the next edition? Visit **www.mysecondcampus.com**

Connecticut

DESTINATION	HOST INSTITUTION	PRGM SEASON	PRGM TYPE	INTERMEDIARY	HOUSING
Jamaica | Montego Bay	Central Connecticut State University	Sum	Self	The George R. Muirhead Center for International Education	n/a
Costs: Sum Costs: T&F: $3,970, R&B: n/a, Ttl: n/a					
Japan | (Multiple)	Central Connecticut State University	Sum	Self	The George R. Muirhead Center for International Education	n/a
Costs: Sum Costs: T&F: $5,150, R&B: n/a, Ttl: n/a					
Mexico | Cuernavaca	Central Connecticut State University	Sum	Self	The George R. Muirhead Center for International Education	n/a
Costs: Sum Costs: T&F: $4,350, R&B: n/a, Ttl: n/a					
Mexico | Merida	Central Connecticut State University	Sum	Self	The George R. Muirhead Center for International Education	n/a
Costs: Sum Costs: T&F: $4,350, R&B: n/a, Ttl: n/a					
Nicaragua | Esteli	Central Connecticut State University	Spr	Self	The George R. Muirhead Center for International Education	n/a
Costs: Spr Costs: T&F: $1,995, R&B: n/a, Ttl: n/a					
Peru | Lima	Central Connecticut State University	Win	Self	The George R. Muirhead Center for International Education	n/a
Costs: Win Costs: T&F: $5,000, R&B: n/a, Ttl: n/a					
Poland | Wroclaw	Central Connecticut State University	Spr	Self	The George R. Muirhead Center for International Education	n/a
Costs: Spr Costs: T&F: $1,995, R&B: n/a, Ttl: n/a					
Scotland | Edinburgh	Central Connecticut State University	Sum	Self	The George R. Muirhead Center for International Education	n/a
Costs: Sum Costs: T&F: $4,350, R&B: n/a, Ttl: n/a					
South Africa | Cape Town	Central Connecticut State University	Sum	Self	The George R. Muirhead Center for International Education	n/a
Costs: Sum Costs: T&F: $7,150, R&B: n/a, Ttl: n/a					
South Korea | Seoul	Central Connecticut State University	Sum	Self	The George R. Muirhead Center for International Education	n/a
Costs: Sum Costs: T&F: n/a, R&B: n/a, Ttl: n/a					
South Korea | Seoul	Central Connecticut State University	Sum	Self	The George R. Muirhead Center for International Education	n/a
Costs: Sum Costs: T&F: $2,395, R&B: n/a, Ttl: n/a					
Spain & Morocco | [City Unspecified]	Central Connecticut State University	Spr	Self	The George R. Muirhead Center for International Education	n/a
Costs: Spr Costs: T&F: $1,995, R&B: n/a, Ttl: n/a					
Spain & Morocco | [City Unspecified]	Central Connecticut State University	Spr	Self	The George R. Muirhead Center for International Education	n/a
Costs: Spr Costs: T&F: $1,995, R&B: n/a, Ttl: n/a					
Spain | Santiago de Compostela	Central Connecticut State University	Sum	Self	The George R. Muirhead Center for International Education	n/a
Costs: Sum Costs: T&F: $4,650, R&B: n/a, Ttl: n/a					
United Arab Emirates | (Multiple)	Central Connecticut State University	Win	Self	The George R. Muirhead Center for International Education	n/a
Costs: Win Costs: T&F: $3,600, R&B: n/a, Ttl: n/a					

© 2011 — Updates? Want to be in the next edition? Visit **www.mysecondcampus.com**

Connecticut

DESTINATION	HOST INSTITUTION	PRGM SEASON	PRGM TYPE	INTERMEDIARY	HOUSING
United States	Honolulu (HI)	Central Connecticut State University	Win	Self	The George R. Muirhead Center for International Education	n/a
Costs: Win Costs: T&F: $4,080, R&B: n/a, Ttl: n/a					

Charter Oak State College

55 Paul J. Manafort Drive
New Britain, CT 06053

860.832.3800
http://www.charteroak.edu/Current/Services/

DESTINATION	HOST INSTITUTION	PRGM SEASON	PRGM TYPE	INTERMEDIARY	HOUSING
(Multiple choices)	(Multiple choices)	Charter Oak State College	n/a	Intermed	Illume	n/a

Connecticut College

Shirley Parson
Director
Office of Study Away
270 Mohegan Avenue
Fanning Hall, 113
New London, CT 06320-4196

sapar@conncoll.edu
860.447.1911
http://www.conncoll.edu/academics/aca_international_programs.htm

DESTINATION	HOST INSTITUTION	PRGM SEASON	PRGM TYPE	INTERMEDIARY	HOUSING
(Multiple choices)	(Multiple choices)	Multiple institutional choices	n/a	Intermed	School for Field Studies	n/a
Argentina	(Multiple choices)	Multiple institutional choices	n/a	Intermed	Institute for Study Abroad	n/a
Argentina	Buenos Aires	IES Abroad Buenos Aires Center	Sum Fall Spr YrRound	Intermed	IES Abroad	n/a
Argentina	Buenos Aires	SIT Study Abroad	n/a	Intermed	SIT Study Abroad	n/a
Australia	Brisbane	University of Queensland	n/a	Intermed	Institute for Study Abroad	n/a
Australia	Byron Bay	SIT Study Abroad	n/a	Intermed	SIT Study Abroad	n/a
Australia	Melbourne	University of Melbourne	n/a	Intermed	Institute for Study Abroad	n/a
Australia	Perth	University of Western Australia	n/a	Intermed	Institute for Study Abroad	n/a
Australia	Sydney	University of New South Wales	n/a	Intermed	Institute for Study Abroad	n/a
Australia	Sydney	University of Sydney	n/a	Intermed	Institute for Study Abroad	n/a
Australia	Townsville	James Cook University	n/a	Intermed	Institute for Study Abroad	n/a
Bolivia	Cochabamba	SIT Study Abroad	n/a	Intermed	SIT Study Abroad	n/a
Cameroon	Yaounde	SIT Study Abroad	n/a	Intermed	SIT Study Abroad	n/a
Chile	Santiago	IES Abroad Santiago Center	Sum Fall Spr YrRound	Intermed	IES Abroad	n/a
Chile	Santiago	Multiple institutional choices	n/a	Intermed	Institute for Study Abroad	n/a
Chile	Santiago	SIT Study Abroad	n/a	Intermed	SIT Study Abroad	n/a
Chile	Santiago	Universidad Adolfo Ibanez	n/a	Intermed	Institute for Study Abroad	n/a
Chile	Valparaiso and Vina del Mar	Universidad Tecnica Federico Santa Maria	n/a	Intermed	Institute for Study Abroad	n/a
China	(Multiple choices)	Multiple institutional choices	n/a	Intermed	Alliance for Global Education	n/a
China	Beijing	Capital University of Economics and Business	n/a	USColl	Hamilton College	n/a

© 2011 — Updates? Want to be in the next edition? Visit www.mysecondcampus.com

Connecticut

DESTINATION	HOST INSTITUTION	PRGM SEASON	PRGM TYPE	INTERMEDIARY	HOUSING
China | Hangzhou	CET Academic Programs	n/a	Intermed	CET Academic Programs	n/a
China | Harbin	CET Academic Programs	n/a	Intermed	CET Academic Programs	n/a
China | Kunming	SIT Study Abroad	n/a	Intermed	SIT Study Abroad	n/a
Costa Rica | Heredia	Universidad Nacional	n/a	Intermed	Institute for Study Abroad	n/a
Costa Rica | San Jose	Universidad de Costa Rica	n/a	Intermed	Institute for Study Abroad	n/a
Czech Republic | Prague	Charles University	n/a	Dir	n/a	n/a
Denmark | Copenhagen	Danish Institute for Study Abroad	n/a	Intermed	Danish Institute for Study Abroad	n/a
Ecuador | Quito	IES Abroad Quito Center	Sum Fall Spr YrRound	Intermed	IES Abroad	n/a
Ecuador | Quito	SIT Study Abroad	n/a	Intermed	SIT Study Abroad	n/a
England | Brighton	University of Sussex	n/a	Intermed	Institute for Study Abroad	n/a
England | Bristol	University of Bristol	n/a	Intermed	Institute for Study Abroad	n/a
England | Cambridge or London	Institute of Economic and Political Studies	n/a	Intermed	Institute of Economic and Political Studies	n/a
England | Canterbury	University of Kent	n/a	Intermed	Institute for Study Abroad	n/a
England | London	British American Drama Academy	n/a	Dir	n/a	n/a
England | London	School of Oriental & African Studies	n/a	Intermed	Institute for Study Abroad	n/a
England | London	University College London	n/a	Intermed	Institute for Study Abroad	n/a
England | Norwich	University of East Anglia	n/a	Intermed	Institute for Study Abroad	n/a
England | Nottingham	University of Nottingham	n/a	Intermed	Institute for Study Abroad	n/a
England | York	University of York	n/a	Intermed	Institute for Study Abroad	n/a
France | Nantes	IES Abroad Nantes Center	Sum Fall Spr YrRound	Intermed	IES Abroad	n/a
France | Paris	IES Abroad Paris Center	Sum Fall Spr YrRound	Intermed	IES Abroad	n/a
France | Paris	Multiple institutional choices	Fall Spr YrRound	USColl	Sweet Briar College Junior Year in France	n/a
Germany | Baden-Wurttemberg	Multiple institutional choices	n/a	Bilat	Baden-Wurttemberg Exchange	n/a
Germany | Berlin	IES Abroad Berlin Center	Fall Spr YrRound	Intermed	IES Abroad	n/a
Germany | Freiburg	IES Abroad European Union	n/a	Intermed	IES Abroad	n/a
Ghana | Accra	SIT Study Abroad	n/a	Intermed	SIT Study Abroad	n/a
Greece | Athens	College Year in Athens	n/a	Intermed	College Year in Athens	n/a
Hungary | Budapest	Technical University of Budapest, College International	n/a	Intermed	Budapest Semesters in Mathematics	n/a
India | Delhi	IES Abroad Delhi Center	Sum Fall Spr YrRound	Intermed	IES Abroad	n/a
India | New Delhi	SIT Study Abroad	n/a	Intermed	SIT Study Abroad	n/a
India | Pune	Fergusson College	n/a	Intermed	Alliance for Global Education	n/a
Ireland | Cork	University College Cork	n/a	Intermed	Institute for Study Abroad	n/a
Ireland | Dublin	IES Abroad Dublin Center	Fall	Intermed	IES Abroad	n/a
Ireland | Dublin	University College Dublin	n/a	Intermed	Institute for Study Abroad	n/a

© 2011 — Updates? Want to be in the next edition? Visit **www.mysecondcampus.com**

Connecticut

DESTINATION	HOST INSTITUTION	PRGM SEASON	PRGM TYPE	INTERMEDIARY	HOUSING
Ireland | Galway	National University of Ireland,	n/a	Intermed	Institute for Study Abroad	n/a
Ireland | Maynooth	National University of Ireland, Maynooth	n/a	Intermed	Institute for Study Abroad	n/a
Italy | Arezzo	Accademia dell'Arte	Fall Spr	USColl	Hendrix College	n/a
Italy | Florence	Instituto at Palazzo Rucellai	n/a	Intermed	Instituto at Palazzo Rucellai	n/a
Italy | Milan	IES Abroad Milan Center	Sum Fall Spr YrRound	Intermed	IES Abroad	n/a
Italy | Perugia	The Umbra Institute	Fall Spr YrRound	Intermed	The Umbra Institute	n/a
Italy | Rome	IES Abroad Rome Center	Sum Fall Spr YrRound	Intermed	IES Abroad	n/a
Italy | Rome	John Cabot University	n/a	Dir	n/a	n/a
Italy | Rome	The Pantheon Institute	n/a	Intermed	The Pantheon Institute	n/a
Italy | Siena	IES Abroad Siena Center	Sum Fall Spr YrRound	Intermed	IES Abroad	n/a
Italy | Siena	Universita per Stranieri de Siena	Sum Fall Spr YrRound	Intermed	CET Academic Programs	n/a
Italy | Venice	Scuola Internazionale di Grafica	n/a	Intermed	Scuola Internazionale di Grafica	n/a
Japan | Kyoto	Doshisha University	YrRound	Consrtm	The Associated Kyoto Program	n/a
Japan | Kyoto	Kyoto Consortium for Japanese Studies	n/a	Intermed	Columbia University	n/a
Japan | Nagoya	Nanzan University	Fall Spr YrRound	Intermed	IES Abroad	n/a
Japan | Tokyo	Sophia University	n/a	Intermed	Council on International Education Exchange (CIEE)	n/a
Kenya | Nairobi	SIT Study Abroad	n/a	Intermed	SIT Study Abroad	n/a
Madagascar | Fort Dauphin	SIT Study Abroad	n/a	Intermed	SIT Study Abroad	n/a
Mali | Bamako	SIT Study Abroad	n/a	Intermed	SIT Study Abroad	n/a
Mexico | Oaxaca	SIT Study Abroad	n/a	Intermed	SIT Study Abroad	n/a
Morocco | Rabat	SIT Study Abroad	n/a	Intermed	SIT Study Abroad	n/a
Nepal | Kathmandu	SIT Study Abroad	n/a	Intermed	SIT Study Abroad	n/a
New Zealand | Auckland	University of Auckland	n/a	Intermed	Institute for Study Abroad	n/a
New Zealand | Christchurch	University of Canterbury	n/a	Intermed	Institute for Study Abroad	n/a
New Zealand | Dunedin	University of Otago	n/a	Intermed	Institute for Study Abroad	n/a
New Zealand | Wellington	Victoria University of Wellington	n/a	Intermed	Institute for Study Abroad	n/a
Nicaragua | Managua	SIT Study Abroad	n/a	Intermed	SIT Study Abroad	n/a
Northern Ireland | Belfast	Queen's University	n/a	Intermed	Institute for Study Abroad	n/a
Peru | Cuzco	SIT Study Abroad	n/a	Intermed	SIT Study Abroad	n/a
Peru | Lima	Pontificia Universidad Catolica del Peru	n/a	Intermed	Institute for Study Abroad	n/a
Russia | (Multiple choices)	Multiple institutional choices	n/a	Intermed	American Council for International Education	n/a
Russia | (Multiple choices)	Multiple institutional choices	n/a	USColl	Middlebury College	n/a
Russia | Moscow	Moscow Art Theater (Connecticut College)	n/a	Self	n/a	n/a
Scotland | Edinburgh	University of Edinburgh	n/a	Intermed	Institute for Study Abroad	n/a

© 2011 — Updates? Want to be in the next edition? Visit **www.mysecondcampus.com**

Connecticut

DESTINATION	HOST INSTITUTION	PRGM SEASON	PRGM TYPE	INTERMEDIARY	HOUSING
Scotland | Glasgow	University of Glasgow	n/a	Intermed	Institute for Study Abroad	n/a
Scotland | St. Andrews	University of St. Andrews	n/a	Intermed	Institute for Study Abroad	n/a
Senegal | Dakar	SIT Study Abroad	n/a	Intermed	SIT Study Abroad	n/a
South Africa | Cape Town	University of Cape Town	n/a	Dir	n/a	n/a
South Africa | Durban	SIT Study Abroad	n/a	Intermed	SIT Study Abroad	n/a
Spain | Barcelona	IES Abroad Barcelona Center	Sum Fall Spr YrRound	Intermed	IES Abroad	n/a
Spain | Granada	IES Abroad Granada Center	Sum Fall Spr YrRound	Intermed	IES Abroad	n/a
Spain | Madrid	IES Abroad Madrid Center	Sum Fall Spr YrRound	Intermed	IES Abroad	n/a
Spain | Salamanca	IES Abroad Salamanca Center	Sum Fall Spr YrRound	Intermed	IES Abroad	n/a
Spain | Seville	International University Studies	n/a	Intermed	International University Studies	n/a
Spain | Seville	The Center for Cross-Cultural Studies	n/a	Intermed	The Center for Cross-Cultural Studies	n/a
Sweden | Stockholm	Stockholm University	n/a	Consrtm	The Swedish Program	n/a
Tanzania | Stone Town (Zanzibar)	SIT Study Abroad	n/a	Intermed	SIT Study Abroad	n/a
Uganda | Gulu	SIT Study Abroad	n/a	Intermed	SIT Study Abroad	n/a

Eastern Connecticut State University

Indira Petoskey
Study Abroad Director
Study Abroad Office, Room 100D
83 Windham Street
Willimantic, CT 06226

petoskeyi@easternct.edu
860.465.5066
http://www.easternct.edu/internationalstudyabroad/index.html

DESTINATION	HOST INSTITUTION	PRGM SEASON	PRGM TYPE	INTERMEDIARY	HOUSING
(Multiple) | [City Unspecified]	Multiple institutional choices	Sum Fall Spr YrRound	Intermed	AustraLearn	n/a
(Multiple) | [City Unspecified]	Multiple institutional choices	Sum Fall Spr YrRound	Intermed	AsiaLearn	n/a
(Multiple) | [City Unspecified]	Multiple institutional choices	Sum Fall Spr YrRound	Intermed	EuroLearn	n/a
(Multiple) | [City Unspecified]	Multiple institutional choices	Sum Fall Spr YrRound	Intermed	Global Student Experience	n/a
(Multiple) | [City Unspecified]	Multiple institutional choices	Sum Fall Spr YrRound	Intermed	Cultural Experiences Abroad	n/a
(Multiple) | [City Unspecified]	Multiple institutional choices	Sum Fall Spr YrRound	Intermed	Education Abroad Network	n/a
(Multiple) | [City Unspecified]	Multiple institutional choices	Sum Fall Spr YrRound	Intermed	American Institution for Foreign Study	n/a
(Multiple) | [City Unspecified]	Multiple institutional choices	Sum Fall Spr YrRound	Intermed	Center for International Studies	n/a
Brazil | [City Unspecified]	University of Santa Catarina	n/a	USColl	Central Connecticut State	n/a
Canada | (Multiple Choices)	Multiple institutional choices	n/a	Self	n/a	n/a

© 2011 — Updates? Want to be in the next edition? Visit **www.mysecondcampus.com**

Connecticut

DESTINATION	HOST INSTITUTION	PRGM SEASON	PRGM TYPE	INTERMEDIARY	HOUSING
Chile | [City Unspecified]	Universidad de Concepcion	n/a	USColl	Central Connecticut State	n/a
China | [City Unspecified]	Multiple institutional choices	n/a	USColl	Central Connecticut State	n/a
Cuba | [City Unspecified]	Eastern Connecticut State	Spr	Self	n/a	n/a
Costs: Spr Costs: T&F: n/a, R&B: n/a, Ttl: $3,950					
Cyprus | [City Unspecified]	Eastern Mediterranean University	n/a	USColl	Central Connecticut State	n/a
England | (Multiple)	Multiple institutional choices	n/a	Self	n/a	n/a
England | London	n/a	Sum	USColl	Midwestern State University, Texas	n/a
England | London	London Metropolitan University	Sum	Self	n/a	n/a
Costs: Sum Costs: T&F: n/a, R&B: n/a, Ttl: $4,500					
France | [City Unspecified]	Universitie Catholique de Lyon	n/a	Self	n/a	n/a
Germany | [City Unspecified]	Multiple institutional choices	n/a	Self	n/a	n/a
Ghana | [City Unspecified]	University of Cape Coast	n/a	USColl	Central Connecticut State	n/a
Greece | (Multiple)	n/a	Sum	Self	n/a	n/a
Greece | [City Unspecified]	n/a	Sum	USColl	Georgia College and State University	n/a
Greece | [City Unspecified]	College of Southeastern Europe	n/a	Self	n/a	n/a
Italy | [City Unspecified]	n/a	Sum	USColl	University of North Carolina Asheville	n/a
Italy | Florence	n/a	Sum	Self	n/a	n/a
Japan | [City Unspecified]	Kansai Gaidai University	n/a	USColl	Central Connecticut State	n/a
Japan | [City Unspecified]	Wakayama University	n/a	Self	n/a	n/a
Nigeria | [City Unspecified]	n/a	Sum	USColl	Georgia College and State University	n/a
Scotland | [City Unspecified]	Queen Margaret University	n/a	Self	n/a	n/a
Scotland | Edinburgh	n/a	Sum	USColl	University of Wisconsin, Superior	n/a
South Korea | [City Unspecified]	Kyung Hee University	n/a	USColl	Central Connecticut State	n/a
Spain | (Multiple)	n/a	Sum	USColl	University of Virginia Wise	n/a
Spain | Alicante	Colegio Internacional, Instituto de Estudios Hispanicos	Sum	Self	n/a	HostFam
Costs: Sum Costs: T&F: n/a, R&B: n/a, Ttl: $4,100					
Thailand | [City Unspecified]	Chiang Mai Rajabhat	n/a	Self	n/a	n/a

Fairfield University

Susan M. Fitzgerald
Associate Dean, International Education
Dolan House, 2nd floor
1073 North Benson Road
Fairfield, CT 06824-5195

studyabroadoffice@fairfield.edu
203.254.4332
http://www.fairfield.edu/studyabroad

DESTINATION	HOST INSTITUTION	PRGM SEASON	PRGM TYPE	INTERMEDIARY	HOUSING
Argentina | Buenos Aires	Multiple institutional choices	n/a	Intermed	Council on International Education Exchange (CIEE)	n/a
Australia | Brisbane	Australian Catholic University	Spr	Dir	n/a	n/a

Connecticut

DESTINATION	HOST INSTITUTION	PRGM SEASON	PRGM TYPE	INTERMEDIARY	HOUSING
Australia	Brisbane	Multiple institutional choices	n/a	Self	n/a	n/a
Belgium	Brussels	Multiple institutional choices	n/a	Intermed	Council on International Education Exchange (CIEE)	n/a
Belgium	Louvain-la-Neuve	Universite Catholique de Louvain	n/a	Bilat	n/a	n/a
Botswana	Gabarone	University of Botswana	n/a	Intermed	Council on International Education Exchange (CIEE)	n/a
Brazil	Rio and Amazonas	Universidade do Amazonas/ Universidade Estadual do Norte Fluminense	n/a	Intermed	Council on International Education Exchange (CIEE)	n/a
Chile	Santiago	Multiple institutional choices	n/a	Intermed	Council on International Education Exchange (CIEE)	n/a
Chile	Valparaiso	Pontificia Universidad Catolica de Valparaiso	n/a	Intermed	Council on International Education Exchange (CIEE)	n/a
China	Beijing	Beijing Center for Chinese Studies	n/a	Intermed	Beijing Center for Chinese Studies	n/a
Costa Rica	Atenas	SFS Center for Sustainable Development Studies	n/a	Intermed	School for Field Studies	n/a
Costa Rica	Monteverde	CIEE Study Center in Monteverde	n/a	Intermed	Council on International Education Exchange (CIEE)	n/a
Costa Rica	San Joaquin de Flores	Instituto San Joaquin de Flores	n/a	Intermed	Academic Programs International	n/a
Czech Republic	Prague	Multiple institutional choices	n/a	Intermed	Council on International Education Exchange (CIEE)	n/a
Dominican Republic	Santiago de los Caballeros	Pontifica Universidad Catolica Madre y Maestra	n/a	Intermed	Council on International Education Exchange (CIEE)	n/a
England	Leeds	University of Leeds	n/a	Dir	n/a	n/a
England	London	London School of Economics and Political Science	n/a	Dir	n/a	n/a
England	London	Regent's American College London	n/a	Dir	n/a	n/a
England	Oxford	Oxford University (Blackfriars Hall)	n/a	Dir	n/a	n/a
Finland	Helsinki	Helsinki Polytechnic	n/a	Bilat	n/a	n/a
France	Aix-en-Provence	Aix Center	n/a	Intermed	Institute for American Universities	n/a
France	Avignon	Le Centre d'Avignon	n/a	Intermed	Institute for American Universities	n/a
France	Paris	CIEE Study Center in Paris	n/a	Intermed	Council on International Education Exchange (CIEE)	n/a
France	Paris	CIEE Study Center in Paris	n/a	Intermed	Council on International Education Exchange (CIEE)	n/a
France	Rennes	Universite de Haute Bretagne	n/a	Intermed	Council on International Education Exchange (CIEE)	n/a
France	Rouen	IFI-Rouen	n/a	Bilat	n/a	n/a
France	Rouen	Rouen Business School	Sum	Dir	n/a	n/a
Germany	(Multiple choices)	Multiple institutional choices	n/a	Bilat	Baden-Wuerttemberg	n/a
Ghana	Legon	University of Ghana	n/a	Intermed	Council on International Education Exchange (CIEE)	n/a

© 2011 — Updates? Want to be in the next edition? Visit **www.mysecondcampus.com**

Connecticut

DESTINATION	HOST INSTITUTION	PRGM SEASON	PRGM TYPE	INTERMEDIARY	HOUSING
Greece | Athens	College Year in Athens	n/a	Intermed	College Year in Athens	n/a
Hungary | Budapest	Corvinus University of Budapest	n/a	Intermed	Council on International Education Exchange (CIEE)	n/a
India | Hyderabad	University of Hyderabad	n/a	Intermed	Council on International Education Exchange (CIEE)	n/a
Ireland | Galway	National University of Ireland Galway	Sum	Dir	n/a	n/a
Costs: Sum Costs: T&F: n/a, R&B: n/a, Ttl: $3,040					
Italy | Florence	Florence University of the Arts	Sum Fall Spr YrRound	Self	n/a	n/a
Italy | Florence	Multiple institutional choices	n/a	Self	n/a	n/a
Italy | Syracuse	Mediterranean Center for Arts and Sciences	Sum	Intermed	n/a	n/a
Costs: Sum Costs: T&F: n/a, R&B: n/a, Ttl: $4,930					
Japan | Kyoto	Doshisha Women's College	n/a	Bilat	n/a	n/a
Japan | Tokyo	Sophia University	n/a	Bilat	n/a	n/a
Jordan | Amman	University of Jordan	n/a	Intermed	Council on International Education Exchange (CIEE)	n/a
Kenya | Kimana	Center for Wildlife Management Studies	n/a	Intermed	School for Field Studies	n/a
Mexico | Baja	Center for Coastal Studies	n/a	Intermed	School for Field Studies	n/a
Mexico | Guanajuato	Universidad de Guanajuato	n/a	Intermed	Council on International Education Exchange (CIEE)	n/a
Netherlands | Amsterdam	University of Amsterdam	n/a	Intermed	Council on International Education Exchange (CIEE)	n/a
Netherlands | Maastricht	University of Maastricht	n/a	Bilat	n/a	n/a
Nicaragua | Managua	Fairfield University	Sum	Self	n/a	n/a
Costs: Sum Costs: T&F: n/a, R&B: n/a, Ttl: $2,850					
Nicaragua | Managua	Fairfield University	Sum	Self	n/a	n/a
Poland | Warsaw	Warsaw School of Economics	n/a	Intermed	Council on International Education Exchange (CIEE)	n/a
Russia | (Multiple choices)	Multiple institutional choices	n/a	Intermed	American Councils for International Program	n/a
Russia | St. Petersburg	Fairfield University	Spr	Self	n/a	n/a
Costs: Spr Costs: T&F: n/a, R&B: n/a, Ttl: $3,300					
Scotland | Edinburgh	University of Edinburgh	n/a	Dir	n/a	n/a
Senegal | Dakar	Suffolk University - Dakar Campus	n/a	Intermed	Council on International Education Exchange (CIEE)	n/a
South Africa | Cape Town	University of the Western Cape	n/a	USColl	Marquette University	n/a
South Africa | Cape Town	University of the Western Cape	n/a	Dir	n/a	n/a
South Africa | Stellenbosch	Stellenbosch University	n/a	Intermed	Council on International Education Exchange (CIEE)	n/a
Spain | Barcelona	IQS Ramon Llull	n/a	Dir	n/a	n/a
Thailand | Khon Kaen	Khon Kaen University	n/a	Intermed	Council on International Education Exchange (CIEE)	n/a

© 2011 — Updates? Want to be in the next edition? Visit **www.mysecondcampus.com**

Connecticut

DESTINATION	HOST INSTITUTION	PRGM SEASON	PRGM TYPE	INTERMEDIARY	HOUSING
Turkey	Istanbul	Koc University	n/a	Intermed	Council on International Education Exchange (CIEE)	n/a
Turks and Caicos	South Caicos	Center for Marine Resource Management Studies	n/a	Intermed	School for Field Studies	n/a
Viet Nam	Ho Chi Minh City	Vietnam National University	n/a	Intermed	Council on International Education Exchange (CIEE)	n/a

Manchester Community College

Joanne Russell
Dean of Academic Affairs
Great Path
P.O. Box 1046
Manchester, CT 06045-1046

jrussell@mcc.commnet.edu
860.512.2603
http://www.mcc.commnet.edu/students/financial/financial.php

DESTINATION	HOST INSTITUTION	PRGM SEASON	PRGM TYPE	INTERMEDIARY	HOUSING
[Country Unspecified]	[City Unspecified]	n/a	n/a	n/a	n/a	n/a

Mitchell College

Kenneth Kuzmich
Department of Global Studies
437 Pequot Avenue
New London, CT 06320-4498

kuzmich_k@mitchell.edu
860.701.7716
http://www.mitchell.edu/Current%20Students/academics/study_abroad.html

DESTINATION	HOST INSTITUTION	PRGM SEASON	PRGM TYPE	INTERMEDIARY	HOUSING
France	Hyeres	E.L.F.C.A. French School	Sum	Self	n/a	n/a
Costs: Sum Costs: T&F: n/a, R&B: n/a, Ttl: $2,950					
Italy	Florence	Leonardo DaVinci Center	Sum	Self	n/a	n/a
Costs: Sum Costs: T&F: n/a, R&B: n/a, Ttl: $2,950					
Mexico	Cuernavaca	Cemanahuac Educational Community	Sum	Self	n/a	n/a
Costs: Sum Costs: T&F: n/a, R&B: n/a, Ttl: $2,950					

Naugatuck Valley Community College

Mirvet Muca
Assistant Professor, Political Science/History/Geography
750 Chase Parkway
Waterbury, CT 06708

MMuca@nvcc.commnet.edu
203.596.2105
http://www.nvcc.commnet.edu/academic/study-abroad.shtml

DESTINATION	HOST INSTITUTION	PRGM SEASON	PRGM TYPE	INTERMEDIARY	HOUSING
Argentina	Buenos Aires	Universidad de Belgrano	Sum Fall Spr	Consrtm	College Consortium for International Studies	n/a
Australia	(Multiple choices)	Multiple institutional choices	Sum Fall Spr	Consrtm	College Consortium for International Studies	n/a
Austria	Salzburg	Salzburg College	Sum Fall Spr	Consrtm	College Consortium for International Studies	n/a
Belize	San Ignacio	Galen University	Sum Fall Spr	Consrtm	College Consortium for International Studies	n/a
Canada	Chicoutimi	University of Quebec Chicoutimi	Sum Fall Spr	Consrtm	College Consortium for International Studies	n/a

Connecticut

DESTINATION	HOST INSTITUTION	PRGM SEASON	PRGM TYPE	INTERMEDIARY	HOUSING
China	Nanjing	Nanjing University	Fall Spr	Consrtm	College Consortium for International Studies	n/a
China	Shanghai	Shanghai University	Sum	Consrtm	College Consortium for International Studies	n/a
Cost Rica	Santa Ana	Centro Linguisto Conversa	Sum Fall Spr	Consrtm	College Consortium for International Studies	n/a
Costa Rica	San Jose	Universidad Veritas	Sum Fall Spr	Consrtm	College Consortium for International Studies	n/a
Czech Republic	Prague	Anglo-American University	Sum Fall Spr	Consrtm	College Consortium for International Studies	n/a
Denmark	Copenhagen	Danish Institute for Study Abroad	Sum Fall Spr	Consrtm	College Consortium for International Studies	n/a
Dominican Republic	Santo Domingo	Pontificia Universidad Catolica Madre y Maestra	Sum Fall Spr	Consrtm	College Consortium for International Studies	n/a
Ecuador	Guayaquil	Universidad Catolica de Santiago de Guayaquil	Sum Fall Spr	Consrtm	College Consortium for International Studies	n/a
Ecuador	Quito	Universidad San Francisco de Quito	Sum Fall Spr	Consrtm	College Consortium for International Studies	n/a
England	(Multiple choices)	Multiple institutional choices	Fall Spr	Consrtm	College Consortium for International Studies	n/a
England	London	Kingston University	Sum	Consrtm	College Consortium for International Studies	n/a
France	(Multiple choices)	Multiple institutional choices	Sum Fall Spr	Consrtm	College Consortium for International Studies	n/a
Germany	(Multiple choices)	Multiple institutional choices	Sum Fall Spr	Consrtm	College Consortium for International Studies	n/a
Greece	Thessaloniki	American College of Thessaloniki	Sum Fall Spr	Consrtm	College Consortium for International Studies	n/a
India	Bangalore	International Center for Management and India Studies	Sum Fall Spr	Consrtm	College Consortium for International Studies	n/a
Ireland	(Multiple choices)	Multiple institutional choices	Sum Fall Spr	Consrtm	College Consortium for International Studies	n/a
Italy	(Multiple choices)	Multiple institutional choices	Sum Fall Spr	Consrtm	College Consortium for International Studies	n/a
Japan	Tokyo	KCP International Language Institute	Sum Fall Spr	Consrtm	College Consortium for International Studies	n/a
Mexico	Guadalajara	Universidad Autonoma de Guadalajara	Sum Fall Spr	Consrtm	College Consortium for International Studies	n/a
Morocco	Ifrane	Al Akhawayn University	Sum Fall Spr	Consrtm	College Consortium for International Studies	n/a
Portugal	Lisbon	CIAL Centro de Linguas	Sum Fall Spr	Consrtm	College Consortium for International Studies	n/a
Russia	Moscow	Institute of Youth	Sum Fall Spr	Consrtm	College Consortium for International Studies	n/a
Scotland	Dundee	University of Dundee	Sum Fall Spr	Consrtm	College Consortium for International Studies	n/a
Scotland	Stirling	University of Stirling	Sum Fall Spr	Consrtm	College Consortium for International Studies	n/a

© 2011 — Updates? Want to be in the next edition? Visit www.mysecondcampus.com

Connecticut

DESTINATION	HOST INSTITUTION	PRGM SEASON	PRGM TYPE	INTERMEDIARY	HOUSING
Spain | Seville	International College of Seville	Sum Fall Spr	Consrtm	College Consortium for International Studies	n/a
Switzerland | Lugano	Franklin College	Sum Fall Spr	Consrtm	College Consortium for International Studies	n/a

Paier College of Art

Rob Hazen Adams
Lecturer in Interior Design
20 Gorham Avenue
Hamden, CT 06514

203.287.3031
http://www.paiercollegeofart.edu/faculty/faculty_index.htm

DESTINATION	HOST INSTITUTION	PRGM SEASON	PRGM TYPE	INTERMEDIARY	HOUSING
[Country Unspecified] | [City Unspecified]	n/a	n/a	n/a	n/a	n/a

Post University

Carole A. Baker
Director of Equine Program
P.O. Box 2450
800 Country Club Road
212 MacDermid Hall, 2nd floor
Waterbury, CT 06723-2540

cbaker@post.edu
203.596.4631
http://www.post.edu/maincampus/equinemanagement.shtml

DESTINATION	HOST INSTITUTION	PRGM SEASON	PRGM TYPE	INTERMEDIARY	HOUSING
England | Gloucester	Hartpury Equine College	n/a	Intermed	Yorkshire Riding Center	n/a

Quinnipiac University

Patrick Frazier
Director of International Education
275 Mount Carmel Avenue
Athletic Center 218
Hamden, CT 06518-1908

patrick.fitzegerald@quinnipiac.edu
203.582.8425
http://www.quinnipiac.edu/x183.xml

DESTINATION	HOST INSTITUTION	PRGM SEASON	PRGM TYPE	INTERMEDIARY	HOUSING
(Multiple choices) | (Multiple choices)	Multiple institutional choices	n/a	Intermed	Academic Programs International	n/a
(Multiple choices) | (Multiple choices)	Multiple institutional choices	n/a	Intermed	Council on International Education	n/a
(Multiple choices) | (Multiple choices)	Multiple institutional choices	n/a	Intermed	American Institute for Foreign Study	n/a
(Multiple choices) | (Multiple choices)	Semester at Sea	n/a	Intermed	Semester at Sea	n/a
Australia | (Multiple choices)	Multiple institutional choices	n/a	Intermed	AustraLearn	n/a
Ireland | Cork	University College Cork	Fall Spr YrRound	Dir	n/a	n/a

© 2011 — Updates? Want to be in the next edition? Visit **www.mysecondcampus.com**

Connecticut

DESTINATION	HOST INSTITUTION	PRGM SEASON	PRGM TYPE	INTERMEDIARY	HOUSING

Sacred Heart University

Marylou Roof
Coordinator, Study Abroad Program
5151 Park Avenue
Academic Building, HC 220
Fairfield, CT 06825-1000

RoofM@sacredheart.edu
203.396.8022
http://www.sacredheart.edu/pages/19_study_abroad.cfm

DESTINATION	HOST INSTITUTION	PRGM SEASON	PRGM TYPE	INTERMEDIARY	HOUSING
(Multiple choices) | (Multiple choices)	Multiple institutional choices	Sum Fall Spr YrRound	Intermed	College Consortium for International Studies	n/a
Australia | Broome	University of Notre Dame Australia	n/a	Dir	n/a	n/a
Australia | Sydney	University of Notre Dame Australia	n/a	Dir	n/a	n/a
Bahamas | Bimini	Dolphin Communication Project	Sum	Dir	n/a	n/a
Bermuda | St. George's	Bermuda Institute of Ocean Sciences	Sum	Dir	n/a	n/a
France | Paris	Institut Catholique	Sum	Intermed	European Studies Association	n/a
Ireland | Dingle	Sacred Heart University	Fall Spr YrRound	Self	n/a	PrivApt
Costs: Fall Costs: T&F: n/a, R&B: n/a, Ttl: $20,608 Spr Costs: T&F: n/a, R&B: n/a, Ttl: $20,608 YrRound Costs: T&F: n/a, R&B: n/a, Ttl: $41,216					
Italy | Bay of Naples	Sacred Heart University	Spr	Self	n/a	Other
Costs: Spr Costs: T&F: n/a, R&B: n/a, Ttl: $3,990					
Italy | Rome	American University of Rome	n/a	Dir	n/a	n/a
Luxembourg | Luxembourg City	Sacred Heart University	n/a	Self	n/a	n/a
Luxembourg | Luxembourg City	Sacred Heart University	Sum	Self	n/a	Other
Costs: Sum Costs: T&F: n/a, R&B: n/a, Ttl: $2,730					
Spain | Granada	University of Granada	n/a	Dir	n/a	n/a

Southern Connecticut State University

Linda Olson
Program Coordinator
501 Crescent Street
Engleman B129
New Haven, CT 06515

olsonl1@southernct.edu
203.392.6975
http://www.southernct.edu/internationalprograms/

DESTINATION	HOST INSTITUTION	PRGM SEASON	PRGM TYPE	INTERMEDIARY	HOUSING
(Multiple choices) | (Multiple choices)	Multiple institutional choices	n/a	USColl	Central Connecticut State	n/a
(Multiple choices) | (Multiple choices)	Multiple institutional choices	n/a	USColl	Eastern Connecticut State	n/a
(Multiple choices) | (Multiple choices)	Multiple institutional choices	n/a	USColl	Western Connecticut State University	n/a
(Multiple choices) | (Multiple choices)	Multiple institutional choices	n/a	Intermed	ISEP	n/a
France | (Multiple choices)	Edhec Business School (ESPEME)	Fall Spr YrRound	Bilat	n/a	n/a

© 2011 — Updates? Want to be in the next edition? Visit **www.mysecondcampus.com**

Connecticut

DESTINATION	HOST INSTITUTION	PRGM SEASON	PRGM TYPE	INTERMEDIARY	HOUSING
France | Paris	Southern Connecticut State	Sum	Self	n/a	n/a
Costs: Sum Costs: T&F: n/a, R&B: n/a, Ttl: $3,525					
Germany | (Multiple Choices)	Multiple institutional choices	n/a	Bilat	Baden-Wurttemberg Exchange	n/a
Greece | Thessaloniki	Southern Connecticut State	Sum	Self	n/a	n/a
Costs: Sum Costs: T&F: n/a, R&B: n/a, Ttl: $5,495					
Guatemala | (Multiple)	Southern Connecticut State	Sum	Self	n/a	n/a
Iceland | Reykjavik	Southern Connecticut State	Sum	Self	n/a	n/a
Costs: Sum Costs: T&F: n/a, R&B: n/a, Ttl: $2,900					
Italy | Montepulciano	Southern Connecticut State	Sum	Self	n/a	n/a
Costs: Sum Costs: T&F: n/a, R&B: n/a, Ttl: $4,800					
Scotland | Edinburgh	Queen Margaret University	Fall Spr YrRound	Bilat	n/a	n/a
Spain | Salamanca	Southern Connecticut State	Sum	Self	n/a	n/a
Costs: Sum Costs: T&F: n/a, R&B: n/a, Ttl: $4,300					

St. Joseph College

Shyamala Raman
Director of International Studies and Programs
1678 Asylum Avenue
Office of International Studies and Programs
Lynch Hall, room 216
West Hartford, CT 06117-2791

sraman@sjc.edu
860.231.5515
http://www.sjc.edu/academics/special_programs/study_abroad/

DESTINATION	HOST INSTITUTION	PRGM SEASON	PRGM TYPE	INTERMEDIARY	HOUSING
Argentina | Buenos Aires	Multiple institutional choices	Fall Spr YrRound	Intermed	Institute for Study Abroad	n/a
Argentina | Buenos Aires	Multiple institutional choices	Fall Spr	USColl	Middlebury College	n/a
Argentina | Cordoba	Universidad Nacional de Cordoba	Sum Fall Spr YrRound	Intermed	Center for Cross Cultural Studies	n/a
Argentina | Mendoza	Multiple institutional choices	Fall Spr YrRound	Intermed	Institute for Study Abroad	n/a
Argentina | Tucuman	Universidad Nacional de Tucuman	Fall Spr	USColl	Middlebury College	n/a
Australia | (Multiple choices)	Multiple institutional choices	n/a	USColl	Arcadia University	n/a
Australia | (Multiple choices)	Multiple institutional choices	n/a	USColl	Ithaca College	n/a
Australia | (Multiple choices)	Multiple institutional choices	n/a	Intermed	Institute for Study Abroad	n/a
Australia | Brisbane	Queensland University	n/a	Dir	n/a	n/a
Australia | Brisbane	Queensland University of	n/a	Dir	n/a	n/a
Australia | Brisbane	University of Queensland	Fall Spr	USColl	Dickinson College	n/a
Australia | Sydney	Macquarie University	n/a	Intermed	Brethren Colleges Abroad	n/a
Austria | Vienna	Multiple institutional choices	Fall Spr	USColl	Central College Abroad	n/a
Belgium | Brussels	Vesalius College	Fall Spr	Intermed	Brethren Colleges Abroad	n/a
Botswana | Gabarone	SIT Study Abroad	Fall Spr	Intermed	SIT Study Abroad	n/a
Brazil | Belo Horizonte	Pontificia Universidade Catolica de Minas Gerais	Fall Spr	USColl	Middlebury College	n/a
Brazil | Niteroi	Universidade Federal Fluminense	Fall Spr	USColl	Middlebury College	n/a

© 2011 — Updates? Want to be in the next edition? Visit **www.mysecondcampus.com**

Connecticut

DESTINATION	HOST INSTITUTION	PRGM SEASON	PRGM TYPE	INTERMEDIARY	HOUSING
Cameroon | Yaounde	Multiple institutional choices	Fall Spr	Intermed	SIT Study Abroad	n/a
Cameroon | Yaounde	University of Yaounde	Spr	USColl	Dickinson College	n/a
	Costs: Spr Costs: T&F: n/a, R&B: n/a, Ttl: $24,930				
Canada | Quebec	Universite Laval	Sum Fall Spr	Dir	n/a	n/a
(Multiple choices) | (Multiple choices)	Michigan State University	n/a	USColl	n/a	n/a
(Multiple choices) | (Multiple choices)	Center for Global Education	n/a	Intermed	n/a	n/a
Chile | Santiago	Universidad Adolfo Ibanez	Fall Spr YrRound	USColl	American University	n/a
Chile | Santiago	Multiple institutional choices	Fall Spr YrRound	Intermed	Institute for Study Abroad	n/a
Chile | Santiago	Pontificia Universidad Catolica de Chile	Fall Spr YrRound	USColl	University of Wisconsin/ University of Michigan	n/a
Chile | Santiago	Universidad Diego Portales	Fall Spr YrRound	USColl	American University	n/a
Chile | Valparaiso	Multiple institutional choices	Fall Spr YrRound	Intermed	Institute for Study Abroad	n/a
China | (Multiple choices)	Hunan Normal University	n/a	Intermed	KIIS	n/a
China | Beijing	Peking University	n/a	USColl	Dickinson College	n/a
China | Dalian	Dongbei University of Finance and Economics or Dalian University for Foreign Language	n/a	Intermed	Brethren Colleges Abroad	n/a
China | Hangzhou	Zhejiang University of Technology	n/a	USColl	Middlebury College	n/a
China | Shanghai	East China Normal University	n/a	USColl	New York University	n/a
Costa Rica | Guacimo de Limon	EARTH University	n/a	USColl	State University of New York Albany	n/a
Costa Rica | Guanacaste	n/a	n/a	USColl	University of Delaware	n/a
Costa Rica | Heredia	Universidad Interamericana	n/a	USColl	University of Delaware	n/a
Costa Rica | Heredia	Heredia Intermediate	Fall Spr	Intermed	Institute for Study Abroad	n/a
Costa Rica | La Suerte	La Suerte Biological Field Station	n/a	Dir	n/a	n/a
Costa Rica | San Jose	Multiple institutional choices	Sum	Intermed	Coalition for Christian Colleges and Universities	n/a
Costa Rica | San Jose	University of Costa Rica	n/a	USColl	State University of New York Albany	n/a
(Multiple choices) | (Multiple choices)	SIT Study Abroad Programs	n/a	Intermed	n/a	n/a
Ecuador | Quito	University of Wisconsin	Sum	USColl	University of Wisconsin/ University of Michigan	n/a
Ecuador | Quito	Ceiba Foundation for Tropical Conservation	Spr	USColl	University of Wisconsin/ University of Michigan	n/a
Ecuador | Quito	Ceiba Foundation for Tropical Conservation	Sum	USColl	University of Wisconsin/ University of Michigan	n/a
Ecuador | Quito	Universidad San Francisco de Quito	Fall Spr	USColl	Boston University	n/a
Ecuador | Quito	University of San Francisco de Quito	Fall Spr YrRound	Intermed	Brethren Colleges Abroad	n/a
Egypt | Cairo	American University in Cairo	n/a	Dir	n/a	n/a
England | (Multiple choices)	Multiple institutional choices	n/a	Intermed	Institute for Study Abroad	n/a

© 2011 — Updates? Want to be in the next edition? Visit **www.mysecondcampus.com**

Connecticut

DESTINATION	HOST INSTITUTION	PRGM SEASON	PRGM TYPE	INTERMEDIARY	HOUSING
England	(Multiple choices)	Multiple institutional choices	n/a	USColl	Arcadia University	n/a
England	[City Unspecified]	n/a	n/a	USColl	Capital University	n/a
England	Ambleside	Saint Martin's College	n/a	Dir	n/a	n/a
England	Cheltenham	University of Gloucestershire	Fall Spr	Intermed	Brethren Colleges Abroad	n/a
England	Lancaster	Saint Martin's College	n/a	Dir	n/a	n/a
England	London	Multiple institutional choices	Fall Spr	Intermed	Central College Abroad	n/a
England	Norwich	University of East Anglia	Fall Spr YrRound	USColl	Dickinson College	n/a
Costs: Fall Costs: T&F: n/a, R&B: n/a, Ttl: $24,930 Spr Costs: T&F: n/a, R&B: n/a, Ttl: $24,930 YrRound Costs: T&F: n/a, R&B: n/a, Ttl: $49,860					
France	Paris	Multiple institutional choices	Fall Spr YrRound	USColl	New York University	n/a
France	Poitiers	Universite de Poitiers	n/a	Intermed	Middlebury College	n/a
France	(Multiple choices)	Multiple institutional choices	Sum Fall Spr YrRound	USColl	University of Kansas	n/a
France	(Multiple choices)	Multiple institutional choices	Sum Fall Spr	Intermed	Institute of European Studies Abroad	n/a
France	Grenoble	Universite de Grenoble	Sum Fall Spr YrRound	USColl	Boston University	n/a
France	Paris	Fall Spr YrRound	n/a	USColl	Vassar/Wesleyan Program in Paris	n/a
France	Paris	Catholic Institute of Paris, the Sorbonne	Fall Spr	Intermed	Central College Abroad	n/a
France	Paris	Le Centre Madeleine	n/a	Intermed	Middlebury College	n/a
France	Paris	University of Paris	Sum Fall Spr YrRound	USColl	University of Connecticut	n/a
France	Rouen	University of Rouen	Spr YrRound	USColl	St. Lawrence University	n/a
France	Strasbourg	University of Strasbourg	Fall Spr	Intermed	Brethren Colleges Abroad	n/a
France	Toulouse	University of Toulouse	Fall Spr YrRound	USColl	Dickinson College	n/a
Germany	Berlin	Freie Universitat Berlin	Fall Spr YrRound	USColl	Middlebury College	n/a
Germany	Bremen	University of Bremen	Spr YrRound	USColl	Dickinson College	n/a
Germany	Mainz	Johannes Gutenberg-Universitat	Fall Spr YrRound	USColl	Middlebury College	n/a
Germany	Marburg	Philipps University	Fall Spr	Intermed	Brethren Colleges Abroad	n/a
Ghana	[City Unspecified]	n/a	n/a	USColl	University of Connecticut	n/a
Ghana	[City Unspecified]	n/a	n/a	USColl	University of Michigan	n/a
Ghana	Accra	n/a	Sum	USColl	Michigan State University	n/a
Ghana	Accra	n/a	Sum	USColl	Michigan State University	n/a
Ghana	Accra	Multiple institutional choices	Fall Spr	Intermed	SIT Study Abroad	n/a
Ghana	Cape Coast	Multiple institutional choices	Fall Spr	Intermed	SIT Study Abroad	n/a
Greece	Athens	Arcadia Center for Hellenic, Mediterranean, and Balkan Studies	Sum Fall Spr	USColl	Arcadia University	n/a
Greece	Athens	City University	Fall Spr	Intermed	Brethren Colleges Abroad	n/a
India	(Multiple choices)	Multiple institutional choices	n/a	USColl	University of Virginia	n/a
India	(Multiple choices)	Multiple institutional choices	n/a	Intermed	SIT Study Abroad	n/a
India	Bangalore	n/a	Spr	USColl	Ramapo College	n/a

Connecticut

DESTINATION	HOST INSTITUTION	PRGM SEASON	PRGM TYPE	INTERMEDIARY	HOUSING
India | Maduri	n/a	n/a	USColl	Dickinson College	n/a
India | New Delhi	Fireflies Ashram	Spr	USColl	Michigan State University	n/a
Ireland | (Multiple choices)	Multiple institutional choices	n/a	Intermed	Institute for Study Abroad	n/a
Ireland | (Multiple choices)	Multiple institutional choices	n/a	USColl	Arcadia University	n/a
Ireland | Derry	Magee College	n/a	Intermed	Brethren Colleges Abroad	n/a
Italy | (Multiple choices)	Multiple institutional choices	n/a	USColl	Arcadia University	n/a
Italy | Bologna	K. Robert Nilsson Center for European Studies, University of Bologna	Fall Spr YrRound	USColl	Dickinson College	n/a
	Costs: Fall Costs: T&F: n/a, R&B: n/a, Ttl: $24,930 Spr Costs: T&F: n/a, R&B: n/a, Ttl: $24,930 YrRound Costs: T&F: n/a, R&B: n/a, Ttl: $49,860				
Italy | Ferrara	Universita degli Studi di Ferrara	Fall Spr YrRound	USColl	Middlebury College	n/a
Italy | Florence	Florence University of the Arts	Fall Spr YrRound	USColl	Fairfield University	n/a
Italy | Florence	Lorenzo d'Medici Institute	Sum Fall Spr YrRound	Dir	n/a	n/a
Italy | Florence	Scuola Lorenzo d'Medici	n/a	USColl	Marist College	n/a
Italy | Florence	Universita degli Studi di Firenze	Fall Spr YrRound	USColl	Middlebury College	n/a
Italy | Rome	John Cabot University	Sum Fall Spr	Dir	n/a	n/a
Italy | Rome	Trinity College Rome Campus	Sum Fall Spr	USColl	Trinity College	n/a
Japan | Iwate	Iwate University	n/a	Dir	n/a	n/a
Japan | Nagoya	Nanzan University	Fall Spr YrRound	USColl	Dickinson College	n/a
Japan | Sapporo	Hokusei Gakuen University	n/a	Intermed	Brethren Colleges Abroad	n/a
Kenya | (Multiple choices)	Multiple institutional choices	n/a	Intermed	School for Field Studies	n/a
Kenya | (Multiple choices)	Multiple institutional choices	n/a	Intermed	Multiple intermediaries choices	n/a
Kenya | Mombasa	SIT Study Abroad	Fall Spr	Intermed	SIT Study Abroad	n/a
Kenya | Nairobi	SIT Study Abroad	Fall Spr	Intermed	SIT Study Abroad	n/a
Madagascar | Antananarivo	SIT Study Abroad	Fall Spr	Intermed	SIT Study Abroad	n/a
Madagascar | Antananarivo	SIT Study Abroad	Sum	Intermed	SIT Study Abroad	n/a
Madagascar | Fort Dauphin	SIT Study Abroad	Fall Spr	Intermed	SIT Study Abroad	n/a
Mexico | Puebla	Universidad de las Americas	Sum Fall Spr	USColl	State University of New York	n/a
Mexico | (Multiple choices)	Multiple institutional choices	Fall Spr YrRound	USColl	University of North Carolina	n/a
Mexico | Cuernavaca	Casa Augsburg	Fall Spr	USColl	Augsburg College Center for Global Education	n/a
Mexico | Guadalajara	Multiple institutional choices	Sum Fall Spr YrRound	Intermed	Northern Illinois University/ CEA Global Education Solutions	n/a
Mexico | Guadalajara	Universidad Jesuita de Guadalajara	Sum	Intermed	Northern Illinois University/ International Studies Abroad	n/a
Mexico | Guadalajara	University of Guadalajara	Fall Spr YrRound	USColl	Middlebury College	n/a
	Costs: Fall Costs: T&F: n/a, R&B: n/a, Ttl: $9,850 Spr Costs: T&F: n/a, R&B: n/a, Ttl: $9,850 YrRound Costs: T&F: n/a, R&B: n/a, Ttl: $19,700				
Mexico | Guadalajara	University of Guadalajara	Sum Fall Spr	USColl	University of Denver	n/a
Mexico | Merida	Autonomous University of the Yucatan	Sum Fall Spr YrRound	Intermed	Institute for Study Abroad	n/a

© 2011 — Updates? Want to be in the next edition? Visit **www.mysecondcampus.com**

Connecticut

DESTINATION	HOST INSTITUTION	PRGM SEASON	PRGM TYPE	INTERMEDIARY	HOUSING
Mexico | Merida	Autonomous University of the Yucatan	Sum Fall Spr YrRound	USColl	Rutgers University	n/a
Mexico | Merida	Autonomous University of the Yucatan	Spr	USColl	DePaul University	n/a
Mexico | Merida	Multiple institutional choices	Fall Spr	USColl	Central College Abroad	n/a
Mexico | Oaxaca	Becari Language School	Fall Spr	Intermed	SIT Study Abroad	n/a
Mexico | Puebla	Universidad de las Americas	Sum	USColl	State University of New York Potsdam	n/a
Mexico | Puebla	Universidad de las Americas	Fall Spr YrRound	USColl	Juniata College	n/a
Mexico | Puebla	Universidad de las Americas	n/a	USColl	Lock Haven University	n/a
Mexico | Queretaro	Universidad Autonoma de Queretaro	Spr	USColl	Dickinson College	n/a
	Costs: Spr Costs: T&F: n/a, R&B: n/a, Ttl: $24,930				
Mexico | Xalapa	Universidad Veracruzana	Fall Spr	Intermed	Brethren Colleges Abroad	n/a
Mexico | Xalapa	Universidad Veracruzana	Fall Spr YrRound	USColl	Middlebury College	n/a
	Costs: Fall Costs: T&F: n/a, R&B: n/a, Ttl: $9,850 Spr Costs: T&F: n/a, R&B: n/a, Ttl: $9,850 YrRound Costs: T&F: n/a, R&B: n/a, Ttl: $19,700				
Namibia | [City Unspecified]	n/a	n/a	USColl	Augsburg College Center for Global Education	n/a
New Zealand | (Multiple choices)	Multiple institutional choices	n/a	Intermed	Institute for Study Abroad	n/a
New Zealand | (Multiple choices)	Multiple institutional choices	n/a	USColl	Arcadia University	n/a
New Zealand | Dunedin	University of Otago	Fall Spr	Intermed	Brethren Colleges Abroad	n/a
Niger | Niamey	n/a	n/a	USColl	Boston University	n/a
Northern Ireland | (Multiple choices)	Multiple institutional choices	n/a	Intermed	Institute for Study Abroad	n/a
Northern Ireland | (Multiple choices)	Multiple institutional choices	n/a	USColl	Arcadia University	n/a
Northern Ireland | Derry	University of Ulster at Magee College	Fall Spr	Intermed	Brethren Colleges Abroad	n/a
Puerto Rico | San Juan	Universidad del Sagrado Corazon	Fall Spr YrRound	USColl	State University of New York Albany	n/a
Russia | (Multiple choices)	Multiple institutional choices	n/a	USColl	Middlebury College	n/a
Russia | Moscow	Russia State University for the Humanities	Fall Spr YrRound	USColl	Dickinson College	n/a
	Costs: Fall Costs: T&F: n/a, R&B: n/a, Ttl: $24,930 Spr Costs: T&F: n/a, R&B: n/a, Ttl: $24,930 YrRound Costs: T&F: n/a, R&B: n/a, Ttl: $49,860				
Scotland | (Multiple choices)	Multiple institutional choices	n/a	Intermed	Institute for Study Abroad	n/a
Scotland | (Multiple choices)	Multiple institutional choices	n/a	USColl	Arcadia University	n/a
South Africa | [City Unspecified]	n/a	n/a	USColl	Michigan State University	n/a
South Africa | [City Unspecified]	n/a	n/a	USColl	Augsburg College Center for Global Education	n/a
South Korea | Seoul	Ewha Women's University	n/a	Dir	n/a	n/a
South Korea | Seoul	Yonsei University	Fall Spr YrRound	USColl	Dickinson College	n/a
Spain | (Multiple choices)	Multiple institutional choices	n/a	USColl	Middlebury College	n/a
Spain | Barcelona	Universidad de Barcelona	Fall Spr YrRound	USColl	Knox College	n/a

© 2011 — Updates? Want to be in the next edition? Visit **www.mysecondcampus.com**

Connecticut

DESTINATION	HOST INSTITUTION	PRGM SEASON	PRGM TYPE	INTERMEDIARY	HOUSING
Spain | Barcelona	University of Barcelona	Sum	USColl	State University of New York Oswego	n/a
	Costs: Sum Costs: T&F: n/a, R&B: n/a, Ttl: $7,257				
Spain | Barcelona	University of Barcelona	Fall Spr	Intermed	Brethren Colleges Abroad	n/a
Spain | Granada	University of Granada	Sum Fall Spr	USColl	University of Delaware	n/a
Spain | Granada	University of Granada	Fall Spr YrRound	USColl	University of Connecticut	n/a
Spain | Granada	University of Granada	Fall Spr	USColl	Central College Abroad	n/a
Spain | Madrid	Alcala University	n/a	USColl	Rider University	n/a
Spain | Madrid	Autonomous University of Madrid	Spr YrRound	USColl	Tufts University	n/a
Spain | Madrid	Centro de Estudios Hispanicos	YrRound	USColl	Hamilton College	n/a
Spain | Madrid	Fundacion Jose Ortega y Gasset	Fall Spr	USColl	Southern Methodist University	n/a
Spain | Madrid	Insituto Internacional; Universidad Autonoma de Madrid	Sum Fall Spr YrRound	USColl	Boston University	n/a
Spain | Madrid	Instituto Internacional	Fall Spr	USColl	Syracuse University	n/a
Spain | Madrid	Instituto Internacional	Fall Spr	USColl	State University of New York Albany	n/a
Spain | Madrid	Marquette University Study Center in Universidad Complutense de Madrid	Sum Fall Spr YrRound	USColl	Marquette University	n/a
	Costs: Sum Costs: T&F: n/a, R&B: n/a, Ttl: $4,550 Fall Costs: T&F: n/a, R&B: n/a, Ttl: $15,990 Spr Costs: T&F: n/a, R&B: n/a, Ttl: $15,990 YrRound Costs: T&F: n/a, R&B: n/a, Ttl: $31,980				
Spain | Madrid	Multiple institutional choices	Sum Fall Spr YrRound	USColl	American University	n/a
Spain | Madrid	Nebrija University	n/a	USColl	Rider University	n/a
Spain | Madrid	New York University Madrid	Fall Spr	USColl	New York University	n/a
Spain | Madrid	The Sede Prim-Middlebury College	YrRound	USColl	Middlebury College	n/a
Spain | Madrid	Universidad Autonoma de Madrid	Fall Spr	USColl	George Washington University	n/a
Spain | Madrid	Universidad Autonoma de Madrid	Spr YrRound	USColl	Skidmore College	n/a
Spain | Malaga	Universidad de Malaga	Fall YrRound	USColl	Dickinson College	n/a
Spain | Oviedo	Universidad de Oviedo	Spr	USColl	University of Massachusetts	n/a
Spain | Salamanca	University of Salamanca	Sum Fall Spr	USColl	James Madison University	n/a
Spain | Salamanca	University of Salamanca	n/a	USColl	Ohio Wesleyan University	n/a
Spain | Salamanca	University of Salamanca	Fall Spr YrRound	USColl	State University of New York Cortland	n/a
Spain | Seville	Center for Cross Cultural Studies Center in Seville	Sum	Intermed	n/a	n/a
Spain | Seville	Universidad de Sevilla	Fall Spr YrRound	USColl	Sweet Briar College	n/a
Spain | Seville	Universidad de Sevilla	Fall Spr YrRound	USColl	State University of New York New Paltz	n/a
Spain | Toledo	Fundacion Jose Ortega y Gasset	Fall Spr YrRound	USColl	Arcadia University	n/a

© 2011 — Updates? Want to be in the next edition? Visit **www.mysecondcampus.com**

Connecticut

DESTINATION	HOST INSTITUTION	PRGM SEASON	PRGM TYPE	INTERMEDIARY	HOUSING
Spain	Toledo	Fundacion Jose Ortega y Gasset	Sum Fall Spr YrRound	USColl	University of Minnesota	n/a
Spain	Valencia	Institute for Spanish Studies	Sum Fall Spr	Intermed	Institute for Spanish Studies	n/a
Spain	Valencia	Universitat de Valencia	Spr YrRound	USColl	Rutgers University	n/a
Spain and Mexico	[City Unspecified]	Knowledge Exchange Institute	n/a	Intermed	n/a	n/a
Tanzania	Arusha	Sokoine University of Agriculture	Fall Spr	Intermed	SIT Study Abroad	n/a
Tanzania	Stone Town, Zanzibar	Institute of Marine Science	Fall Spr	Intermed	SIT Study Abroad	n/a
The Netherlands	Leiden	Leiden University	Fall Spr	USColl	Central College Abroad	n/a
The Netherlands	Nijmegen	Hogeschool van Arnham en Nijmegen	n/a	Dir	n/a	n/a
Uruguay	Montevideo	Multiple institutional choices	Fall Spr	USColl	Middlebury College	n/a
Wales	Bangor	Bangor University	Fall Spr	USColl	Central College Abroad	n/a
Wales	Bangor	Bangor University	Fall Spr YrRound	USColl	Arcadia University	n/a
Wales	Swansea	Swansea University	Fall Spr YrRound	USColl	Arcadia University	n/a
Zimbabwe	[City Unspecified]	n/a	n/a	Intermed	SIT Study Abroad	n/a

Three Rivers Community College

Mark Comeau
Program Coordinator TRCC Architecture & Construction
574 New London Turnpike
Norwich, CT 06360

Mcomeau@trcc.commnet.edu
860.885.2387
http://www.trcc.commnet.edu/News/pages/studyabroad.htm

(Multiple choices)	(Multiple choices)	Multiple institutional choices	n/a	Consrtm	College Consortium for International Studies	n/a

Trinity College

Lisa Sapolis
Acting Director of International Programs
Office of International Programs
66 Vernon Street
Hartford, CT 06106-3100

lisa.sapolis@trincoll.edu
860.297.2436
http://www.trincoll.edu/Academics/StudyAway/

(Multiple)	(Multiple)	International Honors Program	Spr	Intermed	International Honors Program	n/a
(Multiple)	(Multiple)	International Honors Program	YrRound	Intermed	International Honors Program	n/a
(Multiple)	(Multiple)	International Honors Program	Fall Spr	Intermed	International Honors Program	n/a
Argentina	Buenos	Multiple institutional choices	Fall Spr	Intermed	Institute for Study Abroad	n/a
Australia	Brisbane	University of Queensland	Fall Spr YrRound	Dir	n/a	n/a
Australia	Brisbane	University of Queensland	Fall Spr YrRound	Intermed	Institute for Study Abroad	n/a
Australia	Brisbane	University of Queensland	Fall Spr YrRound	USColl	Arcadia University	n/a
Australia	Perth	Curtin University of Technology	Fall Spr YrRound	Dir	n/a	n/a
Australia	Queensland	James Cook University	Fall Spr	USColl	Arcadia University	n/a
Australia	Sydney	University of Sydney	Fall Spr YrRound	Dir	n/a	n/a
Australia	Sydney	University of Sydney	Fall Spr YrRound	Intermed	Institute for Study Abroad	n/a

© 2011 — Updates? Want to be in the next edition? Visit **www.mysecondcampus.com**

Connecticut

DESTINATION	HOST INSTITUTION	PRGM SEASON	PRGM TYPE	INTERMEDIARY	HOUSING
Australia | Sydney	University of Sydney	Fall Spr YrRound	USColl	Arcadia University	n/a
Australia | Yungaburra	Center for Rainforest Studies	Fall Spr	Intermed	School for Field Studies	n/a
Austria | Vienna	University of Vienna	Spr	Self	n/a	n/a
Brazil | Sao Paulo	Pontificia Universidade Catolica de Sao Paulo	Fall Spr	Intermed	Council on International Education Exchange (CIEE)	n/a
Chile | Santiago	Multiple institutional choices	Fall Spr YrRound	Intermed	Council on International Education Exchange (CIEE)	n/a
China | Beijing	Capital University of Economics and Business	Fall Spr YrRound	USColl	Hamilton College	n/a
China | Beijing	IES Abroad Beijing Center	Fall Spr YrRound	Intermed	IES Abroad	n/a
China | Shanghai	East China Normal University	Fall Spr	USColl	New York University	n/a
China | Shanghai	IES Abroad Center	Fall Spr YrRound	Intermed	IES Abroad	n/a
Costa Rica | Atenas	SFS Center for Sustainable Development Studies	Fall Spr	Intermed	School for Field Studies	n/a
Costa Rica | La Cruces and La Selva	Organization for Tropical Studies	Fall Spr	Intermed	Organization for Tropical Studies	n/a
Czech Republic | Prague	Charles University	Fall Spr	Intermed	Council on International Education Exchange (CIEE)	n/a
Denmark | Copenhagen	Danish Institute for Study Abroad (DIS)	Fall Spr	Intermed	Danish Institute for Study Abroad (DIS)	n/a
Dominican Republic | Santiago	Pontificia Universidad Católica Madre y Maestra (PUCMM)	Fall Spr YrRound	Intermed	Council on International Education Exchange (CIEE)	n/a
Dominican Republic | Santo Domingo	Facultad Latinoamericana de Ciencias Sociales (FLACSO)	Fall Spr YrRound	Intermed	Council on International Education Exchange (CIEE)	n/a
Ecuador | Quito	SIT Abroad	Fall Spr	Intermed	SIT Abroad	n/a
Egypt | Cairo	American University in Cairo	Spr YrRound	Dir	n/a	n/a
England | Cambridge or London	Institute of Economics and Political Studies	Fall Spr	Intermed	Institute of Economics and Political Studies	n/a
England | London	Fordham University London Center	Fall Spr YrRound	USColl	Fordham University	n/a
England | London	London School of Economics and Political Science	YrRound	Dir	n/a	n/a
England | London	London School of Economics and Political Science	YrRound	Intermed	Institute for Study Abroad	n/a
England | London	London School of Economics and Political Science	YrRound	USColl	Arcadia University	n/a
England | London	NYU Center in London	Fall Spr	USColl	New York University	n/a
England | London	Queen Mary University	Fall Spr YrRound	Intermed	Institute for Study Abroad	n/a
England | London	Queen Mary University	Fall Spr YrRound	USColl	Arcadia University	n/a
England | London	School of Oriental and African Studies	Fall Spr YrRound	Intermed	Institute for Study Abroad	n/a
England | London	School of Oriental and African Studies	Fall Spr YrRound	USColl	Arcadia University	n/a
England | London	School of Oriental and African Studies	Fall Spr YrRound	Dir	n/a	n/a
England | London	University College London	Fall Spr YrRound	Intermed	Institute for Study Abroad	n/a

© 2011 — Updates? Want to be in the next edition? Visit www.mysecondcampus.com

Connecticut

DESTINATION	HOST INSTITUTION	PRGM SEASON	PRGM TYPE	INTERMEDIARY	HOUSING
England | London	University College London	Fall Spr YrRound	USColl	Arcadia University	n/a
England | Norwich	University of East Anglia	Fall Spr YrRound	Dir	n/a	n/a
England | Norwich	University of East Anglia	Fall Spr YrRound	Intermed	Institute for Study Abroad	n/a
England | Surrey	Royal Holloway University, University of London	Fall Spr YrRound	Intermed	Institute for Study Abroad	n/a
England | Surrey	Royal Holloway University, University of London	Fall Spr YrRound	USColl	Arcadia University	n/a
France | Paris	Internship in Francophone Europe	Fall Spr	Intermed	Internship in Francophone Europe	n/a
France | Paris	Trinity College	Fall Spr YrRound	Self	n/a	n/a
France and United States | Paris and New York City (NY)	Columbia University	YrRound	USColl	Columbia University	n/a
Germany | (Multiple choices)	Multiple institutional choices	n/a	Bilat	Baden-Wurttemberg Exchange	n/a
Germany | Berlin	Humboldt University	Fall	USColl	Duke University	n/a
Germany | Berlin	IES Abroad Berlin Center	Fall Spr YrRound	Intermed	IES Abroad	n/a
Ghana | Accra	Multiple institutional choices	Fall Spr	USColl	New York University	n/a
Ghana | Cape Coast	SIT Abroad	Fall Spr	Intermed	SIT Abroad	n/a
Greece | Athens	Arcadia Center for Hellenic, Balkan and Mediterranean Studies	Fall Spr	USColl	Arcadia University	n/a
Hungary | Budapest	Central European University, Budapest	Fall Spr	USColl	Bard College	n/a
Hungary | Budapest	Technical University of Budapest, College International	Fall Spr	Intermed	Budapest Semester in Mathematics	n/a
India | Delhi	IES Abroad Delhi Center	Fall Spr YrRound	Intermed	IES Abroad	n/a
India | Pune	Fergusson College	Fall Spr	Intermed	Alliance for Global Education	n/a
Ireland | Dublin	Trinity College, University of Dublin	Spr YrRound	Intermed	Institute for Study Abroad	n/a
Ireland | Dublin	Trinity College, University of Dublin	Spr YrRound	USColl	Arcadia University	n/a
Ireland | Dublin	Trinity College, University of Dublin	Spr YrRound	Dir	n/a	n/a
Ireland | Galway	National University of Ireland	Fall Spr YrRound	Dir	n/a	n/a
Ireland | Galway	National University of Ireland	Fall Spr YrRound	USColl	Arcadia University	n/a
Ireland | Galway	National University of Ireland	Fall Spr YrRound	Intermed	Institute for Study Abroad	n/a
Israel | Jerusalem	Hebrew University	Fall Spr YrRound	Dir	n/a	n/a
Israel | Tel Aviv	Tel Aviv University	Fall Spr YrRound	Dir	n/a	n/a
Italy | Arezzo	Accademia dell'Arte	Fall Spr	Intermed	Accademia dell'Arte	n/a
Italy | Florence	SU Florence Center	Fall Spr	USColl	Syracuse University	n/a
Italy | Rome	Trinity College Rome Campus	Fall Spr	Self	n/a	n/a
Italy | Rome, Sicily	Intercollegiate Center for Classical Studies	Fall Spr	USColl	Duke University	n/a
Japan | Nagoya	Nanzan University	Fall Spr YrRound	Intermed	IES Abroad	n/a
Japan | Tokyo	International Christian University	YrRound	Dir	n/a	n/a

Connecticut

DESTINATION	HOST INSTITUTION	PRGM SEASON	PRGM TYPE	INTERMEDIARY	HOUSING
Jordan | Amman	SIT Abroad	Fall Spr	Intermed	SIT Abroad	n/a
Jordan | Amman	University of Jordan	Fall Spr YrRound	Intermed	Council on International Education Exchange (CIEE)	n/a
Kenya | Nairobi	Center for Wildlife Management Studies	Fall Spr	Intermed	School for Field Studies	n/a
Mexico | Baja	Center for Coastal Studies	Fall Spr	Intermed	School for Field Studies	n/a
Morocco | Rabat	Ecole Superieure de Direction et de Gestion	Fall Spr YrRound	Intermed	Council on International Education Exchange (CIEE)	n/a
Netherlands | Amsterdam	University of Amsterdam	Fall Spr YrRound	Intermed	Council on International Education Exchange (CIEE)	n/a
Netherlands | Maastricht	Universiteit Maastricht	Fall Spr YrRound	Dir	n/a	n/a
New Zealand | Dunedin	University of Otago	Fall Spr YrRound	USColl	Arcadia University	n/a
New Zealand | Tikapa Moana	Ecoquest (University of New Hampshire)	Spr	USColl	Ecoquest (University of New Hampshire)	n/a
New Zealand | Wellington	Victoria University of Wellington	Fall Spr YrRound	USColl	Arcadia University	n/a
Northern Ireland | Belfast	Queen's University	Fall Spr YrRound	Dir	n/a	n/a
Northern Ireland | Belfast	Queen's University	Fall Spr YrRound	Intermed	Institute for Study Abroad	n/a
Northern Ireland | Belfast	Queen's University	Fall Spr YrRound	USColl	Arcadia University	n/a
Russia | Moscow	Independent University of Moscow	Fall Spr YrRound	Dir	n/a	n/a
Russia | Moscow	Moscow Art Theater (Connecticut College)	Fall Spr	USColl	Connecticut College	n/a
Russia | Moscow	Russian Language Institute (Russian Academy of Sciences)	Spr	Intermed	Russian Language Institute (Russian Academy of Sciences)	n/a
Scotland | Edinburgh	University of Edinburgh	Fall Spr YrRound	Dir	n/a	n/a
Scotland | Edinburgh	University of Edinburgh	Fall Spr YrRound	Intermed	Institute for Study Abroad	n/a
Scotland | Edinburgh	University of Edinburgh	Fall Spr YrRound	USColl	Arcadia University	n/a
Scotland | Glasgow	University of Glasgow	Fall Spr YrRound	Dir	n/a	n/a
Scotland | Glasgow	University of Glasgow	Fall Spr YrRound	Intermed	Institute for Study Abroad	n/a
Scotland | Glasgow	University of Glasgow	Fall Spr YrRound	USColl	Arcadia University	n/a
Senegal | Dakar	Suffolk University - Dakar Campus	Fall Spr	Intermed	Council on International Education Exchange (CIEE)	n/a
South Africa | Cape Town	University of Cape Town	Fall Spr	Self	n/a	n/a
South Africa | Kruger National Park	Organization for Tropical Studies	Fall Spr	Intermed	Organization for Tropical Studies	n/a
Spain | Barcelona	University of Pompeu Fabra	Fall Spr	Self	n/a	n/a
Spain | Cordoba	University of Cordoba	Fall Spr	Consrtm	Programa de Estudios Hispanicos en Cordoba	n/a
Sweden | Stockholm	Stockholm University	Fall Spr YrRound	Intermed	The Swedish Program	n/a
Trinidad | Port-of-Spain	University of West Indies	Fall Spr	Self	n/a	n/a
Turkey | Istanbul	Bogazici University	Spr	USColl	Duke University	n/a
Turks and Caicos | South Caicos	Center for Marine Resource Management Studies	Fall Spr	Intermed	School for Field Studies	n/a
United States | Beaufort (NC)	Duke University Marine Laboratory	n/a	USColl	Duke University	n/a

© 2011 — Updates? Want to be in the next edition? Visit **www.mysecondcampus.com**

Connecticut

DESTINATION	HOST INSTITUTION	PRGM SEASON	PRGM TYPE	INTERMEDIARY	HOUSING
United States | Mystic (CT)	Williams-Mystic	n/a	USColl	Williams College	n/a
United States | New York (NY)	Trinity/La MaMa Urban Arts Semester in NYC	n/a	Intermed	Trinity/La MaMa Urban Arts Semester in NYC	n/a
United States | Washington (DC)	Washington Semester (American University)	n/a	USColl	Washington Semester (American University)	n/a
United States | Waterford (CT)	O'Neill National Theater Institute (Connecticut College)	n/a	USColl	Connecticut College	n/a
United States | Woods Hole (MA)	Marine Biological Laboratory	n/a	Intermed	Marine Biological Laboratory	n/a
United States | Woods Hole (MA)	Sea Semester	n/a	Intermed	Sea Semester	n/a
Vietnam | Ho Chi Minh City	SIT Abroad	Fall Spr	Intermed	SIT Abroad	n/a

University of Bridgeport

Thomas Ward
International College
126 Park Avenue
Bridgeport, CT 06604

ward@bridgeport.edu
203.576.4966
https://www.bridgeport.edu/pages/3292.asp

DESTINATION	HOST INSTITUTION	PRGM SEASON	PRGM TYPE	INTERMEDIARY	HOUSING
Argentina | (Multiple choices)	Middlebury College	n/a	USColl	Middlebury College	n/a
Argentina | Buenos	Facultad Latinoamericana de Ciencias Sociales	n/a	Intermed	Council on International Education Exchange (CIEE)	n/a
Chile | Santiago	Pontificia Universidad Catolica de Chile or Universidad de Chile	n/a	Intermed	Council on International Education Exchange (CIEE)	n/a
Chile | Valparaiso	Pontificia Universidad Catolica de Valparaiso	n/a	Intermed	Council on International Education Exchange (CIEE)	n/a
China | (Multiple choices)	Middlebury College	n/a	USColl	Middlebury College	n/a
China | Hong Kong	Syracuse University Abroad	n/a	USColl	Syracuse University Abroad	n/a
Dominican Republic | Santiago	Pontificia Universidad Catolica Madre y Maestra	n/a	Intermed	Council on International Education Exchange (CIEE)	n/a
Equador | Quito	Universidad San Francisco de Quito	n/a	USColl	Boston University	n/a
France | (Multiple choices)	Middlebury College	n/a	USColl	Middlebury College	n/a
France | Grenoble	Universite de Grenoble	n/a	USColl	Boston University	n/a
France | Paris	CIEE Study Center	n/a	Intermed	Council on International Education Exchange (CIEE)	n/a
France | Paris	NYU Center in Paris	n/a	USColl	New York University in Paris	n/a
France | Rennes	Universite de Haute Bretagne	n/a	Intermed	Council on International Education Exchange (CIEE)	n/a
France | Strasbourg	Syracuse University Abroad	n/a	USColl	Syracuse University Abroad	n/a
Germany | (Multiple choices)	Middlebury College	n/a	USColl	Middlebury College	n/a
Germany | Dresden	Technische Universitat Dresden	n/a	USColl	Boston University	n/a
Israel | Haifa	University of Haifa	n/a	USColl	Boston University	n/a
Italy | (Multiple choices)	Middlebury College	n/a	USColl	Middlebury College	n/a
Italy | (Multiple choices)	Multiple institutional choices	n/a	USColl	Boston University	n/a
Italy | Florence	Syracuse University Abroad	n/a	USColl	Syracuse University Abroad	n/a

Connecticut

DESTINATION	HOST INSTITUTION	PRGM SEASON	PRGM TYPE	INTERMEDIARY	HOUSING
New Zealand | Auckland	University of Auckland or Auckland University of Technology	n/a	USColl	Boston University	n/a
Niger | Niamey	Universite Abdou Moumouni	n/a	USColl	Boston University	n/a
Russia | (Multiple choices)	Middlebury College	n/a	USColl	Middlebury College	n/a
Spain | (Multiple choices)	Middlebury College	n/a	USColl	Middlebury College	n/a
Spain | Alcala	Universidad de Alcala	n/a	Intermed	Council on International Education Exchange (CIEE)	n/a
Spain | Alicante	Universidad de Alicante	n/a	Intermed	Council on International Education Exchange (CIEE)	n/a
Spain | Barcelona	Multiple institutional choices	n/a	Intermed	Council on International Education Exchange (CIEE)	n/a
Spain | Madrid	Syracuse University Abroad	n/a	USColl	Syracuse University Abroad	n/a
Spain | Madrid	Universidad Autonoma de Madrid	Sum Fall Spr YrRound	USColl	New York University in Madrid	n/a
Spain | Madrid	Universidad Carlos III de Madrid	n/a	Intermed	Council on International Education Exchange (CIEE)	n/a
Spain | Seville	Universidad Pablo de Olavide or Universidad de Sevilla	n/a	Intermed	Council on International Education Exchange (CIEE)	n/a
Taiwan | Taipei	National Chengchi University	n/a	Intermed	Council on International Education Exchange (CIEE)	n/a

University of Connecticut

Ross Lewin
Director
Office of Study Abroad
University of Connecticut
368 Fairfield Road, Unit 2207
Storrs, CT 06269

ross.lewin@uconn.edu
860.486.5022
http://studyabroad.uconn.edu/index.cfm?FuseAction=Abroad.Home

(Multiple choices) | (Multiple choices)	Multiple institutional choices	Fall Spr YrRound	Bilat	Institute of International Education (Global E3 Engineering)	n/a
(Multiple choices) | (Multiple choices)	Semester at Sea	Sum Fall Spr	Intermed	Semester at Sea	n/a
Argentina | Buenos Aires	Facultad Latinoamericana de Ciencias Sociales	Sum	Intermed	Council on International Educational Exchange (CIEE)	n/a
Argentina | Buenos Aires	Facultad Latinoamericana de Ciencias Sociales	Sum	Intermed	Council on International Educational Exchange (CIEE)	n/a
Argentina | Buenos Aires	Favaloro University	YrRound	Bilat	n/a	n/a
Argentina | Buenos Aires	Multiple institutional choices	Fall Spr YrRound	Intermed	Institute for Study Abroad	n/a
Argentina | Buenos Aires	Multiple institutional choices	Fall Spr YrRound	Intermed	Council on International Educational Exchange (CIEE)	n/a
Argentina | Buenos Aires	SIT Study Abroad	Fall Spr	Intermed	SIT Study Abroad	n/a
Argentina | Mendoza	Universidad Nacional de Cuyo	Fall Spr YrRound	Intermed	Institute for Study Abroad	n/a
Armenia | Yerevan	University of Connecticut	Sum	Self	n/a	n/a
Australia | Adelaide	University of Adelaide	Fall Spr YrRound	Bilat	n/a	n/a

© 2011 — Updates? Want to be in the next edition? Visit **www.mysecondcampus.com**

Connecticut

DESTINATION	HOST INSTITUTION	PRGM SEASON	PRGM TYPE	INTERMEDIARY	HOUSING
Australia | Brisbane	University of Queensland	Fall Spr YrRound	Bilat	n/a	n/a
Australia | Byron Bay	SIT Study Abroad	Fall Spr	Intermed	SIT Study Abroad	n/a
Australia | Cairns	SIT Study Abroad	Fall Spr	Intermed	SIT Study Abroad	n/a
Australia | Melbourne	University of Melbourne	Fall Spr YrRound	Bilat	n/a	n/a
Australia | Perth	Murdoch University	Fall Spr YrRound	Intermed	Council on International Educational Exchange (CIEE)	n/a
Australia | Sydney	University of New South Wales	Fall Spr YrRound	Bilat	n/a	n/a
Australia | Wollongong	University of Wollongong	Fall Spr YrRound	Bilat	n/a	n/a
Australia | Yungaburra	Center for Rainforest Studies	Sum Fall Spr	Intermed	School for Field Studies	n/a
Belgium | Brussels	Vesalius University	Fall Spr YrRound	Intermed	Council on International Educational Exchange (CIEE)	n/a
Bolivia | Cochabamba	SIT Study Abroad	Fall Spr	Intermed	SIT Study Abroad	n/a
Bolivia | Cochabamba	SIT Study Abroad	Sum	Intermed	SIT Study Abroad	n/a
Botswana | Gabarone	SIT Study Abroad	Fall Spr	Intermed	SIT Study Abroad	n/a
Botswana | Gabarone	University of Botswana	Fall Spr YrRound	Intermed	Council on International Educational Exchange (CIEE)	n/a
Brazil | (Multiple choices)	SIT Study Abroad	Fall Spr	Intermed	SIT Study Abroad	n/a
Brazil | Belem	SIT Study Abroad	Fall Spr	Intermed	SIT Study Abroad	n/a
Brazil | Salvador de Bahia	SIT Study Abroad	Fall Spr	Intermed	SIT Study Abroad	n/a
Brazil | Salvador de Bahia	Universidade Catolica do Salvador or Universidade Federal da Bahia	Fall Spr YrRound	Intermed	Council on International Educational Exchange (CIEE)	n/a
Brazil | Salvador de Bahia	Universidade Federal da Bahia	Sum	Intermed	Council on International Educational Exchange (CIEE)	n/a
Brazil | Sao Paulo	Pontificia Universidad Catolica de Sao Paulo	Fall Spr YrRound	Intermed	Council on International Educational Exchange (CIEE)	n/a
Cameroon | Yaounde	SIT Study Abroad	Fall Spr	Intermed	SIT Study Abroad	n/a
Canada | Lennoxville	Bishop's University	Fall Spr YrRound	Bilat	n/a	n/a
Canada | Montreal	Concordia University	Fall Spr YrRound	Bilat	n/a	n/a
Canada | Montreal	Ecole Polytechnique	Fall Spr YrRound	Bilat	n/a	n/a
Canada | Montreal	McGill university	Fall Spr YrRound	Bilat	n/a	n/a
Canada | Montreal	University of Montreal	Fall Spr YrRound	Bilat	n/a	n/a
Canada | Quebec	University of Quebec	Fall Spr YrRound	Bilat	n/a	n/a
Canada | Quebec City	Laval University	Fall Spr YrRound	Bilat	n/a	n/a
Canada | Sherbrooke	University of Sherbrooke	Fall Spr YrRound	Bilat	n/a	n/a
Chile | Arica	SIT Study Abroad	Fall Spr	Intermed	SIT Study Abroad	n/a
Chile | Puntas Arenas	University of Connecticut	Fall Spr YrRound	Bilat	University of Magallanes	n/a
Chile | Santiago	IES Abroad Santiago Center	Sum	Intermed	IES Abroad	n/a
Chile | Santiago	Pontificia Universidad Catolica de Chile	Fall Spr YrRound	Bilat	n/a	n/a
Chile | Santiago	SIT Study Abroad	Fall Spr	Intermed	SIT Study Abroad	n/a
Chile | Valparaiso	Pontificia Universidad Catolica de Valparaiso	Fall Spr YrRound	Intermed	Council on International Educational Exchange (CIEE)	n/a
Chile | Valparaiso	SIT Study Abroad	Fall Spr	Intermed	SIT Study Abroad	n/a

© 2011 — Updates? Want to be in the next edition? Visit **www.mysecondcampus.com**

Connecticut

DESTINATION	HOST INSTITUTION	PRGM SEASON	PRGM TYPE	INTERMEDIARY	HOUSING
China	Beijing	CET Academic Programs	Sum Fall Spr	Intermed	CET Academic Programs	n/a
China	Beijing	Peking University	Fall Spr YrRound	Intermed	Council on International Educational Exchange (CIEE)	n/a
China	Hong Kong	University of Hong Kong	Fall Spr YrRound	Bilat	n/a	n/a
China	Kunmimg	SIT Study Abroad	Fall Spr	Intermed	SIT Study Abroad	n/a
China	Kunming	SIT Study Abroad	Sum	Intermed	SIT Study Abroad	n/a
China	Nanjing	Nanjing University	Sum Fall Spr	Intermed	Council on International Educational Exchange (CIEE)	n/a
China	Shanghai	East China Normal University	Sum Fall Spr YrRound	Intermed	Council on International Educational Exchange (CIEE)	n/a
Costa Rica	Atenas	SFS Center for Sustainable Development Studies	Fall Spr	Intermed	School for Field Studies	n/a
Costa Rica	Heredia	Universidad Nacional Autonoma	Fall Spr YrRound	Intermed	Institute for Study Abroad	n/a
Costa Rica	Monteverde	CIEE Study Center	Sum	Intermed	Council on International Educational Exchange (CIEE)	n/a
Costa Rica	Monteverde	CIEE Study Center	Sum Fall Spr	Intermed	Council on International Educational Exchange (CIEE)	n/a
Costa Rica	San Jose	Forester Instituto Internacional	Sum	Intermed	Forester Instituto Internacional	n/a
Costa Rica	San Jose	Universidad de Costa Rica	Fall Spr YrRound	Intermed	Institute for Study Abroad	n/a
Croatia	Zagreb	SIT Study Abroad	Fall Spr	Intermed	SIT Study Abroad	n/a
Czech Republic	Prague	CET Academic Programs	Fall Spr	Intermed	CET Academic Programs	n/a
Czech Republic	Prague	Charles University	Fall Spr YrRound	Dir	n/a	n/a
Czech Republic	Prague	Charles University or Prague Film and Television School of the Academy of the Performing Arts	Fall Spr	Intermed	Council on International Educational Exchange (CIEE)	n/a
Czech Republic	Prague	CIEE Study Center	Sum	Intermed	Council on International Educational Exchange (CIEE)	n/a
Czech Republic	Prague	SIT Study Abroad	Fall Spr	Intermed	SIT Study Abroad	n/a
Denmark	Aarhus	University of Aarhus	Fall Spr YrRound	Bilat	n/a	n/a
Dominican Republic	Santiago	Pontificia Universidad Catolica Madre y Maestra	Sum	Intermed	Council on International Educational Exchange (CIEE)	n/a
Dominican Republic	Santiago	Pontificia Universidad Catolica Madre y Maestra	Fall Spr YrRound	Intermed	Council on International Educational Exchange (CIEE)	n/a
Dominican Republic	Santo Domingo	Multiple institutional choices	Fall Spr YrRound	Intermed	Council on International Educational Exchange (CIEE)	n/a
Ecuador	Quito	IES Abroad Quito Center	Sum	Intermed	IES Abroad	n/a
Ecuador	Quito	IES Abroad Quito Center	Sum	Intermed	IES Abroad	n/a
Ecuador	Quito	SIT Study Abroad	Fall Spr	Intermed	SIT Study Abroad	n/a
Ecuador	Quito	SIT Study Abroad	Fall Spr	Intermed	SIT Study Abroad	n/a
England	Birmingham	University of Birmingham	Fall Spr YrRound	Bilat	n/a	n/a
England	Colchester	University of Essex	Fall Spr YrRound	Bilat	n/a	n/a
England	Edinburgh	University of Edinburgh	YrRound	Bilat	n/a	n/a
England	Liverpool	University of Liverpool	Fall Spr YrRound	Bilat	n/a	n/a
England	Liverpool	University of Liverpool	Sum	Self	n/a	n/a

© 2011 — Updates? Want to be in the next edition? Visit www.mysecondcampus.com

Connecticut

DESTINATION	HOST INSTITUTION	PRGM SEASON	PRGM TYPE	INTERMEDIARY	HOUSING
England	London	Florida State University's London Study Center	Fall Spr	Self	n/a	n/a
England	London	London College of Communications	Fall Spr YrRound	Bilat	n/a	n/a
England	London	University of Connecticut	n/a	Self	n/a	n/a
England	London	University of Connecticut	Fall	Self	n/a	n/a
England	London	University of Connecticut	Sum	Self	n/a	n/a
England	Nottingham	University of Nottingham	Fall Spr YrRound	Bilat	n/a	n/a
England	Warwick	University of Warwick	Fall Spr YrRound	Bilat	n/a	n/a
France	Compiegne	Universite de Technologie de Compiegne	Fall Spr YrRound	Bilat	n/a	n/a
France	Paris	CIEE Study Center	Sum	Intermed	Council on International Educational Exchange (CIEE)	n/a
France	Paris	La Sorbonne - Paris IV	Fall Spr YrRound	Self	n/a	n/a
France	Paris	La Sorbonne - Paris IV	Fall Spr YrRound	Self	n/a	n/a
France	Rennes	Universite de Haute Bretagne	Fall Spr YrRound	Intermed	Council on International Educational Exchange (CIEE)	n/a
France	Toulouse	SIT Study Abroad	Fall Spr	Intermed	SIT Study Abroad	n/a
France	Toulouse	SIT Study Abroad	Fall Spr	Intermed	SIT Study Abroad	n/a
France	Toulouse	Toulouse Language Institute	Sum	Self	n/a	n/a
Germany	Berlin	Freie University	Fall Spr	Dir	n/a	n/a
Germany	Freiburg	University of Freiburg	Fall Spr YrRound	Bilat	Baden-Wurttemburg Exchange Program	n/a
Germany	Heidelberg	University of Heidelberg	Fall Spr YrRound	Bilat	n/a	n/a
Germany	Hohenheim	University of Hohenheim	Fall Spr YrRound	Bilat	n/a	n/a
Germany	Karlsruhe	University of Karlsruhe	Fall Spr YrRound	Bilat	n/a	n/a
Germany	Konstanz	University of Konstanz	Fall Spr YrRound	Bilat	n/a	n/a
Germany	Mannheim	University of Mannheim	Fall Spr YrRound	Bilat	n/a	n/a
Germany	Regensberg	Universitat Regensburg	YrRound	Bilat	n/a	n/a
Germany	Stuttgart	University of Stuttgart	Fall Spr YrRound	Bilat	n/a	n/a
Germany	Tubingen	University of Tubingen	Fall Spr YrRound	Bilat	n/a	n/a
Germany	Ulm	University of Ulm	Fall Spr YrRound	Bilat	n/a	n/a
Ghana	Accra	SIT Study Abroad	Fall Spr	Intermed	SIT Study Abroad	n/a
Ghana	Cape Coast	SIT Study Abroad	Fall Spr	Intermed	SIT Study Abroad	n/a
Ghana	Legon	University of Ghana	Fall Spr YrRound	Intermed	Council on International Educational Exchange (CIEE)	n/a
Greece	Rhodes	Paideia Society at the Center for Hellenic Studies	Sum	Intermed	n/a	n/a
Guatemala	Antigua	University of Connecticut	Sum	Self	n/a	n/a
Hungary	Budapest	CIEE Study Center	Fall Spr YrRound	Intermed	Council on International Educational Exchange (CIEE)	n/a
Iceland	Akureyri	SIT Study Abroad	Sum	Intermed	SIT Study Abroad	n/a
India	(Multiple choices)	American Institute of Indian Studies	Sum	Consrtm	American Institute of Indian Studies	n/a
India	(Multiple choices)	SIT Study Abroad	Sum	Intermed	SIT Study Abroad	n/a

© 2011 — Updates? Want to be in the next edition? Visit **www.mysecondcampus.com**

Connecticut

DESTINATION	HOST INSTITUTION	PRGM SEASON	PRGM TYPE	INTERMEDIARY	HOUSING
India	(Multiple choices)	University of Connecticut	n/a	Self	n/a	n/a
India	Delhi	SIT Study Abroad	Fall Spr	Intermed	SIT Study Abroad	n/a
India	Dharamsala	SIT Study Abroad	Fall Spr	Intermed	SIT Study Abroad	n/a
India	Hyderabad	University of Hyderabad	Fall Spr YrRound	Intermed	Council on International Educational Exchange (CIEE)	n/a
Ireland	Dublin	SIT Study Abroad	Fall Spr	Intermed	SIT Study Abroad	n/a
Ireland	Dublin	University College Dublin	Fall Spr YrRound	Dir	n/a	n/a
Ireland	Dublin	University College Dublin	Fall Spr YrRound	Bilat	n/a	n/a
Israel	Haifa	University of Haifa	Fall Spr YrRound	Self	n/a	n/a
Israel	Jerusalem	Hebrew University of Jerusalem	Fall Spr YrRound	Self	n/a	n/a
Italy	Ascoli-Piceno	University of New Hampshire Ascoli Piceno Center	Sum	Self	n/a	n/a
Italy	Ascoli-Piceno	University of New Hampshire Ascoli Piceno Center	Sum	Self	n/a	n/a
Italy	Florence	Institute for Fine & Liberal Arts	Sum	Self	n/a	n/a
Italy	Florence	University of Connecticut	n/a	Self	n/a	n/a
Italy	Rome	IES Rome Center	Sum	Intermed	IES Abroad	n/a
Japan	Tokyo	Sophia University	Fall Spr YrRound	Bilat	n/a	n/a
Japan	Tokyo	Sophia University	Sum Fall Spr YrRound	Intermed	Council on International Educational Exchange (CIEE)	n/a
Jordan	Amman	SIT Study Abroad	Fall Spr	Intermed	SIT Study Abroad	n/a
Jordan	Amman	SIT Study Abroad	Sum	Intermed	SIT Study Abroad	n/a
Jordan	Amman	University of Jordan	Sum	Intermed	Council on International Educational Exchange (CIEE)	n/a
Kenya	Kimana	Center for Wildlife Management Studies	Fall Spr	Intermed	School for Field Studies	n/a
Kenya	Mombasa	SIT Study Abroad	Fall Spr	Intermed	SIT Study Abroad	n/a
Kenya	Nairobi	SIT Study Abroad	Fall Spr	Intermed	SIT Study Abroad	n/a
Madagascar	Antananarivo	SIT Study Abroad	Fall Spr	Intermed	SIT Study Abroad	n/a
Madagascar	Fort Dauphin	SIT Study Abroad	Fall Spr	Intermed	SIT Study Abroad	n/a
Mali	Bamako	SIT Study Abroad	Fall Spr	Intermed	SIT Study Abroad	n/a
Mexico	Baja	Center for Coastal Studies	Sum	Intermed	School for Field Studies	n/a
Mexico	Guanajuato	University of Guanajuato	Sum	Intermed	Council on International Educational Exchange (CIEE)	n/a
Mexico	Guanajuato	University of Guanajuato	Fall Spr	Intermed	Council on International Educational Exchange (CIEE)	n/a
Mexico	Guanajuato	University of Guanajuato	Fall Spr	Intermed	Council on International Educational Exchange (CIEE)	n/a
Mexico	Merida	Universidad Autonoma de Yucatan	Fall Spr YrRound	Intermed	Institute for Study Abroad	n/a
Mexico	Monterrey	University of Monterrey	Fall Spr YrRound	Bilat	n/a	n/a
Mexico	Oaxaca	Becari Language School	Sum	Self	n/a	n/a
Mexico	Oaxaca	SIT Study Abroad	Fall Spr	Intermed	SIT Study Abroad	n/a
Mexico	Oaxaca	University of Connecticut	Sum	Self	n/a	n/a
Mongolia	Ulaanbaatar	SIT Study Abroad	Fall Spr	Intermed	SIT Study Abroad	n/a

© 2011 — Updates? Want to be in the next edition? Visit **www.mysecondcampus.com**

Connecticut

DESTINATION	HOST INSTITUTION	PRGM SEASON	PRGM TYPE	INTERMEDIARY	HOUSING
Morocco	Rabat	SIT Study Abroad	Sum	Intermed	SIT Study Abroad	n/a
Morocco	Rabat	SIT Study Abroad	Fall Spr	Intermed	SIT Study Abroad	n/a
Netherlands	Amsterdam	SIT Study Abroad	Fall Spr	Intermed	SIT Study Abroad	n/a
Netherlands	Maastricht	University College Maastricht	Fall Spr	Bilat	n/a	n/a
Netherlands	Utrecht	University College Utrecht	Fall Spr	Bilat	n/a	n/a
Nicaragua	Managua	SIT Study Abroad	Fall Spr	Intermed	SIT Study Abroad	n/a
Nicaragua	Managua	Universidad Nacional Autonoma de Nicaragua	Fall Spr YrRound	Intermed	Council on International Educational Exchange (CIEE)	n/a
Norway	Oslo	University of Oslo	Fall Spr YrRound	Bilat	n/a	n/a
Oman	Muscat	SIT Study Abroad	Fall Spr	Intermed	SIT Study Abroad	n/a
Oman	Muscat	SIT Study Abroad	Fall Spr	Intermed	SIT Study Abroad	n/a
Peru	Cuzco	SIT Study Abroad	Fall Spr	Intermed	SIT Study Abroad	n/a
Poland	Krakow	Jagiellonian University	Sum	Intermed	Kosciuszko Foundation	n/a
Poland	Warsaw	Warsaw School of Economics	Fall Spr YrRound	Intermed	Council on International Educational Exchange (CIEE)	n/a
Portugal	Lisbon	Universidade Nova de Lisboa	Fall Spr YrRound	Intermed	Council on International Educational Exchange (CIEE)	n/a
Puerto Rico	San Juan	University of Connecticut	Fall	Self	n/a	n/a
Russia	St. Petersburg	St. Petersburg State University	Sum	Intermed	Council on International Educational Exchange (CIEE)	n/a
Russia	St. Petersburg	St. Petersburg State University	Fall Spr YrRound	Intermed	Council on International Educational Exchange (CIEE)	n/a
Russia	St. Petersburg	St. Petersburg State University	Fall Spr	Intermed	Council on International Educational Exchange (CIEE)	n/a
Samoa	Apia	SIT Study Abroad	Fall Spr	Intermed	SIT Study Abroad	n/a
Scotland	Glasgow	University of Glasgow	Fall Spr YrRound	Bilat	n/a	n/a
Senegal	Dakar	SIT Study Abroad	Fall Spr	Intermed	SIT Study Abroad	n/a
Senegal	Dakar	SIT Study Abroad	Sum	Intermed	SIT Study Abroad	n/a
Singapore	Singapore	National University of Singpore	Fall Spr YrRound	Bilat	n/a	n/a
South Africa	Cape Town	SIT Study Abroad	n/a	Intermed	SIT Study Abroad	n/a
South Africa	Cape Town	University of Connecticut	Spr	Self	n/a	n/a
South Africa	Cape Town	University of Connecticut	Fall	Self	n/a	n/a
South Africa	Durban	SIT Study Abroad	n/a	Intermed	SIT Study Abroad	n/a
South Africa	Durban	SIT Study Abroad	Fall Spr	Intermed	SIT Study Abroad	n/a
South Africa	Durban	SIT Study Abroad	n/a	Intermed	SIT Study Abroad	n/a
South Africa	Entabeni	University of Connecticut Private Game Reserve	Sum	Self	n/a	n/a
South Korea	Seoul	Sogang University	Fall Spr YrRound	Bilat	n/a	n/a
South Korea	Seoul	Yonsei University	Fall Spr YrRound	Bilat	n/a	n/a
Spain	Alicante	Universidad de Alicante	Sum	Intermed	Council on International Educational Exchange (CIEE)	n/a
Spain	Alicante	Universidad de Alicante	Fall Spr YrRound	Intermed	Council on International Educational Exchange (CIEE)	n/a
Spain	Alicante	Universidad de Alicante	Fall Spr	Intermed	Council on International Educational Exchange (CIEE)	n/a

Connecticut

DESTINATION	HOST INSTITUTION	PRGM SEASON	PRGM TYPE	INTERMEDIARY	HOUSING
Spain | Alicante	Universidad de Alicante	Fall Spr	Intermed	Council on International Educational Exchange (CIEE)	n/a
Spain | Barcelona	Escola Superior de Comerc Internacional or Universitat Pompeu Fabra	Fall Spr	Intermed	Council on International Educational Exchange (CIEE)	n/a
Spain | Barcelona	Facultad Latinoamericana de Ciencias Sociales	Fall Spr YrRound	Intermed	Council on International Educational Exchange (CIEE)	n/a
Spain | Barcelona	IES Abroad Barcelona Center	Sum	Intermed	IES Abroad	n/a
Spain | Barcelona	IES Abroad Barcelona Center	Fall Spr YrRound	Intermed	IES Abroad	n/a
Spain | Granada	SIT Study Abroad	Fall Spr	Intermed	SIT Study Abroad	n/a
Spain | Granada	Universidad de Granada	Fall Spr YrRound	Self	n/a	n/a
Spain | Granada	University of Granda	Sum	Self	n/a	n/a
Spain | Madrid	Universidad Carlos III de Madrid	Fall Spr YrRound	Intermed	Council on International Educational Exchange (CIEE)	n/a
Spain | Salamanca	Universidad de Salamanca	Sum	Self	n/a	n/a
Spain | Salamanca	University of Rhode Island	Sum	Intermed	University of Rhode Island	n/a
Spain | Seville	CIEE Study Center	Sum	Intermed	Council on International Educational Exchange (CIEE)	n/a
Spain | Seville	Universidad de Sevilla	Fall Spr	Intermed	Council on International Educational Exchange (CIEE)	n/a
Spain | Seville	Universidad Pablo de Olavide	Fall Spr	Intermed	Council on International Educational Exchange (CIEE)	n/a
Spain | Seville	Universidad Pablo de Olavide or Universidad de Sevilla	Fall Spr YrRound	Intermed	Council on International Educational Exchange (CIEE)	n/a
Spain | Seville	Universidad Pablo de Olavide or Universidad de Sevilla	Fall Spr YrRound	Intermed	Council on International Educational Exchange (CIEE)	n/a
Spain | Seville	Universidad Pablo de Olavide or Universidad de Sevilla	Fall Spr YrRound	Intermed	Council on International Educational Exchange (CIEE)	n/a
Spain | Seville	Universidad Pablo de Olavide or Universidad de Sevilla	Fall Spr YrRound	Intermed	Council on International Educational Exchange (CIEE)	n/a
Sweden | Linkoping	Linkoping University (Institute of Technology)	Fall Spr YrRound	Bilat	n/a	n/a
Sweden | Lund	Lund University	Fall Spr YrRound	Bilat	n/a	n/a
Sweden | Uppsala	Uppsala University	Fall Spr YrRound	Bilat	n/a	n/a
Switzerland | Nyon	SIT Study Abroad	Sum Fall Spr	Intermed	SIT Study Abroad	n/a
Taiwan | Taipei	National Chengchi University	Fall Spr YrRound	Bilat	n/a	n/a
Tanzania | Arusha	SIT Study Abroad	Fall Spr	Intermed	SIT Study Abroad	n/a
Tanzania | Stone Town	SIT Study Abroad	Fall Spr	Intermed	SIT Study Abroad	n/a
Thailand | Khon Kaen	Khon Kaen University	Fall Spr	Intermed	Council on International Educational Exchange (CIEE)	n/a
Turks & Caicos Islands | South Caicos	Center for Marine Resource Management Studies	Sum	Intermed	School for Field Studies	n/a
Uganda | Gulu	SIT Study Abroad	Fall Spr	Intermed	SIT Study Abroad	n/a
Uganda | Kampala	SIT Study Abroad	Fall Spr	Intermed	SIT Study Abroad	n/a
Uganda | Kampala	SIT Study Abroad	Sum	Intermed	SIT Study Abroad	n/a
Vietnam | Can Tho	SIT Study Abroad	Fall Spr	Intermed	SIT Study Abroad	n/a

© 2011 — Updates? Want to be in the next edition? Visit www.mysecondcampus.com

Connecticut

DESTINATION	HOST INSTITUTION	PRGM SEASON	PRGM TYPE	INTERMEDIARY	HOUSING
Vietnam | Hanoi	Vietnam National University	Fall Spr YrRound	Intermed	Council on International Educational Exchange (CIEE)	n/a
Vietnam | Ho Chi Minh City	SIT Study Abroad	Fall Spr	Intermed	SIT Study Abroad	n/a
Wales | Cardiff	Cardiff University	Fall Spr YrRound	Bilat	n/a	n/a

University of Hartford

Susan Carey
Assistant Director for Study Abroad
The International Center
Gengras Student Union, Room 327
200 Bloomfield Avenue
Hartford, CT 06117

sucarey@hartford.edu
860.768.5100
http://uhaweb.hartford.edu/intcenter/studyabroad/

DESTINATION	HOST INSTITUTION	PRGM SEASON	PRGM TYPE	INTERMEDIARY	HOUSING
(Multiple choices) | (Multiple choices)	Multiple institutional choices	n/a	USColl	Antioch University	n/a
Argentina | (Multiple choices)	Multiple institutional choices	n/a	Intermed	Council on International Educational Exchange (CIEE)	n/a
Argentina | [City Unspecified]	Instituto Universitario Nacional de Arte	n/a	Intermed	IES Abroad	n/a
Argentina | [City Unspecified]	Multiple institutional choices	n/a	Intermed	SIT Study Abroad	n/a
Argentina | [City Unspecified]	Multiple institutional choices	n/a	Intermed	Academic Programs International	n/a
Argentina | [City Unspecified]	Multiple institutional choices	n/a	Intermed	Institute for Study Abroad	n/a
Argentina | [City Unspecified]	Multiple institutional choices	n/a	USColl	American University Abroad	n/a
Australia | (Multiple choices)	Multiple institutional choices	n/a	USColl	American University Abroad	n/a
Australia | (Multiple choices)	Multiple institutional choices	n/a	Intermed	Council on International	n/a
Australia | (Multiple choices)	Multiple institutional choices	n/a	Intermed	AustraLearn	n/a
Australia | (Multiple choices)	Multiple institutional choices	n/a	Intermed	IES Abroad	n/a
Australia | (Multiple choices)	Multiple institutional choices	n/a	USColl	Arcadia University	n/a
Australia | (Multiple choices)	Multiple institutional choices	n/a	Intermed	American Institute for Foreign Study	n/a
Australia | (Multiple choices)	Multiple institutional choices	n/a	Intermed	Institute for Study Abroad	n/a
Australia | (Multiple choices)	World Learning Program	n/a	Intermed	SIT Study Abroad	n/a
Australia | Adelaide	n/a	n/a	Intermed	International Partnership for Service-Learning and Leadership	n/a
Austria | Salzburg	University of Salzburg	n/a	Intermed	American Institute for Foreign Study	n/a
Austria | Vienna	University of Vienna	n/a	Intermed	IES Abroad	n/a
Balkans | (Multiple choices)	World Learning Program	n/a	Intermed	SIT Study Abroad	n/a
Bolivia | [City Unspecified]	Multiple institutional choices	n/a	Intermed	SIT Study Abroad	n/a
Bonaire | Bonaire	CIEE Study Center	n/a	Intermed	Council on International Educational Exchange (CIEE)	n/a
Botswana | [City Unspecified]	University of Botswana	n/a	Intermed	Interstudy	n/a
Botswana | [City Unspecified]	University of Botswana	n/a	Intermed	Council on International Educational Exchange (CIEE)	n/a

Connecticut

DESTINATION	HOST INSTITUTION	PRGM SEASON	PRGM TYPE	INTERMEDIARY	HOUSING
Botswana | [City Unspecified]	World Learning Program	n/a	Intermed	SIT Study Abroad	n/a
Brazil | [City Unspecified]	Fundacao Armando Alvares Penteado	n/a	Intermed	American Institute for Foreign Study	n/a
Brazil | [City Unspecified]	Multiple institutional choices	n/a	Intermed	Council on International Educational Exchange (CIEE)	n/a
Brazil | [City Unspecified]	Universidade Federal do Parana and Mato Grosso	n/a	USColl	Antioch University	n/a
Brazil | [City Unspecified]	World Learning Program	n/a	Intermed	SIT Study Abroad	n/a
Brazil | Rio de Janeiro	Pontificia Universidade Catolica do Rio de Janeiro	n/a	USColl	American University Abroad	n/a
Cambodia | [City Unspecified]	Center for Khmer Studies	n/a	Intermed	Council on International Educational Exchange (CIEE)	n/a
Cameroon | [City Unspecified]	World Learning Program	n/a	Intermed	SIT Study Abroad	n/a
Chile | (Multiple choices)	Multiple institutional choices	n/a	Intermed	Institute for Study Abroad	n/a
Chile | (Multiple choices)	Multiple institutional choices	n/a	Intermed	Council on International Educational Exchange (CIEE)	n/a
Chile | (Multiple choices)	Multiple institutional choices	n/a	Intermed	IES Abroad	n/a
Chile | [City Unspecified]	Universidad Diego Portales	n/a	USColl	American University Abroad	n/a
Chile | [City Unspecified]	World Learning Program	n/a	Intermed	SIT Study Abroad	n/a
China | (Multiple choices)	Multiple institutional choices	n/a	Intermed	Council on International Educational Exchange (CIEE)	n/a
China | (Multiple choices)	Multiple institutional choices	n/a	Intermed	Alliance for Global Learning	n/a
China | (Multiple choices)	Multiple institutional choices	n/a	Intermed	American Institute for Foreign Study	n/a
China | (Multiple choices)	Multiple institutional choices	n/a	Intermed	IES Abroad	n/a
China | (Multiple choices)	Multiple institutional choices	n/a	USColl	American University Abroad	n/a
China | (Multiple choices)	World Learning Program	n/a	Intermed	SIT Study Abroad	n/a
China | [City Unspecified]	Nanjing University	n/a	Intermed	American Institute for Foreign Study	n/a
China | [City Unspecified]	Sichuan University	n/a	Intermed	AsiaLearn	n/a
Costa Rica | Heredia	Universidad Nacional	n/a	Intermed	Institute for Study Abroad	n/a
Costa Rica | Heredia	Universidad Nacional	n/a	Intermed	Institute for Study Abroad	n/a
Costa Rica | Monteverde	CIEE Study Center	n/a	Intermed	Council on International Educational Exchange (CIEE)	n/a
Costa Rica | San Joaquin de Flores	Instituto San Joaquin de Flores	n/a	Intermed	Academic Programs International	n/a
Costa Rica | San Jose	Universidad de Costa Rica	n/a	Intermed	Academic Programs International	n/a
Costa Rica | San Jose	Universidad de Costa Rica	n/a	Intermed	Institute for Study Abroad	n/a
Costa Rica | San Jose	Veritas University	n/a	Intermed	American Institute for Foreign Study	n/a
Cuba | Havana	University of Havana	n/a	Intermed	American University Abroad	n/a
Czech Republic | Prague	Charles University	n/a	Intermed	American Institute for Foreign Study	n/a
Czech Republic | Prague	Charles University	n/a	Intermed	Council on International Educational Exchange (CIEE)	n/a

© 2011 — Updates? Want to be in the next edition? Visit **www.mysecondcampus.com**

Connecticut

DESTINATION	HOST INSTITUTION	PRGM SEASON	PRGM TYPE	INTERMEDIARY	HOUSING
Czech Republic and Poland | Prague and Krakow	University of Hartford	Win	Self	n/a	n/a
Costs: Win Costs: T&F: n/a, R&B: n/a, Ttl: $3,899					
Denmark | Copenhagen	Danish Institute for Study Abroad	n/a	Intermed	Danish Institute for Study Abroad	n/a
Dominican Republic | [City Unspecified]	Multiple institutional choices	n/a	Intermed	Council on International Educational Exchange (CIEE)	n/a
Ecuador | (Multiple choices)	Multiple institutional choices	n/a	Intermed	International Partnership for Service-Learning and Leadership	n/a
Ecuador | (Multiple choices)	Multiple institutional choices	n/a	Intermed	IES Abroad	n/a
Ecuador | (Multiple choices)	University of Hartford	Win	Self	n/a	n/a
Costs: Win Costs: T&F: n/a, R&B: n/a, Ttl: $2,745					
Ecuador | (Multiple choices)	World Learning Program	n/a	Intermed	SIT Study Abroad	n/a
Egypt | (Multiple)	American University in Egypt	n/a	USColl	American University Abroad	n/a
Egypt | (Multiple choices)	Multiple institutional choices	n/a	Intermed	Institute for Study Abroad	n/a
England | (Multiple choices)	Multiple institutional choices	n/a	Intermed	Interstudy	n/a
England | (Multiple choices)	Multiple institutional choices	n/a	Intermed	American Institute for Foreign Study	n/a
England | (Multiple choices)	Multiple institutional choices	n/a	Intermed	IES Abroad	n/a
England | (Multiple choices)	Multiple institutional choices	n/a	Intermed	Academic Programs International	n/a
England | (Multiple choices)	Multiple institutional choices	n/a	USColl	Arcadia University	n/a
England | (Multiple choices)	Multiple institutional choices	n/a	Intermed	Institute for Study Abroad	n/a
England | (Multiple choices)	Multiple institutional choices	n/a	Intermed	IES Abroad	n/a
France | (Multiple choices)	Multiple institutional choices	n/a	Intermed	IES Abroad	n/a
France | (Multiple choices)	Multiple institutional choices	n/a	Intermed	International Partnership for Service-Learning and Leadership	n/a
France | (Multiple choices)	Multiple institutional choices	n/a	Intermed	Institute for American Universities	n/a
France | (Multiple choices)	Multiple institutional choices	n/a	Intermed	American Institute for Foreign Study	n/a
France | (Multiple choices)	Multiple institutional choices	n/a	Intermed	Academic Programs International	n/a
France | (Multiple choices)	Multiple institutional choices	n/a	USColl	Arcadia University	n/a
France | (Multiple choices)	World Learning Program	n/a	Intermed	SIT Study Abroad	n/a
France | Paris	SPEOS	n/a	Intermed	SPEOS	n/a
Germany | (Multiple choices)	n/a	n/a	Intermed	IES Abroad	n/a
Germany | [City Unspecified]	n/a	n/a	Bilat	Baden-Wurttemberg Exchange Program	n/a
Germany | Bonn	University of Bonn	n/a	USColl	Arcadia University	n/a
Germany | Tubingen	Tubingen University	n/a	USColl	Antioch University	n/a
Ghana | [City Unspecified]	Multiple institutional choices	n/a	Intermed	Council on International Educational Exchange (CIEE)	n/a
Ghana | [City Unspecified]	World Learning Program	n/a	Intermed	SIT Study Abroad	n/a

Connecticut

DESTINATION	HOST INSTITUTION	PRGM SEASON	PRGM TYPE	INTERMEDIARY	HOUSING
Greece | [City Unspecified]	n/a	n/a	Intermed	Paideia	n/a
Greece | [City Unspecified]	n/a	n/a	USColl	University of Connecticut	n/a
Greece | [City Unspecified]	American College of Thessaloniki	n/a	Dir	n/a	n/a
Greece | [City Unspecified]	Arcadia Center for Hellenic, Mediterranean, and Balkan Studies	Fall Spr YrRound	USColl	Arcadia University	n/a
Holland | (Multiple choices)	Multiple institutional choices	n/a	Intermed	IES Abroad	n/a
Holland | [City Unspecified]	World Learning Program	n/a	Intermed	SIT Study Abroad	n/a
Hungary | Budapest	Corvinus University of Budapest	n/a	Intermed	Academic Programs International	n/a
Iceland | [City Unspecified]	World Learning Program	n/a	Intermed	SIT Study Abroad	n/a
India | [City Unspecified]	n/a	n/a	USColl	Antioch University	n/a
India | [City Unspecified]	n/a	n/a	Intermed	Alliance for Global Learning	n/a
India | [City Unspecified]	Manipal University	n/a	USColl	American University Abroad	n/a
India | [City Unspecified]	World Learning Program	n/a	Intermed	SIT Study Abroad	n/a
India | Abheypur	University of Hartford	Win	Self	n/a	n/a
	Costs: Win Costs: T&F: n/a, R&B: n/a, Ttl: $1,900				
India | Delhi	n/a	n/a	Intermed	IES Abroad	n/a
India | Hyderabad	n/a	n/a	Intermed	American Institute for Foreign Study	n/a
India | Hyderabad	n/a	n/a	Intermed	Council on International Educational Exchange (CIEE)	n/a
India | Kolkata	n/a	n/a	Intermed	International Partnership for Service-Learning and Leadership	n/a
Indonesia | [City Unspecified]	World Learning Program	n/a	Intermed	SIT Study Abroad	n/a
Ireland | (Multiple choices)	Multiple institutional choices	n/a	Intermed	Academic Programs International	n/a
Ireland | (Multiple choices)	Multiple institutional choices	n/a	Intermed	IES Abroad	n/a
Ireland | (Multiple choices)	Multiple institutional choices	n/a	USColl	Arcadia University	n/a
Ireland | (Multiple choices)	Multiple institutional choices	n/a	Intermed	Interstudy	n/a
Ireland | (Multiple choices)	Multiple institutional choices	n/a	Intermed	Institute for Study Abroad	n/a
Ireland | (Multiple choices)	Multiple institutional choices	n/a	Intermed	American Institute for Foreign Study	n/a
Ireland | [City Unspecified]	World Learning Program	n/a	Intermed	SIT Study Abroad	n/a
Israel | (Multiple choices)	Multiple institutional choices	n/a	USColl	American University Abroad	n/a
Israel | Jerusalem	Rothberg International School at Hebrew University of Jerusalem	n/a	Dir	n/a	n/a
Italy | (Multiple choices)	Multiple institutional choices	n/a	Intermed	Academic Programs International	n/a
Italy | (Multiple choices)	Multiple institutional choices	n/a	Intermed	American Institute for Foreign Study	n/a
Italy | (Multiple choices)	Multiple institutional choices	n/a	USColl	Arcadia University	n/a
Italy | (Multiple choices)	Multiple institutional choices	n/a	Intermed	International Partnership for Service-Learning and Leadership	n/a

Connecticut

DESTINATION	HOST INSTITUTION	PRGM SEASON	PRGM TYPE	INTERMEDIARY	HOUSING
Italy	(Multiple choices)	Multiple institutional choices	n/a	Intermed	IES Abroad	n/a
Italy	(Multiple choices)	University of Hartford	Win	Self	n/a	n/a
	Costs: Win Costs: T&F: n/a, R&B: n/a, Ttl: $4,000				
Italy	[City Unspecified]	Instituto at Palazzo Rucellai	n/a	USColl	University of Connecticut	n/a
Italy	Florence	Studio Art Centers International	n/a	USColl	Bowling Green State University	n/a
Jamaica	(Multiple)	University of Hartford	n/a	Self	n/a	n/a
Jamaica	Kingston	n/a	n/a	Intermed	International Partnership for Service-Learning and Leadership	n/a
Japan	[City Unspecified]	n/a	n/a	USColl	Antioch University	n/a
Japan	[City Unspecified]	Multiple institutional choices	n/a	Intermed	IES Abroad	n/a
Japan	[City Unspecified]	Ritsumeikan Asia Pacific University	n/a	Intermed	AsiaLearn	n/a
Japan	[City Unspecified]	Sophia University	n/a	Intermed	Council on International Educational Exchange (CIEE)	n/a
Japan	[City Unspecified]	Waseda University	n/a	USColl	American University Abroad	n/a
Jordan	[City Unspecified]	World Learning Program	n/a	Intermed	SIT Study Abroad	n/a
Jordan	Amman	University of Jordan	n/a	Intermed	Council on International Educational Exchange (CIEE)	n/a
Kenya	[City Unspecified]	American University in Kenya	n/a	USColl	American University Abroad	n/a
Kenya	[City Unspecified]	World Learning Program	n/a	Intermed	SIT Study Abroad	n/a
Madagascar	[City Unspecified]	World Learning Program	n/a	Intermed	SIT Study Abroad	n/a
Malaysia	[City Unspecified]	Swinburne University of Technology	n/a	Intermed	AsiaLearn	n/a
Mali	[City Unspecified]	n/a	n/a	USColl	Antioch University	n/a
Mexico	[City Unspecified]	Multiple institutional choices	n/a	USColl	American University Abroad	n/a
Mexico	[City Unspecified]	World Learning Program	n/a	Intermed	SIT Study Abroad	n/a
Mexico	Guadalajara	Service Learning Program	n/a	Intermed	International Partnership for Service-Learning and Leadership	n/a
Mexico	Guanajuato	Universidad de Guanajuato	n/a	Intermed	Council on International Educational Exchange (CIEE)	n/a
Mexico	Queretero	Universidad Autonoma de Queretero	n/a	Intermed	Academic Programs International	n/a
Mexico	Yucatan	Universidad Autonoma de Yucatan	n/a	Intermed	Institute for Study Abroad	n/a
Mongolia	[City Unspecified]	World Learning Program	n/a	Intermed	SIT Study Abroad	n/a
Morocco	[City Unspecified]	Ecole Superieure de Direction et de Gestion	n/a	Intermed	Council on International Educational Exchange (CIEE)	n/a
Morocco	[City Unspecified]	Mohammed V University	n/a	Intermed	IES Abroad	n/a
Morocco	[City Unspecified]	World Learning Program	n/a	Intermed	SIT Study Abroad	n/a
Nepal	[City Unspecified]	World Learning Program	n/a	Intermed	SIT Study Abroad	n/a
New Zealand	(Multiple choices)	Multiple institutional choices	n/a	Intermed	IES Abroad	n/a
New Zealand	(Multiple choices)	Multiple institutional choices	n/a	Intermed	Institute for Study Abroad	n/a
New Zealand	(Multiple choices)	Multiple institutional choices	n/a	Intermed	AustraLearn	n/a

© 2011 — Updates? Want to be in the next edition? Visit **www.mysecondcampus.com**

Connecticut

DESTINATION	HOST INSTITUTION	PRGM SEASON	PRGM TYPE	INTERMEDIARY	HOUSING
New Zealand	(Multiple choices)	Multiple institutional choices	n/a	USColl	Arcadia University	n/a
New Zealand	Wellington	Victoria University of Wellington	n/a	Intermed	American Institute for Foreign Study	n/a
Nicaragua	[City Unspecified]	Universidad Nacional Autonoma de Nicaragua	n/a	Intermed	Council on International Educational Exchange (CIEE)	n/a
Nicaragua	[City Unspecified]	World Learning Program	n/a	Intermed	SIT Study Abroad	n/a
Nigeria	[City Unspecified]	American University in Nigeria	n/a	USColl	American University Abroad	n/a
Oman	[City Unspecified]	World Learning Program	n/a	Intermed	SIT Study Abroad	n/a
Panama	[City Unspecified]	World Learning Program	n/a	Intermed	SIT Study Abroad	n/a
Peru	(Multiple choices)	Multiple institutional choices	n/a	Intermed	Council on International Educational Exchange (CIEE)	n/a
Peru	[City Unspecified]	Pontificia Universidad Catolica del Peru	n/a	Intermed	Institute for Study Abroad	n/a
Peru	[City Unspecified]	Pontificia Universidad Catolica del Peru	n/a	Intermed	American Institute for Foreign Study	n/a
Peru	[City Unspecified]	World Learning Program	n/a	Intermed	SIT Study Abroad	n/a
Poland	[City Unspecified]	Jagiellonian University	n/a	Intermed	Academic Programs International	n/a
Russia	St. Petersburg	St. Petersburg State Polytechnic University	n/a	Intermed	American Institute for Foreign Study	n/a
Samoa	[City Unspecified]	World Learning Program	n/a	Intermed	SIT Study Abroad	n/a
Scotland	(Multiple choices)	Multiple institutional choices	n/a	USColl	Arcadia University	n/a
Scotland	(Multiple choices)	Multiple institutional choices	n/a	Intermed	Institute for Study Abroad	n/a
Scotland	Glasgow	n/a	n/a	Intermed	International Partnership for Service-Learning and Leadership	n/a
Scotland	Glasgow	Glasgow School of Art	n/a	Intermed	n/a	n/a
Senegal	Dakar	Suffolk University Dakar Campus	n/a	Intermed	Council on International Educational Exchange (CIEE)	n/a
Singapore	[City Unspecified]	James Cook University	n/a	Intermed	AsiaLearn	n/a
South Africa	(Multiple choices)	Multiple institutional choices	n/a	USColl	Arcadia University	n/a
South Africa	(Multiple choices)	Multiple institutional choices	n/a	Intermed	IES Abroad	n/a
South Africa	(Multiple choices)	Multiple institutional choices	n/a	USColl	American University Abroad	n/a
South Africa	(Multiple choices)	Multiple institutional choices	n/a	Intermed	Interstudy	n/a
South Africa	(Multiple choices)	Multiple institutional choices	n/a	Intermed	American Institute for Foreign Study	n/a
South Africa	(Multiple choices)	Multiple institutional choices	n/a	Intermed	Council on International Educational Exchange (CIEE)	n/a
South Africa	(Multiple choices)	World Learning Program	n/a	Intermed	SIT Study Abroad	n/a
South Africa	Cape Town	University of Cape Town	n/a	USColl	Trinity College	n/a
South Korea	(Multiple choices)	Multiple institutional choices	n/a	USColl	American University Abroad	n/a
South Korea	[City Unspecified]	Korea University	n/a	Intermed	AsiaLearn	n/a
Spain	(Multiple choices)	Multiple institutional choices	n/a	Intermed	International Partnership for Service-Learning and Leadership	n/a

© 2011 — Updates? Want to be in the next edition? Visit **www.mysecondcampus.com**

Connecticut

DESTINATION	HOST INSTITUTION	PRGM SEASON	PRGM TYPE	INTERMEDIARY	HOUSING
Spain | (Multiple choices)	Multiple institutional choices	n/a	Intermed	Academic Programs International	n/a
Spain | (Multiple choices)	Multiple institutional choices	n/a	USColl	Arcadia University	n/a
Spain | (Multiple choices)	Multiple institutional choices	n/a	Intermed	American Institute for Foreign Study	n/a
Spain | (Multiple choices)	Multiple institutional choices	n/a	Intermed	IES Abroad	n/a
Spain | [City Unspecified]	World Learning Program	n/a	Intermed	SIT Study Abroad	n/a
St. Vincent | (Multiple)	University of Hartford	Win	Self	n/a	n/a
Costs: Win Costs: T&F: n/a, R&B: n/a, Ttl: $2,250					
Switzerland | [City Unspecified]	World Learning Program	n/a	Intermed	SIT Study Abroad	n/a
Switzerland | Lugano	Franklin College	n/a	Dir	n/a	n/a
Taiwan | [City Unspecified]	Multiple institutional choices	n/a	USColl	American University Abroad	n/a
Taiwan | [City Unspecified]	Tamkang University	n/a	Intermed	Council on International Educational Exchange (CIEE)	n/a
Tanzania | [City Unspecified]	World Learning Program	n/a	Intermed	SIT Study Abroad	n/a
Tanzania | Arusha	Arcadia Center for East African Studies	n/a	USColl	Arcadia University	n/a
Tanzania | Dar es Salaam	University of Dar es Salaam	n/a	Intermed	Council on International Educational Exchange (CIEE)	n/a
Thailand | [City Unspecified]	n/a	n/a	Intermed	International Partnership for Service-Learning and Leadership	n/a
Thailand | [City Unspecified]	Khon Kaen University	n/a	Intermed	Council on International Educational Exchange (CIEE)	n/a
Thailand | [City Unspecified]	Mahidol University	n/a	Intermed	AsiaLearn	n/a
Tunisia | [City Unspecified]	World Learning Program	n/a	Intermed	SIT Study Abroad	n/a
Turkey | [City Unspecified]	Koc University	n/a	Intermed	Council on International Educational Exchange (CIEE)	n/a
Uganda | [City Unspecified]	World Learning Program	n/a	Intermed	SIT Study Abroad	n/a
United Arab Emirates | [City Unspecified]	American University-Sharjah	n/a	USColl	American University Abroad	n/a
Vietnam | (Multiple choices)	Multiple institutional choices	n/a	Intermed	Council on International Educational Exchange (CIEE)	n/a
Vietnam | [City Unspecified]	World Learning Program	n/a	Intermed	SIT Study Abroad	n/a
Wales | (Multiple choices)	Multiple institutional choices	n/a	USColl	Arcadia University	n/a
Wales | [City Unspecified]	Cardiff University	n/a	Intermed	Institute for Study Abroad	n/a

University of New Haven

L. Christie Boronico
Associate Dean for Experiential Education
300 Boston Post Road
Maxcy Hall, MH 205
West Haven, CT 06516

CBoronico@newhaven.edu
203.932.7236
http://www.newhaven.edu/exped/studyabroad/

DESTINATION	HOST INSTITUTION	PRGM SEASON	PRGM TYPE	INTERMEDIARY	HOUSING
(Multiple choices) | (Multiple choices)	Multiple institutional choices	n/a	Intermed	Center for International Studies	n/a

Connecticut

DESTINATION	HOST INSTITUTION	PRGM SEASON	PRGM TYPE	INTERMEDIARY	HOUSING
China | [City Unspecified]	University of New Haven	Sum	Self	n/a	n/a
Costs: Sum Costs: T&F: n/a, R&B: n/a, Ttl: $5,400					
China | Beijing	China Foreign Affairs University	Sum	Self	n/a	n/a
Costs: Sum Costs: T&F: n/a, R&B: n/a, Ttl: $5,400					
China | Beijing, Shanghai, Hong Kong	University of New Haven	Sum	Self	n/a	n/a
Costs: Sum Costs: T&F: n/a, R&B: n/a, Ttl: $5,400					
China | Guangzhou	South China Normal University	Sum	Self	n/a	n/a
Costs: Sum Costs: T&F: n/a, R&B: n/a, Ttl: $5,400					
China | Guangzhou	South China Normal University	Sum	Self	n/a	n/a
Costs: Sum Costs: T&F: n/a, R&B: n/a, Ttl: $4,700					
England | London	Roehampton University	Fall Spr	Self	n/a	n/a
England | London	University of New Haven	Sum	Self	n/a	n/a
Costs: Sum Costs: T&F: n/a, R&B: n/a, Ttl: $6,500					
England | London	University of New Haven	Sum	Self	n/a	n/a
Costs: Sum Costs: T&F: n/a, R&B: n/a, Ttl: $5,400					
England | London	University of New Haven	Sum	Self	n/a	n/a
Costs: Sum Costs: T&F: n/a, R&B: n/a, Ttl: $5,400					
England | London	University of Westminster	Sum	Self	n/a	n/a
Costs: Sum Costs: T&F: n/a, R&B: n/a, Ttl: $6,300					
England and France | London and Dieppe	University of New Haven	Sum	Self	n/a	n/a
Costs: Sum Costs: T&F: n/a, R&B: n/a, Ttl: $5,500					
France | Paris	CEA Global Campus Paris		Intermed	Cultural Experiences Abroad	n/a
France | Paris	University of New Haven	Sum	Self	n/a	n/a
Costs: Sum Costs: T&F: n/a, R&B: n/a, Ttl: $5,400					
France | Paris	University of New Haven	Sum	Self	n/a	n/a
Costs: Sum Costs: T&F: n/a, R&B: n/a, Ttl: $5,400					
France | Paris	University of New Haven	Sum	Self	n/a	n/a
Costs: Sum Costs: T&F: n/a, R&B: n/a, Ttl: $5,400					
Italy | Florence	CEA Global Campus Florence		Intermed	Cultural Experiences Abroad	n/a
Italy | Florence	University of New Haven	Sum	Self	n/a	n/a
Costs: Sum Costs: T&F: n/a, R&B: n/a, Ttl: $5,400					
Italy | Rome, Sorrento, Florence	University of New Haven	Sum	Self	n/a	n/a
Costs: Sum Costs: T&F: n/a, R&B: n/a, Ttl: $5,400					
Middle East | (Multiple)	University of New Haven	Sum	Self	n/a	n/a
Costs: Sum Costs: T&F: n/a, R&B: n/a, Ttl: $5,400					
Poland | Warsaw and Krakow	University of New Haven	Sum	Self	n/a	n/a
Costs: Sum Costs: T&F: n/a, R&B: n/a, Ttl: $5,400					
Romania | (Multiple)	University of New Haven	Sum	Self	n/a	n/a
Costs: Sum Costs: T&F: n/a, R&B: n/a, Ttl: $5,400					

© 2011 — Updates? Want to be in the next edition? Visit **www.mysecondcampus.com**

Connecticut

DESTINATION	HOST INSTITUTION	PRGM SEASON	PRGM TYPE	INTERMEDIARY	HOUSING
Russia	Moscow	Moscow Art Theatre	Sum	Self	n/a	n/a
Costs: Sum Costs: T&F: n/a, R&B: n/a, Ttl: $5,400					
Russia	Moscow	Moscow State University	Sum	Self	n/a	n/a
Costs: Sum Costs: T&F: n/a, R&B: n/a, Ttl: $5,400					
Russia	Moscow, Pskov, St. Petersburg	University of New Haven	Sum	Self	n/a	n/a
Costs: Sum Costs: T&F: n/a, R&B: n/a, Ttl: $5,400					
Russia	Unknown	University of New Haven	Sum	Self	n/a	n/a
Spain	Seville	CEA Global Campus Seville	n/a	Intermed	Cultural Experiences Abroad	n/a
Vietman	Hanoi, Ho Chi Minh, Da Nang	University of New Haven	Sum	Self	n/a	n/a

Wesleyan University

Carolyn Sorkin
Director
Office of International Studies
262 High Street
105 Fisk Hall
Middletown, CT 06459

csorkin@wesleyan.edu
860.685.2550
http://www.wesleyan.edu/ois/studyabroad/index.html

DESTINATION	HOST INSTITUTION	PRGM SEASON	PRGM TYPE	INTERMEDIARY	HOUSING
[Country Unspecified]	[City Unspecified]	n/a	n/a	n/a	n/a	n/a

Western Connecticut State University

Missy Gluckmann
Coordinator
181 White Street
International Services Office
Warner Hall, room 321B
Danbury, CT 06810

gluckmannm@wcsu.edu
203.837.3270
http://www.wcsu.edu/international/abroad.asp

DESTINATION	HOST INSTITUTION	PRGM SEASON	PRGM TYPE	INTERMEDIARY	HOUSING
(Multiple choices)	(Multiple choices)	Multiple institutional choices	n/a	Bilat	International Student Exchange Program	n/a
Italy	Florence	Florence University of the Arts	n/a	Self	n/a	n/a
Puerto Rico	(Multiple)	Western Connecticut State University	Sum	Self	n/a	n/a
Costs: Sum Costs: T&F: n/a, R&B: n/a, Ttl: $1,995					
Spain	Madrid	Western Connecticut State University	Sum	Self	n/a	n/a

© 2011 — Updates? Want to be in the next edition? Visit **www.mysecondcampus.com**

Connecticut

Yale University

Jane Edwards
Associate Dean for International Affairs
Yale College Center for International Experiences
55 Whitney Avenue
3rd floor, room 303
New Haven, CT 06520

jane.edwards@yale.edu
203.432.8680
http://www.yale.edu/yalecollege/international/ opportunities/type/study/index.html

DESTINATION	HOST INSTITUTION	PRGM SEASON	PRGM TYPE	INTERMEDIARY	HOUSING
(Multiple) | (Multiple)	International Honors Program	Fall Spr	Intermed	International Honors Program	n/a
(Multiple) | (Multiple)	International Honors Program	Fall Spr	Intermed	International Honors Program	n/a
(Multiple) | (Multiple)	Multiple institutional choices	Sum	Consrtm	International Alliance of Research Universities	n/a
Amman | Jordan	SIT Study Abroad	Fall Spr	Intermed	SIT Study Abroad	n/a
Argentina | Buenos Aires	Multiple institutional choices	Fall Spr YrRound	Intermed	Institute for Study Abroad	n/a
Argentina | Buenos Aires	IES Abroad Buenos Aires Center	Fall Spr YrRound	Intermed	IES Abroad	n/a
Argentina | Buenos Aires	SIT Study Abroad	Fall Spr	Intermed	SIT Study Abroad	n/a
Argentina | Buenos Aires	SIT Study Abroad	Fall Spr	Intermed	SIT Study Abroad	n/a
Argentina | Buenos Aires	Universidad de Buenos Aires	Sum	Intermed	Institute for Study Abroad	n/a
Argentina | Buenos Aires	Yale University	Sum	Self	n/a	n/
Australia | Adelaide	University of Adelaide	Fall Spr YrRound	Dir	n/a	n/a
Australia | Brisbane	University of Queensland	Fall Spr YrRound	Dir	n/a	n/a
Australia | Byron Bay	SIT Study Abroad	Fall Spr	Intermed	SIT Study Abroad	n/a
Australia | Cairns	SIT Study Abroad	Fall Spr	Intermed	SIT Study Abroad	n/a
Australia | Canberra	Australia National University	Fall Spr YrRound	Dir	n/a	n/a
Australia | Melbourne	University of Melbourne	Fall Spr YrRound	Dir	n/a	n/a
Australia | Northern Queensland	SIT Study Abroad	Sum	Intermed	SIT Study Abroad	n/a
Australia | Perth	University of Western Australia	Fall Spr YrRound	Dir	n/a	n/a
Australia | Sydney	University of New South Wales	Fall Spr YrRound	Dir	n/a	n/a
Australia | Sydney	University of Sydney	Fall Spr YrRound	Dir	n/a	n/a
Australia | Townsville	James Cook University	Fall Spr YrRound	Dir	n/a	n/a
Australia | Yungaburra	Center for Rainforest Studies	Fall Spr	Intermed	School for Field Studies	n/a
Austria | Vienna	IES Abroad Vienna Center	Sum	Intermed	IES Abroad	n/a
Bolivia | Cochabamba	SIT Study Abroad	Sum	Intermed	SIT Study Abroad	n/a
Bolivia | Cochabamba	SIT Study Abroad	Fall Spr	Intermed	SIT Study Abroad	n/a
Botswana | Gabarone	SIT Study Abroad	Fall Spr	Intermed	SIT Study Abroad	n/a
Brazil | Fortaleza	SIT Study Abroad	Fall Spr	Intermed	SIT Study Abroad	n/a
Brazil | Paraty	Yale University	Sum	Self	n/a	n/a
	Costs: Sum Costs: T&F: $5,700, R&B: n/a, Ttl: n/a				
Brazil | Rio de Janeiro	Pontificia Universidade Catolica do Rio de Janeiro	Fall YrRound	USColl	Brown University	n/a
Brazil | Salvador da Bahia	SIT Study Abroad	Fall Spr	Intermed	SIT Study Abroad	n/a
Brazil | Sao Paulo	Pontificia Universidade Catolica de Sao Paulo	Fall Spr YrRound	Intermed	Council on International Education Exchange (CIEE)	n/a

© 2011 — Updates? Want to be in the next edition? Visit **www.mysecondcampus.com**

Connecticut

DESTINATION	HOST INSTITUTION	PRGM SEASON	PRGM TYPE	INTERMEDIARY	HOUSING
Cameroon | Yaounde	SIT Study Abroad	Fall Spr	Intermed	SIT Study Abroad	n/a
Canada | Montreal	McGill University	Sum	Dir	n/a	n/a
Canada | Quebec City	Universite Laval	Sum	Dir	n/a	n/a
Chile | (Multiple choices)	Multiple institutional choices	Fall Spr YrRound	Intermed	Institute for Study Abroad	n/a
Chile | Santiago	IES Abroad Santiago Center	Fall Spr YrRound	Intermed	IES Abroad	n/a
Chile | Santiago	Pontificia Universidad Catolica de Chile	Fall Spr YrRound	Intermed	Council on International Education Exchange (CIEE)	n/a
Chile | Santiago	SIT Study Abroad	Fall Spr	Intermed	SIT Study Abroad	n/a
Chile | Santiago	Yale University	Sum	Self	n/a	n/a
	Costs: Sum Costs: T&F: $2,750, R&B: n/a, Ttl: n/a				
Chile | Valparaiso	SIT Study Abroad	Fall Spr	Intermed	SIT Study Abroad	n/a
China | Beijing	Beijing Language and Culture University	Sum	USColl	Harvard University	n/a
China | Beijing	Beijing Normal University	Sum	USColl	Princeton University	n/a
China | Beijing	Capital University of Economics	Fall Spr YrRound	USColl	Associated Colleges in China/ Hamilton College	n/a
China | Beijing	Capital University of Economics	Sum	USColl	Hamilton College	n/a
China | Beijing	CET Academic Programs	Sum	Intermed	CET Academic Programs	n/a
China | Beijing	Multiple institutional choices	Sum Fall Spr YrRound	USColl	Richard U. Light Fellowship for Language Studies in East Asia (Yale University)	n/a
China | Beijing	Peking University	Fall Spr YrRound	Self	n/a	n/a
China | Beijing	Tsinghua University	Sum Fall Spr YrRound	USColl	University of California, Berkeley	n/a
China | Beijing	University of International Business and Economics	Sum	USColl	Duke University	n/a
China | Beijing	Yale University	Sum	Self	n/a	n/a
	Costs: Sum Costs: T&F: $5,300, R&B: n/a, Ttl: n/a				
China | Beijing	Yale University	Sum	Self	n/a	n/a
	Costs: Sum Costs: T&F: $5,300, R&B: n/a, Ttl: n/a				
China | Hangzhou	Multiple institutional choices	Sum Fall Spr YrRound	USColl	Richard U. Light Fellowship for Language Studies in East Asia (Yale University)	n/a
China | Hanzhou	CET Academic Programs	Sum	Intermed	CET Academic Programs	n/a
China | Harbin	CET Academic Programs	Sum Fall Spr YrRound	Intermed	CET Academic Programs	n/a
China | Harbin	Multiple institutional choices	Sum Fall Spr YrRound	USColl	Richard U. Light Fellowship for Language Studies in East Asia (Yale University)	n/a
China | Hong Kong	Chinese University of Hong Kong	Fall Spr YrRound	Dir	n/a	n/a
China | Kunming	SIT Study Abroad	Sum	Intermed	SIT Study Abroad	n/a
China | Nanjing	Multiple institutional choices	Sum Fall Spr YrRound	USColl	Richard U. Light Fellowship for Language Studies in East Asia (Yale University)	n/a
Costa Rica | (Multiple choices)	Organization for Tropical Studies (Duke University)	Fall Spr	Consrtm	Organization for Tropical Studies (Duke University)	n/a

Connecticut

DESTINATION	HOST INSTITUTION	PRGM SEASON	PRGM TYPE	INTERMEDIARY	HOUSING
Costa Rica	(Multiple choices)	Organization for Tropical Studies (Duke University)	Sum Fall Spr YrRound	Consrtm	Organization for Tropical Studies (Duke University)	n/a
Costa Rica	Atenas	SFS Center for Sustainable Development Studies	Fall Spr	Intermed	School for Field Studies	n/a
Costa Rica	Atenas	SIT Study Abroad	Sum	Intermed	SIT Study Abroad	n/a
Costa Rica	San Jose	University of Costa Rica	Fall Spr YrRound	USColl	University of Kansas	n/a
Croatia	Dubrovnik	Yale University	Sum	Self	n/a	n/a
Costs: Sum Costs: T&F: $5,300, R&B: n/a, Ttl: n/a					
Croatia	Dubrovnik	Yale University	Sum	Self	n/a	n/a
Costs: Sum Costs: T&F: $5,300, R&B: n/a, Ttl: n/a					
Croatia	Zagreb	SIT Study Abroad	Fall Spr	Intermed	SIT Study Abroad	n/a
Czech Republic	Prague	Charles University	Fall Spr YrRound	Intermed	Council on International Education Exchange (CIEE)	n/a
Czech Republic	Prague	Collegium Hieronymi Pragensis	Fall Spr YrRound	Intermed	Collegium Hieronymi Pragensis	n/a
Czech Republic	Prague	Film and Television School of the Academy of Performing Arts	Sum Fall Spr YrRound	Self	n/a	n/a
Czech Republic	Prague	New York University Center Prague	Fall Spr YrRound	USColl	New York University	n/a
Czech Republic	Prague	Yale University	Sum	Self	n/a	n/a
Costs: Sum Costs: T&F: $5,300, R&B: n/a, Ttl: n/a					
Denmark	Copenhagen	Danish Institute for Study Abroad	Sum	Intermed	Danish Institute for Study Abroad	n/a
Denmark	Copenhagen	Danish Institute for Study Abroad	Fall Spr YrRound	Intermed	Danish Institute for Study Abroad	n/a
Dominican Republic	Santiago	Pontificia Universidad Catolica Madre y Maestra	Fall Spr YrRound	Intermed	Council on International Education Exchange (CIEE)	n/a
Dominican Republic	Santiago	Pontificia Universidad Catolica Madre y Maestra	Sum	Intermed	Council on International Education Exchange (CIEE)	n/a
Dominican Republic	Santo Domingo	Multiple institutional choices	Fall Spr YrRound	Intermed	Council on International Education Exchange (CIEE)	n/a
Ecuador	Quito	IES Abroad Quito Center	Fall Spr YrRound	Intermed	IES Abroad	n/a
Ecuador	Quito	SIT Study Abroad	Fall Spr	Intermed	SIT Study Abroad	n/a
Ecuador	Quito	SIT Study Abroad	Fall Spr	Intermed	SIT Study Abroad	n/a
Ecuador	Quito	Universidad San Francisco de Quito	Fall Spr YrRound	Intermed	IES Abroad	n/a
Ecuador	Quito	Yale University	Sum	Self	n/a	n/a
Costs: Sum Costs: T&F: $5,700, R&B: n/a, Ttl: n/a					
Ecuador	Quito	Yale University	Sum	Self	n/a	n/a
Egypt	Alexandria	Alexandria University	Fall Spr YrRound	USColl	Middlebury College	n/a
Egypt	Cairo	American University in Cairo	Sum Fall Spr YrRound	Dir	n/a	n/a
England	Bath	Advanced Studies in England	Sum Fall Spr YrRound	Intermed	Advanced Studies in England	n/a
England	Brighton	University of Sussex	Spr YrRound	Dir	n/a	n/a
England	Bristol	University of Bristol	Fall Spr YrRound	Dir	n/a	n/a

© 2011 — Updates? Want to be in the next edition? Visit **www.mysecondcampus.com**

Connecticut

DESTINATION	HOST INSTITUTION	PRGM SEASON	PRGM TYPE	INTERMEDIARY	HOUSING
England | Cambridge	Cambridge University (Pembroke College)	Sum	Dir	Pembroke-King's Summer Program	n/a
England | Cambridge	Cambridge University (Pembroke College)	Spr YrRound	Dir	n/a	n/a
England | Cambridge	Cambridge University (Pembroke College)	Sum	USColl	The John Thouron Prize (Yale University)	n/a
England | Cardiff	Cardiff University	Spr YrRound	Dir	n/a	n/a
England | Lancaster	Lancaster University	Spr YrRound	Dir	n/a	n/a
England | London	British American Drama Academmcy	Fall YrRound	USColl	Skidmore College	n/a
England | London	British American Drama Academmcy	Fall Spr YrRound	USColl	Sarah Lawrence College	n/a
England | London	Goldsmith's College	Fall Spr YrRound	Dir	n/a	n/a
England | London	King's College London	Fall Spr YrRound	Dir	n/a	n/a
England | London	London Academy of Music and Dramatic Art	Sum Fall Spr YrRound	Dir	n/a	n/a
England | London	London School of Economics	Sum YrRound	Dir	n/a	n/a
England | London	Paul Mellon Centre	Sum Spr	Self	n/a	n/a
England | London	Queen Mary College, University of London	Fall Spr YrRound	Dir	n/a	n/a
England | London	University College London	Fall Spr YrRound	Dir	n/a	n/a
England | London	University of London School of Oriental and African Studies	Fall Spr YrRound	Dir	n/a	n/a
England | Manchester	University of Manchester	Spr YrRound	Dir	n/a	n/a
England | Norwich	University of East Anglia	Fall Spr YrRound	Dir	n/a	n/a
England | Oxford	Oxford University (Wadham College)	YrRound	USColl	Sarah Lawrence College	n/a
England | Oxford	University of Oxford	Spr YrRound	Dir	n/a	n/a
England | Oxford	University of Oxford (Queen's College)	Sum	USColl	Harvard University	n/a
England | St. Andrews	University of St. Andrews	Fall Spr YrRound	Dir	n/a	n/a
England | York	University of York	Fall Spr YrRound	Dir	n/a	n/a
Fiji | Suva	SIT Study Abroad	Fall Spr	Intermed	SIT Study Abroad	n/a
France | Aix-en-Provence	American University Center of Provence	Sum Fall Spr YrRound	Intermed	American University Center of Provence	n/a
France | Aix-en-Provence	Universite de Provence	Fall Spr YrRound	USColl	Wellesley College	n/a
France | Arles	IES Abroad Arles Center	Sum	Intermed	IES Abroad	n/a
France | Auvillar	Institute of Studio Studies	Sum	Self	n/a	n/a
	Costs: Sum Costs: T&F: $5,300, R&B: n/a, Ttl: n/a				
France | Avignon	Bryn Mawr	Sum	USColl	Bryn Mawr	n/a
France | Bordeaux	Universite de Bordeaux	Fall Spr YrRound	USColl	Middlebury College	n/a
France | Grenoble	Swarthmore College	Fall Spr YrRound	USColl	Swarthmore College	n/a
France | Grenoble	Universite de Grenoble	Fall Spr YrRound	USColl	Boston University	n/a
France | Marseille	American University Center of Provence	Fall Spr YrRound	Intermed	American University Center of Provence	n/a

Connecticut

DESTINATION	HOST INSTITUTION	PRGM SEASON	PRGM TYPE	INTERMEDIARY	HOUSING
France | Nantes	IES Abroad Nantes Center	Fall Spr YrRound	Intermed	IES Abroad	n/a
France | Nice	Washington University	Sum	USColl	Washington University	n/a
France | Paris	CIEE Study Center	Fall Spr YrRound	Intermed	Council on International Education Exchange (CIEE)	n/a
France | Paris	Columbia University	Sum	USColl	Columbia University	n/a
France | Paris	Columbia University-Reid Hall	Fall Spr YrRound	USColl	Columbia University	n/a
France | Paris	IES Abroad Paris Center	Sum	Intermed	IES Abroad	n/a
France | Paris	Le Centre Madeleine	Fall Spr YrRound	USColl	Middlebury College	n/a
France | Paris	Multiple institutional choices	Fall Spr YrRound	USColl	Sweet Briar College	n/a
France | Paris	Multiple institutional choices	Fall Spr YrRound	Intermed	Academic Programs Abroad	n/a
France | Paris	Multiple institutional choices	n/a	Intermed	Center for University Programs Abroad	n/a
France | Paris	Vassar-Wesleyan Program	Fall Spr YrRound	USColl	Wesleyan University	n/a
France | Paris	Yale University	Sum	Self	n/a	n/a
France | Poitiers	Universite de Poitiers	Fall Spr YrRound	USColl	Middlebury College	n/a
Germany | (Multiple choices)	Multiple institutional choices	Spr YrRound	USColl	Baden-Württemberg Exchange	n/a
Germany | Berlin	Freie Universitat	Spr YrRound	Consrtm	Berlin Consortium for German Studies (Columbia University)	n/a
Germany | Berlin	Freie Universitat Berlin	Sum	Dir	n/a	n/a
Germany | Berlin	Yale University	Sum	Self	n/a	n/a
	Costs: Sum Costs: T&F: $5,500, R&B: n/a, Ttl: n/a				
Germany | Dresden	Technische Universitat Dresden	Spr	USColl	Boston University	n/a
Germany | Freiburg	IES Abroad Freiburg Center	Fall Spr YrRound	Intermed	IES Abroad	n/a
Germany | Hamburg	Smith College	Spr YrRound	USColl	Smith College	n/a
Germany | Munich	Ludwig Maximillians Universitat Munchen	Spr YrRound	USColl	Wayne State University	n/a
Ghana | Accra	SIT Study Abroad	Fall Spr	Intermed	SIT Study Abroad	n/a
Ghana | Cape Coast	SIT Study Abroad	Fall Spr	Intermed	SIT Study Abroad	n/a
Greece | Athens	Arcadia Center for Hellenic, Balkan and Mediterranean Studies	Fall Spr YrRound	USColl	Arcadia University	n/a
Greece | Athens	College Year in Athens	Fall Spr YrRound	Intermed	College Year in Athens	n/a
Greece | Olympia	Harvard University-Beijing Academy	Sum	USColl	Harvard University	n/a
Guatemala | Antigua	Center for Mesoamerican Research	Sum	USColl	University of Arizona	n/a
Hungary | Budapest	Central European University	Fall Spr YrRound	Dir	n/a	n/a
Hungary | Budapest	Corvinus Univeristy	Fall Spr YrRound	Intermed	Council on International Education Exchange (CIEE)	n/a
Hungary | Budapest	Technical University of Budapest, College International	Fall Spr YrRound	Intermed	Budapest Semesters in Mathematics	n/a
India | (Multiple choices)	American Institute of Indian Studies	Sum	Consrtm	American Institute of Indian Studies	n/a
India | (Multiple choices)	SIT Study Abroad	Sum	Intermed	SIT Study Abroad	n/a

© 2011 — Updates? Want to be in the next edition? Visit **www.mysecondcampus.com**

Connecticut

DESTINATION	HOST INSTITUTION	PRGM SEASON	PRGM TYPE	INTERMEDIARY	HOUSING
India | Bodh Gaya	Burmese Vihar	Fall	USColl	Antioch University	n/a
India | Delhi	IES Abroad Delhi Center	Fall Spr YrRound	Intermed	IES Abroad	n/a
India | Delhi	SIT Study Abroad	Fall Spr	Intermed	SIT Study Abroad	n/a
India | Delhi	St. Stephen's College or Lady Shri Ram College	Fall YrRound	USColl	Brown University	n/a
India | Hyderabad	University of Hyderabad	Fall Spr YrRound	Intermed	Council on International Education Exchange (CIEE)	n/a
India | Mumbai	Yale University	Sum	Self	n/a	n/a
	Costs: Sum Costs: T&F: $5,300, R&B: n/a, Ttl: n/a				
India | Mumbai	Yale University	Sum	Self	n/a	n/a
	Costs: Sum Costs: T&F: $5,300, R&B: n/a, Ttl: n/a				
India | Mysore	Swami Vivekananda Institute of Indian Studies	Fall	USColl	University of Iowa	n/a
India | Pune	Alliance for Global Education	Fall Spr	Intermed	Alliance for Global Education	n/a
India | Varanasi	SIT Study Abroad	Fall Spr	Intermed	SIT Study Abroad	n/a
India | Varanasi	University of Wisconsin	YrRound	USColl	University of Wisconsin	n/a
Indonesia | Bedulu	SIT Study Abroad	Fall Spr	Intermed	SIT Study Abroad	n/a
Ireland | Ballyvaughn	Burren College of Art	Sum	Dir	n/a	n/a
Ireland | Cork	University College Cork	Spr YrRound	Dir	n/a	n/a
Ireland | Dublin	Trinity College Dublin	Spr YrRound	Dir	n/a	n/a
Ireland | Dublin	University College Dublin	Fall Spr YrRound	Dir	n/a	n/a
Ireland | Galway	National University of Ireland, Galway	Fall Spr YrRound	Dir	n/a	n/a
Israel | Beer-Sheva	Ben-Gurion University of the Negev	Fall Spr YrRound	Dir	n/a	n/a
Israel | Haifa	University of Haifa	Fall Spr YrRound	Dir	n/a	n/a
Israel | Jerusalem	Hebrew University	Sum Fall Spr YrRound	Dir	n/a	n/a
Israel | Tel Aviv	Tel Aviv University	Fall Spr YrRound	Dir	n/a	n/a
Israel | Tel Aviv	Tel Aviv University School for Overseas Students	Sum	Dir	n/a	n/a
Italy | Bologna	Universita di Bologna	Fall Spr YrRound	Consrtm	Eastern College Consortium in Bologna (Vassar, Wellesley, Wesleyan)	n/a
Italy | Bologna	University of Bologna	Fall Spr YrRound	USColl	Brown University	n/a
Italy | Catania	University of Catania	Spr	USColl	Sarah Lawrence College	n/a
Italy | Ferrara	Universita degli Studi di Ferrara	Fall Spr YrRound	USColl	Middlebury College	n/a
Italy | Florence	Middlebury College	Fall Spr YrRound	USColl	Middlebury College	n/a
Italy | Florence	Smith College	YrRound	USColl	Smith College	n/a
Italy | Florence	SU Florence Center	Fall Spr YrRound	USColl	Syracuse University	n/a
Italy | Florence	University of Florence	Spr	USColl	Sarah Lawrence College	n/a
Italy | Milan	IES Abroad Milan Center	Sum	Intermed	IES Abroad	n/a
Italy | Milan	IES Abroad Milan Center	Fall Spr YrRound	Intermed	IES Abroad	n/a
Italy | Milan	Universita Bocconi	Fall Spr YrRound	Bilat	n/a	n/a

© 2011 — Updates? Want to be in the next edition? Visit **www.mysecondcampus.com**

Connecticut

DESTINATION	HOST INSTITUTION	PRGM SEASON	PRGM TYPE	INTERMEDIARY	HOUSING
Italy | Naples	Università degli studi di Napoli L'Orientale	Fall Spr YrRound	Intermed	Council on International Education Exchange (CIEE)	n/a
Italy | Padova	Boston University	Sum Fall Spr YrRound	USColl	Boston University	n/a
Italy | Padova	Boston University Center for Italian and European Studies	Fall Spr YrRound	USColl	Boston University	n/a
Italy | Rome	Intercollegiate Center for Classical Studies (Duke University)	Fall Spr YrRound	USColl	Duke University	n/a
Italy | Rome	Yale University	Sum	Self	n/a	n/a
Costs: Sum Costs: T&F: $5,300, R&B: n/a, Ttl: n/a					
Italy | Siena	Yale University	Sum	Self	n/a	n/a
Costs: Sum Costs: T&F: $2,750, R&B: n/a, Ttl: n/a					
Italy | Siena	Yale University	Sum	Self	n/a	n/a
Costs: Sum Costs: T&F: $5,500, R&B: n/a, Ttl: n/a					
Italy | Siena	Yale University	Sum	Self	n/a	n/a
Costs: Sum Costs: T&F: $5,500, R&B: n/a, Ttl: n/a					
Italy | Venice	Ca' Foscari University	Sum	USColl	Columbia University	n/a
Japan | Tokyo	Waseda University	Sum	Self	n/a	n/a
Japan | Hakadote	Multiple institutional choices	Sum Fall Spr YrRound	USColl	Richard U. Light Fellowship for Language Studies in East Asia (Yale University)	n/a
Japan | Hakodate	Hokkaido International Foundation	Sum	Intermed	n/a	n/a
Japan | Ishikawa	Ishikawa Prefectural Government	Sum	USColl	Princeton University	n/a
Japan | Kanazawa	Multiple institutional choices	Sum Fall Spr YrRound	USColl	Richard U. Light Fellowship for Language Studies in East Asia (Yale University)	n/a
Japan | Kyoto	Kyoto Center for Japanese Studies (Doshisha University)	Sum	Consrtm	Kyoto Consortium for Japanese Studies (Columbia University)	n/a
Japan | Kyoto	Kyoto Consortium for Japanese Studies	Fall Spr YrRound	Dir	n/a	n/a
Japan | Kyoto	Multiple institutional choices	Sum Fall Spr YrRound	USColl	Richard U. Light Fellowship for Language Studies in East Asia (Yale University)	n/a
Japan | Nagoya	Multiple institutional choices	Sum Fall Spr YrRound	USColl	Richard U. Light Fellowship for Language Studies in East Asia (Yale University)	n/a
Japan | Nagoya	Nanzan University	Fall Spr YrRound	Dir	n/a	n/a
Japan | Osaka	CET Academic Programs	Sum Fall Spr YrRound	Intermed	CET Academic Programs	n/a
Japan | Tokyo	Multiple institutional choices	Sum Fall Spr YrRound	USColl	Richard U. Light Fellowship for Language Studies in East Asia (Yale University)	n/a
Japan | Tokyo	The Sun Academy	Sum	Intermed	The Sun Academy	n/a
Japan | Tokyo	Yale University	Sum	Self	n/a	n/a
Costs: Sum Costs: T&F: $2,750, R&B: n/a, Ttl: n/a					

© 2011 — Updates? Want to be in the next edition? Visit www.mysecondcampus.com

Connecticut

DESTINATION	HOST INSTITUTION	PRGM SEASON	PRGM TYPE	INTERMEDIARY	HOUSING
Japan | Yokohama	Multiple institutional choices	Sum Fall Spr YrRound	USColl	Richard U. Light Fellowship for Language Studies in East Asia (Yale University)	n/a
Jordan | Amman	University of Jordan	Fall Spr YrRound	Intermed	Council on International Education Exchange (CIEE)	n/a
Jordan | Amman	University of Jordan	Fall Spr YrRound	Intermed	Council on International Education Exchange (CIEE)	n/a
Jordan | Amman	Yale University	Sum	Self	n/a	n/a
	Costs: Sum Costs: T&F: $5,500, R&B: n/a, Ttl: n/a				
Kenya | Koobi Fora	Koobi Kora Field School	Sum	USColl	Rutgers University	n/a
Kenya | Mombasa	SIT Study Abroad	Fall Spr	Intermed	SIT Study Abroad	n/a
Kenya | Mombasa	Yale University	Sum	Self	n/a	n/a
Kenya | Mombasa	Yale University	Sum	Self	n/a	n/a
Kenya | Mombasa	Yale University	Sum	Self	n/a	n/a
Kenya | Nairobi	SIT Study Abroad	Fall Spr	Intermed	SIT Study Abroad	n/a
Kenya | Nairobi	St. Lawrence University	Fall Spr	USColl	St. Lawrence University	n/a
Madagascar | Antananavario	SIT Study Abroad	Fall Spr	Intermed	SIT Study Abroad	n/a
Madagascar | Fort Dauphin	SIT Study Abroad	Fall Spr	Intermed	SIT Study Abroad	n/a
Malaysia | Kota	Harvard University-Beijing Academy	Sum	USColl	Harvard University	n/a
Mali | Banako	SIT Study Abroad	Fall Spr	Intermed	SIT Study Abroad	n/a
Mexico | Baja	Center for Coastal Studies	Fall Spr	Intermed	School for Field Studies	n/a
Mexico | Baja California Sur	SIT Study Abroad	Sum	Intermed	SIT Study Abroad	n/a
Mexico | Cholula	Universidad de las Americas, Puebla	Sum Fall Spr YrRound	Dir	n/a	n/a
Mexico | Guadalajara	Instituto Tecnologico y de Estudios Superiores de Monterrey	Spr	USColl	Boston University	n/a
Mexico | Merida	Universidad Autonoma de Yucatan	Fall Spr YrRound	Intermed	Institute for Study Abroad	n/a
Mexico | Monterrey	Technologico de Monterrey	Fall Spr YrRound	Dir	n/a	n/a
Mexico | Monterrey	Yale University	Sum	Self	n/a	n/a
	Costs: Sum Costs: T&F: $5,300, R&B: n/a, Ttl: n/a				
Morocco | Fez	Arabic Language Institute in Fez	Sum	Dir	n/a	n/a
Morocco | Rabat	AMIDEAST	Sum	Intermed	AMIDEAST	n/a
Morocco | Rabat	Ecole Superieure de Direction et de Gestion	Fall Spr YrRound	Intermed	Council on International Education Exchange (CIEE)	n/a
Morocco | Rabat	SIT Study Abroad	Fall Spr	Intermed	SIT Study Abroad	n/a
Nepal | Kathmandu	Kathmandu University (Centre for Buddhist Studies at Ranjung Yeshe Institute)	Sum	Dir	n/a	n/a
Nepal | Kathmandu	SIT Study Abroad	Fall Spr	Intermed	SIT Study Abroad	n/a
Nepal | Kathmandu	SIT Study Abroad	Fall Spr	Intermed	SIT Study Abroad	n/a
Nepal | Kathmandu	Tribhuvan National University of Nepal	Fall Spr YrRound	USColl	Cornell University	n/a

© 2011 — Updates? Want to be in the next edition? Visit **www.mysecondcampus.com**

Connecticut

DESTINATION	HOST INSTITUTION	PRGM SEASON	PRGM TYPE	INTERMEDIARY	HOUSING
Netherlands | Amsterdam	IES Abroad Amsterdam Center	Fall Spr YrRound	Intermed	IES Abroad	n/a
Netherlands | Amsterdam	SIT Study Abroad	Fall Spr	Intermed	SIT Study Abroad	n/a
New Zealand | Auckland	University of Auckland	Fall Spr YrRound	Dir	n/a	n/a
New Zealand | Christchurch	University of Canterbury	Fall Spr YrRound	Dir	n/a	n/a
New Zealand | Dunedin	University of Otago	Fall Spr YrRound	Dir	n/a	n/a
Nicaragua | Managua	SIT Study Abroad	Fall Spr	Intermed	SIT Study Abroad	n/a
Norway | Oslo	University of Oslo International	Sum	Dir	n/a	n/a
Oman | Muscat	SIT Study Abroad	Fall Spr	Intermed	SIT Study Abroad	n/a
Panama | Bocas del Toro	Yale University	Sum	Self	n/a	n/a
Costs: Sum Costs: T&F: $5,300, R&B: n/a, Ttl: n/a					
Panama | Panama City	SIT Study Abroad	Fall Spr	Intermed	SIT Study Abroad	n/a
Peru | Cuzco	SIT Study Abroad	Fall Spr	Intermed	SIT Study Abroad	n/a
Peru | Lima	Pontificia Catolica del Peru	Fall Spr YrRound	Intermed	Institute for Study Abroad	n/a
Poland | Krakow	Brown University	Sum	USColl	Brown University	n/a
Portugal | Lisbon	Universidade Nova de Lisboa	Fall Spr YrRound	Intermed	Council on International Education Exchange (CIEE)	n/a
Portugal | Lisbon	Universidade Nova de Lisboa	Fall Spr YrRound	Intermed	Council on International Education Exchange (CIEE)	n/a
Portugal | Lisbon	University of Lisbon	Sum	Dir	n/a	n/a
Rome | Italy	Cornell University	Fall Spr YrRound	USColl	Cornell University	n/a
Russia | St. Petersburg	St. Petersburg State University	Fall Spr YrRound	Intermed	Council on International Education Exchange (CIEE)	n/a
Russia | (Multiple)	Multiple institutional choices	Sum Fall Spr YrRound	Intermed	American Councils for International Education	n/a
Costs: Sum Costs: T&F: n/a, R&B: n/a, Ttl: $8,300 Fall Costs: T&F: n/a, R&B: n/a, Ttl: $19,500 Spr Costs: T&F: n/a, R&B: n/a, Ttl: $19,500 YrRound Costs: T&F: n/a, R&B: n/a, Ttl: $33,000					
Russia | Irkutsk	Irkutsk State University	Fall Spr YrRound	USColl	Middlebury College	n/a
Russia | Moscow	Moscow Art Theater	Fall YrRound	USColl	Eugene O'Neill Theater Institute (Connecticut College)	n/a
Russia | Moscow	Moscow State University	Sum	USColl	University of Pittsburgh	n/a
Russia | Moscow	Russian State University for the Humanities	Fall Spr YrRound	USColl	Middlebury College	n/a
Russia | St. Petersburg	Smolny College	Fall Spr YrRound	USColl	Bard College	n/a
Russia | St. Petersburg	Yale University	Sum	Self	n/a	n/a
Costs: Sum Costs: T&F: $5,700, R&B: n/a, Ttl: n/a					
Russia | St. Petersburg	Yale University	Sum	Self	n/a	n/a
Costs: Sum Costs: T&F: $5,700, R&B: n/a, Ttl: n/a					
Scotland | Edinburgh	University of Edinburgh	Fall Spr YrRound	Dir	n/a	n/a
Scotland | Glasgow	University of Glasgow	Fall Spr YrRound	Dir	n/a	n/a
Senegal | Dakar	SIT Study Abroad	Fall Spr	Intermed	SIT Study Abroad	n/a
Senegal | Dakar	Universite Cheikh Anta Diop	Spr	USColl	Mount Holyoke College	n/a
Senegal | Dakar	Universite Cheikh Anta Diop	Fall Spr YrRound	USColl	Wells College	n/a
Singapore | Singapore	Yale University	Sum	Consrtm	International Alliance of Research Universities	n/a
Costs: Sum Costs: T&F: $2,100, R&B: n/a, Ttl: n/a					

Connecticut

DESTINATION	HOST INSTITUTION	PRGM SEASON	PRGM TYPE	INTERMEDIARY	HOUSING
Singapore | Singapore	Yale University	Sum	Consrtm	International Alliance of Research Universities	n/a
	Costs: Sum Costs: T&F: $2,100, R&B: n/a, Ttl: n/a				
South Africa | Cape Town	University of Cape Town	Fall Spr YrRound	Dir	n/a	n/a
South Africa | Durban	SIT Study Abroad	Fall Spr	Intermed	SIT Study Abroad	n/a
South Africa | Durban and Pietermaritzburg	University of KwaZulu-Natal	Fall Spr YrRound	Dir	n/a	n/a
South Korea | Seoul	Multiple institutional choices	Sum Fall Spr YrRound	USColl	Richard U. Light Fellowship for Language Studies in East Asia (Yale University)	n/a
South Korea | Seoul	Seoul National University	Sum	Dir	n/a	n/a
South Korea | Seoul	Sogang University	Sum	Dir	n/a	n/a
Spain | Barcelona	Multiple institutional choices	Fall Spr YrRound	USColl	Brown University	n/a
Spain | Barcelona	Universidad de Barcelona	Spr YrRound	Intermed	Council on International Education Exchange (CIEE)	n/a
Spain | Bilbao	University of Deusto	Spr YrRound	Dir	n/a	n/a
Spain | Bilbao	Yale University	Sum	Self	n/a	n/a
	Costs: Sum Costs: T&F: $5,700, R&B: n/a, Ttl: n/a				
Spain | Bilbao	Yale University	Sum	Self	n/a	n/a
	Costs: Sum Costs: T&F: $5,700, R&B: n/a, Ttl: n/a				
Spain | Cordoba	Universidad de Cordoba	Fall Spr YrRound	USColl	Middlebury College	n/a
Spain | Getafe	Universidad Carlos III de Madrid	Fall Spr YrRound	USColl	Middlebury College	n/a
Spain | Granada	IES Abroad Granada Center	Fall Spr YrRound	Intermed	IES Abroad	n/a
Spain | Leon	Universidad de Leon	Sum	USColl	Hamilton College	n/a
Spain | Logrono	Universidad de la Rioja	Fall Spr YrRound	USColl	Middlebury College	n/a
Spain | Madrid	Hamilton College	Fall Spr YrRound	USColl	Hamilton College	n/a
Spain | Madrid	IES Abroad Madrid Center	Fall Spr YrRound	Intermed	IES Abroad	n/a
Spain | Madrid	IES Abroad Madrid Center	Sum	Intermed	IES Abroad	n/a
Spain | Madrid	Middlebury College	Fall Spr YrRound	USColl	Middlebury College	n/a
Spain | Madrid	Universidad Autonoma de Madrid	Fall Spr YrRound	USColl	Boston University	n/a
Spain | Menorca	Boston University	Sum	USColl	Boston University	n/a
Spain | Salamanca	IES Abroad Salamanca Center	Fall Spr YrRound	Intermed	IES Abroad	n/a
Spain | Seville	Universidad de Sevilla	Fall Spr YrRound	USColl	Sweet Briar College	n/a
Spain | Seville	Universidad de Sevilla	Fall Spr YrRound	Intermed	Academic Programs International	n/a
Spain | Seville	Universidad Pablo de Olavide or Universidad de Sevilla	Fall Spr YrRound	Intermed	Council on International Education Exchange (CIEE)	n/a
Spain | Seville	Universidad Pablo de Olavide or Universidad de Sevilla	Fall Spr YrRound	Intermed	Council on International Education Exchange (CIEE)	n/a
Sweden | Stockholm	Stockhom University	Fall Spr YrRound	Consrtm	The Swedish Program	n/a
Switzerland | Geneva	SIT Study Abroad	Sum	Intermed	SIT Study Abroad	n/a
Switzerland | Geneva	SIT Study Abroad	Fall Spr	Intermed	SIT Study Abroad	n/a
Taiwan | Taichung	Tunghai University	Sum	Dir	n/a	n/a

© 2011 — Updates? Want to be in the next edition? Visit **www.mysecondcampus.com**

Connecticut

DESTINATION	HOST INSTITUTION	PRGM SEASON	PRGM TYPE	INTERMEDIARY	HOUSING
Taiwan | Taichung	Multiple institutional choices	Sum Fall Spr YrRound	USColl	Richard U. Light Fellowship for Language Studies in East Asia (Yale University)	n/a
Taiwan | Taichung	Tunghai University Chinese Language Center	Fall Spr YrRound	Dir	n/a	n/a
Taiwan | Taipei	International Chinese Language Program at National Taiwan University	Sum	Dir	n/a	n/a
Taiwan | Taipei	Multiple institutional choices	Sum Fall Spr YrRound	USColl	Richard U. Light Fellowship for Language Studies in East Asia (Yale University)	n/a
Tanzania | Stone Town	SIT Study Abroad	Fall Spr	Intermed	SIT Study Abroad	n/a
Thailand | Khon Kaen	Khon Kaen University	Fall Spr YrRound	Intermed	Council on International Education Exchange (CIEE)	n/a
The Balkans | (Multiple)	SIT Study Abroad	Sum	Intermed	SIT Study Abroad	n/a
Tunisia | Tunis	University of Tunis El Manar	Sum	Intermed	Bourguiba Institute of Modern Language	n/a
Turkey | Istanbul	Bogazici University	Sum	Dir	n/a	n/a
Turkey | Istanbul	Koc University	Fall Spr YrRound	Intermed	Council on International Education Exchange (CIEE)	n/a
Uganda | Kampala	SIT Study Abroad	Fall Spr	Intermed	SIT Study Abroad	n/a
Uganda | Kampala	SIT Study Abroad	Sum	Intermed	SIT Study Abroad	n/a
Vietnam | Ho Chi Minh City	CET Academic Programs	Sum Fall Spr YrRound	Intermed	CET Academic Programs	n/a
Vietnam | Ho Chi Minh City	Phnom Penh University	Fall Spr YrRound	Intermed	Council on International Education Exchange (CIEE)	n/a
Vietnam | Ho Chi Minh City	SIT Study Abroad	Fall Spr	Intermed	SIT Study Abroad	n/a
Western Samoa | Apia	SIT Study Abroad	Fall Spr	Intermed	SIT Study Abroad	n/a

© 2011 — Updates? Want to be in the next edition? Visit **www.mysecondcampus.com**

Maine

Bowdoin College

Stephen Hall
Director
Office of Off Campus Study
4800 College Station
Brunswick, ME 04011

offcamp@bowdoin.edu
207.725.3473
http://www.bowdoin.edu/ocs/index.shtml

DESTINATION	HOST INSTITUTION	PRGM SEASON	PRGM TYPE	INTERMEDIARY	HOUSING
Argentina | Buenos Aires	IES Abroad Buenos Aires Center	Fall Spr YrRound	Intermed	IES Abroad	HostFam
Argentina | Buenos Aires	Multiple institutional choices	Fall Spr YrRound	Intermed	Institute for Study Abroad	HostFam
Argentina | Mendoza	Universidad Nacional de Cuyo	Fall Spr YrRound	Intermed	Institute for Study Abroad	HostFam
Australia | Byron Bay	SIT Study Abroad	Fall Spr	Intermed	SIT Study Abroad	n/a
Australia | Canberra	Australian National University	Fall Spr YrRound	Dir	n/a	n/a
Australia | Hobart	University of Tasmania	Fall Spr YrRound	Dir	n/a	n/a
Australia | Melbourne	University of Melbourne	Fall Spr YrRound	Dir	n/a	n/a
Australia | Sydney	University of Sydney	Fall Spr YrRound	Dir	n/a	n/a
Australia | Townsville	James Cook University	Fall Spr YrRound	Dir	n/a	n/a
Australia | Yungaburra	Center for Rainforest Studies	Fall Spr	Intermed	School for Field Studies	n/a
Austria | Vienna	IES Abroad Vienna Center	Fall Spr YrRound	Intermed	IES Abroad	HostFam CollRes PrivApt
Botswana | Gaborone	University of Botswana	Fall Spr YrRound	USColl	Pitzer College	HostFam
Cameroon | Yaounde	SIT Study Abroad	Fall Spr	Intermed	SIT Study Abroad	HostFam
Chile | (Multiple choices)	Multiple institutional choices	Fall Spr YrRound	USColl	Middlebury Schools Abroad	HostFam CollRes
Chile | Santiago	Multiple institutional choices	Fall Spr YrRound	Intermed	Institute for Study Abroad	HostFam
Chile | Valparaiso	Multiple institutional choices	Fall Spr YrRound	Intermed	Institute for Study Abroad	HostFam
Chile | Valparaiso	SIT Study Abroad	Fall Spr	Intermed	SIT Study Abroad	HostFam
China | Beijing	Beijing Institute of Education or Capital Normal University	Fall Spr YrRound	Intermed	CET Academic Programs	n/a
China | Beijing	Capital University of Economics and Business	Fall Spr YrRound	USColl	Associated Colleges in China (Hamilton College)	n/a

© 2011 — Updates? Want to be in the next edition? Visit **www.mysecondcampus.com**

Maine

DESTINATION	HOST INSTITUTION	PRGM SEASON	PRGM TYPE	INTERMEDIARY	HOUSING
China | Harbin	Harbin Institute of Technology	Fall Spr YrRound	Intermed	CET Academic Programs	n/a
China | Hong Kong	Chinese University of Hong Kong	Fall Spr YrRound	Dir	n/a	n/a
Costa Rica | La Selva	Organization for Tropical Studies (Duke University)	Fall Spr	Intermed	Organization for Tropical Studies (Duke University)	n/a
Czech Republic | Prague	Collegium Hieronymi Pragensis	Fall Spr	Intermed	Collegium Hieronymi Pragensis	n/a
Denmark | Copenhagen	Danish Institute for Study Abroad (DIS)	Fall Spr YrRound	Intermed	Danish Institute for Study Abroad (DIS)	HostFam CollRes PrivApt
Dominican Republic | Santo Domingo	Multiple institutional choices	Fall Spr YrRound	Intermed	Council on International Education Exchange (CIEE)	HostFam
Ecuador | Quito	SIT Study Abroad	Fall Spr	Intermed	SIT Study Abroad	HostFam
Ecuador | Quito	Universidad Salesiana del Ecuador and Facultad Latinoamericana de Ciencias Sociales (FLACSO)	Fall Spr YrRound	USColl	Duke University	HostFam
Egypt | Cairo	American University in Cairo	Fall Spr YrRound	Dir	n/a	n/a
England | Bristol	University of Bristol	Spr YrRound	Dir	n/a	n/a
England | Cambridge	University of Cambridge	YrRound	Dir	n/a	n/a
England | Lancaster	Lancaster University	Fall Spr YrRound	Dir	n/a	n/a
England | London	British-American Drama Academy	Fall Spr	Intermed	British-American Drama Academy	n/a
England | London	London School of Economics and Political Studies	YrRound	Dir	n/a	n/a
England | London	School of Oriental and African Studies	Spr YrRound	Dir	n/a	n/a
England | London	University College London	Fall Spr YrRound	Dir	n/a	n/a
England | London	University of London, Goldsmiths College	Spr YrRound	Dir	n/a	n/a
England | London	University of London, King's College	Fall Spr YrRound	Dir	n/a	n/a
England | Norwich	University of East Anglia	Fall Spr YrRound	Dir	n/a	n/a
England | Oxford	Oxford University	Spr YrRound	Dir	n/a	n/a
France | Bordeaux	University of Bordeaux	Fall Spr YrRound	USColl	Middlebury College	HostFam
France | Grenoble	Universite de Grenoble	Fall Spr YrRound	USColl	Swarthmore College	HostFam
France | Nantes	IES Abroad Nantes Center	Fall Spr YrRound	Intermed	IES Abroad	HostFam
France | Paris	Multiple institutional choices	Fall Spr YrRound	USColl	Hamilton College	HostFam CollRes
France | Paris	Multiple institutional choices	Fall Spr YrRound	USColl	Middlebury College	HostFam
France | Paris	Multiple institutional choices	Fall Spr YrRound	Consrtm	Wesleyan, Vassar	HostFam
France | Poitiers	University of Poitiers	Fall Spr YrRound	USColl	Middlebury College	HostFam
France | Toulouse	University of Toulouse	Fall Spr YrRound	USColl	Dickenson College	HostFam
Germany | Berlin	IES Abroad Berlin Center	Fall Spr YrRound	Intermed	IES Abroad	HostFam
Germany | Freiburg	IES Abroad EU Center	Fall Spr YrRound	Intermed	IES Abroad	CollRes
Germany | Freiburg	IES Abroad Freiburg Center	Fall Spr YrRound	Intermed	IES Abroad	CollRes
Germany | Munich	Ludwig Maximilians Universitat Munchen	Spr YrRound	USColl	Wayne State University	CollRes

© 2011 — Updates? Want to be in the next edition? Visit **www.mysecondcampus.com**

Maine

DESTINATION	HOST INSTITUTION	PRGM SEASON	PRGM TYPE	INTERMEDIARY	HOUSING
Germany | Tubingen	Eberhard Karls Universitat	Spr YrRound	USColl	Antioch University	PrivApt
Ghana | Accra	Ashesi University	Fall Spr YrRound	Intermed	Council on International Education Exchange (CIEE)	n/a
Ghana | Legon	University of Ghana	Fall Spr YrRound	Intermed	Council on International Education Exchange (CIEE)	n/a
Greece | Athens	College Year in Athens	Fall Spr YrRound	Intermed	College Year in Athens	CollRes
Hungary | Budapest	Technical University of Budapest, College International	Fall Spr YrRound	Intermed	Budapest Semesters in Mathematics	n/a
India | Madurai	South India Term Abroad (George Washington University)	Fall Spr YrRound	Consrtm	South India Term Abroad (George Washington University)	HostFam
Ireland | Cork	University College Cork	Fall Spr YrRound	Dir	n/a	PrivApt
Ireland | Dublin	Trinity College	Fall Spr YrRound	Dir	n/a	CollRes PrivApt
Ireland | Galway	National University of Ireland	Fall Spr YrRound	Dir	n/a	PrivApt
Israel | Jerusalem	Hebrew University of Jerusalem	Fall Spr YrRound	Dir	n/a	n/a
Italy | Bologna	Universita di Bologna	Fall Spr YrRound	Consrtm	Eastern College Consortium in Bologna (Vassar, Wellesley, and Wesleyan)	PrivApt
Italy | Bologna	University of Bologna	Fall Spr YrRound	USColl	Brown University	CollRes
Italy | Ferrara	Universita degli Studi di Ferrara	Spr YrRound	USColl	Middlebury College	n/a
Italy | Florence	NYU in Florence Campus	Fall Spr YrRound	USColl	New York University	HostFam PrivApt
Italy | Milan	IES Abroad Milan Center	Fall Spr YrRound	Intermed	IES Abroad	PrivApt
Italy | Padova	Boston University Center for Italian and European Studies	Fall Spr YrRound	USColl	Boston University	HostFam
Italy | Rome	IES Abroad Rome Center	Fall Spr YrRound	Intermed	IES Abroad	HostFam PrivApt
Italy | Rome	Intercollegiate Center for Classical Studies (Duke University)	Fall Spr	USColl	Duke University	n/a
Italy | Rome	Temple University Rome	Fall Spr YrRound	USColl	Temple University	PrivApt
Italy | Rome	Trinity College Rome Campus	Fall Spr	USColl	Trinity College	CollRes
Italy | Siena	CET Academic Programs	Fall Spr YrRound	Intermed	CET Academic Programs	CollRes
Japan | Hikone	University of Shiga Prefecture or Shiga University	Fall Spr YrRound	Consrtm	Japan Center for Michigan Univerisities	HostFam PrivApt
Japan | Kyoto	Doshisha University	YrRound	Consrtm	Associated Kyoto Program	HostFam
Japan | Kyoto	Kyoto Consortium for Japanese Studies (Columbia University)	Fall Spr YrRound	Consrtm	Kyoto Consortium for Japanese Studies (Columbia University)	HostFam PrivApt
Japan | Nagoya	Nanzan University Center for Japanese Studies	Fall Spr YrRound	Intermed	IES Abroad	HostFam CollRes
Jordan | Amman	University of Jordan	Fall Spr	Intermed	Council on International Education Exchange (CIEE)	HostFam PrivApt
Kenya | Kimana	Center for Wildlife Management Studies	Fall Spr	Intermed	School for Field Studies	n/a
Kenya | Nairobi	St. Lawrence University	Fall Spr	USColl	St. Lawrence University	HostFam
Korea | Seoul	Yonsei University	Fall Spr YrRound	Intermed	Council on International Education Exchange (CIEE)	n/a

Maine

DESTINATION	HOST INSTITUTION	PRGM SEASON	PRGM TYPE	INTERMEDIARY	HOUSING
Korea	Seoul	Yonsei University	Fall Spr YrRound	Dir	n/a	n/a
Madagascar	Fort Dauphin	SIT Study Abroad	Fall Spr	Intermed	SIT Study Abroad	HostFam
Mexico	Cuernavaca	Augsburg College	Fall Spr	USColl	Augsburg College	HostFam
Mexico	Merida	University Autonoma de Yucatan	Fall Spr	Intermed	Institute for Study Abroad	HostFam
Morocco	Rabat	SIT Study Abroad	Fall Spr	Intermed	SIT Study Abroad	HostFam
Namibia	Windhoek	Augsburg College	Fall Spr	USColl	Augsburg College	HostFam
Nepal	Kathmandu	SIT Study Abroad	Fall Spr	Intermed	SIT Study Abroad	HostFam
Nepal	Kathmandu	Tribhuvan University	Fall Spr	USColl	Pitzer College	n/a
New Zealand	Auckland	University of Auckland	Fall Spr YrRound	Dir	n/a	n/a
New Zealand	Dunedin	University of Otago	Fall Spr YrRound	Dir	n/a	n/a
Northern Ireland	Belfast	Queen's University	Fall Spr YrRound	Dir	n/a	n/a
Panama	Panama City	SIT Study Abroad	Fall Spr	Intermed	SIT Study Abroad	HostFam
Peru	Lima	Pontificia Universidad Catolica del Peru	Fall Spr YrRound	Intermed	Institute for Study Abroad	HostFam
Russia	Irkutsk	Irkutsk State University	Fall Spr YrRound	USColl	Middlebury College	HostFam
Russia	Moscow	Moscow International University	Fall Spr YrRound	Intermed	American Councils Study Abroad Programs	HostFam CollRes
Russia	Moscow	Russian State University of the Humanities	Fall Spr YrRound	USColl	Middlebury College	HostFam
Russia	St. Petersburg	Russian State Pedagogical (Gertsen) University	Fall Spr YrRound	Intermed	American Councils Study Abroad Programs	HostFam CollRes
Russia	Vladimir	KORA Center for Russian Language	Fall Spr YrRound	Intermed	American Councils Study Abroad Programs	HostFam CollRes
Russia	Yaroslavl	Yaroslavl State Pedagogical University	Fall Spr YrRound	USColl	Middlebury College	HostFam
Scotland	Brighton	University of Sussex	Fall Spr YrRound	Dir	n/a	n/a
Scotland	Edinburgh	University of Edinburgh	Fall Spr YrRound	Dir	n/a	n/a
Scotland	Glasgow	University of Glasgow	Fall Spr YrRound	Dir	n/a	n/a
Scotland	St. Andrews	University of St. Andrews	Fall Spr YrRound	Dir	n/a	n/a
Senegal	Dakar	L'Universite Cheikh Anta Diop	Fall Spr YrRound	Intermed	Council on International Education Exchange (CIEE)	HostFam
Senegal	Saint Louis	Universite Gaston Berger	YrRound	USColl	University of Wisconsin at Madison	HostFam CollRes
South Africa	Cape Town	University of Cape Town	Fall Spr YrRound	Intermed	Council on International Education Exchange (CIEE)	PrivApt
South Africa	Cape Town	University of Cape Town	Fall Spr YrRound	Intermed	Interstudy	PrivApt
South Africa	Durban	University of KwaZulu-Natal	Fall Spr YrRound	Intermed	Interstudy	n/a
South Africa	Kruger National Park	Organization for Tropical Studies	Fall Spr	Intermed	Organization for Tropical Studies	n/a
Spain	Barcelona	University of Barcelona	Fall Spr YrRound	Intermed	Brethern Colleges Abroad	HostFam
Spain	Granada	IES Abroad Granada Center	Fall Spr YrRound	Intermed	IES Abroad	n/a
Spain	Madrid	IES Abroad Madrid Center	Fall Spr YrRound	Intermed	IES Abroad	HostFam PrivApt
Spain	Salamanca	IES Abroad Salamanca Center	Fall Spr YrRound	Intermed	IES Abroad	HostFam
Spain	Seville	University of Seville	Fall Spr YrRound	USColl	Sweet Briar College	HostFam

© 2011 — Updates? Want to be in the next edition? Visit **www.mysecondcampus.com**

Maine

DESTINATION	HOST INSTITUTION	PRGM SEASON	PRGM TYPE	INTERMEDIARY	HOUSING
Sri Lanka	Kandy	University of Peradeniya	Fall Spr	Consrtm	Intercollegiate Sri Lanka Education	HostFam
Sweden	Stockholm	Stockholm University	Fall Spr YrRound	Consrtm	Swedish Program	n/a
Tanzania	Arusha	SIT Study Abroad	Fall Spr	Intermed	SIT Study Abroad	HostFam
Tanzania	Stonetown (Zanzibar)	SIT Study Abroad	Fall Spr	Intermed	SIT Study Abroad	HostFam
Thailand	Khon Kaen	Khon Kaen University	Fall Spr	Intermed	Council on International Education Exchange (CIEE)	PrivApt
United States	(Multiple choices)	Multiple institutional choices	n/a	Bilat	Twelve College Exchange	n/a
United States	(Multiple choices)	Three Seas Program (Northeastern)	n/a	USColl	Three Seas Program	n/a
United States	Mystic (CT)	Williams-Mystic Seaport Program	n/a	USColl	Williams-Mystic Seaport Program	n/a
United States	Washington (DC)	American University	n/a	USColl	American University	n/a
United States	Waterford (CT)	National Theater Institute	n/a	USColl	Connecticut College	n/a
United States	Woods Hole (MA)	Sea Semester	n/a	Intermed	Sea Semester	n/a
United States	Woods Hole (MA)	Semester in Environmental Science (Marine Biological Laboratory)	n/a	Intermed	Semester in Environmental Science (Marine Biological Laboratory)	n/a

Colby College

Nancy Downey
Director
Off Campus Study
4000 Mayflower Hill
Waterville, ME 04901

ndowney@colby.edu
207.859.4500
http://www.colby.edu/academics_cs/ocs/

DESTINATION	HOST INSTITUTION	PRGM SEASON	PRGM TYPE	INTERMEDIARY	HOUSING
(Multiple)	(Multiple)	International Honors Program	n/a	Intermed	International Honors Program	n/a
(Multiple)	(Multiple)	International Honors Program	n/a	Intermed	International Honors Program	n/a
(Multiple)	(Multiple)	International Honors Program	n/a	Intermed	International Honors Program	n/a
Argentina	Buenos Aires	IES Abroad Buenos Aires Center	n/a	Intermed	IES Abroad	n/a
Argentina	Buenos Aires	Multiple institutional choices	n/a	Intermed	Council on International Educational Exchange (CIEE)	n/a
Australia	Brisbane	University of Queensland	n/a	Dir	n/a	n/a
Australia	Byron Bay	SIT Study Abroad	n/a	Intermed	SIT Study Abroad	n/a
Australia	Cairns	SIT Study Abroad	n/a	Intermed	SIT Study Abroad	n/a
Australia	Canberra	Australian National University	n/a	Dir	n/a	n/a
Australia	Hobart or Launceston	University of Tasmania	n/a	Dir	n/a	n/a
Australia	Melbourne	University of Melbourne	n/a	Dir	n/a	n/a
Australia	Perth	University of Western Australia	n/a	Dir	n/a	n/a
Australia	Sydney	University of New South Wales	n/a	Dir	n/a	n/a
Australia	Sydney	University of Sydney	n/a	Dir	n/a	n/a
Australia	Townsville	James Cook University	n/a	Dir	n/a	n/a
Australia	Yungaburra	Center for Rainforest Studies	n/a	Intermed	School for Field Studies	n/a
Austria	Vienna	IES Abroad Vienna Center	n/a	Intermed	IES Abroad	n/a

Maine

DESTINATION	HOST INSTITUTION	PRGM SEASON	PRGM TYPE	INTERMEDIARY	HOUSING
Belgium	Brussels	Universite Libre de Bruxelles	n/a	Intermed	Council on International Educational Exchange (CIEE)	n/a
Bolivia	Cochabamba	SIT Study Abroad	n/a	Intermed	SIT Study Abroad	n/a
Botswana	Gaborone	SIT Study Abroad	n/a	Intermed	SIT Study Abroad	n/a
Botswana	Gaborone	University of Botswana	n/a	USColl	Pitzer College	n/a
Brazil	Belem	SIT Study Abroad	n/a	Intermed	SIT Study Abroad	n/a
Cameroon	Yaounde	SIT Study Abroad	n/a	Intermed	SIT Study Abroad	n/a
Chile	Santiago	Pontificia Universidad Catolica de Chile	n/a	USColl	Washington University	n/a
Chile	Santiago	SIT Study Abroad	n/a	Intermed	SIT Study Abroad	n/a
Chile	Santiago	SIT Study Abroad	n/a	Intermed	SIT Study Abroad	n/a
Chile	Valparaiso	SIT Study Abroad	n/a	Intermed	SIT Study Abroad	n/a
China	(Multiple choices)	Multiple institutional choices	n/a	Intermed	Alliance for Global Education	n/a
China	Beijing	Capital University of Economics and Business	n/a	USColl	Associated Colleges in China (Hamilton College)	n/a
China	Beijing	Peking University	n/a	Intermed	Beijing Institute of Asian Studies	n/a
China	Beijing	Peking University	n/a	Intermed	Council on International Educational Exchange (CIEE)	n/a
China	Hangzhou	Zhejiang University of Technology	n/a	USColl	Middlebury College	n/a
China	Harbin	CET Academic Programs	n/a	Intermed	CET Academic Programs	n/a
China	Nanjing	Nanjing University	n/a	Intermed	Council on International Educational Exchange (CIEE)	n/a
China	Shanghai	East China Normal University	n/a	Intermed	Council on International Educational Exchange (CIEE)	n/a
China	Shanghai	East China Normal University	n/a	Intermed	Council on International Educational Exchange (CIEE)	n/a
Costa Rica	(Multiple choices)	Organization for Tropical Studies	n/a	Intermed	Organization for Tropical Studies	n/a
Costa Rica	(Multiple choices)	Organization for Tropical Studies	n/a	Intermed	Organization for Tropical Studies	n/a
Costa Rica	Atenas	SFS Center for Sustainable Development Studies	n/a	Intermed	School for Field Studies	n/a
Costa Rica	Monteverde	CIEE Study Center	n/a	Intermed	Council on International Educational Exchange (CIEE)	n/a
Czech Republic	Prague	CET Academic Programs	n/a	Intermed	CET Academic Programs	n/a
Czech Republic	Prague	Charles University or Prague Film and Television School of the Academy of the Performing Arts	n/a	Intermed	Council on International Educational Exchange (CIEE)	n/a
Czech Republic	Prague	Collegium Hieronymi Pragensis	n/a	Intermed	Collegium Hieronymi Pragensis	n/a
Czech Republic	Prague	New York University	n/a	USColl	New York University	n/a
Denmark	Copenhagen	Danish Institute for Study Abroad (DIS)	n/a	Intermed	Danish Institute for Study Abroad (DIS)	n/a

© 2011 — Updates? Want to be in the next edition? Visit **www.mysecondcampus.com**

DESTINATION	HOST INSTITUTION	PRGM SEASON	PRGM TYPE	INTERMEDIARY	HOUSING
Ecuador | Guayaquil	Universidad Espiritu Santo	n/a	Intermed	International Partnership for Service-Learning and Leadership	n/a
Ecuador | Nudo del Azuay	Round River Conservation Studies	n/a	Intermed	Round River Conservation Studies	n/a
Ecuador | Quito	Pontificia Universidad Catolica del Ecuador	n/a	USColl	Pitzer College	n/a
Ecuador | Quito	SIT Study Abroad	n/a	Intermed	SIT Study Abroad	n/a
Ecuador | Quito	SIT Study Abroad	n/a	Intermed	SIT Study Abroad	n/a
Ecuador | Quito	Universidad Politecnica Salesiana or Facultad Latinoamericana de Ciencias Sociales	n/a	USColl	Duke University	n/a
Egypt | Cairo or Alexandria	Multiple institutional choices	n/a	Intermed	Institute for Study Abroad	n/a
England | Brighton	University of Sussex	n/a	Dir	n/a	n/a
England | Bristol	University of Bristol	n/a	Dir	n/a	n/a
England | Cambridge	Cambridge University	n/a	Dir	n/a	n/a
England | London	Birbeck College	n/a	Intermed	Institute for Study Abroad	n/a
England | London	Boston University	n/a	USColl	Boston University	n/a
England | London	King's College	n/a	Dir	n/a	n/a
England | London	London School of Economics and Political Science	n/a	Dir	n/a	n/a
England | London	Royal Holloway	n/a	Dir	n/a	n/a
England | London	School of Oriental and African Studies	n/a	Dir	n/a	n/a
England | London	University College London	n/a	Dir	n/a	n/a
England | Norwich	University of East Anglia	n/a	Dir	n/a	n/a
England | Oxford	Oxford University	n/a	Dir	n/a	n/a
England | York	University of York	n/a	Dir	n/a	n/a
France | Aix-en-Provence	Wellesley College	n/a	USColl	Wellesley College	n/a
France | Dijon	University of Burgundy	Fall	Self	n/a	HostFam
France | Grenoble	Universite de Grenoble	n/a	USColl	Swarthmore College	n/a
France | Paris	Multiple institutional choices	n/a	USColl	Hamilton College	n/a
France | Paris	Multiple institutional choices	n/a	Consrtm	Emory, Duke, Cornell Universities (EDUCO)	n/a
France | Paris	Multiple institutional choices	n/a	USColl	Columbia-Penn Program	n/a
Germany | Berlin	IES Abroad Berlin Center	n/a	Intermed	IES Abroad	n/a
Germany | Freiburg	IES Abroad	n/a	Intermed	IES Abroad	n/a
Germany | Freiburg	IES Abroad Freiburg Center	n/a	Intermed	IES Abroad	n/a
Germany | Munich	Ludwig-Maximilians-Universitat	n/a	USColl	Lewis and Clark College	n/a
Germany | Regensburg	University of Regensburg	n/a	Consrtm	Wesleyan University	n/a
Germany | Tubingen	Eberhard-Karls University	n/a	USColl	Tufts University	n/a
Ghana | Accra	SIT Study Abroad	n/a	Intermed	SIT Study Abroad	n/a
Ghana | Cape Coast	SIT Study Abroad	n/a	Intermed	SIT Study Abroad	n/a

Maine

DESTINATION	HOST INSTITUTION	PRGM SEASON	PRGM TYPE	INTERMEDIARY	HOUSING
Greece | Athens	International Center for Hellenic and Mediterranean Studies	n/a	Intermed	College Year in Athens	n/a
Hungary | Budapest	Technical University of Budapest, College International	n/a	Intermed	Budapest Semesters in Mathematics	n/a
India | Madurai	South India Term Abroad (George Washington University)	n/a	Consrtm	South India Term Abroad (George Washington University)	n/a
India | Pune	Alliance for Global Education	n/a	Intermed	Alliance for Global Education	n/a
Ireland | Cork	University College Cork	n/a	Dir	n/a	n/a
Israel | Beer-Sheva	Ben Gurion University	n/a	Dir	n/a	n/a
Israel | Haifa	University of Haifa	n/a	Dir	n/a	n/a
Israel | Jerusalem	Hebrew University	n/a	Dir	n/a	n/a
Israel | Tel Aviv	Tel Aviv University	n/a	Dir	n/a	n/a
Italy | Bologna	Universita di Bologna	n/a	USColl	Brown University	n/a
Italy | Bologna	Universita di Bologna	n/a	Consrtm	Eastern College Consortium	n/a
Italy | Ferrara	Universita degli Studi di Ferrara	n/a	USColl	Middlebury College	n/a
Italy | Florence	New York University	n/a	USColl	New York University	n/a
Italy | Florence	SU Florence Center	n/a	USColl	Syracuse University	n/a
Italy | Florence	Universita degli Studi di Firenze	n/a	USColl	Middlebury College	n/a
Italy | Padova	Universita degli Studi di Padova	n/a	USColl	Boston University	n/a
Italy | Parma	Universita degli Studi di Parma	n/a	USColl	Pitzer College	n/a
Italy | Rome	Intercollegiate Center for Classical Studies in Rome (Duke University)	n/a	Consrtm	Intercollegiate Center for Classical Studies in Rome (Duke University)	n/a
Italy | Rome	Temple University	n/a	USColl	Temple University	n/a
Italy | Rome	Trinity College (CT)	n/a	USColl	Trinity College (CT)	n/a
Italy | Siena	CET Academic Programs	n/a	Intermed	CET Academic Programs	n/a
Japan | Hirakata City	Kansai Gaidai University	n/a	Dir	n/a	n/a
Japan | Kyoto	Associated Kyoto Program (Doshisha University)	n/a	Intermed	Associated Kyoto Program (Doshisha University)	n/a
Japan | Kyoto	Kyoto Consortium for Japanese Studies (Columbia University)	n/a	Consrtm	Kyoto Consortium for Japanese Studies (Columbia University)	n/a
Japan | Nagasaki	Japan Studies in Nagasaki (JASIN)	n/a	Intermed	Japan Studies in Nagasaki (JASIN)	n/a
Japan | Nagoya	Nagoya University of Foreign Studies	n/a	Dir	n/a	n/a
Jordan | Amman	SIT Study Abroad	n/a	Intermed	SIT Study Abroad	n/a
Jordan | Amman	University of Jordan	n/a	Intermed	Council on International Educational Exchange (CIEE)	n/a
Kenya | Kimana	Center for Wildlife Management Studies	n/a	Intermed	School for Field Studies	n/a
Kenya | Nairobi	SIT Study Abroad	n/a	Intermed	SIT Study Abroad	n/a
Madagascar | Antananarivo	SIT Study Abroad	n/a	Intermed	SIT Study Abroad	n/a
Madagascar | Fort Dauphin	SIT Study Abroad	n/a	Intermed	SIT Study Abroad	n/a

© 2011 — Updates? Want to be in the next edition? Visit **www.mysecondcampus.com**

Maine

DESTINATION	HOST INSTITUTION	PRGM SEASON	PRGM TYPE	INTERMEDIARY	HOUSING
Mexico | Baja	Center for Coastal Studies	n/a	Intermed	School for Field Studies	n/a
Mexico | Guadalajara	Universidad Autonoma de Guadalajara	n/a	Intermed	International Partnership for Service-Learning and Leadership	n/a
Mexico | Mexico City	Universidad Iberoamericana	n/a	USColl	Loyola University New Orleans	n/a
Morocco | Rabat	Ecole Superieure de Direction et de Gestion	n/a	Intermed	Council on International Educational Exchange (CIEE)	n/a
Morocco | Rabat	SIT Study Abroad	n/a	Intermed	SIT Study Abroad	n/a
Namibia | Kunene	Round River Conservation Studies Region	n/a	Intermed	Round River Conservation Studies	n/a
Nepal | Kathmandu	SIT Study Abroad	n/a	Intermed	SIT Study Abroad	n/a
Nepal | Kathmandu	Tribhuvan University	n/a	USColl	Pitzer College	n/a
New Zealand | Auckland	University of Auckland	n/a	Dir	n/a	n/a
New Zealand | Dunedin	University of Otago	n/a	Dir	n/a	n/a
New Zealand | Wellington	Victoria University of Wellington	n/a	Dir	n/a	n/a
Oman | Muscat	SIT Study Abroad	n/a	Intermed	SIT Study Abroad	n/a
Oman | Muscat	SIT Study Abroad	n/a	Intermed	SIT Study Abroad	n/a
Panama | Panama City	SIT Study Abroad	n/a	Intermed	SIT Study Abroad	n/a
Peru | Cusco	Centro Bartolome de las Casas	n/a	Intermed	SIT Study Abroad	n/a
Peru | Lima	Pontificia Universidad Catolica del Peru	n/a	Intermed	Institute for Study Abroad	n/a
Russia | (Multiple choices)	Multiple institutional choices	n/a	Intermed	American Councils for International Education	n/a
Russia | (Multiple choices)	Multiple institutional choices	n/a	USColl	Middlebury College	n/a
Russia | St. Petersburg	St. Petersburg Classical Gymnasium	Fall Spr	Self	n/a	HostFam
Russia | St. Petersburg	St. Petersburg State University	n/a	Intermed	Council on International Educational Exchange (CIEE)	n/a
Scotland | Edinburgh	University of Edinburgh	n/a	Dir	n/a	n/a
Scotland | Glasgow	University of Glasgow	n/a	Dir	n/a	n/a
Scotland | St. Andrews	University of St. Andrews	n/a	Dir	n/a	n/a
Senegal | Dakar	Suffolk University - Dakar Campus	n/a	Intermed	Council on International Educational Exchange (CIEE)	n/a
South Africa | Cape Town	University of Cape Town	n/a	Dir	n/a	n/a
South Africa | Cape Town	University of Cape Town	n/a	Intermed	Council on International Educational Exchange (CIEE)	n/a
South Africa | Durban	SIT Study Abroad	n/a	Intermed	SIT Study Abroad	n/a
South Africa | Johannesburg	University of the Witwatersrand	n/a	USColl	International Human Rights Exchange (Bard College)	n/a
South Africa | Kruger National Park	Organization for Tropical Studies	n/a	Intermed	Organization for Tropical Studies	n/a
Spain | Madrid	Hamilton College	n/a	USColl	Hamilton College	n/a
Spain | Salamanca	Universidad de Salamanca	Fall Spr YrRound	Self	n/a	HostFam
Spain | Salamanca	Universidad de Salamanca	Fall Spr YrRound	Self	n/a	HostFam

Maine

DESTINATION	HOST INSTITUTION	PRGM SEASON	PRGM TYPE	INTERMEDIARY	HOUSING
Sri Lanka	Dangolla	Intercollegiate Sri Lanka Education (Bowdoin College)	n/a	Consrtm	Intercollegiate Sri Lanka Education (Bowdoin College)	n/a
Sweden	Stockholm	Stockholm University	n/a	Consrtm	Swedish Program	n/a
Switzerland	Geneva	Boston University	n/a	USColl	Boston University	n/a
Switzerland	Geneva	SIT Study Abroad	n/a	Intermed	SIT Study Abroad	n/a
Switzerland	Geneva	Universite de Geneve	n/a	USColl	Smith College	n/a
Taiwan	Taipei	National Chengchi University	n/a	Intermed	Council on International Educational Exchange (CIEE)	n/a
Tanzania	Arusha	SIT Study Abroad	n/a	Intermed	SIT Study Abroad	n/a
Tanzania	Dar es Salaam	University of Dar es Salaam	n/a	USColl	Brown University	n/a
Tanzania	Stone Town	SIT Study Abroad	n/a	Intermed	SIT Study Abroad	n/a
Thailand	Chiang Mai	International Sustainable Development Studies Institute	n/a	Intermed	International Sustainable Development Studies Institute	n/a
Turks and Caicos	South Caicos	Center for Marine Resource Management Studies	n/a	Intermed	School for Field Studies	n/a
Uganda	Kampala	SIT Study Abroad	n/a	Intermed	SIT Study Abroad	n/a
United States	Atlanta (GA)	Clark Atlanta University	n/a	Bilat	n/a	n/a
United States	Claremont (CA)	Claremont Colleges	n/a	Bilat	n/a	n/a
United States	Hanover (NH)	Dartmouth College	n/a	Dir	n/a	n/a
United States	Mystic (CT)	Williams-Mystic	n/a	USColl	Williams-Mystic	n/a
United States	Washington (DC)	American University	n/a	Dir	n/a	n/a
United States	Washington (DC)	Howard University	n/a	Bilat	n/a	n/a
United States	Washington (DC)	Washington Center for Internships and Academic Seminars	n/a	Intermed	Washington Center for Internships and Academic Seminars	n/a
United States	Woods Hole (MA)	Marine Biological Laboratory	n/a	Intermed	Semester in Environmental Science	n/a
United States	Woods Hole (MA)	Sea Semester	n/a	Intermed	n/a	n/a
Uruguay	Montevideo	Multiple institutional choices	n/a	USColl	Middlebury College	n/a
Vietnam	Ho Chi Minh City	SIT Study Abroad	n/a	Intermed	SIT Study Abroad	n/a

College of the Atlantic

Andrew Griffiths
Administrative Dean
105 Eden Street
Bar Harbour, ME 04609

agriffiths@coa.edu
207.288.5015
http://www.coa.edu/off-campus-study.htm

DESTINATION	HOST INSTITUTION	PRGM SEASON	PRGM TYPE	INTERMEDIARY	HOUSING
(Multiple choices)	(Multiple choices)	Franklin W. Olin College of Engineering	n/a	Dir	n/a	n/a
(Multiple choices)	(Multiple choices)	Multiple institutional choices	n/a	Consrtm	Ecoleague	n/a
(Multiple choices)	(Multiple choices)	Multiple institutional choices	n/a	Intermed	United World Colleges	n/a
(Multiple choices)	(Multiple choices)	National Outdoor Leadership School	n/a	Intermed	National Outdoor Leadership	n/a

© 2011 — Updates? Want to be in the next edition? Visit **www.mysecondcampus.com**

Maine

DESTINATION	HOST INSTITUTION	PRGM SEASON	PRGM TYPE	INTERMEDIARY	HOUSING
(Multiple choices) | (Multiple choices)	Salt Institute for Documentary Studies	n/a	Intermed	Salt Institute for Documentary Studies	n/a
(Multiple choices) | (Multiple choices)	University of Maine	n/a	Dir	n/a	n/a

Saint Joseph's College of Maine

Vincent J. Kloskowski
Director of The Academic Center
278 White Bridges Road
Standish, ME 04084

vkloskow@sjcme.edu
207.893.7561
http://www.sjcme.edu/TAC/study-abroad

DESTINATION	HOST INSTITUTION	PRGM SEASON	PRGM TYPE	INTERMEDIARY	HOUSING
(Multiple choices) | (Multiple choices)	Multiple institutional choices	n/a	Intermed	International Student Exchange Programs	n/a

Southern Maine Community College

Debra Andrews
Director of Center for Global Opportunities
2 Fort Road
South Portland, ME 04106

dandrews@smccme.edu
207.741.5791
http://www.smccme.edu/academics/study-abroad/

DESTINATION	HOST INSTITUTION	PRGM SEASON	PRGM TYPE	INTERMEDIARY	HOUSING
(Multiple choices) | (Multiple choices)	Multiple institutional choices	n/a	Consrtm	College Consortium for International Studies	n/a
(Multiple choices) | (Multiple choices)	Multiple institutional choices	n/a	Intermed	Academic Programs International	n/a
(Multiple choices) | (Multiple choices)	Multiple institutional choices	n/a	Intermed	Council on International Educational Exchange (CIEE)	n/a
(Multiple choices) | (Multiple choices)	SIT Study Abroad	n/a	Intermed	SIT Study Abroad	n/a
Austria | [City Unspecified]	Southern Maine Community College	Sum Spr	Self	n/a	n/a
Canada | New Brunswick	n/a	n/a	Dir	n/a	n/a
Canada | Ontario	n/a	n/a	Dir	n/a	n/a
Germany | (Multiple choices)	Multiple institutional choices	Sum YrRound	Intermed	CDS International	n/a
Ireland | [City Unspecified]	Southern Maine Community College	Sum Spr	Self	n/a	n/a
Ireland | Cork	Cork Institute of Technology	n/a	Bilat	n/a	n/a
Mexico | [City Unspecified]	Southern Maine Community College	Sum Spr	Self	n/a	n/a
Mexico | Cancun	n/a	n/a	Dir	n/a	n/a
Mexico | Monterrey	n/a	n/a	Dir	n/a	n/a

© 2011 — Updates? Want to be in the next edition? Visit **www.mysecondcampus.com**

Maine

Unity College

Amy Lee Knisley
Senior Vice President for Academic Affairs
North Coop
90 Quaker Hill Road
Unity, ME 04988

AKnisley@unity.edu
207.948.3131 x297
http://www.unity.edu/CareerServices/International/International.aspx

DESTINATION	HOST INSTITUTION	PRGM SEASON	PRGM TYPE	INTERMEDIARY	HOUSING
(Multiple choices)	(Multiple choices)	Global Exchange	n/a	Intermed	Global Exchange	n/a
(Multiple choices)	(Multiple choices)	Multiple institutional choices	n/a	Intermed	AustraLearn	n/a
(Multiple choices)	(Multiple choices)	Multiple institutional choices	n/a	Intermed	International Partnership for Service-Learning and Leadership	n/a
(Multiple choices)	(Multiple choices)	Multiple institutional choices	n/a	Intermed	Council on International Educational Exchange (CIEE)	n/a
(Multiple choices)	(Multiple choices)	Multiple institutional choices	n/a	Intermed	American Institute for Foreign Study	n/a
(Multiple choices)	(Multiple choices)	Multiple institutional choices	n/a	Intermed	Center for Ecological Living and Learning	n/a
(Multiple choices)	(Multiple choices)	Multiple institutional choices	n/a	Intermed	American Universities International Programs	n/a
(Multiple choices)	(Multiple choices)	Multiple institutional choices	n/a	Intermed	Center for Cultural Interchange	n/a
(Multiple choices)	(Multiple choices)	School for Field Studies	n/a	Intermed	School for Field Studies	n/a
(Multiple choices)	(Multiple choices)	SIT Study Abroad	n/a	Intermed	SIT Study Abroad	n/a

University of Maine

Karen Boucias
Director
5782 Winslow Hall, Room 100
Orono, ME 04469

Karen.Boucias@umit.maine.edu
207.581.3433
http://www.umaine.edu/international/

DESTINATION	HOST INSTITUTION	PRGM SEASON	PRGM TYPE	INTERMEDIARY	HOUSING
(Multiple choices)	(Multiple choices)	IES Abroad	n/a	Intermed	IES Abroad	n/a
(Multiple choices)	(Multiple choices)	Multiple Institutional choices	n/a	Consrtm	University Studies Abroad Consortium	n/a
(Multiple choices)	(Multiple choices)	Multiple Institutional choices	n/a	Intermed	AustraLearn	n/a
(Multiple choices)	(Multiple choices)	Multiple Institutional choices	n/a	Intermed	Academic Programs International	n/a
(Multiple choices)	(Multiple choices)	Multiple Institutional choices	n/a	Intermed	Institute for Study Abroad	n/a
(Multiple choices)	(Multiple choices)	Multiple Institutional choices	n/a	Intermed	Center for International Studies	n/a

© 2011 — Updates? Want to be in the next edition? Visit www.mysecondcampus.com

Maine

DESTINATION	HOST INSTITUTION	PRGM SEASON	PRGM TYPE	INTERMEDIARY	HOUSING
(Multiple choices)	(Multiple choices)	Multiple Institutional choices	n/a	Consrtm	College Consortium for International Studies	n/a
(Multiple choices)	(Multiple choices)	Multiple Institutional choices	n/a	Intermed	Council on International Education Exchange (CIEE)	n/a
(Multiple choices)	(Multiple choices)	Multiple Institutional choices	n/a	Intermed	International Studies Abroad	n/a
Australia	Brisbane or Gold Coast	Griffith University	n/a	Dir	n/a	n/a
Australia	Perth	Edith Cowan University	n/a	Dir	n/a	n/a
Austria	Salzburg	University of Salzburg	n/a	Consrtm	New England Universities in Salzburg	n/a
Bulgaria	Blagoevgrad	American University in Bulgaria	n/a	Dir	n/a	n/a
Canada	(Multiple choices)	Multiple Institutions	Fall Spr YrRound	Dir	n/a	n/a
Canada	Burnaby (British Columbia)	Simon Fraser University	Fall Spr YrRound	Bilat	n/a	n/a
Canada	Chicoutimi (Quebec)	Universite du Quebec a Chicoutimi	Sum	Dir	n/a	n/a
Canada	Corner Brook (Newfoundland)	Sir Wilfred Grenfell College	Fall Spr YrRound	Bilat	n/a	n/a
Canada	Fredericton (New Brunswick)	University of New Brunswick	Fall Spr YrRound	Bilat	n/a	n/a
Canada	Fredericton or Saint John	University of New Brunswick	n/a	Dir	n/a	n/a
Canada	Jonquiere (Quebec)	College de Jonquiere	Sum	Dir	n/a	n/a
Canada	Lenoxville (Quebec)	Bishop's University	Fall Spr YrRound	Bilat	n/a	n/a
Canada	Montreal (Quebec)	McGill University	Sum	Dir	n/a	n/a
Canada	Montreal (Quebec)	Universite du Quebec a Montreal	Sum	Dir	n/a	n/a
Canada	Ottawa (Ontario)	University of Ottawa	Sum	Dir	n/a	n/a
Canada	Pointe-de-l'Eglise (Nova Scotia)	Universite Sainte-Anne	Sum Fall Spr YrRound	Dir	n/a	n/a
Canada	Prince George (British Columbia)	University of Northern British Columbia	Fall Spr YrRound	Bilat	n/a	n/a
Canada	Quebec City (Quebec)	College Saint Charles Garnier	Sum	Dir	n/a	n/a
Canada	Quebec City (Quebec)	Universite Laval	Sum Fall Spr YrRound	Dir	n/a	n/a
Canada	Regina (Saskatchewan)	University of Regina	Fall Spr YrRound	Bilat	n/a	n/a
Canada	Riviere du Loup (Quebec)	College de Riviere-du-Loup	Sum	Dir	n/a	n/a
Canada	Sydney (Nova Scotia)	University College of Cape Breton	Fall Spr YrRound	Bilat	n/a	n/a
Canada	Trois-Rivieres (Quebec)	Universite du Quebec a Trois-Rivieres	Sum	Dir	n/a	n/a
Canada	Vancouver (British Columbia)	University of British Columbia	Fall Spr YrRound	Bilat	n/a	n/a
Canada	Victoria (British Columbia)	University of Victoria	Sum	Dir	n/a	n/a
Chile	Santiago	Universidad de Chile	n/a	Dir	n/a	n/a
England	Hull	University of Hull	n/a	Dir	n/a	n/a

© 2011 — Updates? Want to be in the next edition? Visit **www.mysecondcampus.com**

Maine

DESTINATION	HOST INSTITUTION	PRGM SEASON	PRGM TYPE	INTERMEDIARY	HOUSING
England | Lancaster	University of Lancaster	n/a	Dir	n/a	n/a
England | Norwich	University of East Anglia	n/a	Dir	n/a	n/a
England | Sunderland	University of Sunderland	n/a	Dir	n/a	n/a
France | Angers	Universite d'Angers	Fall Spr YrRound	Dir	n/a	n/a
France | Brittany	University of Western Brittany	Fall Spr YrRound	Dir	n/a	n/a
France | Nantes	University of Nantes	Fall Spr YrRound	Dir	n/a	n/a
Germany | Aalen	Aalen University	n/a	Dir	n/a	n/a
Germany | Bonn	Internationale Fachhochschule Bad Honnef	n/a	Dir	n/a	n/a
Japan | Hirosaki	Hirosaki University	n/a	Dir	n/a	n/a
Japan | Kitakyushu or Iizuka	Kyushu Institute of Technology	n/a	Dir	n/a	n/a
Spain | Santiago de Compostela	Universidad de Santiago de Compostela	n/a	Dir	n/a	n/a
Turkey | Ankara	Bilkent University	n/a	Dir	n/a	n/a
United States | Woods Hole (MA)	Sea Semester	n/a	Intermed	Sea Semester	n/a
Wales | Bangor	Bangor University	n/a	Dir	n/a	n/a

University of Maine at Augusta

Joshua Nadel
Provost
46 University Drive
Augusta, ME 04330

nadel@maine.edu
207.621.3360
http://www.uma.maine.edu/

DESTINATION	HOST INSTITUTION	PRGM SEASON	PRGM TYPE	INTERMEDIARY	HOUSING
Germany | [City Unspecified]	Harz University of Applied Studies and Research	n/a	Self	n/a	n/a

University of Maine at Farmington

Allen Berger
Provost
Office of International and Exchange Programs
252 Main Street
Farmington, ME 04938

exchangeprograms@umf.maine.edu
207.778.7122
http://international.umf.maine.edu/

DESTINATION	HOST INSTITUTION	PRGM SEASON	PRGM TYPE	INTERMEDIARY	HOUSING
(Multiple choices) | (Multiple choices)	Multiple institutional choices	n/a	Intermed	Academic Programs International	n/a
(Multiple choices) | (Multiple choices)	Multiple institutional choices	n/a	Intermed	Council on International Educational Exchange (CIEE)	n/a
(Multiple choices) | (Multiple choices)	Multiple institutional choices	n/a	Consrtm	University Studies Abroad Consortium	n/a
(Multiple choices) | (Multiple choices)	Multiple institutional choices	n/a	Consrtm	College Consortium International Studies	n/a
(Multiple choices) | (Multiple choices)	Multiple institutional choices	n/a	Intermed	Institute for Study Abroad	n/a
(Multiple choices) | (Multiple choices)	Multiple institutional choices	n/a	Intermed	American Institute for Foreign Study	n/a
(Multiple choices) | (Multiple choices)	Multiple institutional choices	n/a	Intermed	Global Learning Semesters	n/a

Maine

DESTINATION	HOST INSTITUTION	PRGM SEASON	PRGM TYPE	INTERMEDIARY	HOUSING
(Multiple choices) | (Multiple choices)	Multiple institutional choices	n/a	Intermed	Center for International Studies	n/a
(Multiple choices) | (Multiple choices)	Multiple institutional choices	n/a	Intermed	AustraLearn	n/a
(Multiple choices) | (Multiple choices)	Multiple institutional choices	n/a	Intermed	IES Abroad	n/a
(Multiple choices) | (Multiple choices)	SIT Study Abroad	n/a	Intermed	SIT Study Abroad	n/a
China | Beijing	Beijing University of Technology	n/a	Bilat	n/a	n/a

University of Maine at Fort Kent

Scott Voisine
Dean of Students
Student Affairs Office
23 University Drive
Fort Kent, ME 04743

voisine@maine.edu
207.834.7513
http://www.umfk.maine.edu/studserv/studyabroad/

DESTINATION	HOST INSTITUTION	PRGM SEASON	PRGM TYPE	INTERMEDIARY	HOUSING
Canada | (Multiple choices)	Multiple institutional choices	n/a	Bilat	New England Board of Higher Education	n/a
Canada | Edmunston	Universite de Moncton, Campus d'Edmunston	n/a	Self	SIT Study Abroad	n/a
Canada | Quebec City (Quebec)	University of Laval	Sum	Self	n/a	n/a
France | Angers	University of Angers	Fall Spr YrRound	Consrtm	University of Maine Partnership Maine France Quebec	n/a
France | Brittany	University of Western Brittany	Fall Spr YrRound	Consrtm	University of Maine Partnership Maine France Quebec	n/a
France | Le Mans	Le Mans Fine Arts School	n/a	Consrtm	University of Maine Partnership Maine France Quebec	n/a
France | Le Mans	University of Le Mans	Fall Spr	USColl	University of Maine at Farmington	n/a
France | Le Mans	University of Maine at Le Mans	Fall Spr YrRound	Consrtm	University of Maine Partnership Maine France Quebec	n/a
France | Nantes	The Teacher Formation Institute for the Loire Region	n/a	Consrtm	University of Maine Partnership Maine France Quebec	n/a
France | Nantes	University of Nantes	Fall Spr YrRound	Consrtm	University of Maine Partnership Maine France Quebec	n/a
France | Rennes	Multiple institutional choices	Fall Spr YrRound	Intermed	Council on International Education Exchange (CIEE)	n/a
France | Villeneuve d'Ascq	The Teacher Formation Institute for the Lille Region	n/a	Consrtm	University of Maine Partnership Maine France Quebec	n/a
France | Villeneuve d'Ascq	Theories-Didactique de la Lecture-Ecriture (THEODILE)	n/a	Consrtm	University of Maine Partnership Maine France Quebec	n/a

Maine

DESTINATION	HOST INSTITUTION	PRGM SEASON	PRGM TYPE	INTERMEDIARY	HOUSING

University of Maine at Presque Isle

Michael Sonntag
Vice President for Academic Affairs
181 Main Street
Presque Isle, ME 04769

michael.sonntag@umpi.edu
207.768.9518
http://www.umpi.edu/programs/cas/french/study-abroad

DESTINATION	HOST INSTITUTION	PRGM SEASON	PRGM TYPE	INTERMEDIARY	HOUSING
(Multiple choices)	(Multiple choices)	CELL Program	n/a	Intermed	CELL Program	n/a
(Multiple choices)	(Multiple choices)	Multiple institutional choices	n/a	Consrtm	College Consortium for International Studies	n/a
Canada	Quebec City (Quebec)	University of Laval	Sum	Self	University of Maine Partnership Maine France Quebec	n/a
France	Angers	University of Angers	Fall Spr YrRound	Consrtm	University of Maine Partnership Maine France Quebec	n/a
France	Brittany	University of Western Brittany	Fall Spr YrRound	Consrtm	University of Maine Partnership Maine France Quebec	n/a
France	Le Mans	Theories-Dicactique de la Lecture-Escriture	Fall Spr YrRound	Consrtm	University of Maine Partnership Maine France Quebec	n/a
France	Le Mans	University of Le Mans	Fall Spr YrRound	Consrtm	University of Maine Partnership Maine France Quebec	n/a
France	Le Mans	University of Maine at Le Mans	Fall Spr YrRound	Consrtm	University of Maine Partnership Maine France Quebec	n/a
France	Nantes	The Teacher Formation Institute for the Loire Region	Fall Spr YrRound	Consrtm	University of Maine Partnership Maine France Quebec	n/a
France	Nantes	University of Nantes	Fall Spr YrRound	Consrtm	University of Maine Partnership Maine France Quebec	n/a
France	Villeneuve d'Ascq	The Teacher Formation Institute for the Lille Region	Fall Spr YrRound	Consrtm	University of Maine Partnership Maine France Quebec	n/a

University of New England

Trisha Mason
Director
11 Hills Beach Road
Biddeford, ME 04005

tmason2@une.edu
207.602.2051
http://www.une.edu/international/abroad/

DESTINATION	HOST INSTITUTION	PRGM SEASON	PRGM TYPE	INTERMEDIARY	HOUSING
(Multiple choices)	(Multiple choices)	n/a	n/a	Intermed	ProWorld	n/a
(Multiple choices)	(Multiple choices)	n/a	n/a	Intermed	Experiential Learning International	n/a

© 2011 — Updates? Want to be in the next edition? Visit **www.mysecondcampus.com**

Maine

DESTINATION	HOST INSTITUTION	PRGM SEASON	PRGM TYPE	INTERMEDIARY	HOUSING
(Multiple choices)	(Multiple choices)	n/a	n/a	Intermed	Child Family Health International	n/a
(Multiple choices)	(Multiple choices)	Ausburg College	n/a	USColl	Ausburg College	n/a
(Multiple choices)	(Multiple choices)	Multiple institutional choices	n/a	Intermed	School for Field Studies	n/a
(Multiple choices)	(Multiple choices)	Multiple institutional choices	n/a	Intermed	Academic Programs International	n/a
(Multiple choices)	(Multiple choices)	Multiple institutional choices	n/a	Intermed	Operation Wallacea	n/a
(Multiple choices)	(Multiple choices)	Multiple institutional choices	n/a	Intermed	AustraLearn	n/a
(Multiple choices)	(Multiple choices)	Multiple institutional choices	n/a	Intermed	Lexia	n/a
(Multiple choices)	(Multiple choices)	SIT Study Abroad	n/a	Intermed	SIT Study Abroad	n/a
Brazil	Natal	Federal University of Rio Grandedo Norte	Sum	Self	n/a	n/a
Kenya	[City Unspecified]	University of Nairobi	Spr	Self	n/a	n/a
Mexico	Cuernavaca	Cemanahuac Educational Community	n/a	Intermed	Cemanahuac Educational Community	n/a
Mexico	Cuernavaca	Tecnologico de Monterrey	Spr	Self	n/a	n/a
Republic of Ireland	[City Unspecified]	University of New England	Spr	Self	n/a	n/a
United States	Woods Hole (MA)	Sea Semester	n/a	Intermed	Sea Semester	n/a

University of Southern Maine

Kimbery B. Sinclair
Associate Director of the Office of International Programs
P. O. Box 9300
101 Payson Smith Hall
Portland, ME 04104

ksinc@usm.maine.edu
207.780.4959
http://usm.maine.edu/international/index.htm

DESTINATION	HOST INSTITUTION	PRGM SEASON	PRGM TYPE	INTERMEDIARY	HOUSING
(Multiple choices)	(Multiple choices)	Augsburg College	Fall Spr YrRound	Intermed	Augsburg College	n/a
(Multiple choices)	(Multiple choices)	Multiple institutional choices	n/a	Intermed	Global Learning Semesters	n/a
(Multiple choices)	(Multiple choices)	Multiple institutional choices	n/a	Intermed	AustraLearn	n/a
(Multiple choices)	(Multiple choices)	Multiple institutional choices	n/a	Intermed	EuroLearn	n/a
(Multiple choices)	(Multiple choices)	Multiple institutional choices	n/a	Intermed	Augsburg College	n/a
(Multiple choices)	(Multiple choices)	Multiple institutional choices	n/a	Intermed	Global Learning Semesters	n/a
(Multiple choices)	(Multiple choices)	Multiple institutional choices	n/a	Intermed	The Scholar Ship	n/a

Maine

DESTINATION	HOST INSTITUTION	PRGM SEASON	PRGM TYPE	INTERMEDIARY	HOUSING
(Multiple choices) | (Multiple choices)	Multiple institutional choices	n/a	Intermed	International Studies Abroad	n/a
(Multiple choices) | (Multiple choices)	Multiple institutional choices	n/a	Intermed	American Institute for Foreign Study	n/a
(Multiple choices) | (Multiple choices)	Multiple institutional choices	n/a	Intermed	ProWorld	n/a
(Multiple choices) | (Multiple choices)	Multiple institutional choices	n/a	Intermed	Intern Abroad	n/a
(Multiple choices) | (Multiple choices)	Multiple institutional choices	n/a	Intermed	International Studies Abroad	n/a
(Multiple choices) | (Multiple choices)	Multiple institutional choices	n/a	Intermed	College Consortium of International Studies	n/a
(Multiple choices) | (Multiple choices)	Multiple institutional choices	n/a	Intermed	Center for International Studies	n/a
(Multiple choices) | (Multiple choices)	Multiple institutional choices	n/a	Intermed	Academic Programs International	n/a
(Multiple choices) | (Multiple choices)	Multiple institutional choices	n/a	Intermed	Institute for Study Abroad	n/a
(Multiple choices) | (Multiple choices)	Multiple institutional choices	n/a	Intermed	AsiaLearn	n/a
(Multiple choices) | (Multiple choices)	Multiple institutional choices	Sum	USColl	State University of New York College at Cortland	n/a
(Multiple choices) | (Multiple choices)	Multiple institutional choices	n/a	Intermed	BUNAC	n/a
Argentina | (Multiple choices)	Multiple institutional choices	Sum Fall Spr	Intermed	Institute for Study Abroad	HostFam
Argentina | Buenos Aires	IES Abroad Buenos Aires Center	Fall Spr YrRound	Intermed	IES Abroad	HostFam
Argentina | Buenos Aires	Multiple institutional choices	Fall Spr YrRound	Intermed	Council on International Education Exchange (CIEE)	n/a
Argentina | Buenos Aires	Pontificia Universidad Catolica	Fall Spr YrRound	Intermed	American Institute for Foreign Study	HostFam
Argentina | Buenos Aires	Universidad de Belgrano	Sum Fall Spr YrRound	Intermed	Global Learning Semesters	HostFam PrivApt
Argentina | Buenos Aires	Universidad de Belgrano	Sum Fall Spr YrRound	Intermed	International Studies Abroad	n/a
Argentina | Buenos Aires	Universidad de Belgrano	Sum Fall Spr YrRound	Intermed	Academic Programs International	n/a
Argentina | Buenos Aires	Universidad Torcuato Di Tella	Fall Spr YrRound	Intermed	Academic Program International	HostFam CollRes
Argentina | Cordoba	Universidad Blas Pascal	Fall Spr YrRound	Intermed	Center for Cross Cultural Studies	n/a
Australia | (Multiple choices)	Multiple institutional choices	n/a	Intermed	AustraLearn	n/a
Australia | (Multiple choices)	Multiple institutional choices	n/a	Intermed	College Consortium of International	n/a
Australia | (Multiple choices)	Multiple institutional choices	n/a	Intermed	Council on International Education Exchange (CIEE)	n/a
Australia | (Multiple choices)	Multiple institutional choices	n/a	Intermed	Institute for Study Abroad	n/a
Australia | (Multiple choices)	Multiple institutional choices	n/a	Intermed	Study Australia	n/a

© 2011 — Updates? Want to be in the next edition? Visit **www.mysecondcampus.com**

Maine

DESTINATION	HOST INSTITUTION	PRGM SEASON	PRGM TYPE	INTERMEDIARY	HOUSING
Austria | Salzburg	Salzburg College	Sum Fall Spr YrRound	Intermed	College Consortium of International Studies	HostFam
Austria | Salzburg	University of Salzburg	Fall Spr YrRound	USColl	University of Maine Partnership Maine France Quebec	n/a
Austria | Salzburg	University of Salzburg	Sum Fall Spr YrRound	Intermed	American Institute for Foreign Study	HostFam CollRes
Austria | Vienna	University of Vienna	Sum Fall Spr YrRound	Intermed	IES Abroad	CollRes PrivApt
Belgium | Brussels	Universite Libre de Bruxelles	Fall Spr YrRound	Intermed	Council on International Education Exchange (CIEE)	PrivApt
Belgium | Brussels	University of Southern Maine	Sum	Self	n/a	n/a
	Costs: Sum Costs: T&F: n/a, R&B: n/a, Ttl: $3,256				
Belgium | Brussels	Vesalius College	Sum Fall Spr YrRound	Intermed	Council on International Education Exchange (CIEE)	HostFam PrivApt
Belgium | Brussels	Vesalius College	Sum Fall Spr YrRound	Intermed	International Studies Abroad	HostFam PrivApt
Belize | Belize City and Belmopan	University of Southern Maine	Win	Self	n/a	n/a
	Costs: Win Costs: T&F: n/a, R&B: n/a, Ttl: $3,984				
Belize | San Ignacio	Galen University	Fall Spr YrRound	Intermed	College Consortium of International Studies	Other
Belize | San Ignacio	Galen University	Fall Spr YrRound	Intermed	Global Learning Semesters	Other
Belize | San Ignacio	ProWorld	Sum Fall Spr	Intermed	ProWorld	HostFam
Botswana | Gaborone	SIT Study Abroad	Fall Spr	Intermed	SIT Study Abroad	HostFam CollRes
Botswana | Gaborone	University of Botswana	Sum	Intermed	Council on International Education Exchange (CIEE)	n/a
Botswana | Gaborone	University of Botswana	Sum Fall Spr YrRound	Intermed	Council on International Education Exchange (CIEE)	HostFam CollRes
Brazil | Sao Paulo	Escola de Administracao de Empresas de Sao Paulo da Fundacao Getulio Vargas	Fall Spr YrRound	Intermed	Council on International Education Exchange (CIEE)	HostFam
Brazil | Sao Paulo	Pontificia Universidad Catolica de Sao Paulo	Fall Spr YrRound	Intermed	Council on International Education Exchange (CIEE)	HostFam
Bulgaria | Veliko Turnovo	University of Veliko Turnovo	Sum Fall Spr	Intermed	College Consortium of International Studies	CollRes PrivApt
Cameroon | Yaounde	SIT Study Abroad	Fall Spr	Intermed	SIT Study Abroad	HostFam CollRes
Canada | (Multiple choices)	Multiple institutional choices	n/a	Bilat	University of Maine Partnership Maine France Quebec	n/a
Canada | Abitibi-Temiscamingue (Quebec)	Universite du Quebec en Abitibi-Temiscamingue	n/a	Bilat	n/a	n/a
Canada | Antigonish (Nova Scotia)	Saint Francis Xavier University	n/a	Bilat	n/a	n/a
Canada | Chicoutimi (Quebec)	Universite du Quebec a Chicoutimi	n/a	Bilat	n/a	n/a
Canada | Church Point (Nova Scotia)	Universite Sainte Anne	n/a	Bilat	n/a	n/a
Canada | Fredericton or Saint John (Nova Scotia)	University of New Brunswick School of Law	n/a	Bilat	n/a	n/a

Maine

DESTINATION	HOST INSTITUTION	PRGM SEASON	PRGM TYPE	INTERMEDIARY	HOUSING
Canada | Halifax (Nova Scotia)	Dalhousie School of Law	n/a	Bilat	n/a	n/a
Canada | Halifax (Nova Scotia)	Dalhousie University	n/a	Bilat	n/a	n/a
Canada | Halifax (Nova Scotia)	Mount St. Vincent University	n/a	Bilat	n/a	n/a
Canada | Halifax (Nova Scotia)	Nova Scotia College of Art and Design	n/a	Bilat	n/a	n/a
Canada | Halifax (Nova Scotia)	St. Mary's University	n/a	Bilat	n/a	n/a
Canada | Halifax (Nova Scotia)	St. Mary's University	n/a	Bilat	n/a	n/a
Canada | Halifax (Nova Scotia)	University of King's College	n/a	Bilat	n/a	n/a
Canada | Montreal (Quebec)	Concordia University	n/a	Bilat	n/a	n/a
Canada | Montreal (Quebec)	Ecole des Hautes Etudes Commercials	n/a	Bilat	n/a	n/a
Canada | Montreal (Quebec)	Ecole du technologie superieure	n/a	Bilat	n/a	n/a
Canada | Montreal (Quebec)	Ecole Polytechnique	n/a	Bilat	n/a	n/a
Canada | Montreal (Quebec)	Universite du Quebec a Montreal	n/a	Bilat	n/a	n/a
Canada | Montreal (Quebec)	Universite Montreal	n/a	Bilat	n/a	n/a
Canada | Outaouais (Quebec)	Universite du Quebec en Outaouais	n/a	Bilat	n/a	n/a
Canada | Quebec City (Quebec)	Ecole nationale d'administration publique	n/a	Bilat	n/a	n/a
Canada | Quebec City (Quebec)	Institut national de la recherche scientifique	n/a	Bilat	n/a	n/a
Canada | Quebec City (Quebec)	Tele-universite	n/a	Bilat	n/a	n/a
Canada | Quebec City (Quebec)	Universite Laval	n/a	Bilat	n/a	n/a
Canada | Rimouski (Quebec)	Universite du Quebec a Rimouski	n/a	Bilat	n/a	n/a
Canada | Sherbrooke (Quebec)	Bishop's University	n/a	Bilat	n/a	n/a
Canada | Sydney (Nova Scotia)	University College of Cape Breton	n/a	Bilat	n/a	n/a
Canada | Trois Rivieres (Quebec)	Universite du Quebec a Trois-Rivieres	n/a	Bilat	n/a	n/a
Canada | Truro (Nova Scotia)	Nova Scotia Agricultural College	n/a	Bilat	n/a	n/a
Canada | Truro (Nova Scotia)	Nova Scotia Teachers College	n/a	Bilat	n/a	n/a
Canada | Wolfville (Nova Scotia)	Acadia University	n/a	Bilat	n/a	n/a
Chile | Valparaiso and Vina del Mar	Pontifical Catholic University of Valparaiso or Universidad Adolfo Ibanez	Sum Fall Spr YrRound	Intermed	International Studies Abroad	HostFam CollRes
Chile | Santiago	IES Abroad Santiago Center	Sum Fall Spr YrRound	Intermed	IES Abroad	n/a
Chile | Santiago	Multiple institutional choices	Fall Spr YrRound	Intermed	Institute for Study Abroad	HostFam
Chile | Santiago	Pontificia Universidad Catolica de Chile or Universidad de Santiago	Fall Spr YrRound	Intermed	Council on International Education Exchange (CIEE)	HostFam
Chile | Valparaiso	Multiple institutional choices	Fall Spr YrRound	Intermed	Institute for Study Abroad, Butler University	HostFam
China | (Multiple choices)	Multiple institutional choices	Sum Fall Spr YrRound	Intermed	Alliance for Global Education	n/a

© 2011 — Updates? Want to be in the next edition? Visit **www.mysecondcampus.com**

Maine

DESTINATION	HOST INSTITUTION	PRGM SEASON	PRGM TYPE	INTERMEDIARY	HOUSING
China	(Multiple choices)	Multiple institutional choices	Sum Fall Spr YrRound	Intermed	CET Academic Programs	n/a
China	Beijing	IES Abroad Beijing Center	Sum Fall Spr YrRound	Intermed	IES Abroad	CollRes
China	Beijing	Peking University	n/a	Intermed	Global Learning Semesters	CollRes PrivApt
China	Beijing	University of International Business and Economics	Sum Fall Spr	Intermed	CIS Abroad	HostFam CollRes
China	Beijing	University of International Business Economics or Tsinghua University	Fall Spr YrRound	Intermed	Education Abroad Network	n/a
China	Chengdu	Sichuan University	Fall Spr YrRound	Intermed	AsiaLearn	HostFam CollRes
China	Chengdu	Southwest University for Nationalities	Fall Spr	Intermed	University Studies Abroad Consortium	PrivApt
China	Hong Kong	University of Hong Kong	Sum Fall Spr	Intermed	AsiaLearn	HostFam CollRes
China	Nanjing	Nanjing University	Fall Spr	Intermed	Council on International Education Exchange (CIEE)	n/a
China	Nanjing	Nanjing University	Sum Fall Spr YrRound	Intermed	College Consortium of International Studies	CollRes
China	Nanjing	Nanjing University	Sum Fall Spr YrRound	Intermed	American Institute for Foreign Study	CollRes
China	Shanghai	Fudan University	Sum Fall Spr YrRound	Intermed	Lexia	CollRes
China	Shanghai	Fudan University	Fall Spr YrRound	Intermed	Education Abroad Network	n/a
China	Shanghai	Multiple institutional choices	Sum Fall Spr YrRound	Intermed	IES Abroad	CollRes
Costa Rica	(Multiple choices)	Multiple institutional choices	Fall Spr YrRound	Intermed	Institute for Study Abroad	HostFam
Costa Rica	Heredia	Universidad Latina	Sum Fall Spr	Intermed	International Studies Abroad	HostFam
Costa Rica	Monteverde	CIEE Study Center in Monteverde	Fall Spr YrRound	Intermed	Council on International Education Exchange (CIEE)	n/a
Costa Rica	San Isidro de Penas Blancas	Veritas University	Fall Spr	Intermed	International Studies Abroad	CollRes
Costa Rica	San Joaquin de Flores	Instituto San Joaquin de Flores	Sum Fall Spr YrRound	Intermed	Academic Programs International	HostFam
Costa Rica	San Jose	Veritas University or Latin American University of Science and Technology	Sum Fall Spr	Intermed	College Consortium of International Studies	HostFam
Costa Rica	San Jose	Veritas University or Latin American University of Science and Technology	Sum Fall Spr YrRound	Intermed	International Studies Abroad	HostFam
Cyprus	Nicosia	University of Nicosia	Fall Spr YrRound	Intermed	Global Learning Semesters	PrivApt
Czech Republic	Prague	Anglo-American University	Sum Fall Spr	Intermed	College Consortium of International Studies	PrivApt
Czech Republic	Prague	Charles University	Sum Fall Spr YrRound	Intermed	American Institute for Foreign Study	CollRes PrivApt
Czech Republic	Prague	Charles University	Fall Spr YrRound	Intermed	Lexia	HostFam CollRes
Czech Republic	Prague	Charles University	Fall Spr YrRound	Intermed	International Studies Abroad	PrivApt
Czech Republic	Prague	Charles University	Fall Spr YrRound	Intermed	Council on International Education Exchange (CIEE)	HostFam CollRes

Maine

DESTINATION	HOST INSTITUTION	PRGM SEASON	PRGM TYPE	INTERMEDIARY	HOUSING
Czech Republic | Prague	Prague Film and Television School of the Academy of the Performing Arts	Fall Spr	Intermed	Council on International Education Exchange (CIEE)	PrivApt
Denmark | Copenhagen	Copenhagen School of Business	Sum Fall Spr YrRound	Intermed	University Studies Abroad Consortium	CollRes PrivApt
Denmark | Copenhagen	Danish Institute for Study Abroad (DIS)	Sum Fall Spr YrRound	Intermed	Danish Institute for Study Abroad (DIS)	n/a
Denmark | Copenhagen	Danish Institute for Study Abroad (DIS)	Sum Fall Spr	Intermed	College Consortium of International Studies	HostFam CollRes
Dominican Republic | (Multiple)	University of Southern Maine	Win	Self	n/a	n/a
	Costs: Win Costs: T&F: n/a, R&B: n/a, Ttl: $2,151				
Dominican Republic | Lajas	University of Southern Maine	Sum	Self	n/a	n/a
	Costs: Sum Costs: T&F: n/a, R&B: n/a, Ttl: $2,921				
Dominican Republic | Santiago	Pontificia Universidad Catolica Madre y Maestra	Sum Fall Spr YrRound	Intermed	International Studies Abroad	HostFam
Dominican Republic | Santiago	Pontificia Universidad Catolica Madre y Maestra	Fall Spr YrRound	Intermed	Council on International Education Exchange (CIEE)	n/a
Dominican Republic | Santo Domingo	Pontificia Universidad Catolica Madre y Maestra	n/a	Intermed	College Consortium of International Studies	HostFam
Ecuador | Guayaquil	Universidad Catolica de Santiago de Guayaquil	Fall Spr YrRound	Intermed	College Consortium of International Studies	n/a
Ecuador | Quito	IES Abroad Quito Center	Fall Spr YrRound	Intermed	IES Abroad	n/a
Egypt | Cairo	American University in Cairo	Fall Spr YrRound	Dir	n/a	CollRes
Egypt | Cairo or Alexandria	Multiple institutional choices	Fall Spr YrRound	Intermed	Institute for Study Abroad, Butler University	n/a
England | (Multiple choices)	Multiple institutional choices	Sum Fall Spr YrRound	Intermed	Institute for Study Abroad	n/a
England | (Multiple choices)	Multiple institutional choices	Sum Fall Spr YrRound	Intermed	Arcadia University	n/a
England | Buckingham	University of Buckingham School of Law	n/a	Bilat	n/a	n/a
England | Keele	Keele University	Spr YrRound	Dir	n/a	n/a
England | Keele	Keele University	n/a	Bilat	n/a	n/a
England | Leeds	University of Leeds	Sum Fall Spr YrRound	Intermed	Academic Programs International	n/a
England | London	Boston University	n/a	USColl	Boston University	n/a
England | London	CAPA International Education	Sum Fall Spr YrRound	Intermed	CAPA International Education	n/a
England | London	Kingston University	n/a	Dir	n/a	n/a
England | London	Kingston University	Sum Fall Spr YrRound	Dir	n/a	n/a
England | London	Multiple institutional choices	Sum Fall Spr YrRound	Intermed	International Studies Abroad	n/a
England | London	Multiple institutional choices	Sum Fall Spr YrRound	Intermed	Academic Programs International	n/a
England | London	University of Westmister	Sum Fall Spr	Dir	n/a	n/a

© 2011 — Updates? Want to be in the next edition? Visit **www.mysecondcampus.com**

Maine

DESTINATION	HOST INSTITUTION	PRGM SEASON	PRGM TYPE	INTERMEDIARY	HOUSING
England | Reading	University of Reading	Sum Fall Spr YrRound	Intermed	International Studies Abroad	n/a
England | Winchester	University of Winchester	Fall Spr	Bilat	n/a	n/a
England | Winchester	Winchester University	Fall Spr YrRound	Dir	n/a	n/a
England | Wroxton	University of Southern Maine	Win	Self	n/a	n/a
	Costs: Win Costs: T&F: n/a, R&B: n/a, Ttl: $4,195				
France | (Multiple choices)	Multiple institutional choices	Fall Spr	Self	University of Maine Partnership Maine France Quebec	n/a
France | (Multiple choices)	Multiple institutional choices	n/a	Bilat	University of Maine Partnership Maine France Quebec	n/a
France | Arles	IES Abroad Arles Center	Sum Fall Spr YrRound	Intermed	IES Abroad	HostFam PrivApt
France | Brest	University of Southern Maine	Sum	Self	n/a	n/a
	Costs: Sum Costs: T&F: n/a, R&B: n/a, Ttl: $3,634				
France | Cannes	College International de Cannes	Sum Fall Spr YrRound	Intermed	American Institute for Foreign Study	n/a
France | Cergy-Pointoise	Universite of Cergy-Pointoise	n/a	Bilat	n/a	n/a
France | Grenoble	Centre Universitaire d'Etudes Francaises (CUEF) at Universite Stendhal – Grenoble III	Sum Fall Spr YrRound	Intermed	Academic Programs International	n/a
France | Grenoble	Grenoble School of Management or University of Grenoble	Sum Fall Spr YrRound	Intermed	American Institute for Foreign Study	n/a
France | LeMans	Universite du Maine at LeMans	n/a	Bilat	n/a	n/a
France | Nantes	IES Abroad Nantes Center	Sum Fall Spr YrRound	Intermed	IES Abroad	HostFam PrivApt
France | Paris	IES Abroad Paris French Studies Center	Sum Fall Spr YrRound	Intermed	IES Abroad	HostFam CollRes PrivApt
France | Paris	Multiple institutional choices	Sum Fall Spr YrRound	Intermed	Academic Programs International	n/a
France | Paris	Multiple institutional choices	Sum Fall Spr YrRound	Intermed	International Studies Abroad	n/a
France | Paris	Multiple institutional choices	Sum Fall Spr	Intermed	Global Learning Semesters	HostFam CollRes
France | Paris	Paris Center for Critical Studies	Fall Spr YrRound	Intermed	Council on International Education Exchange (CIEE)	n/a
France | Pau	University of Pau	Sum Fall Spr	Consrtm	University Studies Abroad Consortium	HostFam CollRes
Germany | Berlin	Atelierhaus Mengerzeile	Sum Fall Spr YrRound	Intermed	Lexia	HostFam CollRes
Germany | Berlin	IES Abroad Berlin Center	Sum Fall Spr YrRound	Intermed	IES Abroad	HostFam CollRes
Germany | Heidelberg	Schiller University	Sum Fall Spr YrRound	Intermed	College Consortium of International Studies	CollRes
Germany | Luneburg	Leuphana University	Fall YrRound	Intermed	University Studies Abroad Consortium	HostFam CollRes PrivApt

Maine

DESTINATION	HOST INSTITUTION	PRGM SEASON	PRGM TYPE	INTERMEDIARY	HOUSING
Germany | Marburg	Phillips University	Sum Fall Spr YrRound	Intermed	Abroadco Study Abroad	n/a
Germany | Schwabisch Hall	Fachhochschule Schwabisch Hall School of Art & Design	n/a	Bilat	n/a	n/a
Ghana | Accra	Ashesi University	Fall Spr YrRound	Intermed	Council on International Education Exchange (CIEE)	HostFam CollRes
Ghana | Accra	SIT Study Abroad	Sum	Intermed	SIT Study Abroad	HostFam CollRes
Ghana | Accra	University of Accra	Sum	Consrtm	University Studies Abroad Consortium	CollRes
Ghana | Accra	University of Accra	Fall Spr YrRound	Consrtm	University Studies Abroad Consortium	Other
Ghana | Cape Coast	SIT Study Abroad	Fall Spr	n/a	SIT Study Abroad	HostFam CollRes
Ghana | Legon	University of Ghana	Fall Spr YrRound	Intermed	Council on International Education Exchange (CIEE)	HostFam CollRes
Greece | Athens	Arcadia Center for Hellenic, Mediterranean and Balkan Studies	Sum Fall Spr YrRound	USColl	Arcadia University	PrivApt
Greece | Athens	College Year in Athens	Sum Fall Spr YrRound	Intermed	College Year in Athens	n/a
Greece | Mytilene	University of Southern Maine	Sum	Self	n/a	n/a
Costs: Sum Costs: T&F: n/a, R&B: n/a, Ttl: $4,752					
Greece | Thessaloniki	American College of Thessaloniki	Sum Fall Spr YrRound	Intermed	College Consortium of International Studies	n/a
Hungary | Budapest	Corvinus University of Budapest	Sum Fall Spr YrRound	Intermed	Council on International Education Exchange (CIEE)	CollRes
Hungary | Budapest	Corvinus University of Budapest	Fall Spr YrRound	Intermed	Academic Programs International	CollRes
Hungary | Budapest	Eotvos Collegium	Sum Fall Spr YrRound	Intermed	Lexia	CollRes
India | Bangalore	Christ University	Fall Spr YrRound	Intermed	University Studies Abroad Consortium	PrivApt
India | Dehli	IES Abroad	Fall Spr YrRound	Intermed	IES Abroad	HostFam CollRes
India | Hyderabad	University of Hyderabad	Fall Spr YrRound	Intermed	American Institute for Foreign Study	n/a
India | Hyderabad	University of Hyderabad	Fall Spr YrRound	Intermed	Council on International Education Exchange (CIEE)	HostFam CollRes
India | Pune	Fergusson College	Sum Fall Spr	Intermed	Alliance for Global Education	PrivApt
Ireland | (Multiple choices)	Multiple institutional choices	Sum Fall Spr YrRound	Intermed	Institute for Study Abroad	n/a
Ireland | (Multiple choices)	Multiple institutional choices	Sum Fall Spr YrRound	Intermed	Academic Programs International	n/a
Ireland | Belfast	Queen University Belfast	n/a	Dir	n/a	n/a
Ireland | Galway	National University of Ireland	n/a	Dir	n/a	n/a
Ireland | Galway	University College Galway	n/a	Dir	n/a	n/a
Ireland | Limerick	University of Limerick	Sum Fall Spr YrRound	Intermed	College Consortium of International Studies	n/a

© 2011 — Updates? Want to be in the next edition? Visit www.mysecondcampus.com

Maine

DESTINATION	HOST INSTITUTION	PRGM SEASON	PRGM TYPE	INTERMEDIARY	HOUSING
Ireland | Maynooth	National University of Ireland in Maynooth	Sum Fall Spr YrRound	Intermed	College Consortium of International Studies	n/a
Italy | (Multiple choices)	IES Abroad Center	Sum Fall Spr YrRound	Intermed	IES Abroad	n/a
Italy | (Multiple choices)	Multiple institutional choices	Sum Fall Spr YrRound	Intermed	Academic Programs International	n/a
Italy | (Multiple choices)	Multiple institutional choices	Sum Fall Spr YrRound	Intermed	Center for International Studies	n/a
Italy | (Multiple choices)	Multiple institutional choices	Sum Fall Spr YrRound	Intermed	International Studies Abroad	n/a
Italy | (Multiple choices)	Multiple institutional choices	Sum Fall Spr YrRound	Intermed	College Consortium of International Studies	n/a
Italy | (Multiple choices)	Multiple institutional choices	Sum Fall Spr YrRound	USColl	Arcadia University	n/a
Italy | Florence	American Institute for Foreign Study	Sum Fall Spr YrRound	Intermed	American Institute for Foreign Study	HostFam CollRes
Italy | Florence	CAPA International Education	Sum Fall Spr YrRound	Intermed	CAPA International Education	HostFam CollRes
Italy | Florence	NYU in Florence	Fall Spr YrRound	USColl	New York University	n/a
Italy | Florence	Santa Reparata	Sum Fall Spr YrRound	Intermed	Abroadco Study Abroad	CollRes
Italy | Florence	Studio Art Center International	Sum Fall Spr YrRound	Intermed	Studio Art Center International	PrivApt
Italy | Milan	Universita Cattolica del Sacro Cuore	Fall Spr YrRound	Intermed	EuroLearn	n/a
Italy | Rome	American Institute for Foreign Study	Sum Fall Spr YrRound	Intermed	American Institute for Foreign Study	HostFam CollRes
Italy | Rome	John Cabot University or Pantheon Center	Sum Fall Spr YrRound	Intermed	Abroadco Study Abroad	CollRes
Italy | Torino	University of Torino	Fall Spr YrRound	Intermed	University Studies Abroad Consortium	n/a
Italy | Viterbo	Universita degli Studi della Tuscia	Fall Spr YrRound	Intermed	University Studies Abroad Consortium	n/a
Japan | Beppu	Ritsumeikan Asia Pacific University	Sum Fall Spr	Intermed	AsiaLearn	CollRes
Japan | Hiroshima	Hiroshima University	Sum Fall Spr YrRound	Intermed	University Studies Abroad Consortium	HostFam
Japan | Nagoya	Nanzan University	Sum Fall Spr YrRound	Intermed	IES Abroad	HostFam CollRes
Japan | Osaka	Kwansei Gakuin University	Sum Fall Spr YrRound	Intermed	University Studies Abroad Consortium	HostFam
Japan | Tokyo	IES Abroad Tokyo Center	Sum Fall Spr YrRound	Intermed	IES Abroad	HostFam CollRes
Japan | Tokyo	KCP International Language Institute	Fall Spr	Intermed	College Consortium of International Studies	HostFam
Japan | Tokyo	Sophia University	Fall Spr YrRound	Intermed	Council on International Education Exchange (CIEE)	HostFam CollRes
Jordan | Amman	SIT Study Abroad	Fall Spr YrRound	Intermed	SIT Study Abroad	HostFam

© 2011 — Updates? Want to be in the next edition? Visit www.mysecondcampus.com

Maine

DESTINATION	HOST INSTITUTION	PRGM SEASON	PRGM TYPE	INTERMEDIARY	HOUSING
Jordan | Amman	University of Jordan	Fall Spr YrRound	Intermed	Council on International Education Exchange (CIEE)	n/a
Latvia | Riga	Latvian Academy of Art	n/a	Bilat	n/a	n/a
Latvia | Riga	Latvian Academy of Art	n/a	Dir	n/a	Other
Madagascar | Antananarivo	SIT Study Abroad	Fall Spr	Intermed	SIT Study Abroad	HostFam CollRes
Madagascar | Antananarivo	SIT Study Abroad	Sum	Intermed	SIT Study Abroad	HostFam CollRes
Madagascar | Fort Dauphin	SIT Study Abroad	Fall Spr	Intermed	SIT Study Abroad	HostFam CollRes
Malaysia | Kuching Sarawak	Swinburne University of Technology	Sum Fall Spr	Intermed	AsiaLearn	CollRes
Mali | Bamako	SIT Study Abroad	Fall Spr	Intermed	SIT Study Abroad	HostFam CollRes
Malta | Msida	University of Malta	Fall Spr YrRound	Intermed	University Studies Abroad Consortium	CollRes
Mexico | Cuernavaca	Augsburg College	Sum Fall Spr YrRound	USColl	Augsburg College	HostFam
Mexico | Guadalajara	ITESO; Universidad Jesuita de Guadalajara	Sum Fall Spr YrRound	Intermed	International Studies Abroad	n/a
Mexico | Guadalajara	Universidad Autonoma de Guadalajara	Fall Spr YrRound	Consrtm	College Consortium of International Studies	HostFam
Mexico | Guadalajara	Universidad Autonoma de Guadalajara	Fall Spr YrRound	Intermed	Global Learning Semesters	HostFam PrivApt
Mexico | Guanajuato	Universidad de Guanajuato	Fall Spr YrRound	Intermed	Council on International Education Exchange (CIEE)	n/a
Mexico | Guanajuato	Universidad de Guanajuato	Sum Fall Spr YrRound	Intermed	International Studies Abroad	n/a
Mexico | Merida	Universidad Autonoma de Yucatan	Fall Spr YrRound	Intermed	Institute for Study Abroad	HostFam
Mexico | Oaxaca	ProWorld	Sum Fall Spr YrRound	Intermed	ProWorld	HostFam
Mexico | Oaxaca	Universidad Regional del Sureste	Sum Fall Spr YrRound	Intermed	Academic Programs International	HostFam
Monaco | Monte Carlo	International University of Monaco	Fall Spr YrRound	USColl	Suffolk University	PrivApt
Morocco | Ifrane	Al Akhawayn University	Fall Spr	Intermed	College Consortium of International Studies	HostFam CollRes
Morocco | Meknes	Moulay Ismail University	Sum Fall Spr	Intermed	International Studies Abroad	PrivApt
Morocco | Rabat	Ecole Superieure de Direction et de Gestion	Fall Spr YrRound	Intermed	Council on International Education Exchange (CIEE)	HostFam CollRes
Morocco | Rabat	IES Abroad Rabat Center	n/a	Intermed	IES Abroad	HostFam PrivApt
Namibia | Windhoek	Augsburg College	Fall Spr	Dir	Augsburg College	HostFam CollRes
Namibia | Windhoek	Augsburg College	Sum	Dir	Augsburg College	CollRes
Netherlands | Amsterdam	SIT Study Abroad	n/a	Intermed	SIT Study Abroad	HostFam
Netherlands | Amsterdam	University of Amsterdam	Sum Fall Spr YrRound	Intermed	Council on International Education Exchange (CIEE)	CollRes
Netherlands | Amsterdam	University of Amsterdam	Fall Spr YrRound	Intermed	IES Abroad	PrivApt
Netherlands | Leiden	Leiden University	n/a	Intermed	EuroLearn	PrivApt
Netherlands | Nijmegen	Radboud University	n/a	Intermed	University of Southern Maine	CollRes

© 2011 — Updates? Want to be in the next edition? Visit www.mysecondcampus.com

Maine

DESTINATION	HOST INSTITUTION	PRGM SEASON	PRGM TYPE	INTERMEDIARY	HOUSING
Netherlands | Nijmegen	Radboud University	Fall Spr	Bilat	n/a	n/a
Netherlands | The Hague	Hague University	Fall Spr YrRound	Intermed	University Studies Abroad Consortium	PrivApt
New Zealand | (Multiple choices)	Multiple institutional choices	n/a	Intermed	College Consortium of International Studies	n/a
New Zealand | (Multiple choices)	Multiple institutional choices	n/a	Intermed	Study Australia	n/a
New Zealand | (Multiple choices)	Multiple institutional choices	n/a	Intermed	Institute for Study Abroad	n/a
New Zealand | (Multiple choices)	Multiple institutional choices	n/a	Intermed	Council on International Education Exchange (CIEE)	n/a
New Zealand | (Multiple choices)	Multiple institutional choices	n/a	Intermed	AustraLearn	n/a
Nicaragua | Managua	Universidad Nacional Autonoma de Nicaragua	Fall Spr YrRound	Intermed	Council on International Education Exchange (CIEE)	n/a
Norway | Oslo	University of Oslo	Fall Spr YrRound	Intermed	University Studies Abroad Consortium	CollRes
Oman | Muscat	SIT Study Abroad	n/a	Intermed	SIT Study Abroad	HostFam
Peru | Cusco	Multiple institutional choices	Sum Fall Spr YrRound	Intermed	International Studies Abroad	HostFam
Peru | Lima	Centro Bartolome de las Casas or Universidad San Ignacio de Loyola	Fall Spr YrRound	Intermed	ProWorld	HostFam
Peru | Lima	International Studies Abroad	Sum Fall Spr YrRound	Intermed	International Studies Abroad	HostFam
Peru | Lima	Pontificia Universidad Catolica del Peru	Fall Spr YrRound	Intermed	Institute for Study Abroad, Butler University	HostFam
Peru | Lima	Pontificia Universidad Catolica del Peru	Fall Spr YrRound	Intermed	Council on International Education Exchange (CIEE)	n/a
Poland | Krakow	Jagiellonian University of Krakow	Sum Fall Spr YrRound	Intermed	Academic Programs Insternational	PrivApt
Poland | Krakow	Jagiellonian University of Krakow	Sum Fall Spr YrRound	Intermed	Lexia	CollRes
Poland | Warsaw	Warsaw School of Economics	Fall Spr YrRound	Intermed	Council on International Education Exchange (CIEE)	CollRes
Portugal | Lisbon	Universidade Nova de Lisboa	Sum Fall Spr YrRound	Intermed	Council on International Education Exchange (CIEE)	HostFam CollRes
Puerto Rico | (Multiple choices)	Multiple institutional choices	Fall Spr YrRound	Intermed	National Student Exchange	n/a
Russia | (Multiple choices)	Multiple institutional choices	Sum Fall Spr YrRound	Intermed	American Councils Study Abroad	n/a
Russia | Moscow	Institute of Youth	Sum Fall Spr YrRound	Intermed	College Consortium of International Studies	HostFam
Russia | St. Petersburg	St. Petersburg State Polytechnic University	Sum Fall Spr YrRound	Intermed	American Institute for Foreign Study	HostFam CollRes
Russia | St. Petersburg	St. Petersburg State University:	Sum Fall Spr YrRound	Intermed	Council on International Education Exchange (CIEE)	HostFam
Rwanda & Uganda | Gulu	SIT Study Abroad	Fall Spr	Intermed	SIT Study Abroad	HostFam CollRes
Rwanda & Uganda | Kampala	SIT Study Abroad	Sum	Intermed	SIT Study Abroad	HostFam CollRes
Scotland | (Multiple choices)	Multiple institutional choices	Sum Fall Spr YrRound	Intermed	Institute for Study Abroad	n/a

© 2011 — Updates? Want to be in the next edition? Visit **www.mysecondcampus.com**

Maine

DESTINATION	HOST INSTITUTION	PRGM SEASON	PRGM TYPE	INTERMEDIARY	HOUSING
Scotland | (Multiple choices)	Multiple institutional choices	Sum Fall Spr YrRound	USColl	Arcadia University	n/a
Scotland | St. Andrews	University of St. Andrews	Fall Spr YrRound	Intermed	University Studies Abroad Consortium	n/a
Scotland | Stirling	University of Stirling	Sum Fall Spr YrRound	Intermed	Center for International Studies	n/a
Scotland | Stirling	University of Stirling	Fall Spr YrRound	Intermed	College Consortium of International Studies	n/a
Scotland | Stirling	University of Stirling	Fall Spr YrRound	Intermed	University Studies Abroad Consortium	n/a
Senegal | Dakar	SIT Study Abroad	Sum	Intermed	SIT Study Abroad	HostFam CollRes
Senegal | Dakar	SIT Study Abroad	Fall Spr	Intermed	SIT Study Abroad	HostFam CollRes
Senegal | Dakar	Suffolk University - Dakar Campus	Fall Spr YrRound	Intermed	Council on International Education Exchange (CIEE)	n/a
Singapore | Singapore	James Cook University	Sum Fall Spr YrRound	Intermed	AsiaLearn	PrivApt
South Africa | (Multiple choices)	Multiple institutional choices	Sum Fall Spr YrRound	USColl	Arcadia University	n/a
South Africa | (Multiple)	University of Southern Maine **Costs:** Spr Costs: T&F: n/a, R&B: n/a, Ttl: $5,302	Spr	Self	n/a	n/a
South Africa | Cape Town	University of Cape Town	Fall Spr YrRound	Intermed	Council on International Education Exchange (CIEE)	HostFam CollRes
South Africa | Cape Town	University of Cape Town	Fall Spr YrRound	Intermed	IES Abroad	PrivApt
South Africa | Cape Town	University of Cape Town	Fall Spr	Intermed	Council on International Education Exchange (CIEE)	CollRes
South Africa | Cape Town	University of the Western Cape	Sum	Intermed	Lexia	HostFam
South Africa | Cape Town	University of the Western Cape	Fall Spr YrRound	Intermed	Lexia	HostFam
South Africa | Durban	SIT Study Abroad	Fall Spr YrRound	Intermed	SIT Study Abroad	HostFam
South Africa | Stellenbosch	Univeristy of Stellenbosch	Fall Spr YrRound	Intermed	American Institute for Foreign Study	CollRes
South Africa | Stellenbosch	Univeristy of Stellenbosch	Sum	Intermed	American Institute for Foreign Study	n/a
South Africa | Stellenbosch	University of Stellenbosch	Sum	Intermed	Council on International Education Exchange (CIEE)	CollRes
South Africa | Stellenbosch	University of Stellenbosch	Fall Spr YrRound	Intermed	Council on International Education Exchange (CIEE)	CollRes
South Korea | Seoul	Korea University	Sum Fall Spr YrRound	Intermed	AsiaLearn	CollRes PrivApt
South Korea | Seoul	Sogang University	Fall Spr	Bilat	n/a	n/a
South Korea | Seoul	Sogang University	n/a	USColl	University of Maine Partnership Maine France Quebec	CollRes
Spain | (Multiple choices)	IES Abroad	Sum Fall Spr YrRound	Intermed	IES Abroad	n/a
Spain | (Multiple choices)	Multiple institutional choices	Sum Fall Spr YrRound	Intermed	Academic Programs International	n/a

© 2011 — Updates? Want to be in the next edition? Visit **www.mysecondcampus.com**

Maine

DESTINATION	HOST INSTITUTION	PRGM SEASON	PRGM TYPE	INTERMEDIARY	HOUSING
Spain	(Multiple choices)	Multiple institutional choices	Sum Fall Spr YrRound	Intermed	International Studies Abroad	n/a
Spain	(Multiple choices)	Multiple institutional choices	Sum Fall Spr YrRound	USColl	Arcadia University	n/a
Spain	(Multiple choices)	Multiple institutional choices	Sum Fall Spr YrRound	Intermed	Council on International Education Exchange (CIEE)	n/a
Spain	(Multiple choices)	Multiple institutional choices	Fall Spr YrRound	Intermed	University Studies Abroad Consortium	n/a
Spain	Granada	Universidad de Granada	Sum Fall Spr YrRound	Intermed	Abroadco Study Abroad	HostFam
Spain	Grenada	SIT Study Abroad	Fall Spr	Intermed	SIT Study Abroad	HostFam
Spain	Madrid	Francisco de Vitoria University	Sum Fall Spr YrRound	Intermed	Abroadco Study Abroad	HostFam
Spain	Madrid	NYU in Madrid	Fall Spr YrRound	USColl	New York University	HostFam
Spain	Madrid and Barcelona	Multiple institutional choices	Sum Fall Spr YrRound	Intermed	Center for International Studies	n/a
Spain	Santiago de Compostela	University of Southern Maine	Sum	Self	n/a	n/a
Costs: Sum Costs: T&F: n/a, R&B: n/a, Ttl: $4,782					
Sweden	Stockholm	University of Southern Maine	Sum	Self	n/a	n/a
Costs: Sum Costs: T&F: n/a, R&B: n/a, Ttl: $3,887					
Sweden	Vaxjo	Linneaus University	Sum Fall Spr YrRound	Intermed	University Studies Abroad Consortium	n/a
Switzerland	Geneva and Nyon	SIT Study Abroad	Sum Fall Spr YrRound	Intermed	SIT Study Abroad	CollRes
Switzerland	Lugano	Franklin College	n/a	Intermed	College Consortium of International Studies	n/a
Taiwan	Taipei	National Chengchi University	Fall Spr YrRound	Intermed	Council on International Education Exchange (CIEE)	HostFam PrivApt
Tanzania	Arusha	Arcadia Center for East African Studies	Sum Fall Spr	USColl	Arcadia University	CollRes
Tanzania	Arusha	SIT Study Abroad	Fall Spr	Intermed	SIT Study Abroad	HostFam CollRes
Tanzania	Stone Town (Zanzibar)	SIT Study Abroad	Fall Spr	Intermed	SIT Study Abroad	HostFam CollRes
Thailand	(Multiple)	University of Southern Maine	Sum	Self	n/a	n/a
Costs: Sum Costs: T&F: n/a, R&B: n/a, Ttl: $3,381					
Thailand	Bangkok	Mahidol University	Fall Spr YrRound	Intermed	AsiaLearn	CollRes
Thailand	Bangkok	Mahidol University	Sum Fall Spr YrRound	Intermed	ProWorld	n/a
Thailand	Bangkok	Rangsit University	Fall Spr YrRound	Intermed	University Studies Abroad Consortium	n/a
Thailand	Chiang Mai	Payup University	Sum Fall Spr	Intermed	Lexia	CollRes
Thailand	Chiang Mai	Payup University	n/a	Intermed	Education Abroad Network	n/a
Thailand	Chiang Mai and Nong Khai	Chiang Mai University and First Global Community College	Fall Spr YrRound	Intermed	California Polytechnic State University	PrivApt
Thailand	Khon Kaen	Khon Kaen University	Fall Spr YrRound	Intermed	Council on International Education Exchange (CIEE)	HostFam PrivApt

© 2011 — Updates? Want to be in the next edition? Visit **www.mysecondcampus.com**

Maine

DESTINATION	HOST INSTITUTION	PRGM SEASON	PRGM TYPE	INTERMEDIARY	HOUSING
Turkey	Istanbul	Bogazici University	Sum Fall Spr YrRound	Intermed	Lexia International	HostFam PrivApt
Turkey	Istanbul	Bogazici University	Sum	Intermed	Lexia	n/a
Turkey	Istanbul	Istanbul University	Fall Spr	USColl	Suffolk University	Other
Turkey	Istanbul	Koc University	Fall Spr YrRound	Intermed	Council on International Education Exchange (CIEE)	CollRes
Ukraine	Kharkiv	V.N Karazin Kharkiv National University	n/a	Intermed	n/a	HostFam PrivApt
United Arab Emirates	Dubai	American University in Dubai	Fall Spr YrRound	USColl	State University of New York at Albany	n/a
United States	Washington (DC)	American University Washington College of Law	n/a	USColl	n/a	n/a
Vietnam	Ho Chi Minh City	CET Academic Programs	Sum Fall Spr YrRound	Intermed	CET Academic Programs	n/a
Vietnam	Ho Chi Minh City	Vietnam National University	Fall Spr YrRound	Intermed	Council on International Education Exchange (CIEE)	n/a

© 2011 — Updates? Want to be in the next edition? Visit **www.mysecondcampus.com**

Massachusetts

DESTINATION	HOST INSTITUTION	PRGM SEASON	PRGM TYPE	INTERMEDIARY	HOUSING

American International College

Magdalena Grudzinski-Hall
Director of International Programs
1000 State Street
Springfield, MA 01109

magdalena.hall@aic.edu
413.205.3238
http://www.aic.edu/studyabroad

DESTINATION	HOST INSTITUTION	PRGM SEASON	PRGM TYPE	INTERMEDIARY	HOUSING
[Country Unspecified] | [City Unspecified]	n/a	n/a	n/a	n/a	n/a

Amherst College

Janna Behrens
Director of International Experience
Career Center, College Hall AC 2210
Amherst, MA 01002

jbehrens@amherst.edu
413.542.2265
https://www.amherst.edu/academiclife/study_abroad

DESTINATION	HOST INSTITUTION	PRGM SEASON	PRGM TYPE	INTERMEDIARY	HOUSING
Argentina | Buenos Aires	IES Abroad Buenos Aires Center	Fall Spr YrRound	Intermed	IES Abroad	n/a
Argentina | Buenos Aires	Multiple institutional choices	Fall Spr YrRound	Intermed	Institute for Study Abroad	n/a
Argentina | Mendoza	Universidad Nacional de Cuyo	Fall Spr YrRound	Intermed	Institute for Study Abroad	n/a
Australia | Brisbane	University of Queensland	Fall Spr YrRound	Intermed	Institute for Study Abroad	n/a
Australia | Brisbane	University of Queensland	Fall Spr YrRound	Dir	n/a	n/a
Australia | Brisbane	University of Queensland	Fall Spr YrRound	USColl	Arcadia University	n/a
Australia | Hobart	University of Tasmania	Fall Spr YrRound	Dir	n/a	n/a
Australia | Hobart	University of Tasmania	Fall Spr YrRound	Intermed	Institute for Study Abroad	n/a
Australia | Launceton	University of Tasmania	Fall Spr YrRound	Intermed	Institute for Study Abroad	n/a
Australia | Launceton	University of Tasmania	Fall Spr YrRound	Dir	n/a	n/a
Australia | Melbourne	Monash University	Fall Spr YrRound	Dir	n/a	n/a
Australia | Melbourne	Monash University	Fall Spr YrRound	Intermed	Institute for Study Abroad	n/a
Australia | Melbourne	University of Melbourne	Fall Spr YrRound	Dir	n/a	n/a

© 2011 — Updates? Want to be in the next edition? Visit **www.mysecondcampus.com**

Massachusetts

DESTINATION	HOST INSTITUTION	PRGM SEASON	PRGM TYPE	INTERMEDIARY	HOUSING
Australia | Melbourne	University of Melbourne	Fall Spr YrRound	USColl	Arcadia University	n/a
Australia | Melbourne	University of Melbourne	Fall Spr YrRound	Intermed	Institute for Study Abroad	n/a
Australia | Perth	University of Western Australia	Fall Spr YrRound	Intermed	Institute for Study Abroad	n/a
Australia | Perth	University of Western Australia	Fall Spr YrRound	Dir	n/a	n/a
Australia | Sydney	Macquarie University	Fall Spr YrRound	USColl	Arcadia University	n/a
Australia | Sydney	Macquarie University	Fall Spr YrRound	Dir	n/a	n/a
Australia | Sydney	Macquarie University	Fall Spr YrRound	Intermed	Institute for Study Abroad	n/a
Australia | Sydney	University of Sydney	Fall Spr YrRound	Dir	n/a	n/a
Australia | Sydney	University of Sydney	Fall Spr YrRound	Intermed	Institute for Study Abroad	n/a
Australia | Sydney	University of Sydney	Fall Spr YrRound	USColl	Arcadia University	n/a
Australia | Yungaburra	School for Field Studies	Fall Spr	Intermed	School for Field Studies	n/a
Austria | Vienna	IES Abroad Vienna Center	Fall Spr YrRound	Intermed	IES Abroad	n/a
Barbados | Cave Hill	University of the West Indies	Fall Spr YrRound	Dir	n/a	n/a
Belgium | Leuven	Katholieke University	Fall Spr YrRound	USColl	University of Pennsylvania	n/a
Bolivia | Cochabamba	SIT Study Abroad	Fall Spr	Intermed	SIT Study Abroad	n/a
Botswana | Gaborone	Pitzer College	Fall Spr	USColl	Pitzer College	n/a
Botswana | Gaborone	SIT Study Abroad	Fall Spr	Intermed	SIT Study Abroad	n/a
Brazil | Belem	SIT Study Abroad	Fall Spr	Intermed	SIT Study Abroad	n/a
Brazil | Belo Horizonte	Pontificia Universidade Catolica de Minas Gerais	Fall Spr YrRound	USColl	Middlebury College	n/a
Brazil | Fortaleza	Instituto Brasil/Estados Unidos/ Ceara	Fall Spr	Intermed	SIT Study Abroad	n/a
Brazil | Niteroi	Universidade Federal Fluminense	Fall Spr YrRound	USColl	Middlebury College	n/a
Brazil | Rio de Janeiro	Pontificia Universidade Catolica do Rio de Janeiro	Fall Spr YrRound	USColl	Brown University	n/a
Brazil | Rio de Janeiro	Pontificia Universidade Catolica do Rio de Janeiro	Fall Spr YrRound	USColl	SUNY New Paltz	n/a
Brazil | Sao Paulo	Pontificia Universidade Catolica de Sao Paulo	Fall Spr YrRound	Intermed	Council on International Educational Exchange (CIEE)	n/a
Cameroon | Yaounde	SIT Study Abroad	Fall Spr	Intermed	SIT Study Abroad	n/a
Canada | Montreal	McGill University	Fall Spr YrRound	Dir	n/a	n/a
Canada | Vancouver	University of British Columbia	Fall Spr YrRound	Dir	n/a	n/a
Chile | Santiago	Multiple institutional choices	Fall Spr YrRound	Intermed	Council on International Educational Exchange (CIEE)	n/a
Chile | Santiago	Multiple institutional choices	Fall Spr YrRound	Intermed	Institute for Study Abroad	n/a
Chile | Valparaiso	Multiple institutional choices	Fall Spr YrRound	Intermed	Institute for Study Abroad	n/a
Chile | Valparaiso	SIT Study Abroad	Fall Spr	Intermed	SIT Study Abroad	n/a
China | Beijing	Beijing University of Language and Culture	Fall Spr YrRound	Dir	n/a	n/a
China | Beijing	Capital University of Economics and Business	Fall Spr YrRound	USColl	Associated Colleges in China (Hamilton College)	n/a
China | Beijing	IES Abroad Beijing Center	Fall Spr YrRound	Intermed	IES Abroad	n/a
China | Beijing	Multiple institutional choices	Fall Spr YrRound	Intermed	Council on International Educational Exchange (CIEE)	n/a

© 2011 — Updates? Want to be in the next edition? Visit www.mysecondcampus.com

Massachusetts

DESTINATION	HOST INSTITUTION	PRGM SEASON	PRGM TYPE	INTERMEDIARY	HOUSING
China | Beijing	Peking University	Fall YrRound	Dir	Dickinson College	n/a
China | Beijing	University of International Business and Economics	Sum	USColl	Duke Study in China (Duke University)	n/a
China | Hangzhou	Zhejiang University of Technology	Fall Spr YrRound	USColl	Middlebury College	n/a
China | Nanjing	Nanjing University	Fall Spr YrRound	Intermed	Council on International Educational Exchange (CIEE)	n/a
China | Shanghai	East China Normal University	Fall Spr YrRound	Intermed	Council on International Educational Exchange (CIEE)	n/a
Costa Rica | [City Unspecified]	Organization for Tropical Studies	Fall Spr	Intermed	Organization for Tropical Studies	n/a
Costa Rica | [City Unspecified]	School for Field Studies	Fall Spr	Intermed	School for Field Studies	n/a
Costa Rica | Heredia	Universidad Nacional	Fall Spr YrRound	Intermed	Institute for Study Abroad	n/a
Costa Rica | San Jose	ACM Center	Fall	Consrtm	Associated Colleges of the Midwest (ACM)	n/a
Costa Rica | San Jose	Universidad de Costa Rica	Fall Spr YrRound	USColl	University of Kansas	n/a
Dominican Republic | Santiago	Pontificia Universidad Catolica Madre y Maestra	Fall Spr YrRound	Intermed	Council on International Educational Exchange (CIEE)	n/a
Ecuador | Quito	Pontificia Universidad Catolica del Ecuador	Fall Spr YrRound	USColl	Pitzer College	n/a
Ecuador | Quito	SIT Study Abroad	Fall Spr	Intermed	SIT Study Abroad	n/a
Ecuador | Quito	Universidad San Francisco de Quito	Fall Spr YrRound	USColl	University of Illinois, Urbana-Champaign	n/a
Egypt | Cairo	American University in Cairo	Fall Spr YrRound	Dir	n/a	n/a
Egypt | Cairo	American University in Cairo	Fall Spr YrRound	Dir	n/a	n/a
England | Bath	University of Bath	Fall Spr YrRound	Dir	n/a	n/a
England | Brighton	University of Sussex	Spr YrRound	Dir	n/a	n/a
England | Brighton	University of Sussex	Spr YrRound	USColl	Arcadia University	n/a
England | Brighton	University of Sussex	Spr YrRound	Intermed	Institute for Study Abroad	n/a
England | Bristol	University of Bristol	Fall Spr YrRound	Intermed	Institute for Study Abroad	n/a
England | Bristol	University of Bristol	Fall Spr YrRound	Dir	n/a	n/a
England | Cambridge	Cambridge University	Spr YrRound	Intermed	Institute for Study Abroad	n/a
England | Cambridge	Cambridge University	Spr YrRound	Dir	n/a	n/a
England | Cambridge	Institute of Economic and Political Studies	Fall Spr	Intermed	Institute of Economic and Political Studies	n/a
England | Canterbury	University of Kent	Fall Spr YrRound	Dir	n/a	n/a
England | Canterbury	University of Kent	Fall Spr YrRound	Intermed	Institute for Study Abroad	n/a
England | Colchester	University of Essex	Spr YrRound	Dir	n/a	n/a
England | Colchester	University of Essex	Spr YrRound	USColl	Arcadia University	n/a
England | Colchester	University of Essex	Spr YrRound	Intermed	Institute for Study Abroad	n/a
England | Coventry	University of Warwick	Spr YrRound	Dir	n/a	n/a
England | Exeter	University of Exeter	Fall Spr	Dir	n/a	n/a
England | Lancaster	Lancaster University	Spr YrRound	Dir	n/a	n/a
England | Lancaster	Lancaster University	Spr YrRound	Intermed	Institute for Study Abroad	n/a
England | Lancaster	Lancaster University	Spr YrRound	USColl	Arcadia University	n/a

© 2011 — Updates? Want to be in the next edition? Visit **www.mysecondcampus.com**

Massachusetts

DESTINATION	HOST INSTITUTION	PRGM SEASON	PRGM TYPE	INTERMEDIARY	HOUSING
England | Leeds	University of Leeds	Fall Spr YrRound	Intermed	Institute for Study Abroad	n/a
England | London	Courtauld Institute of Art	YrRound	Dir	n/a	n/a
England | London	Institute of Economic and Political Studies	Fall Spr	Intermed	Institute of Economic and Political Studies	n/a
England | London	King's College	Fall Spr YrRound	USColl	Arcadia University	n/a
England | London	King's College	Fall Spr YrRound	Intermed	Institute for Study Abroad	n/a
England | London	King's College	Fall Spr YrRound	Dir	n/a	n/a
England | London	London School of Economics and Political Science	YrRound	Dir	n/a	n/a
England | London	Queen Mary	Fall Spr YrRound	Intermed	Institute for Study Abroad	n/a
England | London	Royal Holloway	Spr YrRound	Dir	n/a	n/a
England | London	Royal Holloway	Spr YrRound	USColl	Arcadia University	n/a
England | London	School of Oriental and African Studies	Fall Spr YrRound	Dir	n/a	n/a
England | London	School of Oriental and African Studies	Fall Spr YrRound	Intermed	Institute for Study Abroad	n/a
England | London	School of Oriental and African Studies	Fall Spr YrRound	Dir	n/a	n/a
England | London	School of Oriental and African Studies	Fall Spr YrRound	Intermed	Institute for Study Abroad	n/a
England | London	School of Oriental and African Studies	Fall Spr YrRound	USColl	Arcadia University	n/a
England | London	School of Oriental and African Studies	Fall Spr YrRound	USColl	Arcadia University	n/a
England | London	UCL School of Slavonic and East European Studies	YrRound	Dir	n/a	n/a
England | London	University College London	Fall Spr YrRound	USColl	Arcadia University	n/a
England | London	University College London	Fall Spr YrRound	Intermed	Institute for Study Abroad	n/a
England | London	University College London	Fall Spr YrRound	Dir	n/a	n/a
England | Manchester	University of Manchester	Fall Spr YrRound	Dir	n/a	n/a
England | Manchester	University of Manchester	Fall Spr YrRound	USColl	Arcadia University	n/a
England | Norwich	University of East Anglia	Fall Spr YrRound	Intermed	Institute for Study Abroad	n/a
England | Norwich	University of East Anglia	Fall Spr YrRound	Dir	n/a	n/a
England | Oxford	Center for Medieval and Renaissance Studies	Spr YrRound	Intermed	Center for Medieval and Renaissance Studies	n/a
England | Oxford	Oxford University	Spr YrRound	Intermed	Institute for Study Abroad	n/a
England | Oxford	Oxford University	Spr YrRound	USColl	SUNY Brockport	n/a
England | Oxford	Oxford University	Spr YrRound	Dir	n/a	n/a
England | Oxford	Oxford University	Spr YrRound	USColl	Arcadia University	n/a
England | York	University of York	Spr YrRound	Intermed	Institute for Study Abroad	n/a
England | York	University of York	Spr YrRound	Dir	n/a	n/a
England | York	University of York	Spr YrRound	USColl	Arcadia University	n/a
France | Aix-en-Provence	Universite de Provence	Spr YrRound	USColl	Wellesley College	n/a
France | Bordeaux	Universite de Bordeaux 3 and/or d'Etudes Politiques de Bordeaux	Fall Spr YrRound	USColl	Middlebury College	n/a

© 2011 — Updates? Want to be in the next edition? Visit www.mysecondcampus.com

Massachusetts

DESTINATION	HOST INSTITUTION	PRGM SEASON	PRGM TYPE	INTERMEDIARY	HOUSING
France | Grenoble	Universite de Grenoble	Fall Spr	USColl	Swarthmore College	n/a
France | Montpellier	University of Montpellier III	Fall Spr YrRound	USColl	University of North Carolina, Chapel Hill	n/a
France | Nantes	IES Abroad Nantes Center	Fall Spr YrRound	Intermed	IES Abroad	n/a
France | Paris	Academic Programs Abroad (APA)	Fall Spr YrRound	Intermed	Academic Programs Abroad (APA)	n/a
France | Paris	Center for University Programs Abroad (CUPA)	Fall Spr YrRound	Intermed	Center for University Programs Abroad (CUPA)	n/a
France | Paris	Hamilton College	Fall Spr YrRound	USColl	Hamilton College	n/a
France | Paris	IES Abroad Paris Center	Fall Spr YrRound	Intermed	IES Abroad	n/a
France | Paris	Institut d'Etudes Politiques de Paris (Sciences Po)	Fall Spr YrRound	Dir	n/a	n/a
France | Paris	Middlebury College School in Paris	Fall Spr YrRound	USColl	Middlebury College	n/a
France | Paris	Multiple institutional choices	Fall Spr YrRound	USColl	Sweet Briar College	n/a
France | Paris	NYU Center in Paris	Fall Spr YrRound	USColl	New York University	n/a
France | Paris	Smith College	YrRound	USColl	Smith College	n/a
France | Paris	Vassar-Wesleyan Program in Paris	Fall Spr YrRound	USColl	Vassar-Wesleyan Program in Paris	n/a
France | Poitier	Universite de Poitiers	Fall Spr YrRound	USColl	Middlebury College	n/a
France | Strausbourg	Syracuse Center	Fall Spr	USColl	Syracuse University	n/a
Germany | Berlin	Berlin Consortium for German Studies (Columbia University)	Fall Spr YrRound	USColl	Berlin Consortium for German Studies (Columbia University)	n/a
Germany | Berlin	Humboldt University	Fall Spr	USColl	Brown University	n/a
Germany | Berlin	Humboldt University (fall); Freie Universitat (spring)	Fall Spr	USColl	Duke University	n/a
Germany | Freiburg	University of Freiburg	Fall Spr YrRound	USColl	University of Massachusetts at Amherst	n/a
Germany | Gottingen	Gottingen University	YrRound	Bilat	n/a	CollRes
	Costs: YrRound Costs: T&F: $18,500, R&B: n/a, Ttl: n/a				
Germany | Heidelberg	University of Heidelberg	Fall Spr YrRound	USColl	University of Massachusetts at Amherst	n/a
Germany | Heidelberg	University of Heidelberg	Fall Spr YrRound	USColl	Heidelberg University	n/a
Germany | Karlsruhe	Karlsruhe Institute of Technology	Fall Spr YrRound	USColl	University of Massachusetts at Amherst	n/a
Germany | Konstanz	University of Konstanz	Fall Spr YrRound	USColl	University of Massachusetts at Amherst	n/a
Germany | Mannheim	University of Mannheim	Fall Spr YrRound	USColl	University of Massachusetts at Amherst	n/a
Germany | Stuttgart	University of Hohenheim	Fall Spr YrRound	USColl	University of Massachusetts at Amherst	n/a
Germany | Stuttgart	University of Stuttgart	Fall Spr YrRound	USColl	University of Massachusetts at Amherst	n/a
Germany | Tübingen	University of Tübingen	Fall Spr YrRound	USColl	University of Massachusetts at Amherst	n/a

© 2011 — Updates? Want to be in the next edition? Visit **www.mysecondcampus.com**

Massachusetts

DESTINATION	HOST INSTITUTION	PRGM SEASON	PRGM TYPE	INTERMEDIARY	HOUSING
Germany | Ulm	Univeristy of Ulm	Fall Spr YrRound	USColl	University of Massachusetts at Amherst	n/a
Ghana | Accra	Ashesi University	Sum Fall Spr YrRound	Intermed	Council on International Educational Exchange (CIEE)	n/a
Ghana | Accra	University of Ghana	YrRound	USColl	SUNY Brockport	n/a
Ghana | Cape Coast	SIT Study Abroad	Fall Spr	Intermed	SIT Study Abroad	n/a
Honduras | Pueblo Nuevo	Kenyon College	n/a	USColl	Kenyon College	n/a
India | Bodh Gaya	Antioch Education Abroad (Antioch University)	Fall	USColl	Antioch Education Abroad (Antioch University)	n/a
India | Delhi	SIT Study Abroad	Fall Spr	Intermed	SIT Study Abroad	n/a
India | Delhi	St. Stephen's College; Lady Shri Ram College for Women	Fall Spr	USColl	Brown University	n/a
India | Hyderabad	University of Hyderabad	Fall Spr YrRound	Intermed	Council on International Educational Exchange (CIEE)	n/a
India | Madurai	South India Term Abroad (George Washington University)	Fall Spr	Consrtm	South India Term Abroad (George Washington University)	n/a
Ireland | Cork	University College Cork	Fall Spr YrRound	Dir	n/a	n/a
Ireland | Cork	University College Cork	Fall Spr YrRound	USColl	Arcadia University	n/a
Ireland | Cork	University College Cork	Fall Spr YrRound	Intermed	Institute for Study Abroad	n/a
Ireland | Dublin	Trinity College	Spr YrRound	Dir	n/a	n/a
Ireland | Dublin	University College Dublin	Fall Spr YrRound	USColl	Arcadia University	n/a
Ireland | Dublin	University College Dublin	Fall Spr YrRound	Intermed	Institute for Study Abroad	n/a
Italy | Bologna	Indiana University's Bologna Consortial Studies Program	Fall Spr YrRound	Consrtm	Indiana University	n/a
Italy | Bologna	University of Bologna	Fall Spr YrRound	USColl	Brown University	n/a
Italy | Florence	Georgetown University	Fall Spr	USColl	Georgetown University	n/a
Italy | Florence	Multiple institutional choices	Fall Spr YrRound	USColl	Middlebury College	n/a
Italy | Florence	NYU in Florence	Fall Spr YrRound	USColl	New York University	n/a
Italy | Florence	Sarah Lawrence College	Fall Spr YrRound	USColl	Sarah Lawrence College	n/a
Italy | Florence	Smith Center	YrRound	USColl	Smith College	n/a
Italy | Florence	SU Florence Center and/or University of Florence	Fall Spr	USColl	Syracuse University	n/a
Italy | Milan	IES Abroad Milan Center	Fall Spr YrRound	Intermed	IES Abroad	n/a
Italy | Padua	Boston University Center for Italian and European Studies	Fall Spr YrRound	USColl	Boston University	n/a
Italy | Perugia	Umbra Institute and/or Universita per Stranieri	Fall Spr YrRound	USColl	Arcadia University	n/a
Italy | Rome	Cornell University	Fall Spr	USColl	Cornell University	n/a
Italy | Rome	IES Abroad Rome Center	Fall Spr YrRound	Intermed	IES Abroad	n/a
Italy | Rome	Intercollegiate Center for Classical Studies (Duke University)	Fall Spr	Consrtm	Duke University	n/a
Italy | Siena	Siena School for Liberal Arts	Fall Spr	Intermed	Siena School for Liberal Arts	n/a
Japan | Kyoto	Antioch Education Abroad (Antioch University)	Fall	USColl	Antioch Education Abroad (Antioch University)	n/a

© 2011 — Updates? Want to be in the next edition? Visit **www.mysecondcampus.com**

Massachusetts

DESTINATION	HOST INSTITUTION	PRGM SEASON	PRGM TYPE	INTERMEDIARY	HOUSING
Japan | Kyoto	Doshisha University	YrRound	Consrtm	Associated Kyoto Program	n/a
Japan | Kyoto	Kyoto Consortium for Japanese Studies (Columbia University)	Fall Spr YrRound	Consrtm	Kyoto Consortium for Japanese Studies (Columbia University)	n/a
Japan | Nagoya	Nanzan University	Fall Spr	Intermed	IES Abroad	n/a
Japan | Tokyo	International Christian University	Fall Spr YrRound	Dir	n/a	n/a
Japan | Tokyo	Sophia University	Fall Spr YrRound	Intermed	Council on International Educational Exchange (CIEE)	n/a
Japan | Tokyo	Temple University Japan Campus	Fall Spr	USColl	Temple University	n/a
Kenya | Mombasa	SIT Study Abroad	Fall Spr	Intermed	SIT Study Abroad	n/a
Kenya | Nairobi	School for Field Studies	Fall Spr	Intermed	School for Field Studies	n/a
Kenya | Nairobi	SIT Study Abroad	Fall Spr	Intermed	SIT Study Abroad	n/a
Kenya | Nairobi	St. Lawrence University	Fall Spr	USColl	St. Lawrence University	n/a
Kenya | Nairobi	University of Nairobi	Fall	USColl	Kalamazoo College	n/a
Madagascar | Fort Dauphin	SIT Study Abroad	Fall Spr	Intermed	SIT Study Abroad	n/a
Mali | Bamako	Antioch Education Abroad (Antioch University)	Fall Spr	USColl	Antioch Education Abroad (Antioch University)	n/a
Mexico | Baja	School for Field Studies	Fall Spr	Intermed	School for Field Studies	n/a
Mexico | Cuernavaca	Center for Global Education at Augsburg College	Fall Spr	USColl	Center for Global Education at Augsburg College	n/a
Mexico | Guadalajara	Universidad Autonoma de Guadalajara	Fall Spr YrRound	Dir	n/a	n/a
Mexico | Merida	Universidad Autonoma de Yucatan	Fall Spr YrRound	Intermed	Institute for Study Abroad	n/a
Mexico | Mexico City	Universidad Iberoamericana	Fall Spr YrRound	Dir	n/a	n/a
Mexico | Oaxaca	SIT Study Abroad	Fall Spr	Intermed	SIT Study Abroad	n/a
Namibia | Windhoek	Center for Global Education at Augsburg College	Fall Spr	USColl	Center for Global Education at Augsburg College	n/a
Netherlands | Amsterdam	University of Amsterdam	Fall Spr YrRound	Intermed	Council on International Educational Exchange (CIEE)	n/a
Netherlands | Maastricht	Center for European Studies	Fall Spr	Intermed	Center for European Studies	n/a
New Zealand | Auckland	University of Auckland	Fall Spr YrRound	Intermed	Institute for Study Abroad	n/a
New Zealand | Auckland	University of Auckland	Fall Spr	Intermed	Frontiers Abroad Escape Program	n/a
New Zealand | Auckland	University of Auckland	Fall Spr YrRound	Dir	n/a	n/a
New Zealand | Christchurch	University of Canterbury	Fall Spr	Intermed	Frontiers Abroad Escape Program	n/a
New Zealand | Dunedin	University of Otago	Fall Spr YrRound	Dir	n/a	n/a
New Zealand | Dunedin	University of Otago	Fall Spr YrRound	Intermed	Institute for Study Abroad	n/a
New Zealand | Wellington	Victoria University of Wellington	Fall Spr YrRound	Dir	n/a	n/a
New Zealand | Wellington	Victoria University of Wellington	Fall Spr YrRound	Intermed	Institute for Study Abroad	n/a
Nicaragua | Managua	SIT Study Abroad	Fall Spr	Intermed	SIT Study Abroad	n/a
Niger | Niamey	Universite Abdou Moumouni	Fall Spr YrRound	USColl	Boston University	n/a

© 2011 — Updates? Want to be in the next edition? Visit **www.mysecondcampus.com**

Massachusetts

DESTINATION	HOST INSTITUTION	PRGM SEASON	PRGM TYPE	INTERMEDIARY	HOUSING
Russia | Moscow	Moscow International University	Fall Spr YrRound	Intermed	American Councils Study Abroad Programs	n/a
Russia | Moscow	Russian State University of the Humanities	Fall Spr YrRound	USColl	Middlebury College	n/a
Russia | St. Petersburg	Russian State Pedagogical University (Gertsen Institute)	Fall Spr YrRound	Intermed	American Councils Study Abroad Programs	n/a
Russia | St. Petersburg	Smolny College	Fall Spr YrRound	Intermed	Bard-Smolny Study Abroad	n/a
Russia | St. Petersburg	St. Petersburg State University	Fall Spr	USColl	Duke University	n/a
Russia | St. Petersburg	St. Petersburg State University	Fall Spr YrRound	Intermed	Council on International Educational Exchange (CIEE)	n/a
Russia | Vladimir	KORA Center for Russian Language	Fall Spr YrRound	Intermed	American Councils Study Abroad Programs	n/a
Scotland | Aberdeen	University of Aberdeen	Spr YrRound	Dir	n/a	n/a
Scotland | Aberdeen	University of Aberdeen	Spr YrRound	USColl	Arcadia University	n/a
Scotland | Edinburgh	University of Edinburgh	Fall Spr YrRound	Dir	n/a	n/a
Scotland | Edinburgh	University of Edinburgh	Fall Spr YrRound	USColl	Arcadia University	n/a
Scotland | Edinburgh	University of Edinburgh	Fall Spr YrRound	Intermed	Institute for Study Abroad	n/a
Scotland | Glasgow	Glasgow School of Art	Spr YrRound	USColl	Arcadia University	n/a
Scotland | Glasgow	Glasgow School of Art	Spr YrRound	Intermed	Institute for Study Abroad	n/a
Scotland | Glasgow	University of Glasgow	Spr YrRound	USColl	Arcadia University	n/a
Scotland | Glasgow	University of Glasgow	Spr YrRound	Intermed	Institute for Study Abroad	n/a
Scotland | Glasgow	University of Glasgow	Spr YrRound	Dir	n/a	n/a
Scotland | St. Andrews	University of St. Andrews	Fall Spr YrRound	Intermed	Institute for Study Abroad	n/a
Scotland | St. Andrews	University of St. Andrews	Fall Spr YrRound	Dir	n/a	n/a
Scotland | Stirling	University of Stirling	Fall Spr YrRound	Dir	n/a	n/a
Scotland | Stirling	University of Stirling	Fall Spr YrRound	Intermed	Institute for Study Abroad	n/a
Senegal | Dakar	Multiple institutions	Fall Spr	USColl	Wells College	n/a
Senegal | Dakar	Universite Cheikh Anta Diop	Spr	USColl	Mount Holyoke College	n/a
South Africa | Cape Town	SIT Study Abroad	Fall Spr	Intermed	SIT Study Abroad	n/a
South Africa | Cape Town	University of Cape Town	Fall Spr YrRound	Intermed	Council on International Educational Exchange (CIEE)	n/a
South Africa | Cape Town	University of Cape Town	Fall Spr YrRound	Intermed	Interstudy	n/a
South Africa | Durban	University of Kwazulu-Natal	Fall Spr YrRound	Intermed	Interstudy	n/a
South Africa | Johannesburg	University of Witwatersrand	Fall Spr YrRound	Intermed	Interstudy	n/a
South Africa | Kruger National Park	Organization for Tropical Studies	Fall Spr	Intermed	Organization for Tropical Studies	n/a
South Africa | Pietermartizburg	University of Kwazulu-Natal	Fall Spr YrRound	Intermed	Interstudy	n/a
South Korea | Seoul	Yonsei University	Fall Spr YrRound	Intermed	Council on International Educational Exchange (CIEE)	n/a
Spain | Alicante	Universidad de Alicante	Fall Spr YrRound	Intermed	Council on International Educational Exchange (CIEE)	n/a
Spain | Granada	IES Abroad Granada Center	Fall Spr YrRound	Intermed	IES Abroad	n/a
Spain | Madrid	Hamilton College	Fall Spr YrRound	USColl	Hamilton College	n/a

© 2011 — Updates? Want to be in the next edition? Visit **www.mysecondcampus.com**

Massachusetts

DESTINATION	HOST INSTITUTION	PRGM SEASON	PRGM TYPE	INTERMEDIARY	HOUSING
Spain | Madrid	Instituto Internacional; Universidad Autonoma de Madrid	Fall Spr YrRound	USColl	Boston University	n/a
Spain | Madrid	Multiple institutional choices	Fall Spr YrRound	USColl	Middlebury College	n/a
Spain | Madrid	NYU in Madrid	Fall Spr YrRound	USColl	New York University	n/a
Spain | Salamanca	IES Abroad Salamanca Center	Fall Spr YrRound	Intermed	IES Abroad	n/a
Spain | Salamanca	University of Salamanca	Fall Spr YrRound	USColl	Colby College	n/a
Spain | Seville	University of Seville	Fall Spr YrRound	USColl	Sweet Briar College	n/a
Spain | Toledo	Fundacion Jose Ortega y Gasset and/or Universidad de Castilla-La Mancha	Fall Spr YrRound	USColl	Arcadia University	n/a
Taiwan | Taipei	National Chengchi University	Fall Spr YrRound	Intermed	Council on International Educational Exchange (CIEE)	n/a
Tanzania | Arusha	SIT Study Abroad	Fall Spr	Intermed	SIT Study Abroad	n/a
Tanzania | Zanzibar	SIT Study Abroad	Fall Spr	Intermed	SIT Study Abroad	n/a
Trinidad | St. Augustine	University of the West Indies	Fall Spr YrRound	Dir	n/a	n/a
Turks and Caicos | South Caicos	School for Field Studies	Fall Spr	Intermed	School for Field Studies	n/a

Anna Maria College

Stephen Neun
Academic Dean
50 Sunset Lane
Paxton, MA 01612

sneun@annamaria.edu
508.849.3359

DESTINATION	HOST INSTITUTION	PRGM SEASON	PRGM TYPE	INTERMEDIARY	HOUSING
[Country Unspecified] | [City Unspecified]	n/a	n/a	n/a	n/a	n/a

Assumption College

Eloise Knowlton
Dean of Undergraduate Studies
500 Salisbury Street
Worcester, MA 01609

eknowlton@assumption.edu
508.767.7486
http://www1.assumption.edu/acad/opportunities/study_abroad.php

DESTINATION	HOST INSTITUTION	PRGM SEASON	PRGM TYPE	INTERMEDIARY	HOUSING
(Multiple choices) | (Multiple choices)	Multiple institutional choices	n/a	Intermed	American Institute for Foreign Study	n/a
(Multiple choices) | (Multiple choices)	Multiple institutional choices	n/a	Intermed	Institute for Study Abroad	n/a
(Multiple choices) | (Multiple choices)	Semester at Sea	n/a	Intermed	Semester at Sea	n/a
United States | Washington (DC)	Washington Center for Internships and Academic Seminars	n/a	Intermed	Washington Center for Internships and Academic Seminars	n/a

© 2011 — Updates? Want to be in the next edition? Visit **www.mysecondcampus.com**

Massachusetts

| DESTINATION | HOST INSTITUTION | PRGM SEASON | PRGM TYPE | INTERMEDIARY | HOUSING |

Babson College

Elise Beaudin
Associate Director
231 Forest Street
Babson Park, MA 02457

ebeaudin@babson.edu
781.239.4482
http://www3.babson.edu/Centers/Glavin/gps/about.cfm

DESTINATION	HOST INSTITUTION	PRGM SEASON	PRGM TYPE	INTERMEDIARY	HOUSING
(Multiple) | (Multiple)	Babson College	Fall	Self	n/a	n/a
Costs: Fall Costs: T&F: Babson home tuition, R&B: n/a, Ttl: n/a					
Argentina | Buenos Aires	IES Abroad Buenos Aires Center	n/a	Intermed	IES Abroad	n/a
Argentina | Buenos Aires	Multiple institutional choices	n/a	Intermed	Council on International Educational Exchange (CIEE)	n/a
Australia | Clayton	Monash University	Fall Spr	Bilat	n/a	CollRes PrivApt
Costs: Fall Costs: T&F: Babson home tuition, R&B: n/a, Ttl: n/a Spr Costs: T&F: Babson home tuition, R&B: n/a, Ttl: n/a					
Australia | Kensington	University of New South Wales	Fall Spr YrRound	Bilat	n/a	CollRes PrivApt
Costs: Fall Costs: T&F: Babson home tuition, R&B: n/a, Ttl: n/a Spr Costs: T&F: Babson home tuition, R&B: n/a, Ttl: n/a YrRound Costs: T&F: Babson home tuition, R&B: n/a, Ttl: n/a					
Australia | Melbourne	RMIT University	Fall Spr YrRound	Bilat	n/a	HostFam PrivApt Other
Costs: Fall Costs: T&F: Babson home tuition, R&B: n/a, Ttl: n/a Spr Costs: T&F: Babson home tuition, R&B: n/a, Ttl: n/a YrRound Costs: T&F: Babson home tuition, R&B: n/a, Ttl: n/a					
Australia | Sydney	University of Sydney	n/a	USColl	Arcadia University	n/a
Austria | Vienna	Vienna University of Economics and Business Administration	Fall Spr	Bilat	n/a	CollRes PrivApt
Costs: Fall Costs: T&F: Babson home tuition, R&B: n/a, Ttl: n/a Spr Costs: T&F: Babson home tuition, R&B: n/a, Ttl: n/a					
Belgium | Louvain-la-Neuve	Universite Catholique de Louvain	Fall Spr	Bilat	n/a	n/a
Costs: Fall Costs: T&F: Babson home tuition, R&B: $2,517, Ttl: n/a Spr Costs: T&F: Babson home tuition, R&B: $2,517, Ttl: n/a					
Brazil | Sao Paulo	Escola de Administracao de Empresas de Sao Paulo da Fundacao Getulio Vargas	n/a	Intermed	Council on International Educational Exchange (CIEE)	n/a
Brazil | Sao Paulo; Paraty; Rio de Janiero	Fundacao Getulio Vargas	Spr	Self	n/a	n/a
Costs: Spr Costs: T&F: n/a, R&B: n/a, Ttl: $1,800					
Chile | Penalolen	Universidad Adolfo Ibanez	Fall Spr	Bilat	n/a	HostFam PrivApt
Costs: Fall Costs: T&F: Babson home tuition, R&B: n/a, Ttl: n/a Spr Costs: T&F: Babson home tuition, R&B: n/a, Ttl: n/a					
Chile; Peru | Santiago; Lima	Universidad del Desarrollo. CENTRUM Lima	Win	Self	n/a	n/a
Costs: Win Costs: T&F: n/a, R&B: n/a, Ttl: $3,500					
China | Beijing	Beijing Language and Culture University	n/a	Intermed	Alliance for Gllobal Education	n/a
China | Beijing	Tsinghua University	Fall Spr	Bilat	n/a	n/a
Costs: Fall Costs: T&F: Babson home tuition, R&B: $3,000, Ttl: n/a Spr Costs: T&F: Babson home tuition, R&B: $3,000, Ttl: n/a					
China | Beijing; Xi'an; Shanghai	Babson College	Spr	Self	n/a	n/a
Costs: Spr Costs: T&F: n/a, R&B: n/a, Ttl: $2,900					
China | Hong Kong	Chinese University of Hong Kong	Fall Spr	Bilat	n/a	CollRes
Costs: Fall Costs: T&F: Babson home tuition, R&B: n/a, Ttl: n/a Spr Costs: T&F: Babson home tuition, R&B: n/a, Ttl: n/a					

© 2011 — Updates? Want to be in the next edition? Visit **www.mysecondcampus.com**

Massachusetts

DESTINATION	HOST INSTITUTION	PRGM SEASON	PRGM TYPE	INTERMEDIARY	HOUSING
China | Hong Kong	Hong Kong Baptist University	Fall Spr	Bilat	n/a	CollRes
	Costs: Fall Costs: T&F: Babson home tuition, R&B: n/a, Ttl: n/a Spr Costs: T&F: Babson home tuition, R&B: n/a, Ttl: n/a				
China | Nanjing	Nanjing University	n/a	Intermed	Council on International Educational Exchange (CIEE)	n/a
China | Shanghai	Shanghai University of Finance and Economics	n/a	Intermed	Alliance for Gllobal Education	n/a
Costa Rica | Heredia	Universidad Nacional	Fall Spr	Intermed	Institute for Study Abroad	n/a
Czech Republic | Prague	Multiple institutional choices	n/a	Intermed	Council on International Educational Exchange (CIEE)	n/a
England | Cambridge	Cambridge University	n/a	Intermed	Institute for Study Abroad	n/a
England | London	London School of Economics and Political Science	YrRound	Dir	n/a	HostFam CollRes PrivApt
England | London	Queen Mary	n/a	Intermed	Institute for Study Abroad	n/a
England | London	University of Westminster	n/a	Intermed	Institute for Study Abroad	n/a
England | Manchester	Manchester Business School (University of Manchester)	Fall Spr	Bilat	n/a	CollRes PrivApt
	Costs: Fall Costs: T&F: Babson home tuition, R&B: n/a, Ttl: n/a Spr Costs: T&F: Babson home tuition, R&B: n/a, Ttl: n/a				
England | Oxford	Oxford University	n/a	Intermed	Institute for Study Abroad	n/a
France | Nice	Multiple institutional choices	Fall Spr YrRound	USColl	Sweet Briar College	n/a
France | Paris	ESCP-EAP European School of Management	Fall Spr	Bilat	n/a	n/a
	Costs: Fall Costs: T&F: Babson home tuition, R&B: $4,800, Ttl: n/a Spr Costs: T&F: Babson home tuition, R&B: $4,800, Ttl: n/a				
France | Paris	HEC	Fall Spr	Dir	n/a	CollRes
	Costs: Fall Costs: T&F: Babson home tuition, R&B: n/a, Ttl: n/a Spr Costs: T&F: Babson home tuition, R&B: n/a, Ttl: n/a				
France | Paris	IES Abroad Paris Business & International Affairs Program Center	n/a	Intermed	IES Abroad	n/a
France | Paris	University of Paris IV	n/a	Intermed	American Institute for Foreign Study (AIFS)	n/a
France | Rennes	Universite de Haute Bretagne	n/a	Intermed	Council on International Educational Exchange (CIEE)	n/a
Ghana | (Multiple)	Babson College	Win	Self	n/a	n/a
	Costs: Win Costs: T&F: n/a, R&B: n/a, Ttl: $1,000				
Ghana | Accra	University of Ghana	n/a	Intermed	Council on International Educational Exchange (CIEE)	n/a
Greece | Thessaloniki	American College of Thessaloniki	Fall Spr	Dir	n/a	CollRes
India | Hyderabad	University of Hyderabad	n/a	Intermed	Council on International Educational Exchange (CIEE)	n/a
Ireland | Cork	University College Cork	Fall Spr	Bilat	n/a	HostFam CollRes
	Costs: Fall Costs: T&F: Babson home tuition, R&B: n/a, Ttl: n/a Spr Costs: T&F: Babson home tuition, R&B: n/a, Ttl: n/a				
Ireland | Dublin	Trinity College Dublin	YrRound	Bilat	n/a	CollRes
	Costs: YrRound Costs: T&F: Babson home tuition, R&B: n/a, Ttl: n/a				
Italy | Ferrara	University of Ferrara	n/a	Intermed	Council on International Educational Exchange (CIEE)	n/a

© 2011 — Updates? Want to be in the next edition? Visit **www.mysecondcampus.com**

Massachusetts

DESTINATION	HOST INSTITUTION	PRGM SEASON	PRGM TYPE	INTERMEDIARY	HOUSING
Italy | Florence	Richmond, The American International University in London –Florence Center	n/a	Intermed	American Institute for Foreign Study (AIFS)	n/a
Italy | Milan	Bocconi University	Fall Spr	Bilat	n/a	n/a
	Costs: Fall Costs: T&F: Babson home tuition, R&B: n/a, Ttl: n/a Spr Costs: T&F: Babson home tuition, R&B: n/a, Ttl: n/a				
Italy | Milan	SDA Bocconi School of Management	Fall	Bilat	n/a	n/a
	Costs: Fall Costs: T&F: Babson home tuition, R&B: $9,780, Ttl: n/a				
Italy | Perugia	Umbra Institute	n/a	USColl	Arcadia University	n/a
Italy | Rome	Accademia Italiana	n/a	USColl	Arcadia University	n/a
Italy | Rome	Richmond, The American International University in London –Rome Center	n/a	Intermed	American Institute for Foreign Study (AIFS)	n/a
Japan | Tokyo	Sophia University	n/a	Intermed	Council on International Educational Exchange (CIEE)	n/a
Japan | Tokyo	Waseda University	YrRound	Dir	n/a	HostFam CollRes
	Costs: YrRound Costs: T&F: Babson home tuition, R&B: n/a, Ttl: n/a				
Japan; Korea | Nagoya; Seoul	Babson College	Spr	Self	n/a	n/a
	Costs: Spr Costs: T&F: n/a, R&B: n/a, Ttl: $4,000				
Jordan | Amman	University of Jordan	n/a	Intermed	Council on International Educational Exchange (CIEE)	n/a
Mexico | Monterrey	Instituto Tecnologico y Estudios Superiores de Monterrey	Fall Spr	Bilat	n/a	HostFam CollRes PrivApt
	Costs: Fall Costs: T&F: Babson home tuition, R&B: n/a, Ttl: n/a Spr Costs: T&F: Babson home tuition, R&B: n/a, Ttl: n/a				
Netherlands | Maastricht	Maastricht University	Spr	Dir	n/a	CollRes
Netherlands | Rotterdam	Rotterdam School of Management (Erasmus University)	Fall	Bilat	n/a	PrivApt Other
	Costs: Fall Costs: T&F: Babson home tuition, R&B: n/a, Ttl: n/a				
New Zealand | Auckland	University of Auckland	n/a	USColl	Arcadia University	n/a
New Zealand | Dunedin	University of Otago	n/a	USColl	Arcadia University	n/a
New Zealand | Hamilton	University of Waikato	Fall Spr	Bilat	n/a	CollRes PrivApt
	Costs: Fall Costs: T&F: Babson home tuition, R&B: n/a, Ttl: n/a Spr Costs: T&F: Babson home tuition, R&B: n/a, Ttl: n/a				
Northern Ireland | Belfast	Queen's University Belfast	n/a	USColl	Arcadia University	n/a
Norway | Trondheim; Bodo	Norwegian University of Science and Technology	Spr	Self	n/a	n/a
	Costs: Spr Costs: T&F: n/a, R&B: n/a, Ttl: $2,500				
Russia | St. Petersburg	Graduate School of Management (St. Petersburg State University)	Spr	Self	n/a	n/a
	Costs: Spr Costs: T&F: n/a, R&B: n/a, Ttl: $1,700				
Russia | St. Petersburg	St. Petersburg State University	n/a	Intermed	Council on International Educational Exchange (CIEE)	n/a
Scotland | Edinburgh	University of Edinburgh	Fall Spr	Bilat	n/a	CollRes
	Costs: Fall Costs: T&F: Babson home tuition, R&B: n/a, Ttl: n/a Spr Costs: T&F: Babson home tuition, R&B: n/a, Ttl: n/a				
Scotland | St. Andrews	University of St. Andrews	n/a	Intermed	Institute for Study Abroad	n/a

Massachusetts

DESTINATION	HOST INSTITUTION	PRGM SEASON	PRGM TYPE	INTERMEDIARY	HOUSING
Singapore | Singapore	Singapore Management University	Fall Spr	Dir	n/a	n/a
	Costs: Fall Costs: T&F: Babson home tuition, R&B: n/a, Ttl: n/a Spr Costs: T&F: Babson home tuition, R&B: n/a, Ttl: n/a				
South Africa | Cape Town	University of Cape Town	n/a	Intermed	Council on International Educational Exchange (CIEE)	n/a
South Africa | Stellenbosch	Stellenbosch University	n/a	Intermed	Council on International Educational Exchange (CIEE)	n/a
South Korea | Seoul	Yonsei University	n/a	Intermed	Council on International Educational Exchange (CIEE)	n/a
Spain | Alicante	Universidad de Alicante	n/a	Intermed	Council on International Educational Exchange (CIEE)	n/a
Spain | Barcelona	ESADE business school	Fall Spr	Bilat	n/a	n/a
	Costs: Fall Costs: T&F: Babson home tuition, R&B: $5,600, Ttl: n/a Spr Costs: T&F: Babson home tuition, R&B: $5,600, Ttl: n/a				
Spain | Barcelona	Multiple institutional choices	n/a	Intermed	Council on International Educational Exchange (CIEE)	n/a
Spain | Granada	University of Granada	n/a	Intermed	American Institute for Foreign Study (AIFS)	n/a
Spain | Madrid	Instituto de Empresa	Sum Fall	Bilat	n/a	n/a
	Costs: Sum Costs: T&F: Babson home tuition, R&B: Unknown, Ttl: n/a Fall Costs: T&F: Babson home tuition, R&B: $8,680, Ttl: n/a				
Spain | Sant Cugat del Valles	Escuela Superior de Administracion y Direccion de Empresas	Fall Spr	Bilat	n/a	n/a
	Costs: Fall Costs: T&F: Babson home tuition, R&B: n/a, Ttl: n/a Spr Costs: T&F: Babson home tuition, R&B: n/a, Ttl: n/a				
Spain | Seville	Universidad Pablo de Olavide	n/a	Intermed	Council on International Educational Exchange (CIEE)	n/a
Sweden | Jonkoping	Jonkoping International Business School	n/a	Dir	n/a	n/a
Sweden | Lund	Lund University	Fall Spr	Bilat	n/a	CollRes PrivApt
	Costs: Fall Costs: T&F: Babson home tuition, R&B: n/a, Ttl: n/a Spr Costs: T&F: Babson home tuition, R&B: n/a, Ttl: n/a				
Switzerland | St. Gallen	University of St. Gallen	Fall Spr	Dir	n/a	PrivApt
	Costs: Fall Costs: T&F: Babson home tuition, R&B: n/a, Ttl: n/a Spr Costs: T&F: Babson home tuition, R&B: n/a, Ttl: n/a				
Switzerland | St. Gallen	University of St. Gallen	Fall Spr	Bilat	n/a	n/a
	Costs: Fall Costs: T&F: Babson home tuition, R&B: $3,600, Ttl: n/a Spr Costs: T&F: Babson home tuition, R&B: Unknown, Ttl: n/a				
Turkey | Orhanli	Sabanci University	Fall Spr	Bilat	n/a	CollRes
	Costs: Fall Costs: T&F: Babson home tuition, R&B: n/a, Ttl: n/a Spr Costs: T&F: Babson home tuition, R&B: n/a, Ttl: n/a				

Bard College at Simon's Rock

Anne O'Dwyer
Associate Dean of Academic Affairs
84 Alford Road
Great Barrington, MA 01230

aodwyer@simons-rock.edu
413.528.7218

DESTINATION	HOST INSTITUTION	PRGM SEASON	PRGM TYPE	INTERMEDIARY	HOUSING
[Country Unspecified] | [City Unspecified]	n/a	n/a	n/a	n/a	n/a

© 2011 — Updates? Want to be in the next edition? Visit **www.mysecondcampus.com**

Massachusetts

DESTINATION	HOST INSTITUTION	PRGM SEASON	PRGM TYPE	INTERMEDIARY	HOUSING

Bay Path College

Thomas Schorle
Study Abroad Director
Study Abroad Program
588 Longmeadow Street
Longmeadow, MA 01106

tschorle@baypath.edu
413.565.1183
http://www.baypath.edu/UndergraduateExperience/AcademicPrograms/StudyAbroad.aspx

DESTINATION	HOST INSTITUTION	PRGM SEASON	PRGM TYPE	INTERMEDIARY	HOUSING
Australia | Queensland	University of Queensland	n/a	Dir	n/a	n/a
China | Beijing	Beijing Language and Culture University	n/a	Intermed	The Alliance for Global Education	n/a
China | Shanghai	Fudan University	n/a	Dir	n/a	n/a
China | Shanghai	Shanghai University of Finance and Economics (SUFE)	n/a	Dir	n/a	n/a
Denmark | Odense	Tietgen Business College	n/a	Dir	n/a	n/a
England | London	Royal Holloway, University of London	n/a	Dir	n/a	n/a
Netherlands | Leiden	University of Leiden	n/a	Dir	n/a	n/a
South Korea | Seoul	Ewha Womans University	n/a	Dir	n/a	n/a
United States | Honolulu	Chaminade University of Honolulu	Fall Spr	Dir	n/a	CollRes

Becker College

Ken Cameron
Vice President for Academic Affairs
61 Sever Street
Worcester, MA 01609

ken.cameron@becker.edu
774.354.0460
http://www.becker.edu/pages/1177.asp

DESTINATION	HOST INSTITUTION	PRGM SEASON	PRGM TYPE	INTERMEDIARY	HOUSING
(Multiple choices) | (Multiple choices)	Multiple institutional choices	n/a	Intermed	Center for International Studies	n/a

Bentley College

Natalie Schlegel
Director
Education Abroad Office
AAC 161
175 Forest Street
Waltham, MA 02452

nschlegel@bentley.edu
781.891.3474
http://www.bentley.edu/international-ed/index.cfm

DESTINATION	HOST INSTITUTION	PRGM SEASON	PRGM TYPE	INTERMEDIARY	HOUSING
(Multiple) | (Multiple)	Semester at Sea	n/a	Intermed	Semester at Sea	n/a
(Multiple) | (Multiple)	Semester at Sea	Sum	Intermed	Semester at Sea	n/a
Argentina | Buenos Aires	Universidad de San Andres	Sum	Dir	n/a	n/a
Argentina and Peru | (Multiple)	Bentley College	Spr	Self	n/a	n/a
	Costs: Spr Costs: T&F: n/a, R&B: n/a, Ttl: $3,200				
Australia | Gold Coast	Bond University	n/a	Dir	n/a	n/a

© 2011 — Updates? Want to be in the next edition? Visit **www.mysecondcampus.com**

Massachusetts

DESTINATION	HOST INSTITUTION	PRGM SEASON	PRGM TYPE	INTERMEDIARY	HOUSING
Australia | Melbourne	Royal Melbourne Institute of Technology	n/a	Dir	n/a	n/a
Austria | Vienna	Vienna University of Economics and Business	Sum	Dir	n/a	n/a
Austria | Vienna	Vienna University of Economics and Business Administration	n/a	Dir	n/a	n/a
Austria, Hungary, and Czech Republic | (Multiple)	Bentley College	Sum	Self	n/a	n/a
Costs: Sum Costs: T&F: n/a, R&B: n/a, Ttl: $4,200					
Belgium | Brussels	Vesalius College	n/a	Dir	n/a	n/a
Belgium | Brussels	Vesalius College	n/a	Dir	n/a	n/a
Belgium | Brussels	Vesalius College	n/a	Dir	n/a	n/a
Bermuda | (Multiple)	Bentley College	Sum	Self	n/a	n/a
Costs: Sum Costs: T&F: n/a, R&B: n/a, Ttl: $4,600					
Brazil | Sao Paulo	University of Sao Paulo	n/a	Dir	n/a	n/a
Chile | (Multiple)	Bentley College	Win	Self	n/a	n/a
Costs: Win Costs: T&F: n/a, R&B: n/a, Ttl: $3,300					
China | (Multiple)	Bentley College	Sum	Self	n/a	n/a
Costs: Sum Costs: T&F: n/a, R&B: n/a, Ttl: $4,100					
China | (Multiple)	Bentley College	Win	Self	n/a	n/a
Costs: Win Costs: T&F: n/a, R&B: n/a, Ttl: $4,800					
China | Hong Kong	University of Hong Kong	n/a	Dir	n/a	n/a
China | Shanghai	Shanghai University of Finance and Economics	n/a	Intermed	Alliance for Global Education	n/a
China | Shanghai	Shanghai University of Finance and Economics	Sum	Dir	Alliance for Global Education	n/a
Cuba | (Multiple)	Bentley College	Spr	Self	n/a	n/a
Costs: Spr Costs: T&F: n/a, R&B: n/a, Ttl: $4,500					
Denmark | Copenhagen	Copenhagen Business School	n/a	Dir	n/a	n/a
Denmark | Copenhagen	Copenhagen Business School	Sum	Dir	n/a	n/a
Egypt | (Multiple)	Bentley College	Win	Self	n/a	n/a
Costs: Win Costs: T&F: n/a, R&B: n/a, Ttl: $5,500					
Egypt | Cairo	American University in Cairo	n/a	Dir	n/a	n/a
Egypt | Cairo	American University in Cairo	Sum	Dir	n/a	n/a
England | (Multiple)	Bentley College	Spr	Self	n/a	n/a
Costs: Spr Costs: T&F: n/a, R&B: n/a, Ttl: $2,095					
England | London	London School of Economics and Political Science	Sum	Dir	n/a	n/a
England | London	Multiple institutional choices	Sum	Intermed	EUSA	n/a
England | London	Multiple institutional choices	n/a	Intermed	EUSA	n/a
England | London	Royal Holloway	n/a	Dir	n/a	n/a
England | Manchester	University of Manchester	n/a	Dir	n/a	n/a
France | (Multiple)	Bentley College	Sum	Self	n/a	n/a
Costs: Sum Costs: T&F: n/a, R&B: n/a, Ttl: $4,250					

© 2011 — Updates? Want to be in the next edition? Visit **www.mysecondcampus.com**

Massachusetts

DESTINATION	HOST INSTITUTION	PRGM SEASON	PRGM TYPE	INTERMEDIARY	HOUSING
France | Grenoble	Grenoble Graduate School of Business	n/a	Dir	n/a	n/a
France | Rouen	Rouen Business School	n/a	Dir	n/a	n/a
Germany and Czech Republic | (Multiple)	Bentley College	Sum	Self	n/a	n/a
Costs: Sum Costs: T&F: n/a, R&B: n/a, Ttl: $3,395					
Ghana | (Multiple)	Bentley College	Sum	Self	n/a	n/a
Costs: Sum Costs: T&F: n/a, R&B: n/a, Ttl: $5,350					
Ghana | (Multiple)	Bentley College	Win	Self	n/a	n/a
Costs: Win Costs: T&F: n/a, R&B: n/a, Ttl: $4,100					
Ghana | (Multiple)	Bentley College	Spr	Self	n/a	n/a
Costs: Spr Costs: T&F: n/a, R&B: n/a, Ttl: $4,000					
Ghana | Accra	Ashesi University	n/a	Intermed	Council on International Education Exchange (CIEE)	n/a
Greece | Thessaloniki	American College of Thessaloniki	n/a	Dir	n/a	n/a
Greece | Thessaloniki	American College of Thessaloniki	Sum	Dir	n/a	n/a
Hungary | Budapest	Corvinus University of Budapest	n/a	Dir	n/a	n/a
India | Pune	Fergusson College	n/a	Intermed	Alliance for Global Education	n/a
India | Pune	Fergusson College	n/a	Intermed	Alliance for Global Education	n/a
India | Pune	Fergusson College	n/a	Intermed	Alliance for Global Education	n/a
India | Pune	Fergusson College	Sum	Intermed	Alliance for Global Education	n/a
Ireland | (Multiple)	Bentley College	Sum	Self	n/a	n/a
Costs: Sum Costs: T&F: n/a, R&B: n/a, Ttl: $4,100					
Ireland | Dublin	University College Dublin	n/a	Dir	n/a	n/a
Ireland | Dublin	University College Dublin	n/a	Dir	n/a	n/a
Italy | (Multiple)	Bentley College	Spr	Self	n/a	n/a
Costs: Spr Costs: T&F: n/a, R&B: n/a, Ttl: $3,100					
Italy | Florence	Lorenzo de'Medici Institute	n/a	Intermed	Lorenzo de'Medici Institute	n/a
Italy | Florence	Lorenzo de'Medici Institute	Sum	Intermed	Lorenzo de'Medici Institute	n/a
Italy | Milan	IES Abroad Milan Center	n/a	Intermed	IES Study Abroad	n/a
Italy | Rome	Lorenzo de'Medici Institute	n/a	Intermed	Lorenzo de'Medici Institute	n/a
Italy | Rome	Lorenzo de'Medici Institute	Sum	Intermed	Lorenzo de'Medici Institute	n/a
Italy | Tuscania	Lorenzo de'Medici Institute	Sum	Intermed	Lorenzo de'Medici Institute	n/a
Japan | (Multiple)	Bentley College	Sum	Self	n/a	n/a
Costs: Sum Costs: T&F: n/a, R&B: n/a, Ttl: $4,450					
Japan | Tokyo	Sophia University	n/a	Intermed	Council on International Education Exchange (CIEE)	n/a
Mexico | Puebla	Universidad de las Americas	Sum	Dir	n/a	n/a
Morocco | (Multiple)	Bentley College	Sum	Self	n/a	n/a
Costs: Sum Costs: T&F: n/a, R&B: n/a, Ttl: $3,900					
Morocco | Ifrane	Al Akhawayn University	n/a	Dir	n/a	n/a
Morocco | Ifrane	Al Akhawayn University	Sum	Dir	n/a	n/a
New Zealand | (Multiple)	Bentley College	Win	Self	n/a	n/a
Costs: Win Costs: T&F: n/a, R&B: n/a, Ttl: $4,400					

© 2011 — Updates? Want to be in the next edition? Visit **www.mysecondcampus.com**

Massachusetts

DESTINATION	HOST INSTITUTION	PRGM SEASON	PRGM TYPE	INTERMEDIARY	HOUSING
Scotland | Glasgow	University of Glasgow	n/a	Dir	n/a	n/a
Senegal | (Multiple)	Bentley College	Win	Self	n/a	n/a
	Costs: Win Costs: T&F: n/a, R&B: n/a, Ttl: $3,800				
Singapore | Singapore	Nanyang Technological University	n/a	Dir	n/a	n/a
South Africa | Cape Town	Connect-123	n/a	Intermed	Connect-123	n/a
South Africa | Cape Town	University of Cape Town	n/a	Dir	n/a	n/a
South Korea | Seoul	Yonsei University	Sum	Intermed	Council on International Education Exchange (CIEE)	n/a
South Korea | Seoul	Yonsei University	n/a	Intermed	Council on International Education Exchange (CIEE)	n/a
Spain | Barcelona	Universitat Pompeu Fabra	n/a	Dir	n/a	n/a
Spain | Madrid	Suffolk University Madrid Campus	Sum	USColl	Suffolk University	n/a
Spain | Madrid	Universidad Pontificia Comillas	n/a	Dir	n/a	n/a
Spain | Pamplona	Universidad de Navarra	n/a	Dir	n/a	n/a
Spain | Seville	Bentley College	Spr	Self	n/a	n/a
	Costs: Spr Costs: T&F: n/a, R&B: n/a, Ttl: $3,700				
Spain | Seville	Universidad Pablo de Olavide or Universidad de Sevilla	n/a	Intermed	Council on International Education Exchange (CIEE)	n/a
Turkey | (Multiple)	Bentley College	Spr	Self	n/a	n/a
	Costs: Spr Costs: T&F: n/a, R&B: n/a, Ttl: $4,350				
United Arab Emirates and Bahrain | (Multiple)	Bentley College	Win	Self	n/a	n/a
	Costs: Win Costs: T&F: n/a, R&B: n/a, Ttl: $5,100				

Berklee College of Music

Greg Badolato
Assistant Vice President for International Program
International Programs Office
1140 Boylston Street
Boston, MA 02215

gbadolato@berklee.edu
617.747.2700
http://www.berklee.edu/international/intlstudyabroad.html

Germany | Freiburg	International Music College Freiburg	Fall Spr	Dir	n/a	Other
	Costs: Fall Costs: T&F: $15,650, R&B: $7,915, Ttl: $23,565 Spr Costs: T&F: $15,650, R&B: $7,915, Ttl: $23,565				
Greece | Athens	Philipos Nakas Conservatory	Fall Spr	Dir	n/a	Other
	Costs: Fall Costs: T&F: $15,650, R&B: $7,915, Ttl: $23,565 Spr Costs: T&F: $15,650, R&B: $7,915, Ttl: $23,565				

© 2011 — Updates? Want to be in the next edition? Visit **www.mysecondcampus.com**

Massachusetts

DESTINATION	HOST INSTITUTION	PRGM SEASON	PRGM TYPE	INTERMEDIARY	HOUSING

Boston College

Bernd Widdig
Director of the Office of International Programs
Office of International Programs
Hovey House, 140 Commonwealth Avenue
Chestnut Hill, MA 02467

widdig@bc.edu
617.552.3827
http://www.bc.edu/offices/international/

DESTINATION	HOST INSTITUTION	PRGM SEASON	PRGM TYPE	INTERMEDIARY	HOUSING
(Multiple) | Buenos Aires	SIT Study Abroad	n/a	Intermed	SIT Study Abroad	n/a
Argentina | Buenos Aires	Boston College	Sum	Self	n/a	n/a
	Costs: Sum Costs: T&F: $4,000, R&B: $1,500, Ttl: n/a				
Argentina | Buenos Aires	Pontificia Universidad Catolica Argentina	n/a	Dir	n/a	HostFam PrivApt
Argentina | Buenos Aires	Universidad Torcuato Di Tella	n/a	Dir	n/a	HostFam PrivApt
Australia | Brisbane	University of Queensland	Sum Fall Spr YrRound	Intermed	Institute for Study Abroad	n/a
Australia | Fremantle	University of Notre Dame Australia	n/a	Dir	n/a	CollRes PrivApt
Australia | Melbourne	Monash University	n/a	Dir	n/a	CollRes
Australia | Melbourne	University of Melbourne	n/a	Dir	n/a	CollRes PrivApt
Australia | Perth	Murdoch University	n/a	Dir	n/a	CollRes PrivApt
Australia | Sydney	University of New South Wales	n/a	Dir	n/a	PrivApt
Australia | Sydney	University of Sydney	Sum Fall Spr YrRound	Intermed	Institute for Study Abroad	n/a
Austria | Vienna	IES Abroad Vienna Center	n/a	Intermed	IES Abroad	n/a
Brazil | Belem	SIT Study Abroad	n/a	Intermed	SIT Study Abroad	n/a
Brazil | Fortaleza	Instituto Brasil/Estados Unidos/Ceara	n/a	Intermed	SIT Study Abroad	n/a
Brazil | Rio de Janeiro	Pontificia Universidade Catolica do Rio de Janeiro	n/a	Dir	n/a	HostFam
Bulgaria | Blagoevgrad	American University in Bulgaria	n/a	Dir	n/a	n/a
Bulgaria | Veliko Turnovo	University of Veliko Turnovo	n/a	Dir	n/a	CollRes PrivApt
Cameroon | Yaounde	SIT Study Abroad	Spr	Intermed	SIT Study Abroad	n/a
Chile | Santiago	Boston College	Sum	Self	n/a	n/a
	Costs: Sum Costs: T&F: $2,000, R&B: $1,500, Ttl: n/a				
Chile | Santiago	Boston College	Sum	Self	n/a	n/a
	Costs: Sum Costs: T&F: $2,000, R&B: $1,300, Ttl: n/a				
Chile | Santiago	Pontificia Universidad Catolica de Chile	n/a	Dir	n/a	HostFam CollRes PrivApt
Chile | Santiago	Universidad Alberto Hurtado	n/a	Dir	n/a	HostFam CollRes PrivApt
China | Beijing	Beijing Center for Chinese Studies	n/a	Intermed	Beijing Center for Chinese Studies	n/a
China | Beijing	China Studies Institute (Peking University)	n/a	Dir	n/a	CollRes

© 2011 — Updates? Want to be in the next edition? Visit www.mysecondcampus.com

Massachusetts

DESTINATION	HOST INSTITUTION	PRGM SEASON	PRGM TYPE	INTERMEDIARY	HOUSING
China	Hong Kong	Hong Kong University of Science and Technology	n/a	Dir	n/a	CollRes
China	Shanghai	Shanghai University of Finance and Economics	Sum Fall Spr	Intermed	Alliance for Global Education	n/a
Costa Rica	Monteverde	Boston College	Sum	Self	n/a	n/a
	Costs: Sum Costs: T&F: $2,600, R&B: n/a, Ttl: n/a				
Costa Rica	Monteverde	CIEE Study Center in Monteverde	n/a	Intermed	Council on International Educational Exchange (CIEE)	n/a
Costa Rica	San Jose	International Center for Development Studies	n/a	Intermed	International Center for Development Studies	n/a
Czech Republic	Prague	Charles University	Fall Spr YrRound	Intermed	Council on International Educational Exchange (CIEE)	n/a
Czech Republic	Prague	New York University in Prague	Fall Spr YrRound	USColl	New York University	n/a
Denmark	Copenhagen	Copenhagen Business School	n/a	Dir	n/a	CollRes PrivApt
Denmark	Copenhagen	University of Copenhagen	n/a	Dir	n/a	CollRes PrivApt
Ecuador	Quito	Boston College	Sum	Self	n/a	n/a
	Costs: Sum Costs: T&F: $2,000, R&B: $1,200, Ttl: n/a				
Ecuador	Quito	Universidad San Francisco de Quito	n/a	Dir	n/a	HostFam
Egypt	Cairo	American University in Cairo	n/a	Dir	n/a	n/a
Egypt	Cairo	AMIDEAST	Fall Spr YrRound	Intermed	AMIDEAST	n/a
Egypt	Cairo	AMIDEAST	Fall Spr YrRound	Intermed	AMIDEAST	n/a
El Salvador	San Salvador	Santa Clara University	Sum Fall Spr	USColl	Santa Clara University	n/a
England	Bath	Advanced Studies in England (University College, Oxford)	n/a	Dir	n/a	PrivApt
England	Cambridge	Cambridge University	n/a	Intermed	Institute for Study Abroad	n/a
England	Durham	University of Durham	YrRound	Dir	n/a	CollRes
England	Lancaster	Lancaster University	n/a	Dir	n/a	CollRes
England	Liverpool	University of Liverpool	n/a	Dir	n/a	CollRes
England	London	Boston College	Sum	Self	n/a	n/a
	Costs: Sum Costs: T&F: $2,000, R&B: $3,000, Ttl: n/a				
England	London	Boston College	Sum	Self	n/a	n/a
	Costs: Sum Costs: T&F: $2,000, R&B: $2,700, Ttl: n/a				
England	London	British American Drama Academy	Fall Spr YrRound	USColl	Sarah Lawrence College	n/a
England	London	King's College	n/a	Dir	n/a	CollRes PrivApt
England	London	London Center (Boston University)	Sum Fall Spr	USColl	Boston University	n/a
England	London	London School of Economics and Political Science	n/a	Dir	n/a	CollRes PrivApt
England	London	New York University in London	n/a	USColl	New York University	n/a
England	London	Queen Mary	n/a	Dir	n/a	CollRes PrivApt
England	London	Royal Holloway	n/a	Dir	n/a	CollRes PrivApt
England	London	School of Oriental & African Studies	n/a	Dir	n/a	CollRes PrivApt

© 2011 — Updates? Want to be in the next edition? Visit **www.mysecondcampus.com**

Massachusetts

DESTINATION	HOST INSTITUTION	PRGM SEASON	PRGM TYPE	INTERMEDIARY	HOUSING
England | London	University College London	n/a	Dir	n/a	CollRes PrivApt
England | London	University of Westminster	Sum Fall Spr YrRound	Intermed	Institute for Study Abroad	n/a
England | Oxford	Oxford University	n/a	Intermed	Institute for Study Abroad	n/a
France | Aix-en-Provence	Aix Center (IAU)	Sum Fall Spr YrRound	Intermed	Institute for American Universities (IAU)	n/a
France | Bourdeaux	Boston College	Sum	Self	n/a	n/a
	Costs: Sum Costs: T&F: $2,000, R&B: $3,000, Ttl: n/a				
France | Bourdeaux	Boston College	Sum	Self	n/a	n/a
	Costs: Sum Costs: T&F: $4,000, R&B: $3,000, Ttl: n/a				
France | Grenoble	Multiple institutional choices	Sum Fall Spr YrRound	Intermed	Academic Programs International (API)	n/a
France | Montpellier	Paul Valery University	Sum Fall Spr YrRound	USColl	Learning Abroad Center (University of Minnesota)	n/a
France | Paris	Centre Sevres-Facultes jesuites de Paris	n/a	Dir	n/a	HostFam PrivApt
France | Paris	Institut Catholique de Paris	n/a	Dir	n/a	HostFam PrivApt
France | Paris	Institut d'etudes Politiques de Paris (Sciences Po)	n/a	Dir	n/a	HostFam PrivApt
France | Paris	New York University in Paris Center	n/a	USColl	n/a	n/a
France | Paris	University of Paris: Paris VII- Denis Diderot, Paris IV- Sorbonne, Paris IX-Dauphine	n/a	Dir	n/a	HostFam PrivApt
France | Strasbourg	Ecole de Management de Strasbourg	n/a	Dir	n/a	HostFam PrivApt
France | Strasbourg	Institut d'etudes Politiques	n/a	Dir	n/a	HostFam PrivApt
France | Strasbourg	Universite de Strasbourg-Universite Mark Bloch	n/a	Dir	n/a	HostFam PrivApt
Germany | Berlin	Freie Universitat	Sum Fall Spr YrRound	Dir	n/a	n/a
Germany | Berlin	IES Abroad Berlin Center	n/a	Intermed	IES Abroad	n/a
Germany | Eichstatt	Catholic University of Eichstatt	n/a	Dir	n/a	CollRes PrivApt
Germany | Heidelberg	University of Heidelberg	Sum Fall Spr YrRound	USColl	Heidelberg University	n/a
Germany | Unknown	Boston College	Sum	Self	n/a	n/a
	Costs: Sum Costs: T&F: $4,000, R&B: $2,700, Ttl: n/a				
Germany | Vallendar	WHU – Otto Beisheim School of Management	n/a	Dir	n/a	CollRes PrivApt Other
Ghana | Accra	Ashesi University	Fall Spr YrRound	Intermed	Council on International Educational Exchange (CIEE)	n/a
Ghana | Accra	University of Ghana	Fall Spr YrRound	Intermed	Council on International Educational Exchange (CIEE)	n/a
Ghana | Cape Coast	SIT Study Abroad	n/a	Intermed	SIT Study Abroad	Other
Greece | Athens	American College of Greece	n/a	Intermed	American College of Greece	n/a
Greece | Athens	Boston College	Sum	Self	n/a	n/a
	Costs: Sum Costs: T&F: $2,000, R&B: $2,300, Ttl: n/a				

© 2011 — Updates? Want to be in the next edition? Visit **www.mysecondcampus.com**

Massachusetts

DESTINATION	HOST INSTITUTION	PRGM SEASON	PRGM TYPE	INTERMEDIARY	HOUSING
Greece | Athens	College Year in Athens	Sum Fall Spr YrRound	Intermed	College Year in Athens	n/a
Greece | Thessaloniki	American College of Thessaloniki	n/a	Dir	n/a	CollRes
Hungary | Budapest	Corvinus University of Budapest	n/a	Intermed	Academic Programs International (API)	n/a
India | Hyderabad	University of Hyderabad	Sum Fall Spr	Intermed	Council on International Educational Exchange (CIEE)	n/a
India | Mussourie	Boston College	Sum	Self	n/a	n/a
	Costs: Sum Costs: T&F: $2,000, R&B: $1,200, Ttl: n/a				
India | Pune	Fergusson College	Sum Fall Spr	Intermed	Alliance for Global Education	n/a
Indonesia | Ubud (Bali)	Boston College	Sum	Self	n/a	n/a
	Costs: Sum Costs: T&F: $2,000, R&B: $1,500, Ttl: n/a				
Ireland | Cork	University College Cork	n/a	Dir	n/a	HostFam CollRes PrivApt
Ireland | Dublin	Boston College	Sum	Self	n/a	n/a
	Costs: Sum Costs: T&F: $2,000, R&B: $2,800, Ttl: n/a				
Ireland | Dublin	Boston College	Sum	Self	n/a	n/a
	Costs: Sum Costs: T&F: n/a, R&B: $4,700, Ttl: n/a				
Ireland | Dublin	Boston College	Sum	Self	n/a	n/a
	Costs: Sum Costs: T&F: $2,000, R&B: $2,500, Ttl: n/a				
Ireland | Dublin	Boston College	Sum	Self	n/a	n/a
	Costs: Sum Costs: T&F: $2,000, R&B: $2,600, Ttl: n/a				
Ireland | Dublin	Boston College	Sum	Self	n/a	n/a
	Costs: Sum Costs: T&F: $2,000, R&B: $2,500, Ttl: n/a				
Ireland | Dublin	Dublin City University	Sum Fall Spr	USColl	Boston University	n/a
Ireland | Dublin	National University of Ireland, Maynooth	n/a	Dir	n/a	CollRes
Ireland | Dublin	Trinity College	n/a	Dir	n/a	CollRes
Ireland | Dublin	University College Dublin	n/a	Dir	n/a	PrivApt
Ireland | Galway	National University of Ireland	n/a	Dir	n/a	PrivApt
Ireland | Limerick	University of Limerick	Sum Fall Spr YrRound	Intermed	Institute for Study Abroad	n/a
Israel | Jerusalem	Hebrew University of Jerusalem	n/a	Dir	n/a	n/a
Israel | Tel Aviv	Boston College	Sum	Self	n/a	n/a
	Costs: Sum Costs: T&F: $2,000, R&B: n/a, Ttl: n/a				
Italy | Cortona	University of Georgia	Sum Fall Spr	USColl	University of Georgia	n/a
Italy | Florence	Boston College	Sum	Self	n/a	n/a
	Costs: Sum Costs: T&F: $2,000, R&B: $3,200, Ttl: n/a				
Italy | Florence	Boston College	Sum	Self	n/a	n/a
	Costs: Sum Costs: T&F: $2,000, R&B: $3,200, Ttl: n/a				
Italy | Florence	Florence University of the Arts	Fall Spr YrRound	USColl	Fairfield University	n/a
Italy | Florence	New York University in Florence	Sum Fall Spr	USColl	New York University	n/a
Italy | Florence	Syracuse University in Florence	Sum Fall Spr	USColl	Syracuse University	n/a

Massachusetts

DESTINATION	HOST INSTITUTION	PRGM SEASON	PRGM TYPE	INTERMEDIARY	HOUSING
Italy | Milan	Bocconi University	n/a	Bilat	n/a	CollRes PrivApt
Italy | Parma	Boston College	Sum	Self	n/a	n/a
Italy | Parma	University of Parma	n/a	Dir	n/a	HostFam PrivApt
Italy | Rome	American University in Rome	n/a	Dir	n/a	n/a
Italy | Rome	Boston College	Sum	Self	n/a	n/a
	Costs: Sum Costs: T&F: $2,000, R&B: $2,200, Ttl: n/a				
Italy | Rome	Boston College	Sum	Self	n/a	n/a
	Costs: Sum Costs: T&F: $2,000, R&B: $2,400, Ttl: n/a				
Italy | Rome	Intercollegiate Center for Classical Studies in Rome (Duke University)	n/a	Consrtm	Intercollegiate Center for Classical Studies in Rome (Duke University)	n/a
Italy | Rome	John Cabot University	n/a	Dir	n/a	n/a
Italy | Venice	Boston College	Sum	Self	n/a	n/a
	Costs: Sum Costs: T&F: $2,000, R&B: $2,400, Ttl: n/a				
Italy | Venice	Boston College	Sum	Self	n/a	n/a
	Costs: Sum Costs: T&F: $2,000, R&B: $2,400, Ttl: n/a				
Italy | Venice	Boston College	Sum	Self	n/a	n/a
	Costs: Sum Costs: T&F: $2,000, R&B: $2,400, Ttl: n/a				
Italy | Venice	Venice International University	n/a	Dir	n/a	CollRes
Japan | Kyoto	Kyoto Consortium for Japanese Studies	Fall Spr YrRound	Consrtm	Kyoto Consortium for Japanese Studies (Columbia University)	n/a
Japan | Tokyo	Sophia University	n/a	Dir	n/a	HostFam CollRes PrivApt
Japan | Tokyo	Waseda University	n/a	Dir	n/a	HostFam CollRes PrivApt
Jordan | Amman	University of Jordan	Fall Spr YrRound	Intermed	Council on International Educational Exchange (CIEE)	n/a
Kuwait | Kuwait City	Boston College	Sum	Self	n/a	n/a
	Costs: Sum Costs: T&F: $4,000, R&B: $3,300, Ttl: n/a				
Kuwait | Salmiya	American University of Kuwait	n/a	Dir	n/a	HostFam PrivApt
Madagascar | Fort Dauphin	SIT Study Abroad	n/a	Intermed	SIT Study Abroad	n/a
Mali | Bamako	SIT Study Abroad	n/a	Intermed	SIT Study Abroad	n/a
Mexico | Guanajuato	Universidad de Guanajuato	Sum	Intermed	Council on International Educational Exchange (CIEE)	n/a
Mexico | Monterrey	Tecnologico de Monterrey	n/a	Dir	n/a	n/a
Mexico | Nogales	BorderLinks	Sum Fall Spr	Intermed	BorderLinks	n/a
Mexico | Puebla	Universidad Iberoamericana	n/a	Dir	n/a	HostFam
Morocco | Ifrane	Al Akhawayn University	n/a	Dir	n/a	n/a
Morocco | Rabat	AMIDEAST	Fall Spr YrRound	Intermed	AMIDEAST	n/a
Morocco | Rabat	Ecole Superieure de Direction et de Gestion	Fall Spr YrRound	Intermed	Council on International Educational Exchange (CIEE)	n/a
Nepal | Kathmandu	Center for Buddhist Studies (Kathmandu University)	n/a	Dir	n/a	HostFam
Netherlands | Amsterdam	University of Amsterdam	n/a	Dir	n/a	CollRes

© 2011 — Updates? Want to be in the next edition? Visit **www.mysecondcampus.com**

Massachusetts

DESTINATION	HOST INSTITUTION	PRGM SEASON	PRGM TYPE	INTERMEDIARY	HOUSING
Netherlands | Leiden	Leiden University	n/a	Dir	n/a	PrivApt
New Zealand | Dunedin	University of Otago	Sum Fall Spr YrRound	Intermed	Institute for Study Abroad	n/a
Nicaragua | Managua	SIT Study Abroad	n/a	Intermed	SIT Study Abroad	n/a
Nicaragua | Managua	Universidad Centroamericana	n/a	USColl	Fairfield University	n/a
Northern Ireland | Belfast	Queen's University	n/a	Dir	n/a	n/a
Norway | Bergen	University of Bergen	n/a	Dir	n/a	n/a
Oman | Muscat	SIT Study Abroad	n/a	Intermed	SIT Study Abroad	n/a
Panama | Panama City	SIT Study Abroad	n/a	Intermed	SIT Study Abroad	n/a
Philippines | Manila	Ateneo de Manila University	n/a	Dir	n/a	CollRes PrivApt
Poland | Krakow	Jagiellonian University	n/a	Dir	n/a	n/a
Portugal | Lisbon	Universidade Nova de Lisboa	Fall Spr YrRound	Intermed	Council on International Educational Exchange (CIEE)	n/a
Russia | (Multiple)	American Councils for International Education	Sum Fall Spr YrRound	Intermed	American Councils for International Education	n/a
Russia | St. Petersburg	Smolny College of Liberal Arts and Sciences	Sum Fall Spr YrRound	USColl	Bard College	n/a
Russia | St. Petersburg	St. Petersburg State Polytechnic University	Sum Fall Spr YrRound	Intermed	American Institute for Foreign Study (AIFS)	n/a
Scotland | Edinburgh	University of Edinburgh	Fall Spr YrRound	Intermed	Institute for Study Abroad	n/a
Scotland | Glasgow	University of Glasgow	n/a	Dir	n/a	CollRes
Scotland | St. Andrews	University of St. Andrews	Sum Fall Spr YrRound	Intermed	Institute for Study Abroad	n/a
Senegal | Dakar	SIT Study Abroad	n/a	Intermed	SIT Study Abroad	n/a
Singapore | Singapore	National Institute of Education (Nanyang Technical University)	n/a	Dir	n/a	Other
South Africa | Cape Town	University of Cape Town	n/a	Dir	n/a	n/a
South Africa | Grahamstown	Rhodes University	n/a	Dir	n/a	CollRes
South Africa | Unknown	Boston College	Sum	Self	n/a	n/a
	Costs: Sum Costs: T&F: $2,000, R&B: $2,700, Ttl: n/a				
South Korea | Seoul	Sogang University	n/a	Dir	n/a	CollRes
Spain | Alcala de Henares	Universidad de Alcala	Sum Fall Spr YrRound	Intermed	Council on International Educational Exchange (CIEE)	n/a
Spain | Alicante	Universidad de Alicante	Fall Spr	Intermed	Council on International Educational Exchange (CIEE)	n/a
Spain | Barcelona	ESADE	n/a	Dir	n/a	CollRes
Spain | Barcelona	Pompeu Fabra University	n/a	Dir	n/a	CollRes
Spain | Bilbao; San Sebastian	Universidad de Deusto	n/a	Dir	n/a	HostFam CollRes PrivApt
Spain | Cadiz	University of Cadiz	Sum Fall Spr YrRound	Intermed	Academic Programs International (API)	n/a
Spain | Granada	University of Granada	n/a	Dir	n/a	HostFam
Spain | Madrid	Boston College	Sum	Self	n/a	n/a
	Costs: Sum Costs: T&F: $2,000, R&B: $2,100, Ttl: n/a				
Spain | Madrid	Boston College	Sum	Self	n/a	n/a
	Costs: Sum Costs: T&F: $2,000, R&B: $1,800, Ttl: n/a				

Massachusetts

DESTINATION	HOST INSTITUTION	PRGM SEASON	PRGM TYPE	INTERMEDIARY	HOUSING
Spain | Madrid	St. Louis University Madrid Campus	Fall Spr YrRound	USColl	St. Louis University	n/a
Spain | Madrid	Universidad Carlos III	n/a	Dir	n/a	HostFam CollRes PrivApt
Spain | Madrid	Universidad Complutense de Madrid	n/a	Dir	n/a	HostFam CollRes PrivApt
Spain | Madrid	Universidad Pontificia Comillas de Madrid	n/a	Dir	n/a	HostFam CollRes PrivApt
Spain | Salamanca	University of Salamanca	Sum Fall Spr YrRound	Intermed	Academic Programs International (API)	n/a
Spain | Seville	University of Seville	Sum Fall Spr YrRound	Intermed	Academic Programs International (API)	n/a
Sweden | Uppsala	Uppsala University	n/a	Bilat	n/a	Other
Switzerland | Geneva	Boston University	Fall Spr	USColl	Boston University	n/a
Switzerland | Geneva	Kent State University	Fall Spr	USColl	Kent State University	n/a
Switzerland | Geneva	SIT Study Abroad	n/a	Intermed	SIT Study Abroad	n/a
Tanzania | Arusha	Arcadia University	Sum Fall Spr YrRound	USColl	Arcadia University	n/a
Tanzania | Arusha	SIT Study Abroad	n/a	Intermed	SIT Study Abroad	n/a
Turkey | Istanbul	Bogazici University	n/a	Dir	n/a	n/a
Turkey | Istanbul	Boston College	Sum	Self	n/a	n/a
	Costs: Sum Costs: T&F: $2,000, R&B: $2,600, Ttl: n/a				
Uganda | Kampala	SIT Study Abroad	n/a	Intermed	SIT Study Abroad	n/a
United States | Washington (DC)	American University	Fall Spr	USColl	American University	n/a
United States | Washington (DC)	Georgetown University	Fall Spr	USColl	Georgetown University	n/a
United States | Woods Hole (MA)	Sea Semester	n/a	Intermed	Sea Semester	n/a
United States | Woods Hole (MA)	Sea Semester	Sum Fall Spr	Intermed	Sea Semester	n/a
United States | Woods Hole (MA)	Sea Semester	n/a	Intermed	Sea Semester	n/a
United States | Woods Hole (MA)	Sea Semester	Spr	Intermed	Sea Semester	n/a
Wales | Swansea	Swansea University	Fall Spr YrRound	USColl	Arcadia University	n/a

Boston University

Urbain (Ben) DeWinter
Associate Provost
International Programs
888 Commonwealth Avenue
Boston, MA 02215

dewinter@bu.edu
617.353.7113
http://www.bu.edu/abroad/

DESTINATION	HOST INSTITUTION	PRGM SEASON	PRGM TYPE	INTERMEDIARY	HOUSING
Australia | Sydney	Boston University	Sum Fall Spr	Self	n/a	CollRes
	Costs: Sum Costs: T&F: n/a, R&B: n/a, Ttl: $7,300 Fall Costs: T&F: n/a, R&B: n/a, Ttl: $16,550 Spr Costs: T&F: n/a, R&B: n/a, Ttl: $16,550				
Australia | Sydney	Boston University Sydney Center	Sum	Self	n/a	CollRes
	Costs: Sum Costs: T&F: n/a, R&B: n/a, Ttl: $7,300				
Australia | Sydney	Boston University Sydney Center	Sum	Self	n/a	CollRes
	Costs: Sum Costs: T&F: n/a, R&B: n/a, Ttl: $7,300				

© 2011 — Updates? Want to be in the next edition? Visit **www.mysecondcampus.com**

Massachusetts

DESTINATION	HOST INSTITUTION	PRGM SEASON	PRGM TYPE	INTERMEDIARY	HOUSING
Australia | Sydney	University of Sydney	Fall Spr	Dir	n/a	CollRes
Costs: Fall Costs: T&F: n/a, R&B: n/a, Ttl: $22,810 Spr Costs: T&F: n/a, R&B: n/a, Ttl: $22,810					
Australia | Sydney	University of Sydney	Spr	Dir	n/a	CollRes
Costs: Spr Costs: T&F: n/a, R&B: n/a, Ttl: $18,200					
China | Shanghai	Fudan University	Fall Spr	Dir	n/a	CollRes
Costs: Fall Costs: T&F: n/a, R&B: n/a, Ttl: $22,810 Spr Costs: T&F: n/a, R&B: n/a, Ttl: $22,810					
China | Shanghai	Fudan University	Sum	Dir	n/a	CollRes
Costs: Sum Costs: T&F: n/a, R&B: n/a, Ttl: $7,300					
China | Shanghai	Fudan University	Fall Spr YrRound	Dir	n/a	CollRes PrivApt
Costs: Fall Costs: T&F: n/a, R&B: n/a, Ttl: $22,810 Spr Costs: T&F: n/a, R&B: n/a, Ttl: $22,810 YrRound Costs: T&F: n/a, R&B: n/a, Ttl: $45,620					
Denmark | Copenhagen	University of Copenhagen	Fall Spr YrRound	Bilat	n/a	PrivApt
Costs: Fall Costs: T&F: n/a, R&B: n/a, Ttl: $18,955 Spr Costs: T&F: n/a, R&B: n/a, Ttl: $18,955 YrRound Costs: T&F: n/a, R&B: n/a, Ttl: $37,910					
Ecuador | (Multiple)	Universidad San Francisco de Quito (USFQ)	Fall Spr	Self	n/a	HostFam Other
Costs: Fall Costs: T&F: n/a, R&B: n/a, Ttl: $24,879 Spr Costs: T&F: n/a, R&B: n/a, Ttl: $24,879					
Ecuador | Quito	Universidad San Francisco de Quito (USFQ)	Fall Spr YrRound	Dir	n/a	HostFam
Costs: Fall Costs: T&F: n/a, R&B: n/a, Ttl: $24,879 Spr Costs: T&F: n/a, R&B: n/a, Ttl: $24,879 YrRound Costs: T&F: n/a, R&B: n/a, Ttl: $49,758					
England & Switzerland | London & Geneva	Boston University	Sum	Self	n/a	CollRes
Costs: Sum Costs: T&F: n/a, R&B: n/a, Ttl: $7,300					
England | London	Boston University	Fall	Self	n/a	CollRes
Costs: Fall Costs: T&F: n/a, R&B: n/a, Ttl: $22,810					
England | London	Boston University	Sum	Self	n/a	CollRes
Costs: Sum Costs: T&F: n/a, R&B: n/a, Ttl: $7,300					
England | London	Boston University	Sum	Self	n/a	CollRes
Costs: Sum Costs: T&F: n/a, R&B: n/a, Ttl: $19,900					
England | London	Boston University	Sum	Self	n/a	CollRes
Costs: Sum Costs: T&F: n/a, R&B: n/a, Ttl: $7,300					
England | London	Boston University	Sum	Self	n/a	CollRes
Costs: Sum Costs: T&F: n/a, R&B: n/a, Ttl: $7,300					
England | London	Boston University	Sum Fall Spr	Self	n/a	CollRes
Costs: Sum Costs: T&F: n/a, R&B: n/a, Ttl: $12,900 Fall Costs: T&F: n/a, R&B: n/a, Ttl: $16,550 Spr Costs: T&F: n/a, R&B: n/a, Ttl: $16,550					
England | London	Courtauld Institute of Art	Fall	Dir	n/a	CollRes
Costs: Fall Costs: T&F: n/a, R&B: n/a, Ttl: $22,810					
England | London	London Academy of Music and Dramatic Arts (LAMDA)	Spr	Self	n/a	CollRes
Costs: Spr Costs: T&F: n/a, R&B: n/a, Ttl: $22,810					
England | London	Roehampton University	Fall	Self	n/a	PrivApt
Costs: Fall Costs: T&F: n/a, R&B: n/a, Ttl: $22,810					

© 2011 — Updates? Want to be in the next edition? Visit **www.mysecondcampus.com**

Massachusetts

DESTINATION	HOST INSTITUTION	PRGM SEASON	PRGM TYPE	INTERMEDIARY	HOUSING
England | London	Royal College of Music	Fall	Self	n/a	CollRes
Costs: Fall Costs: T&F: n/a, R&B: n/a, Ttl: $22,810					
France | Grenoble	Universite de Grenoble	Sum Fall Spr YrRound	Self	n/a	HostFam
Costs: Sum Costs: T&F: n/a, R&B: n/a, Ttl: $7,300 Fall Costs: T&F: n/a, R&B: n/a, Ttl: $24,879 Spr Costs: T&F: n/a, R&B: n/a, Ttl: $24,879 YrRound Costs: T&F: n/a, R&B: n/a, Ttl: $49,758					
France | Grenoble	Universite de Grenoble	Fall	Self	n/a	HostFam
Costs: Fall Costs: T&F: n/a, R&B: n/a, Ttl: $24,879					
France | Paris	Boston University	Sum Fall Spr	Self	n/a	HostFam CollRes
Costs: Sum Costs: T&F: n/a, R&B: n/a, Ttl: $7,300 Fall Costs: T&F: n/a, R&B: n/a, Ttl: $16,550 Spr Costs: T&F: n/a, R&B: n/a, Ttl: $16,550					
France | Paris	Institut d'Etudes Politiques de Paris (Sciences Po)	YrRound	Bilat	n/a	n/a
Costs: YrRound Costs: T&F: n/a, R&B: n/a, Ttl: $45,620					
Germany | Dresden	Technische Universitat Dresden (TUD)	Fall	Dir	n/a	CollRes
Costs: Fall Costs: T&F: n/a, R&B: n/a, Ttl: $24,879					
Germany | Dresden	Technische Universitat Dresden (TUD)	Fall Spr YrRound	Dir	n/a	CollRes
Costs: Fall Costs: T&F: n/a, R&B: n/a, Ttl: $24,879 Spr Costs: T&F: n/a, R&B: n/a, Ttl: $24,879 YrRound Costs: T&F: n/a, R&B: n/a, Ttl: $49,758					
Germany | Dresden	Technische Universitat Dresden (TUD)	Spr	Dir	n/a	CollRes
Costs: Spr Costs: T&F: n/a, R&B: n/a, Ttl: $24,879					
Germany | Dresden	Technische Universitat Dresden (TUD)	Fall Spr YrRound	Self	n/a	CollRes
Costs: Fall Costs: T&F: n/a, R&B: n/a, Ttl: $24,879 Spr Costs: T&F: n/a, R&B: n/a, Ttl: $24,879 YrRound Costs: T&F: n/a, R&B: n/a, Ttl: $49,758					
Guatemala | Antigua and San Bartolo	Boston University	Spr	Self	n/a	HostFam Other
Costs: Spr Costs: T&F: n/a, R&B: n/a, Ttl: $24,879					
Ireland | Dublin	Dublin City University (DCU)	Sum Fall Spr	Dir	n/a	CollRes
Costs: Sum Costs: T&F: n/a, R&B: n/a, Ttl: $7,300 Fall Costs: T&F: n/a, R&B: n/a, Ttl: $16,500 Spr Costs: T&F: n/a, R&B: n/a, Ttl: $16,550					
Ireland | Dublin	Dublin City University (DCU)	Fall	Dir	n/a	CollRes
Costs: Fall Costs: T&F: n/a, R&B: n/a, Ttl: $22,810					
Israel | Haifa	University of Haifa	Fall Spr	Dir	n/a	CollRes
Costs: Fall Costs: T&F: n/a, R&B: n/a, Ttl: $22,810 Spr Costs: T&F: n/a, R&B: n/a, Ttl: $22,810					
Israel | Tel Aviv	Tel Aviv University (TAU)	Spr	Dir	n/a	CollRes
Costs: Spr Costs: T&F: n/a, R&B: n/a, Ttl: $22,810					
Italy | Arezzo	Accademia dell'Arte	Spr	Dir	n/a	CollRes
Costs: Spr Costs: T&F: n/a, R&B: n/a, Ttl: $24,879					
Italy | Borgo San Lorenzo	Capitignano	Sum	Self	n/a	Other
Costs: Sum Costs: T&F: n/a, R&B: n/a, Ttl: $8,050					
Italy | Milan	Bocconi University	Fall Spr YrRound	Bilat	n/a	CollRes
Costs: Fall Costs: T&F: n/a, R&B: n/a, Ttl: $18,955 Spr Costs: T&F: n/a, R&B: n/a, Ttl: $18,955 YrRound Costs: T&F: n/a, R&B: n/a, Ttl: $37,910					

© 2011 — Updates? Want to be in the next edition? Visit www.mysecondcampus.com

Massachusetts

DESTINATION	HOST INSTITUTION	PRGM SEASON	PRGM TYPE	INTERMEDIARY	HOUSING
Italy | Padova	Universita degli Studi di Padova	Sum Fall Spr YrRound	Self Dir	n/a	HostFam
	Costs: Sum Costs: T&F: n/a, R&B: n/a, Ttl: $7,300 Fall Costs: T&F: n/a, R&B: n/a, Ttl: $24,879 Spr Costs: T&F: n/a, R&B: n/a, Ttl: $24,879 YrRound Costs: T&F: n/a, R&B: n/a, Ttl: $49,758				
Italy | Rome	Intercollegiate Center for Classical Studies in Rome (ICCS)	Fall Spr	Consrtm	Intercollegiate Center for Classical Studies in Rome (Duke University)	CollRes
	Costs: Fall Costs: T&F: n/a, R&B: n/a, Ttl: $24,879 Spr Costs: T&F: n/a, R&B: n/a, Ttl: $24,879				
Italy | Sicily	Intercollegiate Center for Classical Studies in Catania (ICCS-Sicily)	Fall Spr	Consrtm	Intercollegiate Center for Classical Studies in Catania (Duke University)	CollRes
	Costs: Fall Costs: T&F: n/a, R&B: n/a, Ttl: $24,879 Spr Costs: T&F: n/a, R&B: n/a, Ttl: $24,879				
Italy | Venice	Scuola Internazionale di Grafica	Fall Spr	Dir	n/a	PrivApt
	Costs: Fall Costs: T&F: n/a, R&B: n/a, Ttl: $22,810 Spr Costs: T&F: n/a, R&B: n/a, Ttl: $22,810				
Japan | Kyoto	Kyoto Consortium for Japanese Studies (KCJS)	Fall Spr YrRound	Consrtm	n/a	HostFam PrivApt
	Costs: Fall Costs: T&F: n/a, R&B: n/a, Ttl: $18,955 Spr Costs: T&F: n/a, R&B: n/a, Ttl: $18,955 YrRound Costs: T&F: n/a, R&B: n/a, Ttl: $37,910				
Japan | Tokyo	Keio University	Spr YrRound	Bilat	n/a	CollRes PrivApt
	Costs: Spr Costs: T&F: n/a, R&B: n/a, Ttl: $18,955 YrRound Costs: T&F: n/a, R&B: n/a, Ttl: $37,910				
Lebanon | Beirut	American University of Beirut (AUB)	Fall Spr YrRound	Bilat	n/a	CollRes PrivApt
	Costs: Fall Costs: T&F: n/a, R&B: n/a, Ttl: $18,955 Spr Costs: T&F: n/a, R&B: n/a, Ttl: $18,955 YrRound Costs: T&F: n/a, R&B: n/a, Ttl: $37,910				
Mexico | Guadalajara	The Instituto Tecnologico y de Estudios Superiores de Monterrey (ITESM)	Spr	Dir	n/a	CollRes
	Costs: Spr Costs: T&F: n/a, R&B: n/a, Ttl: $22,810				
Morocco | Rabat	Center for Cross Cultural Learning (CCCL)	Fall Spr	Intermed	Center for Cross Cultural Learning (CCCL)	HostFam
	Costs: Fall Costs: T&F: n/a, R&B: n/a, Ttl: $24,879 Spr Costs: T&F: n/a, R&B: n/a, Ttl: $24,879				
Morocco | Rabat	Center for Cross Cultural Learning (CCCL)	Sum	Intermed	Center for Cross Cultural Learning (CCCL)	HostFam
New Zealand | Auckland	University of Auckland; Auckland University of Technology (AUT University)	Fall Spr	Dir	n/a	CollRes
	Costs: Fall Costs: T&F: n/a, R&B: n/a, Ttl: $16,550 Spr Costs: T&F: n/a, R&B: n/a, Ttl: $18,200				
New Zealand | Auckland	University of Auckland; Auckland University of Technology (AUT University)	Fall Spr	Dir	n/a	CollRes
	Costs: Fall Costs: T&F: n/a, R&B: n/a, Ttl: $16,550 Spr Costs: T&F: n/a, R&B: n/a, Ttl: $18,200				
Niger | Niamey	Universite Abdou Moumouni	Fall Spr YrRound	Self	n/a	HostFam PrivApt
	Costs: Fall Costs: T&F: n/a, R&B: n/a, Ttl: $24,879 Spr Costs: T&F: n/a, R&B: n/a, Ttl: $24,879 YrRound Costs: T&F: n/a, R&B: n/a, Ttl: $49,758				
Peru | Lima and Ayacucho	Pontificia Universidad Catolica del Peru; Universidad Nacional de San Cristobal de Huamanga	Sum	Self	n/a	HostFam
	Costs: Sum Costs: T&F: n/a, R&B: n/a, Ttl: $7,300				

© 2011 — Updates? Want to be in the next edition? Visit **www.mysecondcampus.com**

Massachusetts

DESTINATION	HOST INSTITUTION	PRGM SEASON	PRGM TYPE	INTERMEDIARY	HOUSING
Senegal | Dakar	Boston University	Sum	Self	n/a	HostFam
	Costs: Sum Costs: T&F: n/a, R&B: n/a, Ttl: $7,000				
Singapore | Singapore	National University of Singapore	Fall Spr YrRound	Bilat	n/a	CollRes PrivApt
	Costs: Fall Costs: T&F: n/a, R&B: n/a, Ttl: $18,955 Spr Costs: T&F: n/a, R&B: n/a, Ttl: $18,955 YrRound Costs: T&F: n/a, R&B: n/a, Ttl: $37,910				
Spain | Burgos	University of Burgos (UBU)	Spr	Dir	n/a	HostFam CollRes
	Costs: Spr Costs: T&F: n/a, R&B: n/a, Ttl: $24,879				
Spain | Madrid	Instituto Internacional	Fall Spr	Self	n/a	HostFam
	Costs: Fall Costs: T&F: n/a, R&B: n/a, Ttl: $24,879 Spr Costs: T&F: n/a, R&B: n/a, Ttl: $24,879				
Spain | Madrid	Instituto Internacional	Sum Fall Spr YrRound	Self	n/a	HostFam
	Costs: Sum Costs: T&F: n/a, R&B: n/a, Ttl: $7,300 Fall Costs: T&F: n/a, R&B: n/a, Ttl: $24,879 Spr Costs: T&F: n/a, R&B: n/a, Ttl: $24,879 YrRound Costs: T&F: n/a, R&B: n/a, Ttl: $49,758				
Spain | Madrid	Instituto Internacional; Universidad Autonoma de Madrid (UAM)	Sum Fall Spr YrRound	Self	n/a	HostFam
	Costs: Sum Costs: T&F: n/a, R&B: n/a, Ttl: $7,300 Fall Costs: T&F: n/a, R&B: n/a, Ttl: $24,879 Spr Costs: T&F: n/a, R&B: n/a, Ttl: $24,879 YrRound Costs: T&F: n/a, R&B: n/a, Ttl: $49,758				
Spain | Madrid	Instituto Internacional; Universidad Autonoma de Madrid (UAM)	Sum Fall Spr YrRound	Self	n/a	HostFam
	Costs: Sum Costs: T&F: n/a, R&B: n/a, Ttl: $7,300 Fall Costs: T&F: n/a, R&B: n/a, Ttl: $24,879 Spr Costs: T&F: n/a, R&B: n/a, Ttl: $24,879 YrRound Costs: T&F: n/a, R&B: n/a, Ttl: $49,758				
Spain | Madrid	Universidad Autonoma de Madrid (UAM)	Spr	Dir	n/a	HostFam
	Costs: Spr Costs: T&F: n/a, R&B: n/a, Ttl: $24,879				
Spain | Menorca	Boston University	Sum	Self	n/a	Other
	Costs: Sum Costs: T&F: n/a, R&B: n/a, Ttl: $6,900				
Switzerland | Geneva	Boston University	Fall Spr	Self	n/a	CollRes
	Costs: Fall Costs: T&F: n/a, R&B: n/a, Ttl: $22,810 Spr Costs: T&F: n/a, R&B: n/a, Ttl: $22,810				
Syria | Nefilah	Boston University	Sum	Self	n/a	Other
Turkey | Ankara	Middle East Technical University (METU)	Fall Spr YrRound	Bilat	n/a	CollRes
	Costs: Fall Costs: T&F: n/a, R&B: n/a, Ttl: $17,200 Spr Costs: T&F: n/a, R&B: n/a, Ttl: $17,200 YrRound Costs: T&F: n/a, R&B: n/a, Ttl: $34,400				
Turkey | Istabul	Bogazici University	Fall Spr YrRound	Bilat	n/a	CollRes
	Costs: Fall Costs: T&F: n/a, R&B: n/a, Ttl: $17,200 Spr Costs: T&F: n/a, R&B: n/a, Ttl: $17,200 YrRound Costs: T&F: n/a, R&B: n/a, Ttl: $34,400				
United States | Los Angeles (CA)	Boston University	Fall Spr	Self	n/a	PrivApt
	Costs: Fall Costs: T&F: n/a, R&B: n/a, Ttl: $9,900 Spr Costs: T&F: n/a, R&B: n/a, Ttl: $9,900				
United States | Los Angeles (CA)	Boston University	Fall Spr	Self	n/a	PrivApt
	Costs: Fall Costs: T&F: n/a, R&B: n/a, Ttl: $9,900 Spr Costs: T&F: n/a, R&B: n/a, Ttl: $9,900				
United States | Los Angeles (CA)	Boston University	Sum Fall Spr	Self	n/a	PrivApt
	Costs: Sum Costs: T&F: n/a, R&B: n/a, Ttl: $6,700 Fall Costs: T&F: n/a, R&B: n/a, Ttl: $22,810 Spr Costs: T&F: n/a, R&B: n/a, Ttl: $22,810				
United States | Washington (DC)	Boston University Washington	Fall Spr	Self	n/a	CollRes
	Costs: Fall Costs: T&F: n/a, R&B: n/a, Ttl: $22,810 Spr Costs: T&F: n/a, R&B: n/a, Ttl: $22,810				

Massachusetts

DESTINATION	HOST INSTITUTION	PRGM SEASON	PRGM TYPE	INTERMEDIARY	HOUSING
United States | Washington (DC)	Boston University Washington	Sum Fall Spr	Self	n/a	CollRes
Costs: Sum Costs: T&F: n/a, R&B: n/a, Ttl: $7,000 Fall Costs: T&F: n/a, R&B: n/a, Ttl: $22,810 Spr Costs: T&F: n/a, R&B: n/a, Ttl: $22,810					

Brandeis University

J Scott Van Der Meid
Director of Study Abroad
Usdan 127, MS 073
415 South Street
Waltham, MA 02453

svanderm@brandeis.edu
781.736.3483
http://www.brandeis.edu/acserv/abroad/index.html

Argentina | Buenos Aires	Boston University	Sum	USColl	Boston University	n/a
Argentina | Buenos Aires	FLACSO	Sum	Intermed	Council on International Educational Exchange (CIEE)	n/a
Argentina | Buenos Aires	Multiple institutional choices	Fall Spr YrRound	Intermed	Institute for Study Abroad	n/a
Argentina | Buenos Aires	Universidad de Buenos Aires	Sum	Intermed	Institute for Study Abroad	n/a
Argentina | Mendoza	Universidad Nacional de Cuyo	Fall Spr YrRound	Intermed	Institute for Study Abroad	n/a
Australia | Brisbane	University of Queensland	Fall Spr YrRound	Dir	n/a	n/a
Australia | Brisbane	University of Queensland	Fall Spr YrRound	USColl	Arcadia University	n/a
Australia | Brisbane	University of Queensland	Fall Spr YrRound	Intermed	Institute for Study Abroad	n/a
Australia | Canberra	Australia National University	Fall Spr YrRound	Intermed	Institute for Study Abroad	n/a
Australia | Canberra	Australia National University	Fall Spr YrRound	Dir	n/a	n/a
Australia | Canberra	Australia National University	Fall Spr YrRound	USColl	Arcadia University	n/a
Australia | Hobart	University of Tasmania	Fall Spr YrRound	USColl	Arcadia University	n/a
Australia | Hobart	University of Tasmania	Fall Spr YrRound	Dir	n/a	n/a
Australia | Hobart	University of Tasmania	Fall Spr YrRound	Intermed	Institute for Study Abroad	n/a
Australia | Melbourne	Monash University	Fall Spr YrRound	USColl	Arcadia University	n/a
Australia | Melbourne	Monash University	Fall Spr YrRound	Intermed	Institute for Study Abroad	n/a
Australia | Melbourne	Monash University	Fall Spr YrRound	Dir	n/a	n/a
Australia | Melbourne	University of Melbourne	Fall Spr YrRound	Dir	n/a	n/a
Australia | Melbourne	University of Melbourne	Fall Spr YrRound	USColl	Arcadia University	n/a
Australia | Melbourne	University of Melbourne	Fall Spr YrRound	Intermed	Institute for Study Abroad	n/a
Australia | Perth	University of Western Australia	Fall Spr YrRound	Intermed	Institute for Study Abroad	n/a
Australia | Perth	University of Western Australia	Fall Spr YrRound	Dir	n/a	n/a
Australia | Perth	University of Western Australia	Fall Spr YrRound	USColl	Arcadia University	n/a
Australia | Queensland	School for Field Studies	n/a	Intermed	School for Field Studies	n/a
Australia | Sydney	Arcadia University	Sum	USColl	Arcadia University	n/a
Australia | Sydney	Boston University Sydney Center	Sum	USColl	Boston University	n/a
Australia | Sydney	Boston University Sydney Center	Sum	USColl	Boston University	n/a
Australia | Sydney	BU Sydney Center	n/a	USColl	Boston University	n/a
Australia | Sydney	University of Sydney	Fall Spr YrRound	Dir	n/a	n/a
Australia | Sydney	University of Sydney	Fall Spr YrRound	USColl	Arcadia University	n/a
Australia | Sydney	University of Sydney	Fall Spr YrRound	Intermed	Institute for Study Abroad	n/a
Australia | Townsville	James Cook University	Fall Spr YrRound	Intermed	Institute for Study Abroad	n/a

Massachusetts

DESTINATION	HOST INSTITUTION	PRGM SEASON	PRGM TYPE	INTERMEDIARY	HOUSING
Australia | Townsville	James Cook University	Fall Spr YrRound	Dir	n/a	n/a
Australia | Townsville	James Cook University	Fall Spr YrRound	USColl	Arcadia University	n/a
Austria | Vienna	IES Abroad Vienna Center	Sum	Intermed	IES Abroad	n/a
Austria | Vienna	University of Vienna	n/a	Intermed	IES Abroad	n/a
Belgium | Brussels	Universite Libre de Bruxelles	n/a	Intermed	Council on International Educational Exchange (CIEE)	n/a
Bolivia | Cochabamba	SIT Study Abroad	n/a	Intermed	SIT Study Abroad	n/a
Bolivia | Cochabamba	SIT Study Abroad	Sum	Intermed	SIT Study Abroad	n/a
Botswana | Gaborone	SIT Study Abroad	n/a	Intermed	SIT Study Abroad	n/a
Botswana | Gaborone	University of Botswana	Sum	Intermed	Council on International Educational Exchange (CIEE)	n/a
Botswana | Gaborone	University of Botswana	n/a	Intermed	Council on International Educational Exchange (CIEE)	n/a
Brazil | Salvador	SIT Study Abroad	n/a	Intermed	SIT Study Abroad	n/a
Brazil | Salvador da Bahia	Universidade Catolica do Salvador or Universidade Federal da Bahia	n/a	Intermed	Council on International Educational Exchange (CIEE)	n/a
Brazil | Salvador da Bahia	Universidade Federal da Bahia	Sum	Intermed	Council on International Educational Exchange (CIEE)	n/a
Brazil | Sao Paulo	Multiple institutional choices	n/a	Intermed	Council on International Educational Exchange (CIEE)	n/a
Brazil | Sao Paulo	Pontificia Universidad Catolica de Sao Paulo	n/a	Intermed	Council on International Educational Exchange (CIEE)	n/a
Cambodia | Siem Reap	Pannasastra University of Cambodia	Sum	Intermed	Council on International Educational Exchange (CIEE)	n/a
Cameroon | Yaounde	SIT Study Abroad	n/a	Intermed	SIT Study Abroad	n/a
Chile | Arica	SIT Study Abroad	Fall Spr YrRound	Intermed	SIT Study Abroad	n/a
Chile | Santiago	IES Abroad Santiago Center	Sum	Intermed	IES Abroad	n/a
Chile | Santiago	Universidad de Chile; Catolica de Chile	Fall Spr YrRound	Intermed	Institute for Study Abroad	n/a
Chile | Valparaiso	SIT Study Abroad	Fall Spr YrRound	Intermed	SIT Study Abroad	n/a
China | Beijing	Beijing Foreign Studies University	n/a	Intermed	IES Abroad	n/a
China | Beijing	Beijing Institute of Education	n/a	Intermed	CET Academic Programs	n/a
China | Beijing	Beijing Language & Culture University	Sum	Intermed	Alliance for Global Education	n/a
China | Beijing	Capital Normal University	n/a	Intermed	CET Academic Programs	n/a
China | Beijing	CET Academic Programs	Sum	Intermed	CET Academic Programs	n/a
China | Beijing	CET Academic Programs	Sum	Intermed	CET Academic Programs	n/a
China | Beijing	Harvard University	Sum	USColl	Harvard University	n/a
China | Beijing	IES Abroad Beijing Center	Sum	Intermed	IES Abroad	n/a
China | Hangzhou	CET Academic Programs	Sum	Intermed	CET Academic Programs	n/a
China | Harbin	CET Academic Programs	Sum	Intermed	CET Academic Programs	n/a
China | Harbin	Harbin Institute of Technology	n/a	Intermed	CET Academic Programs	n/a
China | Hong Kong	Chinese University of Hong Kong	n/a	Dir	n/a	n/a

© 2011 — Updates? Want to be in the next edition? Visit www.mysecondcampus.com

Massachusetts

DESTINATION	HOST INSTITUTION	PRGM SEASON	PRGM TYPE	INTERMEDIARY	HOUSING
China | Kunming	SIT Study Abroad	Sum	Intermed	SIT Study Abroad	n/a
China | Kunming	SIT Study Abroad	n/a	Intermed	SIT Study Abroad	n/a
China | Shanghai	CET Academic Programs	Sum	Intermed	CET Academic Programs	n/a
China | Shanghai	Fudan University	Sum	Intermed	Alliance for Global Education	n/a
China | Shanghai	Fudan University	Sum	Intermed	Alliance for Global Education	n/a
China | Shanghai	Shanghai University of Finance and Economics	Sum	Intermed	Alliance for Global Education	n/a
China | Shanghai	Shanghai University of Finance and Economics	n/a	Intermed	Alliance for Global Education	n/a
China | Xi'an	Shaanxi Normal University	Sum	Intermed	Alliance for Global Education	n/a
Costa Rica | Atenas	SFS Center for Sustainable Development Studies	n/a	Intermed	School for Field Studies	n/a
Costa Rica | Heredia	Universidad Nacional	n/a	Intermed	Institute for Study Abroad	n/a
Costa Rica | Monteverde	CIEE Study Center in Monteverde	Sum	Intermed	Council on International Educational Exchange (CIEE)	n/a
Costa Rica | San Jose	Institute for Central American Development Studies (ICADS)	n/a	Intermed	Institute for Central American Development Studies (ICADS)	n/a
Croatia | Zagreb	SIT Study Abroad	n/a	Intermed	SIT Study Abroad	n/a
Czech Republic | Prague	CET Academic Programs	n/a	Intermed	CET Academic Programs	n/a
Czech Republic | Prague	CET Academic Programs	Sum	Intermed	CET Academic Programs	n/a
Czech Republic | Prague	CET Academic Programs	n/a	Intermed	CET Academic Programs	n/a
Denmark | Copenhagen	Danish Institute for Study Abroad (DIS)	n/a	Intermed	Danish Institute for Study Abroad (DIS)	n/a
Dominican Republic | Santiago	Pontificia Universidad Catolica Madre y Maestra	n/a	Intermed	Council on International Educational Exchange (CIEE)	n/a
Dominican Republic | Santiago	Pontificia Universidad Catolica Madre y Maestra	Sum	Intermed	Council on International Educational Exchange (CIEE)	n/a
Dominican Republic | Santo Domingo	Facultad Latinoamericana de Ciencias Sociales (FLACSO): Liberal Arts	n/a	Intermed	Council on International Educational Exchange (CIEE)	n/a
Ecuador | Quito	IES Abroad Quito Center	Sum	Intermed	IES Abroad	n/a
Ecuador | Quito	SIT Study Abroad	Fall Spr YrRound	Intermed	SIT Study Abroad	n/a
Ecuador | Quito	SIT Study Abroad	Fall Spr YrRound	Intermed	SIT Study Abroad	n/a
Ecuador | Quito	Universidad San Francisco de Quito	Fall Spr YrRound	Intermed	IES Abroad	n/a
Egypt | Alexandria	Alexandria University	n/a	USColl	Middlebury College	n/a
Egypt | Cairo	American University in Cairo	n/a	Dir	n/a	n/a
England | Bristol	University of Bristol	n/a	Dir	n/a	n/a
England | Bristol	University of Bristol	n/a	Intermed	Institute for Study Abroad	n/a
England | Bristol	University of Bristol	n/a	USColl	Arcadia University	n/a
England | Cambridge	Cambridge University	YrRound	Intermed	Institute for Study Abroad	n/a
England | Cambridge	Cambridge University	Sum	USColl	Arcadia University	n/a
England | Cambridge	Cambridge University	Sum	Intermed	Institute for Study Abroad	n/a
England | Leeds	University of Leeds	n/a	Intermed	Institute for Study Abroad	n/a
England | Leeds	University of Leeds	n/a	Dir	n/a	n/a

© 2011 — Updates? Want to be in the next edition? Visit **www.mysecondcampus.com**

Massachusetts

DESTINATION	HOST INSTITUTION	PRGM SEASON	PRGM TYPE	INTERMEDIARY	HOUSING
England | Leeds	University of Leeds	n/a	USColl	Arcadia University	n/a
England | London	Arcadia University	Sum	USColl	Arcadia University	n/a
England | London	Arcadia University	Sum	USColl	Arcadia University	n/a
England | London	Boston University	Sum	USColl	Boston University	n/a
England | London	Boston University	Sum	USColl	Boston University	n/a
England | London	British American Drama Academy	n/a	USColl	Sarah Lawrence College	n/a
England | London	BU London Center	n/a	USColl	Boston University	n/a
England | London	Goldsmith's College	n/a	Intermed	Institute for Study Abroad	n/a
England | London	Goldsmith's College	n/a	USColl	Arcadia University	n/a
England | London	Goldsmith's College	n/a	Dir	n/a	n/a
England | London	Hansard Society	Sum	Dir	n/a	n/a
England | London	Hansard Society	n/a	Dir	n/a	n/a
England | London	King's College	Fall	Intermed	Institute for Study Abroad	n/a
England | London	King's College	Fall	USColl	Arcadia University	n/a
England | London	King's College	Fall	Dir	n/a	n/a
England | London	London School of Economics and Political Science	YrRound	USColl	Arcadia University	n/a
England | London	London School of Economics and Political Science	YrRound	Intermed	Institute for Study Abroad	n/a
England | London	London School of Economics and Political Science	YrRound	Dir	n/a	n/a
England | London	Queen Mary	Fall	Intermed	Institute for Study Abroad	n/a
England | London	Queen Mary	Fall	USColl	Arcadia University	n/a
England | London	Queen Mary	Fall	Dir	n/a	n/a
England | London	Royal Holloway	n/a	Intermed	Institute for Study Abroad	n/a
England | London	Royal Holloway	n/a	USColl	Arcadia University	n/a
England | London	Royal Holloway	n/a	Dir	n/a	n/a
England | London	School for Oriental and African Studies	Fall	Intermed	Institute for Study Abroad	n/a
England | London	School for Oriental and African Studies	Fall	USColl	Arcadia University	n/a
England | London	School for Oriental and African Studies	Fall	Dir	n/a	n/a
England | London	University College London	Fall	Intermed	Institute for Study Abroad	n/a
England | London	University College London	Fall	USColl	Arcadia University	n/a
England | London	University College London	Fall	Dir	n/a	n/a
England | Norwich	University of East Anglia	Fall	Dir	n/a	n/a
England | Norwich	University of East Anglia	Fall	USColl	Arcadia University	n/a
England | Norwich	University of East Anglia	Fall	Intermed	Institute for Study Abroad	n/a
England | Nottingham	University of Nottingham	n/a	USColl	Arcadia University	n/a
England | Nottingham	University of Nottingham	n/a	Intermed	Institute for Study Abroad	n/a
England | Nottingham	University of Nottingham	n/a	Dir	n/a	n/a
England | Oxford	Oxford University	YrRound	Intermed	Institute for Study Abroad	n/a

Massachusetts

DESTINATION	HOST INSTITUTION	PRGM SEASON	PRGM TYPE	INTERMEDIARY	HOUSING
England | Oxford	Oxford University	YrRound	USColl	Arcadia University	n/a
England | Oxford	Oxford University	YrRound	Dir	n/a	n/a
England | Oxford	Oxford University (St. Peter's)	Sum	Intermed	Institute for Study Abroad	n/a
England | Oxford	Oxford University (Wadham College)	YrRound	Intermed	Sarah Lawrence College	n/a
England | York	University of York	n/a	Dir	n/a	n/a
England | York	University of York	n/a	USColl	Arcadia University	n/a
England | York	University of York	n/a	Intermed	Institute for Study Abroad	n/a
Fiji | Suva	SIT Study Abroad	n/a	Intermed	SIT Study Abroad	n/a
France | Arles	IES Abroad Arles Center	Sum	Intermed	IES Abroad	n/a
France | Grenoble	Universite de Grenoble	n/a	Intermed	Boston University	n/a
France | Montpelier	Paul-Valery University	n/a	USColl	University of Minnesota	n/a
France | Montpelier	Paul-Valery University	n/a	USColl	University of Minnesota	n/a
France | Paris	Academic Programs Abroad	n/a	Intermed	Academic Programs Abroad	n/a
France | Paris	Boston University Paris Center	n/a	USColl	Boston University	n/a
France | Paris	IES Abroad Paris Center	Sum	Intermed	IES Abroad	n/a
France | Paris	IES Abroad Paris Center	Sum	Intermed	IES Abroad	n/a
France | Paris	Middlebury College	n/a	USColl	Middlebury College	n/a
France | Paris	Multiple institutional choices	n/a	USColl	Sweet Briar College	n/a
France | Paris	Reid Hall (Columbia University)	Sum	USColl	Columbia University	n/a
France | Paris	Sarah Lawrence College	n/a	USColl	Sarah Lawrence College	n/a
France | Pont-Aven	Pont-Aven School of Contemporary Art	n/a	Intermed	Pont-Aven School of Contemporary Art	n/a
France | Rennes	Universite de Haute Bretagne	n/a	Intermed	Council on International Educational Exchange (CIEE)	n/a
Germany | Berlin	Humboldt University	n/a	Intermed	IES Abroad	n/a
Germany | Berlin	IES Abroad Berlin Center	Sum	Intermed	IES Abroad	n/a
Germany | Dresden	Technische Universitat Dresden	n/a	USColl	Boston University	n/a
Germany | Dresden	Technische Universitat Dresden	n/a	USColl	Boston University	n/a
Germany | Dresden	Technische Universitat Dresden	n/a	USColl	Boston University	n/a
Germany | Freiburg	Albert Ludwigs University of Freiburg	n/a	Intermed	IES Abroad	n/a
Germany | Freiburg	IES Abroad EU Center	n/a	Intermed	IES Abroad	n/a
Ghana | Accra	SIT Study Abroad	n/a	Intermed	SIT Study Abroad	n/a
Ghana | Accra and Kumasi	SIT Study Abroad	Sum	Intermed	SIT Study Abroad	n/a
Ghana | Cape Coast	SIT Study Abroad	n/a	Intermed	SIT Study Abroad	n/a
Ghana | Legon	University of Ghana	n/a	Intermed	Council on International Educational Exchange (CIEE)	n/a
Greece | Athens	Arcadia Center for Hellenic, Mediterranean and Balkan Studies (Arcadia University)	n/a	USColl	Arcadia University	n/a
Greece | Athens	College Year in Athens	n/a	Intermed	College Year in Athens	n/a
Guatemala | Antigua; San Bartolo	Boston University	n/a	USColl	Boston University	n/a

© 2011 — Updates? Want to be in the next edition? Visit **www.mysecondcampus.com**

Massachusetts

DESTINATION	HOST INSTITUTION	PRGM SEASON	PRGM TYPE	INTERMEDIARY	HOUSING
Hungary | Budapest	Corvinus University of Budapest	n/a	Intermed	Council on International Educational Exchange (CIEE)	n/a
Iceland | Reykjavik	SIT Study Abroad	Sum	Intermed	SIT Study Abroad	n/a
India | Delhi	Jawaharal Nehru University	n/a	Intermed	IES Abroad	n/a
India | Delhi	SIT Study Abroad	n/a	Intermed	SIT Study Abroad	n/a
India | Hyderabad	University of Hyderabad	n/a	Intermed	Council on International Educational Exchange (CIEE)	n/a
India | Jaipur	SIT Study Abroad	n/a	Intermed	SIT Study Abroad	n/a
India | Pune	Fergusson College	n/a	Intermed	Alliance for Global Education	n/a
India | Pune	Fergusson College	Sum	Intermed	Alliance for Global Education	n/a
India | Spiti; Ladakh; Zanskar	SIT Study Abroad	Sum	Intermed	SIT Study Abroad	n/a
Indonesia | Ubud	SIT Study Abroad	n/a	Intermed	SIT Study Abroad	n/a
Ireland | Belfast	Queens University	n/a	Dir	n/a	n/a
Ireland | Belfast	Queens University	n/a	USColl	Arcadia University	n/a
Ireland | Belfast	Queens University	n/a	Intermed	Institute for Study Abroad	n/a
Ireland | Cork	University College Cork	n/a	USColl	Arcadia University	n/a
Ireland | Cork	University College Cork	n/a	Intermed	Institute for Study Abroad	n/a
Ireland | Cork	University College Cork	n/a	Dir	n/a	n/a
Ireland | Dublin	Dublin City University	Sum	USColl	Boston University	n/a
Ireland | Dublin	IES Abroad Dublin Center	Sum	Intermed	IES Abroad	n/a
Ireland | Dublin	Institute of Public Administration (National University of Ireland)	Sum	USColl	Arcadia University	n/a
Ireland | Dublin	Trinity College	n/a	Intermed	Institute for Study Abroad	n/a
Ireland | Dublin	Trinity College	n/a	Dir	n/a	n/a
Ireland | Dublin	Trinity College	n/a	USColl	Arcadia University	n/a
Ireland | Dublin	University College Dublin	n/a	Intermed	Institute for Study Abroad	n/a
Ireland | Dublin	University College Dublin	n/a	USColl	Arcadia University	n/a
Ireland | Dublin	University College Dublin	n/a	Dir	n/a	n/a
Ireland | Galway	National University of Ireland-Galway	n/a	Intermed	Institute for Study Abroad	n/a
Ireland | Galway	National University of Ireland-Galway	n/a	USColl	Arcadia University	n/a
Ireland | Galway	National University of Ireland-Galway	n/a	Dir	n/a	n/a
Ireland | Limerick	University of Limerick	n/a	Intermed	Institute for Study Abroad	n/a
Ireland | Limerick	University of Limerick	n/a	USColl	Arcadia University	n/a
Ireland | Limerick	University of Limerick	n/a	Dir	n/a	n/a
Israel | Beer Sheva	Ben Gurion University	n/a	Dir	n/a	n/a
Israel | Haifa	University of Haifa	n/a	Dir	n/a	n/a
Israel | Jerusalem	Hebrew University	n/a	Dir	n/a	n/a
Israel | Jerusalem	Hebrew University	Sum	Dir	n/a	n/a
Israel | Kibbutz Ketura	Arava Institute for Environmental Studies	n/a	Dir	n/a	n/a
Israel | Tel Aviv	Tel Aviv University	n/a	Dir	n/a	n/a

© 2011 — Updates? Want to be in the next edition? Visit **www.mysecondcampus.com**

Massachusetts

DESTINATION	HOST INSTITUTION	PRGM SEASON	PRGM TYPE	INTERMEDIARY	HOUSING
Italy | Bologna	University of Bologna	n/a	USColl	Indiana University	n/a
Italy | Catania	CET Academic Programs	Sum	Intermed	CET Academic Programs	n/a
Italy | Catania	CET Academic Programs	Sum	Intermed	CET Academic Programs	n/a
Italy | Catania	CET Academic Programs	Sum	Intermed	CET Academic Programs	n/a
Italy | Florence	CET Academic Programs	Sum	Intermed	CET Academic Programs	n/a
Italy | Florence	Sarah Lawrence College	n/a	USColl	Sarah Lawrence College	n/a
Italy | Florence	SU Abroad Florence and Centro di Cultura per Stranieri (University of Florence)	n/a	USColl	Syracuse University	n/a
Italy | Florence	Syracuse University in Florence	Sum	USColl	Syracuse University	n/a
Italy | Florence	University of Florence	n/a	USColl	Syracuse University	n/a
Italy | Milan	IES Abroad Milan Center	n/a	Intermed	IES Abroad	n/a
Italy | Milan	IES Abroad Milan Center	Sum	Intermed	IES Abroad	n/a
Italy | Padova	Boston University Center for Italian and European Studies	n/a	USColl	Boston University	n/a
Italy | Perugia	Umbra Institute	n/a	USColl	Arcadia University	n/a
Italy | Perugia	Umbra Institute	Sum	USColl	Arcadia University	n/a
Italy | Rome	IES Abroad Rome Center	n/a	Intermed	IES Abroad	n/a
Italy | Rome	IES Abroad Rome Center	Sum	Intermed	IES Abroad	n/a
Italy | Rome	Temple University	n/a	USColl	Temple University	n/a
Italy | Siena	CET Academic Programs	n/a	Intermed	CET Academic Programs	n/a
Italy | Siena	IES Abroad Siena Center	n/a	Intermed	IES Abroad	n/a
Italy | Siena	Siena School for Liberal Arts	n/a	Intermed	Siena School for Liberal Arts	n/a
Italy | Tuscany	Boston University	Sum	USColl	Boston University	n/a
Japan | Hakodate	Hokkaido International Foundation	Sum	Intermed	Hokkaido International Foundation	n/a
Japan | Kyoto	Kyoto Consortium for Japanese Studies (Columbia University)	n/a	Consrtm	Kyoto Consortium for Japanese Studies (Columbia University)	n/a
Japan | Nagoya	Nanzan University	n/a	Intermed	IES Abroad	n/a
Japan | Tokyo	IES Abroad Tokyo Center	Sum	Intermed	IES Abroad	n/a
Japan | Tokyo	Kanda University	n/a	Intermed	IES Abroad	n/a
Japan | Tokyo	Sophia University	n/a	Intermed	Council on International Educational Exchange (CIEE)	n/a
Jordan | Amman	SIT Study Abroad	Sum	Intermed	SIT Study Abroad	n/a
Jordan | Amman	SIT Study Abroad	n/a	Intermed	SIT Study Abroad	n/a
Jordan | Amman	SIT Study Abroad	Sum	Intermed	SIT Study Abroad	n/a
Jordan | Amman	University of Amman	n/a	Intermed	Council on International Educational Exchange (CIEE)	n/a
Jordan | Amman	University of Jordan	Sum	Intermed	Council on International Educational Exchange (CIEE)	n/a
Kenya | Nairobi	SFS Center for Wildlife Management Studies	n/a	Intermed	School for Field Studies	n/a
Kenya | Nairobi	SIT Study Abroad	n/a	Intermed	SIT Study Abroad	n/a
Kenya | Nairobi	University of Minnesota	n/a	USColl	University of Minnesota	n/a

© 2011 — Updates? Want to be in the next edition? Visit **www.mysecondcampus.com**

Massachusetts

DESTINATION	HOST INSTITUTION	PRGM SEASON	PRGM TYPE	INTERMEDIARY	HOUSING
Lebanon | Beirut	American University of Beirut	n/a	Dir	n/a	n/a
Madagascar | Fort Dauphin	SIT Study Abroad	n/a	Intermed	SIT Study Abroad	n/a
Mali | Bamako	SIT Study Abroad	n/a	Intermed	SIT Study Abroad	n/a
Mexico | Baja	SFS Center for Coastal Studies	n/a	Intermed	School for Field Studies	n/a
Mexico | Guanajuato	Universidad de Guanajuato	n/a	Intermed	Council on International Educational Exchange (CIEE)	n/a
Mexico | Merida	Universidad Autonoma de Yucatan	Sum	Intermed	Institute for Study Abroad	n/a
Mexico | Merida	Universidad Autonoma de Yucatan	n/a	Intermed	Institute for Study Abroad	n/a
Mongolia | Ulaanbaatar	SIT Study Abroad	n/a	Intermed	SIT Study Abroad	n/a
Morocco | Rabat	AMIDEAST	n/a	Intermed	AMIDEAST	n/a
Morocco | Rabat	Ecole Superieure de Direction et de Gestion	Sum	Intermed	Council on International Educational Exchange (CIEE)	n/a
Morocco | Rabat	SIT Study Abroad	Sum	Intermed	SIT Study Abroad	n/a
Morocco | Rabat	SIT Study Abroad	n/a	Intermed	SIT Study Abroad	n/a
Morocco | Rabat	SIT Study Abroad	n/a	Intermed	SIT Study Abroad	n/a
Nepal | Kathmandu	SIT Study Abroad	n/a	Intermed	SIT Study Abroad	n/a
Netherlands | Amsterdam	SIT Study Abroad	n/a	Intermed	SIT Study Abroad	n/a
Netherlands | Amsterdam	Universiteit van Amsterdam	n/a	Intermed	Council on International Educational Exchange (CIEE)	n/a
Netherlands | Maastricht	University of Maastricht	n/a	Dir	n/a	n/a
Netherlands | The Hague	University of Leiden	Sum	Self	n/a	CollRes
New Zealand | Auckland	University of Auckland	n/a	Dir	n/a	n/a
New Zealand | Auckland	University of Auckland	n/a	USColl	Arcadia University	n/a
New Zealand | Auckland	University of Auckland	n/a	Intermed	Institute for Study Abroad	n/a
New Zealand | Auckland	University of Auckland or Auckland University of Technology	n/a	USColl	Boston University	n/a
New Zealand | Dunedin	University of Otago	n/a	Dir	n/a	n/a
New Zealand | Dunedin	University of Otago	n/a	USColl	Arcadia University	n/a
New Zealand | Dunedin	University of Otago	n/a	Intermed	Institute for Study Abroad	n/a
New Zealand | Wellington	Victoria University of Wellington	n/a	Dir	n/a	n/a
New Zealand | Wellington	Victoria University of Wellington	n/a	USColl	Arcadia University	n/a
New Zealand | Wellington	Victoria University of Wellington	n/a	Intermed	Institute for Study Abroad	n/a
Nicaragua | Managua	SIT Study Abroad	n/a	Intermed	SIT Study Abroad	n/a
Niger | Niamey	Boston University	n/a	USColl	Boston University	n/a
Oman | Muscat	SIT Study Abroad	n/a	Intermed	SIT Study Abroad	n/a
Panama | Panama City	SIT Study Abroad	n/a	Intermed	SIT Study Abroad	n/a
Peru | Lima	Pontificia Universidad Catolica del Peru	n/a	Intermed	Institute for Study Abroad	n/a
Poland | Warsaw	Warsaw School of Economics	n/a	Dir	Council on International Educational Exchange (CIEE)	n/a
Portugal | Lisbon	Universidade Nova de Lisboa	n/a	Dir	Council on International Educational Exchange (CIEE)	n/a

© 2011 — Updates? Want to be in the next edition? Visit **www.mysecondcampus.com**

Massachusetts

DESTINATION	HOST INSTITUTION	PRGM SEASON	PRGM TYPE	INTERMEDIARY	HOUSING
Russia | Moscow	Moscow International University	Sum	Intermed	American Councils for International Program	n/a
Russia | Moscow	Moscow International University	n/a	Intermed	American Councils for International Program	n/a
Russia | St. Petersburg	Russian State Pedagogical (Gertsen) University	Sum	Intermed	American Councils for International Program	n/a
Russia | St. Petersburg	Russian State Pedagogical (Gertsen) University	n/a	Intermed	American Councils for International	n/a
Russia | St. Petersburg	St. Petersburg State University	n/a	Intermed	Council on International Educational Exchange (CIEE)	n/a
Russia | St. Petersburg	St. Petersburg State University	n/a	Intermed	Council on International Educational Exchange (CIEE)	n/a
Russia | St. Petersburg	St. Petersburg State University	Sum	Intermed	Council on International Educational Exchange (CIEE)	n/a
Samoa | Apia	SIT Study Abroad	n/a	Intermed	SIT Study Abroad	n/a
Scotland | Edinburgh	University of Edinburgh	n/a	Intermed	Institute for Study Abroad	n/a
Scotland | Edinburgh	University of Edinburgh	n/a	USColl	Arcadia University	n/a
Scotland | Edinburgh	University of Edinburgh	Fall	Dir	n/a	n/a
Scotland | Glasgow	Glasgow School of Art	n/a	Intermed	Institute for Study Abroad	n/a
Scotland | Glasgow	Glasgow School of Art	n/a	USColl	Arcadia University	n/a
Scotland | Glasgow	Glasgow School of Art	Fall	Dir	n/a	n/a
Scotland | Glasgow	University of Glasgow	n/a	Dir	n/a	n/a
Scotland | Glasgow	University of Glasgow	n/a	USColl	Arcadia University	n/a
Scotland | Glasgow	University of Glasgow	n/a	Intermed	Institute for Study Abroad	n/a
Scotland | St. Andrews	University of St. Andrews	Fall	Dir	n/a	n/a
Scotland | St. Andrews	University of St. Andrews	n/a	USColl	Arcadia University	n/a
Scotland | St. Andrews	University of St. Andrews	n/a	Intermed	Institute for Study Abroad	n/a
Scotland | Stirling	University of Stirling	n/a	USColl	Arcadia University	n/a
Scotland | Stirling	University of Stirling	Fall	Dir	n/a	n/a
Scotland | Stirling	University of Stirling	n/a	Intermed	Institute for Study Abroad	n/a
Senegal | Dakar	Boston University	Sum	USColl	Boston University	n/a
Senegal | Dakar	SIT Study Abroad	Sum	Intermed	SIT Study Abroad	n/a
Senegal | Dakar	Suffolk University - Dakar Campus	n/a	Intermed	Council on International Educational Exchange (CIEE)	n/a
Senegal | Dakar	University of Minnesota	n/a	USColl	University of Minnesota	n/a
Senegal | St. Louis	Universite Gaston Berger	n/a	USColl	University of Wisconsin	n/a
South Africa | Cape Town	University of Cape Town	n/a	Intermed	Council on International Educational Exchange (CIEE)	n/a
South Africa | Durban	SIT Study Abroad	n/a	Intermed	SIT Study Abroad	n/a
South Africa | Durban	SIT Study Abroad	n/a	Intermed	SIT Study Abroad	n/a
South Africa | Durban	SIT Study Abroad	Sum	Intermed	SIT Study Abroad	n/a
South Africa | Durban	University of KwaZulu-Natal, Howard Campus	n/a	Intermed	Interstudy	n/a
South Africa | Johannesburg	University of Witwatersrand	n/a	Intermed	Interstudy	n/a
South Africa | Pietermaritzburg	University of KwaZulu-Natal	n/a	Intermed	Interstudy	n/a

© 2011 — Updates? Want to be in the next edition? Visit **www.mysecondcampus.com**

Massachusetts

DESTINATION	HOST INSTITUTION	PRGM SEASON	PRGM TYPE	INTERMEDIARY	HOUSING
South Africa | Stellenbosch	Stellenbosch University	n/a	Intermed	Council on International Educational Exchange (CIEE)	n/a
South Korea | Seoul	Yonsei University	n/a	Intermed	Council on International Educational Exchange (CIEE)	n/a
South Korea | Seoul	Yonsei University	Sum	Dir	n/a	n/a
South Korea | Seoul	Yonsei University	Sum	Intermed	Council on International Educational Exchange (CIEE)	n/a
Spain | Alcala	Universidad de Alcala	n/a	Intermed	Council on International Educational Exchange (CIEE)	n/a
Spain | Alicante	Universidad de Alicante	n/a	Intermed	Council on International Educational Exchange (CIEE)	n/a
Spain | Alicante	Universidad de Alicante	n/a	Intermed	Council on International Educational Exchange (CIEE)	n/a
Spain | Alicante	Universidad de Alicante	Sum	Intermed	Council on International Educational Exchange (CIEE)	n/a
Spain | Barcelona	Escola Superior de Comerc Internacional or Universitat Pompeu Fabra	n/a	Intermed	Council on International Educational Exchange (CIEE)	n/a
Spain | Barcelona	Universitat de Barcelona	Sum	Intermed	Council on International Educational Exchange (CIEE)	n/a
Spain | Barcelona	Universitat de Barcelona	n/a	Intermed	Council on International Educational Exchange (CIEE)	n/a
Spain | Barcelona	Universitat Pompeu Fabra	n/a	Intermed	Council on International Educational Exchange (CIEE)	n/a
Spain | Burgos	Universidad de Burgos	n/a	USColl	Boston University	n/a
Spain | Granada	Universidad de Granada	n/a	Intermed	IES Abroad	n/a
Spain | Madrid	IES Abroad Madrid Center	Sum	Intermed	IES Abroad	n/a
Spain | Madrid	Instituto Internacional en Espana or Universidad Autonoma de Madrid	Sum	USColl	Boston University	n/a
Spain | Madrid	Universidad Autonoma de Madrid	n/a	USColl	Boston University	n/a
Spain | Madrid	Universidad Autonoma de Madrid	Sum	USColl	Boston University	n/a
Spain | Madrid	Universidad Carlos III de Madrid	n/a	Intermed	Council on International Educational Exchange (CIEE)	n/a
Spain | Madrid	Universidad Carlos III de Madrid	n/a	Intermed	Council on International Educational Exchange (CIEE)	n/a
Spain | Menorca	Boston University	Sum	USColl	Boston University	n/a
Spain | Salamanca	Universidad de Salamanca	n/a	Intermed	IES Abroad	n/a
Spain | Seville	Universidad de Sevilla	n/a	Intermed	Council on International Educational Exchange (CIEE)	n/a
Spain | Seville	Universidad de Sevilla	n/a	USColl	Sweet Briar College	n/a
Spain | Seville	Universidad Pablo de Olavide or Universidad de Sevilla	n/a	Intermed	Council on International Educational Exchange (CIEE)	n/a
Spain | Seville	Universidad Pablo de Olavide or Universidad de Sevilla	n/a	Intermed	Council on International Educational Exchange (CIEE)	n/a
Sweden | Stockholm	Stockholm University	n/a	Consrtm	Swedish Program	n/a

Massachusetts

DESTINATION	HOST INSTITUTION	PRGM SEASON	PRGM TYPE	INTERMEDIARY	HOUSING
Switzerland | Geneva	Boston University	n/a	USColl	Boston University	n/a
Switzerland | Geneva	SIT Study Abroad	n/a	Intermed	SIT Study Abroad	n/a
Switzerland | Geneva	SIT Study Abroad	Sum	Intermed	SIT Study Abroad	n/a
Switzerland | Geneva	University of Geneva	n/a	USColl	Smith College	n/a
Switzerland | Nyon and Geneva	SIT Study Abroad	n/a	Intermed	SIT Study Abroad	n/a
Taiwan | Taipei	National Chengchi University	n/a	Intermed	Council on International Educational Exchange (CIEE)	n/a
Tanzania | Arusha	SIT Study Abroad	n/a	Intermed	SIT Study Abroad	n/a
Tanzania | Dar es Salaam	University of Dar es Salaam	n/a	Intermed	Council on International Educational Exchange (CIEE)	n/a
Tanzania | Zanzibar	SIT Study Abroad	n/a	Intermed	SIT Study Abroad	n/a
Thailand | Khon Kaen	Khon Kaen University	n/a	Intermed	Council on International Educational Exchange (CIEE)	n/a
The Balkans (Montenegro, Kosovo, Macedonia) | (Multiple)	SIT Study Abroad	Sum	Intermed	SIT Study Abroad	n/a
Tibet | Kathmandu	SIT Study Abroad	n/a	Intermed	SIT Study Abroad	n/a
Tunisia | Tunis	SIT Study Abroad	n/a	Intermed	SIT Study Abroad	n/a
Turkey | Istanbul	Bosphorus University	Sum	Dir	n/a	n/a
Turkey | Istanbul	Koc University	n/a	Intermed	Council on International Educational Exchange (CIEE)	n/a
Turks and Caicos | South Caicos	SFS Center for Marine Resource Studies	n/a	Intermed	School for Field Studies	n/a
Uganda | Kampala	SIT Study Abroad	n/a	Intermed	SIT Study Abroad	n/a
Uganda | Kampala	SIT Study Abroad	n/a	Intermed	SIT Study Abroad	n/a
Uganda and Rwanda | Kampala and Kigali	SIT Study Abroad	Sum	Intermed	SIT Study Abroad	n/a
United States | Washington (DC)	American University	n/a	Dir	n/a	n/a
United States | Waterford (CT)	O'Neill National Theater Institute	n/a	Dir	n/a	n/a
United States | Woods Hole (MA)	SEA Semester	n/a	Intermed	SEA Semester	n/a
United States | Woods Hole (MA)	Woods Hole Biological Laboratory	n/a	Intermed	Woods Hole Biological Laboratory	n/a
Vietnam | Cantho	SIT Study Abroad	n/a	Intermed	SIT Study Abroad	n/a
Vietnam | Ho Chi Minh City	CET Academic Programs	Sum	Intermed	CET Academic Programs	n/a
Vietnam | Ho Chi Minh City	SIT Study Abroad	n/a	Intermed	SIT Study Abroad	n/a

Bridgewater State College

Susi Rachouh
Director
Maxwell Library RM 100B
Bridgewater, MA 02325

susan.rachouh@bridgew.edu
508.531.6183
http://www.bridgew.edu/StudyAbroad/

DESTINATION	HOST INSTITUTION	PRGM SEASON	PRGM TYPE	INTERMEDIARY	HOUSING
(Multiple choices) | (Multiple choices)	CAPA International Education	n/a	Intermed	CAPA International Education	n/a
(Multiple choices) | (Multiple choices)	Multiple institutional choices	n/a	Intermed	Academic Programs International	n/a

Massachusetts

DESTINATION	HOST INSTITUTION	PRGM SEASON	PRGM TYPE	INTERMEDIARY	HOUSING
(Multiple choices) | (Multiple choices)	Multiple institutional choices	n/a	Intermed	International Studies Abroad	n/a
(Multiple choices) | (Multiple choices)	Multiple institutional choices	n/a	Intermed	Academic Studies Abroad	n/a
(Multiple choices) | (Multiple choices)	Multiple institutional choices	n/a	Intermed	AustraLearn	n/a
(Multiple choices) | (Multiple choices)	Multiple institutional choices	n/a	Intermed	Center for International Studies	n/a
(Multiple choices) | (Multiple choices)	Multiple institutional choices	n/a	Intermed	The Education Abroad Network	n/a
(Multiple choices) | (Multiple choices)	Multiple institutional choices	n/a	Intermed	EuroLearn	n/a
(Multiple choices) | (Multiple choices)	Multiple institutional choices	n/a	Intermed	AsiaLearn	n/a
Bangladesh | (Multiple)	Bridgewater State College	Win	Self	n/a	n/a
Costs: Win Costs: T&F: n/a, R&B: n/a, Ttl: $3,900					
Brazil | Florianopolis	Universidade do Estado de Santa Catarina	n/a	Bilat	n/a	n/a
Brazil | Porto Alegre	Universidade Federal do Rio Grande do Sul	n/a	Bilat	n/a	n/a
Canada | (Multiple choices)	Multiple institutional choices	n/a	Bilat	n/a	n/a
Canada | (Multiple choices)	Multiple institutional choices	n/a	Bilat	n/a	n/a
China | (Multiple choices)	Bridgewater State College	Sum	Self	n/a	n/a
China | Hong Kong	Hong Kong Institute of Education	n/a	Bilat	n/a	n/a
Egypt | (Multiple)	Bridgewater State College	Win	Self	n/a	n/a
Costs: Win Costs: T&F: n/a, R&B: n/a, Ttl: $4,000					
England | London	Bridgewater State College	Win	Self	n/a	n/a
Costs: Win Costs: T&F: n/a, R&B: n/a, Ttl: $2,500					
England | Manchester	Manchester Metropolitan University	n/a	Bilat	n/a	n/a
Ireland | Limerick	University of Limerick	n/a	Bilat	n/a	n/a
Japan | (Multiple)	Bridgewater State College	Sum	Self	n/a	n/a
Japan | Kansai	Kansai University	n/a	Bilat	n/a	n/a
Japan | Wakayama	Wakayama University	n/a	Bilat	n/a	n/a
Lithuania | (Multiple)	Bridgewater State College	Sum	Self	n/a	n/a
Mexico | (Multiple)	Bridgewater State College	Win	Self	n/a	n/a
Costs: Win Costs: T&F: n/a, R&B: n/a, Ttl: $2,200					
Nicaragua | (Multiple)	Bridgewater State College	Win	Self	n/a	n/a
Costs: Win Costs: T&F: n/a, R&B: n/a, Ttl: $2,200					
Portugal | (Multiple)	Bridgewater State College	Sum	Self	n/a	n/a
Taiwan | (Multiple)	Bridgewater State College	Win	Self	n/a	n/a
Costs: Win Costs: T&F: n/a, R&B: n/a, Ttl: $3,075					
Tanzania | (Multiple)	Bridgewater State College	Sum	Self	n/a	n/a
Turkey | (Multiple)	Bridgewater State College	Sum	Self	n/a	n/a

© 2011 — Updates? Want to be in the next edition? Visit **www.mysecondcampus.com**

Massachusetts

DESTINATION	HOST INSTITUTION	PRGM SEASON	PRGM TYPE	INTERMEDIARY	HOUSING
United States | (Multiple choices)	Multiple institutional choices	n/a	Intermed	National Student Exchange	n/a
(Multiple) | (Multiple)	Semester at Sea	n/a	Intermed	Semester at Sea	n/a
United States | Hawaii	Bridgewater State College	n/a	Self	n/a	n/a

Bunker Hill Community College

Vilma Tafawa
Executive Director
250 New Rutherford Avenue
Boston, MA 02129

vtafawa@bhcc.mass.edu
617.228.2461
http://www.bhcc.mass.edu/inside/186

DESTINATION	HOST INSTITUTION	PRGM SEASON	PRGM TYPE	INTERMEDIARY	HOUSING
Argentina | Buenos Aires	Universidad de Belgrano	Sum	Consrtm	College Consortium for International Studies	n/a
Costs: Sum Costs: T&F: n/a, R&B: n/a, Ttl: $700					
Canada | Chicoutimi (Quebec)	Universite du Quebec a Chicoutimi	Sum	Consrtm	College Consortium for International Studies	n/a
Costs: Sum Costs: T&F: n/a, R&B: n/a, Ttl: $700					
China | Shanghai	Shanghai University	Sum	Consrtm	College Consortium for International Studies	n/a
Costs: Sum Costs: T&F: n/a, R&B: n/a, Ttl: $800					
Costa Rica | (Multiple)	Bunker Hill Community College	Sum	Self	n/a	n/a
Costs: Sum Costs: T&F: n/a, R&B: n/a, Ttl: $500					
Czech Republic | Prague	Anglo-American University	Sum	Consrtm	College Consortium for International Studies	n/a
Costs: Sum Costs: T&F: n/a, R&B: n/a, Ttl: $1,200					
Ecuador | Guayaquil	Universidad Catolica de Santiago de Guayaquil	Sum	Consrtm	College Consortium for International Studies	n/a
Costs: Sum Costs: T&F: n/a, R&B: n/a, Ttl: $870					
England | Kingston	Edge Hill University	Sum	Consrtm	College Consortium for International Studies	n/a
Costs: Sum Costs: T&F: n/a, R&B: n/a, Ttl: $1,400					
France | Chambery	Kingston University	Sum	Consrtm	College Consortium for International Studies	n/a
Costs: Sum Costs: T&F: n/a, R&B: n/a, Ttl: $950					
Greece | Thessaloniki	American College of Thessaloniki	Sum	Consrtm	College Consortium for International Studies	n/a
Costs: Sum Costs: T&F: n/a, R&B: n/a, Ttl: $1,470					
India | Bangalore	International Center for Management and India Studies	Sum	Consrtm	College Consortium for International Studies	n/a
Costs: Sum Costs: T&F: n/a, R&B: n/a, Ttl: $900					
Ireland | Galway	National University of Ireland, Galway	Sum	Consrtm	College Consortium for International Studies	n/a
Costs: Sum Costs: T&F: n/a, R&B: n/a, Ttl: $1,200					
Italy | Venice	Istituto Venezia	Sum	Consrtm	College Consortium for International Studies	n/a
Costs: Sum Costs: T&F: n/a, R&B: n/a, Ttl: $930					

© 2011 — Updates? Want to be in the next edition? Visit **www.mysecondcampus.com**

Massachusetts

DESTINATION	HOST INSTITUTION	PRGM SEASON	PRGM TYPE	INTERMEDIARY	HOUSING
Japan | Tokyo	KCP International Language Institute	Sum	Consrtm	College Consortium for International Studies	n/a
Costs: Sum Costs: T&F: n/a, R&B: n/a, Ttl: $1,670					
Mexico | Guadalajara	Universidad Autonoma de Guadalajara	Sum	Consrtm	College Consortium for International Studies	n/a
Costs: Sum Costs: T&F: n/a, R&B: n/a, Ttl: $550					
Morocco | Ifrane	Al Akhawayn University	Sum	Consrtm	College Consortium for International Studies	n/a
Costs: Sum Costs: T&F: n/a, R&B: n/a, Ttl: $1,080					
Senegal | Unknown	Bunker Hill Community College	Sum	Self	n/a	n/a
Costs: Sum Costs: T&F: n/a, R&B: n/a, Ttl: $500					
Spain | Seville	International College of Seville	Sum	Consrtm	College Consortium for International Studies	n/a
Costs: Sum Costs: T&F: n/a, R&B: n/a, Ttl: $1,130					

Cape Cod Community College

Lore Loftfield De Bower
Dean of Academic Affairs
2240 Iyannough Road
West Barnstable, MA 02668

ldebower@capecod.edu
508.362.2131 x4456
http://www.capecod.edu/web/international

DESTINATION	HOST INSTITUTION	PRGM SEASON	PRGM TYPE	INTERMEDIARY	HOUSING
(Multiple) | (Multiple)	Cape Cod Community College	n/a	Consrtm	College Consortium for International Studies	n/a
France | Montpellier	Cape Cod Community College	Win	Self	n/a	HostFam
Costs: Win Costs: T&F: n/a, R&B: n/a, Ttl: $2,200					
France | Paris	Cape Cod Community College	Spr	Self	n/a	n/a
Costs: Spr Costs: T&F: n/a, R&B: n/a, Ttl: $1,495					
Ireland | Dublin and Galway	Cape Cod Community College	Sum	Self	n/a	n/a
Costs: Sum Costs: T&F: n/a, R&B: n/a, Ttl: $2,000					
Scotland | Unknown	Cape Cod Community College	Sum	Self	n/a	n/a
Costs: Sum Costs: T&F: n/a, R&B: n/a, Ttl: $3,000					

Clark University

Adriane van Gils
Director
Study Abroad and Study Away Programs
Dana Commons, First Floor
950 Main Street
Worcester, MA 01610

avangils@clarku.edu
508.793.7587
http://www.clarku.edu/offices/studyabroad/

DESTINATION	HOST INSTITUTION	PRGM SEASON	PRGM TYPE	INTERMEDIARY	HOUSING
Australia | Hobart and Launceston	University of Tasmania	Fall YrRound	Dir	n/a	n/a
Australia | Perth	Murdoch University	Fall Spr YrRound	Intermed	Council on International	n/a
Australia | Yungaburra	Center for Rainforest Studies	Fall Spr	Intermed	School for Field Studies	n/a
Chile | Santiago	Pontificia Universidad Catolica de Chile or Universidad de Chile	Fall Spr YrRound	Intermed	Council on International Educational Exchange (CIEE)	n/a

Massachusetts

DESTINATION	HOST INSTITUTION	PRGM SEASON	PRGM TYPE	INTERMEDIARY	HOUSING
Chile | Valparaiso	Pontificia Universidad Catolica de Valparaiso	Fall Spr YrRound	Intermed	Council on International Educational Exchange (CIEE)	n/a
China | Beijing	Beijing Institute of Education	Spr	Intermed	CET Academic Programs	n/a
Costa Rica | Atenas	SFS Center for Sustainable Development Studies	Fall Spr	Intermed	School for Field Studies	n/a
Czech Republic | Prague	Charles University	n/a	Intermed	CET Academic Programs	n/a
Czech Republic and Poland | Prague and Terezin	Clark University	n/a	Self	n/a	n/a
Dominican Republic | Santiago	Pontificia Universidad Catolica Madre y Maestra	Fall Spr	Intermed	Council on International Educational Exchange (CIEE)	n/a
Dominican Republic | Santiago	Pontificia Universidad Catolica Madre y Maestra	Fall Spr	Intermed	Council on International Educational Exchange (CIEE)	n/a
Dominican Republic | Santo Domingo	Facultad Latinoamericana de Ciencias Sociales	Fall Spr	Intermed	Council on International Educational Exchange (CIEE)	n/a
England | Brighton	University of Sussex	Fall Spr YrRound	Dir	n/a	n/a
England | London	Birbeck College (University of	Fall Spr YrRound	Dir	n/a	n/a
England | London	London School of Economics and Political Science	YrRound	Dir	n/a	n/a
England | Norwich	University of East Anglia	Fall Spr YrRound	Dir	n/a	n/a
France | Dijon	University of Bourgogne	Spr YrRound	Dir	n/a	n/a
Germany | Trier	University of Trier	Spr YrRound	Dir	n/a	n/a
Japan | Hirakata	Kansai Gaidai University	Fall Spr YrRound	Dir	n/a	n/a
Luxembourg | Luxembourg	Clark University and College of the Holy Cross	Spr	Consrtm	Clark University and College of the Holy Cross	n/a
Mexico | Baja	SFS Center for Coastal Studies	Fall Spr	Intermed	School for Field Studies	n/a
Namibia | Windhoek	Augsburg College	Fall Spr	USColl	Augsburg College	n/a
Netherlands | Leiden	University of Leiden	Spr YrRound	Dir	n/a	n/a
Scotland | Stirling	University of Stirling	Fall Spr YrRound	Bilat	n/a	n/a
Senegal | Dakar	Suffolk University - Dakar Campus	Fall Spr YrRound	Intermed	Council on International Educational Exchange (CIEE)	n/a
South Africa | Cape Town	Students' Health and Welfare Centres Organisation or University of Cape Town	Fall Spr	Intermed	Council on International Educational Exchange (CIEE)	n/a
Spain | Madrid	TANDEM Center	Fall Spr	Intermed	TANDEM Center	n/a
Spain | Seville	Universidad de Sevilla	Spr YrRound	Dir	n/a	n/a
Turkey | Istanbul	Koc University	n/a	Intermed	Council on International Educational Exchange (CIEE)	n/a
Turks and Caicos | South Caicos	Center for Marine Resource Management Studies	Fall Spr	Intermed	School for Field Studies	n/a
Vietnam | Ho Chi Minh City	CET Academic Programs	n/a	Intermed	CET Academic Programs	n/a

© 2011 — Updates? Want to be in the next edition? Visit **www.mysecondcampus.com**

Massachusetts

| DESTINATION | HOST INSTITUTION | PRGM SEASON | PRGM TYPE | INTERMEDIARY | HOUSING |

College of Our Lady of the Elms

Walter Breau
Vice President for Academic Affairs
291 Springfield Street
Chicopee, MA 01013

breauw@elms.edu
413.265.2222
http://www.elms.edu/Academics/Study_Away.xml

DESTINATION	HOST INSTITUTION	PRGM SEASON	PRGM TYPE	INTERMEDIARY	HOUSING
(Multiple choices)	(Multiple choices)	Multiple institutional choices	n/a	Intermed	American Institute for Foreign Study	n/a
China	(Multiple)	College of Our Lady of the Elms	n/a	Self	n/a	n/a
England and France	London and Paris	College of Our Lady of the Elms	n/a	Self	n/a	n/a
Greece	Unknown	College of Our Lady of the Elms	n/a	Self	n/a	n/a
Ireland	Unknown	College of Our Lady of the Elms	n/a	Self	n/a	n/a
Japan	Kochi	Kochi Women's Unviersity	n/a	Bilat	n/a	n/a
United States	Washington (DC)	Washington Center for Internships and Academic Seminars	n/a	Intermed	n/a	n/a

College of the Holy Cross

Mark Lincicome
Director
Study Abroad Office
1 College Street
Worcester, MA 01610

mlincico@holycross.edu
508.793.3082
http://www.holycross.edu/departments/studyabroad/website/index.htm

DESTINATION	HOST INSTITUTION	PRGM SEASON	PRGM TYPE	INTERMEDIARY	HOUSING
Australia	Melbourne	University of Melbourne	Fall Spr	Dir	n/a	n/a
Australia	Yungaburra	School for Field Studies	n/a	Intermed	School for Field Studies	n/a
Cameroon	Yaounde	Universite Catholique de l'Afrique Centrale	n/a	Dir	n/a	n/a
China	Beijing	Beijing Institute of Education	n/a	Dir	n/a	n/a
Costa Rica	Atenas	School for Field Studies	n/a	Intermed	School for Field Studies	n/a
England	Brighton	University of Sussex	YrRound	Dir	n/a	n/a
England	Leicester	University of Leicester	YrRound	Dir	n/a	n/a
England	Oxford	Oxford University (Mansfield)	YrRound	Dir	n/a	n/a
England	Oxford	Oxford University (St. Edmund Hall)	n/a	Dir	n/a	n/a
England	York	University of York	YrRound	Dir	n/a	n/a
France	Dijon	Universite de Bourgogne	YrRound	Dir	n/a	n/a
France	Paris	College of the Holy Cross	Sum	Self	n/a	CollRes
Costs: Sum Costs: T&F: n/a, R&B: n/a, Ttl: $6,500						
France	Strasbourg	Faculte des Sciences Humaines (Strasbourg II Marc Bloch)	YrRound	Dir	n/a	n/a
Germany	Bamberg	Otto-Friedrich-Universitat	YrRound	Dir	n/a	n/a

© 2011 — Updates? Want to be in the next edition? Visit www.mysecondcampus.com

Massachusetts

DESTINATION	HOST INSTITUTION	PRGM SEASON	PRGM TYPE	INTERMEDIARY	HOUSING
Greece | Athens	International Center for Hellenic and Mediterranean Studies	Fall	Intermed	College Year in Athens	n/a
Indonesia | Ubud and Yogyakarta	College of the Holy Cross	Sum	Self	n/a	n/a
	Costs: Sum Costs: T&F: n/a, R&B: n/a, Ttl: $6,500				
Ireland | Cork	University College Cork	YrRound	Dir	n/a	n/a
Ireland | Dublin	Trinity College Dublin	YrRound	Dir	n/a	n/a
Ireland | Galway	National University of Ireland at Galway	YrRound	Dir	n/a	n/a
Israel | Jerusalem	Hebrew University	Sum	Dir	n/a	CollRes
	Costs: Sum Costs: T&F: n/a, R&B: n/a, Ttl: $6,500				
Italy | Bologna	University of Bologna	YrRound	Dir	n/a	n/a
Italy | Florence	University of Florence	YrRound	Dir	n/a	n/a
Italy | Rome	American Institute for Roman Culture	Sum	Self	n/a	PrivApt
	Costs: Sum Costs: T&F: n/a, R&B: n/a, Ttl: $6,500				
Italy | Rome	American Institute for Roman Culture	Fall Spr	Self	n/a	PrivApt
Italy | Rome	Intercollegiate Center for Classical Studies in Rome (Duke University)	Spr	Consrtm	Intercollegiate Center for Classical Studies in Rome (Duke University)	n/a
Japan | Tokyo	Sophia University	Fall	Dir	n/a	n/a
Kenya | Kimana	School for Field Studies	n/a	Intermed	School for Field Studies	n/a
Kenya | Nairobi	Institute for Peace Studies (Hekima College)	Sum	Self	n/a	CollRes
	Costs: Sum Costs: T&F: n/a, R&B: n/a, Ttl: $6,500				
Luxembourg | Mondorf-les-Bains	College of the Holy Cross	Sum	Consrtm	College of Holy Cross and Clark University	n/a
	Costs: Sum Costs: T&F: n/a, R&B: n/a, Ttl: $4,900				
Mexico | Baja	School for Field Studies	n/a	Intermed	School for Field Studies	n/a
Mexico | Puebla	Benemerita Universidad Autonoma de Puebla	n/a	Dir	n/a	n/a
Peru | Lima	Pontificia Universidad Catolica del Perś	Sum	Self	n/a	HostFam
	Costs: Sum Costs: T&F: n/a, R&B: n/a, Ttl: $6,500				
Peru | Lima	Pontificia Universidad de Peru	Fall YrRound	Dir	n/a	n/a
Russia | Moscow	Moscow State Linguistics University	n/a	Dir	n/a	n/a
Russia | St. Petersburg	St. Petersburg University or St. Petersburg State Pedagogical Institute	n/a	Dir	n/a	n/a
Scotland | St. Andrews	St. Andrews University	YrRound	Dir	n/a	n/a
South Africa | (Multiple)	College of the Holy Cross	Sum	Self	n/a	n/a
	Costs: Sum Costs: T&F: n/a, R&B: n/a, Ttl: $6,500				
Spain | La Coruna	Universidad de la Coruna	n/a	Dir	n/a	n/a
Spain | Leon	Universidad de Leon	n/a	Dir	n/a	n/a

© 2011 — Updates? Want to be in the next edition? Visit **www.mysecondcampus.com**

Massachusetts

DESTINATION	HOST INSTITUTION	PRGM SEASON	PRGM TYPE	INTERMEDIARY	HOUSING
Spain | Palma	Universitat de les Illes Balears	YrRound	Dir	n/a	n/a
Sri Lanka | Dangolla	Intercollegiate Sri Lanka Education (Bowdoin College)	n/a	Consrtm	Intercollegiate Sri Lanka Education (Bowdoin College)	n/a
Turks and Caicos | South Caicos Island	School for Field Studies	n/a	Intermed	School for Field Studies	n/a

Curry College

Michelle Perrault
Director
1071 Blue Hill Avenue
Milton, MA 02186

mperraul@curry.edu
617.333.2195

DESTINATION	HOST INSTITUTION	PRGM SEASON	PRGM TYPE	INTERMEDIARY	HOUSING
[Country Unspecified] | [City Unspecified]	n/a	n/a	n/a	n/a	n/a

Eastern Nazarene College

Nancy Ross
Vice President for Academic Affairs
23 East Elm Avenue
Quincy, MA 02170

nancy.ross@enc.edu
617.745.3707
http://www.enc.edu/academics/off_campus_study.html

DESTINATION	HOST INSTITUTION	PRGM SEASON	PRGM TYPE	INTERMEDIARY	HOUSING
(Multiple choices) | (Multiple choices)	Multiple institutional choices	n/a	Intermed	Council for Christian Colleges & Universities	n/a

Emerson College

David Griffin
Director
International Study and External Programs
The Little Building
80 Boylston Street, Suite 121
Boston, MA 02116

David_Griffin@emerson.edu
617.824.8567
http://www.emerson.edu/external_programs/index.cfm

DESTINATION	HOST INSTITUTION	PRGM SEASON	PRGM TYPE	INTERMEDIARY	HOUSING
Czech Republic | Prague	Academy of Performing Arts for Film and Television	Sum	Self	n/a	n/a
Costs: Sum Costs: T&F: n/a, R&B: n/a, Ttl: $10,788					
Netherlands | Well	Kasteel Well	Sum Fall Spr	Self	n/a	Other
Costs: Sum Costs: T&F: n/a, R&B: n/a, Ttl: $6,400 Fall Costs: T&F: n/a, R&B: n/a, Ttl: $24,318 Spr Costs: T&F: n/a, R&B: n/a, Ttl: $24,318					
Taiwan | Taipei	Shih Hsin University	Fall Spr	Dir	n/a	CollRes
Costs: Fall Costs: T&F: n/a, R&B: n/a, Ttl: Emerson home comprehensive fees Spr Costs: T&F: n/a, R&B: n/a, Ttl: Emerson home comprehensive fees					
United States | Washington (DC)	Washington Center	Fall	Intermed	Washington Center	PrivApt
Costs: Fall Costs: T&F: n/a, R&B: n/a, Ttl: $20,023					
United States | Los Angeles (CA)	Emerson College Los Angeles	Sum Fall Spr	Self	n/a	PrivApt
Costs: Sum Costs: T&F: n/a, R&B: n/a, Ttl: $7,279 Fall Costs: T&F: n/a, R&B: n/a, Ttl: $20,613 Spr Costs: T&F: n/a, R&B: n/a, Ttl: $20,613					

© 2011 — Updates? Want to be in the next edition? Visit **www.mysecondcampus.com**

Massachusetts

Emmanuel College

Diane Bissaro
Coordinator of Study Abroad
Room A-324
400 The Fenway
Boston, MA 02115

bissardi@emmanuel.edu
617.735.9713
http://www.emmanuel.edu/Academics/International_Programs.html

DESTINATION	HOST INSTITUTION	PRGM SEASON	PRGM TYPE	INTERMEDIARY	HOUSING
(Multiple choices) | (Multiple choices)	Multiple institutional choices	n/a	Intermed	IES Abroad	n/a
(Multiple choices) | (Multiple choices)	Multiple institutional choices	n/a	Intermed	Study Abroad Italy	n/a
(Multiple choices) | (Multiple choices)	Multiple institutional choices	n/a	Intermed	SIT Study Abroad	n/a
(Multiple choices) | (Multiple choices)	Multiple institutional choices	n/a	Intermed	School for Field Studies	n/a
(Multiple choices) | (Multiple choices)	Multiple institutional choices	n/a	Intermed	International Studies Abroad	n/a
(Multiple choices) | (Multiple choices)	Multiple institutional choices	n/a	Intermed	Interstudy	n/a
(Multiple choices) | (Multiple choices)	Multiple institutional choices	n/a	Intermed	International Honors Program	n/a
(Multiple choices) | (Multiple choices)	Multiple institutional choices	n/a	Intermed	Center for International Studies	n/a
(Multiple choices) | (Multiple choices)	Multiple institutional choices	n/a	Intermed	Institute for Study Abroad	n/a
(Multiple choices) | (Multiple choices)	Multiple institutional choices	n/a	Intermed	Council on International Educational Exchange (CIEE)	n/a
(Multiple choices) | (Multiple choices)	Multiple institutional choices	n/a	Intermed	CET Academic Programs	n/a
(Multiple choices) | (Multiple choices)	Multiple institutional choices	n/a	Intermed	BCA Study Abroad	n/a
(Multiple choices) | (Multiple choices)	Multiple institutional choices	n/a	USColl	Boston University	n/a
(Multiple choices) | (Multiple choices)	Multiple institutional choices	n/a	USColl	Arcadia University	n/a
(Multiple choices) | (Multiple choices)	Multiple institutional choices	n/a	Intermed	American Institute for Foreign Study	n/a
(Multiple choices) | (Multiple choices)	Multiple institutional choices	n/a	Intermed	Academic Programs International	n/a
(Multiple choices) | (Multiple choices)	Multiple institutional choices	n/a	Intermed	Danish Institute for Study Abroad (DIS)	n/a
(Multiple choices) | (Multiple choices)	Semester at Sea	n/a	Intermed	Semester at Sea	n/a

© 2011 — Updates? Want to be in the next edition? Visit **www.mysecondcampus.com**

Massachusetts

| DESTINATION | HOST INSTITUTION | PRGM SEASON | PRGM TYPE | INTERMEDIARY | HOUSING |

Endicott College

April Burriss
Dean of the School of International Education
The School of International Education
1st Floor, Rooms 112-114
376 Hale Street
Beverley, MA 01915

aburriss@endicott.edu
978.232.2272
http://www.endicott.edu/servlet/RetrievePage?site=endicott&page=InternatResourcesStudyAbroadPrograms

DESTINATION	HOST INSTITUTION	PRGM SEASON	PRGM TYPE	INTERMEDIARY	HOUSING
Argentina | Buenos Aires	Facultad Latinoamericana de Ciencias Sociales	n/a	Intermed	Council on International Education Exchange (CIEE)	n/a
Argentina | Buenos Aires	SIT Study Abroad	n/a	Intermed	SIT Study Abroad	n/a
Argentina | Buenos Aires	Universidad de Buenos Aires	n/a	Intermed	Lexia Study Abroad	n/a
Australia | Cairns	SIT Study Abroad	n/a	Intermed	SIT Study Abroad	n/a
Australia | Canberra	Australian National University	n/a	Intermed	AustraLearn	n/a
Australia | Gold Coast	Bond University	n/a	Intermed	AustraLearn	n/a
Australia | Gold Coast or Brisbane	Griffith University	n/a	Intermed	AustraLearn	n/a
Australia | Perth	Murdoch University	n/a	Intermed	Council on International Education Exchange (CIEE)	n/a
Australia | Sydney	Campion College	n/a	Intermed	Athena Study Abroad	n/a
Australia | Sydney	International College of Management	n/a	Intermed	AustraLearn	n/a
Australia | Sydney	Macquarie University	n/a	Intermed	AustraLearn	n/a
Australia | Wollongong	University of Wollongong	n/a	Intermed	Council on International Education Exchange (CIEE)	n/a
Australia | Wollongong	University of Wollongong	n/a	Intermed	AustraLearn	n/a
Belgium | Brussels	Universite Libre de Bruxelles or Vesalius College	n/a	Intermed	Council on International Education Exchange (CIEE)	n/a
Brazil | Salvador	SIT Study Abroad	n/a	Intermed	SIT Study Abroad	n/a
Brazil | Sao Paulo	Escola de Administracao de Empresas de Sao Paulo da Fundacao Getulio Vargas or Pontificia Universidad Catolica de Sao Paulo	n/a	Intermed	Council on International Education Exchange (CIEE)	n/a
Chile | Santiago	Pontificia Universidad Catolica de Chile or Universidad de Chile	n/a	Intermed	Council on International Education Exchange (CIEE)	n/a
China | Beijing	Peking University	n/a	Intermed	Council on International Education Exchange (CIEE)	n/a
China | Shanghai	East China Normal University	n/a	Intermed	Council on International Education Exchange (CIEE)	n/a
China | Shanghai	Fudan University	n/a	Intermed	Lexia Study Abroad	n/a
Costa Rica | Monteverde	CIEE Study Center in Monteverde	n/a	Intermed	Council on International Education Exchange (CIEE)	n/a
Czech Republic | Prague	Charles University or Prague Film and Television School of the Academy of the Performing Arts	n/a	Intermed	Council on International Education Exchange (CIEE)	n/a
Czech Republic | Prague	SIT Study Abroad	n/a	Intermed	SIT Study Abroad	n/a

© 2011 — Updates? Want to be in the next edition? Visit **www.mysecondcampus.com**

Massachusetts

DESTINATION	HOST INSTITUTION	PRGM SEASON	PRGM TYPE	INTERMEDIARY	HOUSING
Dominican Republic | Santo Domingo	Facultad Latinoamericana de Ciencias Sociales	n/a	Intermed	Council on International Education Exchange (CIEE)	n/a
England | London	Academic Solutions	n/a	Intermed	Lexia Study Abroad	n/a
England | London	Marist London Center (Marist	n/a	Intermed	Athena Study Abroad	n/a
Fiji | Suva	SIT Study Abroad	n/a	Intermed	SIT Study Abroad	n/a
France | Paris	CIEE Study Center in Paris	n/a	Intermed	Council on International Education Exchange (CIEE)	n/a
France | Paris	Sorbonne	n/a	Intermed	Lexia Study Abroad	n/a
Germany | Berlin	Multiple institutional choices	n/a	Intermed	Lexia Study Abroad	n/a
Ghana | Accra	Ashesi University	n/a	Intermed	Council on International Education Exchange (CIEE)	n/a
Ghana | Legon	University of Ghana	n/a	Intermed	Council on International Education Exchange (CIEE)	n/a
Greece | Paros Island	Hellenic International Studies in the Arts	n/a	Intermed	Athena Study Abroad	n/a
Hungary | Budapest	Corvinus University of Budapest	n/a	Intermed	Council on International Education Exchange (CIEE)	n/a
Hungary | Budapest	Eotvos Collegium	n/a	Intermed	Lexia Study Abroad	n/a
India | (Multiple choices)	SIT Study Abroad	n/a	Intermed	SIT Study Abroad	n/a
India | Hyderabad	University of Hyderabad	n/a	Intermed	Council on International Education Exchange (CIEE)	n/a
Ireland | Dublin	Dublin City University	n/a	Intermed	Council on International Education Exchange (CIEE)	n/a
Ireland | Dublin	Griffith College	n/a	Intermed	Athena Study Abroad	n/a
Ireland | Dublin	SIT Study Abroad	n/a	Intermed	SIT Study Abroad	n/a
Italy | Florence	Florence University of the Arts or Apicius International School of Hospitality	n/a	Intermed	Study Abroad Italy	n/a
Italy | Florence	Lorenzo de' Medici School	n/a	Intermed	Athena Study Abroad	n/a
Italy | Florence	Studio Art Centers International	n/a	Intermed	Studio Art Centers International	n/a
Italy | Milan	Nuova Accademia di Belle Arti or Domus Academy	n/a	Intermed	Study Abroad Italy	n/a
Italy | Rome	John Cabot University	n/a	Intermed	Study Abroad Italy	n/a
Italy | Rome	Lorenzo de' Medici School	n/a	Intermed	Athena Study Abroad	n/a
Italy | Rome	University of Paris (Sorbonne)	n/a	Intermed	Lexia Study Abroad	n/a
Italy | Sicily	Mediterranean Center for Arts and Sciences	n/a	Intermed	Study Abroad Italy	n/a
Italy | Tuscania	Lorenzo de' Medici School	n/a	Intermed	Athena Study Abroad	n/a
Japan | Tokyo	Sophia University	n/a	Intermed	Council on International Education Exchange (CIEE)	n/a
Jordan | Amman	SIT Study Abroad	n/a	Intermed	SIT Study Abroad	n/a
Kenya | Mombasa	SIT Study Abroad	n/a	Intermed	SIT Study Abroad	n/a
Mexico | Guanajuato	Universidad de Guanajuato	n/a	Intermed	Council on International Education Exchange (CIEE)	n/a
Mexico | Mexico City	Endicott College Mexico	n/a	Self	n/a	n/a

© 2011 — Updates? Want to be in the next edition? Visit **www.mysecondcampus.com**

Massachusetts

DESTINATION	HOST INSTITUTION	PRGM SEASON	PRGM TYPE	INTERMEDIARY	HOUSING
Netherlands | Amsterdam	University of Amsterdam	n/a	Intermed	Council on International Education Exchange (CIEE)	n/a
New Zealand | Auckland	University of Auckland	n/a	Intermed	AustraLearn	n/a
New Zealand | Christchurch	University of Canterbury	n/a	Intermed	AustraLearn	n/a
Nicaragua | Managua	SIT Study Abroad	n/a	Intermed	SIT Study Abroad	n/a
Oman | Muscat	SIT Study Abroad	n/a	Intermed	SIT Study Abroad	n/a
Peru | Lima	Universidad del Pacifico or Pontificia Universidad Catolica del Peru	n/a	Intermed	Council on International Education Exchange (CIEE)	n/a
Poland | Krakow	Jagiellonian University	n/a	Intermed	Lexia Study Abroad	n/a
Poland | Warsaw	Warsaw School of Economics	n/a	Intermed	Council on International Education Exchange (CIEE)	n/a
Russia | St. Petersburg	St. Petersburg State University	n/a	Intermed	Council on International Education Exchange (CIEE)	n/a
Senegal | Dakar	Suffolk University - Dakar Campus	n/a	Intermed	Council on International Education Exchange (CIEE)	n/a
South Africa | Cape Town	University of Cape Town	n/a	Intermed	Council on International Education Exchange (CIEE)	n/a
South Africa | Cape Town	University of the Western Cape	n/a	Intermed	Lexia Study Abroad	n/a
South Africa | Durban	SIT Study Abroad	n/a	Intermed	SIT Study Abroad	n/a
South Africa | Stellenbosch	Stellenbosch University	n/a	Intermed	Council on International Education Exchange (CIEE)	n/a
South Korea | Seoul	Yonsei University	n/a	Intermed	Council on International Education Exchange (CIEE)	n/a
Spain | Madrid	The College of International Studies	n/a	Self	n/a	n/a
Switzerland | Geneva	SIT Study Abroad	n/a	Intermed	SIT Study Abroad	n/a
Thailand | Chiang Mai	Payap University	n/a	Intermed	Lexia Study Abroad	n/a
Thailand | Khon Kaen	Khon Kaen University	n/a	Intermed	Council on International Education Exchange (CIEE)	n/a
Turkey | Istanbul	Bogazici University	n/a	Intermed	Lexia Study Abroad	n/a
Uganda | Kampala	SIT Study Abroad	n/a	Intermed	SIT Study Abroad	n/a
Vietnam | Ho Chi Minh City	Vietnam National University	n/a	Intermed	Council on International Education Exchange (CIEE)	n/a

Fisher College

Susan Dunton
Provost
108 Beacon Street
1st Floor
Boston, MA 02116

sdunton@fisher.edu
617.236.8829
http://www.fisher.edu/academics/studyabroad.html

DESTINATION	HOST INSTITUTION	PRGM SEASON	PRGM TYPE	INTERMEDIARY	HOUSING
Australia | Unknown	Unknown	Sum	n/a	n/a	n/a
Austria | Unknown	Unknown	Sum	n/a	n/a	n/a
England | Unknown	Unknown	Sum	n/a	n/a	n/a
France | Unknown	Unknown	Sum	n/a	n/a	n/a

© 2011 — Updates? Want to be in the next edition? Visit **www.mysecondcampus.com**

Massachusetts

DESTINATION	HOST INSTITUTION	PRGM SEASON	PRGM TYPE	INTERMEDIARY	HOUSING
Ireland | Unknown	Unknown	Sum	n/a	n/a	n/a
Italy | Unknown	Unknown	Sum	n/a	n/a	n/a
Scotland | Unknown	Unknown	Sum	n/a	n/a	n/a
Spain | Unknown	Unknown	Sum	n/a	n/a	n/a

Fitchburg State College

Clare M. O'Brien
Director of International Education
Hammond Building, Room 320
160 Pearl Street
Fitchburg, MA 01420

cmobrien@fsc.edu
978.665.3599
http://www.fsc.edu/intled/studyabroad.cfm

DESTINATION	HOST INSTITUTION	PRGM SEASON	PRGM TYPE	INTERMEDIARY	HOUSING
(Multiple choices) | (Multiple choices)	Multiple institutional choices	n/a	Intermed	Academic Programs International (API)	n/a
(Multiple choices) | (Multiple choices)	Multiple institutional choices	n/a	Intermed	Study Abroad Italy	n/a
(Multiple choices) | (Multiple choices)	Multiple institutional choices	n/a	Intermed	Center for International Studies (CIS)	n/a
(Multiple choices) | (Multiple choices)	Multiple institutional choices	n/a	Intermed	Academic Studies Abroad (ASA)	n/a
(Multiple choices) | (Multiple choices)	Multiple institutional choices	n/a	Intermed	AustraLearn	n/a
China | Hangzhou	Fitchburg State College	Sum	Self	n/a	CollRes
China | Hangzhou	Zhejiang Gongshang University	n/a	Bilat	n/a	n/a
England | London	London Metropolitan University	n/a	Dir	n/a	n/a
France | Grenoble	Fitchburg State College	Sum	Self	n/a	CollRes
Italy | Verona	Fitchburg State College	Sum	Self	n/a	PrivApt
Italy | Verona	University of Verona	n/a	Bilat	n/a	n/a
Spain | (Multiple)	Fitchburg State College	Spr	Self	n/a	Other
Spain | Barcelona	Fitchburg State College	Sum	Self	n/a	PrivApt

Framingham State College

Jane Decatur
Director
100 State Street
Framingham, MA 01701

jdecatur@framingham.edu
508.626.4585
http://www.framingham.edu/study-abroad/

DESTINATION	HOST INSTITUTION	PRGM SEASON	PRGM TYPE	INTERMEDIARY	HOUSING
(Multiple choices) | (Multiple choices)	Bridgewater State College	n/a	USColl	Bridgewater State College	n/a
(Multiple choices) | (Multiple choices)	Fitchburg State College	n/a	USColl	Fitchburg State College	n/a
(Multiple choices) | (Multiple choices)	International Honors Program	n/a	Intermed	International Honors Program	n/a
(Multiple choices) | (Multiple choices)	Salem State College	n/a	USColl	Salem State College	n/a

Massachusetts

DESTINATION	HOST INSTITUTION	PRGM SEASON	PRGM TYPE	INTERMEDIARY	HOUSING
(Multiple choices)	(Multiple choices)	Semester at Sea	n/a	Intermed	Semester at Sea	n/a
(Multiple choices)	(Multiple choices)	Westfield State College	n/a	USColl	Westfield State College	n/a
Argentina	Buenos Aires	American Institute for Foreign Study	n/a	Intermed	American Institute for Foreign Study	n/a
Argentina	Buenos Aires	IES Abroad Buenos Aires Center	n/a	Intermed	IES Abroad	n/a
Argentina	Buenos Aires	Multiple institutional choices	n/a	Intermed	Institute for Study Abroad	n/a
Argentina	Buenos Aires	Universidad de Belgrano	n/a	Intermed	Academic Studies Abroad	n/a
Argentina	Buenos Aires	Universidad de Belgrano or Universidad Torcuato di Tella	n/a	Intermed	Academic Programs International	n/a
Argentina	Mendoza	Universidad Nacional de Cuyo	n/a	Intermed	Institute for Study Abroad	n/a
Australia	(Multiple choices)	Multiple institutional choices	n/a	Intermed	Study Australia (Education Abroad Network)	n/a
Australia	(Multiple choices)	Multiple institutional choices	n/a	Intermed	College Consortium for	n/a
Australia	(Multiple choices)	Multiple institutional choices	n/a	Intermed	Center for International Studies	n/a
Australia	(Multiple choices)	Multiple institutional choices	n/a	Intermed	Institute for Study Abroad	n/a
Australia	(Multiple choices)	Multiple institutional choices	n/a	USColl	Arcadia University	n/a
Australia	(Multiple choices)	Multiple institutional choices	n/a	Intermed	AustraLearn	n/a
Australia	Sydney	CAPA Sydney Center	n/a	Intermed	CAPA International Education	n/a
Australia	Yungaburra	Center for Rainforest Studies	n/a	Intermed	School for Field Studies	n/a
Austria	Salzburg	Salzburg College	n/a	Intermed	College Consortium for International Studies	n/a
Austria	Salzburg	University of Salzburg	n/a	Intermed	American Institute for Foreign Study	n/a
Austria	Vienna	IES Abroad Vienna Center	n/a	Intermed	IES Abroad	n/a
Barbados	Cave Hill	University of the West Indies	n/a	Dir	n/a	n/a
Belgium	Brussels	Universite Libre de Bruxelles or Vesalius College	n/a	Intermed	Council on International Educational Exchange (CIEE)	n/a
Belize	San Ignacio	Galen University	n/a	Consrtm	College Consortium for International Studies	n/a
Bermuda	St. George's	Bermuda Institute of Ocean Sciences	n/a	Dir	n/a	n/a
Bolivia	Cochabamba	SIT Study Abroad	n/a	Intermed	SIT Study Abroad	n/a
Botswana	Gaborone	University of Botswana	n/a	Intermed	Interstudy	n/a
Brazil	Rio de Janeiro	Pontificia Universidade Catolica do Rio de Janeiro	n/a	Intermed	SUNY New Paltz	n/a
Brazil	Salvador	SIT Study Abroad	n/a	Intermed	SIT Study Abroad	n/a
Brazil	Sao Paulo	Pontificia Universidade Catolica de Sao Paulo	n/a	Intermed	Council on International Educational Exchange (CIEE)	n/a
Canada	Antigonish (Nova Scotia)	St. Francis Xavier University	n/a	Bilat	n/a	n/a
Canada	Chicoutimi (Quebec)	Universite du Quebec a Chicoutimi	n/a	Bilat	n/a	n/a
Canada	Church Point (Nova Scotia)	Universite Sainte-Anne	n/a	Bilat	n/a	n/a

Massachusetts

DESTINATION	HOST INSTITUTION	PRGM SEASON	PRGM TYPE	INTERMEDIARY	HOUSING
Canada | Gatineau (Quebec)	Universite du Quebec en Outaouais	n/a	Bilat	n/a	n/a
Canada | Halifax (Nova Scotia)	Dalhousie University	n/a	Bilat	n/a	n/a
Canada | Halifax (Nova Scotia)	Mount Saint Vincent University	n/a	Bilat	n/a	n/a
Canada | Halifax (Nova Scotia)	Nova Scotia College of Art & Design	n/a	Bilat	n/a	n/a
Canada | Halifax (Nova Scotia)	Saint Mary's University	n/a	Bilat	n/a	n/a
Canada | Halifax (Nova Scotia)	University of King's College	n/a	Bilat	n/a	n/a
Canada | Montreal (Quebec)	Concordia University	n/a	Bilat	n/a	n/a
Canada | Montreal (Quebec)	Ecole de technologie superieure	n/a	Bilat	n/a	n/a
Canada | Montreal (Quebec)	Ecole Polytechnique de Montreal	n/a	Bilat	n/a	n/a
Canada | Montreal (Quebec)	McGill University	n/a	Bilat	n/a	n/a
Canada | Montreal (Quebec)	Universite de Montreal	n/a	Bilat	n/a	n/a
Canada | Montreal (Quebec)	Universite du Quebec a Montreal	n/a	Bilat	n/a	n/a
Canada | Quebec City (Quebec)	Ecole nationale d'administration publique	n/a	Bilat	n/a	n/a
Canada | Quebec City (Quebec)	Institut national de la recherche scientifique	n/a	Bilat	n/a	n/a
Canada | Quebec City (Quebec)	Tele-universite (Universite du Quebec a Montreal)	n/a	Bilat	n/a	n/a
Canada | Quebec City (Quebec)	Universite Laval	n/a	Bilat	n/a	n/a
Canada | Rimouski (Quebec)	Universite du Quebec a Rimouski	n/a	Bilat	n/a	n/a
Canada | Rouyn-Noranda (Quebec)	Universite du Quebec en Abitibi-Temiscamingue	n/a	Bilat	n/a	n/a
Canada | Sherbrooke (Quebec)	Bishop's University	n/a	Bilat	n/a	n/a
Canada | Sherbrooke (Quebec)	Universite de Sherbrooke	n/a	Bilat	n/a	n/a
Canada | Trois-Rivieres (Quebec)	Universite du Quebec a Trois-Rivieres	n/a	Bilat	n/a	n/a
Canada | Truro (Nova Scotia)	Nova Scotia Agricultural College	n/a	Bilat	n/a	n/a
Canada | Wolfville (Nova Scotia)	Acadia University	n/a	Bilat	n/a	n/a
Chile | (Multiple)	SIT Study Abroad	n/a	Intermed	SIT Study Abroad	n/a
Chile | Santiago	Multiple institutional choices	n/a	Intermed	Institute for Study Abroad	n/a
Chile | Santiago	Pontificia Universidad Catolica de Chile or Universidad de Chile	n/a	Intermed	n/a	n/a
Chile | Valparaiso	Multiple institutional choices	n/a	Intermed	Institute for Study Abroad	n/a
Chile | Vina del Mar	Universidad de Vina del Mar	n/a	Intermed	Academic Studies Abroad	n/a
China | (Multiple)	Multiple institutional choices	n/a	Intermed	New England Board of Higher Education	n/a
China | Beijing	Beijing Language and Culture University	n/a	Intermed	Alliance for Global Education	n/a
China | Beijing	IES Abroad Beijing Center	n/a	Intermed	IES Abroad	n/a
China | Beijing	Peking University	n/a	Intermed	Council on International Educational Exchange (CIEE)	n/a

Massachusetts

DESTINATION	HOST INSTITUTION	PRGM SEASON	PRGM TYPE	INTERMEDIARY	HOUSING
China	Beijing	University of International Business and Economics	n/a	Intermed	Center for International Studies	n/a
China	Beijing	University of International Business and Economics	n/a	Intermed	Study Asia (Education Abroad Network)	n/a
China	Chengdu	Sichuan University	n/a	Intermed	AsiaLearn	n/a
China	Nanjing	Nanjing University	n/a	Intermed	Council on International Educational Exchange (CIEE)	n/a
China	Shanghai	East China Normal University	n/a	Intermed	Council on International Educational Exchange (CIEE)	n/a
China	Shanghai	Fudan University	n/a	Intermed	Alliance for Global Education	n/a
China	Shanghai	Fudan University	n/a	Intermed	Study Asia (Education Abroad Network)	n/a
China	Shanghai	IES Abroad	n/a	Intermed	IES Abroad	n/a
China	Xi'an	Xi'an International Studies University	n/a	Intermed	Alliance for Global Education	n/a
Costa Rica	Atenas	SFS Center for Sustainable Development Studies	n/a	Intermed	School for Field Studies	n/a
Costa Rica	Heredia	Universidad Nacional	n/a	Intermed	Institute for Study Abroad	n/a
Costa Rica	San Joaquin de Flores	Instituto San Joaquin de Flores	n/a	Intermed	Academic Programs International	n/a
Costa Rica	San Jose	Organization for Tropical Studies (Duke University)	n/a	Intermed	Organization for Tropical Studies (Duke University)	n/a
Czech Republic	Prague	Charles University	n/a	Intermed	American Institute for Foreign Study	n/a
Czech Republic	Prague	Charles University or Prague Film and Television School of the Academy of the Performing Arts	n/a	Intermed	Council on International Educational Exchange (CIEE)	n/a
Denmark	Copenhagen	Danish Institute for Study Abroad (DIS)	n/a	Intermed	Danish Institute for Study Abroad (DIS)	n/a
Dominican Republic	Santiago	Pontificia Universidad Catolica Madre y Maestra	n/a	Intermed	Council on International Educational Exchange (CIEE)	n/a
Ecuador	Guayaquil	La Universidad Catolica de Santiago de Guayaquil	n/a	Consrtm	College Consortium for International Studies	n/a
Ecuador	Quito	SIT Study Abroad	n/a	Intermed	SIT Study Abroad	n/a
Ecuador	Quito	Universidad San Francisco de Quito	n/a	Consrtm	College Consortium for International Studies	n/a
Egypt	(Multiple choices)	Multiple institutional choices	n/a	Intermed	Institute for Study Abroad	n/a
Egypt	Alexandria	Alexandria University	n/a	Intermed	Institute for Study Abroad	n/a
Egypt	Cairo	Multiple institutional choices	n/a	Intermed	Institute for Study Abroad	n/a
England	(Multiple choices)	Multiple institutional choices	n/a	USColl	Arcadia University	n/a
England	(Multiple choices)	Multiple institutional choices	n/a	Intermed	Institute for Study Abroad	n/a
England	(Multiple choices)	Multiple institutional choices	n/a	Intermed	Center for International Studies	n/a
England	(Multiple choices)	Multiple institutional choices	n/a	Intermed	Interstudy	n/a
England	Bath	University of Bath	n/a	Dir	n/a	n/a
England	Brighton	University of Sussex	n/a	Dir	n/a	n/a

© 2011 — Updates? Want to be in the next edition? Visit www.mysecondcampus.com

Massachusetts

DESTINATION	HOST INSTITUTION	PRGM SEASON	PRGM TYPE	INTERMEDIARY	HOUSING
England | Bristol	University of Bristol	n/a	Dir	n/a	n/a
England | Cambridge	Institute of Economic and Political Studies	n/a	Intermed	Institute of Economic and Political Studies	n/a
England | Cambridge	University of Cambridge	n/a	Dir	n/a	n/a
England | Colchester	University of Essex	n/a	Dir	n/a	n/a
England | Coventry	University of Warwick	n/a	Dir	n/a	n/a
England | Exeter	University of Exeter	n/a	Dir	n/a	n/a
England | Kent	University of Kent	n/a	Dir	n/a	n/a
England | Lancaster	University of Lancaster	n/a	Dir	n/a	n/a
England | Leeds	University of Leeds	n/a	Dir	n/a	n/a
England | Leeds	University of Leeds	n/a	Intermed	Academic Programs International	n/a
England | London	American InterContinental University	n/a	Dir	n/a	n/a
England | London	CAPA International Education	n/a	Intermed	CAPA International Education	n/a
England | London	Courtauld Institute of Art	n/a	Dir	n/a	n/a
England | London	Framingham State College	Spr	Self	n/a	n/a
England | London	Institute of Economic and Political Studies	n/a	Intermed	Institute of Economic and Political Studies	n/a
England | London	King's College	n/a	Dir	n/a	n/a
England | London	London School of Economics and Political Science	n/a	Dir	n/a	n/a
England | London	Multiple institutional choices	n/a	Intermed	IES Abroad	n/a
England | London	Multiple institutional choices	n/a	Intermed	Academic Programs International	n/a
England | London	Queen Mary	n/a	Dir	n/a	n/a
England | London	Queen Mary	n/a	Dir	n/a	n/a
England | London	Royal Holloway	n/a	Dir	n/a	n/a
England | London	School of Oriental and African Studies	n/a	Dir	n/a	n/a
England | London	University of Westminster	n/a	Dir	n/a	n/a
England | Manchester	University of Manchester	n/a	Dir	n/a	n/a
England | Norwich	University of East Anglia	n/a	Bilat	n/a	n/a
England | Norwich	University of East Anglia	n/a	Dir	n/a	n/a
England | Nottingham	University of Nottingham	n/a	Dir	n/a	n/a
England | Oxford	St. Catherine's College (University of Oxford)	n/a	Intermed	IES Abroad	n/a
England | Oxford	University of Oxford	n/a	Dir	n/a	n/a
England | Sunderland	University of Sunderland	n/a	Dir	n/a	n/a
England | York	University of York	n/a	Dir	n/a	n/a
Fiji | Suva	SIT Study Abroad	n/a	Intermed	SIT Study Abroad	n/a
Fiji | Suva	University of the South Pacific	n/a	Intermed	AustraLearn	n/a
Finland | Tampere	University of Tampere	n/a	Dir	n/a	n/a
Finland | Turku	University of Turku	n/a	Dir	n/a	n/a

Massachusetts

DESTINATION	HOST INSTITUTION	PRGM SEASON	PRGM TYPE	INTERMEDIARY	HOUSING
France	(Multiple choices)	Multiple institutional choices	n/a	Intermed	American Institute for Foreign Study	n/a
France	(Multiple choices)	Multiple institutional choices	n/a	Intermed	Academic Studies Abroad	n/a
France	Grenoble	Multiple institutional choices	n/a	Intermed	Academic Programs International	n/a
France	Nantes	IES Abroad	n/a	Intermed	IES Abroad	n/a
France	Paris	American Graduate School in Paris; Alliance Francaise	n/a	USColl	Arcadia University	n/a
France	Paris	Internships in Francophone Europe (IFE)	n/a	Intermed	Internships in Francophone Europe (IFE)	n/a
France	Paris	Multiple institutional choices	n/a	Intermed	Academic Programs International	n/a
France, Belgium, and Netherlands	(Multiple)	Framingham State College	Sum	Self	n/a	n/a
Germany	(Multiple choices)	Multiple institutional choices	n/a	USColl	UMass in Baden-Wurttemberg/Germany	n/a
Germany	(Multiple choices)	Multiple institutional choices	n/a	Bilat	German Academic Exchange Service (DAAD)	n/a
Germany	Freiburg	IES Abroad Freiburg Center	n/a	Intermed	IES Abroad	n/a
Ghana	Accra	Ashesi University	n/a	Intermed	Council on International Educational Exchange (CIEE)	n/a
Ghana	Legon	University of Ghana	n/a	Intermed	Council on International Educational Exchange (CIEE)	n/a
Greece	Athens	College Year in Athens	n/a	Intermed	College Year in Athens	n/a
Greece	Athens	The Arcadia Center for Hellenic, Mediterranean and Balkan Studies	n/a	USColl	Arcadia University	n/a
Greece	Thessaloniki	American College of Thessaloniki	n/a	Intermed	College Consortium for International Studies	n/a
Hungary	Budapest	Corvinus University of Budapest	n/a	Intermed	Council on International Educational Exchange (CIEE)	n/a
Hungary	Budapest	Corvinus University of Budapest	n/a	Intermed	Academic Programs International	n/a
Hungary	Budapest	Technical University of Budapest, College International	n/a	Intermed	Budapest Semesters in Mathematics	n/a
India	(Multiple choices)	SIT Study Abroad	n/a	Intermed	SIT Study Abroad	n/a
India	Auroville	Living Routes	n/a	Intermed	Living Routes	n/a
India	Delhi	IES Abroad	n/a	Intermed	IES Abroad	n/a
India	Hyderabad	University of Hyderabad	n/a	Intermed	American Institute for Foreign Study	n/a
India	Hyderabad	University of Hyderabad	n/a	Intermed	Council on International Educational Exchange (CIEE)	n/a
India	Pune	Fergusson College	n/a	Intermed	Alliance for Global Education	n/a
Ireland	(Multiple choices)	Multiple institutional choices	n/a	Intermed	Academic Programs International	n/a
Ireland	(Multiple choices)	Multiple institutional choices	n/a	Intermed	Institute for Study Abroad	n/a
Ireland	(Multiple choices)	Multiple institutional choices	n/a	USColl	Arcadia University	n/a

© 2011 — Updates? Want to be in the next edition? Visit **www.mysecondcampus.com**

Massachusetts

DESTINATION	HOST INSTITUTION	PRGM SEASON	PRGM TYPE	INTERMEDIARY	HOUSING
Ireland | Cork	University College Cork	n/a	Dir	n/a	n/a
Ireland | Dublin	Griffith College Dublin	n/a	Intermed	Academic Studies Abroad	n/a
Ireland | Dublin	Trinity College	n/a	Dir	n/a	n/a
Ireland | Dublin	Trinity College or Dublin City University	n/a	Intermed	Center for International Studies	n/a
Ireland | Dublin	University College Dublin	n/a	Dir	n/a	n/a
Ireland | Galway	National University of Ireland, Galway	n/a	Dir	n/a	n/a
Ireland | Limerick	University of Limerick	n/a	Dir	n/a	n/a
Ireland | Limerick	University of Limerick	n/a	Intermed	Center for International Studies	n/a
Israel | Haifa	University of Haifa	n/a	Intermed	n/a	n/a
Israel | Jerusalem	Hebrew University	n/a	Dir	n/a	n/a
Israel | Kibbutz Lotan	Living Routes	n/a	Dir	Living Routes	n/a
Italy | (Multiple)	Framingham State College	Sum	Self	n/a	n/a
Italy | (Multiple choices)	Multiple institutional choices	n/a	Intermed	Academic Programs International	n/a
Italy | (Multiple choices)	Multiple institutional choices	n/a	USColl	Arcadia University	n/a
Italy | Ferrara	University of Ferrara	n/a	Intermed	Council on International Educational Exchange (CIEE)	n/a
Italy | Florence	CAPA International Education	n/a	Intermed	CAPA International Education	n/a
Italy | Florence	Institute at Palazzo Rucellai	n/a	Intermed	Institute at Palazzo Rucellai	n/a
Italy | Florence	Lorenzo de' Medici	n/a	Intermed	Lorenzo de' Medici	n/a
Italy | Florence or Rome	Accademia Italiana	n/a	Intermed	Accademia Italiana	n/a
Italy | Milan	IES Abroad Milan Center	n/a	Intermed	IES Abroad	n/a
Italy | Rome	Temple University Rome	n/a	Intermed	Temple University	n/a
Jamaica | Mona	University of the West Indies	n/a	Dir	n/a	n/a
Japan | Beppu	Ritsumeikan Asia Pacific University	n/a	Intermed	AsiaLearn	n/a
Japan | Kyoto	Doshisha University	n/a	Consrtm	Associated Kyoto Program	n/a
Japan | Nagoya	Nanzan University	n/a	Intermed	IES Abroad	n/a
Japan | Tokyo	International Christian University	n/a	Dir	n/a	n/a
Japan | Tokyo	Sophia University	n/a	Intermed	Council on International Educational Exchange (CIEE)	n/a
Japan | Tokyo	Temple University	n/a	Dir	n/a	n/a
Jordan | Amman	SIT Study Abroad	n/a	Intermed	SIT Study Abroad	n/a
Jordan | Amman	University of Jordan	n/a	Intermed	Council on International Educational Exchange (CIEE)	n/a
Kenya | Kimana	Center for Wildlife Management Studies	n/a	Intermed	School for Field Studies	n/a
Kenya | Mombasa	SIT Study Abroad	n/a	Intermed	SIT Study Abroad	n/a
Kenya | Nairobi	SIT Study Abroad	n/a	Intermed	SIT Study Abroad	n/a
Madagascar | Fort Dauphin	SIT Study Abroad	n/a	Intermed	SIT Study Abroad	n/a
Malaysia | Kuching	Swinburne University of Technology (Sarawak Campus)	n/a	Intermed	AsiaLearn	n/a

Massachusetts

DESTINATION	HOST INSTITUTION	PRGM SEASON	PRGM TYPE	INTERMEDIARY	HOUSING
Mali | Bamako	SIT Study Abroad	n/a	Intermed	SIT Study Abroad	n/a
Mexico | Baja	Center for Coastal Studies	n/a	Intermed	School for Field Studies	n/a
Mexico | Guadalajara	Universidad Autonoma de Guadalajara	n/a	Intermed	College Consortium for International Studies	n/a
Mexico | Merida	Universidad Autonoma de Yucatan	n/a	Intermed	Institute for Study Abroad	n/a
Mexico | Queretaro	Universidad Autonoma de Queretaro	n/a	Intermed	Academic Programs International	n/a
Morocco | Rabat	Ecole Superieure de Direction et de Gestion	n/a	Intermed	Council on International Educational Exchange (CIEE)	n/a
Netherlands | Amsterdam	IES Abroad Amsterdam Center	n/a	Intermed	IES Abroad	n/a
Netherlands | Amsterdam	University of Amsterdam	n/a	Intermed	Council on International Educational Exchange (CIEE)	n/a
Netherlands | Maastricht	Center for European Studies (University of Maastricht)	n/a	Dir	n/a	n/a
New Zealand | (Multiple choices)	Multiple institutional choices	n/a	Intermed	Study Australia (Education Abroad Network)	n/a
New Zealand | (Multiple choices)	Multiple institutional choices	n/a	Intermed	College Consortium for International Studies	n/a
New Zealand | (Multiple choices)	Multiple institutional choices	n/a	Intermed	Institute for Study Abroad	n/a
New Zealand | (Multiple choices)	Multiple institutional choices	n/a	USColl	Arcadia University	n/a
New Zealand | (Multiple choices)	Multiple institutional choices	n/a	Intermed	AustraLearn	n/a
New Zealand | (Multiple choices)	Multiple institutional choices	n/a	Intermed	Center for International Studies	n/a
New Zealand | Auckland	University of Auckland	n/a	Dir	n/a	n/a
New Zealand | Auckland	University of Auckland	n/a	Intermed	Frontiers Abroad	n/a
New Zealand | Christchurch	University of Canterbury	n/a	Dir	n/a	n/a
New Zealand | Dunedin	University of Otago	n/a	Dir	n/a	n/a
New Zealand | Palmerston North	Massey University	n/a	Dir	n/a	n/a
New Zealand | Tikapa Moana	EcoQuest (University of New Hampshire)	n/a	Intermed	EcoQuest (University of New Hampshire)	n/a
New Zealand | Wellington	Victoria University of Wellington	n/a	Dir	n/a	n/a
Nicaragua | Managua	SIT Study Abroad	n/a	Intermed	SIT Study Abroad	n/a
Northern Ireland | (Multiple)	University of Ulster	n/a	Intermed	Institute for Study Abroad	n/a
Northern Ireland | Belfast	Queen's University	n/a	Intermed	n/a	n/a
Peru | Lima	Pontificia Universidad Catolica del Peru	n/a	Intermed	Institute for Study Abroad	n/a
Poland | Krakow	Jagiellonian University	n/a	Intermed	Academic Programs International	n/a
Portugal | Lisbon	Universidade Nova de Lisboa	n/a	Intermed	Council on International Educational Exchange (CIEE)	n/a
Russia | St. Petersburg	St. Petersburg State Polytechnic University	n/a	Intermed	American Institute for Foreign Study	n/a
Russia | St. Petersburg	St. Petersburg State University	n/a	Intermed	Council on International Educational Exchange (CIEE)	n/a

© 2011 — Updates? Want to be in the next edition? Visit **www.mysecondcampus.com**

Massachusetts

DESTINATION	HOST INSTITUTION	PRGM SEASON	PRGM TYPE	INTERMEDIARY	HOUSING
Scotland	(Multiple choices)	Multiple institutional choices	n/a	Intermed	Center for International Studies	n/a
Scotland	(Multiple)	Multiple institutional choices	n/a	USColl	Arcadia University	n/a
Scotland	(Multiple)	Multiple institutional choices	n/a	Intermed	Institute for Study Abroad	n/a
Scotland	Aberdeen	University of Aberdeen	n/a	Dir	n/a	n/a
Scotland	Dundee	University of Dundee	n/a	Dir	n/a	n/a
Scotland	Dundee	University of Dundee	n/a	Intermed	College Consortium for International Studies	n/a
Scotland	Edinburgh	University of Edinburgh	n/a	Dir	n/a	n/a
Scotland	Findhorn	Living Routes	n/a	Intermed	Living Routes	n/a
Scotland	Glasgow	Glasgow School of Art	n/a	Dir	n/a	n/a
Scotland	Glasgow	University of Glasgow	n/a	Dir	n/a	n/a
Scotland	Glasgow	University of Glasgow	n/a	Dir	n/a	n/a
Scotland	St. Andrews	University of St. Andrews	n/a	Dir	n/a	n/a
Scotland	St. Andrews	University of St. Andrews	n/a	Intermed	Interstudy	n/a
Scotland	Stirling	University of Stirling	n/a	Dir	n/a	n/a
Senegal	Yoff	Living Routes	n/a	Intermed	Living Routes	n/a
Singapore	Singapore	James Cook University (Singapore Campus)	n/a	Intermed	AsiaLearn	n/a
South Africa	(Multiple choices)	Multiple institutional choices	n/a	Intermed	Interstudy	n/a
South Africa	Cape Town	Multiple institutional choices	n/a	USColl	Arcadia University	n/a
South Africa	Cape Town	University of Cape Town	n/a	Dir	n/a	n/a
South Africa	Cape Town	University of Cape Town	n/a	Intermed	Council on International Educational Exchange (CIEE)	n/a
South Africa	Durban	SIT Study Abroad	n/a	Intermed	SIT Study Abroad	n/a
South Korea	Seoul	Korea University	n/a	Intermed	AsiaLearn	n/a
South Korea	Seoul	Yonsei University	n/a	Intermed	Council on International Educational Exchange (CIEE)	n/a
Spain	(Multiple choices)	Multiple institutional choices	n/a	Intermed	Council on International Educational Exchange (CIEE)	n/a
Spain	(Multiple choices)	Multiple institutional choices	n/a	Intermed	IES Abroad	n/a
Spain	(Multiple choices)	Multiple institutional choices	n/a	USColl	Arcadia University	n/a
Spain	(Multiple choices)	Multiple institutional choices	n/a	Intermed	Academic Programs International	n/a
Spain	Valencia	American Institute	n/a	Intermed	Institute for Spanish Studies	n/a
Sweden	Stockholm	The Swedish Program (Stockholm University)	n/a	Consrtm	The Swedish Program (Stockholm University)	n/a
Sweden	Uppsala	Uppsala University	n/a	Intermed	Council on International Educational Exchange (CIEE)	n/a
Switzerland	Geneva	SIT Study Abroad	n/a	Intermed	SIT Study Abroad	n/a
Switzerland	Lugano	Franklin College	n/a	Intermed	College Consortium for International Studies	n/a
Tanzania	Arusha	Arcadia University	n/a	USColl	Arcadia University	n/a
Thailand	Chiang Mai	Chiang Mai University	n/a	Intermed	Study Asia (Education Abroad Network)	n/a

Massachusetts

DESTINATION	HOST INSTITUTION	PRGM SEASON	PRGM TYPE	INTERMEDIARY	HOUSING
Thailand | Khon Kaen	Khon Kaen University	n/a	Intermed	Council on International Educational Exchange (CIEE)	n/a
Trinidad and Tobago | St. Augustine	University of the West Indies	n/a	Dir	n/a	n/a
Turkey | Istanbul	Koc University	n/a	Intermed	Council on International Educational Exchange (CIEE)	n/a
Turks and Caicos | South Caicos	Center for Marine Resource Management Studies	n/a	Intermed	School for Field Studies	n/a
United Arab Emirates | Dubai	Unknown	n/a	Intermed	Institute for Study Abroad	n/a
United States | Washington (DC)	American University	n/a	Dir	n/a	n/a
United States | Washington (DC)	Washington Center for Internships and Academic Seminars	n/a	Intermed	Washington Center for Internships and Academic Seminars	n/a
United States | Woods Hole (MA)	SEA Semester	n/a	Intermed	SEA Semester	n/a
Vietnam | Can Tho	SIT Study Abroad	n/a	Intermed	SIT Study Abroad	n/a
Vietnam | Ho Chi Minh City	SIT Study Abroad	n/a	Intermed	SIT Study Abroad	n/a
Vietnam | Ho Chi Minh City	Vietnam National University	n/a	Intermed	Council on International Educational Exchange (CIEE)	n/a
Wales | Bangor	Bangor University	n/a	USColl	Arcadia University	n/a
Wales | Cardiff	Cardiff University	n/a	Intermed	Institute for Study Abroad	n/a
Wales | Swansea	Swansea University	n/a	USColl	Arcadia University	n/a

Franklin W. Olin College of Engineering

Carol Kelley
Manager of Student Services
Olin Way
Needham, MA 02492

carol.kelley@olin.edu
781.292.2323
http://awayprograms.olin.edu/default.asp

DESTINATION	HOST INSTITUTION	PRGM SEASON	PRGM TYPE	INTERMEDIARY	HOUSING
(Multiple choices) | (Multiple choices)	IES Abroad	n/a	Intermed	IES Abroad	n/a
(Multiple choices) | (Multiple choices)	Multiple institutional choices	n/a	Intermed	Institute for Study Abroad	n/a
(Multiple choices) | (Multiple choices)	Multiple institutional choices	n/a	Intermed	SIT Study Abroad	n/a
(Multiple choices) | (Multiple choices)	Multiple institutional choices	n/a	Intermed	GlobalE3	n/a
(Multiple choices) | (Multiple choices)	Multiple institutional choices	n/a	USColl	Arcadia University	n/a
Australia | Sydney	University of Technology Sydney	n/a	Dir	n/a	n/a
Chile | Santiago	Pontificia Universidad Catolica de Chile	n/a	Bilat	n/a	n/a
Chile | Santiago	Universidad Adolfo Ibanez	n/a	Bilat	n/a	n/a
France | La Rochelle	EIGSI - La Rochelle School of Industrial Systems Engineering	n/a	Bilat	n/a	n/a
France | Metz	Georgia Tech Lorraine	n/a	USColl	Georgia Tech University	n/a
Germany | Regensburg	Hochschule Regensburg School of Applied Sciences	n/a	Bilat	n/a	n/a

Massachusetts

DESTINATION	HOST INSTITUTION	PRGM SEASON	PRGM TYPE	INTERMEDIARY	HOUSING
Hungary | Budapest	Technical University of Budapest, College International	n/a	Intermed	Budapest Semesters in Mathematics	n/a
Scotland | Aberdeen	Robert Gordon University	n/a	Bilat	n/a	n/a
South Korea | Daejon	Korea Advanced Institute of Science and Technology	n/a	Bilat	n/a	n/a
Sweden | Goteborg	Chalmers University of Technology	n/a	Bilat	n/a	n/a
Sweden | Uppsala	Uppsala University	n/a	Bilat	n/a	n/a
Thailand | Bangkok	King Mongkut's University of Technology Thonburi	n/a	Bilat	n/a	n/a
United States | Bar Harbor (ME)	College of the Atlantic	n/a	Bilat	n/a	n/a

Gordon College

Cliff Hersey
Dean of Global Education
255 Grapevine Road
Wenham, MA 01984

cliff.hersey@gordon.edu
978.867.4294
http://www.gordon.edu/geo

DESTINATION	HOST INSTITUTION	PRGM SEASON	PRGM TYPE	INTERMEDIARY	HOUSING
(Multiple choices) | (Multiple choices)	Multiple institutional choices	n/a	Intermed	Council on International Educational Exchange (CIEE)	n/a
Belize | Nabitunich	Gordon College	Fall Spr	Intermed	Creation Care Study Program	Other
Costs: Fall Costs: T&F: n/a, R&B: n/a, Ttl: Gordon home comprehensive fees Spr Costs: T&F: n/a, R&B: n/a, Ttl: Gordon home comprehensive fees					
China | (Multiple)	Gordon College	Sum	Self	n/a	n/a
Costs: Sum Costs: T&F: n/a, R&B: n/a, Ttl: $3,985					
China | Beijing	Peking University	Fall Spr	Intermed	China Studies Institute	HostFam CollRes PrivApt Other
Costs: Fall Costs: T&F: n/a, R&B: n/a, Ttl: Gordon home comprehensive fees Spr Costs: T&F: n/a, R&B: n/a, Ttl: Gordon home comprehensive fees					
China | Xiamen	Xiamen University	Fall Spr	Intermed	Council for Christian Colleges & Universities	CollRes Other
Costs: Fall Costs: T&F: n/a, R&B: n/a, Ttl: Gordon home comprehensive fees Spr Costs: T&F: n/a, R&B: n/a, Ttl: Gordon home comprehensive fees					
Costa Rica | San Jose	Council for Christian Colleges & Universities	Fall Spr	Intermed	Council for Christian Colleges & Universities	HostFam
Costs: Fall Costs: T&F: n/a, R&B: n/a, Ttl: Gordon home comprehensive fees Spr Costs: T&F: n/a, R&B: n/a, Ttl: Gordon home comprehensive fees					
Costa Rica and Romania | Unknown	Gordon College	n/a	Self	n/a	n/a
Croatia | (Multiple)	Gordon College	Sum	Self	n/a	n/a
Egypt | Cairo	Council for Christian Colleges & Universities	Fall Spr	Intermed	Council for Christian Colleges & Universities	PrivApt
Costs: Fall Costs: T&F: n/a, R&B: n/a, Ttl: Gordon home comprehensive fees Spr Costs: T&F: n/a, R&B: n/a, Ttl: Gordon home comprehensive fees					
England | Oxford	Oxford University	YrRound	Intermed	Council for Christian Colleges & Universities	CollRes
Costs: YrRound Costs: T&F: n/a, R&B: n/a, Ttl: Gordon home comprehensive fees					

Massachusetts

DESTINATION	HOST INSTITUTION	PRGM SEASON	PRGM TYPE	INTERMEDIARY	HOUSING
England and Scotland | London and Edinburgh	Gordon College	Sum	Self	n/a	n/a
France | Aix-en-Provence	Institut d'Etudes Francaises pour Etudiants Etrangers	Spr YrRound	Self	n/a	HostFam
	Costs: Spr Costs: T&F: n/a, R&B: n/a, Ttl: Gordon home comprehensive fees YrRound Costs: T&F: n/a, R&B: n/a, Ttl: Gordon home comprehensive fees				
Germany | Heidelberg	University of Heidelberg	Fall Spr	USColl	Heidelberg University	CollRes PrivApt
	Costs: Fall Costs: T&F: n/a, R&B: n/a, Ttl: Gordon home comprehensive fees Spr Costs: T&F: n/a, R&B: n/a, Ttl: Gordon home comprehensive fees				
Greece | (Multiple)	Gordon College	Sum	Self	n/a	n/a
Guatemala | (Multiple)	Gordon College	Sum	Self	n/a	n/a
Honduras or Haiti | Unknown	Gordon College	n/a	Self	n/a	n/a
Hungary | Budapest	Technical University of Budapest, College International	Fall Spr	Intermed	Budapest Semesters in Mathematics	n/a
	Costs: Fall Costs: T&F: n/a, R&B: n/a, Ttl: Gordon home comprehensive fees Spr Costs: T&F: n/a, R&B: n/a, Ttl: Gordon home comprehensive fees				
Israel | Jerusalem	Jerusalem University College	n/a	Dir	n/a	n/a
Israel and Jordan | Jerusalem and Amman	Gordon College	Sum	Self	n/a	n/a
Italy | (Multiple)	Gordon College	Sum	Self	n/a	n/a
Italy | Assisi	Gordon College	Sum	Self	n/a	n/a
Italy | Orvieto	Gordon College	Fall Spr	Self	n/a	PrivApt
	Costs: Fall Costs: T&F: n/a, R&B: n/a, Ttl: Gordon home comprehensive fees Spr Costs: T&F: n/a, R&B: n/a, Ttl: Gordon home comprehensive fees				
Lithuania | Klaipeda	LCC International University	n/a	Bilat	n/a	n/a
New Zealand/Samoa | [City Unspecified]	Gordon College	Fall Spr	Intermed	Creation Care Study Program	HostFam CollRes
	Costs: Fall Costs: T&F: n/a, R&B: n/a, Ttl: Gordon home comprehensive fees Spr Costs: T&F: n/a, R&B: n/a, Ttl: Gordon home comprehensive fees				
Russia | Nizhni Novgorod	Council for Christian Colleges & Universities	Fall Spr	Intermed	Council for Christian Colleges & Universities	HostFam CollRes
	Costs: Fall Costs: T&F: n/a, R&B: n/a, Ttl: Gordon home comprehensive fees Spr Costs: T&F: n/a, R&B: n/a, Ttl: Gordon home comprehensive fees				
Scotland | Edinburgh	University of Edinburgh	Fall Spr	Dir	n/a	n/a
	Costs: Fall Costs: T&F: n/a, R&B: n/a, Ttl: Gordon home comprehensive fees Spr Costs: T&F: n/a, R&B: n/a, Ttl: Gordon home comprehensive fees				
South Africa | (Multiple)	Gordon College	Sum	Self	n/a	n/a
Sri Lanka | Unknown	Gordon College	Sum	Self	n/a	n/a
	Costs: Sum Costs: T&F: n/a, R&B: n/a, Ttl: $3,400				
Thailand | Chiang Mai	Gordon College	Spr	n/a	Spring Semester in Thailand	n/a
	Costs: Spr Costs: T&F: n/a, R&B: n/a, Ttl: Gordon home comprehensive fees				
Uganda | Mukono Town	Uganda Christian University	Fall Spr	Intermed	Council for Christian Colleges & Universities	CollRes
	Costs: Fall Costs: T&F: n/a, R&B: n/a, Ttl: Gordon home comprehensive fees Spr Costs: T&F: n/a, R&B: n/a, Ttl: Gordon home comprehensive fees				

© 2011 — Updates? Want to be in the next edition? Visit **www.mysecondcampus.com**

Massachusetts

DESTINATION	HOST INSTITUTION	PRGM SEASON	PRGM TYPE	INTERMEDIARY	HOUSING
United States | (Multiple choices)	Multiple CCC institutions to choose from	n/a	Consrtm	Christian College Consortium (CCC)	n/a
United States | Boston	Gordon College	Fall Spr	Self	n/a	Other
Costs: Fall Costs: T&F: n/a, R&B: n/a, Ttl: Gordon home comprehensive fees Spr Costs: T&F: n/a, R&B: n/a, Ttl: Gordon home comprehensive fees					
United States | Cascade Mountains	Oregon Extension	Fall	n/a	Oregon Extension	Other
Costs: Fall Costs: T&F: n/a, R&B: n/a, Ttl: Gordon home comprehensive fees					
United States | Washington (DC)	Council for Christian Colleges & Universities	Fall Spr	Intermed	Council for Christian Colleges & Universities	CollRes
Costs: Fall Costs: T&F: n/a, R&B: n/a, Ttl: Gordon home comprehensive fees Spr Costs: T&F: n/a, R&B: n/a, Ttl: Gordon home comprehensive fees					
United States | Gloucester (MA)	Gordon College	Fall	Self	n/a	n/a
United States | Los Angeles	Council for Christian Colleges & Universities	Fall Spr	Intermed	Council for Christian Colleges & Universities	PrivApt
Costs: Fall Costs: T&F: n/a, R&B: n/a, Ttl: Gordon home comprehensive fees Spr Costs: T&F: n/a, R&B: n/a, Ttl: Gordon home comprehensive fees					
United States | Martha's Vineyard	Council for Christian Colleges & Universities	Fall Spr	Intermed	Council for Christian Colleges & Universities	CollRes
Costs: Fall Costs: T&F: n/a, R&B: n/a, Ttl: Gordon home comprehensive fees Spr Costs: T&F: n/a, R&B: n/a, Ttl: Gordon home comprehensive fees					
United States | Salem (MA)	Gordon College	Sum Fall	Self	n/a	n/a
Costs: Sum Costs: T&F: n/a, R&B: n/a, Ttl: Gordon home comprehensive fees Fall Costs: T&F: n/a, R&B: n/a, Ttl: Gordon home comprehensive fees					
United States | San Francisco	Westmont College	n/a	Dir	n/a	n/a

Gordon-Conwell Theological Seminary

Frank James
Provost
130 Essex Street
South Hamilton, MA 01982

fjames@gcts.edu
978.468.7111
http://www.gordonconwell.edu/current_students/global_education_study_abroad

DESTINATION	HOST INSTITUTION	PRGM SEASON	PRGM TYPE	INTERMEDIARY	HOUSING
(Multiple) | (Multiple)	Unknown	n/a	Self	n/a	n/a
Israel | Jerusalem	Jerusalem University College	n/a	Dir	n/a	n/a
United States | (Multiple choices)	Appalachian Ministries Educational Resources Center	n/a	Consrtm	Appalachian Ministries Educational Resources Center	n/a
United States | (Multiple choices)	Multiple institutional choices	n/a	Dir	n/a	n/a
United States | (Multiple choices)	Multiple institutional choices	n/a	Intermed	InterVarsity Christian Fellowship	n/a
United States | (Multiple choices)	Multiple institutional choices	n/a	Consrtm	Boston Theological Institute	n/a
United States | (Multiple choices)	United States Armed Forces	n/a	USColl	United States Armed Forces	n/a
United States | Boston (MA)	Center for Urban Ministerial Education (Gordon-Conwell Theological Seminary)	n/a	Self	n/a	n/a
United States | Charlotte (NC)	Gordon-Conwell Theological Seminary (Charlotte Campus)	n/a	Self	n/a	n/a

Massachusetts

DESTINATION	HOST INSTITUTION	PRGM SEASON	PRGM TYPE	INTERMEDIARY	HOUSING
United States | Dubuque (IA)	Dubuque Theological Seminary and Wartburg Theological Seminary	n/a	Dir	n/a	n/a
United States | Pittsburgh (PA)	Coalition for Christian Outreach	n/a	Intermed	n/a	n/a
United States | South Hamilton (MA)	Center for Advent Christian Studies (Gordon-Conwell Theological Seminary)	n/a	Self	n/a	n/a
United States | Washington (DC)	Wesley Theological Seminary	n/a	Dir	n/a	n/a

Greenfield Community College

David Ram
Dean
One College Drive
Greenfield, MA 01301

ram@gcc.mass.edu
413.775.1811
http://www.gcc.mass.edu/departments/bit/projects.html

DESTINATION	HOST INSTITUTION	PRGM SEASON	PRGM TYPE	INTERMEDIARY	HOUSING
Ireland | Dublin	Dublin Business School	Spr	Dir	n/a	n/a

Hampshire College

Brianna Mercker
Director of Education Abroad
Global Education Office
893 West Street
Amherst, MA 01002

bmercker@hampshire.edu
413.559.5542
http://www.hampshire.edu/geo/goabroad.htm

DESTINATION	HOST INSTITUTION	PRGM SEASON	PRGM TYPE	INTERMEDIARY	HOUSING
(Multiple choices) | (Multiple choices)	Multiple institutional choices	n/a	Bilat	International Student Exchange Program (ISEP)	n/a
Australia | Sydney	Macquarie University	Fall Spr	Bilat	n/a	n/a
China | Hefei	Anhui Academy of Social Science	Sum Fall Spr	Bilat	n/a	n/a
China | Hefei	Anhui Agricultural University	Sum Fall Spr	Bilat	n/a	n/a
China | Hefei	Anhui Agricultural University	Sum	Self	n/a	n/a
Costs: Sum Costs: T&F: n/a, R&B: n/a, Ttl: $3,100					
China | Hefei	Anhui Agricultural University	Sum	Self	n/a	n/a
Costs: Sum Costs: T&F: n/a, R&B: n/a, Ttl: $1,600					
Costa Rica | San Jose	Institute for Central American Development Studies (ICADS)	Fall Spr	Intermed	Institute for Central American Development Studies (ICADS)	n/a
Cuba | Havana	Multiple institutional choices	Spr	Bilat	n/a	n/a
Czech Republic and Poland | Prague and Krakow	Dartmore Institute and Jagiellonian University	Sum	Self	n/a	PrivApt
Costs: Sum Costs: T&F: n/a, R&B: n/a, Ttl: $3,500					
England | London	Goldsmiths College	Fall Spr	Bilat	n/a	n/a
France | Paris	Hampshire College	Sum	Self	n/a	PrivApt
Costs: Sum Costs: T&F: n/a, R&B: n/a, Ttl: $2,300					
France | Paris	Institut d'Etudes Politiques (Sciences Po)	Spr YrRound	Bilat	n/a	n/a
Germany | Berlin	Multiple institutional choices	Spr	Bilat	n/a	n/a

© 2011 — Updates? Want to be in the next edition? Visit **www.mysecondcampus.com**

Massachusetts

DESTINATION	HOST INSTITUTION	PRGM SEASON	PRGM TYPE	INTERMEDIARY	HOUSING
Greece | Corinth	Hampshire College	Sum	Self	n/a	n/a
Costs: Sum Costs: T&F: n/a, R&B: n/a, Ttl: $3,600					
India | Sarnath	Central Institute of Higher Tibetan Studies	n/a	USColl	Smith College	n/a
Ireland | Galway	Hampshire College	Win	Self	n/a	PrivApt
Costs: Win Costs: T&F: n/a, R&B: n/a, Ttl: $1,850					
Ireland | Glenstal Abbey and Dublin	Hampshire College	Sum	Self	n/a	Other
Costs: Sum Costs: T&F: n/a, R&B: n/a, Ttl: $2,300					
Mexico | (Multiple)	Multiple institutional choices	Fall Spr	Intermed	Mexico Solidarity Network	n/a
Netherlands | Hague	Hampshire College	Win	Self	n/a	n/a
Costs: Win Costs: T&F: n/a, R&B: n/a, Ttl: $1,750					
Puerto Rico | San Juan	University of Puerto Rico	Fall Spr	Bilat	n/a	n/a
Scotland | Edinburgh	University of Edinburgh	Fall Spr	Bilat	n/a	n/a
United States | (Multiple choices)	Multiple institutional choices	n/a	Consrtm	Consortium for Innovative Environments in Learning	n/a
United States | New York (NY)	New York Institute for Architecture and Urban Studies	Fall Spr	Bilat	n/a	n/a
United States | Woods Hole (MA)	Semester in Environmental Science	Fall	Intermed	Semester in Environmental Science	n/a

Harvard University

Catherine Winnie
Director
77 Dunster Street
Cambridge, MA 02138

hutchis@fas.harvard.edu
617.384.7521
http://www.fas.harvard.edu/~oip/

DESTINATION	HOST INSTITUTION	PRGM SEASON	PRGM TYPE	INTERMEDIARY	HOUSING
Argentina | Buenos Aires	Instituto de Desarrollo Economico y Social	Sum	Self	n/a	HostFam
Costs: Sum Costs: T&F: n/a, R&B: n/a, Ttl: $5,750					
Argentina | Buenos Aires	Multiple institutional choices	Fall Spr YrRound	Dir	n/a	n/a
Argentina | Buenos Aires	Multiple institutional choices	Fall Spr YrRound	Dir	n/a	n/a
Argentina | Cordoba	Universidad Nacional de Cordoba	Sum	Intermed	Center for Cross-Cultural Study	n/a
Argentina | Victoria	Universidad de San Andres	Sum	Dir	n/a	n/a
Australia | Adelaide	Flinders University	n/a	Intermed	Institute for Study Abroad	n/a
Australia | Adelaide	University of Adelaide	n/a	USColl	Arcadia University	n/a
Australia | Brisbane	Griffith University	n/a	USColl	Arcadia University	n/a
Australia | Brisbane	Queensland University of	n/a	USColl	Arcadia University	n/a
Australia | Brisbane	University of Queensland	n/a	USColl	Arcadia University	n/a
Australia | Brisbane	University of Queensland	n/a	Dir	n/a	n/a
Australia | Byron Bay	SIT Study Abroad	n/a	Intermed	SIT Study Abroad	n/a
Australia | Cairns	James Cook University	n/a	USColl	Arcadia University	n/a
Australia | Cairns	SIT Study Abroad	n/a	Intermed	SIT Study Abroad	n/a

Massachusetts

DESTINATION	HOST INSTITUTION	PRGM SEASON	PRGM TYPE	INTERMEDIARY	HOUSING
Australia | Canberra	Australian National University	n/a	Dir	n/a	n/a
Australia | Canberra	Australian National University	n/a	USColl	Arcadia University	n/a
Australia | Gold Coast	Bond University	n/a	USColl	Arcadia University	n/a
Australia | Gold Coast	Griffith University	n/a	USColl	Arcadia University	n/a
Australia | Hobart	University of Tasmania	n/a	Intermed	Institute for Study Abroad	n/a
Australia | Melbourne	Monash University	n/a	USColl	Arcadia University	n/a
Australia | Melbourne	University of Melbourne	n/a	Dir	n/a	n/a
Australia | Melbourne	University of Melbourne	n/a	USColl	Arcadia University	n/a
Australia | Melbourne	Victorian College of the Arts	n/a	USColl	Arcadia University	n/a
Australia | North Queensland	School for Field Studies	Sum	Intermed	School for Field Studies	n/a
Australia | Perth	Murdoch University	n/a	Intermed	Institute for Study Abroad	n/a
Australia | Perth	University of Western Australia	n/a	Dir	n/a	n/a
Australia | Perth	University of Western Australia	n/a	USColl	Arcadia University	n/a
Australia | Sydney	Boston University Sydney Center	Sum	USColl	Boston University	CollRes
Australia | Sydney	Boston University Sydney Center	Sum	USColl	Boston University	CollRes
Australia | Sydney	Macquarie University	n/a	USColl	Arcadia University	n/a
Australia | Sydney	University of New South Wales	n/a	USColl	Arcadia University	n/a
Australia | Sydney	University of New South Wales	n/a	Dir	n/a	n/a
Australia | Sydney	University of Sydney	n/a	USColl	Arcadia University	n/a
Australia | Sydney	University of Sydney	n/a	Dir	n/a	n/a
Australia | Sydney	University of Technology	n/a	USColl	Arcadia University	n/a
Australia | Townsville	James Cook University	n/a	Dir	n/a	n/a
Australia | Townsville	James Cook University	n/a	USColl	Arcadia University	n/a
Australia | Wollongong	University of Wollongong	n/a	USColl	Arcadia University	n/a
Australia | Yungaburra	School for Field Studies	n/a	Intermed	School for Field Studies	n/a
Austria | Salzburg	University of Salzburg	n/a	Consrtm	New England Universities in Salzburg	n/a
Austria | Vienna	IES Abroad Vienna Center	n/a	Intermed	IES Abroad	n/a
Bolivia | Cochabamba	SIT Study Abroad	Sum	Intermed	SIT Study Abroad	n/a
Botswana | Gaborone	SIT Study Abroad	n/a	Intermed	SIT Study Abroad	HostFam
Botswana | Gaborone	University of Botswana	Spr	Dir	n/a	CollRes
Botswana | Gaborone	University of Botswana	n/a	Intermed	Council on International Educational Exchange (CIEE)	PrivApt
Brazil | Paraty	Yale University	Sum	USColl	Yale University	HostFam
Brazil | Rio de Janeiro	Pontificia Universidade Catolica do Rio de Janeiro	Sum	Self	n/a	n/a
Brazil | Salvador da Bahia	Universidade Federal da Bahia	Sum	Intermed	Council on International Educational Exchange (CIEE)	n/a
Brazil | Sao Paulo	Harvard University	Sum	Self	n/a	HostFam
	Costs: Sum Costs: T&F: n/a, R&B: n/a, Ttl: $3,000				
Cameroon | Yaounde	SIT Study Abroad	n/a	Intermed	SIT Study Abroad	HostFam
Canada | (Multiple)	Multiple institutional choices	n/a	Bilat	n/a	n/a
Canada | Halifax (Nova Scotia)	Dalhousie University	n/a	Dir	n/a	n/a

Massachusetts

DESTINATION	HOST INSTITUTION	PRGM SEASON	PRGM TYPE	INTERMEDIARY	HOUSING
Canada | Hamilton (Ontario)	McMaster University	n/a	Dir	n/a	n/a
Canada | Kingston (Ontario)	Queen's University	n/a	Dir	n/a	n/a
Canada | Montreal (Quebec)	McGill University	n/a	Dir	n/a	n/a
Canada | Montreal (Quebec)	Universite de Montreal	n/a	Dir	n/a	n/a
Canada | Ottawa (Ontario)	University of Ottawa	n/a	Dir	n/a	n/a
Canada | Sackville (New Brunswick)	Mount Allison University	n/a	USColl	n/a	n/a
Canada | St. John's (Newfoundland and Labrador)	Memorial University of Newfoundland	n/a	Dir	n/a	n/a
Canada | Toronto (Ontario)	University of Toronto	n/a	Dir	n/a	n/a
Canada | Toronto (Ontario)	York University	n/a	Dir	n/a	n/a
Canada | Vancouver and Canada	University of British Columbia	n/a	Consrtm	Consortium for Studies in Mexico	n/a
Canada | Wolfville (Nova Scotia)	Acadia University	n/a	Dir	n/a	n/a
Chile | Santiago	Harvard University	Sum	Self	n/a	HostFam
	Costs: Sum Costs: T&F: n/a, R&B: n/a, Ttl: $3,900				
Chile | Santiago	Multiple institutional choices	Fall Spr YrRound	Dir	n/a	HostFam
Chile | Santiago	Multiple institutional choices	Fall Spr YrRound	Dir	n/a	HostFam
Chile | Santiago	University of Chile	Fall Spr	Dir	n/a	n/a
China | Beijing	Beijing Language and Culture University	Sum	Self	n/a	CollRes
	Costs: Sum Costs: T&F: n/a, R&B: n/a, Ttl: $5,250				
China | Beijing	Beijing Language and Culture University	n/a	Intermed	Alliance for Global Education	CollRes
China | Beijing	Beijing University	n/a	Dir	n/a	n/a
China | Beijing	Beijing University	n/a	USColl	Pitzer College	HostFam CollRes
China | Beijing	Capital Normal University	n/a	USColl	Middlebury College and CET	CollRes
China | Beijing	Capital University of Economics and Business	n/a	USColl	Associated Colleges in China (Hamilton College)	n/a
China | Beijing	CET Academic Programs	n/a	Intermed	CET Academic Programs	n/a
China | Beijing	Tsinghua University	n/a	Consrtm	Inter-University Program for Chinese Language Studies (University of California, Berkeley)	n/a
China | Hangzhou	CET Academic Programs	Sum	Intermed	CET Academic Programs	n/a
China | Hangzhou	Zhejiang University	n/a	Dir	n/a	n/a
China | Hangzhou	Zhejiang University	n/a	USColl	Middlebury College and CET	CollRes
China | Harbin	Harbin Institute of Technology	n/a	Intermed	CET Academic Programs	CollRes
China | Hong Kong	Chinese University of Hong Kong	n/a	Dir	n/a	n/a
China | Kunming	SIT Study Abroad	Sum	Intermed	SIT Study Abroad	n/a
China | Kunming	SIT Study Abroad	n/a	Intermed	SIT Study Abroad	HostFam
China | Kunming	Yunnan University	n/a	USColl	Middlebury College and CET	CollRes
China | Shanghai	East China Normal University	n/a	Intermed	Council on International Educational Exchange (CIEE)	HostFam CollRes PrivApt
China | Shanghai	Fudan University	n/a	Dir	n/a	n/a

© 2011 — Updates? Want to be in the next edition? Visit **www.mysecondcampus.com**

Massachusetts

DESTINATION	HOST INSTITUTION	PRGM SEASON	PRGM TYPE	INTERMEDIARY	HOUSING
China | Shanghai	Fudan University	n/a	Intermed	Alliance for Global Education	PrivApt
China | Shanghai	Harvard University	Sum	Self	n/a	CollRes
	Costs: Sum Costs: T&F: n/a, R&B: n/a, Ttl: $7,350				
China | Shanghai	Shanghai University of Finance and Economics	n/a	Intermed	Alliance for Global Education	CollRes
Costa Rica | Monteverde	CIEE Study Center in Monteverde	Sum	Intermed	Council on International Educational Exchange (CIEE)	n/a
Costa Rica | San Jose	Organization for Tropical Studies (Duke University)	Sum	Consrtm	Organization for Tropical Studies (Duke University)	n/a
Croatia | Dubrovnik and Split	University of Zagreb and University of Split	Sum	USColl	Northwestern University	n/a
Cuba | Havana	Universidad de la Habana	Fall	Dir	n/a	PrivApt
Czech Republic | Prague	Charles University	n/a	Dir	n/a	n/a
Czech Republic | Prague	Charles University	n/a	n/a	Council on International Educational Exchange (CIEE)	n/a
Czech Republic | Prague	Harvard University	Sum	Self	n/a	CollRes
	Costs: Sum Costs: T&F: n/a, R&B: n/a, Ttl: $7,500				
Denmark | Copenhagen	Danish Institute for Study Abroad (DIS)	n/a	Intermed	Danish Institute for Study Abroad (DIS)	n/a
Denmark and Sweden | Aarhus and Visby	Harvard University	Sum	Self	n/a	CollRes Other
	Costs: Sum Costs: T&F: n/a, R&B: n/a, Ttl: $7,350				
Dominican Republic | Santiago	Pontificia Universidad Catolica Madre y Maestra	Sum	Intermed	Council on International Educational Exchange (CIEE)	n/a
Ecuador | Quito	Universidad San Francisco de Quito	Sum	USColl	Georgetown University	n/a
Egypt | Alexandria	Alexandria University	n/a	USColl	Middlebury College	CollRes
Egypt | Cairo	American University in Cairo	n/a	Dir	n/a	n/a
Egypt | Cairo	International Language Institute	Sum	Dir	n/a	n/a
England | Brighton	University of Sussex	Sum	Dir	n/a	n/a
England | Cambridge	Cambridge University (Pembroke College)	Sum	Dir	n/a	n/a
England | London	Boston University London Center	Sum	USColl	Boston University	n/a
England | London	Imperial College	Sum	Self	n/a	CollRes
	Costs: Sum Costs: T&F: n/a, R&B: n/a, Ttl: $7,500				
England | Oxford	Oxford University (Queen's College)	Sum	Self	n/a	CollRes
	Costs: Sum Costs: T&F: n/a, R&B: n/a, Ttl: $7,500				
England | Oxford	Oxford University (St. Peter's College)	Sum	Intermed	Institute for Study Abroad	n/a
England | Oxford	Oxford University (Trinity College)	Sum	USColl	University of Massachusetts, Amherst	n/a
France | Aix-en-Provence	Institute for American Universities	Sum	Intermed	Institute for American Universities	n/a
France | Aix-en-Provence	Universite de Provence	n/a	USColl	Wellesley College	n/a
France | Avignon	Bryn Mawr College	Sum	USColl	Bryn Mawr College	n/a

© 2011 — Updates? Want to be in the next edition? Visit **www.mysecondcampus.com**

Massachusetts

DESTINATION	HOST INSTITUTION	PRGM SEASON	PRGM TYPE	INTERMEDIARY	HOUSING
France | Avignon	Institute for American Universities	Sum	Intermed	Institute for American Universities	n/a
France | Bordeaux	Universite Bordeaux 3 - Michel de Montaigne; Sciences Po Bordeaux	n/a	USColl	Middlebury College	HostFam PrivApt
France | Grenoble	Universite de Grenoble	n/a	USColl	Boston University	HostFam CollRes
France | Lyon	Multiple institutional choices	n/a	USColl	Brown University	PrivApt
France | Montpellier	University Paul Valery	n/a	USColl	University of Minnesota	HostFam CollRes PrivApt
France | Nantes	IES Abroad Nantes Center	n/a	Intermed	IES Abroad	n/a
France | Paris	Boston University Paris Center	n/a	USColl	Boston University	n/a
France | Paris	Center for University Programs Abroad	n/a	Intermed	Center for University Programs Abroad	HostFam PrivApt
France | Paris	Center for University Programs Abroad	Sum	USColl	Fordham University	n/a
France | Paris	CIEE Study Center in Paris	n/a	Intermed	Council on International Educational Exchange (CIEE)	n/a
France | Paris	CIEE Study Center in Paris	n/a	Intermed	Council on International Educational Exchange (CIEE)	n/a
France | Paris	Ecole Polytechnique	n/a	Dir	n/a	n/a
France | Paris	Institut Catholique de Paris	Sum	Dir	n/a	n/a
France | Paris	Institut d'Etudes Politiques (Sciences Po)	Spr YrRound	Bilat	n/a	n/a
France | Paris	Internships in Francophone Europe	n/a	Intermed	Internships in Francophone	n/a
France | Paris	Multiple institutional choices	n/a	Consrtm	EDUCO	HostFam CollRes PrivApt
France | Paris	Multiple institutional choices	n/a	USColl	Brown University	PrivApt
France | Paris	Multiple institutional choices	n/a	Intermed	Academic Programs Abroad	n/a
France | Paris	Multiple institutional choices	n/a	USColl	Middlebury College	HostFam CollRes
France | Paris	NYU Center in Paris	Sum	USColl	New York University	CollRes
France | Paris	Reid Hall (Columbia University)	n/a	USColl	Columbia University	n/a
France | Paris	Reid Hall (Columbia University)	Sum	Self	n/a	CollRes
	Costs: Sum Costs: T&F: n/a, R&B: n/a, Ttl: $7,500				
France | Poitiers	University of Poitiers	n/a	USColl	Middlebury College	n/a
France | Strasbourg	Syracuse University	Sum	USColl	Syracuse University	n/a
Germany | (Multiple)	Goethe-Instituts	Sum	Intermed	Goethe-Instituts	n/a
Germany | Berlin	Freie Universitat	Spr	USColl	Duke University	HostFam
Germany | Berlin	Freie Universitat Berlin	n/a	Dir	n/a	n/a
Germany | Berlin	Freie Universitat Berlin	n/a	Consrtm	Berlin Consortium for German Studies (Columbia University)	HostFam
Germany | Berlin	Freie Universitat Berlin International Summer School	Sum	Intermed	Freie Universitat Berlin International Summer School	n/a
Germany | Berlin	Humboldt University	Fall	USColl	Duke University	HostFam
Germany | Berlin	IES Abroad Berlin Center	n/a	Intermed	IES Abroad	n/a

Massachusetts

DESTINATION	HOST INSTITUTION	PRGM SEASON	PRGM TYPE	INTERMEDIARY	HOUSING
Germany | Bonn	University of Bonn	Sum	Self	n/a	CollRes
Costs: Sum Costs: T&F: n/a, R&B: n/a, Ttl: $6,300					
Germany | Dresden	Technische Universitat Dresden	Fall Spr	USColl	Boston University	n/a
Germany | Freiburg	IES Abroad Freiburg Center	n/a	Intermed	IES Abroad	HostFam
Germany | Gottingen	Georg-August-Universitat Gottingen	n/a	Dir	n/a	n/a
Germany | Heidelberg	Collegium Palatium	Sum	Intermed	College Consortium for International Studies	HostFam
Germany | Heidelberg	University of Heidelberg	n/a	USColl	Heidelberg University	CollRes PrivApt
Germany | Heidelberg	University of Heidelberg	n/a	Dir	n/a	n/a
Germany | Munich	Harvard University	Sum	Self	n/a	Other
Costs: Sum Costs: T&F: n/a, R&B: n/a, Ttl: $7,500					
Germany | Munich	Maximilians Universitat München	n/a	USColl	Wayne State University	n/a
Ghana | Accra	Ashesi University	n/a	Intermed	Council on International Educational Exchange (CIEE)	HostFam
Ghana | Accra	SIT Study Abroad	n/a	Intermed	SIT Study Abroad	HostFam
Ghana | Cape Coast	SIT Study Abroad	n/a	Intermed	SIT Study Abroad	HostFam
Ghana | Kumasi	College of Art, Kwame Nkrumah University of Science and	Sum	USColl	North Carolina State University	PrivApt
Ghana | Legon	University of Ghana	n/a	Intermed	Council on International Educational Exchange (CIEE)	HostFam CollRes
Greece | Athens	Arcadia Center for Hellenic, Mediterranean and Balkan Studies	n/a	USColl	Arcadia University	PrivApt
Greece | Athens	College Year in Athens	n/a	Intermed	College Year in Athens	PrivApt
Greece | Olympia and Nafplio	Harvard University	Sum	Self	n/a	Other
Costs: Sum Costs: T&F: n/a, R&B: n/a, Ttl: $7,000					
Guatemala | Antigua	Center for Mesoamerican Research	Sum	Intermed	Center for Mesoamerican Research	n/a
Honduras | Copan	Harvard University	Sum	Self	n/a	Other
Costs: Sum Costs: T&F: n/a, R&B: n/a, Ttl: $5,000					
Hungary | Budapest	Central European University	n/a	USColl	Bard College	n/a
Hungary | Budapest	Technical University of Budapest, College International	n/a	Intermed	Budapest Semesters in Mathematics	HostFam PrivApt
India | (Multiple)	American Institute of Indian Studies	Sum	Consrtm	American Institute of Indian Studies	n/a
India | Bangalore	Centre for Biological Sciences (NCBS), Jawaharlal Nehru Centre for Advanced Scientific Research, and the Indian Institute of Science	Sum	Self	n/a	CollRes
Costs: Sum Costs: T&F: n/a, R&B: n/a, Ttl: $5,250					
India | Bodh Gaya	Antioch University	n/a	USColl	Antioch University	Other
India | Delhi	IES Abroad	n/a	Intermed	IES Abroad	HostFam
India | Delhi	SIT Study Abroad	n/a	Intermed	SIT Study Abroad	n/a

© 2011 — Updates? Want to be in the next edition? Visit **www.mysecondcampus.com**

Massachusetts

DESTINATION	HOST INSTITUTION	PRGM SEASON	PRGM TYPE	INTERMEDIARY	HOUSING
India | Delhi	St. Stephen's College; Lady Shri Ram College for Women	Fall YrRound	USColl	Brown University	n/a
India | Hyderabad	University of Hyderabad	n/a	Intermed	Council on International Educational Exchange (CIEE)	PrivApt
India | Jaipur	SIT Study Abroad	n/a	Intermed	SIT Study Abroad	n/a
India | Jaipur	University of Minnesota	n/a	USColl	University of Minnesota	HostFam
India | Kerala	University of Wisconsin, Madison	Sum	USColl	University of Wisconsin, Madison	n/a
India | Leh	SIT Study Abroad	Sum	Intermed	SIT Study Abroad	n/a
India | Varanasi	University of Wisconsin, Madison	n/a	USColl	University of Wisconsin, Madison	HostFam PrivApt
Indonesia | Bedulu	SIT Study Abroad	n/a	Intermed	SIT Study Abroad	n/a
Ireland | Ballyvaughan	Burren College of Art	n/a	USColl	Arcadia University	n/a
Ireland | Ballyvaughan	Burren College of Art	n/a	Intermed	Institute for Study Abroad	n/a
Ireland | Cork	University College Cork	n/a	Intermed	Institute for Study Abroad	n/a
Ireland | Cork	University College Cork	Fall Spr YrRound	Dir	n/a	n/a
Ireland | Cork	University College Cork	n/a	USColl	Arcadia University	n/a
Ireland | Donegal Gaeltacht	Oideas Gael	Sum	Intermed	Oideas Gael	n/a
Ireland | Dublin	Institute of Public Administration	Sum	USColl	Arcadia University	n/a
Ireland | Dublin	Trinity College Dublin	n/a	USColl	Arcadia University	n/a
Ireland | Dublin	Trinity College Dublin	n/a	Intermed	Institute for Study Abroad	n/a
Ireland | Dublin	Trinity College Dublin	Spr YrRound	Dir	n/a	n/a
Ireland | Dublin	Trinity College Dublin	Sum	Intermed	USIT	HostFam CollRes
Ireland | Dublin	University College Dublin	Fall Spr YrRound	Dir	n/a	n/a
Ireland | Dublin	University College Dublin	n/a	Intermed	Institute for Study Abroad	n/a
Ireland | Dublin	University College Dublin	n/a	USColl	Arcadia University	n/a
Ireland | Galway	National University of Ireland, Galway	Fall Spr YrRound	Dir	n/a	CollRes PrivApt
Ireland | Galway	National University of Ireland, Galway	n/a	USColl	Arcadia University	n/a
Ireland | Galway	National University of Ireland, Galway	n/a	Intermed	Institute for Study Abroad	n/a
Ireland | Galway	National University of Ireland, Galway	Sum	Dir	n/a	n/a
Ireland | Limerick	University of Limerick	Fall Spr YrRound	Dir	n/a	n/a
Ireland | Limerick	University of Limerick	n/a	Intermed	Institute for Study Abroad	n/a
Ireland | Limerick	University of Limerick	n/a	USColl	Arcadia University	n/a
Ireland | Maynooth	National University of Ireland, Maynooth	n/a	Intermed	Institute for Study Abroad	n/a
Israel | Ashkelon	Harvard University	Sum	Self	n/a	Other
	Costs: Sum Costs: T&F: n/a, R&B: n/a, Ttl: $5,000				
Israel | Haifa	University of Haifa (International School)	Sum	Dir	n/a	n/a

Massachusetts

DESTINATION	HOST INSTITUTION	PRGM SEASON	PRGM TYPE	INTERMEDIARY	HOUSING
Israel | Jerusalem	Hebrew University of Jerusalem	Sum	Self	n/a	CollRes
	Costs: Sum Costs: T&F: n/a, R&B: n/a, Ttl: $6,120				
Israel | Jerusalem	Hebrew University of Jerusalem (Rothberg International School)	Sum	Dir	n/a	n/a
Israel | Tel Aviv	Tel Aviv University (School for Overseas Students)	Sum	Dir	n/a	n/a
Italy | Abruzzo	Harvard University	Sum	Self	n/a	Other
	Costs: Sum Costs: T&F: n/a, R&B: n/a, Ttl: $7,300; $7,500				
Italy | Bologna	Universita di Bologna	n/a	USColl	Brown University	PrivApt
Italy | Bologna	Universita di Bologna	n/a	Consrtm	Eastern College Consortium in Bologna (Vassar, Wellesley, and Wesleyan)	CollRes
Italy | Catania	CET Academic Programs	Sum	Intermed	CET Academic Programs	n/a
Italy | Ferrara	Middlebury College	n/a	USColl	Middlebury College	n/a
Italy | Florence	Middlebury College	n/a	USColl	Middlebury College	n/a
Italy | Florence	Syracuse University	n/a	USColl	Syracuse University	n/a
Italy | Milan	IES Abroad Milan Center	Sum	Intermed	IES Abroad	PrivApt
Italy | Milan	Universita' Bocconi	Fall Spr YrRound	Bilat	n/a	n/a
	Costs: Fall Costs: T&F: n/a, R&B: n/a, Ttl: Harvard home comprehensive fees Spr Costs: T&F: n/a, R&B: n/a, Ttl: Harvard home comprehensive fees YrRound Costs: T&F: n/a, R&B: n/a, Ttl: Harvard home comprehensive fees				
Italy | Mugello Valley	Boston University	Sum	USColl	Boston University	Other
Italy | Padova	Boston University Center for Italian and European Studies	n/a	USColl	Boston University	HostFam
Italy | Rome	Accademia Italiana	Sum	USColl	Arcadia University	n/a
Italy | Rome	IES Abroad Rome Center	n/a	Intermed	IES Abroad	HostFam
Italy | Rome	Intercollegiate Center for Classical Studies (Duke University)	n/a	USColl	Duke University	n/a
Italy | Rome	Janiculum Hill (outdoors by Father Reginald Foster)	Sum	n/a	n/a	n/a
Italy | Rome	Temple University	n/a	USColl	Temple University	PrivApt
Italy | Siena	CET Academic Programs	Sum	Intermed	CET Academic Programs	n/a
Italy | Trento	Center for Mind/Brain Sciences (University of Trento)	Sum	Self	n/a	CollRes
	Costs: Sum Costs: T&F: n/a, R&B: n/a, Ttl: $7,500				
Italy | Venice	Ca' Foscari University	Sum	Self	n/a	CollRes
	Costs: Sum Costs: T&F: n/a, R&B: n/a, Ttl: $7,500				
Japan | (Multiple)	Keio University	n/a	Dir	n/a	n/a
Japan | Hakodate	Hokadote International Foundation	Sum	Intermed	Hokadote International Foundation	n/a
Japan | Hikone	Japan Center for Michigan Universities (JCMU)	Sum	USColl	Japan Center for Michigan Universities (JCMU)	n/a
Japan | Kanazawa	Ishikawa Prefectural Government	Sum	USColl	Princeton in Ishikawa (Princeton University)	HostFam
Japan | Kyoto	Doshisha University	Sum	Self	n/a	HostFam
	Costs: Sum Costs: T&F: n/a, R&B: n/a, Ttl: $7,500				

© 2011 — Updates? Want to be in the next edition? Visit **www.mysecondcampus.com**

Massachusetts

DESTINATION	HOST INSTITUTION	PRGM SEASON	PRGM TYPE	INTERMEDIARY	HOUSING
Japan | Kyoto	Kyoto Consortium for Japanese Studies (Columbia University)	Fall Spr YrRound	Consrtm	Kyoto Consortium for Japanese Studies (Columbia University)	n/a
Japan | Kyoto	Ryukoku University	n/a	USColl	Antioch University	n/a
Japan | Nagoya	Nagoya University	n/a	Dir	n/a	n/a
Japan | Nagoya	Nanzan University	n/a	Dir	n/a	n/a
Japan | Tokyo	International Christian University	Sum YrRound	Dir	n/a	n/a
Japan | Tokyo	RIKEN Brain Science Institute	Sum	Self	n/a	CollRes
	Costs: Sum Costs: T&F: n/a, R&B: n/a, Ttl: $5,250				
Japan | Tokyo	Sophia University	Sum	Dir	n/a	n/a
Japan | Tokyo	Sophia University	Sum	Intermed	Council on International Educational Exchange (CIEE)	n/a
Japan | Tokyo	Sophia University	Fall Spr YrRound	Intermed	Council on International Educational Exchange (CIEE)	n/a
Japan | Tokyo	Waseda University	n/a	Dir	n/a	n/a
Japan | Tokyo	Waseda University	n/a	USColl	Oregon State University	n/a
Japan | Tokyo	Waseda University	Sum	Self	n/a	n/a
Japan | Yokohama	RIKEN Center for Allergy and Immunology	Sum	Self	n/a	CollRes
	Costs: Sum Costs: T&F: n/a, R&B: n/a, Ttl: $5,250				
Jordan | Amman	Qasid Institute for Classical and Modern Standard Arabic	Sum	Dir	n/a	PrivApt
Jordan | Irbid	University of Virginia and Yarmouk University	Sum	USColl	University of Virginia	n/a
Kenya | [City Unspecified]	School for Field Studies	n/a	Intermed	School for Field Studies	CollRes
Kenya | Koobi Fora	Koobi Fora Field School	Sum	USColl	Rutgers University	n/a
Kenya | Mombasa	Yale University	Sum	USColl	Yale University	n/a
Kenya | Nairobi	SIT Study Abroad	n/a	Intermed	SIT Study Abroad	HostFam
Kenya | Nairobi	St. Lawrence University	n/a	USColl	St. Lawrence University	HostFam
Madagascar | Ranomafana National Park	SUNY Stony Brook	n/a	USColl	SUNY Stony Brook	Other
Malaysia | Borneo	Harvard University	Sum	Self	n/a	Other
	Costs: Sum Costs: T&F: n/a, R&B: n/a, Ttl: $6,000				
Mali | Bamako	SIT Study Abroad	n/a	Intermed	SIT Study Abroad	HostFam
Mexico | Cuernavaca	Cemanahuac Educational	Sum	USColl	University of Minnesota	n/a
Mexico | Monterrey	Tecnologico de Monterrey	Sum	Dir	n/a	n/a
Mexico | Veracruz	Universidad Veracruzana	Sum	Dir	n/a	n/a
Mexico and Canada | (Multiple)	Multiple institutional choices	n/a	Bilat	n/a	n/a
Mongolia | Ulaanbaatar	SIT Study Abroad	n/a	Intermed	SIT Study Abroad	n/a
Morocco | Fez	Arabic Language Institute in Fez	Sum	Dir	n/a	HostFam
Morocco | Rabat	SIT Study Abroad	n/a	Intermed	SIT Study Abroad	HostFam
Morocco | Rabat	SIT Study Abroad	n/a	Intermed	SIT Study Abroad	n/a
Morocco | Tangier	American Institute for Maghrib Studies	Sum	Intermed	American Institute for Maghrib Studies	n/a

© 2011 — Updates? Want to be in the next edition? Visit **www.mysecondcampus.com**

Massachusetts

DESTINATION	HOST INSTITUTION	PRGM SEASON	PRGM TYPE	INTERMEDIARY	HOUSING
Namibia (and South Africa) | Windhoek	Augsburg College	n/a	USColl	Augsburg College	HostFam
Nepal | Kathmandu	SIT Study Abroad	n/a	Intermed	SIT Study Abroad	n/a
Nepal | Kathmandu	SIT Study Abroad	n/a	Intermed	SIT Study Abroad	n/a
Netherlands | Amsterdam	SIT Study Abroad	n/a	Intermed	SIT Study Abroad	HostFam
Netherlands | Amsterdam	University of Amsterdam	n/a	Intermed	Council on International Educational Exchange (CIEE)	PrivApt
Netherlands | Leiden	Leiden University Language Center	Sum	Dir	n/a	n/a
Netherlands | Utrecht	Utrecht University	Sum	Dir	n/a	n/a
New Zealand | Palmerston North	Massey University	n/a	Intermed	Institute for Study Abroad	n/a
New Zealand | Auckland	University of Auckland	n/a	Dir	n/a	n/a
New Zealand | Auckland	University of Auckland	n/a	USColl	Arcadia University	n/a
New Zealand | Christchurch	University of Canterbury	n/a	USColl	Arcadia University	n/a
New Zealand | Dunedin	University of Otago	n/a	USColl	Arcadia University	n/a
New Zealand | Dunedin	University of Otago	n/a	Dir	n/a	n/a
New Zealand | Wellington	Victoria University of Wellington	n/a	Dir	n/a	n/a
New Zealand | Wellington	Victoria University of Wellington	n/a	USColl	Arcadia University	n/a
Niger | Niamey	Universite Abdou Moumouni	n/a	USColl	Boston University	HostFam CollRes
Norway | Oslo	University of Oslo	n/a	Dir	n/a	n/a
Norway | Oslo	University of Oslo	n/a	Intermed	Oslo Year Program	n/a
Norway | Oslo	University of Oslo International Summer School	Sum	Dir	n/a	CollRes
Peru | Lima	Universidad del Pacifico	Sum	Self	n/a	HostFam
Costs: Sum Costs: T&F: n/a, R&B: n/a, Ttl: $3,700					
Peru | Lima and Ayacucho	Pontificia Universidad Catolica del Peru	Sum	USColl	Boston University	n/a
Peru | San Jose de Moro	Pontificia Universidad Catolica del Peru	Sum	Self	n/a	n/a
Poland | Krakow	Jagiellonian University	Sum	Intermed	Kosciuszko Foundation	n/a
Poland | Krakow	Jagiellonian University	n/a	Dir	n/a	n/a
Poland | Lublin	Catholic University	Sum	Intermed	Kosciuszko Foundation	n/a
Portugal | Lisbon	University of Lisbon	Sum	Dir	n/a	n/a
Puerto Rico | San Juan	Universidad de Puerto Rico	Sum	Dir	n/a	n/a
Russia | Irkutsk	Irkutsk State University	n/a	USColl	Middlebury College	HostFam
Russia | Moscow	Moscow International University	n/a	Intermed	American Councils Study Abroad Programs	HostFam CollRes
Russia | St. Petersburg	Nevsky Institute	Sum	Self	n/a	HostFam
Costs: Sum Costs: T&F: n/a, R&B: n/a, Ttl: $7,350					
Russia | St. Petersburg	Russian State Pedagogical (Gertsen) University	n/a	Intermed	American Councils Study Abroad Programs	HostFam CollRes
Russia | St. Petersburg	Smolny College	n/a	USColl	Bard-Smolny Study Abroad	n/a
Russia | St. Petersburg	St. Petersburg State University	n/a	Intermed	Council on International Educational Exchange (CIEE)	n/a

© 2011 — Updates? Want to be in the next edition? Visit **www.mysecondcampus.com**

Massachusetts

DESTINATION	HOST INSTITUTION	PRGM SEASON	PRGM TYPE	INTERMEDIARY	HOUSING
Russia | St. Petersburg	St. Petersburg State University	n/a	Intermed	Council on International Educational Exchange (CIEE)	HostFam CollRes
Russia | St. Petersburg	St. Petersburg State University	n/a	Intermed	Council on International Educational Exchange (CIEE)	n/a
Russia | St. Petersburg	St. Petersburg State University	Sum	Intermed	Council on International Educational Exchange (CIEE)	n/a
Russia | Vladimir	KORA Center for Russian Language Study	n/a	Intermed	American Councils Study Abroad Programs	HostFam CollRes
Scotland | Edinburgh	University of Edinburgh	Sum	USColl	Arcadia University	CollRes
Scotland | Stirling	University of Stirling	Sum	USColl	Arcadia University	n/a
Senegal | Dakar	Cheikh Anta Diop University	Sum	USColl	Indiana University	CollRes
Senegal | Dakar	SIT Study Abroad	Sum	Intermed	SIT Study Abroad	HostFam
Senegal | Dakar	Suffolk University - Dakar Campus	n/a	Intermed	Council on International Educational Exchange (CIEE)	HostFam
Senegal | Dakar	University of Minnesota	n/a	USColl	University of Minnesota	n/a
Singapore | Singapore	National University of Singapore	n/a	Dir	n/a	n/a
South Africa | Cape Town	SIT Study Abroad	n/a	Intermed	SIT Study Abroad	HostFam
South Africa | Cape Town	University of Cape Town	n/a	Intermed	Interstudy	PrivApt
South Africa | Cape Town	University of Cape Town	n/a	Intermed	Council on International Educational Exchange (CIEE)	CollRes
South Africa | Durban	SIT Study Abroad	Sum	Intermed	SIT Study Abroad	n/a
South Africa | Durban	SIT Study Abroad	n/a	Intermed	SIT Study Abroad	HostFam
South Africa | Durban	University of KwaZulu-Natal (Howard College campus)	n/a	Intermed	Interstudy	CollRes
South Africa | Gauteng Province	Duke University	Sum	USColl	Duke University	n/a
South Africa | Grahamstown	Rhodes University International School	Sum	Dir	n/a	CollRes
South Africa | Pietermaritzburg	University of KwaZulu-Natal	Sum	USColl	University of Pennsylvania	n/a
South Africa | Pietermaritzburg	University of KwaZulu-Natal (Pietermaritzburg campus)	n/a	Intermed	Interstudy	n/a
South Africa | Stellenbosch	Stellenbosch University	n/a	Intermed	Council on International Educational Exchange (CIEE)	CollRes
South Korea | Seoul	Ewha Womans University **Costs:** Sum Costs: T&F: n/a, R&B: n/a, Ttl: $5,775	Sum	Self	n/a	CollRes
South Korea | Seoul	Ewha Womans University	Fall Spr YrRound	Dir	n/a	n/a
South Korea | Seoul	Seoul National University	n/a	Dir	n/a	CollRes
South Korea | Seoul	Sogang University International Summer School	Sum	Dir	n/a	CollRes
South Korea | Seoul	Yonsei University	n/a	Dir	n/a	CollRes
Spain | Alicante	Universidad de Alicante	Sum	Intermed	Council on International Educational Exchange (CIEE)	n/a
Spain | Alicante	Universidad de Alicante	Fall Spr YrRound	Intermed	Center for Cross-Cultural Study	HostFam
Spain | Alicante	University of Pennsylvania	Sum	USColl	University of Pennsylvania	n/a
Spain | Barcelona	CIEE Study Center	Sum	Intermed	Council on International Educational Exchange (CIEE)	n/a

Massachusetts

DESTINATION	HOST INSTITUTION	PRGM SEASON	PRGM TYPE	INTERMEDIARY	HOUSING
Spain | Barcelona	Universidad Pompeu Fabra	Sum	Dir	n/a	n/a
Spain | Barcelona	Universitat Autonoma de Barcelona	Fall Spr YrRound	Consrtm	Consortium for Advanced Studies in Barcelona	n/a
Spain | Barcelona	Universitat de Barcelona	Fall Spr YrRound	Consrtm	Consortium for Advanced Studies in Barcelona	n/a
Spain | Barcelona	Universitat Pompeu Fabra	Fall Spr YrRound	Consrtm	Consortium for Advanced Studies in Barcelona	n/a
Spain | Burgos	University of Burgos	Spr YrRound	USColl	Boston University	n/a
Spain | Granada	University of Granada	Fall Spr YrRound	USColl	Arcadia University	HostFam CollRes
Spain | Leon	Universidad de Leon	Sum	USColl	Hamilton College	n/a
Spain | Madrid	IES Abroad Madrid Center	n/a	Intermed	IES Abroad	n/a
Spain | Madrid	Instituto Internacional	Spr YrRound	USColl	Boston University	n/a
Spain | Madrid	Instituto Internacional	Fall Spr YrRound	USColl	Boston University	n/a
Spain | Madrid	Universidad Autonoma de Madrid	Spr YrRound	USColl	Boston University	n/a
Spain | Madrid	Universidad Autonoma de Madrid	Sum	Dir	n/a	n/a
Spain | Madrid	Universidad Carlos III	Fall Spr YrRound	USColl	Vassar College and Wesleyan University	n/a
Spain | Madrid	Universidad Carlos III de Madrid	Fall Spr YrRound	USColl	Middlebury College	n/a
Spain | Madrid	Universidad Complutense de Madrid or Universidad San Pablo	Fall Spr YrRound	USColl	Hamilton College	n/a
Spain | Madrid	Universidad Pontificia Comillas	Sum	Dir	n/a	n/a
Spain | Malaga	Universidad de Malaga	Sum	Dir	n/a	n/a
Spain | Menorca	Boston University	Sum	USColl	Boston University	n/a
Spain | Salamanca	Universidad de Salamanca	Sum	Dir	n/a	n/a
Spain | Salamanca	University of Rhode Island	Sum	USColl	University of Rhode Island	HostFam CollRes
Spain | Santander	Universidad de Cantabria	Sum	Dir	n/a	n/a
Spain | Seville	Center for Cross-Cultural Study	Sum Fall Spr YrRound	Intermed	Center for Cross-Cultural Study	n/a
Spain | Seville	Universidad de Sevilla	Fall Spr YrRound	Intermed	Council on International Educational Exchange (CIEE)	n/a
Spain | Seville	Universidad Pablo de Olavide or Universidad de Sevilla	Fall Spr YrRound	Intermed	Council on International Educational Exchange (CIEE)	n/a
Spain | Seville	Universidad Pablo de Olavide or Universidad de Sevilla	Fall Spr YrRound	Intermed	Council on International Educational Exchange (CIEE)	n/a
Spain | Toledo	Fundacion Jose Ortega y Gasset	Sum Fall Spr YrRound	USColl	Arcadia University	n/a
Spain | Valencia	Universidad de Valencia	Sum	Dir	n/a	n/a
Sweden | Stockholm	Stockholm University	Fall Spr	Consrtm	Swedish Program	HostFam CollRes
Sweden | Uppsala	Uppsala International Summer Session	Sum	Intermed	Uppsala International Summer Session	n/a
Sweden | Uppsala	Uppsala University	Fall Spr YrRound	Bilat	n/a	n/a
Switzerland | Berne	World Trade Institute	Sum	Dir	n/a	n/a
Switzerland | Geneva	Boston University	n/a	USColl	Boston University	n/a
Switzerland | Geneva	SIT Study Abroad	n/a	Intermed	SIT Study Abroad	n/a

© 2011 — Updates? Want to be in the next edition? Visit **www.mysecondcampus.com**

Massachusetts

DESTINATION	HOST INSTITUTION	PRGM SEASON	PRGM TYPE	INTERMEDIARY	HOUSING
Switzerland	Zurich	ETH Zurich	n/a	Dir	n/a	n/a
Syria	Damascus	University of Damascus	Sum	Dir	n/a	n/a
Taiwan	Taipei	Mandarin Training Center (National Taiwan Normal University)	Sum	Dir	n/a	n/a
Taiwan	Taipei	National Chengchi University	n/a	Intermed	Council on International Educational Exchange (CIEE)	n/a
Tanzania	Arusha	SIT Study Abroad	n/a	Intermed	SIT Study Abroad	n/a
Tanzania	Dar es Salaam	Georgetown University	Sum	USColl	Georgetown University	CollRes
Tanzania	Dar es Salaam	University of Dar es Salaam	n/a	USColl	Brown University	PrivApt
Tanzania	Stone Town	SIT Study Abroad	n/a	Intermed	SIT Study Abroad	n/a
Thailand	Khon Kaen	Khon Kaen University	n/a	Intermed	Council on International Educational Exchange (CIEE)	n/a
Turkey	Ankara	Bilkent University	n/a	Dir	n/a	n/a
Turkey	Istanbul	Bogazici University	n/a	Dir	n/a	n/a
Turkey	Istanbul	Harvard University	Sum	Self	n/a	n/a
Turks and Caicos	South Caicos Island	Center for Marine Resource Studies	Sum	Intermed	School for Field Studies	n/a
United States	Lansing (MI)	Summer Cooperative African Language Institute (Michigan State University)	Sum	USColl	Summer Cooperative African Language Institute (Michigan State University)	n/a
United States	Middlebury (VT)	Middlebury College	Sum	Dir	n/a	n/a
United States	Middlebury (VT)	Middlebury College	Sum	Dir	n/a	n/a
United States	Woods Hole (MT)	Sea Semester	Sum	Intermed	Sea Semester	n/a
Uruguay	Montevideo	Technology Laboratory of Uruguay	Sum	Self	n/a	CollRes
	Costs: Sum Costs: T&F: n/a, R&B: n/a, Ttl: $5,750				
Venezuela	Merida	VENUSA Institute of International Studies	Sum	USColl	University of Minnesota	n/a
Vietnam	Ho Chi Minh City	CET Academic Programs	n/a	Intermed	CET Academic Programs	Other
Vietnam	Ho Chi Minh City	SIT Study Abroad	n/a	Intermed	SIT Study Abroad	HostFam
Vietnam	Ho Chi Minh City	Vietnamese Language Studies Saigon	Sum	Consrtm	Vietnamese Advanced Summer Institute - Center for Southeast Asia Studies (University of California, Berkeley)	n/a
Yemen	Sana'a	Yemen Language Center	Sum	Dir	n/a	n/a

Hellenic College-Holy Cross Greek Orthodox School

Nicholas Triantafilou
President
50 Goddard Avenue
Brookline, MA 02445

development@hchc.edu
617.731.3500

DESTINATION	HOST INSTITUTION	PRGM SEASON	PRGM TYPE	INTERMEDIARY	HOUSING
[Country Unspecified]	[City Unspecified]	n/a	n/a	n/a	n/a	n/a

Massachusetts

DESTINATION	HOST INSTITUTION	PRGM SEASON	PRGM TYPE	INTERMEDIARY	HOUSING

Lasell College

Tessa LeRoux
Director of International Programs
1844 Commonwealth Avenue
Newton, MA 02466

tleroux@lasell.edu
617.243.2104
http://www.lasell.edu/about/study_abroad.asp

DESTINATION	HOST INSTITUTION	PRGM SEASON	PRGM TYPE	INTERMEDIARY	HOUSING
Ecuador	(Multiple)	Lasell College	n/a	Self	n/a	n/a
Mexico	(Multiple)	Lasell College	n/a	Self	n/a	HostFam
Nicaragua	San Juan del Sur	Lasell College	Spr	Self	n/a	n/a

Lesley University

Martha McKenna
Provost
29 Everett Street
Cambridge, MA 02138

mckenna2@lesley.edu
617.349.8518
http://www.lesley.edu/services/study_abroad/index.html

DESTINATION	HOST INSTITUTION	PRGM SEASON	PRGM TYPE	INTERMEDIARY	HOUSING
(Multiple choices)	(Multiple choices)	Multiple institutional choices	n/a	Intermed	Academic Programs International	n/a
(Multiple choices)	(Multiple choices)	Multiple institutional choices	n/a	Intermed	International Partnership for Service Learning	n/a
(Multiple choices)	(Multiple choices)	Multiple institutional choices	n/a	Intermed	AustraLearn	n/a
(Multiple choices)	(Multiple choices)	Multiple institutional choices	n/a	Intermed	American Institute for Foreign Study	n/a
(Multiple choices)	(Multiple choices)	Multiple institutional choices	n/a	Intermed	SIT Study Abroad	n/a
France	Paris	American University in Paris	n/a	Dir	n/a	n/a
France	Paris	Parsons Paris School of Art and Design	n/a	Intermed	Parsons Paris School of Art and Design	n/a
France	Paris	School of Visual Communication	n/a	Dir	n/a	n/a
Germany	Bremen	University for the Arts	n/a	Dir	n/a	n/a
Italy	(Multiple choices)	Lorenzo de Medici Institute	n/a	Intermed	Lorenzo de Medici Institute	n/a
Netherlands	Rotterdam	William de Kooning Academy	n/a	Dir	n/a	n/a
Sweden	Orebro	Orebro University	n/a	Dir	n/a	n/a
United States	Arizona	Lesley University	n/a	Self	n/a	n/a
United States	Washington (DC)	American University	n/a	USColl	American University	n/a

© 2011 — Updates? Want to be in the next edition? Visit **www.mysecondcampus.com**

Massachusetts

| DESTINATION | HOST INSTITUTION | PRGM SEASON | PRGM TYPE | INTERMEDIARY | HOUSING |

Massachusetts Bay Community College

Marie Lourdes Elgirus
Director, International Education and Study Abroad
Community and Corporate Education Suite, Room C
First Floor
50 Oakland Street
Welleley Hills, MA 02481

melgirus@massbay.edu
781.239.3140
http://www.massbay.edu/Academics/StudyAbroad.aspx

DESTINATION	HOST INSTITUTION	PRGM SEASON	PRGM TYPE	INTERMEDIARY	HOUSING
(Multiple choices) | (Multiple choices)	Multiple institutional choices	n/a	Consrtm	College Consortium on International Studies	n/a

Massachusetts College of Art and Design

Natalie Vinski
Director, International Education
Office of International Education Programs
Kennedy Building, 2nd floor
621 Huntington Avenue
Boston, MA 02115

natalie.vinski@massart.edu
617.879.7702
http://inside.massart.edu/x910.xml

DESTINATION	HOST INSTITUTION	PRGM SEASON	PRGM TYPE	INTERMEDIARY	HOUSING
Australia | Melbourne	Melbourne University / Victorian College of Art	n/a	Bilat	n/a	n/a
China | (Multiple)	Massachusetts College of Art and Design	Sum	Self	n/a	n/a
China | Beijing	The Central Academy of Fine Arts	n/a	Bilat	n/a	n/a
China | Unknown	Massachusetts College of Art and Design	Spr	Self	n/a	n/a
Costs: Spr Costs: T&F: $3,500, R&B: n/a, Ttl: n/a					
Egypt | Unknown	Massachusetts College of Art and Design	Spr	Self	n/a	n/a
Costs: Spr Costs: T&F: $3,500, R&B: n/a, Ttl: n/a					
England | Maidstone	University College for the Creative Arts	n/a	Bilat	n/a	n/a
England and Ireland | London and Dublin	Massachusetts College of Art and Design	Spr	Self	n/a	n/a
England and Scotland | [City Unspecified]	Massachusetts College of Art and Design	Spr	Self	n/a	n/a
Costs: Spr Costs: T&F: $3,500, R&B: n/a, Ttl: n/a					
France | Paris	Massachusetts College of Art and Design	n/a	Self	n/a	n/a
Germany | Cologne	Massachusetts College of Art and Design	Sum	Self	n/a	n/a
Guatemala | (Multiple)	Massachusetts College of Art and Design	Spr	Self	n/a	n/a
Italy | Rome	Massachusetts College of Art and Design	Spr	Self	n/a	n/a
Costs: Spr Costs: T&F: $3,500, R&B: n/a, Ttl: n/a					

Massachusetts

DESTINATION	HOST INSTITUTION	PRGM SEASON	PRGM TYPE	INTERMEDIARY	HOUSING
Italy	Venice	Massachusetts College of Art and Design	Spr	Self	n/a	n/a
Japan	Kyoto	Osaka Seikei University	n/a	Bilat	n/a	n/a
Mexico	Mexico City, Puebla, and Cholula	Massachusetts College of Art and Design	Spr	Self	n/a	n/a
Netherlands	Amsterdam	Gerrit Reitveld	n/a	Bilat	n/a	n/a
Netherlands	Enschede	AKI	n/a	Bilat	n/a	n/a
Netherlands	Rotterdam	Willem de Kooning	n/a	Bilat	n/a	n/a
Scotland	Edinburgh	Edinburgh College of Art	n/a	Bilat	n/a	n/a
Scotland	Glasgow	Glasgow School of Art	n/a	Bilat	n/a	n/a
Spain	Barcelona	University of Barcelona	n/a	Bilat	n/a	n/a
Turkey	Istanbul	Massachusetts College of Art and Design	Spr	Self	n/a	n/a

Costs: Spr Costs: T&F: $3,500, R&B: n/a, Ttl: n/a

Massachusetts College of Liberal Arts

Sharron Zavattaro
Director of Career Services Center/Study Broad Programs
375 Church Street
North Adams, MA 01247

szavattaro@mcla.edu
413.662.5332
http://www.mcla.edu/Academics/academicresources/career/travelcourses/

DESTINATION	HOST INSTITUTION	PRGM SEASON	PRGM TYPE	INTERMEDIARY	HOUSING
(Multiple choices)	(Multiple choices)	Multiple institutional choices	n/a	Consrtm	Massachusetts Council for International Education (MaCIE)	n/a
(Multiple choices)	(Multiple choices)	Multiple institutional choices	n/a	Intermed	College Consortium for International Studies (CCIS)	n/a
China	(Multiple)	Massachusetts College of Liberal Arts	Spr	Self	n/a	Other
England	(Multiple)	Massachusetts College of Liberal Arts	Spr	Self	n/a	Other
Ireland	(Multiple)	Massachusetts College of Liberal Arts	Spr	Self	n/a	Other
Japan	(Multiple)	Massachusetts College of Liberal Arts	Spr	Self	n/a	Other
Spain	(Multiple)	Massachusetts College of Liberal Arts	n/a	Intermed	n/a	Other
United States	Woods Hole (MA)	Semester at Sea	n/a	Intermed	Semester at Sea	n/a

Massachusetts College of Pharmacy & Health

Julie Donlon
Director of International Programs
179 Longwood Avenue
Boston, MA 02115

julie.donlon@mcphs.edu
617.879.5905
http://www.mcphs.edu/about_mcphs/offices_and_services/international_programs/study_abroad.html

DESTINATION	HOST INSTITUTION	PRGM SEASON	PRGM TYPE	INTERMEDIARY	HOUSING
(Multiple choices)	(Multiple choices)	Multiple institutional choices	n/a	Intermed	The Education Abroad Network	n/a

© 2011 — Updates? Want to be in the next edition? Visit **www.mysecondcampus.com**

Massachusetts

DESTINATION	HOST INSTITUTION	PRGM SEASON	PRGM TYPE	INTERMEDIARY	HOUSING
(Multiple choices) | (Multiple choices)	Multiple institutional choices	n/a	Intermed	Study Abroad Italy	n/a
(Multiple choices) | (Multiple choices)	Multiple institutional choices	n/a	Intermed	CAPA International Education	n/a
(Multiple choices) | (Multiple choices)	Multiple institutional choices	n/a	Intermed	Council on International Education Exchange (CIEE)	n/a
(Multiple choices) | (Multiple choices)	Multiple institutional choices	n/a	Intermed	Academic Studies Abroad	n/a
(Multiple choices) | (Multiple choices)	Multiple institutional choices	n/a	Intermed	International Studies Abroad	n/a
(Multiple choices) | (Multiple choices)	Multiple institutional choices	n/a	Intermed	Academic Programs International	n/a
(Multiple choices) | (Multiple choices)	Multiple institutional choices	n/a	Intermed	Center for International Studies	n/a
(Multiple choices) | (Multiple choices)	Multiple institutional choices	n/a	Intermed	Institute For Study Abroad	n/a
Denmark | Copenhagen	Danish Institute for Study Abroad (DIS)	n/a	Intermed	Danish Institute for Study Abroad (DIS)	n/a

Massachusetts Institute of Technology

Malgorzata Hedderick
Associate Dean for Global Education
Global Education Office
Room 12-189
Cambridge, MA 02139

malrh@mit.edu
617.253.9358
http://web.mit.edu/studyabroad/

DESTINATION	HOST INSTITUTION	PRGM SEASON	PRGM TYPE	INTERMEDIARY	HOUSING
(Multiple choices) | (Multiple choices)	Multiple institutional choices	n/a	Dir	n/a	n/a
China | Hong Kong	Hong Kong University	n/a	Bilat	n/a	n/a
England | Cambridge	Cambridge University (Cambridge-MIT Exchange)	YrRound	Bilat	n/a	n/a
	Costs: YrRound Costs: T&F: MIT home tuition & fees, R&B: n/a, Ttl: n/a				
England | London	Imperial College of Science and Technology	n/a	Bilat	n/a	n/a
England | Oxford	Oxford University	n/a	Bilat	n/a	n/a
France | Toulouse	Ecole Centrale Superieure de l'Aeronautique at de l'Espace (ENSAE)	n/a	Bilat	n/a	n/a
Germany | (Multiple)	IAP-Germany Program (MIT)	n/a	Self	n/a	n/a
Germany | Stuttgart	University of Stuttgart	n/a	Bilat	n/a	n/a
Israel | Haifa	Technion University	Spr YrRound	Dir	n/a	n/a
Netherlands | Delft	Delft University of Technology	n/a	Bilat	n/a	n/a
Spain | Madrid	Escuela Tecnica Superior de Ingenieros Aeronauticos (ETSIA)	n/a	Bilat	n/a	n/a
Spain | Madrid	IAP-Madrid Program (MIT)	n/a	Self	n/a	n/a

© 2011 — Updates? Want to be in the next edition? Visit **www.mysecondcampus.com**

Massachusetts

DESTINATION	HOST INSTITUTION	PRGM SEASON	PRGM TYPE	INTERMEDIARY	HOUSING
Spain | Madrid	Universidad Politecnica de Madrid or Universidad Complutense de Madrid	Spr	Self	n/a	HostFam
	Costs: Spr Costs: T&F: n/a, R&B: n/a, Ttl: $9,125				
Sweden | Stockholm	Royal Technical Institute of Sweden (KTH)	n/a	Bilat	n/a	n/a
Switzerland | Zurich	Swiss Federal Institute of Technology (ETH)	n/a	Bilat	n/a	n/a

Merrimack College

Lauren Gannon
Director
315 Turnpike Street
North Andover, MA 01845

lauren.gannon@merrimack.edu
978.837.5250
http://warrior.merrimack.edu/academics/EngagedLearning/StudyAbroad/Pages/default.aspx

DESTINATION	HOST INSTITUTION	PRGM SEASON	PRGM TYPE	INTERMEDIARY	HOUSING
(Multiple choices) | (Multiple choices)	SIT Study Abroad	n/a	Intermed	SIT Study Abroad	n/a
Argentina | (Multiple choices)	Multiple institutional choices	n/a	Intermed	Institute for Study Abroad	n/a
Australia | (Multiple choices)	Multiple institutional choices	n/a	Intermed	Study Australia	n/a
Australia | (Multiple choices)	Multiple institutional choices	n/a	Intermed	AustraLearn	n/a
Australia | (Multiple choices)	Multiple institutional choices	n/a	Intermed	Council on International Educational Exchange (CIEE)	n/a
Australia | (Multiple choices)	Multiple institutional choices	n/a	Intermed	Center for International Studies	n/a
Austria | Vienna	University of Vienna	n/a	Intermed	IES Abroad	n/a
Brazil | (Multiple choices)	Multiple institutional choices	n/a	Intermed	Council on International Educational Exchange (CIEE)	n/a
Chile | (Multiple choices)	Multiple institutional choices	n/a	Intermed	Council on International Educational Exchange (CIEE)	n/a
Chile | (Multiple choices)	Multiple institutional choices	n/a	Intermed	Institute for Study Abroad	n/a
Chile | (Multiple choices)	Multiple institutional choices	n/a	Intermed	International Studies Abroad (ISA)	n/a
China | Beijing	Beijing Language and Culture University	n/a	Intermed	American Institute for Foreign Study (AIFS)	n/a
China | Beijing	Beijing Language and Culture University	n/a	Intermed	Alliance for Global Education	n/a
China | Beijing	Multiple institutional choices	n/a	Intermed	Council on International Educational Exchange (CIEE)	n/a
Costa Rica | Monteverde	Multiple institutional choices	n/a	Intermed	Council on International Educational Exchange (CIEE)	n/a
Czech Republic | Prague	Center for Economic Research and Graduate Education-Economics Institute (Charles University)	n/a	Dir	n/a	n/a
Czech Republic | Prague	Charles University	n/a	Intermed	Council on International Educational Exchange (CIEE)	n/a
Czech Republic | Prague	Unknown	n/a	USColl	New York University	n/a

© 2011 — Updates? Want to be in the next edition? Visit **www.mysecondcampus.com**

Massachusetts

DESTINATION	HOST INSTITUTION	PRGM SEASON	PRGM TYPE	INTERMEDIARY	HOUSING
Denmark | Copenhagen	Danish Institute for Study Abroad (DIS)	n/a	Intermed	Danish Institute for Study Abroad (DIS)	n/a
Dominican Republic | (Multiple choices)	Multiple institutional choices	n/a	Intermed	Council on International Educational Exchange (CIEE)	n/a
Egypt | Cairo	American University of Cairo	n/a	Dir	n/a	n/a
England | (Multiple choices)	Multiple institutional choices	n/a	Intermed	American Institute for Foreign Study (AIFS)	n/a
England | (Multiple choices)	Multiple institutional choices	n/a	Intermed	International Studies Abroad (ISA)	n/a
England | (Multiple choices)	Multiple institutional choices	n/a	USColl	Arcadia University	n/a
England | (Multiple choices)	Multiple institutional choices	n/a	Intermed	Institute for Study Abroad	n/a
England | Bath	Advanced Studies in England	n/a	Intermed	Advanced Studies in England	n/a
England | Brighton	University of Sussex	n/a	Dir	n/a	n/a
England | Brighton	University of Sussex	n/a	USColl	Arcadia University	n/a
England | Brighton	University of Sussex	n/a	Intermed	Institute for Study Abroad	n/a
England | Manchester	University of Manchester	n/a	Dir	n/a	n/a
England | Oxford	Oxford University	n/a	Intermed	Institute for Study Abroad	n/a
France | (Multiple	Multiple institutional choices	n/a	Intermed	Academic Programs International	n/a
France | Angers	CIDEF (L'Universite Catholique de l'Ouest)	n/a	Dir	n/a	n/a
Germany | (Multiple	IES Abroad Center	n/a	Intermed	IES Abroad	n/a
Ghana | Accra and Legon	Multiple institutional choices	n/a	Intermed	Council on International Educational Exchange (CIEE)	n/a
Ghana | Cape Coast or Accra	SIT Study Abroad	n/a	Intermed	SIT Study Abroad	n/a
Greece | Athens	College Year in Athens	n/a	Intermed	n/a	n/a
Greece | Thessaloniki	American College of Thessaloniki	n/a	Dir	n/a	n/a
Hungary | Budapest	Corvinus University of Budapest	n/a	Intermed	Council on International Educational Exchange (CIEE)	n/a
Hungary | Budapest	Corvinus University of Budapest	n/a	Intermed	Academic Programs International	n/a
India | Delhi	IES Abroad Delhi Center	n/a	Intermed	IES Abroad	n/a
India | Hyderabad	University of Hyderabad	n/a	Intermed	Council on International Educational Exchange (CIEE)	n/a
Ireland | (Multiple choices)	Multiple institutional choices	n/a	Intermed	Academic Programs International	n/a
Italy | (Multiple choices)	Multiple institutional choices	n/a	Intermed	Academic Programs International	n/a
Italy | Florence	CAPA International Education	n/a	Intermed	CAPA International Education	n/a
Italy | Florence	Unknown	n/a	USColl	Fairfield University	n/a
Japan | Tokyo	IES Abroad Tokyo Center	n/a	Intermed	IES Abroad	n/a
Mexico | Guanajuato	Universidad de Guanajuato	n/a	Intermed	Council on International Educational Exchange (CIEE)	n/a
Mexico | Oaxaca	SIT Study Abroad	n/a	Intermed	SIT Study Abroad	n/a
Mexico | Queretaro	Universidad Autonoma de Queretaro	n/a	Intermed	Academic Programs International	n/a

© 2011 — Updates? Want to be in the next edition? Visit **www.mysecondcampus.com**

Massachusetts

DESTINATION	HOST INSTITUTION	PRGM SEASON	PRGM TYPE	INTERMEDIARY	HOUSING
Morocco | Rabat	Ecole Superieure de Direction et de Gestion	n/a	Intermed	Council on International Educational Exchange (CIEE)	n/a
Netherlands | Amsterdam	University of Amsterdam	n/a	Intermed	Council on International Educational Exchange (CIEE)	n/a
New Zealand | (Multiple choices)	Multiple institutional choices	n/a	Intermed	AustraLearn	n/a
New Zealand | (Multiple choices)	Multiple institutional choices	n/a	Intermed	Center for International Studies	n/a
New Zealand | (Multiple choices)	Multiple institutional choices	n/a	Intermed	Study Australia	n/a
Nicaragua | Unknown	Unknown	n/a	USColl	Fairfield University	n/a
Northern Ireland | Unknown	Unknown	n/a	Intermed	Academic Programs International	n/a
Poland | Krakow	Jagiellonian University	n/a	Intermed	Academic Programs International	n/a
Portugal | Lisbon	Universidade Nova de Lisboa	n/a	Intermed	Council on International Educational Exchange (CIEE)	n/a
Russia | St. Petersburg	University of St. Petersburg	n/a	Intermed	CEA Global Education	n/a
Scotland | St. Andrews	University of St. Andrews	n/a	Dir	n/a	n/a
Scotland | St. Andrews	University of St. Andrews	n/a	Intermed	Institute for Study Abroad	n/a
South Africa | Cape Town	University of Cape Town	n/a	Intermed	Council on International Educational Exchange (CIEE)	n/a
South Africa | Stellenbosch	Stellenbosch University	n/a	Intermed	American Institute for Foreign Study (AIFS)	n/a
Spain | (Multiple choices)	IES Abroad Center	n/a	Intermed	IES Abroad	n/a
Spain | (Multiple)	Merrimack College	Sum	Self	n/a	n/a
Spain | (Multiple choices)	Multiple institutional choices	n/a	Intermed	Academic Programs International	n/a
Spain | (Multiple choices)	Multiple institutional choices	n/a	Intermed	Council on International Educational Exchange (CIEE)	n/a
Thailand | Khon Kaen	Khon Kaen University	n/a	Intermed	Council on International Educational Exchange (CIEE)	n/a
United Arab Emirates | Unknown	American Intercontinental University	n/a	USColl	American Intercontinental	n/a

Middlesex Community College

Pat Demaras
Assistant Dean of International/Multicultural Studies
3rd floor, Lowell Campus
33 Kearney Square
Lowell, MA 01852

demarasp@middlesex.mass.edu
978.656.3256
https://www.middlesex.mass.edu/international/opportunities.html

DESTINATION	HOST INSTITUTION	PRGM SEASON	PRGM TYPE	INTERMEDIARY	HOUSING
Belize | (Multiple)	Unknown	n/a	Self	n/a	PrivApt
China | (Multiple)	Unknown	n/a	Self	n/a	Other
Ireland | (Multiple)	Unknown	n/a	Self	n/a	PrivApt

© 2011 — Updates? Want to be in the next edition? Visit **www.mysecondcampus.com**

Massachusetts

Montserrat College of Art

Marjorie Augenbraum
Assistant Dean of Academic Affairs
23 Essex Street
Beverly, MA 01915

maugenbraum@montserrat.edu
978.921.4242 x1603
http://www.montserrat.edu/academics/study-abroad/

DESTINATION	HOST INSTITUTION	PRGM SEASON	PRGM TYPE	INTERMEDIARY	HOUSING
Canada | Calgary (Alberta)	Alberta College of Art and Design	n/a	Dir	n/a	n/a
Canada | Halifax (Nova Scotia)	Nova Scotia College of Art and Design	n/a	Dir	n/a	n/a
Canada | Toronto (Ontario)	Ontario College of Art and Design	n/a	Dir	n/a	n/a
Canada | Vancouver (British Columbia)	Emily Carr Institute of Art and Design	n/a	Dir	n/a	n/a
Italy | Viterbo	Accademia di Belle Arti	Sum	Self	n/a	PrivApt
Costs: Sum Costs: T&F: n/a, R&B: n/a, Ttl: $5,375					
Japan | Niigata	Niigata College of Art and Design	Sum	Self	n/a	HostFam
Costs: Sum Costs: T&F: n/a, R&B: n/a, Ttl: $5,600					
Mali | Segou	Montserrat College of Art	n/a	Self	n/a	n/a
Puerto Rico | Vieques	Montserrat College of Art	Win	Self	n/a	PrivApt
Costs: Win Costs: T&F: n/a, R&B: n/a, Ttl: $2,950					
United States | Baltimore (MD)	Maryland Institute	n/a	Dir	n/a	n/a
United States | Boston (MA)	Art Institute of Boston	n/a	Dir	n/a	n/a
United States | Boston (MA)	Massachusetts College of Art	n/a	Dir	n/a	n/a
United States | Boston (MA)	School of the Museum of Fine Arts	n/a	Dir	n/a	n/a
United States | Chicago (IL)	School of the Art Institute of Chicago	n/a	Dir	n/a	n/a
United States | Cincinnati (OH)	Art Academy of Cincinnati	n/a	Dir	n/a	n/a
United States | Cleveland (OH)	Cleveland Institute of Art	n/a	Dir	n/a	n/a
United States | Columbus (OH)	Columbus College of Art and Design	n/a	Dir	n/a	n/a
United States | Detroit (MI)	College for Creative Studies	n/a	Dir	n/a	n/a
United States | Kansas City (MO)	Kansas City Art Institute	n/a	Dir	n/a	n/a
United States | Laguna Beach (CA)	Laguna College of Art and Design	n/a	Dir	n/a	n/a
United States | Los Angeles (CA)	Otis College of Art and Design	n/a	Dir	n/a	n/a
United States | Memphis (TN)	Memphis College of Art	n/a	Dir	n/a	n/a
United States | Milwaukee (WI)	Milwaukee Institute of Art and Design	n/a	Dir	n/a	n/a
United States | Minneapolis (MN)	Minneapolis College of Art and Design	n/a	Dir	n/a	n/a
United States | New York (NY)	Cooper Union School of Art	n/a	Dir	n/a	n/a

© 2011 — Updates? Want to be in the next edition? Visit **www.mysecondcampus.com**

Massachusetts

DESTINATION	HOST INSTITUTION	PRGM SEASON	PRGM TYPE	INTERMEDIARY	HOUSING
United States	New York (NY)	Parsons School of Design	n/a	Dir	n/a	n/a
United States	Oakland (CA)	California College of the Arts	n/a	Dir	n/a	n/a
United States	Old Lyme (CT)	Lyme Academy of Fine Arts	n/a	Dir	n/a	n/a
United States	Philadelphia (PA)	Moore College of Art and Design	n/a	Dir	n/a	n/a
United States	Philadelphia (PA)	Pennsylvania Academy of Fine Arts	n/a	Dir	n/a	n/a
United States	Philadelphia (PA)	University of the Arts	n/a	Dir	n/a	n/a
United States	Portland (ME)	Maine College of Art	n/a	Dir	n/a	n/a
United States	Portland (OR)	Oregon College of Arts and Craft	n/a	Dir	n/a	n/a
United States	Portland (OR)	Pacific Northwest College of Art	n/a	Dir	n/a	n/a
United States	Providence (RI)	Rhode Island School of Design	n/a	Dir	n/a	n/a
United States	San Francisco (CA)	San Francisco Art Institute	n/a	Dir	n/a	n/a
United States	Sarasota (FL)	Ringling School of Art and Design	n/a	Dir	n/a	n/a
United States	Washington (DC)	Corcoran School of Art & Design	n/a	Dir	n/a	n/a

Mount Holyoke College

Joanne M. Picard
Dean of International Studies
McCulloch Center for Global Initiatives
50 College Street
South Hadley, MA 01075

jpicard@mtholyoke.edu
413.538.2072
http://www.mtholyoke.edu/global/15870.shtml

DESTINATION	HOST INSTITUTION	PRGM SEASON	PRGM TYPE	INTERMEDIARY	HOUSING
(Multiple choices)	(Multiple choices)	IES Abroad Center	n/a	Intermed	IES Abroad	n/a
(Multiple choices)	(Multiple choices)	Intercollegiate Center for Classical Studies (Duke University)	n/a	Consrtm	Intercollegiate Center for Classical Studies (Duke University)	n/a
(Multiple choices)	(Multiple choices)	Sweet Briar College	n/a	USColl	Sweet Briar College	n/a
Argentina	La Plata	Home English School	Sum	Self	n/a	n/a
Belgium	Brussels	Committee of the Regions – European Union	Sum	Self	n/a	n/a
Chile	Santiago	Solidarity and Social Investment Fund of Chile	Sum	Self	n/a	n/a
Chile	Santiago	Universidad Alberto Hurtado	Fall Spr YrRound	Bilat	n/a	HostFam PrivApt
Chile	Santiago	University of Hurtado	Sum	Self	n/a	n/a
China	Hong Kong	University of Hong Kong	Fall Spr YrRound	Bilat	n/a	CollRes
China	Ningbo	Ningbo University of Technology	Sum	Self	n/a	n/a
China	Shenzhen	Shenzhen Diguang Electronics Co. Ltd.	Sum	Self	n/a	n/a
Costa Rica	Mount Verde	Monteverde Institute	Spr	Consrtm	Mount Holyoke and Goucher	HostFam
	Costs: Spr Costs: T&F: n/a, R&B: n/a, Ttl: $13,600				
Costa Rica	San Jose	La Universidad de Costa Rica	Fall Spr YrRound	Bilat	n/a	HostFam PrivApt
Costa Rica	San Jose	Rainforest Alliance	Sum	Self	n/a	n/a

© 2011 — Updates? Want to be in the next edition? Visit **www.mysecondcampus.com**

Massachusetts

DESTINATION	HOST INSTITUTION	PRGM SEASON	PRGM TYPE	INTERMEDIARY	HOUSING
Denmark | Copenhagen	Danish Institute for Study Abroad (DIS)	n/a	Intermed	Danish Institute for Study Abroad (DIS)	n/a
Egypt | Cairo	Daily News Egypt	Sum	Self	n/a	n/a
England | Brighton	University of Sussex	Fall Spr YrRound	Bilat	n/a	CollRes
England | Brighton	University of Sussex	n/a	Dir	n/a	n/a
England | Bristol	University of St. Andrews	n/a	Dir	n/a	n/a
England | Cambridge	Cambridge University (Murray Edwards College)	n/a	Dir	n/a	n/a
England | Canterbury	University of Kent	YrRound	Bilat	n/a	CollRes PrivApt
England | Canterbury	University of Kent	Fall Spr	Dir	n/a	n/a
England | Colchester	University of Essex	YrRound	Bilat	n/a	CollRes
England | Colchester	University of Essex	Spr	Dir	n/a	n/a
England | London	London School of Economics	n/a	Dir	n/a	n/a
England | London	Royal Holloway, University of	Fall Spr YrRound	Bilat	n/a	CollRes
England | London	Royal Holloway, University of	n/a	Dir	n/a	n/a
England | London	University College London	n/a	Dir	n/a	n/a
England | Oxford	Oxford University (St. Anne's College)	n/a	Dir	n/a	n/a
England | York	University of York	YrRound	Bilat	n/a	CollRes PrivApt
England | York	University of York	Spr	Dir	n/a	n/a
France | Chantilly	Chateau de Chantilly	Sum	Self	n/a	n/a
France | Montpellier	Universite Paul Valery	Fall Spr YrRound	Dir	n/a	HostFam PrivApt
France | Paris	Institut d'Etudes Politiques de Paris (Sciences Po)	Spr YrRound	Bilat	n/a	n/a
France | Paris	University of Bristol	n/a	Dir	n/a	n/a
France | Sceaux	International Institute of Women in Engineering (IIWE)	Sum	Self	n/a	n/a
Germany | Berlin	Berlin School of Economics and Law	n/a	Bilat	n/a	n/a
Germany | Bonn	University of Bonn	Spr YrRound	Dir	n/a	n/a
	Costs: Spr Costs: T&F: n/a, R&B: n/a, Ttl: $5,857 YrRound Costs: T&F: n/a, R&B: n/a, Ttl: $9,440				
Germany | Bonn	University of Bonn	Spr YrRound	Bilat	n/a	CollRes
Germany | Leipzig	University of Leipzig	Spr YrRound	Dir	n/a	n/a
Germany | Leipzig	University of Leipzig	Spr YrRound	Bilat	n/a	CollRes PrivApt
Germany | Potsdam	University of Potsdam	Spr YrRound	Bilat	n/a	CollRes
Ghana | Accra	African Women's Development Fund (AWDF)	n/a	Self	n/a	n/a
India | New Delhi	Centre for Science and Environment	Sum	Self	n/a	n/a
Italy | Bologna	Unknown	n/a	Consrtm	Bologna Consortial Studies	n/a
Italy | Rome	School for Field Studies	n/a	Intermed	School for Field Studies	n/a
Japan | Kyoto	Doshisha University	YrRound	Consrtm	n/a	HostFam
	Costs: YrRound Costs: T&F: n/a, R&B: n/a, Ttl: Comprehensive fee at home institution ($50,576 at Mt. Holyoke)				
Japan | Tokyo	Japan Women's University	YrRound	Bilat	n/a	HostFam CollRes PrivApt

Massachusetts

DESTINATION	HOST INSTITUTION	PRGM SEASON	PRGM TYPE	INTERMEDIARY	HOUSING
Japan	Tokyo	Tokyo Woman's Christian University	Sum	Self	n/a	n/a
Lebanon	Beirut	The Daily Star	Sum	Self	n/a	n/a
Senegal	Dakar	Universite Cheikh Anta Diop (UCAD)	Spr	Dir	n/a	HostFam
Costs: Spr Costs: T&F: n/a, R&B: n/a, Ttl: $13,000					
South Korea	Seoul	Ewha Womans University	Fall Spr YrRound	Bilat	n/a	CollRes
South Korea	Seoul	Research Institute of Asian Women (RIAW)	Sum	Self	n/a	n/a
South Korea	Seoul	Sookmyung Women's University	Fall Spr YrRound	Bilat	n/a	CollRes
South Korea	Seoul	Sookmyung Women's University	Sum	Self	n/a	n/a
Spain	Cordoba	Universidad de Cordoba	n/a	Bilat	n/a	n/a
Spain	Seville	Center for Cross-Cultural Study	Sum	Self	n/a	n/a
Thailand	Bangkok	UNICEF	Sum	Self	n/a	n/a
Uganda	Gulu Town	Straight Talk Foundation	n/a	Self	n/a	n/a
Uganda	Kampala	Mango Tree Educational Enterprises	n/a	Self	n/a	n/a
United States	San Francisco (CA)	Global Fund for Women	Sum	Self	n/a	n/a
Vietnam	Hanoi	Gioi Publishing	Sum	Self	n/a	n/a
Vietnam	Hanoi	Vietnam Veterans of America Foundation (VVAF)	Sum	Self	n/a	n/a

Mount Ida College

Jane Howard
Director of International Student Affairs
777 Dedham Street
Newton, MA 02459

jhoward@mountida.edu
617.928.4624
http://www.mountida.edu/sp.cfm?pageid=1049

DESTINATION	HOST INSTITUTION	PRGM SEASON	PRGM TYPE	INTERMEDIARY	HOUSING
(Multiple choices)	(Multiple choices)	American InterContinental University	n/a	Intermed	American InterContinental University	n/a
(Multiple choices)	(Multiple choices)	Multiple institutional choices	n/a	Intermed	Academic Programs International	n/a
(Multiple choices)	(Multiple choices)	Multiple institutional choices	n/a	Intermed	American Institute for Foreign Study	n/a
England	London	Regent's College	n/a	Intermed	Academic Studies Abroad	n/a
United States	Charlottesville (VA)	Semester at Sea	n/a	Intermed	Semester at Sea	n/a

Mount Wachusett Community College

Melissa A. Fama
Vice President for Academic Affairs
444 Green Street
Gardner, MA 01440

mfama@mwcc.mass.edu
978.630.9288
http://www.mwcc.edu/catalog/alternate.html

DESTINATION	HOST INSTITUTION	PRGM SEASON	PRGM TYPE	INTERMEDIARY	HOUSING
(Multiple choices)	(Multiple choices)	Multiple institutional choices	n/a	Consrtm	College Consortium for International Studies (CCIS)	n/a

© 2011 — Updates? Want to be in the next edition? Visit **www.mysecondcampus.com**

Massachusetts

| DESTINATION | HOST INSTITUTION | PRGM SEASON | PRGM TYPE | INTERMEDIARY | HOUSING |

New England College of Optometry

Bina Patel
Director of CIAO
Center for the International Advancement of Optometry
424 Beacon Street
Boston, MA 02115

patelb@neco.edu
617.266.2030 x5293
http://www.neco.edu/international-programs/index.html

DESTINATION	HOST INSTITUTION	PRGM SEASON	PRGM TYPE	INTERMEDIARY	HOUSING
China | Unknown	Unknown	n/a	n/a	n/a	n/a
Germany | Unknown	Unknown	n/a	n/a	n/a	n/a
Israel | Unknown	Unknown	n/a	n/a	n/a	n/a
South Africa | Unknown	Unknown	n/a	n/a	n/a	n/a
Spain | Unknown	Unknown	n/a	n/a	n/a	n/a

New England School of Law

Philip K. Hamilton
Director, New England Galway Summer Program
154 Stuart Street
Boston, MA 02116

phamilton@nesl.edu
617.451.0010
http://www.nesl.edu/exceptional/international_opportunities.cfm

DESTINATION	HOST INSTITUTION	PRGM SEASON	PRGM TYPE	INTERMEDIARY	HOUSING
Cambodia | Phnom Penh	Office of the Co-prosecutors of the Extraordinary Chambers in the Courts of Cambodia	Sum Fall Spr	n/a	n/a	n/a
Chile | Santiago	University of Heidelberg	Sum	Consrtm	Consortium for Innovative Legal Education	n/a
Czech Republic | Prague	Charles University	Sum	Consrtm	Consortium for Innovative Legal Education	n/a
Denmark | Aarhus	University of Aarhus	Fall Spr	Bilat	n/a	n/a
England | London	BPP Law School	Sum	Consrtm	Consortium for Innovative Legal Education	n/a
France | Paris	University of Paris X-Nanterre	Fall Spr	Dir	n/a	n/a
Ireland | Galway	National University of Ireland	Sum	Consrtm	Consortium for Innovative Legal Education	n/a
Malta | Valletta	University of Malta	Sum	Consrtm	Consortium for Innovative Legal Education	n/a
Netherlands | Hague	Appeals Chambers (International Criminal Tribunals for former Yugoslavia and Rwanda)	Sum Fall Spr	n/a	n/a	n/a
Netherlands | Hague	International Criminal Court	Sum Fall Spr	n/a	n/a	n/a
Netherlands | Hague	International Criminal Tribunal for Rwanda	Sum Fall Spr	n/a	n/a	n/a
Netherlands | Hague	International Criminal Tribunal for the former Yugoslavia	Sum Fall Spr	n/a	n/a	n/a
Netherlands | Hague	Special Court for Sierra Leone	Sum Fall Spr	n/a	n/a	n/a
Netherlands | Hague	University of Leiden	Sum	Consrtm	Consortium for Innovative Legal Education	n/a

© 2011 — Updates? Want to be in the next edition? Visit **www.mysecondcampus.com**

Massachusetts

DESTINATION	HOST INSTITUTION	PRGM SEASON	PRGM TYPE	INTERMEDIARY	HOUSING
Netherlands | Leiden	University of Leiden School of Law	Fall Spr	Dir	n/a	n/a

Nichols College

Len Harmon　　　　　　　　　　　　　　　Len.Harmon@nichols.edu
Director　　　　　　　　　　　　　　　　　　508.213.2230
Robert C. Fischer Policy & Cultural Institute　　http://www.nichols.edu/currentstudents/academicresources/abroad/
124 Center Road
Dudley, MA 01571

DESTINATION	HOST INSTITUTION	PRGM SEASON	PRGM TYPE	INTERMEDIARY	HOUSING
China | Hong Kong	European University	n/a	Dir	n/a	n/a
England | London	European University	n/a	Dir	n/a	n/a
England | London	Regent's College	n/a	Dir	n/a	n/a
Germany | Munich	European University	n/a	Dir	n/a	n/a
Greece | Athens	European University	n/a	Dir	n/a	n/a
Singapore | Singapore	European University	n/a	Dir	n/a	n/a
Spain | Barcelona	European University	n/a	Dir	n/a	n/a
Switzerland | Geneva	European University	n/a	Dir	n/a	n/a
Switzerland | Montreux	European University	n/a	Dir	n/a	n/a

North Shore Community College

Paul Frydrych　　　　　　　　　　　　　　pfrydryc@northshore.edu
Vice President for Academic Affairs　　　　　978.762.4000 x5516
1 Ferncroft Road
Danvers, MA 01923

DESTINATION	HOST INSTITUTION	PRGM SEASON	PRGM TYPE	INTERMEDIARY	HOUSING
(Multiple choices) | (Multiple choices)	Multiple institutional choices	n/a	Consrtm	College Consortium for International Studies	n/a

Northeastern University

William T. Hyndman III　　　　　　　　　　w.hyndman@neu.edu
Director　　　　　　　　　　　　　　　　　　617.373.2090
360 Huntington Avenue　　　　　　　　　　http://www.northeastern.edu/oisp/
10 BV
Boston, MA 02115

DESTINATION	HOST INSTITUTION	PRGM SEASON	PRGM TYPE	INTERMEDIARY	HOUSING
(Multiple choices) | (Multiple choices)	Multiple institutional choices	Fall Spr	Bilat	n/a	HostFam CollRes PrivApt Other
	Costs: Fall Costs: T&F: $19,400, R&B: n/a, Ttl: n/a Spr Costs: T&F: $19,400, R&B: n/a, Ttl: n/a				
Argentina | Buenos Aires	Universidad del Salvador	Fall Spr	Dir	n/a	HostFam CollRes PrivApt
	Costs: Fall Costs: T&F: $19,400, R&B: n/a, Ttl: n/a Spr Costs: T&F: $19,400, R&B: n/a, Ttl: n/a				
Argentina | Unknown	Northeastern University	Sum	Self	n/a	n/a
Armenia | Unknown	Northeastern University	Sum	Self	n/a	n/a
Australia | Canberra	Australian National University	Fall Spr	Dir	n/a	CollRes
	Costs: Fall Costs: T&F: n/a, R&B: n/a, Ttl: $21,400 Spr Costs: T&F: n/a, R&B: n/a, Ttl: $21,400				

© 2011 — Updates? Want to be in the next edition? Visit **www.mysecondcampus.com**

Massachusetts

DESTINATION	HOST INSTITUTION	PRGM SEASON	PRGM TYPE	INTERMEDIARY	HOUSING
Australia | Gold Coast	Bond University	Fall Spr	Dir	n/a	CollRes Other
Costs: Fall Costs: T&F: n/a, R&B: n/a, Ttl: $21,400 Spr Costs: T&F: n/a, R&B: n/a, Ttl: $21,400					
Australia | Melbourne	Monash University	Fall Spr	Dir	n/a	CollRes
Costs: Fall Costs: T&F: n/a, R&B: n/a, Ttl: $21,400 Spr Costs: T&F: n/a, R&B: n/a, Ttl: $21,400					
Australia | Melbourne	Swinburne University of Technology	Fall Spr	Dir	n/a	PrivApt
Costs: Fall Costs: T&F: n/a, R&B: n/a, Ttl: $21,400 Spr Costs: T&F: n/a, R&B: n/a, Ttl: $21,400					
Australia | Perth	Curtin University	Fall Spr	Dir	n/a	CollRes
Costs: Fall Costs: T&F: n/a, R&B: n/a, Ttl: $21,400 Spr Costs: T&F: n/a, R&B: n/a, Ttl: $21,400					
Australia | Sydney	University of Sydney	Fall Spr	Dir	n/a	PrivApt
Costs: Fall Costs: T&F: n/a, R&B: n/a, Ttl: $21,400 Spr Costs: T&F: n/a, R&B: n/a, Ttl: $21,400					
Australia | Unknown	Northeastern University	Sum	Self	n/a	n/a
Balkans | Unknown	Northeastern University	Sum	Self	n/a	n/a
Belgium | Leuven	Katholieke Universiteit Leuven	Fall Spr	Bilat	n/a	CollRes PrivApt
Costs: Fall Costs: T&F: $19,400, R&B: n/a, Ttl: n/a Spr Costs: T&F: $19,400, R&B: n/a, Ttl: n/a					
Belgium | Leuven & Brussels	Louvain Institute for Ireland in	Fall Spr	Dir	n/a	CollRes
Costs: Fall Costs: T&F: n/a, R&B: n/a, Ttl: $21,400 Spr Costs: T&F: n/a, R&B: n/a, Ttl: $21,400					
Benin/France | Unknown	Northeastern University	Sum	Self	n/a	n/a
Brazil | Salvador da Bahia	Universidade Federal da Bahia; Universidade Catolica do Salvador	Fall Spr	Intermed	Council on International Educational Exchange (CIEE)	HostFam
Costs: Fall Costs: T&F: n/a, R&B: n/a, Ttl: $21,400 Spr Costs: T&F: n/a, R&B: n/a, Ttl: $21,400					
Brazil | Sao Paulo	Fundacao Armando Alvares Penteado; Pontificia Universidade Catolica de Sao Paulo	Fall Spr	Intermed	Council on International Educational Exchange (CIEE)	HostFam
Costs: Fall Costs: T&F: n/a, R&B: n/a, Ttl: $21,400 Spr Costs: T&F: n/a, R&B: n/a, Ttl: $21,400					
Brazil | Unknown	Northeastern University	Sum	Self	n/a	n/a
Canada | Vancouver	Simon Fraser University	Fall Spr	Dir	n/a	CollRes
Costs: Fall Costs: T&F: $19,400, R&B: n/a, Ttl: n/a Spr Costs: T&F: $19,400, R&B: n/a, Ttl: n/a					
Central Europe | Unknown	Northeastern University	Sum	Self	n/a	n/a
Chile | Santiago	Pontificia Universidad Catolica de Chile	Fall Spr	Dir	n/a	HostFam CollRes PrivApt
Costs: Fall Costs: T&F: $19,400, R&B: n/a, Ttl: n/a Spr Costs: T&F: $19,400, R&B: n/a, Ttl: n/a					
Chile | Unknown	Northeastern University	Sum	Self	n/a	n/a
China | Beijing	Beijing Foreign Studies University	Fall Spr	Intermed	IES Abroad	HostFam CollRes
Costs: Fall Costs: T&F: n/a, R&B: n/a, Ttl: $21,400 Spr Costs: T&F: n/a, R&B: n/a, Ttl: $21,400					
China | Hong Kong	Chinese University of Hong Kong	Fall Spr	Dir	n/a	CollRes
Costs: Fall Costs: T&F: n/a, R&B: n/a, Ttl: $21,400 Spr Costs: T&F: n/a, R&B: n/a, Ttl: $21,400					
China | Nanjing	Northeastern University	Sum	Self	n/a	n/a
China | Shanghai	East China Normal University	Fall Spr	Intermed	Council on International Educational Exchange (CIEE)	HostFam CollRes
Costs: Fall Costs: T&F: n/a, R&B: n/a, Ttl: $21,400 Spr Costs: T&F: n/a, R&B: n/a, Ttl: $21,400					

© 2011 — Updates? Want to be in the next edition? Visit **www.mysecondcampus.com**

Massachusetts

DESTINATION	HOST INSTITUTION	PRGM SEASON	PRGM TYPE	INTERMEDIARY	HOUSING
China	Unknown	Northeastern University	Sum	Self	n/a	n/a
China	Unknown	Northeastern University	Sum	Self	n/a	n/a
China	Xiamen	Xiamen University	Fall Spr	Bilat	n/a	CollRes PrivApt
Costs: Fall Costs: T&F: $19,400, R&B: n/a, Ttl: n/a Spr Costs: T&F: $19,400, R&B: n/a, Ttl: n/a					
Costa Rica	Monteverde	Monteverde Institute	Fall Spr	Intermed	Council on International Educational Exchange (CIEE)	Other
Costs: Fall Costs: T&F: n/a, R&B: n/a, Ttl: $21,400 Spr Costs: T&F: n/a, R&B: n/a, Ttl: $21,400					
Costa Rica	San Jose	International Center for Development Studies	Sum	Intermed	International Center for Development Studies	HostFam
Costs: Sum Costs: T&F: n/a, R&B: n/a, Ttl: $10,700					
Costa Rica	San Jose	International Center for Development Studies	Fall Spr	Intermed	International Center for Development Studies	HostFam
Costs: Fall Costs: T&F: n/a, R&B: n/a, Ttl: $21,400 Spr Costs: T&F: n/a, R&B: n/a, Ttl: $21,400					
Cuba	Havana	Casa de las Americas	Fall Spr	Intermed	Casa de las Americas	CollRes
Costs: Fall Costs: T&F: n/a, R&B: n/a, Ttl: $21,400 Spr Costs: T&F: n/a, R&B: n/a, Ttl: $21,400					
Czech Republic	Prague	Charles University	Fall Spr	Dir	n/a	CollRes
Costs: Fall Costs: T&F: n/a, R&B: n/a, Ttl: $21,400 Spr Costs: T&F: n/a, R&B: n/a, Ttl: $21,400					
Dominican Republic	Santiago	Pontificia Universidad Catolica Madre y Maestra	Fall Spr	Intermed	Council on International Educational Exchange (CIEE)	HostFam
Costs: Fall Costs: T&F: n/a, R&B: n/a, Ttl: $21,400 Spr Costs: T&F: n/a, R&B: n/a, Ttl: $21,400					
Dominican Republic	Santo Domingo	Facultad Latinoamericana de Ciencias Sociales	Fall Spr	Intermed	Council on International Educational Exchange (CIEE)	HostFam
Costs: Fall Costs: T&F: n/a, R&B: n/a, Ttl: $21,400 Spr Costs: T&F: n/a, R&B: n/a, Ttl: $21,400					
Dominican Republic	Unknown	Northeastern University	Sum	Self	n/a	n/a
Egypt	Cairo	American University of Cairo	Fall Spr	Dir	n/a	CollRes
Costs: Fall Costs: T&F: n/a, R&B: n/a, Ttl: $21,400 Spr Costs: T&F: n/a, R&B: n/a, Ttl: $21,400					
Egypt	Unknown	Northeastern University	Sum	Self	n/a	n/a
Egypt	Unknown	Northeastern University	Sum	Self	n/a	n/a
Egypt	Unknown	Northeastern University	Sum	Self	n/a	n/a
England	Cambridge	Cambridge University	Sum	Dir	n/a	CollRes
Costs: Sum Costs: T&F: n/a, R&B: n/a, Ttl: $19,400					
England	London	Goldsmiths College	Fall Spr	Dir	n/a	CollRes
Costs: Fall Costs: T&F: n/a, R&B: n/a, Ttl: $21,400 Spr Costs: T&F: n/a, R&B: n/a, Ttl: $21,400					
England	London	Hansard Scholars Program	Fall Spr	Dir	n/a	PrivApt
Costs: Fall Costs: T&F: n/a, R&B: n/a, Ttl: $21,400 Spr Costs: T&F: n/a, R&B: n/a, Ttl: $21,400					
France	Grenoble	University Stendhal	Fall Spr	Intermed	Academic Programs International	HostFam
Costs: Fall Costs: T&F: n/a, R&B: n/a, Ttl: $21,400 Spr Costs: T&F: n/a, R&B: n/a, Ttl: $21,400					
France	Paris	American University of Paris	Fall Spr	Dir	n/a	HostFam PrivApt
Costs: Fall Costs: T&F: $19,400, R&B: n/a, Ttl: n/a Spr Costs: T&F: $19,400, R&B: n/a, Ttl: n/a					
France	Paris	Multiple institutional choices	Fall Spr	Intermed	Academic Programs International	HostFam CollRes PrivApt
Costs: Fall Costs: T&F: n/a, R&B: n/a, Ttl: $21,400 Spr Costs: T&F: n/a, R&B: n/a, Ttl: $21,400					
France	Unknown	Northeastern University	Sum	Self	n/a	n/a

© 2011 — Updates? Want to be in the next edition? Visit **www.mysecondcampus.com**

Massachusetts

DESTINATION	HOST INSTITUTION	PRGM SEASON	PRGM TYPE	INTERMEDIARY	HOUSING
France | Unknown	Northeastern University	Sum	Self	n/a	n/a
Germany | Unknown	Northeastern University	Sum	Self	n/a	n/a
Ghana | Legon	University of Ghana	Fall Spr	Intermed	Council on International Educational Exchange (CIEE)	CollRes
Costs: Fall Costs: T&F: n/a, R&B: n/a, Ttl: $21,400 Spr Costs: T&F: n/a, R&B: n/a, Ttl: $21,400					
Ghana | Unknown	Northeastern University	Sum	Self	n/a	n/a
Greece | Thessaloniki	American College of Thessaloniki	Fall Spr	Dir	n/a	CollRes
Costs: Fall Costs: T&F: n/a, R&B: n/a, Ttl: $21,400 Spr Costs: T&F: n/a, R&B: n/a, Ttl: $21,400					
Greece | Unknown	Northeastern University	Sum	Self	n/a	n/a
Hungary | Budapest	Corvinus University of Budapest	Fall Spr	Intermed	Council on International Educational Exchange (CIEE)	HostFam PrivApt
Costs: Fall Costs: T&F: n/a, R&B: n/a, Ttl: $21,400 Spr Costs: T&F: n/a, R&B: n/a, Ttl: $21,400					
Hungary | Budapest	Technical University of Budapest, College International	Fall Spr	Intermed	Budapest Semesters in Mathematics	n/a
Costs: Fall Costs: T&F: $19,400, R&B: n/a, Ttl: n/a Spr Costs: T&F: $19,400, R&B: n/a, Ttl: n/a					
Iceland | Unknown	Northeastern University	Sum	Self	n/a	n/a
Iceland | Unknown	Northeastern University	Sum	Self	n/a	n/a
India | Hyderabad	University of Hyderabad	Fall Spr	Intermed	Council on International Educational Exchange (CIEE)	HostFam CollRes PrivApt
Costs: Fall Costs: T&F: n/a, R&B: n/a, Ttl: $21,400 Spr Costs: T&F: n/a, R&B: n/a, Ttl: $21,400					
India | Unknown	Northeastern University	Fall	Self	n/a	n/a
Ireland | Dublin	Dublin City University	Fall Spr	Intermed	Council on International Educational Exchange (CIEE)	HostFam CollRes
Costs: Fall Costs: T&F: n/a, R&B: n/a, Ttl: $21,400 Spr Costs: T&F: n/a, R&B: n/a, Ttl: $21,400					
Ireland | Dublin	Gaiety School of Acting	Sum	Dir	n/a	Other
Costs: Sum Costs: T&F: n/a, R&B: n/a, Ttl: $19,400					
Ireland | Dublin	Institute of Public Administration	Fall Spr	Dir	n/a	HostFam
Costs: Fall Costs: T&F: n/a, R&B: n/a, Ttl: $21,400 Spr Costs: T&F: n/a, R&B: n/a, Ttl: $21,400					
Ireland | Unknown	Northeastern University	Sum	Self	n/a	n/a
Israel | Unknown	Northeastern University	Sum	Self	n/a	n/a
Italy | Florence	Studio Art Center International	Fall Spr	Intermed	Studio Art Center International	PrivApt
Costs: Fall Costs: T&F: n/a, R&B: n/a, Ttl: $21,400 Spr Costs: T&F: n/a, R&B: n/a, Ttl: $21,400					
Italy | Perugia	Umbra Institute	Fall Spr	USColl	Arcadia University	PrivApt
Costs: Fall Costs: T&F: n/a, R&B: n/a, Ttl: $21,400 Spr Costs: T&F: n/a, R&B: n/a, Ttl: $21,400					
Italy | Rome	Academic Initiatives Abroad	Fall Spr	Intermed	Academic Initiatives Abroad	PrivApt
Costs: Fall Costs: T&F: $19,400, R&B: n/a, Ttl: n/a Spr Costs: T&F: $19,400, R&B: n/a, Ttl: n/a					
Italy | Rome	John Cabot University	Sum	Dir	n/a	PrivApt
Costs: Sum Costs: T&F: n/a, R&B: n/a, Ttl: $10,700					
Italy | Rome	John Cabot University	Fall Spr	Dir	n/a	PrivApt
Costs: Fall Costs: T&F: n/a, R&B: n/a, Ttl: $21,400 Spr Costs: T&F: n/a, R&B: n/a, Ttl: $21,400					
Italy | Unknown	Northeastern University	Sum	Self	n/a	n/a
Italy | Unknown	Northeastern University	Sum	Self	n/a	n/a

Massachusetts

DESTINATION	HOST INSTITUTION	PRGM SEASON	PRGM TYPE	INTERMEDIARY	HOUSING
Italy | Unknown	Northeastern University	Sum	Self	n/a	n/a
Italy | Unknown	Northeastern University	Sum	Self	n/a	n/a
Italy | Unknown	Northeastern University	Sum	Self	n/a	n/a
Italy | Unknown	Northeastern University	Sum	Self	n/a	n/a
Japan | Tokyo	J. F. Oberlin University	Fall Spr	Dir	n/a	HostFam PrivApt
Costs: Fall Costs: T&F: n/a, R&B: n/a, Ttl: $21,400 Spr Costs: T&F: n/a, R&B: n/a, Ttl: $21,400					
Japan | Tokyo	Meiji University	Fall Spr	Dir	n/a	CollRes
Costs: Fall Costs: T&F: $19,400, R&B: n/a, Ttl: n/a Spr Costs: T&F: $19,400, R&B: n/a, Ttl: n/a					
Japan | Unknown	Northeastern University	Sum	Self	n/a	n/a
Japan | Unknown	Northeastern University	Sum	Self	n/a	n/a
Kenya | Unknown	Northeastern University	Sum	Self	n/a	n/a
Korea | Seoul	Yonsei University	Fall Spr	Intermed	Council on International Educational Exchange (CIEE)	CollRes
Costs: Fall Costs: T&F: n/a, R&B: n/a, Ttl: $21,400 Spr Costs: T&F: n/a, R&B: n/a, Ttl: $21,400					
Lebanon | Beirut	American University of Beirut	Fall Spr	Dir	n/a	CollRes
Costs: Fall Costs: T&F: n/a, R&B: n/a, Ttl: $21,400 Spr Costs: T&F: n/a, R&B: n/a, Ttl: $21,400					
Mexico | Puebla	Universidad de las Americas Puebla	Fall Spr	Dir	n/a	HostFam CollRes
Costs: Fall Costs: T&F: n/a, R&B: n/a, Ttl: $21,400 Spr Costs: T&F: n/a, R&B: n/a, Ttl: $21,400					
Mexico/Costa Rica | Unknown	Northeastern University	Sum	Self	n/a	n/a
Morocco | Unknown	Northeastern University	Sum	Self	n/a	n/a
Netherlands | Amsterdam	Vrije Universiteit Amsterdam	Fall Spr	Bilat	n/a	CollRes
Costs: Fall Costs: T&F: $19,400, R&B: n/a, Ttl: n/a Spr Costs: T&F: $19,400, R&B: n/a, Ttl: n/a					
Netherlands | Rotterdam	Erasmus University Rotterdam	Fall Spr	Bilat	n/a	PrivApt
Costs: Fall Costs: T&F: $19,400, R&B: n/a, Ttl: n/a Spr Costs: T&F: $19,400, R&B: n/a, Ttl: n/a					
Netherlands | Unknown	Northeastern University	Sum	Self	n/a	n/a
New Zealand | Auckland	University of Auckland	Fall Spr	Dir	n/a	CollRes
Costs: Fall Costs: T&F: n/a, R&B: n/a, Ttl: $21,400 Spr Costs: T&F: n/a, R&B: n/a, Ttl: $21,400					
New Zealand | Christchurch	University of Canterbury	Fall Spr	Dir	n/a	CollRes
Costs: Fall Costs: T&F: n/a, R&B: n/a, Ttl: $21,400 Spr Costs: T&F: n/a, R&B: n/a, Ttl: $21,400					
Northern Ireland | Belfast	Queen's University Belfast	Fall Spr	Dir	n/a	CollRes
Costs: Fall Costs: T&F: n/a, R&B: n/a, Ttl: $21,400 Spr Costs: T&F: n/a, R&B: n/a, Ttl: $21,400					
Northern Ireland | Unknown	Northeastern University	Sum	Self	n/a	n/a
Peru | Lima	Pontificia Universidad Catolica del Peru	Fall Spr	Intermed	Council on International Educational Exchange (CIEE)	HostFam
Costs: Fall Costs: T&F: n/a, R&B: n/a, Ttl: $21,400 Spr Costs: T&F: n/a, R&B: n/a, Ttl: $21,400					
Peru | Unknown	Northeastern University	Sum	Self	n/a	n/a
Poland | Bialystok	University of Bialystok	Fall Spr	Bilat	n/a	CollRes
Costs: Fall Costs: T&F: $19,400, R&B: n/a, Ttl: n/a Spr Costs: T&F: $19,400, R&B: n/a, Ttl: n/a					
Scotland | Edinburgh	University of Edinburgh	Fall Spr	Dir	n/a	CollRes
Costs: Fall Costs: T&F: n/a, R&B: n/a, Ttl: $21,400 Spr Costs: T&F: n/a, R&B: n/a, Ttl: $21,400					
Senegal | Dakar	Suffolk University-Dakar Campus	Fall Spr	Intermed	Council on International Educational Exchange (CIEE)	HostFam
Costs: Fall Costs: T&F: n/a, R&B: n/a, Ttl: $21,400 Spr Costs: T&F: n/a, R&B: n/a, Ttl: $21,400					

© 2011 — Updates? Want to be in the next edition? Visit **www.mysecondcampus.com**

Massachusetts

DESTINATION	HOST INSTITUTION	PRGM SEASON	PRGM TYPE	INTERMEDIARY	HOUSING
Singapore | Singapore	Nanyang Technological University	Fall Spr	Dir	n/a	CollRes
	Costs: Fall Costs: T&F: n/a, R&B: n/a, Ttl: $21,400 Spr Costs: T&F: n/a, R&B: n/a, Ttl: $21,400				
Singapore | Singapore	Singapore Management University	Sum Fall Spr	Dir	n/a	PrivApt Other
	Costs: Sum Costs: T&F: $19,400, R&B: n/a, Ttl: n/a Fall Costs: T&F: $19,400, R&B: n/a, Ttl: n/a Spr Costs: T&F: $19,400, R&B: n/a, Ttl: n/a				
Singapore and Thailand | Unknown	Northeastern University	Sum	Self	n/a	n/a
South Africa | Cape Town	University of Cape Town	Fall Spr	Intermed	Council on International Educational Exchange (CIEE)	PrivApt
	Costs: Fall Costs: T&F: n/a, R&B: n/a, Ttl: $21,400 Spr Costs: T&F: n/a, R&B: n/a, Ttl: $21,400				
South Africa | Stellenbosch	Stellenbosch University	Fall Spr	Intermed	Council on International Educational Exchange (CIEE)	CollRes
	Costs: Fall Costs: T&F: n/a, R&B: n/a, Ttl: $21,400 Spr Costs: T&F: n/a, R&B: n/a, Ttl: $21,400				
South Africa | Unknown	Northeastern University	Sum	Self	n/a	n/a
South Africa | Unknown	Northeastern University	Sum	Self	n/a	n/a
Spain | Alicante	Universidad de Alicante	Fall Spr	Intermed	Council on International Educational Exchange (CIEE)	HostFam PrivApt
	Costs: Fall Costs: T&F: n/a, R&B: n/a, Ttl: $21,400 Spr Costs: T&F: n/a, R&B: n/a, Ttl: $21,400				
Spain | Barcelona	Multiple institutional choices	Fall Spr	Intermed	Council on International Educational Exchange (CIEE)	HostFam CollRes
	Costs: Fall Costs: T&F: n/a, R&B: n/a, Ttl: $21,400 Spr Costs: T&F: n/a, R&B: n/a, Ttl: $21,400				
Spain | Barcelona	Universitat Politecnica de Catalunya	Fall Spr	Bilat	n/a	n/a
	Costs: Fall Costs: T&F: $19,400, R&B: n/a, Ttl: n/a Spr Costs: T&F: $19,400, R&B: n/a, Ttl: n/a				
Spain | Seville	Universidad de Sevilla	Fall Spr	Intermed	Council on International Educational Exchange (CIEE)	HostFam CollRes
	Costs: Fall Costs: T&F: n/a, R&B: n/a, Ttl: $21,400 Spr Costs: T&F: n/a, R&B: n/a, Ttl: $21,400				
Spain | Unknown	Northeastern University	Sum	Self	n/a	n/a
Spain | Unknown	Northeastern University	Sum	Self	n/a	n/a
Spain | Unknown	Northeastern University	Sum	Self	n/a	n/a
Spain | Unknown	Northeastern University	Sum	Self	n/a	n/a
Switzerland | Geneva	Northeastern University	Sum	Self	n/a	n/a
Syria | Unknown	Northeastern University	Sum	Self	n/a	n/a
Thailand | Khon Kaen	Khon Kaen University	Fall Spr	Intermed	Council on International Educational Exchange (CIEE)	PrivApt
	Costs: Fall Costs: T&F: n/a, R&B: n/a, Ttl: $21,400 Spr Costs: T&F: n/a, R&B: n/a, Ttl: $21,400				
Thailand | Unknown	Northeastern University	Sum	Self	n/a	n/a
Trinidad & Tobago | Unknown	Northeastern University	Sum	Self	n/a	n/a
Turkey | Istanbul	Koc University	Fall Spr	Intermed	Council on International Educational Exchange (CIEE)	CollRes
	Costs: Fall Costs: T&F: n/a, R&B: n/a, Ttl: $21,400 Spr Costs: T&F: n/a, R&B: n/a, Ttl: $21,400				
Turkey | Unknown	Northeastern University	Sum	Self	n/a	n/a

© 2011 — Updates? Want to be in the next edition? Visit **www.mysecondcampus.com**

Massachusetts

DESTINATION	HOST INSTITUTION	PRGM SEASON	PRGM TYPE	INTERMEDIARY	HOUSING
United States | Woods Hole & Other Locations	Sea Education Association	Sum Fall Spr	Intermed	Sea Education Association	CollRes Other
Costs: Sum Costs: T&F: n/a, R&B: n/a, Ttl: $19,400 Fall Costs: T&F: n/a, R&B: n/a, Ttl: $21,400 Spr Costs: T&F: n/a, R&B: n/a, Ttl: $21,400					
United States | Woods Hole & Other Locations	Sea Education Association	Sum	Intermed	Sea Education Association	CollRes Other
Costs: Sum Costs: T&F: n/a, R&B: n/a, Ttl: $19,400					
Venezuela | Unknown	Northeastern University	Sum	Self	n/a	n/a
Vietnam | Ho Chi Minh City	SIT Study Abroad	Fall Spr	Intermed	SIT Study Abroad	HostFam CollRes PrivApt Other
Costs: Fall Costs: T&F: n/a, R&B: n/a, Ttl: $21,400 Spr Costs: T&F: n/a, R&B: n/a, Ttl: $21,400					

Northern Essex Community College

Elizabeth Wilcoxson
Director of International Studies
Spurk Classroom Building
C314X
Haverhill, MA 01830

ewilcoxson@necc.mass.edu
978.556.3967
http://www.necc.mass.edu/InternationalStudies/

Argentina | Unknown	Unknown	n/a	n/a	n/a	n/a
Australia | Unknown	Unknown	n/a	n/a	n/a	n/a
Austria | Unknown	Unknown	n/a	n/a	n/a	n/a
Bulgaria | Unknown	Unknown	n/a	n/a	n/a	n/a
Canada | Unknown	Unknown	n/a	n/a	n/a	n/a
China | Unknown	Unknown	n/a	n/a	n/a	n/a
Costa Rica | Unknown	Unknown	n/a	n/a	n/a	n/a
Cyprus | Unknown	Unknown	n/a	n/a	n/a	n/a
Dominican Republic | Unknown	Unknown	n/a	n/a	n/a	n/a
Ecuador | Unknown	Unknown	n/a	n/a	n/a	n/a
England | Unknown	Unknown	n/a	n/a	n/a	n/a
France | Unknown	Unknown	n/a	n/a	n/a	n/a
Germany | Unknown	Unknown	n/a	n/a	n/a	n/a
Greece | Unknown	Unknown	n/a	n/a	n/a	n/a
Hungary | Unknown	Unknown	n/a	n/a	n/a	n/a
Ireland | Unknown	Unknown	n/a	n/a	n/a	n/a
Israel | Unknown	Unknown	n/a	n/a	n/a	n/a
Italy | Unknown	Unknown	n/a	n/a	n/a	n/a
Japan | Unknown	Unknown	n/a	n/a	n/a	n/a
Mexico | Unknown	Unknown	n/a	n/a	n/a	n/a
Morocco | Unknown	Unknown	n/a	n/a	n/a	n/a
New Zealand | Unknown	Unknown	n/a	n/a	n/a	n/a
Northern Ireland | Unknown	Unknown	n/a	n/a	n/a	n/a
Peru | Unknown	Unknown	n/a	n/a	n/a	n/a
Portugal | Unknown	Unknown	n/a	n/a	n/a	n/a

© 2011 — Updates? Want to be in the next edition? Visit **www.mysecondcampus.com**

Massachusetts

DESTINATION	HOST INSTITUTION	PRGM SEASON	PRGM TYPE	INTERMEDIARY	HOUSING
Russia | Unknown	Unknown	n/a	n/a	n/a	n/a
Scotland | Unknown	Unknown	n/a	n/a	n/a	n/a
South Korea | Unknown	Unknown	n/a	n/a	n/a	n/a
Spain | Unknown	Unknown	n/a	n/a	n/a	n/a
Switzerland | Unknown	Unknown	n/a	n/a	n/a	n/a

Pine Manor College

Nia Lane Chester
Vice President for Academic Affairs
400 Heath Street
Chestnut Hill, MA 02467

chestern@pmc.edu
617.731.7106

DESTINATION	HOST INSTITUTION	PRGM SEASON	PRGM TYPE	INTERMEDIARY	HOUSING
United States | Washington (DC)	American University	n/a	USColl	American University	n/a

Quinsigamond Community College

Patricia Toney
Vice President of Academic Affairs
670 West Boylston Street
Worcester, MA 01606

patt@qcc.mass.edu
508.854.4425

DESTINATION	HOST INSTITUTION	PRGM SEASON	PRGM TYPE	INTERMEDIARY	HOUSING
Greece | Unknown	Unknown	n/a	n/a	n/a	n/a

Regis College

Sarah Barrett
Associate Vice President, Academic Affairs
235 Wellesley Street
Weston, MA 02493

sarah.barrett@regiscollege.edu
781.768.7162

DESTINATION	HOST INSTITUTION	PRGM SEASON	PRGM TYPE	INTERMEDIARY	HOUSING
[Country Unspecified] | [City Unspecified]	n/a	n/a	n/a	n/a	n/a

Roxbury Community College

Brenda Mercomes
Vice President for Academic Affairs
Administration Building 2, Room 301
1234 Columbus Avenue
Roxbury Crossing, MA 02120

Brendam@rcc.mass.edu
617.541.5304

DESTINATION	HOST INSTITUTION	PRGM SEASON	PRGM TYPE	INTERMEDIARY	HOUSING
Nigeria | Owerri	Unknown	n/a	n/a	n/a	n/a

© 2011 — Updates? Want to be in the next edition? Visit **www.mysecondcampus.com**

Massachusetts

DESTINATION	HOST INSTITUTION	PRGM SEASON	PRGM TYPE	INTERMEDIARY	HOUSING

Salem State College

Donald F. Ross, Jr.
Director
Center for International Education
352 Lafayette Street
Salem, MA 01970

dross@salemstate.edu
978.542.6351
http://www.salemstate.edu/academics/4428.php

DESTINATION	HOST INSTITUTION	PRGM SEASON	PRGM TYPE	INTERMEDIARY	HOUSING
(Multiple choices) | (Multiple choices)	Multiple institutional choices	n/a	Intermed	Centers for Academic Programs Abroad	n/a
(Multiple choices) | (Multiple choices)	Multiple institutional choices	n/a	Intermed	Institute for Study Abroad	n/a
(Multiple choices) | (Multiple choices)	Multiple institutional choices	n/a	Intermed	American Institute for Foreign Study	n/a
(Multiple choices) | (Multiple choices)	Multiple institutional choices	n/a	Intermed	Center for International Studies	n/a
(Multiple choices) | (Multiple choices)	Multiple institutional choices	n/a	Consrtm	College Consortium for International Studies	n/a
(Multiple choices) | (Multiple choices)	Multiple institutional choices	n/a	Intermed	AustraLearn	n/a
(Multiple choices) | (Multiple choices)	Multiple institutional choices	n/a	Intermed	Academic Programs International	n/a
(Multiple choices) | (Multiple choices)	Multiple institutional choices	n/a	Intermed	Study Abroad Italy	n/a
Canada | Quebec City	Universite Laval	n/a	Dir	n/a	n/a
Italy | Florence	University of Florence	n/a	Dir	n/a	n/a
Spain | Oviedo	Universidad de Oviedo	n/a	Dir	n/a	n/a

School of the Museum of Fine Arts-Boston

Susan Lush
Associate Dean for Academic Affairs
230 The Fenway
Boston, MA 02115

slush@smfa.edu
617.369.3833
http://www.smfa.edu/exchange-programs

DESTINATION	HOST INSTITUTION	PRGM SEASON	PRGM TYPE	INTERMEDIARY	HOUSING
[Country Unspecified] | [City Unspecified]	n/a	n/a	n/a	n/a	n/a

Simmons College

Hilary Wilson
Education Abroad Program Manager
Education Abroad Office
Room C-313
300 The Fenway
Boston, MA 02135

hilary.wilson@simmons.edu
617.521.2128

DESTINATION	HOST INSTITUTION	PRGM SEASON	PRGM TYPE	INTERMEDIARY	HOUSING
(Multiple choices) | (Multiple choices)	Multiple institutional choices	n/a	Intermed	Danish Institute for Study Abroad (DIS)	n/a

© 2011 — Updates? Want to be in the next edition? Visit **www.mysecondcampus.com**

Massachusetts

DESTINATION	HOST INSTITUTION	PRGM SEASON	PRGM TYPE	INTERMEDIARY	HOUSING
(Multiple choices) | (Multiple choices)	Multiple institutional choices	n/a	Intermed	IES Abroad	n/a
(Multiple choices) | (Multiple choices)	Multiple institutional choices	n/a	Intermed	Study Abroad Italy	n/a
(Multiple choices) | (Multiple choices)	Multiple institutional choices	n/a	Intermed	SIT Study Abroad	n/a
(Multiple choices) | (Multiple choices)	Multiple institutional choices	n/a	Intermed	School for Field Studies	n/a
(Multiple choices) | (Multiple choices)	Multiple institutional choices	n/a	Intermed	International Studies Abroad	n/a
(Multiple choices) | (Multiple choices)	Multiple institutional choices	n/a	Intermed	Interstudy	n/a
(Multiple choices) | (Multiple choices)	Multiple institutional choices	n/a	Intermed	Institute for Study Abroad	n/a
(Multiple choices) | (Multiple choices)	Multiple institutional choices	n/a	Intermed	American Institute for Foreign Study	n/a
(Multiple choices) | (Multiple choices)	Multiple institutional choices	n/a	Intermed	Center for International Studies	n/a
(Multiple choices) | (Multiple choices)	Multiple institutional choices	n/a	Intermed	CET Academic Programs	n/a
(Multiple choices) | (Multiple choices)	Multiple institutional choices	n/a	Intermed	International Honors Program	n/a
(Multiple choices) | (Multiple choices)	Multiple institutional choices	n/a	Intermed	BCA Study Abroad	n/a
(Multiple choices) | (Multiple choices)	Multiple institutional choices	n/a	USColl	Boston University	n/a
(Multiple choices) | (Multiple choices)	Multiple institutional choices	n/a	Intermed	Academic Studies Abroad	n/a
(Multiple choices) | (Multiple choices)	Multiple institutional choices	n/a	USColl	Arcadia University	n/a
(Multiple choices) | (Multiple choices)	Multiple institutional choices	n/a	Intermed	Academic Programs International	n/a
(Multiple choices) | (Multiple choices)	Semester at Sea	n/a	Intermed	Semester at Sea	n/a
France | Paris	Simmons College	Spr	Self	n/a	n/a
Costs: Spr Costs: T&F: n/a, R&B: n/a, Ttl: $2,600					
Germany and Russia | Berlin, St. Petersburg, and Moscow	Simmons College	Spr	Self	n/a	n/a
Costs: Spr Costs: T&F: n/a, R&B: n/a, Ttl: $3,200					
Japan | Kyoto	Ritsumeikan University	n/a	Bilat	n/a	n/a
Japan | Tokyo, Kyoto and Hiroshima	Simmons College	Spr	Self	n/a	HostFam
Costs: Spr Costs: T&F: n/a, R&B: n/a, Ttl: $3,106					
Nicaragua | San Juan del Sur	Simmons College	Win	Self	n/a	HostFam
Costs: Win Costs: T&F: n/a, R&B: n/a, Ttl: $2,349					
Nicaragua | San Juan del Sur	Simmons College	Win	Self	n/a	HostFam
Costs: Win Costs: T&F: n/a, R&B: n/a, Ttl: $1,888					

© 2011 — Updates? Want to be in the next edition? Visit **www.mysecondcampus.com**

Massachusetts

DESTINATION	HOST INSTITUTION	PRGM SEASON	PRGM TYPE	INTERMEDIARY	HOUSING
Nicaragua | San Juan del Sur and Isla de Ometepe	Simmons College	Spr	Self	n/a	Other
Costs: Spr Costs: T&F: n/a, R&B: n/a, Ttl: $2,558					
Spain | Granada	Simmons College	Spr	Self	n/a	HostFam
Costs: Spr Costs: T&F: n/a, R&B: n/a, Ttl: $3,846					
Thailand | Bangkok	Simmons College	Spr	Self	n/a	Other
Costs: Spr Costs: T&F: n/a, R&B: n/a, Ttl: $4,574					
Uganda | Kampala	Simmons College	Sum	Self	n/a	n/a
Costs: Sum Costs: T&F: n/a, R&B: n/a, Ttl: $4,280					
United Arab Emirates | Dubai and Abu Dhabi	Simmons College	Spr	Self	n/a	n/a
Costs: Spr Costs: T&F: n/a, R&B: n/a, Ttl: $3,200					
United States | California	Simmons College	Spr	Self	n/a	n/a
Costs: Spr Costs: T&F: n/a, R&B: n/a, Ttl: $1,591					
United States | New York (NY)	Simmons College	Spr	Self	n/a	n/a
Costs: Spr Costs: T&F: n/a, R&B: n/a, Ttl: $2,855					

Smith College

Leslie M. Hill
Associate Dean, International Study
Office for International Study
Neilson Library Neon Archway
Northampton, MA 01063

lhill@smith.edu
413.585.4905
http://www.smith.edu/studyabroad/index.php

Argentina | Buenos Aires	Multiple institutional choices	n/a	Intermed	Institute for Study Abroad	n/a
Argentina | Buenos Aires	SIT Study Abroad	n/a	Intermed	SIT Study Abroad	n/a
Argentina | Buenos Aires	SIT Study Abroad	n/a	Intermed	SIT Study Abroad	n/a
Argentina | Buenos Aires	Universidad de Buenos Aires	n/a	Intermed	Council on International Educational Exchange (CIEE)	n/a
Australia | Byron Bay	SIT Study Abroad	n/a	Intermed	SIT Study Abroad	n/a
Australia | Cairns	SIT Study Abroad	n/a	Intermed	SIT Study Abroad	n/a
Australia | Hobart	University of Tasmania	n/a	Dir	n/a	n/a
Australia | Melbourne	University of Melbourne	n/a	Dir	n/a	n/a
Australia | Wollongong	University of Wollongong	n/a	Dir	n/a	n/a
Australia | Yungaburra	Center for Rainforest Studies	n/a	Intermed	School for Field Studies	n/a
Austria | Vienna	IES Abroad Vienna Center	n/a	Intermed	IES Abroad	n/a
Bolivia | Cochabamba	SIT Study Abroad	n/a	Intermed	SIT Study Abroad	n/a
Botswana | Gaborone	SIT Study Abroad	n/a	Intermed	SIT Study Abroad	n/a
Brazil | Belem	SIT Study Abroad	n/a	Intermed	SIT Study Abroad	n/a
Brazil | Fortaleza	SIT Study Abroad	n/a	Intermed	SIT Study Abroad	n/a
Brazil | Rio de Janeiro	Pontificia Universidade Catolica	n/a	USColl	Brown University	n/a
Brazil | Salvador	SIT Study Abroad	n/a	Intermed	SIT Study Abroad	n/a
Brazil | Sao Paolo	Universidade de Sao Paulo	n/a	Intermed	Council on International Educational Exchange (CIEE)	n/a

© 2011 — Updates? Want to be in the next edition? Visit **www.mysecondcampus.com**

Massachusetts

DESTINATION	HOST INSTITUTION	PRGM SEASON	PRGM TYPE	INTERMEDIARY	HOUSING
Cameroon | Dschang and Yaounde	SIT Study Abroad	n/a	Intermed	SIT Study Abroad	n/a
Canada | Montreal	McGill University	n/a	Dir	n/a	n/a
Canada | Toronto	University of Toronto	n/a	Dir	n/a	n/a
Chile | Santiago	Pontificia Universidad Catolica de Chile or Universidad de Chile	n/a	Intermed	Council on International Educational Exchange (CIEE)	n/a
Chile | Santiago	SIT Study Abroad	n/a	Intermed	SIT Study Abroad	n/a
Chile | Santiago	SIT Study Abroad	n/a	Intermed	SIT Study Abroad	n/a
Chile | Valparaiso	SIT Study Abroad	n/a	Intermed	SIT Study Abroad	n/a
China | Beijing	Beijing Language and Culture University	n/a	Intermed	Alliance for Global Education	n/a
China | Beijing	Capital University of Economics and Business	n/a	USColl	Associated Colleges in China (Hamilton College)	n/a
China | Beijing	Tsinghua University	n/a	Consrtm	Inter-University Program for Chinese Language Studies (University of California, Berkeley)	n/a
China | Hangzhou	Zhejiang University of Technology	n/a	USColl	Middlebury College	n/a
China | Kunming	SIT Study Abroad	n/a	Intermed	SIT Study Abroad	n/a
China | Shanghai	Fudan University	n/a	Intermed	Alliance for Global Education	n/a
Costa Rica | (Multiple)	Organization for Tropical Studies	n/a	Intermed	Organization for Tropical Studies	n/a
Costa Rica | Atenas	SFS Center for Sustainable Development Studies	n/a	Intermed	School for Field Studies	n/a
Costa Rica | San Jose	University of Costa Rica	n/a	USColl	University of Kansas	n/a
Czech Republic | Prague	CET Academic Programs	n/a	Intermed	CET Academic Programs	n/a
Czech Republic | Prague	SIT Study Abroad	n/a	Intermed	SIT Study Abroad	n/a
Denmark | Copenhagen	Danish Institute for Study Abroad (DIS)	n/a	Intermed	Danish Institute for Study Abroad (DIS)	n/a
Dominican Republic | Santo Domingo	Facultad Latinoamericana de Ciencias Sociales (FLACSO)	n/a	Intermed	Council on International Educational Exchange (CIEE)	n/a
Ecuador | Quito	SIT Study Abroad	n/a	Intermed	SIT Study Abroad	n/a
Ecuador | Quito	SIT Study Abroad	n/a	Intermed	SIT Study Abroad	n/a
Ecuador | Quito	Universidad Politecnica Salesiana or Facultad Latinoamericana de Ciencias Sociales (FLACSO)	n/a	USColl	Duke University	n/a
England | Brighton	University of Sussex	n/a	Dir	n/a	n/a
England | Bristol	University of Bristol	n/a	Dir	n/a	n/a
England | Cambridge	Cambridge University (Pembroke College)	n/a	Dir	n/a	n/a
England | London	British American Drama Academy (BADA)	n/a	USColl	Sarah Lawrence College	n/a
England | London	King's College London	n/a	Dir	n/a	n/a
England | London	London Academy of Music and Dramatic Arts (LAMDA)	n/a	Dir	n/a	n/a

© 2011 — Updates? Want to be in the next edition? Visit **www.mysecondcampus.com**

Massachusetts

DESTINATION	HOST INSTITUTION	PRGM SEASON	PRGM TYPE	INTERMEDIARY	HOUSING
England | London	London School of Economics and Political Science	n/a	Dir	n/a	n/a
England | London	Queen Mary	n/a	Dir	n/a	n/a
England | London	Royal Holloway	n/a	Dir	n/a	n/a
England | London	School of Oriental and African Studies	n/a	Dir	n/a	n/a
England | Manchester	University of Manchester	n/a	Dir	n/a	n/a
England | Norwich	University of East Anglia	n/a	Dir	n/a	n/a
England | Oxford	Oxford University (Hertford College)	n/a	Dir	n/a	n/a
England | Oxford	Oxford University (Lady Margaret Hall)	n/a	Dir	n/a	n/a
England | Oxford	Oxford University (St. Catherine's College)	n/a	Dir	n/a	n/a
England | Oxford	Oxford University (St. Edmund Hall)	n/a	Dir	n/a	n/a
England | York	University of York	n/a	Dir	n/a	n/a
Germany | Hamburg	Universitat Hamburg and Technische Universitat Hamburg-Harburg	Fall Spr YrRound	Self	n/a	CollRes
	Costs: Fall Costs: T&F: n/a, R&B: n/a, Ttl: $25,066 Spr Costs: T&F: n/a, R&B: n/a, Ttl: $25,066 YrRound Costs: T&F: n/a, R&B: n/a, Ttl: $50,132				
Ghana | Accra and Kumasi	SIT Study Abroad	n/a	Intermed	SIT Study Abroad	n/a
Ghana | Cape Coast	SIT Study Abroad	n/a	Intermed	SIT Study Abroad	n/a
Greece | Athens	International Center for Hellenic & Mediterranean Studies (College Year in Athens)	n/a	Intermed	College Year in Athens	n/a
Hungary | Budapest	Central European University	n/a	USColl	Bard College	n/a
Hungary | Budapest	Technical University of Budapest, College International	n/a	Intermed	Budapest Semesters in Mathematics	n/a
India | (Multiple choices)	University of Wisconsin, Madison	n/a	USColl	University of Wisconsin, Madison	n/a
India | Bodhi Gaya	Antioch University	n/a	USColl	Antioch University	n/a
India | Madras	South India Term Abroad (George Washington University)	n/a	Consrtm	South India Term Abroad (George Washington University)	n/a
India | Pune	Fergusson College	n/a	Intermed	Alliance for Global Education	n/a
India | Sarnath	Central Institute of Higher Tibetan Studies	n/a	Dir	n/a	n/a
Ireland | Cork	University College Cork	n/a	Dir	n/a	n/a
Ireland | Dublin	University College Dublin	n/a	Dir	n/a	n/a
Ireland | Galway	National University of Ireland, Galway	n/a	Dir	n/a	n/a
Israel | Beer Sheva	Ben-Gurion University of the Negev	n/a	Dir	n/a	n/a
Israel | Eilot	Arava Institute for Environmental Studies	n/a	Dir	n/a	n/a

© 2011 — Updates? Want to be in the next edition? Visit **www.mysecondcampus.com**

Massachusetts

DESTINATION	HOST INSTITUTION	PRGM SEASON	PRGM TYPE	INTERMEDIARY	HOUSING
Israel | Haifa	Haifa University	n/a	Dir	n/a	n/a
Israel | Jerusalem	Hebrew University	n/a	Dir	n/a	n/a
Israel | Tel Aviv	Tel Aviv University	n/a	Dir	n/a	n/a
Israel | Tel Aviv	Tel Aviv University	n/a	USColl	Boston University	n/a
Italy | Florence	Multiple institutional choices	YrRound	Self	n/a	HostFam
	Costs: YrRound Costs: T&F: n/a, R&B: n/a, Ttl: $50,132				
Italy | Rome	Intercollegiate Center for Classical Studies (Duke University)	n/a	USColl	Duke University	n/a
Japan | Kyoto	Doshisha University	n/a	Consrtm	Associated Kyoto Program	n/a
Japan | Nagoya	Nanzan University	n/a	Intermed	IES Abroad	n/a
Japan | Tokyo	Sophia University	n/a	Intermed	Council on International Educational Exchange (CIEE)	n/a
Jordan | Amman	SIT Study Abroad	n/a	Intermed	SIT Study Abroad	n/a
Jordan | Amman	University of Jordan	n/a	Intermed	Council on International Educational Exchange (CIEE)	n/a
Kenya | Kimana	Center for Wildlife Management Studies	n/a	Intermed	School for Field Studies	n/a
Kenya | Mombasa	SIT Study Abroad	n/a	Intermed	SIT Study Abroad	n/a
Kenya | Nairobi	St. Lawrence University	n/a	USColl	St. Lawrence University	n/a
Madagascar | Antananarivo	SIT Study Abroad	n/a	Intermed	SIT Study Abroad	n/a
Madagascar | Fort Dauphin	SIT Study Abroad	n/a	Intermed	SIT Study Abroad	n/a
Mexico | Baja	Center for Coastal Studies	n/a	Intermed	School for Field Studies	n/a
Mexico | Guadalajara	Instituto Tecnologico y de Estudios Superiores de Monterrey	n/a	USColl	Boston University	n/a
Mexico | Puebla	Benemerita Universidad Autonoma de Puebla	n/a	Consrtm	Oberlin, Smith, Wellesley, and Wheaton Colleges	n/a
Mongolia | Ulaanbaatar	SIT Study Abroad	n/a	Intermed	SIT Study Abroad	n/a
Morocco | Rabat	SIT Study Abroad	n/a	Intermed	SIT Study Abroad	n/a
Morocco | Rabat	SIT Study Abroad	n/a	Intermed	SIT Study Abroad	n/a
Morocco | Rabat	SIT Study Abroad	n/a	Intermed	SIT Study Abroad	n/a
Morocco | Rabat	SIT Study Abroad	n/a	Intermed	SIT Study Abroad	n/a
Netherlands | Amsterdam	SIT Study Abroad	n/a	Intermed	SIT Study Abroad	n/a
Netherlands | Utrecht	University College Utrecht	n/a	Dir	n/a	n/a
New Zealand | Auckland	University of Auckland	n/a	Dir	n/a	n/a
New Zealand | Christchurch	University of Canterbury	n/a	Dir	n/a	n/a
New Zealand | Dunedin	University of Otago	n/a	Dir	n/a	n/a
Nicaragua | Managua	SIT Study Abroad	n/a	Intermed	SIT Study Abroad	n/a
Poland | Warsaw	Warsaw School of Economics	n/a	Intermed	Council on International Educational Exchange (CIEE)	n/a
Portugal | Lisbon	Universidade Nova de Lisboa	n/a	Intermed	Council on International Educational Exchange (CIEE)	n/a
Russia | (Multiple choices)	Multiple institutional choices	n/a	Intermed	American Councils Study Abroad Programs	n/a

Massachusetts

DESTINATION	HOST INSTITUTION	PRGM SEASON	PRGM TYPE	INTERMEDIARY	HOUSING
Russia | (Multiple choices)	Multiple institutional choices	n/a	USColl	Middlebury College	n/a
Russia | St. Petersburg	Smolny College	n/a	USColl	Bard-Smolny Study Abroad	n/a
Samoa | Apia	SIT Study Abroad	n/a	Intermed	SIT Study Abroad	n/a
Scotland | Edinburgh	University of Edinburgh	n/a	Dir	n/a	n/a
Scotland | Edinburgh	University of Edinburgh	n/a	Dir	n/a	n/a
Scotland | Glasgow	University of Glasgow	n/a	Dir	n/a	n/a
Scotland | St. Andrews	University of St. Andrews	n/a	Dir	n/a	n/a
Senegal | Dakar	SIT Study Abroad	n/a	Intermed	SIT Study Abroad	n/a
Senegal | Dakar	Universite Cheikh Anta Diop	n/a	USColl	Kalamazoo College	n/a
South Africa | Cape Town	SIT Study Abroad	n/a	Intermed	SIT Study Abroad	n/a
South Africa | Cape Town	University of Cape Town	n/a	Intermed	Council on International Educational Exchange (CIEE)	n/a
South Africa | Durban	SIT Study Abroad	n/a	Intermed	SIT Study Abroad	n/a
South Africa | Durban	SIT Study Abroad	n/a	Intermed	SIT Study Abroad	n/a
South Africa | Durban	University of KwaZulu-Natal, Pietermartzburg Campus	n/a	Intermed	Interstudy	n/a
South Africa | Johannesburg	University of Witwatersrand	n/a	Intermed	International Human Rights Exchange (Bard College)	n/a
South Africa | Pietermaritzburg	University of KwaZulu-Natal, Pietermartzburg Campus	n/a	Intermed	Interstudy	n/a
South Korea | Seoul	Ewha Woman's University	n/a	Dir	n/a	n/a
South Korea | Seoul	Yonsei University	n/a	Intermed	Council on International Educational Exchange (CIEE)	n/a
Spain | Barcelona	Universitat de Barcelona	n/a	USColl	Knox College	n/a
Spain | Cordoba	Universidad de Cordoba	n/a	Consrtm	Programa de Estudios Hispanicos en Cordoba (PRESHCO)	n/a
Spain | Madrid	Universidad Autonoma de Madrid or University of Alcala	n/a	USColl	Tufts University	n/a
Spain | Madrid	Universidad Complutense de Madrid or Universidad San Pablo	n/a	USColl	Hamilton College	n/a
Switzerland | Geneva	Universite de Geneve	Fall Spr YrRound	Self	n/a	CollRes
	Costs: Fall Costs: T&F: n/a, R&B: n/a, Ttl: $25,066 Spr Costs: T&F: n/a, R&B: n/a, Ttl: $25,066 YrRound Costs: T&F: n/a, R&B: n/a, Ttl: $50,132				
Tanzania | Arusha	SIT Study Abroad	n/a	Intermed	SIT Study Abroad	n/a
Tanzania | Zanzibar	SIT Study Abroad	n/a	Intermed	SIT Study Abroad	n/a
Thailand | Kohn Kaen	Kohn Kaen University	n/a	Intermed	Council on International Educational Exchange (CIEE)	n/a
Turks and Caicos | South Caicos	Center for Marine Resource Management Studies	n/a	Intermed	School for Field Studies	n/a
Uganda | Kampala	SIT Study Abroad	n/a	Intermed	SIT Study Abroad	n/a
Vietnam | Ho Chi Minh City	CET Academic Programs	n/a	Intermed	CET Academic Programs	n/a
Vietnam | Ho Chi Minh City	SIT Study Abroad	n/a	Intermed	SIT Study Abroad	n/a
Wales | Bangor	Bangor University	n/a	Dir	n/a	n/a
Wales | Cardiff	Cardiff University	n/a	Dir	n/a	n/a
Wales | Swansea	University of Swansea	n/a	Dir	n/a	n/a

© 2011 — Updates? Want to be in the next edition? Visit **www.mysecondcampus.com**

Massachusetts

DESTINATION	HOST INSTITUTION	PRGM SEASON	PRGM TYPE	INTERMEDIARY	HOUSING

Springfield College

Joyce Szewczynski
Associate Director of Study Abroad Programming
263 Alden Street
Springfield, MA 01109

jszewczy@spfldcol.edu
413.748.3215
http://www.spfldcol.edu/homepage/dept.nsf/BC81220B343BE6788525738E005FDA74/ B633760A197EAC448525707D0048EEF3

DESTINATION	HOST INSTITUTION	PRGM SEASON	PRGM TYPE	INTERMEDIARY	HOUSING
Australia | Newcastle	University of Newcastle	n/a	Dir	n/a	n/a
Australia | Wollongong	University of Wollongong	n/a	Dir	n/a	n/a
China | Beijing	University of International Business and Economics	n/a	Intermed	Center for International Studies	n/a
England | London	Center for International Studies	n/a	Intermed	Center for International Studies	n/a
England | York	York St. John University	n/a	Dir	n/a	n/a
France | Grenoble	Centre Universitaire d'Etudes Francaises (CUEF) at Universite Stendhal	n/a	Intermed	Academic Programs International	n/a
France | Grenoble	Grenoble Ecole de Management	n/a	Intermed	Academic Programs International	n/a
France | Paris	Universite de Paris and Institut Catholique de Paris	n/a	Intermed	Academic Programs International	n/a
Hungary | Budapest	Corvinus University of Budapest	n/a	Intermed	Academic Programs International	n/a
Ireland | Dublin	Center for International Studies	n/a	Intermed	Center for International Studies	n/a
Ireland | Dublin	Dublin City University	n/a	Intermed	Center for International Studies	n/a
Ireland | Limerick	University of Limerick	n/a	Intermed	Academic Programs International	n/a
Italy | (Multiple choices)	Scuola Lorenzo de' Medici	n/a	Intermed	Academic Programs International	n/a
Italy | Rome	John Cabot University	n/a	Intermed	Academic Programs International	n/a
Italy | Syracuse	Mediterranean Center for Arts and Sciences	n/a	Intermed	Academic Programs International	n/a
New Zealand | Auckland	University of Auckland	n/a	Intermed	Center for International Studies	n/a
New Zealand | Dunedin	University of Otago	n/a	Intermed	Center for International Studies	n/a
New Zealand | Wellington	Victoria University of Wellington	n/a	Intermed	Center for International Studies	n/a
Poland | Krakow	Jagiellonian University of Krakow	n/a	Intermed	Academic Programs International	n/a
Scotland | Edinburgh	Napier University	n/a	Intermed	Center for International Studies	n/a
Scotland | Stirling	University of Stirling	n/a	Intermed	Center for International Studies	n/a
Spain | Alcala	Universidad de Alcala	n/a	Intermed	n/a	n/a

© 2011 — Updates? Want to be in the next edition? Visit **www.mysecondcampus.com**

Massachusetts

DESTINATION	HOST INSTITUTION	PRGM SEASON	PRGM TYPE	INTERMEDIARY	HOUSING
Spain	Madrid	Suffolk University Madrid	n/a	Intermed	Center for International Studies	n/a
Spain	Salamanca	Universidad de Salamanca	n/a	Intermed	Academic Programs International	n/a

Springfield Technical Community College

Steven Keller
Vice President for Academic Affairs
1 Armory Square
P.O. Box 9000
Springfield, MA 01102

keller@stcc.edu
413.755.4440
http://www.stcc.edu/academics/foreignlang.asp

DESTINATION	HOST INSTITUTION	PRGM SEASON	PRGM TYPE	INTERMEDIARY	HOUSING
Argentina	Buenos Aires	Universidad de Buenos Aires	Sum Fall Spr	n/a	n/a	n/a
Italy	Urbino	University of Urbino	Sum Fall Spr	n/a	n/a	n/a
Spain	Madrid	King Juan Carlos University	Sum Fall Spr	n/a	n/a	n/a

Stonehill College

Alice M. Cronin
Director of International Programs
Office of International Programs
320 Washington Street
Easton, MA 02357

acronin@stonehill.edu
508.565.1021
http://www.stonehill.edu/x14103.xml

DESTINATION	HOST INSTITUTION	PRGM SEASON	PRGM TYPE	INTERMEDIARY	HOUSING
(Multiple choices)	(Multiple choices)	SIT Study Abroad	n/a	Intermed	SIT Study Abroad	n/a
Argentina	Buenos Aires	Universidad Catolica de Argentina	n/a	Intermed	Institute for Study Abroad	n/a
Argentina	Buenos Aires	Universidad de Buenos Aires	n/a	Intermed	Institute for Study Abroad	n/a
Argentina	Buenos Aires	Universidad del Salvador	n/a	Intermed	Institute for Study Abroad	n/a
Argentina	Buenos Aires	Universidad Torcuato Di Tella	n/a	Intermed	Institute for Study Abroad	n/a
Australia	Adelaide	Flinders University	n/a	Intermed	Institute for Study Abroad	n/a
Australia	Adelaide	University of Adelaide	n/a	Intermed	Institute for Study Abroad	n/a
Australia	Brisbane	Griffith University	n/a	Intermed	Institute for Study Abroad	n/a
Australia	Brisbane	University of Queensland	n/a	Intermed	Institute for Study Abroad	n/a
Australia	Cairns or Townsville	James Cook University	n/a	Intermed	Institute for Study Abroad	n/a
Australia	Canberra	Australian National University	n/a	Intermed	Institute for Study Abroad	n/a
Australia	Hobart or Launceston	University of Tasmania	n/a	Intermed	Institute for Study Abroad	n/a
Australia	Lismore	Southern Cross University	n/a	Intermed	Institute for Study Abroad	n/a
Australia	Melbourne	Monash University	n/a	Intermed	Institute for Study Abroad	n/a
Australia	Melbourne	University of Melbourne	n/a	Intermed	Institute for Study Abroad	n/a
Australia	Perth	Murdoch University	n/a	Intermed	Institute for Study Abroad	n/a
Australia	Perth	University of Western Australia	n/a	Intermed	Institute for Study Abroad	n/a
Australia	Sydney	Macquarie University	n/a	Intermed	Institute for Study Abroad	n/a
Australia	Sydney	University of New South Wales	n/a	Intermed	Institute for Study Abroad	n/a
Australia	Sydney	University of Sydney	n/a	Intermed	Institute for Study Abroad	n/a

© 2011 — Updates? Want to be in the next edition? Visit **www.mysecondcampus.com**

Massachusetts

DESTINATION	HOST INSTITUTION	PRGM SEASON	PRGM TYPE	INTERMEDIARY	HOUSING
Australia	Sydney	University of Technology	n/a	Intermed	Institute for Study Abroad	n/a
Australia	Wollongong	University of Wollongong	n/a	Intermed	Institute for Study Abroad	n/a
Austria	Salzburg	University of Salzburg	n/a	Intermed	American Institute for Foreign Study	n/a
Brazil	(Multiple choices)	SIT Study Abroad	n/a	Intermed	SIT Study Abroad	n/a
Canada	(Multiple choices)	Universite du Quebec	n/a	Dir	n/a	n/a
Canada	Montreal	Concordia University	n/a	Dir	n/a	n/a
Canada	Montreal	Ecole Polytechnique	n/a	Dir	n/a	n/a
Canada	Montreal	McGill University	n/a	Dir	n/a	n/a
Canada	Montreal	Universite de Montreal	n/a	Dir	n/a	n/a
Canada	Quebec City	Universite Laval	n/a	Dir	n/a	n/a
Canada	Sherbrooke	Bishop's University	n/a	Dir	n/a	n/a
Canada	Sherbrooke	Universite de Sherbrooke	n/a	Dir	n/a	n/a
Chile	Santiago	Multiple institutional choices	n/a	Intermed	Institute for Study Abroad	n/a
Chile	Santiago	Pontificia Universidad Catolica de Chile	n/a	Intermed	Institute for Study Abroad	n/a
Chile	Santiago	Universidad Adolfo Ibanez	n/a	Intermed	Institute for Study Abroad	n/a
Chile	Santiago	Universidad de Chile	n/a	Intermed	Institute for Study Abroad	n/a
Chile	Santiago	Universidad Diego Portales	n/a	Intermed	Institute for Study Abroad	n/a
Chile	Valparaiso	Pontificia Universidad Catolica de Valparaiso	n/a	Intermed	Institute for Study Abroad	n/a
Chile	Valparaiso	Universidad de Valparaiso	n/a	Intermed	Institute for Study Abroad	n/a
Chile	Valparaiso and Vina del Mar	Multiple institutional choices	n/a	Intermed	Institute for Study Abroad	n/a
Chile	Valparaiso and Vina del Mar	Universidad Tecnica Federico Santa Maria	n/a	Intermed	Institute for Study Abroad	n/a
China	Beijing	Beijing Center for Chinese Studies	n/a	USColl	Loyola University Chicago	n/a
Costa Rica	Heredia	Universidad Nacional	n/a	Intermed	Institute for Study Abroad	n/a
Costa Rica	Heredia	Universidad Nacional	n/a	Intermed	Institute for Study Abroad	n/a
Costa Rica	San Jose	Universidad de Costa Rica	n/a	Intermed	Institute for Study Abroad	n/a
Denmark	Copenhagen	Danish Institute for Study Abroad (DIS)	n/a	Intermed	Danish Institute for Study Abroad (DIS)	n/a
Ecuador	Quito	SIT Study Abroad	n/a	Intermed	SIT Study Abroad	n/a
Egypt	Cairo	American University in Cairo	n/a	Dir	n/a	n/a
England	Brighton	University of Sussex	n/a	USColl	Arcadia University	n/a
England	Cambridge	Cambridge University	n/a	Intermed	Institute for Study Abroad	n/a
England	Essex	University of Essex	n/a	USColl	Arcadia University	n/a
England	Glasgow	Glasgow School of Art	n/a	USColl	Arcadia University	n/a
England	Lancaster	Lancaster University	n/a	USColl	Arcadia University	n/a
England	Leeds	University of Leeds	n/a	Intermed	Academic Programs International	n/a
England	London	Birbeck College	Fall Spr	Self	n/a	PrivApt

Costs: Fall Costs: T&F: n/a, R&B: n/a, Ttl: Stonehill home comprehensive fees Spr Costs: T&F: n/a, R&B: n/a, Ttl: Stonehill home comprehensive fees

Massachusetts

DESTINATION	HOST INSTITUTION	PRGM SEASON	PRGM TYPE	INTERMEDIARY	HOUSING
England | London	City University	n/a	USColl	Arcadia University	n/a
England | London	Goldsmiths College	n/a	USColl	Arcadia University	n/a
England | London	King's College London	n/a	USColl	Arcadia University	n/a
England | London	London School of Economics and Political Science	n/a	USColl	Arcadia University	n/a
England | London	Middlesex University	n/a	USColl	Arcadia University	n/a
England | London	Queen Mary	n/a	USColl	Arcadia University	n/a
England | London	Richmond University	n/a	Intermed	American Institute for Foreign Study	n/a
England | London	Royal Holloway	n/a	Dir	n/a	n/a
England | London	University College London	n/a	USColl	Arcadia University	n/a
England | London	University of Greenwich	n/a	USColl	Arcadia University	n/a
England | London	University of Westminster	n/a	USColl	Arcadia University	n/a
England | Manchester	University of Manchester	n/a	USColl	Arcadia University	n/a
England | Nottingham	University of Nottingham	n/a	USColl	Arcadia University	n/a
England | Oxford	Oxford University	n/a	Intermed	Institute for Study Abroad	n/a
England | York	University of York	n/a	USColl	Arcadia University	n/a
France | Cannes	College International de Cannes	n/a	Intermed	American Institute for Foreign Study	n/a
France | Grenoble	Grenoble Ecole de Management	n/a	Intermed	Academic Programs International	n/a
France | Grenoble	Universite Stendhal – Grenoble III	n/a	Intermed	Academic Programs International	n/a
France | Paris	Institut Catholique de Paris	n/a	Intermed	Academic Programs International	n/a
France | Paris	Stone Hill College	Fall Spr	Self	n/a	HostFam
	Costs: Fall Costs: T&F: n/a, R&B: n/a, Ttl: Stonehill home comprehensive fees Spr Costs: T&F: n/a, R&B: n/a, Ttl: Stonehill home comprehensive fees				
France | Paris	Universite Paris – Sorbonne	n/a	Intermed	Academic Programs International	n/a
Germany | Bonn	University of Bonn	n/a	Dir	n/a	n/a
Germany | Heidelberg	University of Heidelberg	n/a	USColl	Heidelberg University	n/a
Ghana | (Multiple choices)	SIT Study Abroad	n/a	Intermed	SIT Study Abroad	n/a
Greece | Athens	Arcadia Center for Hellenic, Mediterranean, and Balkan Studies	n/a	USColl	Arcadia University	n/a
Greece | Athens	College Year in Athens	n/a	Intermed	College Year in Athens	n/a
India | (Multiple choices)	SIT Study Abroad	n/a	Intermed	SIT Study Abroad	n/a
Ireland | (Multiple choices)	University of Ulster	n/a	USColl	Arcadia University	n/a
Ireland | Ballyvaughn	Burren College of Art	n/a	USColl	Arcadia University	n/a
Ireland | Belfast	Queen's University	n/a	USColl	Arcadia University	n/a
Ireland | Cork	University College Cork	n/a	USColl	Arcadia University	n/a
Ireland | Dublin	Stone Hill College	Fall Spr	Self	n/a	PrivApt
	Costs: Fall Costs: T&F: n/a, R&B: n/a, Ttl: Stonehill home comprehensive fees Spr Costs: T&F: n/a, R&B: n/a, Ttl: Stonehill home comprehensive fees				

© 2011 — Updates? Want to be in the next edition? Visit **www.mysecondcampus.com**

Massachusetts

DESTINATION	HOST INSTITUTION	PRGM SEASON	PRGM TYPE	INTERMEDIARY	HOUSING
Ireland | Dublin	Trinity College Dublin	n/a	USColl	Arcadia University	n/a
Ireland | Dublin	University College Dublin (Quinn School of Business)	n/a	USColl	Arcadia University	n/a
Ireland | Dublin	University College Dublin (School of Arts)	n/a	USColl	Arcadia University	n/a
Ireland | Galway	National University of Ireland,	Fall Spr YrRound	Self	n/a	PrivApt
Ireland | Limerick	University of Limerick	n/a	USColl	Arcadia University	n/a
Ireland | Maynooth	National University of Ireland, Maynooth	n/a	USColl	Arcadia University	n/a
Italy | Florence	Scuola Lorenzo de' Medici	n/a	Intermed	Academic Programs International	n/a
Italy | Perugia	Umbra Institute	n/a	USColl	Arcadia University	n/a
Italy | Rome	John Cabot University	n/a	Intermed	Academic Programs International	n/a
Italy | Syracuse	Mediterranean Center for Arts and Sciences	n/a	Intermed	Academic Programs International	n/a
Japan | Tokyo	Sophia University	n/a	Intermed	Council on International Educational Exchange (CIEE)	n/a
Mexico | Guanajuato	Universidad de Guanajuato	n/a	Intermed	Council on International Educational Exchange (CIEE)	n/a
Mexico | Merida	Universidad Autonoma de Yucatan	n/a	Intermed	Institute for Study Abroad	n/a
Mexico | Merida	Universidad Autonoma de Yucatan	n/a	Intermed	Institute for Study Abroad	n/a
Mexico | Oaxaca	SIT Study Abroad	n/a	Intermed	SIT Study Abroad	n/a
Mexico and Peru | (Multiple)	Institute for Study Abroad	n/a	Intermed	Institute for Study Abroad	n/a
Morocco | Rabat	SIT Study Abroad	n/a	Intermed	SIT Study Abroad	n/a
Netherlands | Amsterdam	SIT Study Abroad	n/a	Intermed	SIT Study Abroad	n/a
New Zealand | Palmerston North	Massey University	n/a	Intermed	Institute for Study Abroad	n/a
New Zealand | Auckland	University of Auckland	n/a	Intermed	Institute for Study Abroad	n/a
New Zealand | Christchurch	University of Canterbury	n/a	Intermed	Institute for Study Abroad	n/a
New Zealand | Dunedin	University of Otago	n/a	Intermed	Institute for Study Abroad	n/a
New Zealand | Wellington	Victoria University of Wellington	n/a	Intermed	Institute for Study Abroad	n/a
Oman | Muscat	SIT Study Abroad	n/a	Intermed	SIT Study Abroad	n/a
Panama | Panama City	SIT Study Abroad	n/a	Intermed	SIT Study Abroad	n/a
Peru | Lima	Pontificia Universidad Catolica del Peru	n/a	Intermed	Institute for Study Abroad	n/a
Russia | St. Petersburg	St. Petersburg State Polytechnic University	n/a	Intermed	American Institute for Foreign Study	n/a
Scotland | Aberdeen	University of Aberdeen	n/a	USColl	Arcadia University	n/a
Scotland | Edinburgh	University of Edinburgh	n/a	USColl	Arcadia University	n/a
Scotland | Glasgow	University of Glasgow	n/a	Dir	n/a	n/a
Scotland | St. Andrews	University of St. Andrews	n/a	USColl	Arcadia University	n/a
Scotland | Stirling	University of Stirling	n/a	USColl	Arcadia University	n/a
South Africa | Cape Town	SIT Study Abroad	n/a	Intermed	SIT Study Abroad	n/a

© 2011 — Updates? Want to be in the next edition? Visit **www.mysecondcampus.com**

Massachusetts

DESTINATION	HOST INSTITUTION	PRGM SEASON	PRGM TYPE	INTERMEDIARY	HOUSING
South Africa | Cape Town	University of Cape Town	n/a	USColl	Arcadia University	n/a
South Africa | Stellenbosch	University of Stellenbosch	n/a	Intermed	American Institute for Foreign Study	n/a
South Korea | Seoul	Yonsei University	n/a	Intermed	Council on International Educational Exchange (CIEE)	n/a
Spain | Barcelona	University of Barcelona	n/a	Intermed	Academic Programs International	n/a
Spain | Granada	Granada Institute of International Studies	n/a	Intermed	Granada Institute of International Studies	n/a
Spain | Madrid	Stone Hill College	Fall Spr	Self	n/a	HostFam PrivApt
Costs: Fall Costs: T&F: n/a, R&B: n/a, Ttl: Stonehill home comprehensive fees Spr Costs: T&F: n/a, R&B: n/a, Ttl: Stonehill home comprehensive fees					
Spain | Madrid	University Complutense of Madrid	n/a	Intermed	Academic Programs International	n/a
Spain | Salamanca	University of Salamanca	n/a	Intermed	Academic Programs International	n/a
Spain | Seville	University of Seville or Pablo de Olavide University	n/a	Intermed	Academic Programs International	n/a
Spain | Toledo	Fundacion Jose Ortega y Gasset	n/a	USColl	Arcadia University	n/a
Switzerland | Geneva	SIT Study Abroad	n/a	Intermed	SIT Study Abroad	n/a
Tanzania | (Multiple choices)	SIT Study Abroad	n/a	Intermed	SIT Study Abroad	n/a
United States | Portland (OR)	University of Portland	n/a	Bilat	n/a	n/a
Vietnam | (Multiple)	SIT Study Abroad	n/a	Intermed	SIT Study Abroad	n/a
Wales | Bangor	Bangor University	n/a	USColl	Arcadia University	n/a

Suffolk University

Youmna Hinnawi
Director
Center for International Education
Study Abroad Programs
8 Ashburton Place
Boston, MA 02108

yhinnawi@suffolk.edu
617.573.8072
http://www.suffolk.edu/33115.html

DESTINATION	HOST INSTITUTION	PRGM SEASON	PRGM TYPE	INTERMEDIARY	HOUSING
Argentina | Buenos Aires	Lincoln University College	n/a	Dir	n/a	n/a
Australia | Melbourne	La Trobe University	n/a	Dir	Center for International Studies	n/a
Australia | Newcastle	Newcastle University	n/a	Dir	Center for International Studies	n/a
Australia | Robina	Bond University	n/a	Dir	Center for International Studies	n/a
Australia | Sydney	Macquarie University	n/a	Dir	Center for International Studies	n/a
Austria | Vienna	Austria-Illinois Exchange Program (University of Illinois, Urbana-Champaign)	n/a	USColl	Austria-Illinois Exchange Program (University of Illinois, Urbana-Champaign)	n/a
China | Shanghai	Shanghai Normal University	Sum	Self	n/a	n/a

© 2011 — Updates? Want to be in the next edition? Visit **www.mysecondcampus.com**

Massachusetts

DESTINATION	HOST INSTITUTION	PRGM SEASON	PRGM TYPE	INTERMEDIARY	HOUSING
Costa Rica | San Jose	International Center for Development Studies	n/a	Intermed	International Center for Development Studies	n/a
Czech Republic | Prague	Charles University	Sum	Self	n/a	n/a
Czech Republic | Prague	Charles University	n/a	Dir	n/a	n/a
Czech Republic and Poland | Unknown	Unknown	Sum	Self	n/a	n/a
Denmark | Aalborg	Aalborg University	n/a	Dir	n/a	n/a
Denmark | Aarhus	Aarhus School of Business	n/a	Dir	n/a	n/a
Denmark | Copenhagen	Copenhagen Business School	n/a	Dir	n/a	n/a
England | London	European Business School (Regent's College)	n/a	Dir	n/a	n/a
England | London	Regent's American College (Regent's College)	n/a	Dir	n/a	n/a
France | Marseille	EUROMED Marseille Ecole de Management	n/a	Dir	n/a	n/a
France | Marseille	Institute Universitaire de Technologie de Marseilles	n/a	Dir	n/a	n/a
France | Paris	Ecole Superieure de Gestion (Paris Graduate School of Management)	n/a	Dir	n/a	n/a
France | Paris	Pole Universitaire Leonard de Vinci	n/a	Dir	n/a	n/a
France | Paris	University Paris-Sorbonne (Paris IV)	n/a	Dir	n/a	n/a
Germany | Giessen	Justus Liebig University	n/a	Dir	n/a	n/a
Greece | Thessaloniki	American College of Thessaloniki	n/a	Dir	n/a	n/a
Ireland | Cork	University College Cork	n/a	Dir	n/a	n/a
Italy | (Multiple)	Lorenzo de Medici	Sum	Self	n/a	n/a
Italy | (Multiple)	Scuola Lorenzo de Medici	n/a	Intermed	Scuola Lorenzo de Medici	n/a
Italy | Florence	Florence University of the Arts	n/a	Intermed	Study Abroad Italy (SAI)	n/a
Italy | Florence	Studio Art Centers International (SACI)	n/a	Intermed	Studio Art Centers International (SACI)	n/a
Italy | Rome	John Cabot University	n/a	Intermed	Study Abroad Italy (SAI)	n/a
Italy | Syracuse	Mediterranean Center for Arts and Sciences	n/a	Intermed	Study Abroad Italy (SAI)	n/a
Italy | Unknown	Unknown	Sum	Self	n/a	n/a
Japan | Osaka	Kansai Gadai University	n/a	Dir	n/a	n/a
Japan | Tokyo	Sophia University	n/a	Dir	n/a	n/a
Mexico | Mexico City	Tecnologico de Monterrey	n/a	Dir	n/a	n/a
Mexico | Mexico City	Universidad Iberoamericana	n/a	Dir	n/a	n/a
Monaco | Monte Carlo	International University of Monaco	n/a	Dir	n/a	n/a
New Zealand | Auckland	University of Auckland	n/a	Intermed	Center for International Studies	n/a
New Zealand | Wellington	Victoria University	n/a	Intermed	Center for International Studies	n/a

Massachusetts

DESTINATION	HOST INSTITUTION	PRGM SEASON	PRGM TYPE	INTERMEDIARY	HOUSING
Norway | Aalesund	Aalesund University College	n/a	Dir	n/a	n/a
Senegal | Dakar	Suffolk University (Dakar Campus)	Fall Spr YrRound	Self	n/a	HostFam
South Korea | Seoul	Yonsei University	n/a	Dir	n/a	n/a
Spain | Madrid	Suffolk University (Madrid Campus)	Sum Fall Spr YrRound	Self	n/a	HostFam CollRes PrivApt
	Costs: Sum Costs: T&F: n/a, R&B: n/a, Ttl: $7,137 Fall Costs: T&F: n/a, R&B: n/a, Ttl: $16,600 Spr Costs: T&F: n/a, R&B: n/a, Ttl: $16,600 YrRound Costs: T&F: n/a, R&B: n/a, Ttl: $33,200				
Sweden | Stockholm	Stockholm University School of Business	n/a	Dir	n/a	n/a
Taiwan | Taipei	Tamkang University	n/a	Dir	n/a	n/a
Turkey | Istanbul	Yeditepe University	n/a	Dir	n/a	n/a
Vietnam | Ho Chi Minh City	Hoa Sen University	n/a	Dir	n/a	n/a

The New England Institute of Art

Amy Sanford
10 Brookline Place West
Brookline, MA 02445

asanford@aii.edu
617.582.4495

DESTINATION	HOST INSTITUTION	PRGM SEASON	PRGM TYPE	INTERMEDIARY	HOUSING
[Country Unspecified] | [City Unspecified]	n/a	n/a	n/a	n/a	n/a

Tufts University

Sheila Bayne
Director, Programs Abroad
Tufts Office of Programs Abroad
Dowling Hall
Medford, MA 02155

sheila.bayne@tufts.edu
617.627.2000
http://uss.tufts.edu/studyabroad/

DESTINATION	HOST INSTITUTION	PRGM SEASON	PRGM TYPE	INTERMEDIARY	HOUSING
Argentina | Buenos Aires	IES Abroad	n/a	Intermed	IES Abroad	n/a
Argentina | Buenos Aires	Multiple institutional choices	n/a	Intermed	Council on International Educational Exchange (CIEE)	n/a
Argentina | Buenos Aires	Multiple institutional choices	n/a	Intermed	Institute for Study Abroad	n/a
Argentina | Mendoza	Multiple institutional choices	n/a	Intermed	Institute for Study Abroad	n/a
Australia | (Multiple choices)	IES Abroad	n/a	Intermed	IES Abroad	n/a
Australia | (Multiple choices)	Multiple institutional choices	n/a	USColl	Arcadia University	n/a
Australia | (Multiple choices)	Multiple institutional choices	n/a	Intermed	AustraLearn	PrivApt
Australia | (Multiple choices)	Multiple institutional choices	n/a	Intermed	Institute for Study Abroad	n/a
Australia | (Multiple choices)	Multiple institutional choices	n/a	Intermed	Council on International Educational Exchange (CIEE)	n/a
Australia | (Multiple choices)	SIT Study Abroad	n/a	Intermed	SIT Study Abroad	n/a
Australia | Yungaburra	Center for Rainforest Studies	n/a	Intermed	School for Field Studies	n/a
Austria | Vienna	IES Abroad Vienna Center	n/a	Intermed	IES Abroad	n/a
Belgium | Brussels	American University	n/a	USColl	American University	n/a
Bolivia | Cochabamba	SIT Study Abroad	n/a	Intermed	SIT Study Abroad	n/a

Massachusetts

DESTINATION	HOST INSTITUTION	PRGM SEASON	PRGM TYPE	INTERMEDIARY	HOUSING
Botswana | Gaborone	SIT Study Abroad	n/a	Intermed	SIT Study Abroad	n/a
Brazil | Campinas	Campinas State University	n/a	USColl	SUNY Albany	n/a
Brazil | Fortaleza	Instituto Brasil/Estados Unidos/Ceara	n/a	Intermed	SIT Study Abroad	n/a
Brazil | Sao Paulo	Pontificia Universidad Catolica de Sao Paulo or Escola de Administracao de Empresas de Sao Paulo da Fundacao Getulio Vargas	n/a	Intermed	Council on International Educational Exchange (CIEE)	n/a
Cameroon | Yaounde	SIT Study Abroad	n/a	Intermed	SIT Study Abroad	n/a
Chile | (Multiple choices)	Multiple institutional choices	n/a	Intermed	Institute for Study Abroad	n/a
Chile | (Multiple choices)	Multiple institutional choices	n/a	Intermed	Council on International Educational Exchange (CIEE)	n/a
Chile | (Multiple)	SIT Study Abroad	n/a	Intermed	SIT Study Abroad	n/a
Chile | Santiago	IES Abroad Santiago Center	n/a	Intermed	IES Abroad	n/a
Chile | Santiago	University of Chile	Fall YrRound	Self	n/a	HostFam
Costs: Fall Costs: T&F: n/a, R&B: n/a, Ttl: $25,898 YrRound Costs: T&F: n/a, R&B: n/a, Ttl: $51,796					
Chile | Valparaiso	Multiple institutional choices	n/a	USColl	Middlebury College	n/a
China | Beijing	Associated Colleges in China (Hamilton College)	n/a	USColl	Associated Colleges in China (Hamilton College)	n/a
China | Beijing	Capital Normal University	n/a	USColl	SUNY Oswego	n/a
China | Beijing	CET Academic Programs	n/a	Intermed	CET Academic Programs	n/a
China | Beijing	IES Abroad Beijing Center	n/a	Intermed	IES Abroad	n/a
China | Beijing	Peking University or Minzu University of China	n/a	Intermed	Council on International Educational Exchange (CIEE)	n/a
China | Hangzhou	Zhejiang University	Fall	Self	n/a	CollRes
Costs: Fall Costs: T&F: n/a, R&B: n/a, Ttl: $25,898					
China | Harbin	CET Academic Programs	n/a	Intermed	CET Academic Programs	n/a
China | Hong Kong	Chinese University of Hong Kong	n/a	Dir	n/a	n/a
China | Hong Kong	University of Hong Kong	Spr	Self	n/a	CollRes
Costs: Spr Costs: T&F: n/a, R&B: n/a, Ttl: $25,898					
China | Nanjing	Nanjing University	n/a	Intermed	Council on International Educational Exchange (CIEE)	n/a
Costa Rica | [City Unspecified]	Organization for Tropical Studies	n/a	Intermed	Organization for Tropical Studies	n/a
Costa Rica | Atenas	SFS Center for Sustainable Development Studies	n/a	Intermed	School for Field Studies	n/a
Costa Rica | Heredia	Universidad Nacional	n/a	Intermed	Institute for Study Abroad	n/a
Costa Rica | San Jose	Universidad de Costa Rica	n/a	Intermed	Institute for Study Abroad	n/a
Costa Rica | San Jose	Universidad de Costa Rica	n/a	USColl	University of Kansas	n/a
Costa Rica | San Jose	Universidad de Costa Rica	n/a	USColl	SUNY Albany	n/a
Czech Republic | Prague	CET Academic Programs	n/a	Intermed	CET Academic Programs	n/a
Czech Republic | Prague	Charles University or Prague Film and Television School of the Academy of the Performing Arts	n/a	Intermed	Council on International Educational Exchange (CIEE)	n/a

© 2011 — Updates? Want to be in the next edition? Visit **www.mysecondcampus.com**

Massachusetts

DESTINATION	HOST INSTITUTION	PRGM SEASON	PRGM TYPE	INTERMEDIARY	HOUSING
Czech Republic | Prague	NYU Center	n/a	USColl	New York University	n/a
Czech Republic | Prague	SIT Study Abroad	n/a	Intermed	SIT Study Abroad	n/a
Denmark | Copenhagen	Danish Institute for Study Abroad	n/a	Intermed	Danish Institute for Study Abroad	n/a
Dominican Republic | (Multiple choices)	Multiple institutional choices	n/a	Intermed	Council on International Educational Exchange (CIEE)	n/a
Ecuador | Quito	SIT Study Abroad	n/a	Intermed	SIT Study Abroad	n/a
Egypt | Cairo	American University in Cairo	n/a	Dir	n/a	n/a
England | (Multiple choices)	Multiple institutional choices	n/a	Intermed	Institute for Study Abroad	n/a
England | (Multiple choices)	Multiple institutional choices	n/a	USColl	Arcadia University	n/a
England | London	British American Drama Academy	n/a	USColl	Skidmore College	n/a
England | London	British American Drama Academy	n/a	USColl	Sarah Lawrence College	n/a
England | London	London School of Economics and Political Science	n/a	Dir	n/a	n/a
England | London	Multiple institutional choices	n/a	Intermed	Interstudy	n/a
England | London	Royal Academy of Dramatic Art	n/a	USColl	New York University	n/a
England | London	University College London or School of Oriental and African Studies	YrRound	Self	n/a	CollRes
	Costs: YrRound Costs: T&F: n/a, R&B: n/a, Ttl: $51,796				
England | Oxford	Oxford University (Wadham College)	n/a	USColl	Sarah Lawrence College	n/a
England | Oxford	Oxford University (Pembroke College)	YrRound	Self	n/a	CollRes
	Costs: YrRound Costs: T&F: n/a, R&B: n/a, Ttl: $51,796				
France | Aix-en-Provence	Institute for American Universities	n/a	Intermed	Institute for American Universities	n/a
France | Aix-en-Provence	University of Provence (Aix-Marseille I)	n/a	USColl	Wellesley College	n/a
France | Grenoble	Universite de Grenoble	n/a	USColl	Swarthmore College	n/a
France | Nantes	IES Abroad Nantes Center	n/a	Intermed	IES Abroad	n/a
France | Paris	IES Abroad Paris French Studies Center	n/a	Intermed	IES Abroad	n/a
France | Paris	Le Centre Madeleine	n/a	USColl	Middlebury College	n/a
France | Paris	Multiple institutional choices	n/a	USColl	Columbia University	n/a
France | Paris	Multiple institutional choices	n/a	USColl	Sarah Lawrence College	n/a
France | Paris	Multiple institutional choices	n/a	USColl	Sweet Briar College	n/a
France | Paris	Multiple institutional choices	n/a	USColl	Vassar College and Wesleyan University	n/a
France | Paris	Multiple institutional choices	n/a	Intermed	Center for University Programs Abroad (CUPA)	n/a
France | Paris	Multiple institutional choices	Fall Spr YrRound	Self	n/a	HostFam
	Costs: Fall Costs: T&F: n/a, R&B: n/a, Ttl: $25,898 Spr Costs: T&F: n/a, R&B: n/a, Ttl: $25,898 YrRound Costs: T&F: n/a, R&B: n/a, Ttl: $51,796				

© 2011 — Updates? Want to be in the next edition? Visit **www.mysecondcampus.com**

Massachusetts

DESTINATION	HOST INSTITUTION	PRGM SEASON	PRGM TYPE	INTERMEDIARY	HOUSING
France | Paris	NYU Center	n/a	USColl	New York University	n/a
France | Toulouse	University of Toulouse	n/a	USColl	Dickinson College	n/a
France | Tours	University of Tours - Universite Francois Rabelais	n/a	USColl	Rutgers University	n/a
France | Tours	University of Tours - Universite Francois Rabelais	n/a	USColl	Davidson College	n/a
Germany | Berlin	IES Abroad Berlin Center	n/a	Intermed	IES Abroad	n/a
Germany | Freiburg	IES Abroad Freiburg Center	n/a	Intermed	IES Abroad	n/a
Germany | Hamburg	Universitat Hamburg or Technische Universitat Hamburg-Harburg	n/a	USColl	Smith College	n/a
Germany | Konstanz	University of Konstanz	n/a	USColl	Rutgers University	n/a
Germany | Mainz	Johannes-Gutenberg Universitat	n/a	USColl	Middlebury College	n/a
Germany | Munich	Ludwig-Maximilians-Universitat Munchen	n/a	USColl	Wayne State University	n/a
Germany | Tubingen	Eberhard-Karls University	Sum YrRound	Self	n/a	CollRes
	Costs: Sum Costs: T&F: n/a, R&B: n/a, Ttl: $25,898 YrRound Costs: T&F: n/a, R&B: n/a, Ttl: $51,796				
Ghana | Accra	SIT Study Abroad	n/a	Intermed	SIT Study Abroad	n/a
Ghana | Accra	University of Ghana	Fall	Self	n/a	Other
	Costs: Fall Costs: T&F: n/a, R&B: n/a, Ttl: $25,898				
Ghana | Cape Coast	SIT Study Abroad	n/a	Intermed	SIT Study Abroad	n/a
Greece | Athens	College Year in Athens	n/a	Intermed	College Year in Athens	n/a
Greece | Athens	The Arcadia Center for Hellenic, Mediterranean and Balkan Studies	n/a	USColl	Arcadia University	n/a
Hungary | Budapest	Corvinus University of Budapest	n/a	Intermed	Council on International Educational Exchange (CIEE)	n/a
Hungary | Budapest	Technical University of Budapest, College International	n/a	Intermed	Budapest Semesters in Mathematics	n/a
India | (Multiple choices)	Multiple institutional choices	n/a	USColl	University of Wisconsin	n/a
India | Bodh Gaya	Antioch University	n/a	USColl	Antioch University	n/a
India | Jaipur	SIT Study Abroad	n/a	Intermed	SIT Study Abroad	n/a
Indonesia | Bedulu	SIT Study Abroad	n/a	Intermed	SIT Study Abroad	n/a
Ireland | (Multiple choices)	Multiple institutional choices	n/a	USColl	Arcadia University	n/a
Ireland | (Multiple choices)	Multiple institutional choices	n/a	Intermed	Institute for Study Abroad	n/a
Ireland | (Multiple choices)	Multiple institutional choices	n/a	Intermed	Interstudy	n/a
Ireland | Dublin	IES Abroad Dublin Center	n/a	Intermed	IES Abroad	n/a
Israel | Beer Sheba	Ben Gurion University	n/a	Dir	n/a	n/a
Israel | Haifa	University of Haifa	n/a	Dir	n/a	n/a
Israel | Jerusalem	Hebrew University	n/a	Dir	n/a	n/a
Israel | Tel Aviv	Tel Aviv University	n/a	Dir	n/a	n/a
Italy | Bologna	K. Robert Nilsson Center for European Studies	n/a	USColl	Dickinson College	n/a
Italy | Bologna	Universita di Bologna	n/a	Consrtm	Bologna Consortial Studies Program (Indiana University)	n/a

© 2011 — Updates? Want to be in the next edition? Visit **www.mysecondcampus.com**

Massachusetts

DESTINATION	HOST INSTITUTION	PRGM SEASON	PRGM TYPE	INTERMEDIARY	HOUSING
Italy | Bologna	Universita di Bologna	n/a	Consrtm	Eastern College Consortium	n/a
Italy | Bologna	University of Bologna	n/a	USColl	Brown University	n/a
Italy | Ferrara	Universita degli Studi di Ferrara	n/a	USColl	Middlebury College	n/a
Italy | Florence	Middlebury Sede	n/a	USColl	Middlebury College	n/a
Italy | Florence	Sarah Lawrence College	n/a	USColl	Sarah Lawrence College	n/a
Italy | Florence	Smith College	n/a	USColl	Smith College	n/a
Italy | Florence	SU Florence Center	n/a	USColl	Syracuse University	n/a
Italy | Florence	Universita degli Studi di Firenze	n/a	USColl	Rutgers University	n/a
Italy | Milan	IES Abroad Milan Center	n/a	Intermed	IES Abroad	n/a
Italy | Padova	University of Padova	n/a	USColl	Boston University	n/a
Italy | Perugia	Umbra Institute	n/a	USColl	Arcadia University	n/a
Italy | Rome	Temple University	n/a	USColl	Temple University	n/a
Italy | Rome	Trinity College Rome Campus	n/a	USColl	Trinity College	n/a
Italy | Rome	University of Rome	n/a	USColl	SUNY Stony Brook	n/a
Italy | Siena	CET Academic Programs	n/a	Intermed	CET Academic Programs	n/a
Italy | Siena	Universita per Stranieri Siena	n/a	USColl	University of Massachusetts, Amherst	n/a
Italy | Urbino	University of Urbino	n/a	USColl	SUNY New Paltz	n/a
Italy | Venice	Scuola Internazionale di Grafica	n/a	USColl	Boston University	n/a
Japan | Kanazawa	Kanazawa University	YrRound	Self	n/a	PrivApt
	Costs: YrRound Costs: T&F: n/a, R&B: n/a, Ttl: $51,796				
Japan | Kyoto	Associated Kyoto Program (Doshisha University)	n/a	Intermed	Associated Kyoto Program (Doshisha University)	n/a
Japan | Kyoto	Kyoto Consortium for Japanese Studies (Columbia University)	n/a	Consrtm	Kyoto Consortium for Japanese Studies (Columbia University)	n/a
Japan | Nagoya	Nanzan University	n/a	USColl	IES Abroad	n/a
Japan | Nishinomiya	Kwansei Gakuin University	n/a	USColl	Southern Methodist University	n/a
Japan | Osaka	Kansai Gadai University	n/a	Dir	n/a	n/a
Japan | Tokyo	IES Abroad Tokyo Center	n/a	USColl	IES Abroad	n/a
Japan | Tokyo	International Christian University	n/a	Dir	n/a	n/a
Japan | Tokyo	Waseda University	n/a	USColl	Earlham College	n/a
Kenya | Mombasa	SIT Study Abroad	n/a	Intermed	SIT Study Abroad	n/a
Kenya | Nairobi	Center for Wildlife Management Studies	n/a	Intermed	School for Field Studies	n/a
Kenya | Nairobi	SIT Study Abroad	n/a	Intermed	SIT Study Abroad	n/a
Kenya | Nairobi	St. Lawrence University	n/a	USColl	St. Lawrence University	n/a
Kenya | Nairobi	University of Nairobi	n/a	USColl	Kalamazoo College	n/a
Madagascar | Antananarivo	SIT Study Abroad	n/a	Intermed	SIT Study Abroad	n/a
Madagascar | Fort Dauphin	SIT Study Abroad	n/a	Intermed	SIT Study Abroad	n/a
Mexico | Baja	Center for Coastal Studies	n/a	Intermed	School for Field Studies	n/a
Mexico | Merida	Universidad Autonoma de Yucatan	n/a	USColl	Rutgers University	n/a

© 2011 — Updates? Want to be in the next edition? Visit **www.mysecondcampus.com**

Massachusetts

DESTINATION	HOST INSTITUTION	PRGM SEASON	PRGM TYPE	INTERMEDIARY	HOUSING
Mexico | Mexico City	Universidad Iberoamericana	n/a	Intermed	n/a	n/a
Mexico | Oaxaca	SIT Study Abroad	n/a	Intermed	SIT Study Abroad	n/a
Morocco | Rabat	SIT Study Abroad	n/a	Intermed	SIT Study Abroad	n/a
Nepal | Kathmandu	SIT Study Abroad	n/a	Intermed	SIT Study Abroad	n/a
Netherlands | Maastricht	University of Maastricht	n/a	Dir	n/a	n/a
New Zealand | (Multiple choices)	Multiple institutional choices	n/a	USColl	Arcadia University	n/a
New Zealand | (Multiple choices)	Multiple institutional choices	n/a	Intermed	Institute for Study Abroad	n/a
Niger | Niamey	Universite Abdou Moumouni	n/a	USColl	Boston University	n/a
Russia | (Multiple choices)	Multiple institutional choices	n/a	USColl	Middlebury College	n/a
Russia | (Multiple choices)	Multiple institutional choices	n/a	Intermed	American Councils Study Abroad Programs	n/a
Russia | St. Petersburg	St. Petersburg State University	n/a	Intermed	Council on International Educational Exchange (CIEE)	n/a
Scotland | (Multiple choices)	Multiple institutional choices	n/a	Intermed	Institute for Study Abroad	n/a
Scotland | (Multiple choices)	Multiple institutional choices	n/a	USColl	Arcadia University	n/a
Scotland | St. Andrews	University of St. Andrews	n/a	Intermed	Interstudy	n/a
Senegal | Dakar	Universite Cheikh Anta Diop	n/a	USColl	Kalamazoo College	n/a
South Africa | (Multiple choices)	Multiple institutional choices	n/a	Intermed	Interstudy	n/a
South Africa | Durban	SIT Study Abroad	n/a	Intermed	SIT Study Abroad	n/a
South Africa | Kruger National Park	Organization for Tropical Studies	n/a	Intermed	Organization for Tropical Studies	n/a
South Korea | Seoul	Yonsei University	n/a	Dir	n/a	n/a
Spain | (Multiple choices)	Multiple institutional choices	n/a	Intermed	Council on International Educational Exchange (CIEE)	n/a
Spain | Alcala	University of Alcala	Fall Spr YrRound	Self	n/a	HostFam
	Costs: Fall Costs: T&F: n/a, R&B: n/a, Ttl: $25,898 Spr Costs: T&F: n/a, R&B: n/a, Ttl: $25,898 YrRound Costs: T&F: n/a, R&B: n/a, Ttl: $51,796				
Spain | Barcelona	BCA Study Abroad	n/a	Intermed	BCA Study Abroad	n/a
Spain | Barcelona	Universitat de Barcelona	n/a	USColl	Knox College	n/a
Spain | Madrid	Autonomous University of Madrid	Spr YrRound	Self	n/a	HostFam
	Costs: Spr Costs: T&F: n/a, R&B: n/a, Ttl: $25,898 YrRound Costs: T&F: n/a, R&B: n/a, Ttl: $51,796				
Spain | Madrid	Centro Universitario de Estudios Hispanicos de Hamilton College	n/a	USColl	Hamilton College	n/a
Spain | Madrid	IES Abroad Madrid Center	n/a	Intermed	IES Abroad	n/a
Spain | Madrid	Instituto Internacional	n/a	USColl	SUNY Albany	n/a
Spain | Madrid	New York University	n/a	USColl	New York University	n/a
Spain | Madrid	Sede Prim	n/a	USColl	Middlebury College	n/a
Spain | Madrid	SU Center in Madrid	n/a	USColl	Syracuse University	n/a
Spain | Salamanca	IES Abroad Salamanca Center	n/a	Intermed	IES Abroad	n/a
Spain | Seville	Universidad de Sevilla	n/a	USColl	Sweet Briar College	n/a
Sweden | Stockholm	Stockholm University	n/a	Consrtm	Swedish Program	n/a
Switzerland | Fribourg	University of Fribourg	n/a	Intermed	American College Program	n/a
Switzerland | Geneva	John Knox International Centre	n/a	USColl	Kent State University	n/a

Massachusetts

DESTINATION	HOST INSTITUTION	PRGM SEASON	PRGM TYPE	INTERMEDIARY	HOUSING
Switzerland | Geneva	SIT Study Abroad	n/a	Intermed	SIT Study Abroad	n/a
Switzerland | Geneva	Universite de Geneve	n/a	USColl	Smith College	n/a
Taiwan | Taichung	Tunghai University	n/a	USColl	University of Massachusetts, Amherst	n/a
Taiwan | Taipei	National Chengchi University	n/a	Intermed	Council on International Educational Exchange (CIEE)	n/a
Taiwan | Taipei	Taipei Language Institute	n/a	Intermed	Taipei Language Institute	n/a
Tanzania | (Multiple)	SIT Study Abroad	n/a	Intermed	SIT Study Abroad	n/a
Thailand | Khon Kaen	Khon Kaen University	n/a	Intermed	Council on International Educational Exchange (CIEE)	n/a
Turks and Caicos | South Caicos	Center for Marine Resource Management Studies	n/a	Intermed	School for Field Studies	n/a
United States | Atlanta (GA)	Spelman College	n/a	Dir	n/a	n/a
United States | Philadelphia (PA)	Swarthmore College	n/a	Dir	n/a	n/a
United States | Washington (DC)	American University	n/a	Dir	n/a	n/a
Vietnam | (Multiple choices)	SIT Study Abroad	n/a	Intermed	SIT Study Abroad	n/a
Wales | (Multiple choices)	Multiple institutional choices	n/a	USColl	Arcadia University	n/a
Wales | (Multiple choices)	Multiple institutional choices	n/a	Intermed	Institute for Study Abroad	n/a
Wales | Swansea	Swansea	n/a	Intermed	Interstudy	n/a

University of Massachusetts Amherst

Erika L. Schluntz
Director of Education Abroad
William S. Clark International Center
International Programs Office
467 Hills South, 4th Floor
Amherst, MA 01003

schluntz@ipo.umass.edu
413.545.2710
http://www.umass.edu/ipo/

Argentina | Buenos Aires	IES Abroad Buenos Aires Center	Fall Spr YrRound	Intermed	IES Abroad	n/a
Argentina | Buenos Aires	Multiple institutional choices	Fall Spr YrRound	Intermed	Council on International Educational Exchange (CIEE)	n/a
Argentina | Buenos Aires	Multiple institutional choices	Fall Spr YrRound	Intermed	Institute for Study Abroad	n/a
Argentina | Buenos Aires	SIT Study Abroad	Fall Spr	Intermed	SIT Study Abroad	n/a
Argentina | Buenos Aires	Universidad de Belgrano	Fall Spr	Intermed	AmeriSpan Study Abroad	n/a
Argentina | Buenos Aires	Universidad Torcuato di Tella or University of Belgrano	Fall Spr YrRound	Intermed	Academic Programs International	n/a
Argentina | Buenos Aires	University of Belgrano	Fall Spr YrRound	Intermed	International Studies Abroad	n/a
Australia | Adelaide	University of Adelaide	Fall Spr YrRound	Bilat	n/a	n/a
Australia | Brisbane	Multiple institutional choices	n/a	Intermed	Study Australia	n/a
Australia | Brisbane	University of Queensland	Fall Spr YrRound	Intermed	AustraLearn	n/a
Australia | Brisbane	University of Queensland	Fall Spr YrRound	Bilat	n/a	n/a
Australia | Byron Bay	SIT Study Abroad	Fall Spr	Intermed	SIT Study Abroad	n/a
Australia | Cairns	James Cook University	Fall Spr YrRound	Intermed	AustraLearn	n/a
Australia | Cairns	James Cook University	n/a	Intermed	Study Australia	n/a
Australia | Cairns	SIT Study Abroad	Fall Spr	Intermed	SIT Study Abroad	n/a

Massachusetts

DESTINATION	HOST INSTITUTION	PRGM SEASON	PRGM TYPE	INTERMEDIARY	HOUSING
Australia | Canberra	Multiple institutional choices	Sum Fall Spr	Intermed	AustraLearn	n/a
Australia | Gold Coast	Bond University or Griffith University	n/a	Intermed	AustraLearn	n/a
Australia | Gold Coast	Bond University or Griffith University	n/a	Intermed	Study Australia	n/a
Australia | Lismore	Southern Cross University	Fall Spr YrRound	Bilat	n/a	n/a
Australia | Melbourne	Deakin University: Burwood Campus	Fall Spr YrRound	Bilat	n/a	n/a
Australia | Melbourne	Multiple institutional choices	Fall Spr YrRound	Intermed	AustraLearn	n/a
Australia | Melbourne	Multiple institutional choices	n/a	Intermed	Study Australia	n/a
Australia | Melbourne	Swinburne University of Technology or La Trobe University	Sum Fall Spr YrRound	Intermed	Center for International Studies (CIS)	n/a
Australia | Newcastle	University of Newcastle	n/a	Intermed	AustraLearn	n/a
Australia | Newcastle	University of Newcastle	Sum Fall Spr YrRound	Intermed	Center for International Studies (CIS)	n/a
Australia | Perth	Multiple institutional choices	n/a	Intermed	AustraLearn	n/a
Australia | Perth	Multiple institutional choices	n/a	Intermed	Study Australia	n/a
Australia | Perth	Murdoch University	Sum Fall Spr YrRound	Intermed	Center for International Studies (CIS)	n/a
Australia | Sydney	CAPA Sydney Center	Sum Fall Spr	Intermed	CAPA International Education	n/a
Australia | Sydney	Macquarie University	Sum Fall Spr YrRound	Intermed	Center for International Studies (CIS)	n/a
Australia | Sydney	Multiple institutional choices	n/a	Intermed	AustraLearn	n/a
Australia | Sydney	Multiple institutional choices	n/a	Intermed	Study Australia	n/a
Australia | Toowoomba	University of Southern Queensland	Sum Fall Spr YrRound	Intermed	Center for International Studies (CIS)	n/a
Australia | Townsville	James Cook University	Fall Spr YrRound	Intermed	AustraLearn	n/a
Australia | Townsville	James Cook University	n/a	Intermed	Study Australia	n/a
Australia | Wollongong	University of Wollongong	Fall Spr YrRound	Bilat	n/a	n/a
Australia | Wollongong	University of Wollongong	n/a	Intermed	Study Australia	n/a
Australia | Yungaburra	Center for Rainforest Studies (School for Field Studies)	Sum Fall Spr	Intermed	School for Field Studies	n/a
Bolivia | Cochabamba	SIT Study Abroad	Fall Spr	Intermed	SIT Study Abroad	n/a
Botswana | Gaborone	SIT Study Abroad	Fall Spr	Intermed	SIT Study Abroad	n/a
Brazil | Belem	SIT Study Abroad	Fall Spr	Intermed	SIT Study Abroad	n/a
Brazil | Curitiba	Universidade Federal do Parana	Fall Spr YrRound	Bilat	n/a	n/a
Brazil | Fortaleza	SIT Study Abroad	Fall Spr	Intermed	SIT Study Abroad	n/a
Brazil | Rio de Janeiro	Pontificia Universidade Catolica do Rio de Janeiro	Fall Spr YrRound	Bilat	n/a	n/a
Brazil | Salvador	SIT Study Abroad	Fall Spr	Intermed	SIT Study Abroad	n/a
Brazil | Salvador	Universidade Catolica do Salvador or Universidade Federal da Bahia	Fall Spr YrRound	Intermed	Council on International Educational Exchange (CIEE)	n/a
Cameroon | Yaounde	SIT Study Abroad	Fall Spr	Intermed	SIT Study Abroad	n/a

Massachusetts

DESTINATION	HOST INSTITUTION	PRGM SEASON	PRGM TYPE	INTERMEDIARY	HOUSING
Canada | Abitibi-Temiscamingue	Universite du Quebec	Fall Spr YrRound	Bilat	n/a	n/a
Canada | Chicoutimi	Universite du Quebec	Fall Spr YrRound	Bilat	n/a	n/a
Canada | Lennoxville	Bishop's University	Fall Spr YrRound	Bilat	n/a	n/a
Canada | Montreal	Concordia University	Fall Spr YrRound	Bilat	n/a	n/a
Canada | Montreal	Ecole Polytechnique-Montreal	Fall Spr YrRound	Bilat	n/a	n/a
Canada | Montreal	McGill University	Fall Spr YrRound	Bilat	n/a	n/a
Canada | Montreal	Universite de Montreal	Fall Spr YrRound	Bilat	n/a	n/a
Canada | Montreal	Universite du Quebec	Fall Spr YrRound	Bilat	n/a	n/a
Canada | Outaouais	Universite du Quebec	Fall Spr YrRound	Bilat	n/a	n/a
Canada | Quebec City	Universite Laval	Fall Spr YrRound	Bilat	n/a	n/a
Canada | Rimouski	Universite du Quebec	Fall Spr YrRound	Bilat	n/a	n/a
Canada | Sherbrooke	Universite de Sherbrooke	Fall Spr YrRound	Bilat	n/a	n/a
Canada | Trois-Riviere	Universite du Quebec	Fall Spr YrRound	Bilat	n/a	n/a
Chile | Arica	SIT Study Abroad	Fall Spr	Intermed	SIT Study Abroad	n/a
Chile | Santiago	Multiple institutional choices	Fall Spr YrRound	Intermed	Institute for Study Abroad	n/a
Chile | Santiago	SIT Study Abroad	Fall Spr	Intermed	SIT Study Abroad	n/a
Chile | Santiago	Universidad Andres Bello	Fall Spr YrRound	Consrtm	University Studies Abroad Consortium (USAC)	n/a
Chile | Valparaiso	SIT Study Abroad	Fall Spr	Intermed	SIT Study Abroad	n/a
Chile | Valparaiso/Vina del Mar	Multiple institutional choices	Fall Spr YrRound	Intermed	Institute for Study Abroad	n/a
Chile | Valparaiso/Vina del Mar	Pontifical Catholic University or Adolfo Ibanez University	Sum Fall Spr YrRound	Intermed	International Studies Abroad	n/a
China | Beijing	Beijing Foreign Studies University	Sum Fall Spr	Intermed	IES Abroad	n/a
China | Beijing	Beijing Language and Culture University	Sum Fall Spr YrRound	Intermed	Alliance for Global Education	n/a
China | Beijing	Beijing University	Sum Fall Spr YrRound	Intermed	Council on International Educational Exchange (CIEE)	n/a
China | Beijing	Central University of Nationalities	Fall Spr YrRound	Intermed	Council on International Educational Exchange (CIEE)	n/a
China | Beijing	CET Academic Programs	Sum Fall Spr YrRound	Intermed	CET Academic Programs	n/a
China | Beijing	CET Academic Programs	Sum Fall Spr YrRound	Intermed	CET Academic Programs	n/a
China | Chengdu	Southwest University for Nationalities	Fall Spr YrRound	Consrtm	University Studies Abroad Consortium (USAC)	n/a
China | Hangzhou	CET Academic Programs	Sum	Intermed	CET Academic Programs	n/a
China | Harbin	CET Academic Programs	Sum Fall Spr YrRound	Intermed	CET Academic Programs	n/a
China | Hong Kong	Chinese University of Hong Kong	Sum Fall Spr YrRound	Bilat	n/a	n/a
China | Hong Kong	Chinese University of Hong Kong	Sum	Dir	n/a	n/a
China | Hong Kong	Hong Kong University of Science and Technology	Fall Spr YrRound	Bilat	n/a	n/a
China | Kunming	SIT Study Abroad	Fall Spr	Intermed	SIT Study Abroad	n/a

Massachusetts

DESTINATION	HOST INSTITUTION	PRGM SEASON	PRGM TYPE	INTERMEDIARY	HOUSING
China | Nanjing	Nanjing University	Fall Spr YrRound	Intermed	Council on International Educational Exchange (CIEE)	n/a
China | Shanghai	CET Academic Programs	Sum Fall Spr YrRound	Intermed	CET Academic Programs	n/a
China | Shanghai	East China Normal University	Fall Spr YrRound	Intermed	Council on International Educational Exchange (CIEE)	n/a
China | Shanghai	East China Normal University	Fall Spr YrRound	Intermed	Council on International Educational Exchange (CIEE)	n/a
China | Shanghai	East China Normal University	Sum Fall Spr YrRound	Intermed	Council on International Educational Exchange (CIEE)	n/a
China | Shanghai	IES Abroad Shanghai Center	Sum Fall Spr YrRound	Intermed	IES Abroad	n/a
China | Shanghai	Shanghai University	Fall Spr YrRound	Consrtm	University Studies Abroad Consortium (USAC)	n/a
China | Shanghai	Shanghai University of Finance and Economics	Sum Fall Spr YrRound	Intermed	Alliance for Global Education	n/a
China | Xian	Xi'an International Studies University	Sum Fall Spr YrRound	Intermed	Alliance for Global Education	n/a
Costa Rica | Atenas	Center for Sustainable Development Studies (School for Field Studies)	Sum Fall Spr	Intermed	School for Field Studies	n/a
Costa Rica | Heredia	Inter-American University	Sum Fall Spr YrRound	Intermed	International Studies Abroad	n/a
Costa Rica | Heredia	Universidad Nacional de Costa Rica	Fall Spr YrRound	Consrtm	University Studies Abroad Consortium (USAC)	n/a
Costa Rica | Puntarenas	Universidad Nacional de Costa Rica	Sum Fall Spr	Consrtm	University Studies Abroad Consortium (USAC)	n/a
Costa Rica | San Joaquin de Flores	Instituto San Joaquin de Flores	Fall Spr YrRound	Intermed	Academic Programs International	n/a
Costa Rica | San Jose	Institute for Central American Developments Studies	Sum Fall Spr	Intermed	Institute for Central American Developments Studies	n/a
Costa Rica | San Jose	Institute for Central American Developments Studies	Fall Spr	Intermed	Institute for Central American Developments Studies	n/a
Costa Rica | San Jose	Institute for Central American Developments Studies	Fall Spr	Intermed	Institute for Central American Developments Studies	n/a
Costa Rica | San Jose	Universidad de Costa Rica	Fall Spr YrRound	Intermed	Academic Programs International	n/a
Costa Rica | San Jose	Veritas University	Sum Fall Spr YrRound	Intermed	International Studies Abroad	n/a
Denmark | Copenhagen	Danish Institute for Study Abroad (DIS)	Sum	Intermed	Danish Institute for Study Abroad (DIS)	n/a
Denmark | Copenhagen	Danish Institute for Study Abroad (DIS)	Fall Spr	Intermed	Danish Institute for Study Abroad (DIS)	n/a
Denmark | Copenhagen	Danish Institute for Study Abroad (DIS)	Fall Spr	Intermed	Danish Institute for Study Abroad (DIS)	n/a
Denmark | Copenhagen	University of Copenhagen	Fall Spr YrRound	Bilat	n/a	n/a

© 2011 — Updates? Want to be in the next edition? Visit **www.mysecondcampus.com**

Massachusetts

DESTINATION	HOST INSTITUTION	PRGM SEASON	PRGM TYPE	INTERMEDIARY	HOUSING
Ecuador | Puerto Baquerizo Moreno	Galapagos Academic Institute for the Arts and Sciences (Universidad San Francisco de Quito)	Sum Fall Spr	Dir	n/a	n/a
Ecuador | Quito	SIT Study Abroad	Fall Spr	Intermed	SIT Study Abroad	n/a
Ecuador | Quito	Universidad San Francisco de Quito	Fall Spr YrRound	Bilat	n/a	n/a
Egypt | Cairo	American University in Cairo	Sum Fall Spr YrRound	Bilat	n/a	n/a
England | Brighton	University of Sussex	Fall Spr YrRound	Bilat	n/a	n/a
England | Bristol	University of Bristol	Sum Fall Spr YrRound	Intermed	Institute for Study Abroad	n/a
England | Cambridge	Cambridge University	Sum Fall Spr YrRound	Intermed	Arcadia University	n/a
England | Cambridge	Cambridge University	Sum Fall Spr YrRound	Intermed	Institute for Study Abroad	n/a
England | Canterbury	University of Kent	Fall Spr YrRound	Bilat	n/a	n/a
England | Colchester	University of Essex	Sum Fall Spr YrRound	Intermed	Arcadia University	n/a
England | Colchester	University of Essex	Sum Fall Spr YrRound	Intermed	Institute for Study Abroad	n/a
England | Coventry	University of Warwick	Fall YrRound	Dir	n/a	n/a
England | Hull	University of Hull	Fall Spr YrRound	Bilat	n/a	n/a
England | Lancaster	Lancaster University	Fall Spr YrRound	Bilat	n/a	n/a
England | Leeds	University of Leeds	Fall Spr YrRound	Bilat	n/a	n/a
England | London	CAPA London Center	Fall Spr	Intermed	CAPA International Education	n/a
England | London	Multiple institutional choices	Sum Fall Spr YrRound	USColl	Arcadia University	n/a
England | London	Multiple institutional choices	Sum Fall Spr YrRound	Intermed	Institute for Study Abroad	n/a
England | London	University College London	Fall Spr YrRound	Bilat	n/a	n/a
England | London	University of Westminster	Sum Fall Spr YrRound	Intermed	Center for International Studies (CIS)	n/a
England | London-Egham	Royal Holloway	Fall Spr YrRound	Bilat	n/a	n/a
England | Manchester	Manchester Business School	Fall Spr YrRound	Bilat	n/a	n/a
England | Manchester	University of Manchester	Fall Spr YrRound	Bilat	n/a	n/a
England | Norwich	University of East Anglia	Fall Spr YrRound	Bilat	n/a	n/a
England | Nottingham	University of Nottingham	Sum Fall Spr YrRound	USColl	Arcadia University	n/a
England | Nottingham	University of Nottingham	Sum Fall Spr YrRound	Intermed	Center for International Studies (CIS)	n/a
England | Nottingham	University of Nottingham	Sum Fall Spr YrRound	Intermed	Institute for Study Abroad	n/a
England | Oxford	Oxford Brookes University	Fall Spr	Bilat	n/a	n/a
England | Oxford	Oxford University	Sum Fall Spr YrRound	USColl	Arcadia University	n/a

© 2011 — Updates? Want to be in the next edition? Visit www.mysecondcampus.com

Massachusetts

DESTINATION	HOST INSTITUTION	PRGM SEASON	PRGM TYPE	INTERMEDIARY	HOUSING
England | Oxford	Oxford University	Sum Fall Spr YrRound	Intermed	Institute for Study Abroad	n/a
England | Oxford	Oxford University (Trinity College)	Sum	Self	n/a	n/a
	Costs: Sum Costs: T&F: n/a, R&B: n/a, Ttl: $6,500				
England | Roehampton	Roehampton University	Sum Fall Spr YrRound	Intermed	Center for International Studies (CIS)	n/a
England | York	University of York	Sum Fall Spr YrRound	USColl	Arcadia University	n/a
England | York	University of York	Sum Fall Spr YrRound	Intermed	Institute for Study Abroad	n/a
Fiji | Suva	SIT Study Abroad	Fall Spr	Intermed	SIT Study Abroad	n/a
France | Grenoble	Centre Universitaire d'Etudes Francaises - Universite Grenoble III	Sum Fall Spr YrRound	Intermed	Academic Programs International	n/a
France | Grenoble	Centre Universitaire d'Etudes Francaises - Universite Grenoble III	Sum Fall Spr YrRound	Intermed	Academic Programs International	n/a
France | Grenoble	Grenoble Management School	Sum Fall Spr YrRound	Intermed	Academic Programs International	n/a
France | Paris	Engineering Institute of Information Technology and Management	Sum	Bilat	n/a	n/a
France | Paris	Institut Catholique de Paris	Fall Spr YrRound	Intermed	Academic Programs International	n/a
France | Paris	Institut Catholique de Paris	Fall Spr YrRound	Intermed	Academic Programs International	n/a
France | Paris	Universite de Paris - Cours de Civilisation Francaise de la	Sum Fall Spr YrRound	Intermed	Academic Programs International	n/a
France | Paris	Universite Paris Dauphine or Universite Paris Diderot	n/a	Intermed	Academic Programs International	n/a
France | Paris	Universite Paris Sorbonne-Paris IV	Sum Fall Spr YrRound	Intermed	Academic Programs International	n/a
France | Pau	University of Pau	Sum Fall Spr YrRound	Consrtm	University Studies Abroad Consortium (USAC)	n/a
Germany | (Multiple choices)	Multiple institutional choices	YrRound	Bilat	German Academic Exchange Service (DAAD)	n/a
Germany | (Multiple choices)	Multiple institutional choices	n/a	Intermed	Research Internships in Science and Engineering (DAAD-RISE)	n/a
Germany | Berlin	Technical University of Berlin	Spr YrRound	Bilat	n/a	n/a
Germany | Darmstadt	Technische Universitat Darmstadt	Sum Spr YrRound	Bilat	n/a	n/a
Germany | Freiburg	Albert-Ludwigs-Universitat Freiburg	Fall Spr YrRound	Bilat	n/a	n/a
Germany | Heidelburg	Ruprecht-Karls-Universitat Heidelberg	Fall Spr YrRound	Bilat	n/a	n/a
Germany | Hohenheim	Universitat Hohenheim	Fall Spr YrRound	Bilat	n/a	n/a

Massachusetts

DESTINATION	HOST INSTITUTION	PRGM SEASON	PRGM TYPE	INTERMEDIARY	HOUSING
Germany | Karlsruhe	Universitat Karlsruhe	Fall Spr YrRound	Bilat	n/a	n/a
Germany | Konstanz	Universitat Konstanz	Fall Spr YrRound	Bilat	n/a	n/a
Germany | Mannheim	Universitat Mannheim	Fall Spr YrRound	Bilat	n/a	n/a
Germany | Stuttgart	Universitat Stuttgart	Fall Spr YrRound	Bilat	n/a	n/a
Germany | Tubingen	Eberhard-Karls-Universitat Tubingen	Fall Spr YrRound	Bilat	n/a	n/a
Germany | Ulm	Universitat Ulm	Fall Spr YrRound	Bilat	n/a	n/a
Germany | Ulm	Universitat Ulm	Sum	Bilat	n/a	n/a
Ghana | Accra	University of Ghana	Sum Fall Spr YrRound	Consrtm	University Studies Abroad Consortium (USAC)	n/a
Ghana | Accra & Kumasi	SIT Study Abroad	Fall Spr	Intermed	SIT Study Abroad	n/a
Ghana | Cape Coast	SIT Study Abroad	Fall Spr	Intermed	SIT Study Abroad	n/a
Ghana | Kopeyia	Dagbe Cultural Center	Sum	Self	n/a	n/a
Costs: Sum Costs: T&F: n/a, R&B: n/a, Ttl: $2,450					
Ghana | Kumasi	Kwame Nkrumah University of Science and Technology	Fall Spr YrRound	Dir	n/a	n/a
Greece | Athens	Arcadia Center for Hellenic, Mediterranean and Balkan Studies	Sum Fall Spr YrRound	USColl	Arcadia University	n/a
Greece | Athens	International Center for Hellenic & Mediterranean Studies (College Year in Athens)	Sum Fall Spr YrRound	Intermed	College Year in Athens	n/a
Hungary | Budapest	Corvinus University	Fall Spr YrRound	Intermed	Academic Programs International	n/a
India | Auroville	Living Routes	Fall Spr	Intermed	Living Routes	n/a
India | Bangalore	Christ College	Fall Spr YrRound	Consrtm	University Studies Abroad Consortium (USAC)	n/a
India | Chennai	Unknown	n/a	Bilat	n/a	n/a
India | Delhi	IES Abroad Delhi Center	Fall Spr YrRound	Intermed	IES Abroad	n/a
India | Delhi	Indian Institute of Technology, Delhi	Spr YrRound	Bilat	n/a	n/a
India | Delhi	SIT Study Abroad	Fall Spr	Intermed	SIT Study Abroad	n/a
India | Dharamsala	SIT Study Abroad	Fall Spr	Intermed	SIT Study Abroad	n/a
India | Jaipur	SIT Study Abroad	Fall Spr	Intermed	SIT Study Abroad	n/a
India | Madurai	Unknown	n/a	Bilat	n/a	n/a
India | Mumbai	Unknown	n/a	USColl	Wells College	n/a
India | Pune	Fergusson College	Sum Fall Spr YrRound	Intermed	Alliance for Global Education	n/a
Indonesia | Bedulu	SIT Study Abroad	Fall Spr	Intermed	SIT Study Abroad	n/a
Ireland | Ballyvaughn	Burren College of Art	Fall Spr YrRound	USColl	Arcadia University	n/a
Ireland | Cork	University College Cork	Fall Spr YrRound	Dir	n/a	n/a
Ireland | Dublin	Dublin City University	Fall Spr YrRound	Intermed	Center for International Studies (CIS)	n/a
Ireland | Dublin	Trinity College Dublin	n/a	Intermed	Center for International Studies (CIS)	n/a

© 2011 — Updates? Want to be in the next edition? Visit **www.mysecondcampus.com**

Massachusetts

DESTINATION	HOST INSTITUTION	PRGM SEASON	PRGM TYPE	INTERMEDIARY	HOUSING
Ireland | Dublin	Trinity College Dublin	YrRound	Dir	n/a	n/a
Ireland | Galway	National University of Ireland at Galway	Sum Fall Spr YrRound	Intermed	Academic Programs International	n/a
Ireland | Limerick	University of Limerick	Fall Spr YrRound	Dir	n/a	n/a
Ireland | Maynooth	National University of Ireland at Maynooth	Fall Spr YrRound	USColl	Arcadia University	n/a
Israel | Beer Sheva	Ben Gurion University	Fall Spr YrRound	Dir	n/a	n/a
Israel | Haifa	University of Haifa	Sum Fall Spr YrRound	Dir	n/a	n/a
Israel | Jerusalem	Hebrew University	Sum Fall Spr YrRound	Dir	n/a	n/a
Israel | Kibbutz Lotan	Living Routes	Fall Spr	Intermed	Living Routes	n/a
Israel | Tel Aviv	Tel Aviv University	Spr	USColl	Boston University	n/a
Israel | Tel Aviv	Tel Aviv University	Sum Fall Spr YrRound	Dir	n/a	n/a
Italy | Bologna	University of Bologna-Forli	Fall Spr YrRound	Bilat	n/a	n/a
Italy | Florence	Accademia Italiana	Sum Fall Spr YrRound	USColl	Arcadia University	n/a
Italy | Florence	Accademia Italiana	Sum Fall Spr YrRound	USColl	Arcadia University	n/a
Italy | Florence	CAPA Florence Center	Sum Fall Spr YrRound	Intermed	CAPA International Education	n/a
Italy | Florence	Scuola Lorenzo de' Medici	Sum Fall Spr YrRound	Intermed	Academic Programs International	n/a
Italy | Lecce	Universita del Salento	Sum Fall Spr YrRound	USColl	Arcadia University	n/a
Italy | Perugia	Umbra Institute	Sum Fall Spr YrRound	USColl	Arcadia University	n/a
Italy | Perugia	Umbra Institute	Sum Fall Spr YrRound	Intermed	Center for International Studies (CIS)	n/a
Italy | Perugia	Umbra Institute or Universita per Stranieri di Perugia	Sum Fall Spr YrRound	USColl	Arcadia University	n/a
Italy | Rome	Accademia Italiana	Fall Spr YrRound	USColl	Arcadia University	n/a
Italy | Rome	Accademia Italiana	Fall Spr YrRound	USColl	Arcadia University	n/a
Italy | Rome	American University of Rome	Sum Fall Spr YrRound	Intermed	International Studies Abroad	n/a
Italy | Rome	Intercollegiate Center for Classical Studies (Duke University)	Fall Spr YrRound	Consrtm	Intercollegiate Center for Classical Studies (Duke University)	n/a
Italy | Rome	John Cabot University	Fall Spr YrRound	Intermed	Academic Programs International	n/a
Italy | Rome	Pantheon Institute	Sum Fall Spr YrRound	Intermed	Center for International Studies (CIS)	n/a
Italy | Rome	Scuola Lorenzo de' Medici	Sum Fall Spr YrRound	Intermed	Academic Programs International	n/a
Italy | Siena	Universita per Stranieri di Siena	Spr	Dir	n/a	n/a

© 2011 — Updates? Want to be in the next edition? Visit **www.mysecondcampus.com**

Massachusetts

DESTINATION	HOST INSTITUTION	PRGM SEASON	PRGM TYPE	INTERMEDIARY	HOUSING
Italy | Syracuse	Mediterranean Center for Arts and Sciences	n/a	USColl	Arcadia University	n/a
Italy | Syracuse	Mediterranean Center for Arts and Sciences	Fall Spr YrRound	Intermed	Academic Programs International	n/a
Italy | Torino	University of Torino	Sum Fall Spr YrRound	Consrtm	University Studies Abroad Consortium (USAC)	n/a
Italy | Tuscania	Scuola Lorenzo de' Medici	Fall Spr YrRound	Intermed	Academic Programs International	n/a
Italy | Venice	Scuola Internazionale di Grafica Venezia	Fall Spr YrRound	Dir	n/a	n/a
Italy | Viterbo	Universita Degli Studi della Tuscia	Sum Fall Spr YrRound	Consrtm	University Studies Abroad Consortium (USAC)	n/a
Japan | Hikone	Japan Center for Michigan Universities	Sum	Consrtm	Japan Center for Michigan Universities	n/a
Japan | Hikone	Japan Center for Michigan Universities	Fall Spr YrRound	Consrtm	Japan Center for Michigan Universities	n/a
Japan | Hikone	Japan Center for Michigan Universities	Sum	Consrtm	Japan Center for Michigan Universities	n/a
Japan | Hikone	Japan Center for Michigan Universities	Sum	Consrtm	Japan Center for Michigan Universities	n/a
Japan | Hikone	Japan Center for Michigan Universities	Sum	Consrtm	Japan Center for Michigan Universities	n/a
Japan | Hirakata	Kansai Gaidai University	Fall Spr YrRound	Bilat	n/a	n/a
Japan | Japan	Sophia University	Spr YrRound	Bilat	n/a	n/a
Japan | Nagasaki	Nagasaki University of Foreign Studies	Spr YrRound	Consrtm	University Studies Abroad Consortium (USAC)	n/a
Japan | Nagoya	Nanzan University	Fall Spr YrRound	Bilat	n/a	n/a
Japan | Nishinomiya	Kwansei Gakuin University	Fall Spr YrRound	Bilat	n/a	n/a
Japan | Osaka	CET Academic Programs	Sum	Intermed	CET Academic Programs	n/a
Japan | Osaka	CET Academic Programs	Fall Spr	Intermed	CET Academic Programs	n/a
Japan | Sapporo	Hokkaido University HUSTEP (Short Term Exchange Program)	Fall YrRound	Bilat	n/a	n/a
Japan | Sapporo	Hokkaido University Nikken	YrRound	Bilat	n/a	n/a
Japan | Sapporo	Hokkaido University of Education	Spr YrRound	Bilat	n/a	n/a
Japan | Sapporo	Hokkaido University Summer	Sum	Bilat	n/a	n/a
Japan | Tokyo	International Christian University	YrRound	Bilat	n/a	n/a
Japan | Tokyo	International Christian University	Sum	Dir	n/a	n/a
Japan | Tokyo	Sophia University	Sum	Dir	n/a	n/a
Japan | Tokyo	Temple University (branch campus in Japan)	Sum Fall Spr YrRound	Dir	n/a	n/a
Japan | Tokyo	Temple University (branch campus in Japan)	Sum	Dir	n/a	n/a
Japan | Tsukuba	University of Tsukuba	YrRound	Bilat	n/a	n/a
Jordan | Amman	SIT Study Abroad	Fall Spr	Intermed	SIT Study Abroad	n/a

© 2011 — Updates? Want to be in the next edition? Visit **www.mysecondcampus.com**

Massachusetts

DESTINATION	HOST INSTITUTION	PRGM SEASON	PRGM TYPE	INTERMEDIARY	HOUSING
Jordan | Amman	University of Jordan	Fall Spr YrRound	Intermed	Council on International Educational Exchange (CIEE)	n/a
Kenya | Mombasa	SIT Study Abroad	Fall Spr	Intermed	SIT Study Abroad	n/a
Kenya | Nairobi	Center for Wildlife Management Studies (School for Field Studies)	Sum Fall Spr	Intermed	School for Field Studies	n/a
Kenya | Nairobi	SIT Study Abroad	Fall Spr	Intermed	SIT Study Abroad	n/a
Kenya | Nairobi	University of Minnesota	Fall Spr YrRound	USColl	University of Minnesota	n/a
Lebanon | Beirut	American University of Beirut	Sum Fall Spr YrRound	Dir	n/a	n/a
Madagascar | Antananarivo	SIT Study Abroad	Fall Spr	Intermed	SIT Study Abroad	n/a
Madagascar | Fort Dauphin	SIT Study Abroad	Fall Spr	Intermed	SIT Study Abroad	n/a
Mali | Bamako	Antioch University	Fall Spr	USColl	Antioch University	n/a
Mali | Bamako	SIT Study Abroad	Fall Spr	Intermed	SIT Study Abroad	n/a
Mexico | Bahia Magdalena	Center for Coastal Studies (School for Field Studies)	Sum Fall Spr	Intermed	School for Field Studies	n/a
Mexico | Cuernavaca	Instituto Tecnologico y de Estudios Superiores de Monterrey, Cuernavaca	Fall Spr YrRound	Bilat	n/a	n/a
Mexico | Estado de Mexico	Instituto Tecnologico y de Estudios Superiores de Monterrey, Estado de Mexico	Fall Spr YrRound	Bilat	n/a	n/a
Mexico | Guadalajara	Instituto Tecnologico y de Estudios Superiores de Monterrey, Guadalajara	Sum Fall Spr YrRound	Bilat	n/a	n/a
Mexico | Huehuecoyotl	Living Routes	Spr	Intermed	Living Routes	n/a
Mexico | Mazatlan	Instituto Tecnologico y de Estudios Superiores de Monterrey, Mazatlan	n/a	Bilat	n/a	n/a
Mexico | Monterrey	Instituto Tecnologico y de Estudios Superiores de Monterrey, Monterrey	Sum Fall Spr YrRound	Bilat	n/a	n/a
Mexico | Oaxaca	SIT Study Abroad	Fall Spr	Intermed	SIT Study Abroad	n/a
Mexico | Puebla	Instituto Tecnologico y de Estudios Superiores de Monterrey, Puebla	Fall Spr YrRound	Bilat	n/a	n/a
Mexico | Puebla	Universidad Iberoamericana	Sum Fall Spr YrRound	Consrtm	University Studies Abroad Consortium (USAC)	n/a
Mexico | Queretaro	Instituto Tecnologico y de Estudios Superiores de Monterrey, Queretaro	Fall Spr YrRound	Bilat	n/a	n/a
Mexico | San Luis Potosi	Instituto Tecnologico y de Estudios Superiores de Monterrey, San Luis Potosi	Fall Spr YrRound	Bilat	n/a	n/a
Mexico | Toluca	Instituto Tecnologico y de Estudios Superiores de Monterrey, Toluca	Fall Spr YrRound	Bilat	n/a	n/a
Mongolia | Ulaanbaatar	SIT Study Abroad	Fall Spr	Intermed	SIT Study Abroad	n/a

© 2011 — Updates? Want to be in the next edition? Visit **www.mysecondcampus.com**

Massachusetts

DESTINATION	HOST INSTITUTION	PRGM SEASON	PRGM TYPE	INTERMEDIARY	HOUSING
Morocco | Meknes	ISA Morocco	Fall Spr YrRound	Intermed	International Studies Abroad	n/a
Morocco | Rabat	SIT Study Abroad	Fall Spr	Intermed	SIT Study Abroad	n/a
Namibia | Windhoek	Augsburg College	Fall Spr	USColl	Augsburg College	n/a
Nepal | Kathmandu	SIT Study Abroad	Fall Spr	Intermed	SIT Study Abroad	n/a
Netherlands | Leiden	Leiden University	Fall Spr YrRound	Dir	n/a	n/a
New Zealand | (Multiple choices)	Multiple institutional choices	Sum Fall Spr YrRound	Intermed	AustraLearn	n/a
New Zealand | Christchurch	Lincoln University or University of Canterbury	Sum Fall Spr YrRound	Intermed	AustraLearn	n/a
New Zealand | Dunedin	University of Otago	Sum Fall Spr YrRound	Intermed	AustraLearn	n/a
New Zealand | Hamilton	University of Waikato	Sum Fall Spr YrRound	Intermed	AustraLearn	n/a
New Zealand | Palmerston North	Massey University	Sum Fall Spr YrRound	Intermed	AustraLearn	n/a
New Zealand | Queenstown	Queenstown Resort College	Sum Fall Spr YrRound	Intermed	AustraLearn	n/a
New Zealand | Wellington	Massey University or Victoria University of Wellington	Sum Fall Spr	Intermed	AustraLearn	n/a
Nicaragua | Managua	SIT Study Abroad	Fall Spr	Intermed	SIT Study Abroad	n/a
Northern Ireland | Belfast	Queen's University Belfast	Fall Spr YrRound	USColl	Arcadia University	n/a
Northern Ireland | Londonderry	University of Ulster	Fall Spr YrRound	Bilat	n/a	n/a
Oman | Muscat	SIT Study Abroad	Fall Spr	Intermed	SIT Study Abroad	n/a
Panama | Panama City	SIT Study Abroad	Fall Spr	Intermed	SIT Study Abroad	n/a
Peru | Cuzco	ProWorld	Fall Spr	Intermed	ProWorld	n/a
Peru | Cuzco	SIT Study Abroad	Fall Spr	Intermed	SIT Study Abroad	n/a
Peru | High Amazon	Living Routes	Spr	Intermed	Living Routes	n/a
Peru | Lima	Pontificia Universidad Catolica	Fall Spr YrRound	Intermed	Institute for Study Abroad	n/a
Poland | Krakow	Jagiellonian University	Fall Spr YrRound	Intermed	Academic Programs International	n/a
Scotland | Aberdeen	University of Aberdeen	Sum Fall Spr YrRound	USColl	Arcadia University	n/a
Scotland | Edinburgh	Edinburgh College of Art	Fall Spr YrRound	Dir	n/a	n/a
Scotland | Edinburgh	Napier University	Sum Fall Spr YrRound	Intermed	Center for International Studies (CIS)	n/a
Scotland | Edinburgh	University of Edinburgh	Sum Fall Spr YrRound	USColl	Arcadia University	n/a
Scotland | Edinburgh	University of Edinburgh	Sum Fall Spr YrRound	Intermed	Institute for Study Abroad	n/a
Scotland | Edinburgh	Unknown	Sum	Self	n/a	n/a
Scotland | Forres	Living Routes	Fall Spr YrRound	Intermed	Living Routes	n/a
Scotland | Glasgow	University of Glasgow or Glasgow School of Art	Sum Fall Spr YrRound	USColl	Arcadia University	n/a
Scotland | St. Andrews	University of St. Andrews	Sum Fall Spr YrRound	USColl	Arcadia University	n/a

© 2011 — Updates? Want to be in the next edition? Visit **www.mysecondcampus.com**

Massachusetts

DESTINATION	HOST INSTITUTION	PRGM SEASON	PRGM TYPE	INTERMEDIARY	HOUSING
Scotland | St. Andrews	University of St. Andrews	Sum Fall Spr YrRound	Intermed	Institute for Study Abroad	n/a
Scotland | Stirling	University of Stirling	Fall Spr YrRound	Bilat	n/a	n/a
Senegal | Dakar	Living Routes	Spr	Intermed	Living Routes	n/a
Senegal | Dakar	SIT Study Abroad	Fall Spr	Intermed	SIT Study Abroad	n/a
Senegal | Dakar	Universite Cheikh Anta Diop	Fall Spr YrRound	USColl	Wells College	n/a
Senegal | Dakar	University of Minnesota	Fall Spr YrRound	USColl	University of Minnesota	n/a
South Africa | Cape Town	SIT Study Abroad	Fall Spr	Intermed	SIT Study Abroad	n/a
South Africa | Cape Town	University of Cape Town	Fall Spr YrRound	Bilat	n/a	n/a
South Africa | Cape Town	University of the Western Cape	Fall Spr YrRound	USColl	Arcadia University	n/a
South Africa | Durban	SIT Study Abroad	Fall Spr	Intermed	SIT Study Abroad	n/a
South Africa | Durban	University of KwaZulu Natal		Intermed	Interstudy	n/a
South Korea | Seoul	Yonsei University	Fall Spr YrRound	Bilat	n/a	n/a
South Korea | Seoul	Yonsei University	Sum	Dir	n/a	n/a
Spain | Alcala de Henares	Universidad de Alcala	Fall Spr YrRound	Intermed	Council on International Educational Exchange (CIEE)	n/a
Spain | Alicante	Universidad de Alicante	Fall Spr YrRound	Intermed	Council on International Educational Exchange (CIEE)	n/a
Spain | Alicante	Universidad de Alicante	Sum Fall Spr YrRound	Consrtm	University Studies Abroad Consortium (USAC)	n/a
Spain | Barcelona	IES Abroad Barcelona Center	Fall Spr YrRound	Intermed	IES Abroad	n/a
Spain | Barcelona	Multiple institutional choices	Sum Fall Spr YrRound	Intermed	Academic Programs International	n/a
Spain | Barcelona	Multiple institutional choices	Fall Spr YrRound	Intermed	Council on International Educational Exchange (CIEE)	n/a
Spain | Barcelona	Multiple institutional choices	Sum Fall Spr YrRound	Intermed	International Studies Abroad	n/a
Spain | Bilbao	University of Deusto	Sum Fall Spr YrRound	Intermed	International Studies Abroad	n/a
Spain | Bilbao	University of Deusto or University of the Basque Country	Sum Fall Spr YrRound	Intermed	Academic Programs International	n/a
Spain | Bilbao	University of the Basque Country	Sum Fall Spr YrRound	Consrtm	University Studies Abroad Consortium (USAC)	n/a
Spain | Cadiz	University of Cadiz	Sum Fall Spr YrRound	Intermed	Academic Programs International	n/a
Spain | Granada	University of Granada	Sum Fall Spr YrRound	Intermed	Academic Programs International	n/a
Spain | Granada	University of Granada	Sum Fall Spr YrRound	Intermed	International Studies Abroad	n/a
Spain | Madrid	Antonio de Nebrija University or Complutense University of Madrid	Sum Fall Spr YrRound	Intermed	International Studies Abroad	n/a
Spain | Madrid	Multiple institutional choices	Sum Fall Spr YrRound	Intermed	Academic Programs International	n/a
Spain | Madrid	Universidad Carlos III de Madrid	Fall Spr YrRound	Intermed	Council on International Educational Exchange (CIEE)	n/a

© 2011 — Updates? Want to be in the next edition? Visit **www.mysecondcampus.com**

Massachusetts

DESTINATION	HOST INSTITUTION	PRGM SEASON	PRGM TYPE	INTERMEDIARY	HOUSING
Spain | Madrid	Universidad Rey Juan Carlos	n/a	Consrtm	University Studies Abroad Consortium (USAC)	n/a
Spain | Malaga	University of Malaga	Sum Fall Spr YrRound	Intermed	International Studies Abroad	n/a
Spain | Oviedo	Universidad de Oviedo	Spr	Self	n/a	n/a
	Costs: Spr Costs: T&F: n/a, R&B: n/a, Ttl: $10,350				
Spain | Palma de Mallorca	Universitat de les Illes Balears	Fall Spr YrRound	Intermed	Council on International Educational Exchange (CIEE)	n/a
Spain | Salamanca	Colegio Hispano Continental	Sum	Self	n/a	n/a
	Costs: Sum Costs: T&F: n/a, R&B: n/a, Ttl: $3,200				
Spain | Salamanca	University of Salamanca	Sum Fall Spr YrRound	Intermed	Academic Programs International	n/a
Spain | Salamanca	University of Salamanca	Sum Fall Spr YrRound	Intermed	International Studies Abroad	n/a
Spain | Salamanca	University of Salamanca	Sum Spr	USColl	University of Connecticut	n/a
Spain | San Sebastian	University of Deusto	Sum Fall Spr YrRound	Intermed	International Studies Abroad	n/a
Spain | San Sebastian	University of the Basque Country	n/a	Consrtm	University Studies Abroad Consortium (USAC)	n/a
Spain | Santander	Menendez Pelayo International University or University of Cantabria	Sum Fall Spr YrRound	Intermed	International Studies Abroad	n/a
Spain | Seville	Multiple institutional choices	Sum Fall Spr YrRound	Intermed	International Studies Abroad	n/a
Spain | Seville	Pablo de Olavide University or University of Seville	Sum Fall Spr YrRound	Intermed	Academic Programs International	n/a
Spain | Seville	Spanish-American Institute of International Education	Fall Spr YrRound	USColl	University of Wisconsin	n/a
Spain | Seville	Universidad Pablo de Olavide or Universidad de Sevilla	Fall Spr YrRound	Intermed	Council on International Educational Exchange (CIEE)	n/a
Spain | Seville	University of Seville and International College of Seville	Fall Spr YrRound	Intermed	CCIS Study Abroad	n/a
Spain | Valencia	AIP Language Institute	Fall Spr YrRound	USColl	SUNY Albany	n/a
Spain | Valencia	Universidad Politecnica de Valencia	Fall Spr YrRound	Bilat	n/a	n/a
Spain | Valencia	University of Valencia	Sum Fall Spr YrRound	Intermed	International Studies Abroad	n/a
Sweden | Linkoping	Linkoping University	Fall Spr YrRound	Bilat	n/a	n/a
Sweden | Uppsala	Uppsala University	Fall Spr YrRound	Bilat	n/a	n/a
Switzerland | Geneva	John Knox International Centre	Fall Spr YrRound	USColl	Kent State University	n/a
Switzerland | Vitznau	DCT Swiss Hotel & Business Management School	Fall Spr YrRound	Dir	n/a	n/a
Taiwan | Taichung	Tunghai University	Fall Spr YrRound	Bilat	n/a	n/a
Taiwan | Taichung	Tunghai University	Sum	Bilat	n/a	n/a
Taiwan | Taipei	National Chengchi University	Fall Spr YrRound	Intermed	Council on International Educational Exchange (CIEE)	n/a
Tanzania | Arusha	SIT Study Abroad	Fall Spr	Intermed	SIT Study Abroad	n/a

© 2011 — Updates? Want to be in the next edition? Visit **www.mysecondcampus.com**

Massachusetts

DESTINATION	HOST INSTITUTION	PRGM SEASON	PRGM TYPE	INTERMEDIARY	HOUSING
Tanzania	Stone Town; Zanzibar	SIT Study Abroad	Fall Spr	Intermed	SIT Study Abroad	n/a
Thailand	Bangkok	Rangsit University	Sum	Consrtm	University Studies Abroad Consortium (USAC)	n/a
Thailand	Bangkok	Rangsit University	Fall Spr YrRound	Consrtm	University Studies Abroad Consortium (USAC)	n/a
Thailand	Khon Kaen	Khon Kaen University	Fall Spr	Intermed	Council on International Educational Exchange (CIEE)	n/a
Tunisia	Tunis	SIT Study Abroad	Fall Spr	Intermed	SIT Study Abroad	n/a
Turks and Caicos	South Caicos	Center for Marine Resource Management Studies (School for Field Studies)	Sum Fall Spr	Intermed	School for Field Studies	n/a
Uganda	Kampala	SIT Study Abroad	Fall Spr	Intermed	SIT Study Abroad	n/a
Uganda and Rwanda	Kampala and Kigali	SIT Study Abroad	Fall Spr	Intermed	SIT Study Abroad	n/a
United States	Apia Samoa	SIT Study Abroad	Fall Spr	Intermed	SIT Study Abroad	n/a
United States	Woods Hole (MA)	Sea Semester	Sum Fall Spr	Dir	Sea Semester	n/a
Vietnam	Can Tho	SIT Study Abroad	Fall Spr	Intermed	SIT Study Abroad	n/a
Vietnam	Ho Chi Minh City	CET Academic Programs	Sum Fall Spr YrRound	Intermed	CET Academic Programs	n/a
Vietnam	Ho Chi Minh City	SIT Study Abroad	Fall Spr	Intermed	SIT Study Abroad	n/a
Vietnam	Ho Chi Minh	Vietnam National University	Fall Spr YrRound	Intermed	Council on International Educational Exchange (CIEE)	n/a
Wales	Bangor	Bangor University	Sum Fall Spr YrRound	USColl	Arcadia University	n/a
Wales	Swansea	University of Wales Swansea	Fall Spr YrRound	Bilat	n/a	n/a

University of Massachusetts-Dartmouth

Kirsten Kalbrener
Office of International & Exchange Study Programs
Pine Hall, Suite 7123A
285 Old Westport Road
North Dartmouth, MA 02747

kkalbrener@umassd.edu
508.910.6506
http://www.umassd.edu/ipo/studyabroad/

DESTINATION	HOST INSTITUTION	PRGM SEASON	PRGM TYPE	INTERMEDIARY	HOUSING
Argentina	Buenos Aires	Facultad Latinoamericana de Ciencias Sociales; Pontificia Universidad Catolica; Universidad de Buenos Aires; Instituto Universitario Nacional de Arte	Fall Spr YrRound	Intermed	Council on International Educational Exchange (CIEE)	n/a
Australia	(Multiple choices)	Multiple institutional choices	Sum Fall Spr YrRound	Intermed	Center for International Studies (CIS)	n/a
Australia	(Multiple choices)	Multiple institutional choices	Fall Spr YrRound	Intermed	Australearn	n/a
Bahamas / Carribean	Bonaire	CIEE Study Center	Fall Spr	Intermed	Council on International Educational Exchange (CIEE)	n/a
Belgium	Brussels	Universite Libre de Bruxelles	Fall Spr YrRound	Intermed	Council on International Educational Exchange (CIEE)	n/a
Belgium	Brussels	Vesalius College	Fall Spr YrRound	Intermed	Council on International Educational Exchange (CIEE)	n/a

Massachusetts

DESTINATION	HOST INSTITUTION	PRGM SEASON	PRGM TYPE	INTERMEDIARY	HOUSING
Botswana | Gaborone	University of Botswana	Fall Spr YrRound	Intermed	Council on International Educational Exchange (CIEE)	n/a
Brazil | Salvador da Bahia	Universidade Catolica do Salvador; Universidade Federal da Bahia	Fall Spr YrRound	Intermed	Council on International Educational Exchange (CIEE)	n/a
Brazil | Sao Paulo	Escola de Administracao de Empresas de Sao Paulo da Fundacao Getulio Vargas	Fall Spr YrRound	Intermed	Council on International Educational Exchange (CIEE)	n/a
Brazil | Sao Paulo	Pontificia Universidad Catolica de Sao Paulo	Fall Spr YrRound	Intermed	Council on International Educational Exchange (CIEE)	n/a
Cambodia | Siem Reap	Center for Khmer Studies	Sum	Intermed	Council on International Educational Exchange (CIEE)	n/a
Canada | (Multiple choices)	Multiple institutional choices	n/a	Intermed	New England Board of Higher Education	n/a
Chile | Santiago	Pontificia Universidad Catolica de Chile; Universidad de Chile; or Universidad de Santiago	Fall Spr YrRound	Intermed	Council on International Educational Exchange (CIEE)	n/a
Chile | Valparaiso	Pontificia Universidad Catolica de Valparaiso	Fall Spr YrRound	Intermed	Council on International Educational Exchange (CIEE)	n/a
China | Nanjing	Nanjing University	Fall Spr YrRound	Intermed	Council on International Educational Exchange (CIEE)	n/a
Costa Rica | Monteverde	CIEE Study Center in Monteverde	Fall Spr	Intermed	Council on International Educational Exchange (CIEE)	n/a
Costa Rica | Monteverde	CIEE Study Center in Monteverde	Fall Spr	Intermed	Council on International Educational Exchange (CIEE)	n/a
Czech Republic | Prague	Charles University	Fall Spr YrRound	Intermed	Council on International Educational Exchange (CIEE)	n/a
Dominican Republic | Santiago	Pontificia Universidad Catolica Madre y Maestra	Fall Spr	Intermed	Council on International Educational Exchange (CIEE)	n/a
Dominican Republic | Santiago	Pontificia Universidad Catolica Madre y Maestra	Fall Spr YrRound	Intermed	Council on International Educational Exchange (CIEE)	n/a
Ecuador | Galapagos Island	University of Massachusetts-Dartmouth	n/a	Self	n/a	n/a
England | London	Goldsmiths College, University of London	Sum Fall Spr YrRound	Intermed	Council on International Educational Exchange (CIEE)	n/a
England | London	Middlesex University	Sum	Intermed	Center for International Studies (CIS)	n/a
England | London	Roehampton University	Fall Spr	Intermed	Center for International Studies (CIS)	n/a
England | London	University College London	Sum Fall Spr YrRound	Intermed	Council on International Educational Exchange (CIEE)	n/a
England | London	University of Westminster	Fall Spr YrRound	Intermed	Center for International Studies (CIS)	n/a
England | London	University of Westminster	Sum Fall Spr YrRound	Intermed	Council on International Educational Exchange (CIEE)	n/a
England | Nottingham	Nottingham University	Fall Spr	Intermed	Center for International Studies (CIS)	n/a
England | Sunderland	University of Sunderland	Fall Spr YrRound	Intermed	Center for International Studies (CIS)	n/a

© 2011 — Updates? Want to be in the next edition? Visit **www.mysecondcampus.com**

Massachusetts

DESTINATION	HOST INSTITUTION	PRGM SEASON	PRGM TYPE	INTERMEDIARY	HOUSING
Fiji | Suva or Nadi	Unknown	Fall Spr YrRound	Intermed	Australearn	n/a
France | Montpellier	Unknown	n/a	Bilat	n/a	n/a
France | Mulhouse	Ecole Nationale Superieure d'Ingenieurs Sud Alsace (ENSISA)	n/a	Bilat	n/a	n/a
France | Paris	Paris Center for Critical Studies (CIEE Study Center)	Fall Spr YrRound	Intermed	Council on International Educational Exchange (CIEE)	n/a
France | Pont Aven	Rhode Island School of Design at Pont Aven School of Contemporary Art	Sum Spr	Intermed	Rhode Island School of Design at Pont Aven School of Contemporary Art	n/a
France | Renne	Universite de Haute Bretagne	Fall Spr YrRound	Intermed	Council on International Educational Exchange (CIEE)	n/a
Germany | Darmstadt	Darmstadt Technical University	Sum Fall Spr YrRound	Bilat	n/a	n/a
Germany | Darmstadt	University of Applied Science Darmstadt	Sum Fall Spr YrRound	Bilat	n/a	n/a
Germany | Frankfurt	Applied University for Music and Performing Arts	Sum Fall Spr YrRound	Bilat	n/a	n/a
Germany | Frankfurt	Johann Wolfgang Goethe University Frankfurt	Sum Fall Spr YrRound	Bilat	n/a	n/a
Germany | Frankfurt	University of Applied Science Frankfurt am Main	Sum Fall Spr YrRound	Bilat	n/a	n/a
Germany | Fulda	University of Applied Science Fulda	Sum Fall Spr YrRound	Bilat	n/a	n/a
Germany | Giessen	Justus-Liebig University Giessen	Sum Fall Spr YrRound	Bilat	n/a	n/a
Germany | Giessen	University of Applied Science Giessen-Friedberg	Sum Fall Spr YrRound	Bilat	n/a	n/a
Germany | Kassel	University of Kassel	Sum Fall Spr YrRound	Bilat	n/a	n/a
Germany | Marburg	Philipps-University Marburg	Sum Fall Spr YrRound	Bilat	n/a	n/a
Germany | Offenbach	Academy of Arts and Design	Sum Fall Spr YrRound	Bilat	n/a	n/a
Germany | Wiesbaden	University of Applied Science Wiesbaden	Sum Fall Spr YrRound	Bilat	n/a	n/a
Ghana | Accra	Ashesi University	Fall Spr YrRound	Intermed	Council on International Educational Exchange (CIEE)	n/a
Ghana | Legon	University of Ghana	Fall Spr YrRound	Intermed	Council on International Educational Exchange (CIEE)	n/a
Hungary | Budapest	Corvinus University	Fall Spr YrRound	Intermed	Council on International Educational Exchange (CIEE)	n/a
India | Hyderabad	University of Hyderabad	Fall Spr YrRound	Intermed	Council on International Educational Exchange (CIEE)	n/a
Ireland | Dublin	Dublin City University	Fall Spr YrRound	Intermed	Council on International Educational Exchange (CIEE)	n/a
Ireland | Dublin	Dublin City University	Fall Spr	Intermed	Center for International Studies (CIS)	n/a

Massachusetts

DESTINATION	HOST INSTITUTION	PRGM SEASON	PRGM TYPE	INTERMEDIARY	HOUSING
Ireland | Dublin	Dublin City University	Sum	Intermed	Council on International Educational Exchange (CIEE)	n/a
Ireland | Dublin	Trinity College	Fall Spr YrRound	Intermed	Center for International Studies (CIS)	n/a
Ireland | Dublin	Unknown	Sum	Intermed	Center for International Studies (CIS)	n/a
Ireland | Limerick	University of Limerick	Fall Spr	Intermed	Center for International Studies (CIS)	n/a
Italy | Florence	Institute at Palazzo Rucellai	Sum Fall Spr YrRound	Intermed	Center for International Studies (CIS)	n/a
Italy | Florence	Studio Art Centers International (SACI)	Sum Fall Spr YrRound	Intermed	Studio Art Centers International (SACI)	n/a
Italy | Perugia	The Umbra Institute	Sum Fall Spr YrRound	Intermed	Center for International Studies (CIS)	n/a
Japan | Tokyo	Sophia University	Fall Spr YrRound	Intermed	Council on International Educational Exchange (CIEE)	n/a
Japan | Unknown	Unknown	Sum	n/a	n/a	n/a
Jordan | Amman	University of Jordan	Fall Spr YrRound	Intermed	Council on International Educational Exchange (CIEE)	n/a
Mexico | Guanajuato	Universidad de Guanajuato	Fall Spr YrRound	Intermed	Council on International Educational Exchange (CIEE)	n/a
Mexico | Guanajuato	Universidad de Guanajuato	Fall Spr YrRound	Intermed	Council on International Educational Exchange (CIEE)	n/a
Morocco | Rabat	Ecole Superieure de Direction et de Gestion	Fall Spr YrRound	Intermed	Council on International Educational Exchange (CIEE)	n/a
Netherlands | Amsterdam	University of Amsterdam	Fall Spr YrRound	Intermed	Council on International Educational Exchange (CIEE)	n/a
New Zealand | (Multiple choices)	Multiple institutional choices	Sum Fall Spr YrRound	Intermed	Australearn	n/a
Peru | Lima	Pontificia Universidad Catolica del Peru	Fall Spr YrRound	Intermed	Council on International Educational Exchange (CIEE)	n/a
Peru | Lima	Universidad del Pacifico	Fall Spr YrRound	Intermed	Council on International Educational Exchange (CIEE)	n/a
Poland | Warsaw	Warsaw School of Economics	Fall Spr	Intermed	Council on International Educational Exchange (CIEE)	n/a
Portugal | Lisbon	Universidade Nova de Lisboa	Fall Spr YrRound	Intermed	Council on International Educational Exchange (CIEE)	n/a
Portugal | Lisbon	University of Massachusetts-Dartmouth **Costs:** Sum Costs: T&F: n/a, R&B: n/a, Ttl: $3,500	Sum	Self	n/a	Other
Scotland | Edinburgh	Edinburgh Napier University	Fall Spr	Intermed	Center for International Studies (CIS)	n/a
Scotland | Stirling	University of Stirling	Sum Fall Spr	Intermed	Center for International Studies (CIS)	n/a
Senegal | Dakar	Suffolk University - Dakar Campus	Fall Spr YrRound	Intermed	Council on International Educational Exchange (CIEE)	n/a
South Africa | Cape Town	University of Cape Town	Fall Spr	Intermed	Council on International Educational Exchange (CIEE)	n/a

© 2011 — Updates? Want to be in the next edition? Visit **www.mysecondcampus.com**

Massachusetts

DESTINATION	HOST INSTITUTION	PRGM SEASON	PRGM TYPE	INTERMEDIARY	HOUSING
South Africa | Cape Town	University of Cape Town	Fall Spr YrRound	Intermed	Council on International Educational Exchange (CIEE)	n/a
South Africa | Stellenbosch	Stellenbosch University	Fall Spr YrRound	Intermed	Council on International Educational Exchange (CIEE)	n/a
South Korea | Seoul	Yonsei University	Fall Spr YrRound	Intermed	Council on International Educational Exchange (CIEE)	n/a
Spain | Alcala de Henares	University of Alcala	Fall Spr YrRound	Intermed	Council on International Educational Exchange (CIEE)	n/a
Spain | Alicante	University of Alicante	Fall Spr YrRound	Intermed	Council on International Educational Exchange (CIEE)	n/a
Spain | Alicante	University of Alicante	Fall Spr	Intermed	Council on International Educational Exchange (CIEE)	n/a
Spain | Alicante	University of Alicante	Fall Spr	Intermed	Council on International Educational Exchange (CIEE)	n/a
Spain | Madrid	Universidad Carlos III de Madrid	Fall Spr YrRound	Intermed	Council on International Educational Exchange (CIEE)	n/a
Spain | Seville	Universidad Pablo de Olavide (UPO)	Fall Spr YrRound	Intermed	Council on International Educational Exchange (CIEE)	n/a
Spain | Seville	Universidad Pablo de Olavide (UPO)	Fall Spr YrRound	Intermed	Council on International Educational Exchange (CIEE)	n/a
Spain | Seville	Universidad Pablo de Olavide (UPO)	Fall Spr YrRound	Intermed	Council on International Educational Exchange (CIEE)	n/a
Taiwan | Taipei	National Chengchi University	Fall Spr YrRound	Intermed	Council on International Educational Exchange (CIEE)	n/a
Thailand | Khon Kaen	Khon Kaen University	Fall Spr	Intermed	Council on International Educational Exchange (CIEE)	n/a
Turkey | Istanbul	Koc University	Fall Spr YrRound	Intermed	Council on International Educational Exchange (CIEE)	n/a
Vietnam | Ho Chi Minh City	Vietnam National University	Fall Spr YrRound	Intermed	Council on International Educational Exchange (CIEE)	n/a

University of Massachusetts-Lowell

Kristen Rhyner
Study Abroad Advisor
Centers for Learning, Southwick 308
One University Avenue
Lowell, MA 01854

Kristen_Rhyner@uml.edu
978.934.2920
http://www.uml.edu/class/Study_Abroad_Program/study_abroad.html

DESTINATION	HOST INSTITUTION	PRGM SEASON	PRGM TYPE	INTERMEDIARY	HOUSING
(Multiple choices) | (Multiple choices)	Multiple institutional choices	n/a	Intermed	International Studies Abroad	n/a
(Multiple choices) | (Multiple choices)	Multiple institutional choices	n/a	Intermed	AsiaLearn	n/a
(Multiple choices) | (Multiple choices)	Multiple institutional choices	n/a	Intermed	Academic Programs International	n/a
(Multiple choices) | (Multiple choices)	Multiple institutional choices	n/a	Intermed	AustraLearn	n/a
(Multiple choices) | (Multiple choices)	Multiple institutional choices	n/a	Intermed	Center for International Studies	n/a

© 2011 — Updates? Want to be in the next edition? Visit **www.mysecondcampus.com**

Massachusetts

DESTINATION	HOST INSTITUTION	PRGM SEASON	PRGM TYPE	INTERMEDIARY	HOUSING
(Multiple choices)	(Multiple choices)	Multiple institutional choices	n/a	Intermed	Council on International Educational Exchange (CIEE)	n/a
(Multiple)	(Multiple)	Semester at Sea	n/a	Intermed	Semester at Sea	n/a
China	Beijing	Tsinghua University	n/a	Bilat	n/a	n/a
Germany	(Multiple choices)	Multiple institutional choices	n/a	Bilat	Hessen-Massachusetts Program	n/a
Germany	Darmstadt	Hochschule Darmstadt	n/a	Bilat	n/a	n/a
Germany	Darmstadt	Technische Universitat Darmstadt	n/a	Bilat	n/a	n/a
Germany	Frankfurt	Fachhochschule Frankfurt am Main	n/a	Bilat	n/a	n/a
Germany	Frankfurt	Hochschule fur Musik und Darstellende Kunst	n/a	Bilat	n/a	n/a
Germany	Frankfurt	Johann Wolfgang Goethe Universitat Frankfurt	n/a	Bilat	n/a	n/a
Germany	Freiburg im Breisgau	University of Freiburg	n/a	Bilat	n/a	n/a
Germany	Friedberg, Giessen, and Wetzlar	Fachhochschule Giessen-Friedberg	n/a	Bilat	n/a	n/a
Germany	Fulda	Hochschule Fulda	n/a	Bilat	n/a	n/a
Germany	Giessen	Justus-Liebig Universitat Giessen	n/a	Bilat	n/a	n/a
Germany	Heidelberg	University of Heidelberg	n/a	Bilat	n/a	n/a
Germany	Karlsruhe	University of Karlsruhe	n/a	Bilat	n/a	n/a
Germany	Kassel	Universitat Kassel	n/a	Bilat	n/a	n/a
Germany	Konstanz	University of Konstanz	n/a	Bilat	n/a	n/a
Germany	Mannheim	University of Mannheim	n/a	Bilat	n/a	n/a
Germany	Marburg	Philipps-Universitat Marburg	n/a	Bilat	n/a	n/a
Germany	Offenbach am Main	Hochschule für Gestaltung	n/a	Bilat	n/a	n/a
Germany	Stuttgart	University of Hohenheim	n/a	Bilat	n/a	n/a
Germany	Stuttgart	University of Stuttgart	n/a	Bilat	n/a	n/a
Germany	Tubingen	University of Tubingen	n/a	Bilat	n/a	n/a
Germany	Ulm	University of Ulm	n/a	Bilat	n/a	n/a
Germany	Wiesbaden	Fachhochschule Wiesbaden	n/a	Bilat	n/a	n/a
Japan	Hokkaido	Hokkaido University	n/a	Bilat	n/a	n/a
Liberia	Monrovia	University of Liberia	n/a	Bilat	n/a	n/a
South Africa	Cape Town	University of Cape Town	n/a	Bilat	n/a	n/a
South Africa	Cape Town	University of Western Cape	n/a	Bilat	n/a	n/a
South Africa	Pietermaritzburg	University of KwaZulu-Natal	n/a	Bilat	n/a	n/a

© 2011 — Updates? Want to be in the next edition? Visit **www.mysecondcampus.com**

Massachusetts

Wellesley College

Jennifer Thomas-Starck
Director of International Studies
Office of International Studies
Green Hall, Room 337
106 Central Street
Wellesley, MA 02481

jthomass@wellesley.edu
781.283.3532
http://www.wellesley.edu/OIS/index.html

DESTINATION	HOST INSTITUTION	PRGM SEASON	PRGM TYPE	INTERMEDIARY	HOUSING
(Multiple) | (Multiple)	George Mason University	n/a	USColl	George Mason University	n/a
(Multiple) | (Multiple)	International Honors Program	n/a	Intermed	International Honors Program	n/a
(Multiple) | (Multiple)	International Honors Program	n/a	Intermed	International Honors Program	n/a
(Multiple) | (Multiple)	International Honors Program	n/a	Intermed	International Honors Program	n/a
Argentina | Buenos Aires	Multiple institutional choices	n/a	Intermed	Council on International Educational Exchange (CIEE)	n/a
Argentina | Buenos Aires	Multiple institutional choices	n/a	Intermed	Institute for Study Abroad	n/a
Argentina | Buenos Aires	SIT Study Abroad	n/a	Intermed	SIT Study Abroad	n/a
Argentina | Buenos Aires	Universidad de Belgrano	Sum	Intermed	Academic Programs International	n/a
Argentina | Buenos Aires	Universidad de San Andres	Sum	Dir	n/a	n/a
Argentina | Mendoza	Universidad Nacional de Cuyo	n/a	Intermed	Institute for Study Abroad	n/a
Argentina and Uruguay | Buenos Aires and Montevideo	CUNY (Brooklyn College)	n/a	USColl	CUNY (Brooklyn College)	n/a
Argentina, Brazil, Paraguay, and Uruguay | (Multiple)	SIT Study Abroad	n/a	Intermed	SIT Study Abroad	n/a
Australia | Brisbane	University of Queensland	n/a	Intermed	Institute for Study Abroad	n/a
Australia | Melbourne	University of Melbourne	n/a	Intermed	Institute for Study Abroad	n/a
Australia | North Queensland	School for Field Studies	Sum	Intermed	School for Field Studies	n/a
Australia | Sydney	Boston University Sydney Center	Sum	USColl	Boston University	n/a
Australia | Sydney	Macquarie University	n/a	Intermed	Institute for Study Abroad	n/a
Australia | Sydney	University of Sydney	n/a	Intermed	Institute for Study Abroad	n/a
Australia | Yungaburra	Center for Rainforest Studies (School for Field Studies)	n/a	Intermed	School for Field Studies	n/a
Austria | Vienna	University of Vienna	Spr YrRound	Self	n/a	PrivApt
Austria | Vienna	University of Vienna	Sum	Dir	n/a	n/a
Austria | Vienna	Wellesley College	n/a	Self	n/a	n/a
Bahamas | San Salvador Island	SUNY (Brockport)	n/a	USColl	SUNY (Brockport)	n/a
Bangladesh | Dhaka	Independent University Bangladesh	n/a	Consrtm	Higher Education Consortium for Urban Affairs (HECUA)	n/a
Belgium | Brussels	Universite Libre de Bruxelles	n/a	Intermed	Council on International Educational Exchange (CIEE)	n/a
Belize and Costa Rica | [City Unspecified]	Wellesley College	n/a	Self	n/a	n/a
Bolivia | Cochabamba	SIT Study Abroad	n/a	Intermed	SIT Study Abroad	n/a
Botswana | Gaborone	SIT Study Abroad	n/a	Intermed	SIT Study Abroad	n/a

© 2011 — Updates? Want to be in the next edition? Visit **www.mysecondcampus.com**

Massachusetts

DESTINATION	HOST INSTITUTION	PRGM SEASON	PRGM TYPE	INTERMEDIARY	HOUSING
Brazil | Belem	SIT Study Abroad	n/a	Intermed	SIT Study Abroad	n/a
Brazil | Fortaleza	Instituto Brasil/Estados Unidos/Ceara	n/a	Intermed	SIT Study Abroad	n/a
Brazil | Salvador	SIT Study Abroad	n/a	Intermed	SIT Study Abroad	n/a
Brazil | Salvador da Bahia	Universidade Catolica do Salvador or Universidade Federal da Bahia	n/a	Intermed	Council on International Educational Exchange (CIEE)	n/a
Cameroon | Yaounde	SIT Study Abroad	n/a	Intermed	SIT Study Abroad	n/a
Canada | London (Ontario)	University of Western Ontario	n/a	Dir	n/a	n/a
Canada | Montreal	McGill University	n/a	Dir	n/a	n/a
Canada | Montreal	University of Montreal	n/a	Dir	n/a	n/a
Canada | Toronto	University of Toronto	n/a	Dir	n/a	n/a
Canada | Vancouver	University of British Columbia	n/a	Dir	n/a	n/a
Canada | Vancouver	University of British Columbia	n/a	Bilat	n/a	n/a
Chile | Santiago	IES Abroad Santiago Center	Sum	Intermed	IES Abroad	n/a
Chile | Santiago	Multiple institutional choices	n/a	Intermed	Council on International Educational Exchange (CIEE)	n/a
Chile | Santiago	SIT Study Abroad	n/a	Intermed	SIT Study Abroad	n/a
Chile | Santiago	SUNY (University of Albany)	n/a	USColl	SUNY (University of Albany)	n/a
Chile | Valparaiso	Multiple institutional choices	n/a	Intermed	Institute for Study Abroad	n/a
Chile | Valparaiso	SIT Study Abroad	n/a	Intermed	SIT Study Abroad	n/a
China | (Multiple)	SUNY (University of Albany)	n/a	USColl	SUNY (University of Albany)	n/a
China | Beijing	Associated Colleges in China (Hamilton College)	n/a	USColl	Associated Colleges in China (Hamilton College)	n/a
China | Beijing	Beijing Center	n/a	USColl	Loyola Marymount University	n/a
China | Beijing	Beijing Language and Culture University	n/a	Intermed	Alliance for Global Education	n/a
China | Beijing	Beijing Normal University	Sum	USColl	Princeton University	n/a
China | Beijing	CET Academic Programs	n/a	Intermed	CET Academic Programs	n/a
China | Beijing	Columbia University	Sum	USColl	Columbia University	n/a
China | Beijing	Peking University	Sum	Dir	London School of Economics and Political Science	n/a
China | Beijing	Tsinghua University	n/a	USColl	Columbia University	n/a
China | Beijing	Tsinghua University	Sum	Consrtm	Inter-University Program for Chinese Language Studies (University of California at Berkeley)	n/a
China | Hangzhou	C.V. Starr-Middlebury School	n/a	USColl	CET Academic Programs	n/a
China | Harbin	CET Academic Programs	n/a	Intermed	CET Academic Programs	n/a
China | Hong Kong	Cooperative Center for Study Abroad (Northern Kentucky University)	n/a	Consrtm	Cooperative Center for Study Abroad (Northern Kentucky University)	n/a
China | Hong Kong	University of Hong Kong	n/a	Bilat	n/a	n/a
China | Shanghai	East China Normal University	Sum	Intermed	Council on International Educational Exchange (CIEE)	n/a

Massachusetts

DESTINATION	HOST INSTITUTION	PRGM SEASON	PRGM TYPE	INTERMEDIARY	HOUSING
China	Shanghai	Fudan University	n/a	Intermed	Alliance for Global Education	n/a
China	Xi'an	Xi'an International Studies University	Sum	Intermed	Alliance for Global Education	n/a
Costa Rica	[City Unspecified]	Organization for Tropical Studies (Duke University)	n/a	Consrtm	Organization for Tropical Studies (Duke University)	n/a
Costa Rica	Atenas	School for Field Studies	n/a	Intermed	School for Field Studies	n/a
Costa Rica	Atenas	School for Field Studies	Sum	Intermed	School for Field Studies	n/a
Costa Rica	Heredia	Universidad Nacional	n/a	Intermed	Institute for Study Abroad	n/a
Costa Rica	Monteverde	CIEE Study Center	Sum	Intermed	Council on International Educational Exchange (CIEE)	n/a
Costa Rica	San Jose	Instituto San Joaquin de Flores	Sum	Intermed	Council on International Educational Exchange (CIEE)	n/a
Croatia	Zagreb	SIT Study Abroad	n/a	Intermed	SIT Study Abroad	n/a
Czech Republic	Prague	Anglo-American University	n/a	Intermed	Central European Education and Cultural Exchange (CEECE)	n/a
Czech Republic	Prague	CET Academic Programs	n/a	Intermed	CET Academic Programs	n/a
Czech Republic	Prague	CET Academic Programs	Sum	Intermed	CET Academic Programs	n/a
Czech Republic	Prague	Charles University	n/a	Intermed	Council on International Educational Exchange (CIEE)	n/a
Czech Republic	Prague	CIEE Study Center	Sum	Intermed	Council on International Educational Exchange (CIEE)	n/a
Denmark	Copenhagen	Danish Institute for Study Abroad (DIS)	n/a	Intermed	Danish Institute for Study Abroad (DIS)	n/a
Dominican Republic	Santiago	Pontificia Universidad Catolica Madre y Maestra	Sum	Intermed	Council on International Educational Exchange (CIEE)	n/a
Dominican Republic	Santo Domingo	Facultad Latinoamericana de Ciencias Sociales	n/a	Intermed	Council on International Educational Exchange (CIEE)	n/a
Ecuador	Quito	Higher Education Consortium for Urban Affairs (HECUA)	n/a	Consrtm	Higher Education Consortium for Urban Affairs (HECUA)	n/a
Ecuador	Quito	IES Abroad Quito Center	Sum	Intermed	IES Abroad	n/a
Ecuador	Quito	Pontificia Universidad Catolica del Ecuador or Facultad Latinoamericana de Ciencias	n/a	Intermed	IES Abroad	n/a
Ecuador	Quito	SIT Study Abroad	n/a	Intermed	SIT Study Abroad	n/a
Ecuador	Quito	SIT Study Abroad	n/a	Intermed	SIT Study Abroad	n/a
Ecuador	Quito	Universidad de San Francisco de Quito; Instituto Santiago de Quito	n/a	USColl	University of Maryland	n/a
Ecuador	Riobamba	IES Abroad Center	n/a	Intermed	IES Abroad	n/a
Egypt	Alexandria	Alexandria University	n/a	USColl	Middlebury College	n/a
Egypt	Cairo	American University in Cairo	Sum	Dir	n/a	n/a
Egypt	Unknown	University of Maryland	n/a	USColl	University of Maryland	n/a
England	Bristol	University of Bristol	n/a	Dir	n/a	n/a
England	Cambridge	Cambridge University (Pembroke College)	n/a	Dir	n/a	n/a
England	Lancaster	Lancaster University	n/a	Dir	n/a	n/a

© 2011 — Updates? Want to be in the next edition? Visit **www.mysecondcampus.com**

Massachusetts

DESTINATION	HOST INSTITUTION	PRGM SEASON	PRGM TYPE	INTERMEDIARY	HOUSING
England | Leeds	University of Leeds	Sum	Dir	n/a	n/a
England | London	British American Drama Academy	n/a	USColl	Sarah Lawrence College	n/a
England | London	British American Drama Academy	n/a	USColl	Skidmore College	n/a
England | London	Cooperative Center for Study Abroad (Northern Kentucky University)	n/a	Consrtm	Cooperative Center for Study Abroad (Northern Kentucky University)	n/a
England | London	Courtauld Institute of Art	n/a	Dir	n/a	n/a
England | London	King's College London	n/a	Dir	n/a	n/a
England | London	London Academy of Music and Dramatic Art	n/a	Dir	n/a	n/a
England | London	London School of Economics and Political Science	n/a	Dir	n/a	n/a
England | London	Queen Mary	n/a	Dir	n/a	n/a
England | London	Royal Holloway	n/a	Dir	n/a	n/a
England | London	Slade School of Fine Art	n/a	Dir	n/a	n/a
England | London	SUNY (New Paltz)	n/a	USColl	SUNY (New Paltz)	n/a
England | London	SUNY (New Paltz)	n/a	USColl	SUNY (New Paltz)	n/a
England | London	University College London	n/a	Dir	n/a	n/a
England | London	University of Roehampton	n/a	Dir	n/a	n/a
England | Manchester	University of Manchester	Sum	Dir	n/a	n/a
England | Manchester	University of Manchester	n/a	Bilat	n/a	n/a
England | Norwich	University of East Anglia	n/a	Dir	n/a	n/a
England | Oxford	Oxford University (Lady Margaret Hall)	n/a	Dir	n/a	n/a
England | Oxford	Oxford University (Mansfield College)	n/a	Dir	n/a	n/a
England | Oxford	Oxford University (St. Peter's College)	n/a	Dir	n/a	n/a
England | York	University of York	n/a	Dir	n/a	n/a
France | Aix-en-Provence	University of Provence (Aix-Marseille I)	Fall Spr YrRound	Self	n/a	HostFam PrivApt
	Costs: Fall Costs: T&F: n/a, R&B: n/a, Ttl: $23,870 Spr Costs: T&F: n/a, R&B: n/a, Ttl: $23,870 YrRound Costs: T&F: n/a, R&B: n/a, Ttl: $47,740				
France | Avignon	Institut d'etudes francaises d'Avignon (Bryn Mawr College)	Sum	USColl	Bryn Mawr College	n/a
France | Grenoble	Universite Stendhal – Grenoble III	Sum	Intermed	Academic Programs International	n/a
France | Paris	American Graduate School in Paris; Alliance Francaise	Sum	USColl	Arcadia University	n/a
France | Paris	Columbia University	n/a	USColl	Columbia University	n/a
France | Paris	Cours de Civilisation Francaise de la Sorbonne	Sum	Intermed	Academic Programs International	n/a
France | Paris	Multiple institutional choices	n/a	USColl	Sweet Briar College	n/a
France | Paris	Sciences Po	n/a	Bilat	n/a	n/a

© 2011 — Updates? Want to be in the next edition? Visit **www.mysecondcampus.com**

Massachusetts

DESTINATION	HOST INSTITUTION	PRGM SEASON	PRGM TYPE	INTERMEDIARY	HOUSING
France | Paris	Sciences Po	n/a	Consrtm	n/a	n/a
France | Paris	Sweet Briar College	Sum	USColl	Sweet Briar College	n/a
France | Paris	Wellesley College	n/a	Self	n/a	n/a
France | Strasbourg	Syracuse Center	n/a	USColl	Syracuse University	n/a
Georgia | Tbilisi	Wellesley College	n/a	Self	n/a	n/a
Germany | Berlin	Atelierhaus Mengerzeile	Sum	Intermed	Lexia Study Abroad	n/a
Germany | Berlin	Freie Universitet	n/a	USColl	Columbia University	n/a
Germany | Berlin	Freie Universitet	Sum	USColl	Duke University	n/a
Germany | Freiburg	IES Abroad EU Center	n/a	Intermed	IES Abroad	n/a
Germany | Munich	Ludwig Maximilians Universitat München	n/a	USColl	Wayne State University	n/a
Germany | Tubingen	Unknown	n/a	USColl	Tufts University	n/a
Ghana | Accra	University of Ghana	n/a	USColl	SUNY (Brockport)	n/a
Ghana | Legon	University of Ghana	n/a	Intermed	Council on International Educational Exchange (CIEE)	n/a
Greece | Athens	Arcadia Center for Hellenic, Mediterranean & Balkan Studies	Sum	Intermed	Arcadia University	n/a
Greece | Athens	College Year in Athens	n/a	Intermed	College Year in Athens	n/a
Guatemala | Antigua	Centro Linguistico Maya	Sum	USColl	Augsburg College	n/a
Hungary | Budapest	Central European University	Sum	USColl	Bard College	n/a
Hungary | Budapest	Corvinus University of Budapest	n/a	Intermed	Council on International Educational Exchange (CIEE)	n/a
Hungary | Budapest	Technical University of Budapest, College International	n/a	Intermed	Budapest Semesters in Mathematics	n/a
India | [City Unspecified]	Wellesley College	n/a	Self	n/a	n/a
India | Hyderabad	University of Hyderabad	n/a	Intermed	Council on International Educational Exchange (CIEE)	n/a
India | Jaipur	SIT Study Abroad	n/a	Intermed	SIT Study Abroad	n/a
India | Leh	Central Institute of Buddhist Studies	Sum	Intermed	SIT Study Abroad	n/a
India | New Delhi	SIT Study Abroad	n/a	Intermed	SIT Study Abroad	n/a
India | Unknown	Cooperative Center for Study Abroad (Northern Kentucky University)	n/a	Consrtm	Cooperative Center for Study Abroad (Northern Kentucky University)	n/a
India | Varanasi	University of Wisconsin at Madison	n/a	USColl	University of Wisconsin at Madison	n/a
Ireland | Ballyvaughan	Burren College of Art	n/a	Dir	n/a	n/a
Ireland | Cork	National University of Ireland at Cork	n/a	Dir	n/a	n/a
Ireland | Dublin	Trinity College Dublin	Sum	USColl	New York University	n/a
Ireland | Dublin	Trinity College Dublin	n/a	Dir	n/a	n/a
Ireland | Dublin	University College Dublin	n/a	Dir	n/a	n/a
Ireland | Galway	National University of Ireland at Galway	n/a	Dir	n/a	n/a
Ireland | Limerick	University of Limerick	Sum	USColl	Arcadia University	n/a

© 2011 — Updates? Want to be in the next edition? Visit **www.mysecondcampus.com**

Massachusetts

DESTINATION	HOST INSTITUTION	PRGM SEASON	PRGM TYPE	INTERMEDIARY	HOUSING
Israel | Beer-Sheva	Ben Gurion University	n/a	Dir	n/a	n/a
Israel | Jerusalem	Hebrew University	n/a	Dir	n/a	n/a
Israel | Tel Aviv	Tel Aviv University	n/a	Dir	n/a	n/a
Italy | Bologna	University of Bologna	Fall Spr	Consrtm	Eastern College Consortium (ECC)	CollRes
	Costs: Fall Costs: T&F: n/a, R&B: n/a, Ttl: $24,000 Spr Costs: T&F: n/a, R&B: n/a, Ttl: $24,000				
Italy | Catania	CET Academic Programs	Sum	Intermed	CET Academic Programs	n/a
Italy | Catania	Intercollegiate Center for Classical Studies (Duke University)	n/a	Consrtm	Intercollegiate Center for Classical Studies (Duke University)	n/a
Italy | Cotorna	John D. Kehoe Center (University of Georgia)	Sum	USColl	University of Georgia	n/a
Italy | Florence	SU Florence Center	n/a	USColl	Syracuse University	n/a
Italy | Milan	IES Abroad Milan Center	n/a	Intermed	IES Abroad	n/a
Italy | Mugello Valey	Capitignano Estate	Sum	USColl	Boston University	n/a
Italy | Rome	Brown University	Sum	USColl	Brown University	n/a
Italy | Rome	IES Abroad Rome Center	n/a	Intermed	IES Abroad	n/a
Italy | Rome	Intercollegiate Center for Classical Studies (Duke University)	n/a	Consrtm	Intercollegiate Center for Classical Studies (Duke University)	n/a
Italy | Rome	Wellesley College	n/a	Self	n/a	n/a
Italy | Siena	Siena School for Liberal Arts	n/a	Intermed	Siena School for Liberal Arts	n/a
Italy | Siena	Siena School for Liberal Arts	Sum	Intermed	Siena School for Liberal Arts	n/a
Italy | Syracuse	Mediterranean Center for Arts and Sciences	Sum	Intermed	Academic Programs International	n/a
Japan | Hakodate	Hokkaido International Foundation	Sum	Intermed	Hokkaido International Foundation	n/a
Japan | Kyoto	Doshisha University	YrRound	Consrtm	Associated Kyoto Program	HostFam
	Costs: YrRound Costs: T&F: n/a, R&B: n/a, Ttl: Wellesley home comprehensive fees				
Japan | Kyoto	Kyoto Consortium for Japanese Studies (Columbia University)	n/a	Consrtm	Kyoto Consortium for Japanese Studies (Columbia University)	n/a
Japan | Mitaka City	International Christian University	Sum	Dir	n/a	n/a
Japan | Nagoya	Nanzan University	n/a	Dir	n/a	n/a
Japan | Osaka	CET Academic Programs	Sum	Intermed	CET Academic Programs	n/a
Japan | Tokyo	Japan Women's University	n/a	Bilat	n/a	n/a
Japan | Tokyo	Keio University	Sum	Dir	n/a	n/a
Japan | Tokyo	Sophia University	Sum	Dir	n/a	n/a
Japan | Tokyo	Waseda University	n/a	Dir	n/a	n/a
Jordan | Amman	SIT Study Abroad	n/a	Intermed	SIT Study Abroad	n/a
Jordan | Amman	University of Jordan	n/a	Intermed	Council on International Educational Exchange (CIEE)	n/a
Jordan | Amman	University of Jordan	n/a	Intermed	Council on International Educational Exchange (CIEE)	n/a

Massachusetts

DESTINATION	HOST INSTITUTION	PRGM SEASON	PRGM TYPE	INTERMEDIARY	HOUSING
Kenya | Nairobi	Center for Wildlife Management Studies	n/a	Intermed	School for Field Studies	n/a
Kenya | Nairobi	SIT Study Abroad	n/a	Intermed	SIT Study Abroad	n/a
Lebanon | Beirut	American University of Beirut	Sum	Dir	n/a	n/a
Madagascar | Antananarivo	SIT Study Abroad	n/a	Intermed	SIT Study Abroad	n/a
Mali | Bamako	SIT Study Abroad	n/a	Intermed	SIT Study Abroad	n/a
Mexico | Baja	Center for Coastal Studies	n/a	Intermed	School for Field Studies	n/a
Mexico | Baja	Center for Coastal Studies	Sum	Intermed	School for Field Studies	n/a
Mexico | Cuernavaca	Augsburg College	Sum	USColl	Augsburg College	n/a
Mexico | Cuernavaca	Augsburg College	Sum	USColl	Augsburg College	n/a
Mexico | Cuernavaca	Augsburg College	Sum	USColl	Augsburg College	n/a
Mexico | Cuernavaca	Universal	Sum	Intermed	Universal	n/a
Mexico | Oaxaca	Universidad Autonoma de Queretaro	Sum	Intermed	Academic Programs International	n/a
Mexico | Puebla	Benemerita Universidad Autonoma de Puebla	Fall Spr YrRound	Consrtm	Program for Mexican Culture and Society in Puebla (PMCSP)	HostFam
	Costs: Fall Costs: T&F: n/a, R&B: n/a, Ttl: Wellesley home comprehensive fees Spr Costs: T&F: n/a, R&B: n/a, Ttl: Wellesley home comprehensive fees YrRound Costs: T&F: n/a, R&B: n/a, Ttl: Wellesley home comprehensive fees				
Mongolia | Ulaanbaatar	SIT Study Abroad	n/a	Intermed	SIT Study Abroad	n/a
Morocco | Fez	Arabic Language Institute	Sum	USColl	Wake Forest University	n/a
Morocco | Rabat	Center for Cross-cultural Learning	n/a	Self	n/a	n/a
Morocco | Rabat	Ecole Superieure de Direction et de Gestion	n/a	Intermed	Council on International Educational Exchange (CIEE)	n/a
Morocco | Rabat	SIT Study Abroad	n/a	Intermed	SIT Study Abroad	n/a
Morocco | Rabat	SIT Study Abroad	n/a	Intermed	SIT Study Abroad	n/a
Morocco | Rabat	SIT Study Abroad	Sum	Intermed	SIT Study Abroad	n/a
Namibia | Windhoek	Augsburg College	Sum	USColl	Augsburg College	n/a
Nepal | Kathmandu	SIT Study Abroad	n/a	Intermed	SIT Study Abroad	n/a
Netherlands | Amsterdam	IES Abroad Amsterdam Center	n/a	Intermed	IES Abroad	n/a
Netherlands | Amsterdam	Institute at the International School for Humanities and Social Sciences (University of Amsterdam)	Sum	Dir	n/a	n/a
New Zealand | (Multiple)	SUNY (Brockport)	n/a	USColl	SUNY (Brockport)	n/a
New Zealand | [City Unspecified]	Wellesley College	n/a	Self	n/a	n/a
Nicaragua | Managua	SIT Study Abroad	n/a	Intermed	SIT Study Abroad	n/a
Northern Ireland | Belfast	Queen's University Belfast	n/a	Dir	n/a	n/a
Oman | Muscat	SIT Study Abroad	n/a	Intermed	SIT Study Abroad	n/a
Panama | Panama City	SIT Study Abroad	n/a	Intermed	SIT Study Abroad	n/a
Peru | (Multiple)	University of Maryland	n/a	USColl	University of Maryland	n/a
Poland | Krakow	Jagiellonian University	n/a	Intermed	Academic Programs International	n/a

Massachusetts

DESTINATION	HOST INSTITUTION	PRGM SEASON	PRGM TYPE	INTERMEDIARY	HOUSING
Russia | (Multiple)	Multiple institutional choices	Sum	Intermed	American Councils for International Education	n/a
Russia | Irkutsk	Irkutsk State University	n/a	USColl	Middlebury College	n/a
Russia | Moscow	O'Neill Moscow Art Theatre (Connecticut College)	n/a	USColl	O'Neill Moscow Art Theatre (Connecticut College)	n/a
Russia | Moscow	Russian State University of the Humanities	n/a	USColl	Middlebury College	n/a
Russia | Moscow	Wellesley College	n/a	Self	n/a	n/a
Russia | St. Petersburg	Smolny College	n/a	Intermed	Bard-Smolny Study Abroad	n/a
Russia | St. Petersburg	St. Petersburg State University	Sum	Intermed	Council on International Educational Exchange (CIEE)	n/a
Russia | Yaroslavl	Yaroslavl State Pedagogical University	n/a	USColl	Middlebury College	n/a
Scotland | Edinburgh	Scottish Universities' International Summer School (University of Edinburgh)	Sum	Dir	Scottish Universities' International Summer School (University of Edinburgh)	n/a
Scotland | Edinburgh	University of Edinburgh	n/a	Dir	n/a	n/a
Scotland | Glasgow	Glasgow University	n/a	Dir	n/a	n/a
Scotland | St. Andrews	St. Andrew's University	n/a	Dir	n/a	n/a
Senegal | Dakar	SIT Study Abroad	n/a	Intermed	SIT Study Abroad	n/a
Senegal | Dakar	Suffolk University-Dakar Campus	n/a	Intermed	Council on International Educational Exchange (CIEE)	n/a
Senegal | Dakar	University of Maryland	n/a	USColl	University of Maryland	n/a
South Africa | Cape Town	University of Cape Town	n/a	Intermed	Council on International Educational Exchange (CIEE)	n/a
South Africa | Cape Town	University of Cape Town	Sum	Intermed	Council on International Educational Exchange (CIEE)	n/a
South Africa | Cape Town and Johannesburg	University of Maryland	n/a	USColl	University of Maryland	n/a
South Africa | Durban	SIT Study Abroad	Sum	Intermed	SIT Study Abroad	n/a
South Africa | Johannesburg	University of the Witwatersrand	n/a	USColl	International Human Rights Exchange (Bard College)	n/a
South Africa | Kruger National Park	Organization for Tropical Studies (Duke University)	n/a	Intermed	Organization for Tropical Studies (Duke University)	n/a
South Korea | Seoul	Ewha Womans University	n/a	Bilat	n/a	n/a
South Korea | Seoul	Ewha Womans University	Sum	Dir	n/a	n/a
South Korea | Seoul	Ewha Womans University	n/a	USColl	Wellesley College	n/a
South Korea | Seoul	Seoul National University	Sum	Dir	n/a	n/a
South Korea | Seoul	Yonsei University	Sum	Dir	n/a	n/a
South Korea | Seoul	Yonsei University	n/a	Intermed	Council on International Educational Exchange (CIEE)	n/a
South Korea | Seoul	Yonsei University	Sum	Intermed	Council on International Educational Exchange (CIEE)	n/a
Spain | Alcala de Henares	Universidad de Alcala	Sum	Intermed	Council on International Educational Exchange (CIEE)	n/a

Massachusetts

DESTINATION	HOST INSTITUTION	PRGM SEASON	PRGM TYPE	INTERMEDIARY	HOUSING
Spain | Barcelona	CIEE Study Center	Sum	Intermed	Council on International Educational Exchange (CIEE)	n/a
Spain | Barcelona	IES Abroad Barcelona Center	Sum	Intermed	IES Abroad	n/a
Spain | Barcelona	Universitat Pompeu Fabra	n/a	Intermed	Council on International Educational Exchange (CIEE)	n/a
Spain | Barcelona	Wellesley College	n/a	Self	n/a	n/a
Spain | Bilbao	Universidad del Pais Vasco or University of Deusto	Sum	Intermed	Academic Programs International	n/a
Spain | Cadiz	University of Cadiz	Sum	Intermed	Academic Programs International	n/a
Spain | Cordoba	Universidad de Cordoba	Fall Spr	Consrtm	Programa de Estudios Hispanicos en Cordoba (PRESHCO)	CollRes PrivApt

Costs: Fall Costs: T&F: n/a, R&B: n/a, Ttl: Wellesley home comprehensive fees Spr Costs: T&F: n/a, R&B: n/a, Ttl: Wellesley home comprehensive fees

DESTINATION	HOST INSTITUTION	PRGM SEASON	PRGM TYPE	INTERMEDIARY	HOUSING
Spain | Granada	IES Abroad Granada Center	n/a	Intermed	IES Abroad	n/a
Spain | Leon	University of Leon	Sum	Intermed	Summer Institute of Hispanic Studies	n/a
Spain | Madrid	IES Abroad Madrid Center	Sum	Intermed	IES Abroad	n/a
Spain | Madrid	Universidad Carlos III de Madrid	n/a	Intermed	Council on International Educational Exchange (CIEE)	n/a
Spain | Salamanca	Colegio Hispano Continental	Sum	USColl	University of Massachusetts at Amherst	n/a
Spain | Salamanca	IES Abroad Center	Sum	Intermed	IES Abroad	n/a
Spain | Salamanca	Universidad de Salamanca	n/a	Intermed	Academic Programs International	n/a
Spain | Seville	CIEE Study Center	Sum	Intermed	Council on International Educational Exchange (CIEE)	n/a
Switzerland | Geneva	Boston University	n/a	USColl	Boston University	n/a
Switzerland | Geneva	University of Geneva	n/a	Dir	n/a	n/a
Switzerland and England | Geneva and London	Boston University Centers in Geneva and London	Sum	USColl	Boston University	n/a
Taiwan | Taipei	International Chinese Language Program (National Taiwan Normal University)	Sum	Dir	n/a	n/a
Taiwan | Taipei	Mandarin Training Center (National Taiwan Normal University)	Sum	Dir	n/a	n/a
Tanzania | Arusha	SIT Study Abroad	n/a	Intermed	SIT Study Abroad	n/a
Tanzania | Arusha	SIT Study Abroad	n/a	Intermed	SIT Study Abroad	n/a
Thailand | Khon Kaen	Khon Kaen University	n/a	Intermed	Council on International Educational Exchange (CIEE)	n/a
Turkey | Alanya	McGhee Center for Eastern Mediterranean Studies (Georgetown University)	n/a	USColl	Georgetown University	n/a
Turkey | Unknown	University of Maryland	n/a	USColl	University of Maryland	n/a
Turks and Caicos | South Caicos	Center for Marine Resource Management Studies	n/a	Intermed	School for Field Studies	n/a

© 2011 — Updates? Want to be in the next edition? Visit **www.mysecondcampus.com**

Massachusetts

DESTINATION	HOST INSTITUTION	PRGM SEASON	PRGM TYPE	INTERMEDIARY	HOUSING
Uganda | Kampala	SIT Study Abroad	n/a	Intermed	SIT Study Abroad	n/a
United States | (Multiple choices)	Multiple institutional choices	n/a	Bilat	n/a	n/a
United States | South Carolina	Wellesley College	n/a	Self	n/a	n/a
Vietnam | Can Tho	SIT Study Abroad	n/a	Intermed	SIT Study Abroad	n/a
Vietnam | Ho Chi Minh City	SIT Study Abroad	n/a	Intermed	SIT Study Abroad	n/a
Vietnam | Ho Chi Minh City	Vietnam National University	n/a	Intermed	Council on International Educational Exchange (CIEE)	n/a

Wentworth Institute of Technology

Glenn Wiggins
Head of Architecture Department
550 Huntington Avenue
Boston, MA 02115

wigginsg@wit.edu
617.989.4470
http://www.wit.edu/arch/wit_web_site/programs_study_abroad.html

DESTINATION	HOST INSTITUTION	PRGM SEASON	PRGM TYPE	INTERMEDIARY	HOUSING
Germany | Berlin	Fachhochschule fur Technik und Wirtschaft (FHTW)	n/a	Self	n/a	n/a
Venezuela | Caracas	Universidad Central de Venezuela in Caracas	n/a	Bilat	n/a	n/a

Western New England College

Saeed Ghahramani
Director of the Study Abroad Program
1215 Wilbraham Road
Springfield, MA 01119

ghahram@wnec.edu
413.782.1218
http://www1.wnec.edu/admissions/index.cfm?selection=doc.202

DESTINATION	HOST INSTITUTION	PRGM SEASON	PRGM TYPE	INTERMEDIARY	HOUSING
England | London	Western New England College	Fall	Self	n/a	n/a
	Costs: Fall Costs: T&F: n/a, R&B: n/a, Ttl: Western New England home comprehensive fees				
Greece and Italy | Unknown	Western New England College	Sum	Self	n/a	n/a
Ireland | Unknown	Western New England College	Spr	Self	n/a	n/a

Westfield State College

Cynthia Siegler
Director of International Programs
Parenzo Hall 130
577 Western Avenue
Westfield, MA 01085

csiegler@wsc.ma.edu
413.572.8545
http://wsc.ma.edu/educationabroad/

DESTINATION	HOST INSTITUTION	PRGM SEASON	PRGM TYPE	INTERMEDIARY	HOUSING
Belize | Monkey Bay Wildlife Sanctuary	Westfield State College	Win	Self	n/a	CollRes
	Costs: Win Costs: T&F: n/a, R&B: n/a, Ttl: $3,550				
China | Beijing	Capital Normal University	Fall Spr YrRound	Bilat	n/a	n/a
China | Zhuhai	United International College	Fall Spr YrRound	Bilat	n/a	n/a
Costa Rica | San Jose and Monteverde	Westfield State College	Spr	Self	n/a	Other
	Costs: Spr Costs: T&F: n/a, R&B: n/a, Ttl: $3,550				

© 2011 — Updates? Want to be in the next edition? Visit **www.mysecondcampus.com**

Massachusetts

DESTINATION	HOST INSTITUTION	PRGM SEASON	PRGM TYPE	INTERMEDIARY	HOUSING
Greece | Athens	Westfield State College	Spr	Self	n/a	Other
Costs: Spr Costs: T&F: n/a, R&B: n/a, Ttl: $4,550					
India | (Multiple)	Westfield State College	Win	Self	n/a	PrivApt Other
Costs: Win Costs: T&F: n/a, R&B: n/a, Ttl: $4,950					
Israel | (Multiple)	Westfield State College	Spr	Self	n/a	Other
Costs: Spr Costs: T&F: n/a, R&B: n/a, Ttl: $4,550					
Kenya | Nairobi	Westfield State College	Win	Self	n/a	CollRes Other
Costs: Win Costs: T&F: n/a, R&B: n/a, Ttl: $4,950					
Mexico | Merida	Westfield State College	Win	Self	n/a	Other
Costs: Win Costs: T&F: n/a, R&B: n/a, Ttl: $3,550					
Puerto Rico | Ponce and San Juan	Westfield State College	Win	Self	n/a	CollRes
Costs: Win Costs: T&F: n/a, R&B: n/a, Ttl: $3,550					
Puerto Rico | Ponce and San Juan	Westfield State College	Win	Self	n/a	CollRes
Costs: Win Costs: T&F: n/a, R&B: n/a, Ttl: $3,550					
Spain | Madrid and Granada	Westfield State College	Win	Self	n/a	HostFam Other
Costs: Win Costs: T&F: n/a, R&B: n/a, Ttl: $3,950					
Vietnam | (Multiple)	Westfield State College	Win	Self	n/a	Other
Costs: Win Costs: T&F: n/a, R&B: n/a, Ttl: $5,250					

Wheaton College

Alfredo Varela
Dean
Center for Global Education
26 East Main Street
Norton, MA 02766

varela_alfredo@wheatonma.edu
508.286.4950
http://wheatoncollege.edu/global/study/study-programs/

DESTINATION	HOST INSTITUTION	PRGM SEASON	PRGM TYPE	INTERMEDIARY	HOUSING
(Multiple choices) | (Multiple choices)	Multiple institutional choices	n/a	Intermed	SIT Study Abroad	n/a
Argentina | Buenos Aires	Multiple institutional choices	Fall Spr YrRound	Intermed	Institute for Study Abroad	n/a
Argentina | Mendoza	Universidad Nacional de Cuyo	Fall Spr YrRound	Intermed	Institute for Study Abroad	n/a
Australia | Cairn	James Cook University	Fall Spr YrRound	Dir	n/a	n/a
Australia | Sydney	Boston University	Fall	USColl	Boston University	n/a
Australia | Townsville	James Cook University	Fall Spr YrRound	Dir	n/a	n/a
Australia | Wollongong	University of Wollongong	Fall Spr YrRound	Dir	n/a	n/a
Austria | Vienna	IES Abroad Vienna Center	Fall Spr	Intermed	IES Abroad	n/a
Botswana | Gaborone	University of Botswana	Fall Spr YrRound	Dir	n/a	n/a
Chile | Santiago	Multiple institutional choices	Fall Spr YrRound	Intermed	Institute for Study Abroad	n/a
Chile | Valparaiso	Multiple institutional choices	Fall Spr YrRound	Intermed	Institute for Study Abroad	n/a
China | Hong Kong	Chinese University of Hong Kong	Fall Spr	Dir	n/a	n/a
Costa Rica | Heredia	La Universidad Nacional Autonoma	Fall Spr YrRound	Intermed	Institute for Study Abroad	n/a
Costa Rica | San Jose	Organization for Tropical Studies	Fall Spr	Intermed	Organization for Tropical Studies	n/a

Massachusetts

DESTINATION	HOST INSTITUTION	PRGM SEASON	PRGM TYPE	INTERMEDIARY	HOUSING
Costa Rica | San Jose	Unversidad de Costa Rica	Fall Spr YrRound	Intermed	Institute for Study Abroad	n/a
Denmark | Copenhagen	Danish Institute for Study Abroad (DIS)	Fall Spr YrRound	Intermed	Danish Institute for Study Abroad (DIS)	n/a
Egypt | Cairo	American University in Cairo	Fall Spr YrRound	Dir	n/a	n/a
England | Brighton	University of Sussex	YrRound	Dir	n/a	n/a
England | London	Boston University	Fall	USColl	Boston University	n/a
England | London	London School of Economics and Political Science	YrRound	Dir	n/a	n/a
England | Oxford	Oxford University	n/a	Intermed	Institute for Study Abroad	n/a
France | Paris	Boston University	Fall	USColl	Boston University	n/a
France | Paris	Multiple institutional choices	Fall Spr YrRound	USColl	Sweet Briar College	n/a
Germany | Berlin	Freie Universitat Berlin	Fall Spr	Dir	n/a	n/a
Germany | Regensburg	University of Regensburg	Fall Spr	Consrtm	Vanderbilt and Wesleyan Universities	n/a
Greece | Athens	International Center for Hellenic & Mediterranean Studies (College Year in Athens)	Fall Spr YrRound	Intermed	College Year in Athens	n/a
India | Delhi	IES Abroad Delhi Center	Fall Spr YrRound	Intermed	IES Abroad	n/a
Ireland | Cork	University College Cork	Fall Spr	Dir	n/a	n/a
Ireland | Dublin	Dublin City University	Fall	USColl	Boston University	n/a
Italy | Cortona	John D. Kehoe Center (University of Georgia)	Fall Spr YrRound	USColl	University of Georgia	n/a
Italy | Ferrara	University of Ferrara	Fall Spr YrRound	USColl	Middlebury College	n/a
Italy | Florence	Universita degli Studi di Firenze	Fall Spr YrRound	USColl	Middlebury College	n/a
Italy | Rome	IES Abroad Rome Center	Fall Spr YrRound	Intermed	IES Abroad	n/a
Japan | Nagoya	Nanzan University	n/a	Intermed	IES Abroad	n/a
Japan | Tokyo	IES Abroad Tokyo Center	n/a	Intermed	IES Abroad	n/a
Mexico | Puebla	Benemerita Universidad Autonoma de Puebla	Fall Spr YrRound	Consrtm	Program for Mexican Culture and Society in Puebla (PMCSP)	n/a
New Zealand | Auckland	University of Auckland	Fall Spr	Dir	n/a	n/a
New Zealand | Christchurch	University of Canterbury	Fall Spr YrRound	Dir	n/a	n/a
Russia | Irkutsk	Irkutsk State University	Fall Spr YrRound	USColl	Middlebury College	n/a
Russia | Moscow	Russian State University of the Humanities	Fall Spr YrRound	USColl	Middlebury College	n/a
Russia | Yaroslavl	Yaroslavl State Pedagogical University	Fall Spr YrRound	USColl	Middlebury College	n/a
Scotland | Edinburgh	University of Edinburgh	Fall Spr YrRound	Dir	n/a	n/a
Scotland | Edinburgh	University of Edinburgh	Fall Spr	Dir	n/a	n/a
Scotland | Glasgow	Glasgow School of Art	Fall	Dir	n/a	n/a
South Africa | Grahamstown	Rhodes University	Fall Spr YrRound	Dir	n/a	n/a
Spain | Cordoba	Universidad de Cordoba	Fall Spr	Consrtm	Programa de Estudios Hispanicos en Cordoba	n/a

© 2011 — Updates? Want to be in the next edition? Visit **www.mysecondcampus.com**

Massachusetts

DESTINATION	HOST INSTITUTION	PRGM SEASON	PRGM TYPE	INTERMEDIARY	HOUSING

Wheelock College

Joan M. Bergstrom jbergstrom@wheelock.edu
Professor of Education and Director 617.879.2227
Center for International Education, Leadership, and Innovation
200 The Riverway
Boston, MA 02215

DESTINATION	HOST INSTITUTION	PRGM SEASON	PRGM TYPE	INTERMEDIARY	HOUSING
[Country Unspecified] | [City Unspecified]	n/a	n/a	n/a	n/a	n/a

Williams College

Laura McKeon laura.b.mckeon@williams.edu
Associate Dean 413.597.3131
880 Main Street http://www.williams.edu/dean/sa.php
Hopkins Hall 3rd floor
P.O. Box 624
Williamstown, MA 01267

DESTINATION	HOST INSTITUTION	PRGM SEASON	PRGM TYPE	INTERMEDIARY	HOUSING
(Multiple) | (Multiple)	Antioch College	Fall	USColl	Antioch College	n/a
(Multiple) | (Multiple)	International Honors Program	Fall	Intermed	International Honors Program	n/a
Argentina | Buenos Aires	IES Abroad Buenos Aires Center	Fall Spr YrRound	Intermed	IES Abroad	n/a
Argentina | Buenos Aires	Multiple institutional choices	Fall Spr YrRound	USColl	Middlebury College	n/a
Argentina | Buenos Aires	Multiple institutional choices	Fall Spr YrRound	Intermed	Institute for Study Abroad	n/a
Argentina | Buenos Aires	Multiple institutional choices	Fall Spr YrRound	Intermed	Council on International Educational Exchange (CIEE)	n/a
Argentina | Mendoza	Universidad Nacional de Cuyo	Fall Spr YrRound	Intermed	Institute for Study Abroad	n/a
Australia | (Multiple choices)	Multiple institutional choices	Fall Spr YrRound	USColl	Arcadia University	n/a
Australia | (Multiple choices)	Multiple institutional choices	Fall Spr YrRound	Intermed	Institute for Study Abroad	n/a
Australia | Cairns	SIT Study Abroad	Fall Spr	Intermed	SIT Study Abroad	n/a
Australia | Melbourne	Multiple institutional choices	Fall Spr YrRound	Intermed	IES Abroad	n/a
Australia | Rockhampton	Central Queensland Conservatorium of Music	Fall Spr YrRound	Dir	n/a	n/a
Australia | Yungaburra	Center for Rainforest Studies	Fall Spr	Intermed	School for Field Studies	n/a
Austria | Graz	Karl-Franzens-Universitat	Fall Spr YrRound	Dir	n/a	n/a
Austria | Vienna	IES Abroad Vienna Center	Fall Spr YrRound	Intermed	IES Abroad	n/a
Austria | Vienna	University of Vienna	YrRound	Dir	n/a	n/a
Bangladesh | Dhaka	Independent University Bangladesh	Spr	Intermed	Higher Education Consortium for Urban Affairs (HECUA)	n/a
Belgium | Antwerp	University of Antwerp	Fall Spr	Dir	n/a	n/a
Belgium | Brussels	Universite Libre de Bruxelles	Fall Spr	Dir	n/a	n/a
Belgium | Brussels	Universite Libre de Bruxelles or Vesalius College	Fall Spr YrRound	Intermed	Council on International Educational Exchange (CIEE)	n/a
Belgium | Leuven	Katholieke Universiteit Leuven	Fall Spr YrRound	Dir	n/a	n/a
Bolivia | Cochabamba	SIT Study Abroad	Fall Spr	Intermed	SIT Study Abroad	n/a

Massachusetts

DESTINATION	HOST INSTITUTION	PRGM SEASON	PRGM TYPE	INTERMEDIARY	HOUSING
Botswana	Gaborone	SIT Study Abroad	Fall Spr	Intermed	SIT Study Abroad	n/a
Botswana	Gaborone	University of Botswana	Fall Spr YrRound	USColl	Pitzer College	n/a
Brazil	Belem	SIT Study Abroad	Fall Spr	Intermed	SIT Study Abroad	n/a
Brazil	Belo Horizonte	Pontificia Universidade Catolica de Minas Gerais	Fall Spr YrRound	USColl	Middlebury College	n/a
Brazil	Fortaleza	Instituto Brasil/Estados Unidos/Ceara	Fall Spr	Intermed	SIT Study Abroad	n/a
Brazil	Rio de Janeiro	Pontificia Universidade Catolica	Fall YrRound	USColl	Brown University	n/a
Brazil	Salvador da Bahia	Universidade Catolica do Salvador or Universidade Federal da Bahia	Fall Spr YrRound	Intermed	Council on International Educational Exchange (CIEE)	n/a
Brazil	Sao Paulo	Escola de Administracao de Empresas de Sao Paulo da Fundacao Getulio Vargas or Pontificia Universidad Catolica de Sao Paulo	Fall Spr YrRound	Intermed	Council on International Educational Exchange (CIEE)	n/a
Brazil	Sao Paulo	Universidade Estadual de Campinas	Fall Spr YrRound	USColl	SUNY Albany	n/a
Canada	(Multiple choices)	Multiple institutional choices	n/a	Dir	n/a	n/a
Chile	Santiago	IES Abroad Santiago Center	Fall Spr YrRound	Intermed	IES Abroad	n/a
Chile	Santiago	Multiple institutional choices	Fall Spr YrRound	Intermed	Institute for Study Abroad	n/a
Chile	Santiago	Pontificia Universidad Catolica de Chile or Universidad de Chile	Fall Spr YrRound	Intermed	Council on International Educational Exchange (CIEE)	n/a
Chile	Santiago	SIT Study Abroad	Fall Spr	Intermed	SIT Study Abroad	n/a
Chile	Valparaiso	Multiple institutional choices	Fall Spr YrRound	Intermed	Institute for Study Abroad	n/a
China	Beijing	Associated Colleges in China (Hamilton College)	Fall Spr YrRound	USColl	Associated Colleges in China (Hamilton College)	n/a
China	Beijing	Beijing Language and Culture University	Fall Spr YrRound	Intermed	Alliance for Global Education	n/a
China	Beijing	CET Academic Programs	Fall Spr YrRound	Intermed	CET Academic Programs	n/a
China	Beijing	IES Abroad Beijing Center	Fall Spr YrRound	Intermed	IES Abroad	n/a
China	Beijing	Peking University or Minzu University of China	Fall Spr	Intermed	Council on International Educational Exchange (CIEE)	n/a
China	Beijing	Tsinghua University	Fall Spr YrRound	Consrtm	Inter-University Program for Chinese Language Studies (University of California, Berkeley)	n/a
China	Beijing	Tsinghua University	Fall Spr YrRound	USColl	Columbia University	n/a
China	Hangzhou	Zhejiang University of Technology	Fall Spr YrRound	USColl	Middlebury College	n/a
China	Harbin	CET Academic Programs	Fall Spr YrRound	Intermed	CET Academic Programs	n/a
China	Hong Kong	Chinese University of Hong Kong	Fall Spr YrRound	Dir	n/a	n/a
China	Hong Kong	Chinese University of Hong Kong	Fall Spr YrRound	USColl	Yale University	n/a
China	Hong Kong	SU Hong Kong Center	Fall Spr YrRound	USColl	Syracuse University	n/a
China	Hong Kong	University of Hong Kong	Fall Spr YrRound	Dir	n/a	n/a
China	Hong Kong	University of Hong Kong	Fall Spr YrRound	Intermed	AsiaLearn	n/a

© 2011 — Updates? Want to be in the next edition? Visit **www.mysecondcampus.com**

Massachusetts

DESTINATION	HOST INSTITUTION	PRGM SEASON	PRGM TYPE	INTERMEDIARY	HOUSING
China	Kunming	SIT Study Abroad	Fall Spr	Intermed	SIT Study Abroad	n/a
China	Kunming	Yunnan Normal University	Spr	USColl	Duke University	n/a
China	Nanjing	Nanjing University	Fall Spr	Intermed	Council on International Educational Exchange (CIEE)	n/a
China	Shanghai	CET Academic Programs	Fall Spr YrRound	Intermed	CET Academic Programs	n/a
China	Shanghai	Fudan University	Fall Spr YrRound	Intermed	Alliance for Global Education	n/a
China	Shanghai	Shanghai University of Finance and Economics	Fall Spr YrRound	Intermed	Alliance for Global Education	n/a
China	Xi'an	Xi'an International Studies University	Fall Spr YrRound	Intermed	Alliance for Global Education	n/a
Colombia	Bogota	Universidad de los Andes	Fall Spr YrRound	Dir	n/a	n/a
Costa Rica	(Multiple choices)	Institute for Central American Developments Studies (ICADS)	Fall Spr YrRound	Intermed	Institute for Central American Developments Studies (ICADS)	n/a
Costa Rica	(Multiple choices)	Institute for Central American Developments Studies (ICADS)	Fall Spr YrRound	Intermed	Institute for Central American Developments Studies (ICADS)	n/a
Costa Rica	Heredia	Universidad Nacional	Fall Spr YrRound	Intermed	Institute for Study Abroad	n/a
Costa Rica	San Jose	Organization for Tropical Studies (Duke University)	Fall Spr	Consrtm	Organization for Tropical Studies (Duke University)	n/a
Croatia	Zagreb	SIT Study Abroad	n/a	Intermed	SIT Study Abroad	n/a
Czech Republic	Prague	Center for Economic Research and Graduate Education Economics Institute (CERGE-EI)	Fall Spr YrRound	Dir	n/a	n/a
Czech Republic	Prague	CET Academic Programs	Fall Spr	Intermed	CET Academic Programs	n/a
Czech Republic	Prague	Charles University or Prague Film and Television School of the Academy of the Performing Arts	Fall Spr YrRound	Intermed	Council on International Educational Exchange (CIEE)	n/a
Czech Republic	Prague	NYU Center	Fall Spr YrRound	USColl	New York University	n/a
Czech Republic	Prague	SIT Study Abroad	Fall Spr	Intermed	SIT Study Abroad	n/a
Denmark	Copenhagen	Danish Institute for Study Abroad (DIS)	Fall Spr YrRound	Intermed	Danish Institute for Study Abroad (DIS)	n/a
Dominican Republic	Santiago	Pontificia Universidad Catolica Madre y Maestra	Fall Spr YrRound	Intermed	Council on International Educational Exchange (CIEE)	n/a
Dominican Republic	Santo Domingo	Facultad Latinoamericana de Ciencias Sociales	Fall Spr YrRound	Intermed	Council on International Educational Exchange (CIEE)	n/a
Ecuador	Quito	Higher Education Consortium for Urban Affairs (HECUA)	Fall Spr	Intermed	Higher Education Consortium for Urban Affairs (HECUA)	n/a
Ecuador	Quito	Pontificia Universidad Catolica del Ecuador	Fall Spr YrRound	USColl	Pitzer College	n/a
Ecuador	Quito	Pontificia Universidad Catolica del Ecuador	Fall Spr YrRound	Dir	n/a	n/a
Ecuador	Quito	SIT Study Abroad	Fall Spr YrRound	Intermed	SIT Study Abroad	n/a
Ecuador	Quito	Universidad Salesiana del Ecuador and Facultad Latinoamericana de Ciencias Sociales (FLACSO)	n/a	USColl	Duke University	n/a

© 2011 — Updates? Want to be in the next edition? Visit **www.mysecondcampus.com**

Massachusetts

DESTINATION	HOST INSTITUTION	PRGM SEASON	PRGM TYPE	INTERMEDIARY	HOUSING
Ecuador	Quito	Universidad San Francisco de Quito	YrRound	USColl	Kalamazoo College	n/a
Ecuador	Quito	Universidad San Francisco de Quito	YrRound	USColl	Kalamazoo College	n/a
Egypt	Alexandria	Alexandria University	Fall Spr YrRound	Intermed	Middlebury College	n/a
Egypt	Cairo	American University in Cairo	Fall Spr YrRound	Intermed	n/a	n/a
El Salvador	(Multiple choices)	Augsburg College	Fall Spr	USColl	Augsburg College	n/a
England	(Multiple choices)	Multiple institutional choices	Fall Spr YrRound	USColl	Arcadia University	n/a
England	(Multiple choices)	Multiple institutional choices	Fall Spr YrRound	Intermed	Institute for Study Abroad	n/a
England	Bath and Oxford	Advanced Studies in England	Fall Spr YrRound	Intermed	Advanced Studies in England	n/a
England	London	London Academy of Music and Dramatic Art (LAMDA)	Fall Spr	Dir	n/a	n/a
England	London	London School of Economics and Political Science	YrRound	Intermed	n/a	n/a
England	Oxford	Oxford University (Exeter College)	YrRound	Self	Williams-Exeter Programme (Williams College)	CollRes
	Costs: YrRound Costs: T&F: Williams home tuition & fees, R&B: Williams home room & board, Ttl: Williams home comprehensive fees				
Ethiopia	Addis Abba	Jimma University and Haramaya University	Fall YrRound	USColl	Brown University	n/a
Fiji	Suva	SIT Study Abroad	Fall Spr	Intermed	SIT Study Abroad	n/a
France	Aix-en-Provence	American University Center of Provence	Fall Spr YrRound	Intermed	American University Center of Provence	n/a
France	Aix-en-Provence	Universite de Provence	Spr YrRound	USColl	Wellesley College	n/a
France	Bordeaux	University of Bordeaux	Fall Spr YrRound	USColl	Middlebury College	n/a
France	Grenoble	Universite de Grenoble	Fall Spr YrRound	USColl	Swarthmore College	n/a
France	Nantes	IES Abroad Nantes Center	Fall Spr YrRound	Intermed	IES Abroad	n/a
France	Paris	CIEE Study Center in Paris	Fall Spr YrRound	Intermed	Council on International Educational Exchange (CIEE)	n/a
France	Paris	IES Abroad Paris Center	Fall Spr YrRound	Intermed	IES Abroad	n/a
France	Paris	Le Centre Madeleine	Fall Spr YrRound	USColl	Middlebury College	n/a
France	Paris	Multiple institutional choices	YrRound	USColl	Smith College	n/a
France	Paris	Multiple institutional choices	Fall Spr YrRound	Intermed	Center for University Programs Abroad (CUPA)	n/a
France	Paris	Multiple institutional choices	Fall Spr YrRound	USColl	Columbia University	n/a
France	Paris	Multiple institutional choices	Fall Spr YrRound	USColl	Sweet Briar College	n/a
France	Paris	NYU Center	Fall Spr YrRound	USColl	New York University	n/a
France	Paris	Reid Hall (Columbia University)	YrRound	USColl	Hamilton College	n/a
France	Paris	Tufts University	Spr	USColl	Tufts University	n/a
France	Paris	Wesleyan University	Fall Spr YrRound	USColl	Wesleyan University	n/a
France	Poitiers	Universite de Poitiers	Fall Spr YrRound	USColl	Middlebury College	n/a
France	Rennes	Universite de Haute Bretagne	Fall Spr YrRound	Intermed	Council on International Educational Exchange (CIEE)	n/a
France	Strasbourg	Syracuse Center	Fall Spr	USColl	Syracuse University	n/a
France	Toulouse	Institut Catholique Toulouse	Fall Spr YrRound	Intermed	SIT Study Abroad	n/a

© 2011 — Updates? Want to be in the next edition? Visit **www.mysecondcampus.com**

Massachusetts

DESTINATION	HOST INSTITUTION	PRGM SEASON	PRGM TYPE	INTERMEDIARY	HOUSING
France | Tours	University of Tours - Universite Francois Rabelais	Fall Spr YrRound	USColl	Davidson College	n/a
Germany | Berlin	Freie Universitat Berlin	Fall Spr YrRound	USColl	Middlebury College	n/a
Germany | Berlin	IES Abroad Berlin Center	Fall Spr YrRound	Intermed	IES Abroad	n/a
Germany | Berlin	Lexia Study Abroad	Fall Spr YrRound	Intermed	Lexia Study Abroad	n/a
Germany | Berlin	Multiple institutional choices	Fall Spr YrRound	USColl	Columbia University	n/a
Germany | Freiburg	IES Abroad Freiburg Center	Fall Spr YrRound	Intermed	IES Abroad	n/a
Germany | Hamburg	Multiple institutional choices	Fall Spr YrRound	USColl	Smith College	n/a
Germany | Mainz	Johannes Gutenberg-Universitat	Fall Spr YrRound	USColl	Middlebury College	n/a
Ghana | Accra	SIT Study Abroad	Fall Spr	Intermed	SIT Study Abroad	n/a
Ghana | Accra	University of Ghana	YrRound	Intermed	SUNY Brockport	n/a
Greece | Athens	Arcadia Center for Hellenic, Mediterranean and Balkan Studies	Fall Spr YrRound	USColl	Arcadia University	n/a
Greece | Athens	College Year in Athens	Fall Spr YrRound	Intermed	College Year in Athens	n/a
Guatemala | (Multiple choices)	Augsburg College	Fall Spr	USColl	Augsburg College	n/a
Hungary | Budapest	Central European University	Fall Spr YrRound	USColl	Bard College	n/a
Hungary | Budapest	Corvinus University of Budapest	Fall Spr YrRound	Intermed	Council on International Educational Exchange (CIEE)	n/a
Hungary | Budapest	Technical University of Budapest, College International	Fall Spr YrRound	Intermed	Budapest Semesters in Mathematics	n/a
India | Bodh Gaya	Antioch Education Abroad (Antioch University)	Fall	USColl	Antioch Education Abroad (Antioch University)	n/a
India | Delhi	SIT Study Abroad	Fall Spr	Intermed	SIT Study Abroad	n/a
India | Delhi	St. Stephen's College and Lady Shri Ram College for Women	Fall YrRound	USColl	Brown University	n/a
India | Dharamsala	Emory University	Spr	USColl	Emory University	n/a
India | Jaipur	SIT Study Abroad	Fall Spr	Intermed	SIT Study Abroad	n/a
India | Madurai	SITA Center	Fall Spr YrRound	Consrtm	South India Term Abroad (SITA)	n/a
India | Pune	Alliance for Global Education	Fall Spr YrRound	Intermed	Alliance for Global Education	n/a
India | Varanasi	University of Wisconsin, Madison	YrRound	USColl	University of Wisconsin, Madison	n/a
Indonesia | Bedulu	SIT Study Abroad	Fall Spr	Intermed	SIT Study Abroad	n/a
Ireland | (Multiple choices)	Multiple institutional choices	Fall Spr YrRound	Intermed	Interstudy	n/a
Ireland | (Multiple choices)	Multiple institutional choices	Fall Spr YrRound	USColl	Arcadia University	n/a
Ireland | (Multiple choices)	Multiple institutional choices	Fall Spr YrRound	Intermed	Institute for Study Abroad	n/a
Ireland | Ballyvaughan	Burren College of Art	Fall Spr YrRound	Intermed	Burren College of Art	n/a
Ireland | Dublin	IES Abroad Dublin Center	Fall Spr YrRound	Intermed	IES Abroad	n/a
Ireland | Dublin	SIT Study Abroad	Fall Spr	Intermed	SIT Study Abroad	n/a
Israel | Eilot	Arava Institute for Environmental Studies	Fall Spr	Dir	n/a	n/a
Israel | Haifa	Haifa University	Fall Spr YrRound	Dir	n/a	n/a
Israel | Jerusalem	Hebrew University	Fall Spr	USColl	Wesleyan University	n/a
Israel | Jerusalem	Hebrew University	Spr YrRound	Dir	n/a	n/a

Massachusetts

DESTINATION	HOST INSTITUTION	PRGM SEASON	PRGM TYPE	INTERMEDIARY	HOUSING
Israel | Tel Aviv	Tel Aviv University	Fall Spr YrRound	Dir	n/a	n/a
Italy | Bologna	K. Robert Nilsson Center for European Studies	YrRound	USColl	Dickinson College	n/a
Italy | Bologna	Universita di Bologna	Fall Spr YrRound	Consrtm	ECCO (Vassar, Wesleyan, and Wellesley)	n/a
Italy | Bologna	University of Bologna	Fall Spr YrRound	USColl	Brown University	n/a
Italy | Bologna	University of Bologna	YrRound	Consrtm	Bologna Consorial Studies Program (Indiana University)	n/a
Italy | Catania	CET Academic Programs	Fall Spr YrRound	Intermed	CET Academic Programs	n/a
Italy | Ferrara	Universita degli Studi di Ferrara	Fall Spr YrRound	USColl	Middlebury College	n/a
Italy | Florence	Accademia Italiana	Fall Spr YrRound	USColl	Arcadia University	n/a
Italy | Florence	Sarah Lawrence College	Spr YrRound	USColl	Sarah Lawrence College	n/a
Italy | Florence	Smith College	YrRound	USColl	Smith College	n/a
Italy | Florence	Studio Art Centers International (SACI)	Fall Spr YrRound	Intermed	Studio Art Centers International (SACI)	n/a
Italy | Florence	Syracuse University	Fall Spr YrRound	USColl	Syracuse University	n/a
Italy | Florence	Universita degli Studi di Firenze	Fall Spr YrRound	USColl	Middlebury College	n/a
Italy | Milan	IES Abroad Milan Center	Fall Spr YrRound	Intermed	IES Abroad	n/a
Italy | Orvieto	University of Arizona Orvieto Institute	Fall Spr YrRound	USColl	University of Arizona	n/a
Italy | Padova	BU Center for Italian and European Studies (CIES)	Fall Spr YrRound	USColl	Boston University	n/a
Italy | Parma	Universita degli Studi di Parma	Fall Spr	USColl	Pitzer College	n/a
Italy | Rome	Accademia Italiana	Fall Spr YrRound	USColl	Arcadia University	n/a
Italy | Rome	Cornell University	Fall Spr YrRound	USColl	Cornell University	n/a
Italy | Rome	IES Abroad Rome Center	Fall Spr YrRound	Intermed	IES Abroad	n/a
Italy | Rome	Intercollegiate Center for Classical Studies (ICCS)	Fall Spr YrRound	USColl	Duke University	n/a
Italy | Rome	Trinity College Rome Campus	Fall Spr YrRound	USColl	Trinity College	n/a
Italy | Siena	CET Academic Programs	Fall Spr YrRound	Intermed	CET Academic Programs	n/a
Italy | Siena	Siena School for Liberal Arts	Fall Spr YrRound	Intermed	Siena School for Liberal Arts	n/a
Italy | Syracuse	Mediterranean Center for Arts and Sciences	Fall Spr	Intermed	Mediterranean Center for Arts and Sciences	n/a
Italy | Venice	Scuola Internazionale di Grafica	Fall Spr YrRound	USColl	Boston University	n/a
Japan | Hikone	Japan Center for Michigan Universities (JCMU)	Fall Spr YrRound	Intermed	Japan Center for Michigan Universities (JCMU)	n/a
Japan | Hirakata	Kansai Gaidai University	Fall Spr YrRound	Dir	n/a	n/a
Japan | Kyoto	Associated Kyoto Program (Doshisha University)	YrRound	Intermed	Associated Kyoto Program (Doshisha University)	n/a
Japan | Kyoto	Kyoto Consortium for Japanese Studies (Columbia University)	Fall Spr YrRound	Consrtm	Kyoto Consortium for Japanese Studies (Columbia University)	n/a
Japan | Kyoto	Ryukoku University	Fall	USColl	Antioch Education Abroad (Antioch University)	n/a
Japan | Nagoya	Nanzan University	Fall Spr YrRound	Intermed	IES Abroad	n/a

Massachusetts

DESTINATION	HOST INSTITUTION	PRGM SEASON	PRGM TYPE	INTERMEDIARY	HOUSING
Japan | Tokyo	IES Abroad Tokyo Center	Fall Spr YrRound	Intermed	IES Abroad	n/a
Japan | Tokyo	Sophia University	Fall Spr YrRound	Intermed	Council on International Educational Exchange (CIEE)	n/a
Japan | Tokyo	Waseda University	Fall Spr YrRound	Dir	n/a	n/a
Jordan | Amman	SIT Study Abroad	Fall Spr	Intermed	SIT Study Abroad	n/a
Jordan | Amman	University of Jordan	Fall Spr YrRound	Intermed	Council on International Educational Exchange (CIEE)	n/a
Kenya | Mombasa	SIT Study Abroad	Fall Spr	Intermed	SIT Study Abroad	n/a
Kenya | Nairobi	Center for Wildlife Management Studies	Fall Spr	Intermed	School for Field Studies	n/a
Kenya | Nairobi	SIT Study Abroad	Fall Spr	Intermed	SIT Study Abroad	n/a
Kenya | Nairobi	St. Lawrence University	Fall Spr	USColl	St. Lawrence University	n/a
Kenya | Nairobi	University of Nairobi	Fall Spr YrRound	USColl	Bryan Mawr College	n/a
Kenya | Nairobi	University of Nairobi	YrRound	USColl	Kalamazoo College	n/a
Lebanon | Beirut	American University of Beirut	Fall Spr YrRound	Dir	n/a	n/a
Madagascar | Antananarivo	SIT Study Abroad	Fall Spr	Intermed	SIT Study Abroad	n/a
Mexico | Baja	Center for Coastal Studies	Fall Spr	Intermed	School for Field Studies	n/a
Mexico | Cuernavaca	Augsburg College	Fall Spr	USColl	Augsburg College	n/a
Mexico | Guadalajara	Universidad Autonoma de Guadalajara	Spr YrRound	Dir	n/a	n/a
Mexico | Guadalajara	Universidad de Guadalajara	Fall Spr YrRound	USColl	Middlebury College	n/a
Mexico | Merida	Universidad Autonoma de Yucatan	Fall Spr YrRound	Intermed	Institute for Study Abroad	n/a
Mexico | Merida	Universidad Autonoma de Yucatan	Fall Spr YrRound	USColl	Rutgers University	n/a
Mexico | Mexico City	Centro de Investigacion y Docencia Economicas (CIDE)	Fall Spr YrRound	Dir	n/a	n/a
Mexico | Oaxaca	SIT Study Abroad	Fall Spr	Intermed	SIT Study Abroad	n/a
Mexico | Oaxaca	University of Pennsylvania	Fall YrRound	USColl	University of Pennsylvania	n/a
Mexico | Puebla	Benemerita Universidad Autonoma de Puebla	Fall Spr YrRound	Consrtm	Program for Mexican Culture and Society in Puebla (Oberlin, Smith, Wellesley, and Wheaton)	n/a
Mexico | Xalapa	University of Veracruz	Fall Spr YrRound	Intermed	BCA Study Abroad	n/a
Mongolia | Ulaanbaatar	SIT Study Abroad	Fall Spr	Intermed	SIT Study Abroad	n/a
Morocco | Rabat	SIT Study Abroad	Fall Spr	Intermed	SIT Study Abroad	n/a
Namibia | Windhoek	Augsburg College	Fall Spr	USColl	Augsburg College	n/a
Nepal | Kathmandu	SIT Study Abroad	Fall Spr	Intermed	SIT Study Abroad	n/a
Nepal | Kathmandu	SIT Study Abroad	Fall Spr	Intermed	SIT Study Abroad	n/a
Nepal | Kathmandu	Tribhuvan University	Fall Spr	USColl	Pitzer College	n/a
Netherlands | Amsterdam	IES Abroad Amsterdam Center	Fall Spr YrRound	Intermed	IES Abroad	n/a
Netherlands | Amsterdam	SIT Study Abroad	Fall Spr	Intermed	SIT Study Abroad	n/a
Netherlands | Amsterdam	University of Amsterdam	Fall Spr YrRound	Intermed	Council on International Educational Exchange (CIEE)	n/a
New Zealand | (Multiple choices)	Multiple institutional choices	Fall Spr YrRound	Intermed	Institute for Study Abroad	n/a

Massachusetts

DESTINATION	HOST INSTITUTION	PRGM SEASON	PRGM TYPE	INTERMEDIARY	HOUSING
Nicaragua	(Multiple choices)	Augsburg College	Fall Spr	USColl	Augsburg College	n/a
Nicaragua	(Multiple choices)	Institute for Central American Developments Studies (ICADS)	Fall Spr	Intermed	Institute for Central American Developments Studies (ICADS)	n/a
Nicaragua	Managua	SIT Study Abroad	Fall Spr	Intermed	SIT Study Abroad	n/a
Northern Ireland	Belfast	University of Ulster	Fall Spr	Intermed	Higher Education Consortium for Urban Affairs (HECUA)	n/a
Norway	Bo	Scandinavian Seminar	Fall Spr YrRound	Intermed	Scandinavian Seminar	n/a
Norway	Oslo	University of Oslo	Fall Spr	Intermed	Higher Education Consortium for Urban Affairs (HECUA)	n/a
Norway	Trondheim	Norwegian University of Science and Technology	Fall Spr YrRound	Dir	n/a	n/a
Oman	Muscat	SIT Study Abroad	Fall Spr	Intermed	SIT Study Abroad	n/a
Panama	Panama City	SIT Study Abroad	Fall Spr	Intermed	SIT Study Abroad	n/a
Peru	Cuzco	Centro Bartolome de las Casas	Fall Spr	Intermed	SIT Study Abroad	n/a
Poland	Krakow	Jagiellonian University	Fall Spr YrRound	Intermed	Lexia Study Abroad	n/a
Poland	Warsaw	Warsaw School of Economics	Fall Spr YrRound	Intermed	Council on International Educational Exchange (CIEE)	n/a
Portugal	Coimbra	Universidade de Coimbra	YrRound	USColl	University of Wisconsin, Madison	n/a
Puerto Rico	San Juan	Universidad del Sagrado Corazon	Fall Spr YrRound	USColl	SUNY Albany	n/a
Russia	(Multiple choices)	Multiple institutional choices	Fall Spr YrRound	USColl	Middlebury College	n/a
Russia	Moscow	Independent University of Moscow	Fall Spr	Intermed	Math in Moscow	n/a
Russia	Moscow	Moscow International University	Fall Spr	Intermed	American Councils for International Education	n/a
Russia	St. Petersburg	Smolny College	Fall Spr YrRound	Intermed	Bard-Smolny Study Abroad	n/a
Russia	St. Petersburg	St. Petersburg State University	Fall Spr YrRound	Intermed	Council on International Educational Exchange (CIEE)	n/a
Russia	St. Petersburg	St.Petersburg State Theatre Arts Academy	Fall Spr YrRound	Dir	n/a	n/a
Russia	St. Petersburg	Vassar College	Fall	USColl	Vassar College	n/a
Scotland	(Multiple choices)	Multiple institutional choices	Fall Spr YrRound	USColl	Arcadia University	n/a
Scotland	(Multiple choices)	Multiple institutional choices	Fall Spr YrRound	Intermed	Institute for Study Abroad	n/a
Scotland	St. Andrews	University of St. Andrews	Fall Spr YrRound	Intermed	Interstudy	n/a
Senegal	Dakar	SIT Study Abroad	Fall Spr	Intermed	SIT Study Abroad	n/a
Senegal	Dakar	Suffolk University-Dakar Campus	Fall Spr YrRound	Intermed	Council on International Educational Exchange (CIEE)	n/a
Senegal	Dakar	Universite Cheikh Anta Diop	YrRound	USColl	Kalamazoo College	n/a
Senegal	Dakar	Universite Cheikh Anta Diop	Spr YrRound	USColl	Mount Holyoke College	n/a
Singapore	Singapore	National University of Singapore	Fall Spr YrRound	Dir	n/a	n/a
South Africa	(Multiple choices)	Multiple institutional choices	Fall Spr YrRound	Intermed	Interstudy	n/a
South Africa	Cape Town	SIT Study Abroad	Fall Spr	Intermed	SIT Study Abroad	n/a

© 2011 — Updates? Want to be in the next edition? Visit **www.mysecondcampus.com**

Massachusetts

DESTINATION	HOST INSTITUTION	PRGM SEASON	PRGM TYPE	INTERMEDIARY	HOUSING
South Africa | Cape Town	University of Cape Town or Students' Health and Welfare Centres Organisation	Fall Spr YrRound	Intermed	Council on International Educational Exchange (CIEE)	n/a
South Africa | Cape Town	Williams College	n/a	Self	Williams in Africa Initiative (Williams College)	n/a
South Africa | Durban	SIT Study Abroad	Fall Spr	Intermed	SIT Study Abroad	n/a
South Africa | Kruger National Park	Organization for Tropical Studies (Duke University)	Fall Spr	Consrtm	Organization for Tropical Studies (Duke University)	n/a
South Korea | Seoul	Ewha Women's University	Fall Spr YrRound	Dir	n/a	n/a
South Korea | Seoul	Seoul National University	Fall Spr YrRound	Dir	n/a	n/a
South Korea | Seoul	Yonsei University	Fall Spr YrRound	Dir	n/a	n/a
Spain | (Multiple choices)	IES Abroad	Fall Spr YrRound	Intermed	IES Abroad	n/a
Spain | (Multiple choices)	Multiple institutional choices	Fall Spr YrRound	USColl	Arcadia University	n/a
Spain | (Multiple choices)	Multiple institutional choices	Fall Spr YrRound	USColl	Middlebury College	n/a
Spain | Alicante	Center for Cross-Cultural Study	Fall Spr YrRound	Intermed	Center for Cross-Cultural Study	n/a
Spain | Barcelona	Multiple institutional choices	YrRound	USColl	University of Illinois, Urbana-Champaign	n/a
Spain | Barcelona	Multiple institutional choices	Spr YrRound	Intermed	Council on International Educational Exchange (CIEE)	n/a
Spain | Barcelona	Universitat de Barcelona	Fall Spr YrRound	Intermed	BCA Study Abroad	n/a
Spain | Burgos	Universidad de Burgos	Fall Spr YrRound	USColl	Boston University	n/a
Spain | Granada	SIT Study Abroad	Fall Spr	Intermed	SIT Study Abroad	n/a
Spain | Madrid	Hamilton College	Fall Spr YrRound	USColl	Hamilton College	n/a
Spain | Madrid	Instituto Internacional or Universidad Autonoma de Madrid	Fall Spr YrRound	USColl	Boston University	n/a
Spain | Madrid	SU Center	Fall Spr YrRound	USColl	Syracuse University	n/a
Spain | Madrid	Universidad de San Pablo - CEU	Fall Spr YrRound	USColl	Duke University	n/a
Spain | Salamanca	Universidad de Salamanca	Fall Spr YrRound	USColl	Emory University	n/a
Spain | Salamanca	Universidad de Salamanca	Fall Spr YrRound	USColl	Colby College	n/a
Spain | Seville	Center for Cross-Cultural Study	Fall Spr YrRound	Intermed	Center for Cross-Cultural Study	n/a
Spain | Seville	Universidad de Sevilla	Spr YrRound	USColl	Sweet Briar College	n/a
Spain | Seville	Universidad de Sevilla or Universidad Pablo de Olavide	Spr YrRound	Intermed	Council on International Educational Exchange (CIEE)	n/a
Spain | Seville	University of North Carolina, Chapel Hill	Fall Spr YrRound	USColl	University of North Carolina, Chapel Hill	n/a
Spain | Valencia	University of Virginia	Fall Spr YrRound	USColl	University of Virginia	n/a
Sweden | Stockholm	Stockholm University	Fall Spr YrRound	Consrtm	Swedish Program	n/a
Switzerland | Geneva	Boston University	Fall Spr	USColl	Boston University	n/a
Switzerland | Geneva	Multiple institutional choices	YrRound	USColl	Smith College	n/a
Switzerland | Geneva	SIT Study Abroad	Fall Spr	Intermed	SIT Study Abroad	n/a
Switzerland | Geneva	Universite de Geneve	Fall	Dir	n/a	n/a
Switzerland | Lausanne	Swiss Federal Institute of Technology	Spr YrRound	USColl	Iowa State University	n/a

© 2011 — Updates? Want to be in the next edition? Visit **www.mysecondcampus.com**

Massachusetts

DESTINATION	HOST INSTITUTION	PRGM SEASON	PRGM TYPE	INTERMEDIARY	HOUSING
Syria | Damascus	Higher Language Institute (University of Damascus)	Fall Spr YrRound	Dir	n/a	n/a
Taiwan | Taipei	International Chinese Language Program (National Taiwan Normal University)	YrRound	Dir	n/a	n/a
Taiwan | Taipei	Mandarin Training Center (National Taiwan Normal University)	Fall Spr YrRound	Dir	n/a	n/a
Taiwan | Taipei	National Chengchi University	Fall Spr YrRound	Intermed	Council on International Educational Exchange (CIEE)	n/a
Tanzania | Arusha	SIT Study Abroad	Fall Spr	Intermed	SIT Study Abroad	n/a
Tanzania | Zanzibar	SIT Study Abroad	Fall Spr	Intermed	SIT Study Abroad	n/a
Thailand | Chiang Mai	Chiang Mai University	YrRound	USColl	University of Wisconsin, Madison	n/a
Thailand | Khon Kaen	Khon Kaen University	Fall Spr	Intermed	Council on International Educational Exchange (CIEE)	n/a
Trinidad and Tobago | St. Augustine	University of the West Indies	Fall Spr YrRound	Dir	n/a	n/a
Turkey | Alanya	McGhee Center for Eastern Mediterranean Studies	Spr	USColl	Georgetown University	n/a
Turkey | Istanbul	Bogazici University	Spr	USColl	Duke University	n/a
Turkey | Istanbul	Bosphorus University	Fall Spr YrRound	USColl	SUNY Binghamton	n/a
Turks and Caicos | South Caicos	Center for Marine Resource Management Studies	Fall Spr	Intermed	School for Field Studies	n/a
Turks and Caicos | South Caicos	Center for Marine Resource Management Studies	Fall Spr	Intermed	School for Field Studies	n/a
United States | Mystic (CT)	Williams-Mystic Seaport Program	Fall Spr	Self	Williams-Mystic Seaport Program	Other
Costs: Fall Costs: T&F: $20,870, R&B: $4,080, Ttl: $24,950 Spr Costs: T&F: $20,870, R&B: $4,080, Ttl: $24,950					
United States | Woods Hole (MA)	Marine Biological Laboratory	n/a	Dir	Marine Biological Laboratory	n/a
Vietnam | Ho Chi Minh City	CET Academic Programs	Fall Spr	Intermed	CET Academic Programs	n/a
Vietnam | Ho Chi Minh City	SIT Study Abroad	Fall Spr	Intermed	SIT Study Abroad	n/a
Wales | Swansea	Swansea University	Fall Spr YrRound	Intermed	Interstudy	n/a

Worcester Polytechnic Institute

John A. Orr
Provost and Senior Vice President
100 Institute Road
Worcester, MA 01609

orr@wpi.edu
508.831.5222
http://www.wpi.edu/academics/catalogs/ugrad/global.html#oncampus

DESTINATION	HOST INSTITUTION	PRGM SEASON	PRGM TYPE	INTERMEDIARY	HOUSING
Australia | Melbourne	Worcester Polytechnic Institute	Spr	Self	n/a	n/a
Canada | Edmonton (Alberta)	Worcester Polytechnic Institute	Fall Spr	Self	n/a	n/a
China | (Multiple)	Worcester Polytechnic Institute	Sum	Self	n/a	n/a
China | Hong Kong	Worcester Polytechnic Institute	Spr	Self	n/a	n/a
China | Shanghai	Worcester Polytechnic Institute	Fall	Self	n/a	n/a
Costa Rica | San Jose	Worcester Polytechnic Institute	Fall	Self	n/a	n/a

© 2011 — Updates? Want to be in the next edition? Visit **www.mysecondcampus.com**

Massachusetts

DESTINATION	HOST INSTITUTION	PRGM SEASON	PRGM TYPE	INTERMEDIARY	HOUSING
Denmark	Copenhagen	Worcester Polytechnic Institute	Spr	Self	n/a	n/a
England	London	Worcester Polytechnic Institute	Sum	Self	n/a	n/a
England	London	Worcester Polytechnic Institute	Sum Spr	Self	n/a	n/a
France	Nancy	Worcester Polytechnic Institute	Spr	Self	n/a	n/a
Hungary	Budapest	Worcester Polytechnic Institute	Spr	Self	n/a	n/a
Ireland	Limerick	Worcester Polytechnic Institute	Fall	Self	n/a	n/a
Italy	Venice	Worcester Polytechnic Institute	Fall	Self	n/a	n/a
Morocco	Ifrane	Worcester Polytechnic Institute	Fall	Self	n/a	n/a
Namibia	Windhoek	Worcester Polytechnic Institute	Spr	Self	n/a	n/a
Panama	Panama City	Worcester Polytechnic Institute	Fall	Self	n/a	n/a
Puerto Rico	San Juan	Worcester Polytechnic Institute	Spr	Self	n/a	n/a
South Africa	Cape Town	Worcester Polytechnic Institute	Fall	Self	n/a	n/a
Thailand	Bangkok	Worcester Polytechnic Institute	Spr	Self	n/a	n/a
United States	(Multiple choices)	Worcester Polytechnic Institute	n/a	Self	n/a	n/a
United States	(Multiple choices)	Worcester Polytechnic Institute	n/a	Self	n/a	n/a
United States	Boston (MA)	Worcester Polytechnic Institute	Fall	Self	n/a	n/a
United States	Nantucket Island (MA)	Worcester Polytechnic Institute	Fall	Self	n/a	n/a
United States	New York (NY)	Worcester Polytechnic Institute	Fall	Self	n/a	n/a
United States	Santa Fe (NM)	Worcester Polytechnic Institute	Spr	Self	n/a	n/a
United States	Silicon Valley (CA)	Worcester Polytechnic Institute	Spr	Self	n/a	n/a
United States	Washington (DC)	Worcester Polytechnic Institute	Fall	Self	n/a	n/a
United States	Worcester (MA)	Worcester Polytechnic Institute	Fall Spr	Self	n/a	n/a

Worcester State College

Steve Chao
Director of the International Programs Office
International Programs Office
486 Chandler Street
Worcester, MA 01602

schao@worcester.edu
508.929.8747
http://www.worcester.edu/ip/Shared%20Documents/StudyAbroad.aspx

DESTINATION	HOST INSTITUTION	PRGM SEASON	PRGM TYPE	INTERMEDIARY	HOUSING
(Multiple choices)	(Multiple choices)	Multiple institutional choices	n/a	Intermed	International Partnership for Service-Learning and Leadership	n/a
(Multiple choices)	(Multiple choices)	Multiple institutional choices	n/a	USColl	SUNY Brockport	n/a
(Multiple choices)	(Multiple choices)	Multiple institutional choices	n/a	Intermed	Sol Education Abroad	n/a
(Multiple choices)	(Multiple choices)	Multiple institutional choices	n/a	Intermed	Global Student Experience	n/a
(Multiple choices)	(Multiple choices)	Multiple institutional choices	n/a	Intermed	Center for International Studies	n/a
(Multiple choices)	(Multiple choices)	Multiple institutional choices	n/a	Intermed	Australearn	n/a

© 2011 — Updates? Want to be in the next edition? Visit **www.mysecondcampus.com**

Massachusetts

DESTINATION	HOST INSTITUTION	PRGM SEASON	PRGM TYPE	INTERMEDIARY	HOUSING
(Multiple choices)	(Multiple choices)	Multiple institutional choices	n/a	Intermed	American Institute for Foreign Study	n/a
(Multiple choices)	(Multiple choices)	Multiple institutional choices	n/a	Intermed	Cultural Experiences Abroad	n/a
(Multiple choices)	(Multiple choices)	Multiple institutional choices	n/a	Consrtm	College Consortium for International Studies	n/a
(Multiple choices)	(Multiple choices)	Multiple institutional choices	n/a	Intermed	Council on International Education Exchange (CIEE)	n/a
(Multiple choices)	(Multiple choices)	Multiple institutional choices	n/a	Intermed	International Studies Abroad	n/a
(Multiple choices)	(Multiple choices)	Multiple institutional choices	n/a	Consrtm	University Studies Abroad Consortium (USAC)	n/a
(Multiple choices)	(Multiple choices)	Multiple institutional choices	n/a	Intermed	Academic Programs International	n/a
(Multiple choices)	(Multiple choices)	Semester at Sea	n/a	Intermed	Semester at Sea	n/a
(Multiple)	Dublin	American College Dublin	n/a	Intermed	American College Dublin	n/a
Belize	Unknown	Worcester State College	Sum Spr	Self	n/a	n/a
Costa Rica	(Multiple choices)	Worcester State College	n/a	Self	n/a	n/a
Ecuador	(Multiple choices)	Worcester State College	n/a	Self	n/a	n/a
England	Worcester	University of Worcester	n/a	Bilat	n/a	n/a
Nicaragua	Unknown	Worcester State College	Spr	Self	n/a	n/a
Puerto Rico	Cayey	University of Puerto Rico, Cayey	n/a	Bilat	n/a	n/a

© 2011 — Updates? Want to be in the next edition? Visit **www.mysecondcampus.com**

New Hampshire

DESTINATION	HOST INSTITUTION	PRGM SEASON	PRGM TYPE	INTERMEDIARY	HOUSING

Antioch University New England

Katherine Clarke
Vice President for Academic Affairs
40 Avon Street
Keene, NH 03431

kclarke@antioch.edu
603.283.2150

DESTINATION	HOST INSTITUTION	PRGM SEASON	PRGM TYPE	INTERMEDIARY	HOUSING
[Country Unspecified]	[City Unspecified]	n/a	n/a	n/a	n/a	n/a

Chester College of New England

Laura Ives
Dean of the College, Chief Academic Officer
40 Chester Street
Chester, NH 03036

laura.ives@chestercollege.edu
603.887.7403
http://chestercollege.edu/learn/study-abroad/

DESTINATION	HOST INSTITUTION	PRGM SEASON	PRGM TYPE	INTERMEDIARY	HOUSING
Greece	Paros	Aegean Center for the Fine Arts	Fall Spr	Intermed	Aegean Center for the Fine Arts	n/a
Italy	Florence	Firenze Arti Visive	Sum Fall Spr	Intermed	Firenze Arti Visive	n/a

Colby-Sawyer College

Kathy Taylor
Director of Career and Academic Advising
541 Main Street
New London, NH 03257

ktaylor@colby-sawyer.edu
603.526.3766
http://www.colby-sawyer.edu/academics/experience/abroad/index.html

DESTINATION	HOST INSTITUTION	PRGM SEASON	PRGM TYPE	INTERMEDIARY	HOUSING
(Multiple choices)	(Multiple choices)	Multiple institutional choices	n/a	Intermed	Academic Programs International	n/a
(Multiple choices)	(Multiple choices)	Multiple institutional choices	n/a	Intermed	American Institute of Foreign Study	n/a

© 2011 — Updates? Want to be in the next edition? Visit **www.mysecondcampus.com**

New Hampshire

DESTINATION	HOST INSTITUTION	PRGM SEASON	PRGM TYPE	INTERMEDIARY	HOUSING
(Multiple choices) | (Multiple choices)	Multiple institutional choices	n/a	Intermed	Center for International Studies	n/a
(Multiple choices) | (Multiple choices)	Multiple institutional choices	n/a	Intermed	Education Abroad Network	n/a
(Multiple choices) | (Multiple choices)	School for Field Studies	n/a	Intermed	School for Field Studies	n/a

Dartmouth College

John G. Tansey
Director
Off-Campus Programs
44 North College Street, Suite 6102
Hanover, NH 03755

John.G.Tansey@Dartmouth.EDU
603.646.1202
http://ocp-prod.dartmouth.edu/ocp/prod/

DESTINATION	HOST INSTITUTION	PRGM SEASON	PRGM TYPE	INTERMEDIARY	HOUSING
Argentina | Buenos Aires	Universidad Argentina de la Empresa	Spr	Self	n/a	HostFam
Austria | Vienna	Dartmouth College	Spr	Self	n/a	PrivApt
Brazil | Salvador	Associacao Cultural Brasil-Estados Unidos	Sum	Self	n/a	HostFam
Brazil | Salvador	Associacao Cultural Brasil-Estados Unidos	Sum	Self	n/a	HostFam
Canada | Montreal	McGill University	Fall	Bilat	n/a	CollRes
Cayman Islands | Little Cayman Research Center	Dartmouth College	n/a	Self	n/a	CollRes Other
China | Beijing	Beijing Normal University	Sum Fall	Self	n/a	CollRes
Costa Rica | (Multiple)	Dartmouth College	n/a	Self	n/a	CollRes Other
Czech Republic | Prague	Charles University	Spr	Self	n/a	PrivApt
Denmark | Copenhagen	University of Copenhagen	Fall	Bilat	n/a	CollRes
England | London	Dartmouth College	Fall	Self	n/a	PrivApt
England | London	London Academy of Music and Dramatic Art	Sum	Self	n/a	PrivApt
England | London	London School of Economics and Political Science	Fall	Self	n/a	PrivApt
England | Oxford	Oxford University (Keble College)	Fall Spr YrRound	Bilat	n/a	CollRes
France | Lyon	University of Lyon	Spr	Self	n/a	HostFam
France | Paris	Dartmouth College	Fall Spr	Self	n/a	HostFam
France | Toulouse	University of Toulouse	Spr	Self	n/a	HostFam
Germany | (Multiple choices)	Multiple institutional choices	YrRound	Bilat	n/a	CollRes
Germany | Berlin	Dartmouth College	Sum Spr	Self	n/a	HostFam
Germany | Berlin	Dartmouth College	Fall	Self	n/a	HostFam
Greece | (Multiple)	Dartmouth College	Spr	Self	n/a	Other
India | Hyderabad	University of Hyderabad	n/a	Self	n/a	CollRes
Ireland | Dublin	Trinity College Dublin	Fall	Self	n/a	PrivApt
Italy | Milan	Bocconi University	Fall	Bilat	n/a	CollRes

© 2011 — Updates? Want to be in the next edition? Visit **www.mysecondcampus.com**

New Hampshire

DESTINATION	HOST INSTITUTION	PRGM SEASON	PRGM TYPE	INTERMEDIARY	HOUSING
Italy | Rome	Dartmouth College	Spr	Self	n/a	PrivApt
Italy | Rome	Dartmouth College	Fall	Self	n/a	HostFam
Italy | Rome	Dartmouth College	Spr	Self	n/a	HostFam
Italy | Rome	Dartmouth College	Fall	Self	n/a	PrivApt Other
Japan | Makuhari and Chiba	Kanda University of International Studies	Fall Spr YrRound	Bilat	n/a	CollRes PrivApt
Japan | Tokyo	Kanda University of International Studies	Sum	Self	n/a	HostFam
Japan | Tokyo	Keio University	YrRound	Bilat	n/a	HostFam CollRes PrivApt
Mexico | Cholula	Universidad de las Americas	Spr	Self	n/a	HostFam
Morocco | Fez	American/Arabic Language Institute	Spr	Self	n/a	HostFam Other
Morocco | Tangier	Tangier American School; Tangier American Legation Museum	Fall	Self	n/a	HostFam CollRes
New Zealand | Auckland	University of Auckland	n/a	Self	n/a	HostFam CollRes
Russia | St. Petersburg	University of St. Petersburg	Sum	Self	n/a	HostFam
Scotland | Edinburgh	University of Edinburgh	Fall	Self	n/a	CollRes
Scotland | Edinburgh	University of Edinburgh	Fall	Self	n/a	PrivApt
Scotland | Glasgow	University of Glasgow	Fall	Self	n/a	CollRes
South Africa | Pretoria	University of Pretoria	Fall	Self	n/a	HostFam Other
South Korea | Seoul	Yonsei University	Fall	Bilat	n/a	CollRes
Spain | Barcelona	University of Barcelona	Fall Spr	Self	n/a	HostFam
Spain | Madrid	Universidad Complutense de Madrid	Fall	Self	n/a	HostFam
Thailand | Bangkok	Chulalongkorn University	Spr	Bilat	n/a	CollRes
Trinidad and Tobago | St. Augustine	University of the West Indies (St. Augustine Campus)	Fall	Self	n/a	CollRes
United States | Amherst (MA)	Amherst College	Fall Spr	Bilat	n/a	n/a
United States | Atlanta (GA)	Morehouse College	Fall	Bilat	n/a	CollRes
United States | Atlanta (GA)	Spelman College	Fall	Bilat	n/a	CollRes
United States | Hartford (CT)	Trinity College	Fall Spr	Bilat	n/a	CollRes
United States | Middletown (CT)	Wesleyan University	Fall Spr	Bilat	n/a	CollRes
United States | Mystic (CT)	Williams College (Mystic Maritime Studies)	Fall Spr	Bilat	n/a	CollRes
United States | New Brunswick (ME)	Bowdoin College	Fall Spr	Bilat	n/a	CollRes
United States | New London (CT)	Connecticut College	Fall Spr	Bilat	n/a	CollRes
United States | Northampton (MA)	Smith College	Fall Spr	Bilat	n/a	CollRes
United States | Norton (MA)	Wheaton College	Fall Spr	Bilat	n/a	CollRes
United States | Poughkeepsie (NY)	Vassar College	Fall Spr	Bilat	n/a	CollRes

© 2011 — Updates? Want to be in the next edition? Visit **www.mysecondcampus.com**

New Hampshire

DESTINATION	HOST INSTITUTION	PRGM SEASON	PRGM TYPE	INTERMEDIARY	HOUSING
United States | San Diego (CA)	University of California at San Diego	Fall Spr	Bilat	n/a	CollRes
United States | South Hadley (MA)	Mount Holyoke College	Fall Spr YrRound	Bilat	n/a	CollRes
United States | Washington (DC)	Dartmouth College	Spr	Self	n/a	PrivApt
United States | Waterford (CT)	O'Neill National Theater Institute	Fall Spr YrRound	Bilat	n/a	CollRes
United States | Wellesley (MA)	Wellesley College	Fall Spr	Bilat	n/a	CollRes
United States | Western United States	Dartmouth College	Fall	Self	n/a	Other

Franklin Pierce Law Center

Debra Beauregard
Director of Graduate Programs
Two White Street
Concord, NH 03301

dbeauregard@piercelaw.edu
603.513.5173
http://www.piercelaw.edu/summer/index.php#chipsi

China | Beijing	Tsinghua University School of Law	Sum	Self	n/a	Other
	Costs: Sum Costs: T&F: $5,200, R&B: $2,739, Ttl: $7,939				
Ireland | Cork	University College Cork	Sum	Self	n/a	PrivApt
	Costs: Sum Costs: T&F: $3,900, R&B: $1,378, Ttl: $5,278				

Franklin Pierce University

Stella van Renesse-Walling
Director of International Programs
40 University Drive
Rindge, NH 03461

stella@franklinpierce.edu
603.899.4147
http://franklinpierce.edu/academics/studyabroad/index.htm

Austria | Vienna	Theresianum Academy	Fall Spr	Self	n/a	PrivApt
	Costs: Fall Costs: T&F: n/a, R&B: n/a, Ttl: $39,000 plus program fees. Spr Costs: T&F: n/a, R&B: n/a, Ttl: $39,000 plus program fees				
Greece | Athens		Fall Spr	n/a	n/a	n/a
	Costs: Fall Costs: T&F: n/a, R&B: n/a, Ttl: $43,800. Spr Costs: T&F: n/a, R&B: n/a, Ttl: $43,800				

Keene State College

Skye Stephenson
Director
Global Education Office
229 Main Street
Keene, NH 03435

sstephenson@keene.edu
603.358.2348
http://www.keene.edu/niec/

Australia | Melbourne	La Trobe University	Fall Spr	Dir	n/a	n/a
Australia | Melbourne	Swinburne University of Technology	Fall Spr	Dir	n/a	n/a
Australia | Newcastle	University of Newcastle	Fall Spr	Dir	n/a	n/a

New Hampshire

DESTINATION	HOST INSTITUTION	PRGM SEASON	PRGM TYPE	INTERMEDIARY	HOUSING
Australia | Robina	Bond University	Fall Spr	Dir	n/a	n/a
Australia | Sydney	Macquarie University	Fall Spr	Dir	n/a	n/a
Australia | Wollongong	University of Wollongong	Fall Spr	Dir	n/a	n/a
Canada | Chicoutimi	Universite du Quebec a Chicoutimi	Fall Spr	Dir	n/a	n/a
Canada | Montreal	Concordia University	Fall Spr	Dir	n/a	n/a
Canada | Montreal	McGill University	Fall Spr	Dir	n/a	n/a
Canada | Montreal	Universite de Montreal	Fall Spr	Dir	n/a	n/a
Canada | Montreal	Universite du Quebec a Montreal	Fall Spr	Dir	n/a	n/a
Canada | Quebec City	Universite Laval	Fall Spr	Dir	n/a	n/a
Canada | Sherbrooke	Bishop's University	Fall Spr	Dir	n/a	n/a
Canada | Sherbrooke	Universite de Sherbrooke	Fall Spr	Dir	n/a	n/a
Canada | Trois-Rivieres	Universite du Quebec a Trois-Rivieres	Fall Spr	Dir	n/a	n/a
Ecuador | Cumbaya	Universidad San Francisco de Quito	Fall Spr	Dir	n/a	n/a
Ecuador | Galapagos Islands	Galapagos Academic Institute for the Arts and Sciences	Fall Spr	Dir	n/a	n/a
Ecuador | Quito	Pontifica Universidad Catolica del Ecuador	Fall Spr	Dir	n/a	n/a
England | Derby	University of Derby	n/a	Dir	n/a	n/a
England | Wolverhampton	University of Wolverhampton	n/a	Dir	n/a	n/a
England | York	York St. John University	n/a	Dir	n/a	n/a
France | Rennes	Universite of Rennes 2 Haute-Bretagne	Fall Spr	Dir	n/a	n/a
Ireland | Dublin	Dublin City University	Fall Spr	Dir	n/a	n/a
Ireland | Limerick	University of Limerick	Fall Spr	Dir	n/a	n/a
Italy | Florence	Lorenzo de' Medici Art Institute	Fall Spr	Intermed	Lorenzo de' Medici Art Institute	n/a
New Zealand | Auckland	University of Auckland	Fall Spr	Dir	n/a	n/a
New Zealand | Wellington	Victoria University of Wellington	Fall Spr	Dir	n/a	n/a
New Zealand | Wellington	Victoria University of Wellington	Fall Spr	Dir	n/a	n/a
Peru | Cusco	ProWorld	Fall Spr	Intermed	ProWorld	n/a
Scotland | Edinburgh	Napier University	Fall Spr	Dir	n/a	n/a
Scotland | Stirling	University of Stirling	Fall Spr	Dir	n/a	n/a
Spain | Madrid	Suffolk University (Madrid Campus)	Fall Spr	Dir	n/a	n/a
Spain | Seville	Center for Cross-Cultural Studies	Fall Spr	Intermed	Center for Cross-Cultural Studies	n/a
United States | Charlottesville (VA)	Semester at Sea	n/a	Intermed	Semester at Sea	n/a

© 2011 — Updates? Want to be in the next edition? Visit **www.mysecondcampus.com**

New Hampshire

| DESTINATION | HOST INSTITUTION | PRGM SEASON | PRGM TYPE | INTERMEDIARY | HOUSING |

New Hampshire Institute of Art

Loula Kalampalikis
Director of Student Services
148 Concord Street
Manchester, NH 03104

lkalampalikis@nhia.edu
603.836.2527
http://www.nhia.edu/study-abroad/

DESTINATION	HOST INSTITUTION	PRGM SEASON	PRGM TYPE	INTERMEDIARY	HOUSING
[Country Unspecified] | [City Unspecified]	n/a	n/a	n/a	n/a	n/a

NHTI-Concord's Community College

Dawn Comito
NHTI Academic Travel Coordinator
31 College Drive
Concord, NH 03301

dcomito@ccsnh.edu
603.271.7122
http://www.nhti.edu/continuingeducation/dceedabroad.html

DESTINATION	HOST INSTITUTION	PRGM SEASON	PRGM TYPE	INTERMEDIARY	HOUSING
Costa Rica | (Multiple)	Saint Anselm College	Spr	Self	n/a	n/a
Costs: Spr Costs: T&F: n/a, R&B: n/a, Ttl: Up to $2,195					
France | Paris	Saint Anselm College	Spr	Self	n/a	n/a
Costs: Spr Costs: T&F: n/a, R&B: n/a, Ttl: $2,095					

Plymouth State University

Debra A. Regan
Director
Global Education Office
Bagley House, MSC44, 17 High Street
Plymouth, NH 03264

dregan@plymouth.edu
603.535.2336
http://www.plymouth.edu/services/study-abroad/

DESTINATION	HOST INSTITUTION	PRGM SEASON	PRGM TYPE	INTERMEDIARY	HOUSING
(Multiple choices) | (Multiple choices)	American College Dublin	n/a	Dir	n/a	n/a
(Multiple choices) | (Multiple choices)	American University in Cairo	n/a	Dir	n/a	n/a
(Multiple choices) | (Multiple choices)	Cambridge University (Gonville and Caius College)	n/a	USColl	University of New Hampshire	n/a
(Multiple choices) | (Multiple choices)	Hawaii Pacific University	n/a	Intermed	Study Abroad Hawaii	n/a
(Multiple choices) | (Multiple choices)	IES Abroad	n/a	Intermed	IES Abroad	n/a
(Multiple choices) | (Multiple choices)	Kansai Gaidai University	n/a	Bilat	n/a	n/a
(Multiple choices) | (Multiple choices)	Living Routes	n/a	Intermed	Living Routes	n/a
(Multiple choices) | (Multiple choices)	Middlesex University	n/a	Dir	n/a	n/a
(Multiple choices) | (Multiple choices)	Multiple institutional choices	n/a	Intermed	Study Abroad Italy	n/a

© 2011 — Updates? Want to be in the next edition? Visit **www.mysecondcampus.com**

New Hampshire

DESTINATION	HOST INSTITUTION	PRGM SEASON	PRGM TYPE	INTERMEDIARY	HOUSING
(Multiple choices) | (Multiple choices)	Multiple institutional choices	n/a	Intermed	Lexia	n/a
(Multiple choices) | (Multiple choices)	Multiple institutional choices	n/a	Intermed	Knowledge Exchange Institute	n/a
(Multiple choices) | (Multiple choices)	Multiple institutional choices	n/a	Intermed	AustraLearn	n/a
(Multiple choices) | (Multiple choices)	Multiple institutional choices	n/a	Intermed	American Institute for Foreign Study	n/a
(Multiple choices) | (Multiple choices)	Multiple institutional choices	n/a	Intermed	Academic Programs International	n/a
(Multiple choices) | (Multiple choices)	Multiple institutional choices	n/a	Intermed	Center for International Studies	n/a
(Multiple choices) | (Multiple choices)	Multiple institutional choices	n/a	USColl	Arcadia University	n/a
(Multiple choices) | (Multiple choices)	Multiple institutional choices	n/a	Intermed	Interstudy	n/a
(Multiple choices) | (Multiple choices)	Multiple institutional choices	n/a	Intermed	Council on International Exchange (CIEE)	n/a
(Multiple choices) | (Multiple choices)	Semester at Sea	n/a	Intermed	Semester at Sea	n/a
(Multiple choices) | (Multiple choices)	SIT Study Abroad	n/a	Intermed	SIT Study Abroad	n/a
(Multiple choices) | (Multiple choices)	University of Winchester	n/a	Dir	n/a	n/a
Canada | Pointe-de-l'Église (Nova Scotia)	Universite Sainte Anne	n/a	Dir	n/a	n/a
Canada | Sherbrooke	Bishops University	n/a	Bilat	n/a	n/a
Ireland | Limerick	University of Limerick	n/a	Self	n/a	n/a
Mexico | Cuernavaca	Universal (Centro de Lengua y Comunicacion Social)	n/a	Intermed	Universal (Centro de Lengua y Comunicacion Social)	n/a
Spain | (Multiple choices)	Center for Cross-Cultural Study	n/a	Intermed	Center for Cross-Cultural Study	n/a

Saint Anselm College

Donald Cox
Director Education Abroad Programs
100 Saint Anselm Drive
Manchester, NH 03102

doncox@anselm.edu
603.641.7371
http://www.anselm.edu/Academics/Study-Abroad.htm

DESTINATION	HOST INSTITUTION	PRGM SEASON	PRGM TYPE	INTERMEDIARY	HOUSING
Greece | (Multiple)	Saint Anselm College	Sum	Self	n/a	n/a
Italy | Castel Viscardo	Saint Anselm College	Sum	Self	n/a	n/a

© 2011 — Updates? Want to be in the next edition? Visit **www.mysecondcampus.com**

New Hampshire

DESTINATION	HOST INSTITUTION	PRGM SEASON	PRGM TYPE	INTERMEDIARY	HOUSING

Southern New Hampshire University

Study Abroad Office
2500 North River Road
Manchester, NH 03106

studyabroad@snhu.edu
603.645.9608
http://www.snhu.edu/895.asp

DESTINATION	HOST INSTITUTION	PRGM SEASON	PRGM TYPE	INTERMEDIARY	HOUSING
(Multiple choices)	(Multiple choices)	Multiple institutional choices	n/a	Intermed	University Studies Abroad Consortium	n/a
(Multiple choices)	(Multiple choices)	Multiple institutional choices	n/a	Intermed	AustraLearn	n/a
(Multiple choices)	(Multiple choices)	Multiple institutional choices	n/a	Intermed	American Institute for Foreign Study	n/a
(Multiple choices)	(Multiple choices)	Multiple institutional choices	n/a	Intermed	Academic Programs International	n/a

University of New Hampshire-Main Campus

Stacy D. VanDeveer
Director
223 Hood House
89 Main Street
Durham, NH 03824

Stacy.Vandeveer@unh.edu
603.862.2399
http://www.unh.edu/cie/studyabroad/

DESTINATION	HOST INSTITUTION	PRGM SEASON	PRGM TYPE	INTERMEDIARY	HOUSING
(Multiple choices)	(Multiple choices)	American University in Cairo	n/a	Dir	n/a	n/a
(Multiple choices)	(Multiple choices)	Danish Institute for Study Abroad	n/a	Intermed	Danish Institute for Study Abroad	n/a
(Multiple choices)	(Multiple choices)	International Honors Program	n/a	Intermed	International Honors Program	n/a
(Multiple choices)	(Multiple choices)	Living Routes	n/a	Intermed	Living Routes	n/a
(Multiple choices)	(Multiple choices)	Multiple institutional choices	n/a	Intermed	Academic Programs International	n/a
(Multiple choices)	(Multiple choices)	Multiple institutional choices	n/a	Intermed	Academic Studies Abroad	n/a
(Multiple choices)	(Multiple choices)	Multiple institutional choices	n/a	USColl	Arcadia University	n/a
(Multiple choices)	(Multiple choices)	Multiple institutional choices	n/a	Intermed	AustraLearn	n/a
(Multiple choices)	(Multiple choices)	Multiple institutional choices	n/a	USColl	Boston University	n/a
(Multiple choices)	(Multiple choices)	Multiple institutional choices	n/a	Intermed	Institute for Study Abroad	n/a
(Multiple choices)	(Multiple choices)	Multiple institutional choices	n/a	Intermed	Lexia	n/a
(Multiple choices)	(Multiple choices)	Multiple institutional choices	n/a	Intermed	InterStudy	n/a

New Hampshire

DESTINATION	HOST INSTITUTION	PRGM SEASON	PRGM TYPE	INTERMEDIARY	HOUSING
(Multiple choices) | (Multiple choices)	Multiple institutional choices	n/a	Intermed	Council on International Educational Exchange (CIEE)	n/a
(Multiple choices) | (Multiple choices)	Multiple institutional choices	n/a	Intermed	Global Learning Semesters	n/a
(Multiple choices) | (Multiple choices)	Multiple institutional choices	n/a	Intermed	IES Abroad	n/a
(Multiple choices) | (Multiple choices)	Multiple institutional choices	n/a	Intermed	International Studies Abroad	n/a
(Multiple choices) | (Multiple choices)	Multiple institutional choices	n/a	Intermed	Center for International Studies	n/a
(Multiple choices) | (Multiple choices)	Multiple institutional choices	n/a	USColl	Syracuse University	n/a
(Multiple choices) | (Multiple choices)	Multiple institutional choices	n/a	Consrtm	Universities Studies Abroad Consortium	n/a
(Multiple choices) | (Multiple choices)	Multiple institutional choices	n/a	Intermed	Study Abroad Italy	n/a
(Multiple choices) | (Multiple choices)	Multiple institutional choices	n/a	Intermed	Study Australia	n/a
(Multiple choices) | (Multiple choices)	Multiple institutional choices	n/a	Intermed	American Institute for Foreign Study	n/a
(Multiple choices) | (Multiple choices)	National Outdoor Leadership School	n/a	Intermed	National Outdoor Leadership	n/a
(Multiple choices) | (Multiple choices)	Round River Conservation Studies	n/a	Intermed	Round River Conservation Studies	n/a
(Multiple choices) | (Multiple choices)	School for Field Studies	n/a	Intermed	School for Field Studies	n/a
(Multiple choices) | (Multiple choices)	School for International Training	n/a	Intermed	SIT Study Abroad	n/a
(Multiple choices) | (Multiple choices)	University of Arizona Russian Abroad	n/a	Intermed	University of Arizona Russian Abroad	n/a
(Multiple choices) | (Multiple choices)	University of Salzburg	n/a	Consrtm	New England Universities in Salzburg	n/a
England | Cambridge	Cambridge University (Gonville and Caius College)	Sum	Self	n/a	CollRes
	Costs: Sum Costs: T&F: n/a, R&B: n/a, Ttl: $9,093				
England | Lancaster	Lancaster University	Fall Spr YrRound	Bilat	n/a	n/a
England | London	Regent's College	Fall Spr YrRound	Self	n/a	n/a
	Costs: Fall Costs: T&F: Up to $12,350, R&B: $5,572, Ttl: Up to $17,922. Spr Costs: T&F: Up to $12,350, R&B: $5,572, Ttl: Up to $17,922. YrRound Costs: T&F: $24,700, R&B: $11,144, Ttl: $35,844				
France | Aix-en-Provence or Avignon	Institute for American Universities	n/a	Intermed	Institute for American Universities	n/a
France | Brest	Centre International d'Etude des Langues	Sum	Self	n/a	HostFam
	Costs: Sum Costs: T&F: n/a, R&B: n/a, Ttl: New Hampshire comprehensive fees				
France | Dijon	Université de Bourgogne or Centre International d'Etudes Franēaises	YrRound	Self	n/a	HostFam
	Costs: YrRound Costs: T&F: n/a, R&B: n/a, Ttl: Up to $36,694				

New Hampshire

DESTINATION	HOST INSTITUTION	PRGM SEASON	PRGM TYPE	INTERMEDIARY	HOUSING
Greece | Athens	College Year Athens	n/a	Intermed	College Year Athens	n/a
Hungary | Budapest	Budapest University of Technology and Economics	Fall	Self	n/a	n/a
Costs: Fall Costs: T&F:n/a, R&B:n/a, Ttl:Up to $17,922					
Hungary | Budapest	Corvinus University	Fall	Self	n/a	n/a
Costs: Fall Costs: T&F:New Hampshire home tuition, R&B:$2,500 (housing) + cost for food, Ttl:n/a					
Hungary | Budapest	Corvinus University	Fall	Self	n/a	n/a
Costs: Fall Costs: T&F:New Hampshire home tuition, R&B:Cost for food and housing at local rate, Ttl:n/a					
Italy | Ascoli Piceno	UNH-in-Italy Ascoli Piceno Center	Sum Fall Spr YrRound	Self	n/a	PrivApt
Italy | Florence	Institute at Palazzo Rucellai	Sum	Self	n/a	PrivApt
Costs: Sum Costs: T&F:n/a, R&B:n/a, Ttl:$3,750					
Italy | Pollenzo	University of Gastronomic Sciences	Fall	Self	n/a	n/a
Italy | Rome	Intercollegiate Center for Classical Studies (Duke)	n/a	Consrtm	Intercollegiate Center for Classical Studies (Duke)	n/a
Japan | Osaka	CET Academic Programs	n/a	Intermed	CET Academic Programs	n/a
Mexico | Cholula	La Universidad de las Américas	Sum	Self	n/a	HostFam CollRes
Costs: Sum Costs: T&F: n/a, R&B: n/a, Ttl: Up to $3,846					
New Zealand | (Multiple)	EcoQuest	Sum Fall Spr	Self	n/a	Other
Costs: Sum Costs: T&F: n/a, R&B: n/a, Ttl: $4,850. Fall Costs: T&F: n/a, R&B: n/a, Ttl: $16,500. Spr Costs: T&F: n/a, R&B: n/a, Ttl: $16,500					
Scotland | Edinburgh	Heriot-Watt University	Spr	Bilat	n/a	n/a
Spain | (Multiple choices)	Center for Cross Cultural Study	n/a	Intermed	Center for Cross Cultural Study	n/a
Spain | Granada	Universidad de Granada	Fall Spr YrRound	Self	n/a	HostFam
Costs: Fall Costs: T&F: n/a, R&B: n/a, Ttl: Up to $18,347. Spr Costs: T&F: n/a, R&B: n/a, Ttl: Up to $18,347. YrRound Costs: T&F: n/a, R&B: n/a, Ttl: Up to $36,694					
Syria | Aleppo	CET Academic Programs	n/a	Intermed	CET Academic Programs	n/a
The Netherlands | Utrecht	University College Utrecht	Fall Spr	Bilat	n/a	n/a
The Netherlands | Utrecht	Utrecht University	Spr	Bilat	n/a	n/a
United States | Charlottesville (VA)	Semester at Sea	n/a	Intermed	Semester at Sea	n/a
United States | Woods Hole (MA)	SEA Semester	n/a	Intermed	SEA Semester	n/a

© 2011 — Updates? Want to be in the next edition? Visit **www.mysecondcampus.com**

Rhode Island

DESTINATION	HOST INSTITUTION	PRGM SEASON	PRGM TYPE	INTERMEDIARY	HOUSING

Brown University

Kendall Brostuen
Director
Office of International Programs
J Walter Wilson, Suite 420
Box 1973, 69 Brown Street
Providence, RI 02912

Kendall_Brostuen@brown.edu
401.863.3555
http://www.brown.edu/Administration/OIP/

DESTINATION	HOST INSTITUTION	PRGM SEASON	PRGM TYPE	INTERMEDIARY	HOUSING
Argentina | Buenos Aires	Multiple institutional choices	n/a	Intermed	Council on International Educational Exchange (CIEE)	n/a
Argentina | Buenos Aires	Multiple institutional choices	n/a	Intermed	Institute for Study Abroad	n/a
Argentina | Buenos Aires	Universidad Torcuato di Tella	n/a	Intermed	IES Abroad	n/a
Argentina | Mendoza	Universidad Nacional de Cuyo	n/a	Intermed	Institute for Study Abroad	n/a
Australia | Brisbane	University of Queensland	n/a	Dir	n/a	n/a
Australia | Cairns	SIT Study Abroad	n/a	Intermed	SIT Study Abroad	n/a
Australia | Canberra	Australian National University	n/a	Dir	n/a	n/a
Australia | Caulfield	Monash University, Caulfield	n/a	Dir	n/a	n/a
Australia | Clayton	Monash University, Clayton	n/a	Dir	n/a	n/a
Australia | Hobart	University of Tasmania, Hobart	n/a	Dir	n/a	n/a
Australia | Launceston	University of Tasmania, Launceston	n/a	Dir	n/a	n/a
Australia | Melbourne	University of Melbourne	n/a	Dir	n/a	n/a
Australia | Perth	University of Western Australia	n/a	Dir	n/a	n/a
Australia | Sydney	University of New South Wales	n/a	Dir	n/a	n/a
Australia | Sydney	University of Sydney	n/a	Dir	n/a	n/a
Australia | Wollongong	University of Wollongong	n/a	Dir	n/a	n/a
Australia | Yungaburra	Center for Rainforest Studies	n/a	Intermed	School for Field Studies	n/a
Barbados | Bridgetown	University of the West Indies	n/a	Dir	n/a	n/a

© 2011 — Updates? Want to be in the next edition? Visit **www.mysecondcampus.com**

Rhode Island

DESTINATION	HOST INSTITUTION	PRGM SEASON	PRGM TYPE	INTERMEDIARY	HOUSING
Belgium	Brussels	Universite Libre de Bruxelles	n/a	Intermed	Council on International Educational Exchange (CIEE)	n/a
Botswana	Gaborone	SIT Study Abroad	n/a	Intermed	SIT Study Abroad	n/a
Brazil	Belem	SIT Study Abroad	n/a	Intermed	SIT Study Abroad	n/a
Brazil	Rio de Janeiro	Pontificia Universidade Catolica	n/a	Bilat	n/a	n/a
Cameroon	Yaounde	SIT Study Abroad	n/a	Intermed	SIT Study Abroad	n/a
Canada	Halifax	Dalhousie University	n/a	Dir	n/a	n/a
Canada	Montreal	McGill University	n/a	Dir	n/a	n/a
Canada	Quebec City	Universite Laval	n/a	Dir	n/a	n/a
Canada	Toronto	University of Toronto	n/a	Dir	n/a	n/a
Canada	Vancouver	University of British Columbia	n/a	Dir	n/a	n/a
Chile	Santiago	IES Abroad Santiago Center	n/a	Intermed	IES Abroad	n/a
Chile	Santiago	Pontificia Universidad Catolica de Chile or Universidad de Chile	n/a	Intermed	Council on International Educational Exchange (CIEE)	n/a
Chile	Valparaiso	Universidad Catolica de Valparaiso	n/a	Intermed	Institute for Study Abroad	n/a
China	(Multiple)	International Honors Program	n/a	Intermed	International Honors Program	n/a
China	Beijing	Capital University of Economics and Business	n/a	USColl	Associated Colleges in China (Hamilton College)	n/a
China	Beijing	CET Academic Programs	n/a	Intermed	CET Academic Programs	n/a
China	Beijing	IES Abroad Beijing Center	n/a	Intermed	IES Abroad	n/a
China	Beijing	IES Abroad Beijing Center	n/a	Intermed	IES Abroad	n/a
China	Beijing	Tsinghua University	n/a	Consrtm	Inter-University Program for Chinese Language Studies (University of California, Berkeley)	n/a
China	Harbin	CET Academic Programs	n/a	Intermed	CET Academic Programs	n/a
China	Hong Kong	Chinese University of Hong Kong	n/a	Dir	n/a	n/a
China	Shanghai	Fudan University	n/a	Intermed	Alliance for Global Education	n/a
Costa Rica	Atenas	SFS Center for Sustainable Development Studies	n/a	Intermed	School for Field Studies	n/a
Costa Rica	(Multiple choices)	Organization for Tropical Studies (Duke University)	n/a	Consrtm	Organization for Tropical Studies (Duke University)	n/a
Costa Rica	San Jose	Universidad de Costa Rica	n/a	USColl	University of Kansas	n/a
Cuba	Havana	Casa de Las Americas	n/a	Dir	n/a	n/a
Czech Republic	Prague	Collegium Hieronymi Pragensis	n/a	Intermed	n/a	n/a
Czech Republic	Prague	Film and Television School of the Academy of Performing Arts	n/a	Intermed	CET Academic Programs	n/a
Denmark	Copenhagen	Danish Institute for Study Abroad (DIS)	n/a	Intermed	n/a	n/a
Dominican Republic	Santiago	Pontificia Universidad Catolica Madre y Maestra	n/a	Intermed	Council on International Educational Exchange (CIEE)	n/a
Dominican Republic	Santiago	Pontificia Universidad Catolica Madre y Maestra	n/a	Consrtm	Committee on Institutional Cooperation (Big Ten universities and University of Chicago)	n/a

© 2011 — Updates? Want to be in the next edition? Visit **www.mysecondcampus.com**

Rhode Island

DESTINATION	HOST INSTITUTION	PRGM SEASON	PRGM TYPE	INTERMEDIARY	HOUSING
Dominican Republic | Santo Domingo	Facultad Latinoamericana de Ciencias Sociales	n/a	Intermed	Council on International Educational Exchange (CIEE)	n/a
Ecuador | Quito	SIT Study Abroad	n/a	Intermed	SIT Study Abroad	n/a
Ecuador | Quito	SIT Study Abroad	n/a	Intermed	SIT Study Abroad	n/a
Ecuador | Quito	Universidad San Francisco de Quito	n/a	USColl	Boston University	n/a
Ecuador | Quito	Universidad San Francisco de Quito	n/a	Intermed	BCA Study Abroad	n/a
Egypt | Alexandria	Alexandria University	n/a	USColl	Middlebury College	n/a
England | Birmingham	University of Birmingham	n/a	Dir	n/a	n/a
England | Brighton	University of Sussex	n/a	Dir	n/a	n/a
England | Bristol	University of Bristol	n/a	Dir	n/a	n/a
England | Cambridge	Cambridge University (New College Hall)	n/a	Dir	n/a	n/a
England | Cambridge	Cambridge University (Pembroke College)	n/a	Dir	n/a	n/a
England | Coventry	University of Warwick	n/a	Dir	n/a	n/a
England | Durham	University of Durham	n/a	Dir	n/a	n/a
England | Lancaster	University of Lancaster	n/a	Dir	n/a	n/a
England | Leeds	University of Leeds	n/a	Dir	n/a	n/a
England | London	Architectural Association School of Architecture	n/a	Dir	n/a	n/a
England | London	British American Drama Academy	n/a	USColl	Sarah Lawrence College	n/a
England | London	Goldsmiths College	n/a	Dir	n/a	n/a
England | London	Imperial College	n/a	Dir	n/a	n/a
England | London	King's College	n/a	Dir	n/a	n/a
England | London	London Dramatic Academy	n/a	USColl	Marymount College	n/a
England | London	London School of Economics and Political Science	n/a	Dir	n/a	n/a
England | London	Queen Mary	n/a	Dir	n/a	n/a
England | London	Royal Holloway	n/a	Dir	n/a	n/a
England | London	School of Oriental and African Studies	n/a	Dir	n/a	n/a
England | London	Slade School of Fine Art	n/a	Dir	n/a	n/a
England | London	University College London	n/a	Dir	n/a	n/a
England | Manchester	University of Manchester	n/a	Dir	n/a	n/a
England | Oxford	Oxford University (Lady Margaret Hall)	n/a	Dir	n/a	n/a
England | Oxford	Oxford University (Mansfield College)	n/a	Dir	n/a	n/a
England | Oxford	Oxford University (Pembroke College)	n/a	Dir	n/a	n/a
England | Oxford	Oxford University (St. Anne's College)	n/a	Dir	n/a	n/a

© 2011 — Updates? Want to be in the next edition? Visit **www.mysecondcampus.com**

Rhode Island

DESTINATION	HOST INSTITUTION	PRGM SEASON	PRGM TYPE	INTERMEDIARY	HOUSING
England | Oxford	Oxford University (St. Edmund Hall)	n/a	Dir	n/a	n/a
England | Oxford	Oxford University (St. Peter's College)	n/a	Dir	n/a	n/a
England | Reading	University of Reading	n/a	Dir	n/a	n/a
England | York	University of York	n/a	Dir	n/a	n/a
France | Aix-en-Provence	Universite de Provence	n/a	USColl	Wellesley College	n/a
France | Lyon	Universite Louis Lumiere (Lyon II)	n/a	Bilat	n/a	n/a
France | Nantes	IES Abroad Nantes Center	n/a	Intermed	IES Abroad	n/a
France | Paris	CIEE Study Center	n/a	Intermed	Council on International Educational Exchange (CIEE)	n/a
France | Paris	Columbia University	n/a	USColl	Columbia University	n/a
France | Paris	Internships in Francophone Europe	n/a	Intermed	Internships in Francophone	n/a
France | Paris	Universite de Paris (Institut d'Etudes Politiques)	n/a	Bilat	n/a	n/a
France | Paris	Universite de Paris I (Pantheon Sorbonne)	n/a	Bilat	n/a	n/a
France | Paris	Universite de Paris III (La Sorbonne Nouvelle)	n/a	Bilat	n/a	n/a
France | Paris	Universite de Paris IV (La Sorbonne)	n/a	Bilat	n/a	n/a
France | Paris	Universite de Paris VI (Pierre et Marie Curie)	n/a	Bilat	n/a	n/a
France | Pont Aven	Pont Aven School of Contemporary Art	n/a	Intermed	Pont Aven School of Contemporary Art	n/a
France | Saint Denis	Universite de Paris VIII (Vincennes - Saint-Denis)	n/a	Bilat	n/a	n/a
Germany | Berlin	Humboldt Universitat	n/a	Bilat	n/a	n/a
Germany | Dresden	Technische Universitat Dresden	n/a	USColl	Boston University	n/a
Germany | Tubingen	Eberhard-Karls Universitat	n/a	Bilat	n/a	n/a
Ghana | Cape Coast	SIT Study Abroad	n/a	Intermed	SIT Study Abroad	n/a
Ghana | Legon	University of Ghana	n/a	Intermed	Council on International Educational Exchange (CIEE)	n/a
Greece | Athens	Arcadia Center for Hellenic, Mediterranean and Balkan Studies	n/a	USColl	Arcadia University	n/a
Greece | Athens	College Year in Athens	n/a	Intermed	College Year in Athens	n/a
Greece | Athens	Helenic Education and Research Center	n/a	Intermed	Helenic Education and Research Center	n/a
Hungary | Budapest	Technical University of Budapest, College International	n/a	Intermed	Budapest Semesters in Mathematics	n/a
India | (Multiple)	International Honors Program	n/a	Intermed	International Honors Program	n/a
India | Bodh Gaya	Antioch University	n/a	USColl	Antioch University	n/a
India | Madras	Madras Christian College	n/a	USColl	Davidson College	n/a

© 2011 — Updates? Want to be in the next edition? Visit **www.mysecondcampus.com**

Rhode Island

DESTINATION	HOST INSTITUTION	PRGM SEASON	PRGM TYPE	INTERMEDIARY	HOUSING
India | New Delhi	Lady Shri Ram College for Women	n/a	Bilat	n/a	n/a
India | New Delhi	St. Stephen's College	n/a	Bilat	n/a	n/a
India | Varanasi	University of Wisconsin, Madison	n/a	USColl	University of Wisconsin, Madison	n/a
Indonesia | Bali	SIT Study Abroad	n/a	Intermed	SIT Study Abroad	n/a
Ireland | Cork	University College Cork	n/a	USColl	Arcadia University	n/a
Ireland | Cork	University College Cork	n/a	Intermed	Interstudy	n/a
Ireland | Cork	University College Cork	n/a	Intermed	Institute for Study Abroad	n/a
Ireland | Dublin	Trinity College	n/a	USColl	Arcadia University	n/a
Ireland | Dublin	Trinity College	n/a	Intermed	Institute for Study Abroad	n/a
Ireland | Dublin	University College Dublin	n/a	USColl	Arcadia University	n/a
Ireland | Dublin	University College Dublin	n/a	Intermed	Institute for Study Abroad	n/a
Ireland | Galway	National University of Ireland, Galway	n/a	Intermed	Institute for Study Abroad	n/a
Ireland | Galway	National University of Ireland, Galway	n/a	Intermed	Interstudy	n/a
Ireland | Galway	National University of Ireland, Galway	n/a	USColl	Arcadia University	n/a
Israel | Beer-Sheva	Ben Gurion University	n/a	Dir	n/a	n/a
Israel | Haifa	Technion Israel Institute of Technology	n/a	Dir	n/a	n/a
Israel | Haifa	University of Haifa	n/a	Dir	n/a	n/a
Israel | Hevel Eilot	Arava Institute for Environmental Studies	n/a	Dir	n/a	n/a
Israel | Jerusalem	Hebrew University	n/a	Dir	n/a	n/a
Israel | Tel Aviv	Tel Aviv University	n/a	Dir	n/a	n/a
Italy | Bologna	Universita di Bologna	n/a	Bilat	n/a	n/a
Italy | Florence	SU Florence Center	n/a	USColl	Syracuse University	n/a
Italy | Florence	Universita degli Studi di Firenze	n/a	USColl	Middlebury College	n/a
Italy | Rome	Cornell University	n/a	USColl	Cornell University	n/a
Italy | Rome	Intercollegiate Center for Classical Studies (Duke University)	n/a	USColl	Duke University	n/a
Italy | Rome	Temple University	n/a	USColl	Temple University	n/a
Japan | Kyoto	Kyoto University	n/a	Consrtm	Kyoto Consortium for Japanese Studies (Columbia University)	n/a
Japan | Nagoya	Nanzan University	n/a	Intermed	IES Abroad	n/a
Japan | Tokyo	International Christian University	n/a	Dir	n/a	n/a
Japan | Tokyo	Keio University	n/a	Bilat	n/a	n/a
Japan | Tokyo	Sophia University	n/a	Intermed	Council on International Educational Exchange (CIEE)	n/a
Jordan | Amman	SIT Study Abroad	n/a	Intermed	SIT Study Abroad	n/a

© 2011 — Updates? Want to be in the next edition? Visit **www.mysecondcampus.com**

Rhode Island

DESTINATION	HOST INSTITUTION	PRGM SEASON	PRGM TYPE	INTERMEDIARY	HOUSING
Jordan | Amman	University of Jordan	n/a	Intermed	Council on International Educational Exchange (CIEE)	n/a
Jordan | Amman	University of Jordan	n/a	Intermed	Council on International Educational Exchange (CIEE)	n/a
Madagascar | Fort Dauphin	SIT Study Abroad	n/a	Intermed	SIT Study Abroad	n/a
Mexico | Baja	Center for Coastal Studies	n/a	Intermed	School for Field Studies	n/a
Mexico | Guadalajara	Instituto Tecnologico y de Estudios Superiores de Monterrey	n/a	USColl	Boston University	n/a
Mexico | Merida	Universidad Autonoma de Yucatan	n/a	Intermed	Institute for Study Abroad	n/a
Mexico | Xalapa	Universidad Veracruzana	n/a	Intermed	BCA Study Abroad	n/a
Morocco | Ifrane	Al Akhawayn University	n/a	USColl	SUNY Binghamton	n/a
Morocco | Rabat	SIT Study Abroad	n/a	Intermed	SIT Study Abroad	n/a
Netherlands | Amsterdam	University of Amsterdam	n/a	Intermed	Council on International Educational Exchange (CIEE)	n/a
Netherlands | Leiden	University of Leiden	n/a	Dir	n/a	n/a
New Zealand | Auckland	University of Auckland	n/a	Dir	n/a	n/a
New Zealand | Dunedin	University of Otago	n/a	Dir	n/a	n/a
Nicaragua | Managua	SIT Study Abroad	n/a	Intermed	SIT Study Abroad	n/a
Niger | Niamey	Boston University	n/a	USColl	Boston University	n/a
Northern Ireland | Belfast	Queen's University Belfast	n/a	Intermed	Institute for Study Abroad	n/a
Peru | Lima	Pontificia Universidad Catolica del Peru	n/a	Intermed	Institute for Study Abroad	n/a
Russia | Irkutsk	Irkutsk State University	n/a	USColl	Middlebury College	n/a
Russia | Moscow	Moscow International University	n/a	USColl	American Councils Study Abroad Programs	n/a
Russia | Moscow	Moscow International University	n/a	Intermed	American Councils Study Abroad Programs	n/a
Russia | Moscow	Russian State University for the Humanities	n/a	Intermed	Middlebury College	n/a
Russia | St. Petersburg	European University	n/a	USColl	Vassar College	n/a
Russia | St. Petersburg	Russian State Pedagogical	n/a	Intermed	American Councils Study Abroad Programs	n/a
Russia | St. Petersburg	Russian State Pedagogical	n/a	Intermed	American Councils Study Abroad Programs	n/a
Russia | St. Petersburg	St. Petersburg State University	n/a	Intermed	Council on International Educational Exchange (CIEE)	n/a
Russia | Yaroslavl	Yaroslavl State Pedagogical University	n/a	USColl	Middlebury College	n/a
Scotland | Edinburgh	University of Edinburgh	n/a	Dir	n/a	n/a
Scotland | Glasgow	Glasgow School of Art	n/a	Dir	n/a	n/a
Scotland | Glasgow	University of Glasgow	n/a	Dir	n/a	n/a
Scotland | Glasgow	University of Strathclyde	n/a	Dir	n/a	n/a
Scotland | St. Andrews	University of St. Andrews	n/a	Dir	n/a	n/a
Senegal | Dakar	Universite Cheikh Anta Diop	n/a	USColl	Wells College	n/a

© 2011 — Updates? Want to be in the next edition? Visit **www.mysecondcampus.com**

Rhode Island

DESTINATION	HOST INSTITUTION	PRGM SEASON	PRGM TYPE	INTERMEDIARY	HOUSING
Senegal | Dakar	Universite Cheikh Anta Diop	n/a	USColl	Mount Holyoke College	n/a
Singapore | Singapore	National University of Singapore	n/a	Dir	n/a	n/a
South Africa | (Multiple)	International Honors Program	n/a	Intermed	International Honors Program	n/a
South Africa | Cape Town	University of Cape Town	n/a	Intermed	Council on International Educational Exchange (CIEE)	n/a
South Korea | Seoul	Ewha Womans University	n/a	Dir	n/a	n/a
Spain | Barcelona	Multiple institutional choices	n/a	Consrtm	Consortium for Advanced Studies in Barcelona (CASB)	n/a
Spain | Madrid	Instituto Internacional en Espana	n/a	USColl	Boston University	n/a
Spain | Madrid	Universidad Autonoma de Madrid	n/a	Intermed	IES Abroad	n/a
Spain | Salamanca	Universidad de Sevilla	n/a	USColl	Colby College	n/a
Spain | Seville	Universidad de Sevilla	n/a	USColl	Sweet Briar College	n/a
Sweden | Stockholm	Stockholm University	n/a	Consrtm	Swedish Program	n/a
Switzerland | Geneva	Universite de Geneve	n/a	USColl	Smith College	n/a
Taiwan | Taipei	National Chengchi University	n/a	Intermed	Council on International Educational Exchange (CIEE)	n/a
Tanzania | Arusha	SIT Study Abroad	n/a	Intermed	SIT Study Abroad	n/a
Thailand | Khon Kaen	Khon Kaen University	n/a	Intermed	Council on International Educational Exchange (CIEE)	n/a
Tunisia | Tunis	SIT Study Abroad	n/a	Intermed	SIT Study Abroad	n/a
Turkey | Istanbul	Koc University	n/a	Intermed	Council on International Educational Exchange (CIEE)	n/a
Turks and Caicos | South Caicos Island	Center for Marine Resource Management Studies	n/a	Intermed	School for Field Studies	n/a
Vietnam | Ho Chi Minh City	Ho Chi Minh International University	n/a	Intermed	Council on International Educational Exchange (CIEE)	n/a
Vietnam | Ho Chi Minh City	SIT Study Abroad	n/a	Intermed	SIT Study Abroad	n/a
Wales | Aberystwyth	University of Wales at Aberystwyth	n/a	Dir	n/a	n/a

Bryant University

Beth Engwall
Assistant Director
Study Abroad Office
1150 Douglas Pike
Smithfield, RI 02917

saoffice@bryant.edu
401.232.6209
http://studyabroad.bryant.edu

DESTINATION	HOST INSTITUTION	PRGM SEASON	PRGM TYPE	INTERMEDIARY	HOUSING
Argentina | Buenos Aires	IES Abroad Buenos Aires Center	n/a	Intermed	IES Abroad	n/a
Argentina | Buenos Aires	Multiple institutional choices	n/a	Intermed	Council on International Educational Exchange (CIEE)	n/a
Argentina | Buenos Aires	University of Belgrano	n/a	Intermed	International Studies Abroad	n/a
Australia | (Multiple choices)	Multiple institutional choices	n/a	USColl	Arcadia University	n/a
Australia | (Multiple choices)	Multiple institutional choices	n/a	Intermed	IES Abroad	n/a

© 2011 — Updates? Want to be in the next edition? Visit **www.mysecondcampus.com**

Rhode Island

DESTINATION	HOST INSTITUTION	PRGM SEASON	PRGM TYPE	INTERMEDIARY	HOUSING
Australia | (Multiple choices)	Multiple institutional choices	n/a	Intermed	Council on International Educational Exchange (CIEE)	n/a
Belgium | Brussels	Multiple institutional choices	n/a	Intermed	Council on International Educational Exchange (CIEE)	n/a
Botswana | Gaborone	University of Botswana	n/a	Intermed	Council on International Educational Exchange (CIEE)	n/a
Brazil | (Multiple choices)	Multiple institutional choices	n/a	Intermed	Council on International Educational Exchange (CIEE)	n/a
Cambodia | Siem Reap	Pannasastra University of Cambodia	n/a	Intermed	Council on International Educational Exchange (CIEE)	n/a
Chile | (Multiple choices)	Multiple institutional choices	n/a	Intermed	Council on International Educational Exchange (CIEE)	n/a
Chile | Santiago	IES Abroad Santiago Center	n/a	Intermed	IES Abroad	n/a
Chile | Valparaiso and Vina del Mar	Pontifical Catholic University of Valparaiso	n/a	Intermed	International Studies Abroad	n/a
China | (Multiple)	Bryant University	Win	Self	n/a	n/a
	Costs: Win Costs: T&F: n/a, R&B: n/a, Ttl: $3,500				
China | (Multiple)	Multiple institutional choices	n/a	Self	n/a	n/a
China | (Multiple)	Multiple institutional choices	n/a	Self	n/a	n/a
China | (Multiple choices)	Multiple institutional choices	n/a	Intermed	IES Abroad	n/a
China | (Multiple choices)	Multiple institutional choices	n/a	Intermed	Council on International Educational Exchange (CIEE)	n/a
China | Beijing	Beijing Language and Culture University	n/a	Intermed	Alliance for Global Education	n/a
China | Shanghai	Multiple institutional choices	n/a	Intermed	Alliance for Global Education	n/a
Costa Rica | (Multiple choices)	Multiple institutional choices	n/a	Intermed	International Studies Abroad	n/a
Costa Rica | Monteverde	CIEE Study Center	n/a	Intermed	Council on International Educational Exchange (CIEE)	n/a
Costa Rica | San Joaquin de Flores or San Jose	Multiple institutional choices	n/a	Intermed	Academic Programs International	n/a
Costa Rica and Panama | (Multiple)	Bryant University	Win	Self	n/a	n/a
	Costs: Win Costs: T&F: n/a, R&B: n/a, Ttl: $3,500				
Czech Republic | Prague	Multiple institutional choices	n/a	Intermed	Council on International Educational Exchange (CIEE)	n/a
Dominican Republic | (Multiple choices)	Multiple institutional choices	n/a	Intermed	Council on International Educational Exchange (CIEE)	n/a
Dominican Republic | Santiago	Pontifical Catholic University - Madre y Maestra	n/a	Intermed	International Studies Abroad	n/a
England | (Multiple choices)	Multiple institutional choices	n/a	Intermed	IES Abroad	n/a
England | (Multiple choices)	Multiple institutional choices	n/a	Intermed	Academic Programs International	n/a
England | (Multiple choices)	Multiple institutional choices	n/a	USColl	Arcadia University	n/a
England | (Multiple choices)	Multiple institutional choices	n/a	Intermed	International Studies Abroad	n/a
England | London	Multiple institutional choices	n/a	USColl	Arcadia University	n/a

© 2011 — Updates? Want to be in the next edition? Visit **www.mysecondcampus.com**

Rhode Island

DESTINATION	HOST INSTITUTION	PRGM SEASON	PRGM TYPE	INTERMEDIARY	HOUSING
England	London	Multiple institutional choices	n/a	Intermed	Council on International Educational Exchange (CIEE)	n/a
European Union	Freiburg	IES Abroad EU Center	n/a	Intermed	IES Abroad	n/a
France	(Multiple choices)	Multiple institutional choices	n/a	Intermed	IES Abroad	n/a
France	(Multiple choices)	Multiple institutional choices	n/a	Intermed	Council on International Educational Exchange (CIEE)	n/a
France	(Multiple choices)	Multiple institutional choices	n/a	Intermed	Institute for American Universities	n/a
France	Grenoble or Paris	Multiple institutional choices	n/a	Intermed	Academic Programs International	n/a
France	Paris	Multiple institutional choices	n/a	Intermed	International Studies Abroad	n/a
Germany	(Multiple choices)	Multiple institutional choices	n/a	Intermed	IES Abroad	n/a
Germany and Greece	(Multiple)	Bryant University	Win	Self	n/a	n/a
	Costs: Win Costs: T&F: n/a, R&B: n/a, Ttl: $3,500				
Ghana	(Multiple choices)	Multiple institutional choices	n/a	Intermed	Council on International Educational Exchange (CIEE)	n/a
Greece	Athens	Arcadia Center for Hellenic, Mediterranean, and Balkan Studies	n/a	USColl	Arcadia University	n/a
Hungary	Budapest	Corvinus University of Budapest	n/a	Intermed	Council on International Educational Exchange (CIEE)	n/a
Hungary	Budapest	Corvinus University of Budapest	n/a	Intermed	Academic Programs International	n/a
India	Hyderabad	University of Hyderabad	n/a	Intermed	Council on International Educational Exchange (CIEE)	n/a
Ireland	(Multiple choices)	Multiple institutional choices	n/a	Intermed	Academic Programs International	n/a
Ireland	(Multiple choices)	Multiple institutional choices	n/a	USColl	Arcadia University	n/a
Ireland	Dublin	Dublin City University	n/a	Intermed	Council on International Educational Exchange (CIEE)	n/a
Ireland	Dublin	Multiple institutional choices	n/a	USColl	Arcadia University	n/a
Ireland	Dublin	Multiple institutional choices	n/a	Intermed	IES Abroad	n/a
Italy	(Multiple)	Bryant University	Sum	Self	n/a	n/a
	Costs: Sum Costs: T&F: n/a, R&B: n/a, Ttl: $3,500				
Italy	(Multiple choices)	Multiple institutional choices	n/a	Intermed	International Studies Abroad	n/a
Italy	(Multiple choices)	Multiple institutional choices	n/a	Intermed	Council on International Educational Exchange (CIEE)	n/a
Italy	(Multiple choices)	Multiple institutional choices	n/a	USColl	Arcadia University	n/a
Italy	(Multiple choices)	Multiple institutional choices	n/a	Intermed	Academic Programs International	n/a
Italy	(Multiple choices)	Multiple institutional choices	n/a	Intermed	IES Abroad	n/a
Italy	Rome and Florence	Bryant University	n/a	Self	n/a	n/a
Japan	(Multiple choices)	Multiple institutional choices	n/a	Intermed	IES Abroad	n/a
Japan	Osaka	Kansai-Gaidai University	n/a	Bilat	n/a	n/a
Japan	Tokyo	Sophia University	n/a	Intermed	Council on International Educational Exchange (CIEE)	n/a

Rhode Island

DESTINATION	HOST INSTITUTION	PRGM SEASON	PRGM TYPE	INTERMEDIARY	HOUSING
Jordan | Amman	University of Jordan	n/a	Intermed	Council on International Educational Exchange (CIEE)	n/a
Mexico | (Multiple choices)	Multiple institutional choices	n/a	Intermed	International Studies Abroad	n/a
Mexico | Guanajuato	Universidad de Guanajuato	n/a	Intermed	Council on International Educational Exchange (CIEE)	n/a
Mexico | Queretaro	Universidad Autonoma de Queretaro	n/a	Intermed	Academic Programs International	n/a
Netherlands | Amsterdam	Multiple institutional choices	n/a	Intermed	Council on International Educational Exchange (CIEE)	n/a
Netherlands | Amsterdam	Multiple institutional choices	n/a	Intermed	IES Abroad	n/a
New Zealand | (Multiple choices)	Multiple institutional choices	n/a	USColl	Arcadia University	n/a
Peru | (Multiple choices)	Multiple institutional choices	n/a	Intermed	International Studies Abroad	n/a
Peru | Lima	Multiple institutional choices	n/a	Intermed	Council on International Educational Exchange (CIEE)	n/a
Poland | Krakow	Jagiellonian University	n/a	Intermed	Academic Programs International	n/a
Poland | Warsaw	Warsaw School of Economics	n/a	Intermed	Council on International Educational Exchange (CIEE)	n/a
Portugal | Lisbon	Universidade Nova de Lisboa	n/a	Intermed	Council on International Educational Exchange (CIEE)	n/a
Russia | St. Petersburg	St. Petersburg State University	n/a	Intermed	Council on International Educational Exchange (CIEE)	n/a
Scotland | (Multiple choices)	Multiple institutional choices	n/a	USColl	Arcadia University	n/a
Senegal | Dakar	Suffolk University - Dakar Campus	n/a	Intermed	Council on International Educational Exchange (CIEE)	n/a
South Africa | (Multiple choices)	Multiple institutional choices	n/a	Intermed	Council on International Educational Exchange (CIEE)	n/a
South Korea | Seoul	Yonsei University	n/a	Intermed	Council on International Educational Exchange (CIEE)	n/a
Spain | (Multiple choices)	Multiple institutional choices	n/a	USColl	Arcadia University	n/a
Spain | (Multiple choices)	Multiple institutional choices	n/a	Intermed	International Studies Abroad	n/a
Spain | (Multiple choices)	Multiple institutional choices	n/a	Intermed	IES Abroad	n/a
Spain | (Multiple choices)	Multiple institutional choices	n/a	Intermed	Council on International Educational Exchange (CIEE)	n/a
Spain | (Multiple choices)	Multiple institutional choices	n/a	Intermed	Academic Programs International	n/a
Spain | Leon	Universidad de Leon	n/a	Bilat	n/a	n/a
Sweden | Uppsala	Uppsala University	n/a	Intermed	Council on International Educational Exchange (CIEE)	n/a
Taiwan | Taipei	National Chengchi University	n/a	Intermed	Council on International Educational Exchange (CIEE)	n/a
Thailand | Khon Kaen	Khon Kaen University	n/a	Intermed	Council on International Educational Exchange (CIEE)	n/a
Turkey | Istanbul	Koc University	n/a	Intermed	Council on International Educational Exchange (CIEE)	n/a
Vietnam | Ho Chi Minh City	Vietnam National University	n/a	Intermed	Council on International Educational Exchange (CIEE)	n/a

Rhode Island

DESTINATION	HOST INSTITUTION	PRGM SEASON	PRGM TYPE	INTERMEDIARY	HOUSING
Wales | (Multiple)	Multiple institutional choices	n/a	USColl	Arcadia University	n/a
Wales | Pontypridd	University of Glamorgan	n/a	Bilat	n/a	n/a

Community College of Rhode Island

Deborah Notarianni-Girard
Coordinator
400 East Avenue
Warwick, RI 02886

dnotariannigir@ccri.edu
401.825.2254
http://www.ccri.edu/studyabroad/

DESTINATION	HOST INSTITUTION	PRGM SEASON	PRGM TYPE	INTERMEDIARY	HOUSING
(Multiple choices) | (Multiple choices)	Multiple institutional choices	n/a	Consrtm	n/a	n/a

Johnson & Wales University

Erin Fitzgerald
Dean, International Programs & Development
8 Abbott Park Place
Providence, RI 02903

erin.fitzgerald@jwu.edu
401.598.1406
http://www.jwu.edu/content.aspx?id=9314

DESTINATION	HOST INSTITUTION	PRGM SEASON	PRGM TYPE	INTERMEDIARY	HOUSING
England and Scotland | (Multiple)	Cambridge University (Fitzwilliams College)	Sum	Self	n/a	CollRes
	Costs: Sum Costs: T&F: n/a, R&B: n/a, Ttl: $6,798				
France | La Rochelle	Ecole Superieure de Commerce	Spr	Dir	n/a	HostFam
	Costs: Spr Costs: T&F: Johnson & Wales home tuition, R&B: $1,913, Ttl: n/a				
Germany | (Multiple choices)	Goethe Institute	Spr	Dir	n/a	CollRes
	Costs: Spr Costs: T&F: Johnson & Wales home tuition, R&B: $3,083, Ttl: n/a				
Spain | Seville	Centro de Lenguas e Intercambio Cultural	Spr	Dir	n/a	HostFam
	Costs: Spr Costs: T&F: Johnson & Wales home tuition, R&B: $3,439, Ttl: n/a				
Sweden | Goteborg	IHM Business School	Spr	Self	n/a	Other
	Costs: Spr Costs: T&F: Johnson & Wales home tuition, R&B: $3,461, Ttl: n/a				

Providence College

Adrian Beaulieu
Dean
Harkins Hall 336
Providence, RI 02918

abeaulie@providence.edu
401.865.2114
http://www.providence.edu/CIS/Study+Abroad/

DESTINATION	HOST INSTITUTION	PRGM SEASON	PRGM TYPE	INTERMEDIARY	HOUSING
(Multiple) | (Multiple)	International Honors Program	n/a	Intermed	International Honors Program	n/a
(Multiple) | (Multiple)	International Honors Program	n/a	Intermed	International Honors Program	n/a
(Multiple) | [City Unspecified]	Antioch College	n/a	USColl	Antioch College	n/a
Argentina | Buenos Aires	Facultad Latinoamericana de Ciencias Sociales	n/a	Intermed	Council on International Educational Exchange (CIEE)	n/a
Argentina | Buenos Aires	IES Abroad Buenos Aires Center	n/a	Intermed	IES Abroad	n/a
Argentina | Buenos Aires	IES Abroad Buenos Aires Center	n/a	Intermed	IES Abroad	n/a
Argentina | Buenos Aires	Multiple institutional choices	n/a	Intermed	Institute for Study Abroad	n/a

Rhode Island

DESTINATION	HOST INSTITUTION	PRGM SEASON	PRGM TYPE	INTERMEDIARY	HOUSING
Argentina | Buenos Aires	SIT Study Abroad	n/a	Intermed	SIT Study Abroad	n/a
Argentina | Buenos Aires	SIT Study Abroad	n/a	Intermed	SIT Study Abroad	n/a
Argentina | Buenos Aires	Universidad Torcuato di Tella	n/a	Intermed	IES Abroad	n/a
Australia | Brisbane	Queensland University of Technology	n/a	USColl	Arcadia University	n/a
Australia | Byron Bay	SIT Study Abroad	n/a	Intermed	SIT Study Abroad	n/a
Australia | Cairns	SIT Study Abroad	n/a	Intermed	SIT Study Abroad	n/a
Australia | Canberra	Australian National University	n/a	USColl	Arcadia University	n/a
Australia | Canberra	Australian National University	n/a	USColl	Arcadia University	n/a
Australia | Canberra	Australian National University	n/a	Intermed	Institute for Study Abroad	n/a
Australia | Sydney	Arcadia University	n/a	USColl	Arcadia University	n/a
Australia | Sydney	Boston University Sydney Center	n/a	USColl	Boston University	n/a
Australia | Sydney	Macquarie University	n/a	Intermed	Institute for Study Abroad	n/a
Australia | Sydney	Macquarie University	n/a	USColl	Arcadia University	n/a
Australia | Sydney	University of Technology	n/a	USColl	Arcadia University	n/a
Australia | Sydney	University of Technology	n/a	Intermed	Institute for Study Abroad	n/a
Australia | Wollongong	University of Wollongong	n/a	USColl	Arcadia University	n/a
Australia | Wollongong	University of Wollongong	n/a	Intermed	Institute for Study Abroad	n/a
Australia | Yungaburra	Center for Rainforest Studies	n/a	Intermed	School for Field Studies	n/a
Austria | Vienna	IES Abroad Vienna Center	n/a	Intermed	IES Abroad	n/a
Bolivia | Cochabamba	SIT Study Abroad	n/a	Intermed	SIT Study Abroad	n/a
Bolivia | Cochabamba	SIT Study Abroad	n/a	Intermed	SIT Study Abroad	n/a
Bolivia | La Paz	SIT Study Abroad	n/a	Intermed	SIT Study Abroad	n/a
Botswana | Gabarone	SIT Study Abroad	n/a	Intermed	SIT Study Abroad	n/a
Brazil | Belem	SIT Study Abroad	n/a	Intermed	SIT Study Abroad	n/a
Brazil | Fortaleza	Instituto Brasil/Estados Unidos/Ceara	n/a	Intermed	SIT Study Abroad	n/a
Brazil | Salvador	SIT Study Abroad	n/a	Intermed	SIT Study Abroad	n/a
Cameroon | Yaounde	SIT Study Abroad	n/a	Intermed	SIT Study Abroad	n/a
Chile | (Multiple)	SIT Study Abroad	n/a	Intermed	SIT Study Abroad	n/a
Chile | Arica	SIT Study Abroad	n/a	Intermed	SIT Study Abroad	n/a
Chile | Santiago	IES Abroad	n/a	Intermed	IES Abroad	n/a
Chile | Santiago	Multiple institutional choices	n/a	Intermed	Institute for Study Abroad	n/a
Chile | Santiago	SIT Study Abroad	n/a	Intermed	SIT Study Abroad	n/a
Chile | Valparaiso	SIT Study Abroad	n/a	Intermed	SIT Study Abroad	n/a
China | Beijing	Beijing Language and Culture University	n/a	Intermed	Alliance for Global Education	n/a
China | Kunming	SIT Study Abroad	n/a	Intermed	SIT Study Abroad	n/a
China | Shanghai	Shanghai University of Finance and Economics	n/a	Intermed	Alliance for Global Education	n/a
China | Shanghai	Shanghai University of Finance and Economics	n/a	Intermed	Alliance for Global Education	n/a
Costa Rica | (Multiple)	Multiple institutional choices	n/a	Intermed	Institute for Study Abroad	n/a

© 2011 — Updates? Want to be in the next edition? Visit **www.mysecondcampus.com**

Rhode Island

DESTINATION	HOST INSTITUTION	PRGM SEASON	PRGM TYPE	INTERMEDIARY	HOUSING
Costa Rica | Atenas	SFS Center for Sustainable Development Studies	n/a	Intermed	School for Field Studies	n/a
Croatia | Zagreb	SIT Study Abroad	n/a	Intermed	SIT Study Abroad	n/a
Czech Republic | Prague	SIT Study Abroad	n/a	Intermed	SIT Study Abroad	n/a
Denmark | Copenhagen	Danish Institute for Study Abroad (DIS)	n/a	Intermed	Danish Institute for Study Abroad (DIS)	n/a
Dominican Republic | Santiago	Pontificia Universidad Catolica Madre y Maestra	n/a	Intermed	Council on International Educational Exchange (CIEE)	n/a
Dominican Republic | Santiago	Pontificia Universidad Catolica Madre y Maestra	n/a	Intermed	Council on International Educational Exchange (CIEE)	n/a
Dominican Republic | Santo Domingo	Multiple institutional choices	n/a	Intermed	Council on International Educational Exchange (CIEE)	n/a
Dominican Republic | Santo Domingo	Multiple institutional choices	n/a	Intermed	Council on International Educational Exchange (CIEE)	n/a
Ecuador | Quito	Multiple institutional choices	n/a	Intermed	IES Abroad	n/a
Ecuador | Quito	Universidad Politecnica Salesiana or Facultad Latinoamericana de Ciencias Sociales (FLACSO)	n/a	USColl	Duke University	n/a
England | London	Arcadia University	n/a	USColl	Arcadia University	n/a
England | London	Arcadia University	n/a	USColl	Arcadia University	n/a
England | London	Boston University	n/a	USColl	Boston University	n/a
England | London	Boston University	n/a	USColl	Boston University	n/a
England | London	CAPA International Education	n/a	Intermed	CAPA International Education	n/a
England | London	London School of Economics and Political Science	n/a	USColl	Arcadia University	n/a
England | London	London School of Economics and Political Science	n/a	Intermed	Institute for Study Abroad	n/a
England | London	Michigan State University	n/a	USColl	Michigan State University	n/a
England | London	Royal Holloway	n/a	USColl	Arcadia University	n/a
England | London	Royal Holloway	n/a	Intermed	Institute for Study Abroad	n/a
France | Aix-en-Provence	American University Center for Provence	n/a	Intermed	American University Center for Provence	n/a
France | Brest	ESC Bretagne	n/a	Bilat	n/a	n/a
France | Grenoble	Grenoble School of Management	n/a	Intermed	American Institute for Foreign Study	n/a
France | Paris	CIEE Study Center	n/a	Intermed	Council on International Educational Exchange (CIEE)	n/a
France | Paris	CIEE Study Center	n/a	Intermed	Council on International Educational Exchange (CIEE)	n/a
France | Paris	Hamilton College	n/a	USColl	Hamilton College	n/a
France | Paris	IES Abroad Paris Center	n/a	Intermed	IES Abroad	n/a
France | Paris	Internships in Francophone Europe	n/a	Intermed	Internships in Francophone	n/a
France | Paris	Internships in Francophone Europe	n/a	Intermed	Internships in Francophone	n/a

Rhode Island

DESTINATION	HOST INSTITUTION	PRGM SEASON	PRGM TYPE	INTERMEDIARY	HOUSING
France | Paris	Internships in Francophone Europe	n/a	Intermed	Internships in Francophone	n/a
France | Paris	Multiple institutional choices	n/a	USColl	Sweet Briar College	n/a
France | Paris	Multiple institutional choices	n/a	Consrtm	Vassar College and Wesleyan University	n/a
France | Paris	Multiple institutional choices	n/a	USColl	Sarah Lawrence College	n/a
France | Paris	Multiple institutional choices	n/a	USColl	Columbia University	n/a
France | Paris	Multiple institutional choices	n/a	Intermed	Center for University Programs Abroad	n/a
France | Reims	Reims School of Management	n/a	Bilat	n/a	n/a
France | Toulouse	University of Toulouse	n/a	USColl	Dickinson College	n/a
Germany | Berlin	Freie Universitat or Humboldt Universitat	n/a	USColl	Duke University	n/a
Germany | Heidelberg	Heidelberg University	n/a	Intermed	Heidelberg University	n/a
Germany | Tubingen	Tubingen University	n/a	USColl	Antioch University	n/a
Ghana | Accra	SIT Study Abroad	n/a	Intermed	SIT Study Abroad	n/a
Ghana | Cape Coast	SIT Study Abroad	n/a	Intermed	SIT Study Abroad	n/a
Ghana | Legon	University of Ghana	n/a	Intermed	Council on International Educational Exchange (CIEE)	n/a
Hungary | Budapest	Corvinus University of Budapest	n/a	Intermed	Council on International Educational Exchange (CIEE)	n/a
India | Delhi	SIT Study Abroad	n/a	Intermed	SIT Study Abroad	n/a
India | Pune	Fergusson College	n/a	Intermed	Alliance for Global Education	n/a
India | Rajasthan	SIT Study Abroad	n/a	Intermed	SIT Study Abroad	n/a
Ireland | Dublin	Dublin City University	n/a	USColl	Boston University	n/a
Ireland | Dublin	Dublin City University	n/a	USColl	Boston University	n/a
Ireland | Dublin	Institute for Public Administration	n/a	USColl	Arcadia University	n/a
Ireland | Dublin	SIT Study Abroad	n/a	Intermed	SIT Study Abroad	n/a
Ireland | Dublin	University College Dublin	n/a	Intermed	Institute for Study Abroad	n/a
Ireland | Dublin	University College Dublin	n/a	USColl	Arcadia University	n/a
Ireland | Limerick	University of Limerick	n/a	Intermed	Institute for Study Abroad	n/a
Ireland | Limerick	University of Limerick	n/a	USColl	Arcadia University	n/a
Israel | Haifa	University of Haifa	n/a	USColl	Boston University	n/a
Israel | Haifa	University of Haifa	n/a	USColl	Boston University	n/a
Italy | Catania	CET Academic Programs	n/a	Intermed	CET Academic Programs	n/a
Italy | Ferrara	University of Ferrara	n/a	Intermed	Council on International Educational Exchange (CIEE)	n/a
Italy | Florence	CAPA International Education	n/a	Intermed	CAPA International Education	n/a
Italy | Florence	Fairfield University	n/a	USColl	Fairfield University	n/a
Italy | Florence	Middlebury College	n/a	USColl	Middlebury College	n/a
Italy | Florence	University of Florence	n/a	USColl	Rutgers University	n/a
Italy | Milan	IES Abroad Milan Center	n/a	Intermed	IES Abroad	n/a
Italy | Milan	IES Abroad Milan Center	n/a	Intermed	IES Abroad	n/a

© 2011 — Updates? Want to be in the next edition? Visit **www.mysecondcampus.com**

Rhode Island

DESTINATION	HOST INSTITUTION	PRGM SEASON	PRGM TYPE	INTERMEDIARY	HOUSING
Italy | Perugia	Umbra Institute	n/a	USColl	Arcadia University	n/a
Italy | Rome	Accademia Italiana	n/a	USColl	Arcadia University	n/a
Italy | Rome	CEA Global Campus	n/a	Intermed	Cultural Experiences Abroad (CEA Global Education)	n/a
Italy | Rome	IES Abroad Rome Center	n/a	Intermed	IES Abroad	n/a
Italy | Rome	St. John's University - Rome Campus	n/a	USColl	St. John's University	n/a
Italy | Rome	Trinity College - Rome Campus	n/a	USColl	Trinity College	n/a
Italy | Urbino	Rutgers University	n/a	USColl	Rutgers University	n/a
Italy | Venice	Venice International University	n/a	Consrtm	Duke University	n/a
Jordan | Amman	SIT Study Abroad	n/a	Intermed	SIT Study Abroad	n/a
Jordan | Amman	University of Jordan	n/a	Intermed	Council on International Educational Exchange (CIEE)	n/a
Kenya | Kimana	Center for Wildlife Management Studies	n/a	Intermed	School for Field Studies	n/a
Kenya | Nairobi	SIT Study Abroad	n/a	Intermed	SIT Study Abroad	n/a
Madagascar | Antananarivo	SIT Study Abroad	n/a	Intermed	SIT Study Abroad	n/a
Mali | Bamako	SIT Study Abroad	n/a	Intermed	SIT Study Abroad	n/a
Mali | Bamako	SIT Study Abroad	n/a	Intermed	SIT Study Abroad	n/a
Mexico | Cuernavaca	Augsburg College	n/a	USColl	Augsburg College	n/a
Mexico | Merida	Universidad Autonoma de Yucatan	n/a	Intermed	Institute for Study Abroad	n/a
Mexico | Puebla	Benemerita Universidad Autonoma de Puebla	n/a	Consrtm	Program for Mexican Culture and Society in Puebla (Oberlin, Smith, Wellesley, and Wheaton)	n/a
Morocco | Rabat	SIT Study Abroad	n/a	Intermed	SIT Study Abroad	n/a
Netherlands | Amsterdam	SIT Study Abroad	n/a	Intermed	SIT Study Abroad	n/a
Netherlands | Amsterdam	SIT Study Abroad	n/a	Intermed	SIT Study Abroad	n/a
New Zealand | Auckland	Auckland University of Technology	n/a	USColl	Boston University	n/a
New Zealand | Auckland	University of Auckland	n/a	USColl	Boston University	n/a
New Zealand | Auckland	University of Auckland	n/a	USColl	Arcadia University	n/a
Nicaragua | Managua	SIT Study Abroad	n/a	Intermed	SIT Study Abroad	n/a
Nicaragua | Managua	Universidad Nacional Autonoma de Nicaragua	n/a	Intermed	Council on International Educational Exchange (CIEE)	n/a
Niger | Niamey	Faculte des Lettres et Sciences Humaines de l'Universite Abdou Moumouni	n/a	USColl	Boston University	n/a
Niger | Niamey	Faculte des Lettres et Sciences Humaines de l'Universite Abdou Moumouni	n/a	USColl	Boston University	n/a
Oman | Muscat	SIT Study Abroad	n/a	Intermed	SIT Study Abroad	n/a
Peru | Cusco	SIT Study Abroad	n/a	Intermed	SIT Study Abroad	n/a
Peru | Lima	Pontificia Universidad Catolica del Peru	n/a	Intermed	Council on International Educational Exchange (CIEE)	n/a

© 2011 — Updates? Want to be in the next edition? Visit **www.mysecondcampus.com**

Rhode Island

DESTINATION	HOST INSTITUTION	PRGM SEASON	PRGM TYPE	INTERMEDIARY	HOUSING
Peru | Lima	Pontificia Universidad Catolica del Peru	n/a	Intermed	Institute for Study Abroad	n/a
Peru | Lima	Pontificia Universidad Catolica del Peru	n/a	Intermed	Council on International Educational Exchange (CIEE)	n/a
Peru | Lima	Universidad del Pacifico	n/a	Intermed	Council on International Educational Exchange (CIEE)	n/a
Scotland | Edinburgh	University of Edinburgh	n/a	USColl	Arcadia University	n/a
Scotland | Edinburgh	University of Edinburgh	n/a	USColl	Arcadia University	n/a
Scotland | Edinburgh	University of Edinburgh	n/a	Intermed	Institute for Study Abroad	n/a
Scotland | Glasgow	University of Glasgow	n/a	Intermed	Institute for Study Abroad	n/a
Scotland | Glasgow	University of Glasgow	n/a	USColl	Arcadia University	n/a
Senegal | Dakar	Suffolk University - Dakar Campus	n/a	Intermed	Council on International Educational Exchange (CIEE)	n/a
Senegal | Dakar	Suffolk University - Dakar Campus	n/a	Intermed	Council on International Educational Exchange (CIEE)	n/a
South Africa | Cape Town	SIT Study Abroad	n/a	Intermed	SIT Study Abroad	n/a
South Africa | Cape Town	Students' Health and Welfare Centres Organisation (University of Cape Town)	n/a	USColl	Arcadia University	n/a
South Africa | Durban	SIT Study Abroad	n/a	Intermed	SIT Study Abroad	n/a
South Africa | Stellenbosch	University of Stellenbosch	n/a	Intermed	American Institute for Foreign Study	n/a
Spain | Alicante	Universidad de Alicante	n/a	Intermed	Council on International Educational Exchange (CIEE)	n/a
Spain | Alicante	Universidad de Alicante	n/a	Intermed	Council on International Educational Exchange (CIEE)	n/a
Spain | Barcelona	Multiple institutional choices	n/a	Intermed	Council on International Educational Exchange (CIEE)	n/a
Spain | Barcelona	Multiple institutional choices	n/a	Intermed	Council on International Educational Exchange (CIEE)	n/a
Spain | Barcelona	Universitat de Barcelona	n/a	Intermed	Council on International Educational Exchange (CIEE)	n/a
Spain | Barcelona	Universitat Pompeu Fabra	n/a	Intermed	Council on International Educational Exchange (CIEE)	n/a
Spain | Granada	Centro de Lenguas y Educacion Intercultural	n/a	Intermed	SIT Study Abroad	n/a
Spain | Madrid	Centro Universitario de Estudios Hispanicos de Hamilton College	n/a	Consrtm	Hamilton, Williams, Swarthmore	n/a
Spain | Madrid	Instituto Internacional en Espana	n/a	USColl	Boston University	n/a
Spain | Madrid	Instituto Internacional or the Universidad Autonoma de Madrid	n/a	USColl	Boston University	n/a
Spain | Madrid	Universidad Autonoma de Madrid	n/a	USColl	Boston University	n/a
Spain | Madrid	Universidad Autonoma de Madrid	n/a	USColl	Boston University	n/a

© 2011 — Updates? Want to be in the next edition? Visit **www.mysecondcampus.com**

Rhode Island

DESTINATION	HOST INSTITUTION	PRGM SEASON	PRGM TYPE	INTERMEDIARY	HOUSING
Spain | Madrid	Universidad Carlos III de Madrid	n/a	Consrtm	Vassar College and Wesleyan University	n/a
Spain | Madrid	Universidad Carlos III de Madrid	n/a	Intermed	Council on International Educational Exchange (CIEE)	n/a
Spain | Madrid	Universidad Carlos III de Madrid	n/a	Intermed	Council on International Educational Exchange (CIEE)	n/a
Spain | Sevilla	Multiple institutional choices	n/a	Intermed	Council on International Educational Exchange (CIEE)	n/a
Spain | Sevilla	Multiple institutional choices	n/a	Intermed	Council on International Educational Exchange (CIEE)	n/a
Spain | Sevilla	Multiple institutional choices	n/a	Intermed	Council on International Educational Exchange (CIEE)	n/a
Spain | Sevilla	Universidad de Sevilla	n/a	USColl	Sweet Briar College	n/a
Spain | Sevilla	Universidad de Sevilla	n/a	Intermed	Council on International Educational Exchange (CIEE)	n/a
Spain | Sevilla	Universidad Pablo de Olavide	n/a	Intermed	Council on International Educational Exchange (CIEE)	n/a
Spain | Toledo	Fundacion Jose Ortega y Gasset	n/a	USColl	Arcadia University	n/a
Switzerland | Geneva	Boston University	n/a	USColl	Boston University	n/a
Switzerland | Geneva	SIT Study Abroad	n/a	Intermed	SIT Study Abroad	n/a
Switzerland and England | Geneva and London	Boston University	n/a	USColl	Boston University	n/a
Thailand | Khon Kaen	Khon Kaen University	n/a	Intermed	Council on International Educational Exchange (CIEE)	n/a
Tunisia | Tunis	SIT Study Abroad	n/a	Intermed	SIT Study Abroad	n/a
Uganda | Gulu	SIT Study Abroad	n/a	Intermed	SIT Study Abroad	n/a
Uganda | Kampala	SIT Study Abroad	n/a	Intermed	SIT Study Abroad	n/a
Vietnam | Ho Chi Minh City	CET Academic Programs	n/a	Intermed	CET Academic Programs	n/a
Vietnam | Ho Chi Minh City	SIT Study Abroad	n/a	Intermed	SIT Study Abroad	n/a

Rhode Island College

Gale Goodwin Gomez
Director
600 Mount Pleasant Avenue
Providence, RI 02908

ggoodwin@ric.edu
401.456.9623
http://www.ric.edu/studyabroad/

Australia | Townsville or Cairns	James Cook University	n/a	Dir	n/a	n/a
Ecuador | Quito	Facultad Latinoamericana de Ciencias Sociales	n/a	Self	n/a	n/a
Ecuador | Quito	PUCE University	n/a	Dir	n/a	n/a
England | Carlisle	University of Cumbria	n/a	Dir	n/a	n/a
England | Carlisle	University of Cumbria	n/a	Bilat	n/a	n/a
Mexico | Cuernavaca	Universal	Win	Self	n/a	n/a
	Costs: Win Costs: T&F: n/a, R&B: n/a, Ttl: $1,600				
United States | Morris (MN)	University of Minnesota, Morris	n/a	Dir	n/a	n/a

Rhode Island

DESTINATION	HOST INSTITUTION	PRGM SEASON	PRGM TYPE	INTERMEDIARY	HOUSING

Rhode Island School of Design

Two College Street
Providence, RI 02903

oip@risd.edu
401.454.6754
http://www.risd.edu/risdabroad.cfm

DESTINATION	HOST INSTITUTION	PRGM SEASON	PRGM TYPE	INTERMEDIARY	HOUSING
(Multiple choices) | (Multiple choices)	Rhode Island School of Design	n/a	Self	n/a	n/a
Australia | Canberra	Canberra School of Art	n/a	Bilat	n/a	n/a
Australia | Melbourne	RMIT University	n/a	Bilat	n/a	n/a
Australia | Sydney	Sydney College of the Arts	n/a	Bilat	n/a	n/a
China | Beijing	Central Academy of Fine Art	n/a	Bilat	n/a	n/a
Czech Republic | Prague	Academy of Arts, Architecture and Design	n/a	Bilat	n/a	n/a
Denmark | Copenhagen	Denmarks Designskole	n/a	Bilat	n/a	n/a
Denmark | Copenhagen	Rhode Island School of Design	Sum	Self	n/a	n/a
Costs: Sum Costs: T&F: n/a, R&B: n/a, Ttl: $3,350					
Denmark | Copenhagen	Royal Danish Academy	n/a	Bilat	n/a	n/a
England | London	Chelsea College of Art & Design	n/a	Bilat	n/a	n/a
England | London	University of Westminster	n/a	Bilat	n/a	n/a
Estonia | Tallinn	Estonian Academy of the Arts	n/a	Bilat	n/a	n/a
Finland | Helsinki	University of Art & Design	n/a	Bilat	n/a	n/a
Finland | Helsinki	University of Technology	n/a	Bilat	n/a	n/a
France | Paris	ESAG Penninghen	n/a	Bilat	n/a	n/a
France | Paris	Les Ateliers	n/a	Bilat	n/a	n/a
France | Sevres	Strate College	n/a	Bilat	n/a	n/a
Germany | Berlin	Universitat der Kunste Berlin	n/a	Bilat	n/a	n/a
Germany | Koln	Koln International School of Design	n/a	Bilat	n/a	n/a
Germany | Munich	Technicshe Universitat Munchen	n/a	Bilat	n/a	n/a
Germany | Pforzheim	Fachhochschule, Pforzheim	n/a	Bilat	n/a	n/a
Germany | Stuttgart	Fachhochschule, Stuttgart	n/a	Bilat	n/a	n/a
India | [City Unspecified]	n/a	n/a	Bilat	n/a	n/a
India | [City Unspecified]	n/a	n/a	Bilat	n/a	n/a
Ireland | [City Unspecified]	n/a	n/a	Bilat	n/a	n/a
Israel | [City Unspecified]	n/a	n/a	Bilat	n/a	n/a
Israel | [City Unspecified]	n/a	n/a	Bilat	n/a	n/a
Italy | [City Unspecified]	n/a	n/a	Bilat	n/a	n/a
Italy | [City Unspecified]	n/a	n/a	Bilat	n/a	n/a
Italy | Rome	Rhode Island School of Design	Sum	Self	n/a	n/a
Italy | Rome	Rhode Island School of Design	Fall Spr	Self	n/a	n/a
Switzerland | [City Unspecified]	Rhode Island School of Design	Sum	Self	n/a	n/a
Costs: Sum Costs: T&F: n/a, R&B: n/a, Ttl: $3,850					

© 2011 — Updates? Want to be in the next edition? Visit **www.mysecondcampus.com**

Rhode Island

DESTINATION	HOST INSTITUTION	PRGM SEASON	PRGM TYPE	INTERMEDIARY	HOUSING

Roger Williams University

Guilan Wang
Assistant Provost for Global Affairs
One Old Ferry Road
Bristol, RI 02809

gwang@rwu.edu
401.254.3899
http://www.rwu.edu/academics/undergraduate/studyabroad.htm

DESTINATION	HOST INSTITUTION	PRGM SEASON	PRGM TYPE	INTERMEDIARY	HOUSING
Argentina | Mendoza	Universidad Nacional de Cuyo	n/a	Intermed	Institute for Study Abroad	n/a
Australia | Brisbane	Griffith University	n/a	Intermed	Institute for Study Abroad	n/a
Australia | Cairns	James Cook University	n/a	USColl	Arcadia University	n/a
Australia | Wollongong	University of Wollongong	n/a	USColl	Arcadia University	n/a
Bahamas | [City Unspecified]	Roger Williams University	Sum	Self	n/a	n/a
	Costs: Sum Costs: T&F: n/a, R&B: n/a, Ttl: $2,265				
Belize | (Multiple)	Roger Williams University	Win	Self	n/a	Other
	Costs: Win Costs: T&F: n/a, R&B: n/a, Ttl: $3,535				
Bermuda | [City Unspecified]	Bermuda Institute of Ocean Sciences	n/a	Dir	n/a	n/a
Chile | Santiago	Pontifica Universidad Catolica de Chile	n/a	Intermed	Institute for Study Abroad	n/a
China | [City Unspecified]	Roger Williams University	Sum	Self	n/a	n/a
	Costs: Sum Costs: T&F: n/a, R&B: n/a, Ttl: $2,475				
China | Hong Kong	Lingnan University	n/a	Dir	n/a	n/a
China | Hong Kong	Lingnan University	Sum	Self	n/a	n/a
China | Shanghai	East China Normal University	n/a	Intermed	Council on International Educational Exchange (CIEE)	n/a
Costa Rica | Heredia	Universidad Nacional	n/a	Intermed	Institute for Study Abroad	n/a
Costa Rica | Monteverde	CIEE Study Center	n/a	Intermed	Council on International Educational Exchange (CIEE)	n/a
Czech Republic | Prague	Charles University	n/a	Intermed	Council on International Educational Exchange (CIEE)	n/a
Ecuador | Guayaquil	Universidad Espiritu Santo	n/a	Intermed	International Partnership for Service Learning	n/a
Egypt | (Multiple)	Roger Williams University	n/a	Self	n/a	n/a
England | London	Roger Williams University	n/a	Self	n/a	Other
England | London	University of London, Birkbeck	n/a	Intermed	Institute for Study Abroad	n/a
England | London	University of Westminster	n/a	Dir	n/a	n/a
England and France | London and Paris	Roger Williams University	Sum	Self	n/a	n/a
	Costs: Sum Costs: T&F: n/a, R&B: n/a, Ttl: $2,815				
France | Paris	CIEE Study Center	n/a	Intermed	Council on International Educational Exchange (CIEE)	n/a
France | Paris	Roger Williams University	Spr	Self	n/a	n/a
	Costs: Spr Costs: T&F: n/a, R&B: n/a, Ttl: $2,560				
France | Rouen	Roger Williams University	Sum	Self	n/a	n/a
	Costs: Sum Costs: T&F: n/a, R&B: n/a, Ttl: $3,530				

Rhode Island

DESTINATION	HOST INSTITUTION	PRGM SEASON	PRGM TYPE	INTERMEDIARY	HOUSING
Germany	Berlin	Freie Universitat Berlin	n/a	Intermed	Council on International Educational Exchange (CIEE)	n/a
Greece	Athens	Arcadia Center for Hellenic, Mediterranean and Balkan Studies	n/a	USColl	Arcadia University	n/a
Guatemala	(Multiple)	Roger Williams University	Sum	Self	n/a	n/a
Costs: Sum Costs: T&F: n/a, R&B: n/a, Ttl: $4,995					
India	Hyderabad	University of Hyderabad	n/a	Intermed	Council on International Educational Exchange (CIEE)	n/a
Ireland	Dublin	Dublin City University	n/a	Intermed	Council on International Educational Exchange (CIEE)	n/a
Ireland	Dublin	Roger Williams University	n/a	Self	n/a	n/a
Ireland	Galway	National University of Ireland, Galway	n/a	USColl	Arcadia University	n/a
Italy	Florence	Roger Williams University	Sum	Self	n/a	n/a
Italy	Florence	Roger Williams University	Self	n/a	PrivApt	
Italy	Sicily	Roger Williams University	Sum	Self	n/a	n/a
Costs: Sum Costs: T&F: n/a, R&B: n/a, Ttl: $2,500					
Jamaica	Kingston	University of Technology	n/a	Intermed	International Partnership for Service Learning	n/a
Japan	Tokyo	Sophia University	n/a	Intermed	Council on International Educational Exchange (CIEE)	n/a
Jordan	Amman	University of Jordan	n/a	Intermed	Council on International Educational Exchange (CIEE)	n/a
Mexico	Cuernavaca	Roger Williams University	Win	Self	n/a	n/a
Costs: Win Costs: T&F: n/a, R&B: n/a, Ttl: $3,270					
Mexico	Guadalajara	Universidad Autonoma de Guadalajara	n/a	Intermed	International Partnership for Service Learning	n/a
Netherlands	Amsterdam and Rotterdam	Roger Williams University	Sum	Self	n/a	n/a
Costs: Sum Costs: T&F: n/a, R&B: n/a, Ttl: $2,645					
Netherlands	Leiden	Central College	n/a	USColl	Central College	n/a
New Zealand	Auckland	University of Auckland	n/a	USColl	Arcadia University	n/a
New Zealand	Palmerston North	Massey University	n/a	Intermed	Institute for Study Abroad	n/a
Northern Ireland	(Multiple choices)	University of Ulster	n/a	Intermed	Institute for Study Abroad	n/a
Panama	(Multiple)	Roger Williams University	Win	Self	n/a	n/a
Costs: Win Costs: T&F: n/a, R&B: n/a, Ttl: $3,024					
Portugal	Lisbon	Universidade Nova de Lisboa	n/a	Intermed	Council on International Educational Exchange (CIEE)	n/a
Scotland	Stirling and Edinburgh	University of Stirling and University of Edinburg	n/a	USColl	Arcadia University	n/a
Senegal	Dakar	Suffolk University - Dakar Campus	n/a	Intermed	Council on International Educational Exchange (CIEE)	n/a
South Africa	Cape Town	University of Cape Town	n/a	USColl	Arcadia University	n/a

© 2011 — Updates? Want to be in the next edition? Visit **www.mysecondcampus.com**

Rhode Island

DESTINATION	HOST INSTITUTION	PRGM SEASON	PRGM TYPE	INTERMEDIARY	HOUSING
Spain | Barcelona	Arcadia Center for Catalan, Spanish & Mediterranean Studies	n/a	USColl	Arcadia University	n/a
Spain | Granada	Central College	n/a	USColl	Central College	n/a
Thailand | Chiang Mai	Payap University	n/a	Intermed	International Partnership for Service Learning	n/a
Turkey | (Multiple)	Roger Williams University	Sum	Self	n/a	n/a
	Costs: Sum Costs: T&F: n/a, R&B: n/a, Ttl: $3,500				
Turkey | Istanbul	Koc University	n/a	Intermed	Council on International Educational Exchange (CIEE)	n/a

Roger Williams University School of Law

Ten Metacom Avenue
Bristol, RI 02809

lawinternational@rwu.edu
401.254.4522
http://law.rwu.edu/academics/study-abroad

England | London	Roger Williams University	Sum	Self	n/a	CollRes
	Costs: Sum Costs: T&F: n/a, R&B: n/a, Ttl: $4,900				

Salve Regina University

George P. Antone
Director
Office of International Programs - Gatehouse
100 Ochre Point Avenue
Newport, RI 02840

antoneg@salve.edu
401.341.2372
http://www.salve.edu/programs/ipsa/

(Multiple choices) | (Multiple choices)	Multiple institutional choices	n/a	USColl	Webster University	n/a
(Multiple choices) | (Multiple choices)	Multiple institutional choices	n/a	Intermed	Cultural Experiences Abroad	n/a
(Multiple choices) | (Multiple choices)	Multiple institutional choices	n/a	Intermed	Center for International Studies	n/a
(Multiple choices) | (Multiple choices)	Multiple institutional choices	n/a	Intermed	Global Student Experience	n/a
(Multiple choices) | (Multiple choices)	Multiple institutional choices	n/a	Intermed	American Institute for Foreign Study	n/a
(Multiple choices) | (Multiple choices)	Multiple institutional choices	n/a	Intermed	Center for Cross-Cultural Study	n/a
(Multiple choices) | (Multiple choices)	Multiple institutional choices	n/a	Intermed	Council on International Educational Exchange (CIEE)	n/a
(Multiple choices) | (Multiple choices)	Multiple institutional choices	n/a	Intermed	AustraLearn	n/a
(Multiple choices) | (Multiple choices)	Multiple institutional choices	n/a	USColl	Arcadia University	n/a
(Multiple choices) | (Multiple choices)	Multiple institutional choices	n/a	Intermed	Academic Programs International	n/a
Argentina | [City Unspecified]	Salve Regina University	Sum	Self	n/a	n/a

Rhode Island

DESTINATION	HOST INSTITUTION	PRGM SEASON	PRGM TYPE	INTERMEDIARY	HOUSING
Australia	(Multiple choices)	Australian Catholic University	n/a	Dir	n/a	n/a
Australia	Sippy Downs	University of the Sunshine Coast	n/a	Bilat	n/a	n/a
Belize	[City Unspecified]	Salve Regina University	Sum	Self	n/a	n/a
Belize	[City Unspecified]	Salve Regina University	n/a	Self	n/a	n/a
Belize	[City Unspecified]	Salve Regina University	n/a	Self	n/a	n/a
Egypt	[City Unspecified]	Salve Regina University	n/a	Self	n/a	n/a
England	Lincoln or Hull	University of Lincoln	n/a	Dir	n/a	n/a
England	Oxford	Salve Regina University	Sum	Self	n/a	n/a
England	Oxford	St. Clare's, Oxford	n/a	Intermed	St. Clare's, Oxford	n/a
England or France	London or Paris	American InterContinental University	n/a	USColl	American InterContinental University	n/a
France	Angers	Universite d'Angers	n/a	Bilat	n/a	n/a
France	Lyon	IDRAC Lyon	n/a	Bilat	n/a	n/a
France	Paris	American University of Paris	n/a	Dir	n/a	n/a
France	Paris	Salve Regina University	n/a	Self	n/a	n/a
Galapagos	[City Unspecified]	Salve Regina University	Sum	Self	n/a	n/a
Greece	Thessaloniki	American College of Thessaloniki	n/a	Bilat	n/a	n/a
Ireland	[City Unspecified]	Salve Regina University	Spr	Self	n/a	n/a
Ireland	[City Unspecified]	Salve Regina University	Sum	Self	n/a	n/a
Ireland	Cork	University College Cork	n/a	Bilat	n/a	n/a
Ireland	Limerick	Mary Immaculate College	n/a	Bilat	n/a	n/a
Israel	[City Unspecified]	Salve Regina University	Sum	Self	n/a	n/a
Italy	Florence	Salve Regina University	Spr	Self	n/a	n/a
Italy	Rome	American University of Rome	n/a	Dir	n/a	n/a
Italy	Rome	Salve Regina University	Sum	Self	n/a	n/a
Japan	Kashiwa	Reitaku University	n/a	Bilat	n/a	n/a
Spain	Alicante	University of Alicante	n/a	Bilat	n/a	n/a
Turkey	[City Unspecified]	Salve Regina University	Spr	Self	n/a	n/a
United States	Washington (DC)	American University	n/a	Dir	n/a	n/a
United States	Woods Hole (MA)	Sea Semester	n/a	Intermed	Sea Semester	n/a
Vienna	[City Unspecified]	Salve Regina University	Spr	Self	n/a	n/a

University of Rhode Island

Dania Brandford-Calvo
Director
Office of International Education
9 Lippitt Road & 107 Taft Hall
Kingston, RI 02881

brandford@uri.edu
401.874.2395
http://www.uri.edu/international/study_abroad.html

DESTINATION	HOST INSTITUTION	PRGM SEASON	PRGM TYPE	INTERMEDIARY	HOUSING
(Multiple choices)	(Multiple choices)	Danish Institute for Study Abroad	n/a	Intermed	Danish Institute for Study Abroad	n/a
(Multiple choices)	(Multiple choices)	Multiple institutional choices	n/a	Intermed	Education Abroad Network	n/a

© 2011 — Updates? Want to be in the next edition? Visit **www.mysecondcampus.com**

Rhode Island

DESTINATION	HOST INSTITUTION	PRGM SEASON	PRGM TYPE	INTERMEDIARY	HOUSING
(Multiple choices) | (Multiple choices)	Multiple institutional choices	n/a	Intermed	American Institute for Foreign Study	n/a
(Multiple choices) | (Multiple choices)	Multiple institutional choices	n/a	Intermed	Academic Programs International	n/a
(Multiple choices) | (Multiple choices)	Multiple institutional choices	n/a	Intermed	Interstudy	n/a
(Multiple choices) | (Multiple choices)	Multiple institutional choices	Sum	Self	n/a	n/a
(Multiple choices) | (Multiple choices)	Multiple institutional choices	n/a	Consrtm	College Consortium for International Studies	n/a
(Multiple choices) | (Multiple choices)	Multiple institutional choices	n/a	Intermed	Council on International Education Exchange (CIEE)	n/a
(Multiple choices) | (Multiple choices)	Multiple institutional choices	n/a	Intermed	GlobaLinks Learning Abroad	n/a
(Multiple) | Florence or Rome	Accademia Italiana	n/a	Intermed	Accademia Italiana	n/a
(Multiple) | London or Paris	American InterContinental University	n/a	Intermed	American InterContinental University	n/a
Belize | [City Unspecified]	University of Rhode Island	Sum	Self	n/a	n/a
	Costs: Sum Costs: T&F: n/a, R&B: n/a, Ttl: $2,600				
Bermuda | Sandys	University of Rhode Island	Sum	Self	n/a	n/a
	Costs: Sum Costs: T&F: n/a, R&B: n/a, Ttl: $2,750				
Bermuda | St. George	Bermuda Institute of Ocean Sciences	n/a	Dir	n/a	n/a
Canada | Nova Scotia (Multiple choices)	Multiple institutional choices	n/a	Bilat	n/a	n/a
Canada | Quebec (Multiple choices)	Multiple institutional choices	n/a	Bilat	n/a	n/a
Canada | Quebec City	Universite Laval	n/a	Bilat	n/a	n/a
Cape Verde | Praia	University of Rhode Island	Sum	Self	n/a	n/a
	Costs: Sum Costs: T&F: n/a, R&B: n/a, Ttl: $2,915				
Dominican Republic | Santo Domingo	University of Rhode Island	Sum	Self	n/a	n/a
England | Norwich	University of East Anglia	n/a	Bilat	n/a	n/a
England | Reading	University of Reading	n/a	Bilat	n/a	n/a
France | Le Havre	University of Le Havre	n/a	Bilat	n/a	n/a
France | Marseille	EUROMED Marseille Ecole de Management	n/a	Bilat	n/a	n/a
France | Nanterre	University of Paris Ouest Nanterre	n/a	Bilat	n/a	n/a
Germany | Braunschweig	Technische Universitat	n/a	Bilat	n/a	n/a
Germany | Hamburg	Hamburg University of Applied Sciences	n/a	Bilat	n/a	n/a
Ghana | Cape Coast	University of Cape Coast	Sum	Self	n/a	n/a
	Costs: Sum Costs: T&F: n/a, R&B: n/a, Ttl: $5,028				
Greece | (Multiple choices)	Multiple institutional choices	n/a	Intermed	Paideia Study Abroad Programs	n/a

Rhode Island

DESTINATION	HOST INSTITUTION	PRGM SEASON	PRGM TYPE	INTERMEDIARY	HOUSING
Greece and Italy | (Multiple)	University of Rhode Island	Sum	Self	n/a	n/a
Costs: Sum Costs: T&F: n/a, R&B: n/a, Ttl: $4,761					
India | [City Unspecified]	University of Rhode Island	Sum	Self	n/a	n/a
Costs: Sum Costs: T&F: n/a, R&B: n/a, Ttl: $2,000					
Japan | Fukuoka	Seinan Gakuin University	n/a	Bilat	n/a	n/a
Japan | Hirakata City	Kansai Gaidai University	n/a	Dir	n/a	n/a
Mexico | Monterrey or Toluca	Instituto Tecnologico y de Estudios Superiores de Monterrey	n/a	Bilat	n/a	n/a
Norway | Honefoss, Kongsberg, or Drammen	Buskerud University College	n/a	Bilat	n/a	n/a
South Korea | Daegu	Keimyung University	n/a	Bilat	n/a	n/a
South Korea | Incheon	INHA University	n/a	Bilat	n/a	n/a
Spain | Salamanca	University of Rhode Island	Sum	Self	n/a	n/a
Costs: Sum Costs: T&F: n/a, R&B: n/a, Ttl: $3,300					
Spain | San Sebastian	Universidad de Navarra	n/a	Bilat	n/a	n/a
Spain | Valladolid	Universidad de Valladolid	n/a	Bilat	n/a	n/a
Spain | Zaragoza	Universidad de Zaragoza	n/a	Bilat	n/a	n/a
United States | (Multiple choices)	Multiple institutional choices	n/a	Bilat	National Student Exchange	n/a
United States | Woods Hole (MA)	Sea Semester	n/a	Intermed	Sea Semester	n/a

© 2011 — Updates? Want to be in the next edition? Visit **www.mysecondcampus.com**

Vermont

| DESTINATION | HOST INSTITUTION | PRGM SEASON | PRGM TYPE | INTERMEDIARY | HOUSING |

Bennington College

Tammy Fraser
Director of Field Work Team
1 College Drive
Bennington, VT 05201

Tfraser@bennington.edu
802.44.4321
http://www.bennington.edu/go/academics/field-work-term

DESTINATION	HOST INSTITUTION	PRGM SEASON	PRGM TYPE	INTERMEDIARY	HOUSING
(Multiple choices)	(Multiple choices)	Multiple institutional choices	Fall Spr YrRound	Self	n/a	n/a

Burlington College

Sandra Baird
Director of International Studies
95 North Avenue
Burlington, VT 05401

sbaird@burlington.edu
802.862.9616
http://www.burlington.edu/academics/index1.php?subj=17

DESTINATION	HOST INSTITUTION	PRGM SEASON	PRGM TYPE	INTERMEDIARY	HOUSING
Bahamas	South Andros Island	Burlington College	Spr	Self	n/a	n/a
Cuba	Havana	University of Havana	n/a	Self	n/a	n/a
Italy	(Multiple choices)	Multiple institutional choices	n/a	Intermed	Study Abroad Italy	n/a

Castleton State College

Renny Harrigan
Associate Academic Dean
Woodruff Hall
Castleton, VT 05735

renny.harrigan@castleton.edu
802.468.5237
http://www.castleton.edu/travel/index.htm

DESTINATION	HOST INSTITUTION	PRGM SEASON	PRGM TYPE	INTERMEDIARY	HOUSING
Belize	(Multiple)	Castleton State College	Spr	Self	n/a	n/a
Bhutan	(Multiple)	Various temples and monasteries	Sum	Intermed	Wisdom Tours	n/a
Cambodia	[City Unspecified]	Wisdom Tours	Spr	Intermed	Wisdom Tours	n/a

© 2011 — Updates? Want to be in the next edition? Visit **www.mysecondcampus.com**

Vermont

DESTINATION	HOST INSTITUTION	PRGM SEASON	PRGM TYPE	INTERMEDIARY	HOUSING
England	London	Roehampton University	Fall	Self	n/a	CollRes
Galapagos Islands	Multiple	Castleton State College	Win	Self	n/a	Other
India	Multiple	Various temples and monasteries	Win	Intermed	Wisdom Tours	n/a
Peru	Multiple	Castleton State College	Sum	Self	n/a	n/a
Costs: Sum Costs: T&F: n/a, R&B: n/a, Ttl: $3,575					
St. John	Maho Bay	Castleton State College	Fall	Self	n/a	n/a
Tibet	Multiple	Various temples and monasteries	Sum	Intermed	Wisdom Tours	n/a
United States	Mojave Desert (CA)	Castleton State College	Sum	Self	n/a	n/a
United States	Santa Fe (NM)	Castleton State College	Fall	Self	n/a	n/a
Costs: Fall Costs: T&F: Castleton home tuition, R&B: Castleton home room fees and $1,350 for food, Ttl: n/a					

Champlain College

Noah Goldblatt
Study Abroad Coordinator
195 South Willard Street
Burlington, VT 05402

ngoldblatt@champlain.edu
802.865.6464
http://www.champlain.edu/Office-of-International-Education.html

DESTINATION	HOST INSTITUTION	PRGM SEASON	PRGM TYPE	INTERMEDIARY	HOUSING
Canada	Montreal	Champlain College	Fall Spr YrRound	Self	n/a	n/a
China	Beijing	Beijing Language and Culture University	Fall Spr	Intermed	American Institute for Foreign Study	n/a
China	Shanghai	Multiple institutional choices	n/a	Intermed	Council on International Education Exchange (CIEE)	n/a
Costa Rica	San Jose	Veritas University	Fall Spr YrRound	Intermed	Cultural Experiences Abroad	n/a
Czech Republic	Prague	Anglo-American University	Sum Fall Spr YrRound	Intermed	Cultural Experiences Abroad	n/a
England	London	Richmond, the American International University in London	Sum Fall Spr YrRound	Intermed	American Institute for Foreign Study	n/a
France	French Riviera	SKEMA-EAI	Sum Fall Spr YrRound	Intermed	Cultural Experiences Abroad	n/a
France	Rennes	ESC Rennes School of Business	Fall Spr	Bilat	Champlain College	n/a
Hungary	Budapest	Corvinus University	Fall Spr YrRound	Intermed	Academic Programs International	n/a
Ireland	Dublin	Champlain College	Fall Spr YrRound	Self	n/a	n/a
Italy	Florence	Multiple institutional choices	Sum Fall Spr YrRound	Intermed	Academic Programs International	n/a
Italy	Rome	Multiple institutional choices	Sum Fall Spr YrRound	Intermed	Academic Programs International	n/a
Japan	Tokyo	Sophia University	Sum Fall Spr YrRound	Intermed	Council on International Education Exchange (CIEE)	n/a
Japan	Beppu	Ritsumeikan Asia Pacific University	Sum Fall Spr YrRound	Intermed	AsiaLearn	n/a
Netherlands	Amsterdam	HES School of Economics and Business	Fall Spr	Bilat	Champlain College	n/a

© 2011 — Updates? Want to be in the next edition? Visit **www.mysecondcampus.com**

Vermont

DESTINATION	HOST INSTITUTION	PRGM SEASON	PRGM TYPE	INTERMEDIARY	HOUSING
Spain	Madrid	Multiple institutional choices	Sum Fall Spr YrRound	Intermed	Academic Programs International	n/a
Sweden	Skovde	University of Skovde	Fall Spr	Bilat	Champlain College	n/a
Thailand	Khon Kaen	n/a	n/a	Intermed	Council on International Education Exchange (CIEE)	n/a

Goddard College

Lucinda Garthwaite
Academic Dean
123 Pitkin Road
Plainfield, VT 05667

Lucinda.garthwaite@goddard.edu
802.322.1655
http://www.goddard.edu/

DESTINATION	HOST INSTITUTION	PRGM SEASON	PRGM TYPE	INTERMEDIARY	HOUSING
Mexico	Morelos	Goddard College	n/a	Self	n/a	n/a

Green Mountain College

Anne Colpitts
Director, International Programs
1 Brennan Circle
Withey 152
Poultney, VT 05764

colpittsa@greenmtn.edu
802.287.8306
http://www.greenmtn.edu/travel.aspx

DESTINATION	HOST INSTITUTION	PRGM SEASON	PRGM TYPE	INTERMEDIARY	HOUSING
(Multiple)	[City Unspecified]	n/a	n/a	Intermed	The Eco League	n/a
Argentina	Rosario	Universidad del Centro Educativo Latinamericano	n/a	Self	Green Mountain College	n/a
France	Montpellier	L'Institute Mediterraneen d'Etudes Francaises	n/a	Self	Green Mountain College	n/a
Italy	[City Unspecified]	Brunnenburg Castle	Spr	Self	Green Mountain College	n/a
Japan	Nagoya	Nagoya University School of Law	Fall Spr YrRound	Bilat	Green Mountain College	n/a
Korea	[City Unspecified]	Hannan University	Spr	Bilat	Green Mountain College	n/a
Wales	Aberystwyth	University of Wales-Aberystwyth	n/a	Bilat	Green Mountain College	n/a

Johnson State College

Sara Kinerson
Director, Advising and Career Center
337 College Hill
Johnson, VT 05656

sara.kinerson@jsc.edu
802.635.1257
http://www.jsc.edu/Academics/StudyAbroad/default.aspx

DESTINATION	HOST INSTITUTION	PRGM SEASON	PRGM TYPE	INTERMEDIARY	HOUSING
(Multiple)	[City Unspecified]	n/a	n/a	n/a	n/a	n/a

© 2011 — Updates? Want to be in the next edition? Visit **www.mysecondcampus.com**

Vermont

| DESTINATION | HOST INSTITUTION | PRGM SEASON | PRGM TYPE | INTERMEDIARY | HOUSING |

Landmark College

Kathleen Fortier
Office Manager, Academic Affairs & Executive Assistant
River Road South
EAB, room 208
PAutney, VT 05346

kfortier@landmark.edu
802.387.6712
http://www.landmark.edu/programs/study_abroad/index.html

DESTINATION	HOST INSTITUTION	PRGM SEASON	PRGM TYPE	INTERMEDIARY	HOUSING
Costa Rica	San Jose	Landmark College	Win	Self	n/a	n/a
Costs: Win Costs: T&F: n/a, R&B: n/a, Ttl: $5,500					
Greece	Nauplion	Landmark College	Sum	Self	n/a	n/a
Costs: Sum Costs: T&F: n/a, R&B: n/a, Ttl: $6,000					
Ireland	Galway	Landmark College	Sum	Self	n/a	n/a
Costs: Sum Costs: T&F: n/a, R&B: n/a, Ttl: $11,000					

Lyndon State College

Jonathan Davis
Associate Dean for Student Affairs
P.O. Box 919
Lyndonville, VT 05851

jonathan.davis@lyndonstate.edu
802.626.6418
http://www.lyndonstate.edu

DESTINATION	HOST INSTITUTION	PRGM SEASON	PRGM TYPE	INTERMEDIARY	HOUSING
[Country Unspecified]	[City Unspecified]	n/a	n/a	n/a	n/a	n/a

Marlboro College

Beverly Berhmann
World Studies Office
2582 South Road
Marlboro, VT 05344

berhmann@marlboro.edu
802.258.9220
http://www.marlboro.edu/academics/international/

DESTINATION	HOST INSTITUTION	PRGM SEASON	PRGM TYPE	INTERMEDIARY	HOUSING
(Multiple)	[City Unspecified]	n/a	n/a	n/a	n/a	n/a

Middlebury College

Jeffrey Cason
Dean of International Programs
Sunderland Language Center
1st floor
Middlebury, VT 05753

cason@middlebury.edu
802.443.5745
http://www.middlebury.edu/international/sa/programs

DESTINATION	HOST INSTITUTION	PRGM SEASON	PRGM TYPE	INTERMEDIARY	HOUSING
(Multiple)	[City Unspecified]	Multiple institutional choices	Spr	Dir	International Honors Program	n/a
Argentina	Buenos Aires	Multiple institutional choices	Fall Spr YrRound	Self	n/a	n/a
Australia	(Multiple choices)	Griffith University	Fall Spr YrRound	Dir	n/a	n/a
Australia	(Multiple choices)	James Cook University	Fall Spr YrRound	Dir	n/a	n/a
Australia	(Multiple choices)	University of New South Wales	Fall Spr YrRound	Dir	n/a	n/a
Australia	Adelaide	Flinders University	Fall Spr YrRound	Dir	n/a	n/a

© 2011 — Updates? Want to be in the next edition? Visit **www.mysecondcampus.com**

Vermont

DESTINATION	HOST INSTITUTION	PRGM SEASON	PRGM TYPE	INTERMEDIARY	HOUSING
Australia | Adelaide	University of Adelaide	Fall Spr YrRound	Dir	n/a	n/a
Australia | Hobart	Tasmania School of Art	Fall Spr YrRound	Dir	n/a	n/a
Australia | Melbourne	Monash University	Fall Spr YrRound	Dir	n/a	n/a
Australia | Melbourne	University of Melbourne	Fall Spr YrRound	Dir	n/a	n/a
Australia | New South Wales	University of Wollongong	Fall Spr YrRound	Dir	n/a	n/a
Australia | Perth	Murdoch University	Fall Spr YrRound	Dir	n/a	n/a
Australia | Perth	University of Western Australia	Fall Spr YrRound	Dir	n/a	n/a
Australia | Queensland	University of Queensland	Fall Spr YrRound	Dir	n/a	n/a
Australia | Sydney	Macquarie University	Fall Spr YrRound	Dir	n/a	n/a
Australia | Sydney	University of Sydney	Fall Spr YrRound	Dir	n/a	n/a
Australia | Sydney	University of Tasmania	Fall Spr YrRound	Dir	n/a	n/a
Australia | Victoria	La Trobe University	Fall Spr YrRound	Dir	n/a	n/a
Bolivia | Cochabamba	SIT Study Abroad	Fall Spr	Intermed	SIT Study Abroad	n/a
Botswana | Gabarone	Multiple institutional choices	Fall Spr	Intermed	SIT Study Abroad	n/a
Botswana | Gabarone	University of Botswana	Fall Spr YrRound	Intermed	SIT Study Abroad	n/a
Brazil | (Multiple)	C.V. Starr-Middlebury School for Language	Fall Spr YrRound	Self	n/a	n/a
Cameroon | Yaounde	Multiple institutional choices	Fall Spr	Intermed	SIT Study Abroad	n/a
Chile | (Multiple)	Multiple institutional choices	Fall Spr YrRound	Self	C.V. Starr-Middlebury Language School	n/a
China | (Multiple)	C.V. Starr-Middlebury School for Language	Fall Spr	Self	n/a	n/a
Costa Rica | [City Unspecified]	Organization for Tropical Studies	n/a	Intermed	Organization for Tropical Studies	n/a
Costa Rica | [City Unspecified]	Organization for Tropical Studies	Sum Fall Spr	Intermed	Organization for Tropical Studies	n/a
Costa Rica | San Jose	Universidad de Costa Rica	Fall Spr	Intermed	University of Kansas	n/a
Croatia | Zagreb	SIT Study Abroad	Fall Spr	Intermed	SIT Study Abroad	n/a
Czech Republic | Prague	SIT Study Abroad	Fall Spr	Intermed	SIT Study Abroad	n/a
Czech Republic | Prague	Charles University	Sum Fall Spr	Intermed	CET Academic Programs	n/a
Czech Republic | Prague	Charles University	Fall Spr YrRound	Intermed	Council on International Education Exchange (CIEE)	n/a
Czech Republic | Prague	Charles University	n/a	Intermed	Center for Economic Research and Graduate Education, Economics Institute	n/a
Czech Republic | Prague	New York University Center in Prague	Fall Spr	USColl	New York University	n/a
Denmark | [City Unspecified]	Danish Institute for Study Abroad	n/a	Dir	n/a	n/a
Denmark | Copenhagen	Danish Institute for Study Abroad	Fall Spr	Dir	n/a	n/a
Dominican Republic | Santiago	Pontificia Universidad Catolica Madre y Maestra	Fall Spr YrRound	Intermed	Council on International Education Exchange (CIEE)	n/a
Dominican Republic | Santo Domingo	Multiple institutional choices	Fall Spr YrRound	Intermed	Council on International Education Exchange (CIEE)	n/a

© 2011 — Updates? Want to be in the next edition? Visit www.mysecondcampus.com

Vermont

DESTINATION	HOST INSTITUTION	PRGM SEASON	PRGM TYPE	INTERMEDIARY	HOUSING
Ecuador | Quito	Universidad San Francisco de Quito	Fall Spr	Intermed	International Partnership for Service-Learning and Leadership	n/a
Ecuador | Quito	SIT Study Abroad	Fall Spr	Intermed	SIT Study Abroad	n/a
Ecuador | Quito	Multiple institutional choices	Fall Spr	Intermed	SIT Study Abroad	n/a
Ecuador | Quito	Universidad San Francisco de Quito	Fall Spr YrRound	Intermed	Brethren Colleges Abroad	n/a
Egypt | Alexandria	Alexandria University	Fall Spr YrRound	Self	n/a	n/a
England | Birmingham	University of Birmingham	Fall Spr YrRound	Dir	n/a	n/a
England | Brighton	University of Sussex	Fall Spr YrRound	Dir	n/a	n/a
England | Bristol	University of Bristol	Fall Spr YrRound	Dir	n/a	n/a
England | Bristol	University of Bristol	n/a	Dir	n/a	n/a
England | Durham	Durham University	n/a	Dir	n/a	n/a
England | Lancaster	Lancaster University	Fall Spr YrRound	Dir	n/a	n/a
England | Leeds	University of Leeds	Fall Spr YrRound	Dir	n/a	n/a
England | London	Goldsmiths-University of London	Fall Spr YrRound	Dir	n/a	n/a
England | London	King's College London	Fall Spr YrRound	Dir	n/a	n/a
England | London	London School of Economics	YrRound	Dir	n/a	n/a
England | London	Queen Mary-University of London	Fall Spr YrRound	Dir	n/a	n/a
England | London	School of Oriental and African Studies-University of London	Fall Spr YrRound	Dir	n/a	n/a
England | London	Slade School of Fine Art	Fall Spr YrRound	Dir	n/a	n/a
England | London	University College London	Fall Spr YrRound	Dir	n/a	n/a
England | Manchester	University of Manchester	Fall Spr YrRound	Dir	n/a	n/a
England | Norwich	University of East Anglia	Fall Spr YrRound	Bilat	n/a	n/a
England | Nottingham	University of Nottingham	Fall Spr YrRound	Bilat	n/a	n/a
England | Oxford	Lincoln College-University of Oxford	YrRound	Bilat	n/a	n/a
England | Surrey	Royal Holloway-University of London	Fall Spr YrRound	Dir	n/a	n/a
England | Warwick	University of Warwick	Fall Spr YrRound	Dir	n/a	n/a
England | York	University of York	Fall Spr YrRound	Dir	n/a	n/a
Fiji | Suva	SIT Study Abroad	Fall Spr	Intermed	SIT Study Abroad	n/a
France | (Multiple)	C.V. Starr-Middlebury School for Language	Fall Spr YrRound	Self	n/a	n/a
Germany | (Multiple)	C.V. Starr-Middlebury School for Language	Fall Spr YrRound	Self	n/a	n/a
Ghana | Accra	SIT Study Abroad	Fall Spr	Intermed	SIT Study Abroad	n/a
Ghana | Cape Coast	SIT Study Abroad	Fall Spr	Intermed	SIT Study Abroad	n/a
Ghana | Legon	University of Ghana	Fall Spr YrRound	Intermed	Council on International Education Exchange (CIEE)	n/a

© 2011 — Updates? Want to be in the next edition? Visit **www.mysecondcampus.com**

Vermont

DESTINATION	HOST INSTITUTION	PRGM SEASON	PRGM TYPE	INTERMEDIARY	HOUSING
Greece | Athens	Center for Hellenic, Mediterranean and Balkan Studies	Fall Spr YrRound	USColl	Arcadia University	n/a
Greece | Athens	City University	Fall Spr YrRound	Intermed	Brethren Colleges Abroad	n/a
Greece | Athens	International Center for Hellenic and Mediterranean Studies	Fall Spr YrRound	Intermed	College Year Athens	n/a
Hungary | Budapest	Budapest Semesters in Mathematics	Fall Spr	USColl	St. Olaf College	n/a
Hungary | Budapest	Corvinus University	Fall Spr YrRound	Intermed	Council on International Education Exchange (CIEE)	n/a
India | (Multiple choices)	Multiple institutional choices	Sum Fall Spr YrRound	USColl	University of Wisconsin-Madison	n/a
India | Delhi	St. Stephen's College	Fall YrRound	USColl	Rutgers University	n/a
India | Delhi	St. Stephen's College/Lady Shri Ram College	Fall YrRound	USColl	Brown University	n/a
India | Hyderabad	University of Hyderabad	Fall Spr YrRound	Intermed	Council on International Education Exchange (CIEE)	n/a
India | Jaipur	SIT Study Abroad	Fall Spr	Intermed	SIT Study Abroad	n/a
India | New Delhi	SIT Study Abroad	Fall Spr	Intermed	SIT Study Abroad	n/a
Indonesia | Bedulu	SIT Study Abroad	Fall Spr	Intermed	SIT Study Abroad	n/a
Ireland | Cork	University College Cork	Fall Spr YrRound	Dir	n/a	n/a
Ireland | Dublin	Trinity College Dublin	Fall Spr YrRound	Dir	n/a	n/a
Ireland | Dublin	University College Dublin	Fall Spr YrRound	Dir	n/a	n/a
Ireland | Galway	National University of Ireland, Galway	Fall Spr YrRound	Dir	n/a	n/a
Ireland | Limerick	University of Limerick	Fall Spr YrRound	Dir	n/a	n/a
Israel | [City Unspecified]	Ben-Gurion University of the Negev	n/a	Intermed	Ginsburg-Ingerman Overseas Student Program	n/a
Israel | D.N. Hevel Eilot	Ben Gurion University	Fall Spr YrRound	Intermed	Arava Institute for Environmental Studies	n/a
Israel | Haifa	University of Haifa	Fall Spr YrRound	Dir	n/a	n/a
Israel | Jerusalem	Hebrew University of Jerusalem-Rothberg International School	Fall Spr YrRound	Dir	n/a	n/a
Israel | Ramat Gan	Bar-Ilan University	YrRound	Dir	n/a	n/a
Israel | Tel Aviv	Tel Aviv University	n/a	Intermed	School for Overseas Students	n/a
Italy | (Multiple choices)	C.V. Starr-Middlebury School for Language	Fall Spr YrRound	Self	n/a	n/a
Italy | Rome	Intercollegiate Center for Classical Studies (Duke University)	Fall Spr	Consrtm	Duke University	n/a
Japan | Tokyo	International Christian University	Fall Spr	Self	C.V. Starr-Middlebury Language School	n/a
Kenya | [City Unspecified]	St. Lawrence University	Fall Spr	USColl	St. Lawrence University	n/a
Kenya | Mombasa	SIT Study Abroad	Fall Spr	Intermed	SIT Study Abroad	n/a
Kenya | Nairobi	SIT Study Abroad	Fall Spr	Intermed	SIT Study Abroad	n/a
Madagascar | Antananarivo	SIT Study Abroad	Fall Spr	Intermed	SIT Study Abroad	n/a

© 2011 — Updates? Want to be in the next edition? Visit **www.mysecondcampus.com**

Vermont

DESTINATION	HOST INSTITUTION	PRGM SEASON	PRGM TYPE	INTERMEDIARY	HOUSING
Madagascar | Fort Dauphin	SIT Study Abroad	Fall Spr	Intermed	SIT Study Abroad	n/a
Mali | Bamako	SIT Study Abroad	Fall Spr	Intermed	SIT Study Abroad	n/a
Mexico | Guadalajara	Universidad de Guadalajara	Fall Spr YrRound	Self	n/a	n/a
Mongolia | Ulaanbaatar	SIT Study Abroad	Fall Spr	Intermed	SIT Study Abroad	n/a
Nepal | Kathmandu	SIT Study Abroad	Fall Spr	Intermed	SIT Study Abroad	n/a
Nepal | Kathmandu	SIT Study Abroad	Fall Spr	Intermed	SIT Study Abroad	n/a
Nepal | Kathmandu	Tribhuvan University	Fall Spr	USColl	Pitzer College	n/a
Netherlands | Amsterdam	University of Amsterdam	Fall Spr YrRound	Intermed	Council on International Education Exchange (CIEE)	n/a
New Zealand | Auckland	University of Auckland	Fall Spr YrRound	Dir	n/a	n/a
New Zealand | Christchurch	Lincoln University	Fall Spr YrRound	Dir	n/a	n/a
New Zealand | Christchurch	University of Canterbury	Fall Spr YrRound	Dir	n/a	n/a
New Zealand | Dunedin	University of Otago	Fall Spr YrRound	Dir	n/a	n/a
New Zealand | Hamilton	University of Waikato	Fall Spr YrRound	Dir	n/a	n/a
New Zealand | Wellington	Victoria University of Wellington	Fall Spr YrRound	Dir	n/a	n/a
Nicaragua | Managua	SIT Study Abroad	Fall Spr	Intermed	SIT Study Abroad	n/a
Niger | Niamey	Faculte des Lettres et Sciences Humaines de l'Universite Abdou Moumouni	Fall Spr YrRound	USColl	Boston University	n/a
North Ireland | Belfast	Queen's University Belfast	Fall Spr YrRound	Dir	n/a	n/a
Norway | Oslo	University of Oslo	Fall	Intermed	Higher Education Consortium for Urban Affairs	n/a
Panama | Panama City	SIT Study Abroad	Fall Spr	Intermed	SIT Study Abroad	n/a
Peru | Cuzco	Colegio Andino	Fall Spr	Intermed	SIT Study Abroad	n/a
Peru | Lima	Universidad Antonio Ruiz de	Sum Fall Spr	USColl	University of Virginia	n/a
Poland | Warsaw	Warsaw School of Economics	Fall Spr	Intermed	Council on International Education Exchange (CIEE)	n/a
Russia | (Multiple)	C.V. Starr-Middlebury School for Language	Fall Spr YrRound	Self	n/a	n/a
Samoa | Apia	SIT Study Abroad	Fall Spr	Intermed	SIT Study Abroad	n/a
Scotland | Aberdeen	University of Aberdeen	Fall Spr YrRound	Dir	n/a	n/a
Scotland | Edinburgh	University of Edinburgh	Fall Spr YrRound	Dir	n/a	n/a
Scotland | Fife	University of St. Andrew's	Fall Spr YrRound	Dir	n/a	n/a
Scotland | Glasgow	Glasgow School of Art	Fall Spr YrRound	Dir	n/a	n/a
Scotland | Stirling	University of Stirling	Fall Spr YrRound	Dir	n/a	n/a
Senegal | Dakar	SIT Study Abroad	Fall Spr	Intermed	SIT Study Abroad	n/a
South Africa | (Multiple choices)	Multiple institutional choices	n/a	Intermed	InterStudy	n/a
South Africa | Cape Town	Council on International Education Exchange (CIEE)	Fall Spr	Intermed	Council on International Education Exchange (CIEE)	n/a
South Africa | Cape Town	Council on International Education Exchange (CIEE)	Fall Spr	Intermed	Council on International Education Exchange (CIEE)	n/a
South Africa | Cape Town	SIT Study Abroad	Fall Spr	Intermed	SIT Study Abroad	n/a
South Africa | Cape Town	University of Cape Town	Fall Spr	Dir	n/a	n/a
South Africa | Durban	SIT Study Abroad	Fall Spr	Intermed	SIT Study Abroad	n/a

© 2011 — Updates? Want to be in the next edition? Visit **www.mysecondcampus.com**

Vermont

DESTINATION	HOST INSTITUTION	PRGM SEASON	PRGM TYPE	INTERMEDIARY	HOUSING
South Africa | Durban	SIT Study Abroad	Fall Spr	Intermed	SIT Study Abroad	n/a
South Africa | Stellenbosch	Stellenbosch University	Fall Spr YrRound	Intermed	Council on International Education Exchange (CIEE)	n/a
South Korea | Seoul	Yonsei University	n/a	Self	n/a	n/a
Spain | (Multiple choices)	C.V. Starr-Middlebury School for Language	Fall Spr YrRound	Self	n/a	n/a
Sweden | Stockholm	Stockholm University	n/a	USColl	Hamilton College	n/a
Tanzania | Arusha	SIT Study Abroad	Fall Spr	Intermed	SIT Study Abroad	n/a
Tanzania | Dar es Salaam	University of Dar es Salaam	Fall Spr YrRound	Intermed	Council on International Education Exchange (CIEE)	n/a
Tanzania | Zanzibar	SIT Study Abroad	Fall Spr	Intermed	SIT Study Abroad	n/a
Thailand | Khon Kaen	Khon Kaen University	Fall Spr	Intermed	Council on International Education Exchange (CIEE)	n/a
Turkey | Istanbul	Bogazici University	n/a	Dir	n/a	n/a
Turkey | Istanbul	Koc University	Fall Spr YrRound	Intermed	Council on International Education Exchange (CIEE)	n/a
Uganda | Kampala	SIT Study Abroad	Fall Spr	Intermed	SIT Study Abroad	n/a
Uruguay | Montevideo	Multiple institutional choices	Fall Spr YrRound	Self	n/a	n/a
Vietnam | Can Tho	SIT Study Abroad	Fall Spr	Intermed	SIT Study Abroad	n/a
Vietnam | Ho Chi Minh City	Sum Fall Spr	n/a	Intermed	CET Academic Programs	n/a
Vietnam | Ho Chi Minh City	SIT Study Abroad	Fall Spr	Intermed	SIT Study Abroad	n/a
Vietnam | ho Chi Minh City	Vietnam National University	Fall Spr YrRound	Intermed	Council on International Education Exchange (CIEE)	n/a
Wales | Aberystwyth	Aberystwyth University	Fall Spr YrRound	Dir	n/a	n/a
Wales | Bangor	Bangor University	Fall Spr YrRound	Dir	n/a	n/a
Wales | Cardiff	University of Cardiff	Fall Spr YrRound	Dir	n/a	n/a
Wales | Ceredigion	University of Wales Lampeter	Fall Spr YrRound	Dir	n/a	n/a
Wales | Swansea	Swansea University	Fall Spr YrRound	Dir	n/a	n/a

New England Culinary Institute

Mark Molinaro
Executive Chef
56 College Street
Montpelier, VT 05602

mark.molinaro@neci.edu
877.223.6324
http://www.neci.edu/admissions

[Country Unspecified] | [City Unspecified]	n/a	n/a	n/a	n/a	n/a

Norwich University

School of Graduate Studies
P.O. Box 367
Northfield, VT 05663-0367

info@grad.norwich.edu
800.460.5597
http://graduate.norwich.edu/contact/

[Country Unspecified] | [City Unspecified]	n/a	n/a	n/a	n/a	n/a

© 2011 — Updates? Want to be in the next edition? Visit **www.mysecondcampus.com**

Vermont

DESTINATION	HOST INSTITUTION	PRGM SEASON	PRGM TYPE	INTERMEDIARY	HOUSING

Southern Vermont College

Albert DeCiccio
Provost
982 Mansion Drive
Bennington, VT 05201-6002

adeciccio@svc.edu
802.447.6303
http://www.svc.edu/academics/study_abroad.html

| [Country Unspecified] \| [City Unspecified] | n/a | n/a | n/a | n/a | n/a |

St. Michael's College

Peggy Imai
Director
Office of Study Abroad
1 Winooski Park, Box 112
Klein Commons 118
Colchester, VT 05439

pimai@smcvt.edu
802.654.2803
http://www.smcvt.edu/studyabroad/default.asp

| [Country Unspecified] \| [City Unspecified] | n/a | n/a | n/a | n/a | n/a |

Sterling College

Pavel Cenkl
Dean of Academics
P.O. Box 72
Craftsbury Common, VT 05827

pcenkl@sterlingcollege.edu
802.586.7711 x 240
http://sterlingcollege.edu/gfs.html

DESTINATION	HOST INSTITUTION	PRGM SEASON	PRGM TYPE	INTERMEDIARY	HOUSING
(Multiple) | [City Unspecified]	Sterling College	Sum	Self	n/a	n/a
Costs: Sum Costs: T&F: n/a, R&B: n/a, Ttl: $4,000					
Bahamas | San	Sterling College	Win	Self	n/a	n/a
Costs: Win Costs: T&F: n/a, R&B: n/a, Ttl: $2,000					
Canada | Newfoundland	Sterling College	n/a	Self	n/a	n/a
Canada | Quebec	Sterling College	n/a	Self	n/a	n/a
Iceland | [City Unspecified]	Sterling College	n/a	Self	n/a	n/a
Japan | Hokkaido	Sterling College	n/a	Self	n/a	n/a

University of Vermont

Kim Howard
Director of International Education
633 Main Street
Office of International Education
Living/Learning Center, B-162
Burlington, VT 05405

kimberly.howard@uvm.edu
802.656.4296
http://www.uvm.edu/~oies/?Page=sa_index.php&SM=samenu.html

| [Country Unspecified] \| [City Unspecified] | n/a | n/a | n/a | n/a | n/a |

© 2011 — Updates? Want to be in the next edition? Visit **www.mysecondcampus.com**

www.ingramcontent.com/pod-product-compliance
Lightning Source LLC
Chambersburg PA
CBHW080729300426
44114CB00019B/2530